Nonprofit
MANAGEMENT
Principles and Practice
Fourth Edition

Nonprofit
MANAGEMENT
Principles and Practice

Fourth Edition

Michael J. Worth
The George Washington University

Los Angeles | London | New Delhi
Singapore | Washington DC

Los Angeles | London | New Delhi
Singapore | Washington DC

FOR INFORMATION:

SAGE Publications, Inc.
2455 Teller Road
Thousand Oaks, California 91320
E-mail: order@sagepub.com

SAGE Publications Ltd.
1 Oliver's Yard
55 City Road
London EC1Y 1SP
United Kingdom

SAGE Publications India Pvt. Ltd.
B 1/I 1 Mohan Cooperative Industrial Area
Mathura Road, New Delhi 110 044
India

SAGE Publications Asia-Pacific Pte. Ltd.
3 Church Street
#10-04 Samsung Hub
Singapore 049483

Acquisitions Editor: Maggie Stanley
Associate Editor: Abbie Rickard
eLearning Editor: Katie Bierach
Editorial Assistant: Nicole Mangona
Production Editor: Libby Larson
Copy Editors: Diane DiMura and Melinda Masson
Typesetter: Hurix Systems Pvt. Ltd.
Proofreader: Dennis W. Webb
Indexer: Jeanne Busemeyer
Cover Designer: Candice Harman
Marketing Manager: Ashlee Blunk

Copyright © 2017 by SAGE Publications, Inc.

Printed in the United States of America

Library of Congress Cataloging-in-Publication Data

Names: Worth, Michael J., author.

Title: Nonprofit management : principles and practice / Michael J. Worth.

Description: Fourth edition. | Los Angeles : SAGE, [2017] | Includes bibliographical references and index.

Identifiers: LCCN 2015040089 | ISBN 9781483375991 (pbk. : alk. paper)

Subjects: LCSH: Nonprofit organizations—Management.

Classification: LCC HD62.6 .W675 2017 | DDC 658/.048—dc23
LC record available at http://lccn.loc.gov/2015040089

This book is printed on acid-free paper.

SUSTAINABLE FORESTRY INITIATIVE
Certified Chain of Custody
Promoting Sustainable Forestry
www.sfiprogram.org
SFI-01268
SFI label applies to text stock

17 18 19 20 10 9 8 7 6 5 4 3 2

Brief Contents

PART V. Special Topics 409

Detailed Contents

3 Theories of the Nonprofit Sector and Nonprofit Organizations   49

PART II. Governing and Leading Nonprofit Organizations   73

4 Nonprofit Governing Boards   75

5 Executive Leadership   107

PART III. Managing the Nonprofit Organization   133

6   Ensuring Accountability and Measuring Performance   135

7   Developing Strategy and Building Capacity   171

11 Advocacy and Lobbying   285

PART IV. Obtaining and Managing Resources   303

12 Financial Management   305

13   Philanthropic Fundraising   333

14   Earned-Income Strategies   371

15   Government Grants and Contracts 397

PART V. Special Topics 409

16   Social Entrepreneurship and Innovation 411

17 Governing and Managing International and Global Organizations   429

Acknowledgments

Writing a book is a collective enterprise, even when the book has one author. Any author builds on the work of others, and this text reflects the wisdom of the many scholars and practitioners who are cited throughout it.

I am grateful to my SAGE editor, Maggie Stanley, who encouraged me to undertake this fourth edition.

I am grateful as well to the following reviewers, whose frank comments have added immeasurably to this revision:

Ann Marie Kinnell, University of Southern Mississippi

Becky J. Starnes, Austin Peay State University

Beth Gazley, Indiana University

Catherine E. Wilson, Villanova University

Chandra Commuri, California State University, Bakersfield

Christine W. Cugliari, High Point University

Christopher Klingeman, Southern Illinois University

David A. Coplan, University of Pittsburgh

Deborah Harley-McClaskey, East Tennessee State University

Eunice V. Akoto, North Carolina Central University

Jessica E. Sowa, University of Colorado Denver

John Conahan, Kutztown University

Lynn W. Clemons, Mercer University

Marilyn L. Grady, University of Nebraska-Lincoln

Marjorie Carlson Hurst, Liberty University

Robert Dibie, Indiana University Kokomo

Robert C. Teitelbaum, State University of New York, Empire State College

Sylvia Ramierz Benatti, University of the District of Columbia

Thomas L. Winter, Abilene Christian University

Tory S. Vornholt, Agnes Scott College

I have learned immensely from my students at The George Washington University, from my faculty colleagues, and from the many nonprofit executives who have participated in various classes of mine over the years. I thank them for the education they have provided me and hope that they will find this book to be a useful contribution to the field. I am grateful to Gretchen Wieland, my graduate assistant at The George Washington University during 2015–2016, who provided invaluable assistance to me in producing this fourth edition. Finally, I express my deepest gratitude to my family and friends for their patience over the months of my effort with this project, as I have undertaken the many revisions that are encompassed in this fourth edition.

Michael J. Worth
Professor of Nonprofit Management
The George Washington University
Washington, DC

Preface

The first edition of *Nonprofit Management: Principles and Practice* was published by SAGE in 2009, the second edition in 2012, and the third edition in 2014. It is striking how much the landscape of the nonprofit sector has continued to change over the years, requiring frequent updates to stay current with the state of the field in nonprofit management.

Changes reflected in this fourth edition of the book include, most obviously, certain data, but also trends, new concepts and research, and new cases that have drawn attention since the third edition was completed. The inevitable lag between research and writing and publication often means that readers should be alert to changes that may have occurred during the process of updating the book. Thus, even this fourth edition may have some obsolescence by the time it reaches the reader. There are reminders of this reality throughout the book, and it is recommended that students consult referenced websites and other resources on points that seem subject to change.

It is, of course, impossible to know what economic conditions will prevail when this book reaches its readers. The recession that began in 2007, what some people called the Great Recession, took a significant toll on many nonprofit organizations, resulting in decreased financial resources at a time when the demand for services was increasing. By 2015, the economy had recovered by many measures. Perhaps by the time this fourth edition reaches its readers, the economy will have continued to grow. Or, perhaps, it will again have slipped into recession. It is impossible to predict. In any case, effects of the financial crisis that occurred at the end of the preceding decade are likely to linger. It produced a heightened awareness of financial uncertainty, the need for nonprofits to use resources efficiently and effectively, and the importance of achieving diverse revenue sources to weather various economic scenarios. Those lessons have brought permanent change to our thinking about the management of nonprofit organizations. It seems likely the nonprofit sector will continue to face new opportunities and challenges in the years ahead.

New to This Edition

This fourth edition includes a number of changes from the third. First, chapter topics continued from the previous edition all have been updated to reflect new data, new research, and recent events. For example, new principles and standards released by Maryland Nonprofits in 2014 and by Independent Sector in 2015 are reflected in the chapters concerning governance (Chapter 4) and accountability (Chapter 6). In response to reviewer comments, some topics from the previous edition have been reorganized and expanded. For example, new material has been included on managing governing boards, including board development and the role of board professionals; the use of social networks and social media in marketing; fundraising on the Internet; risk management; crisis communications; human resource management; and employment law, among other topics.

The chapter on developing strategy and building capacity (Chapter 7) brings together topics that appeared in various sections of the third edition. In addition, coverage of those topics has been thoroughly updated and expanded. This reorganization provides a more even flow to the text. A new chapter (Chapter 8) discusses collaboration, partnerships, and mergers among nonprofits, reflecting the growing importance of such relationships. Among new material in this chapter is an expanded discussion of cross-sector collaborations and collective impact. The chapter on financial management (Chapter 12) has been relocated earlier in the text, consistent with the order in which some reviewers cover the topic in their courses. Chapters on social entrepreneurship and innovation (Chapter 16) and on international and global organizations (Chapter 17) have been substantially revised from the third edition. The chapter on social entrepreneurship has been expanded to include a discussion of how existing nonprofit organizations can develop and maintain a culture of continuous innovation. Learning objectives related to each chapter are a new feature in this edition.

New cases have been developed for this fourth edition, encompassing recent events and new approaches. New cases related to specific chapters include Brian Gallagher's leadership of change at United Way; the merger of N Street Village and Miriam's House; the Corcoran Gallery of Art and Corcoran School of the Arts and Design; and Aspire CoffeeWorks. Cases retained from the third edition all have been updated to reflect new developments. Some reviewers of the third edition suggested including longer cases that could be used in discussions that would cut across chapters. In response to that useful idea, a new feature in this edition is an Appendix that includes three longer, more comprehensive case studies regarding organizations in different subsectors: New York City Opera, Share Our Strength, and the Y (YMCA).

Philosophy of This Book

A Balanced Approach

Students reading this book are likely to have varied backgrounds. Some may be undergraduates who do not yet have substantial work experience and perhaps wish to explore nonprofit management as a possible career direction. Others may be graduate students who have an interest in nonprofit careers but have not previously studied management. Still others might have studied management but may have limited knowledge of the unique values, characteristics, and circumstances of the nonprofit sector or how the management principles they know can be applied in the nonprofit environment. Yet others may be individuals with considerable experience working in nonprofit organizations who are pursuing further study to increase and broaden their understanding and professional skills.

Some students reading this book may be undergraduates taking a course that is an introduction to the nonprofit sector. Others may be enrolled in a program leading to a master's degree in nonprofit management. Some may be pursuing a master's degree in business, social work, public administration, or public policy, with a concentration in nonprofit management. Still others may be taking only one course in nonprofit management as an elective in their undergraduate or graduate degree program, seeking only a broad and general orientation to the field.

Given this diversity of backgrounds and goals often found among students taking a course in nonprofit management, a textbook that seeks to provide an overview of the field must include both theoretical concepts and practical applications; it must cover some basics as well as intellectually stimulating issues; it must be both rigorous and accessible to students of varied academic backgrounds; and it must provide both a foundation of knowledge that may serve as a springboard to more advanced study and a comprehensive overview for those students whose one experience with the field will consist of a single course.

This book strives to address all these diverse needs and interests, with the author's humble recognition that it may not succeed in meeting all of them for all students. It attempts to provide a comprehensive exposure to topics relevant to the field of nonprofit management, but it obviously must be selective in its discussion of those topics. This intended balance between comprehensiveness in topics and selectivity in their treatment may frustrate some readers. Some may find their appetites whetted but unsatisfied by the quick tour provided in some parts of the book. It is possible that others may find that some chapters include ideas they have seen before in other courses.

Students are encouraged to tailor their use of the book to their own interests and backgrounds. Readers who, for example, already have studied some of the organizational and management theories we will discuss are encouraged to read relevant sections as a refresher but to pay closer attention to material that is new to them. Those to whom the theories are new, and who find their discussion in this book to be too brief, are encouraged to explore the additional resources suggested throughout the book. In sum, it is hoped that this book may provide a kind of comprehensive menu, from which students may select the topics or approaches on which they wish to "click" for more information. Both novices and more experienced individuals may find it a foundation on which they can build, seeking appropriate avenues for further information and learning. And, in all likelihood, professors also will elaborate on some topics and skip lightly over others, as they sense the tempo of their individual classes.

Focus on Charitable Nonprofits

As will be discussed in Chapter 2, the nonprofit sector encompasses an amazing array of organizations with different characteristics, structures, and purposes. This book focuses primarily on that category known as charitable nonprofits and, in particular, those that provide services, such as education and research, health care, arts and cultural programs, and social and legal services. The following chapters also will sometimes mention member-serving organizations—for example, trade and professional associations—but primarily as points of contrast with charitable nonprofits. Religious congregations make up a significant component of the overall nonprofit sector, but religion is the subsector that is the least professionalized—that is, it employs relatively few professional managers. Thus, this book does not devote significant discussion to the management of churches, synagogues, mosques, or other religious congregations. We will discuss foundations, but primarily as sources of support for service-providing nonprofits; we will not discuss the management of foundations per se. This book does not exclude, but also does not emphasize, those nonprofits that are primarily advocacy organizations, also known as social welfare organizations. While they are nonprofits, they are also different from charitable nonprofits in important ways, as we will discuss further in Chapter 2. Of course, some principles of governance, leadership, and management discussed in this book apply to all nonprofits and will be of relevance to students intending to work in any component of the nonprofit world.

Focus on U.S. Nonprofits

This book includes a chapter on nonprofits in the global environment, but it primarily addresses the management of nonprofit organizations in the United States. The American nonprofit sector is the largest in the world; it operates under unique cultural, economic, and legal circumstances. It is where most American students of nonprofit management will pursue their careers. In addition, as governments around the world seek to reduce their expenditures and devolve many functions to nonprofit organizations, many also are looking to relevant aspects of the American model in developing their own nonprofit sectors. Thus, even for students primarily interested in working on the international stage, an understanding of nonprofit management in the United States is both relevant and useful. Indeed, I have been gratified to learn that previous editions of this book were adopted by professors in countries outside of the United States.

Overview of the Book

The first three chapters of this book provide an orientation to the nonprofit sector and a theoretical foundation for the more applied topics considered later. Chapter 1 provides an introduction to nonprofit management, both as a profession and as an academic field of study, and offers a justification for studying the topic as distinct from management in government or business. Chapter 2 offers a look at the structure, boundaries, and characteristics of the nonprofit sector and establishes some basic definitions. Chapter 3 expands our understanding of the nonprofit sector by reviewing theories that explain its existence and its role in relation to government and business. That chapter also examines selected theories that describe the nature of nonprofit organizations and explain their behavior.

The next two chapters, Chapters 4 and 5, consider the roles and responsibilities of governing boards and nonprofit chief executive officers (CEOs) and the ways in which these two vital actors interact in leading organizations. The nonprofit governing board has functional, moral, and legal responsibilities. Nonprofit chief executives, whether titled "executive director," "president," "CEO," or something else, lead their organizations in a complex and dynamic environment that will be described. The partnership between the CEO and the board is critical to a well-operating and effective organization.

The next six chapters focus on applied aspects of nonprofit management. Chapter 6 reviews the increasing demands for nonprofit accountability and various approaches to measuring the performance of nonprofit organizations. Chapter 7 discusses the development of organizational strategy and the tools of strategic planning and strategic management now employed by many nonprofits. Strategic planning is often the first step in the larger undertaking of building the organization's capacity or its ability to achieve the goals identified in the plan; thus capacity building also is considered in this chapter. Chapter 8 explores collaborations and partnerships among nonprofit organizations and those that cross the sectors. In addition, recent years have brought mergers of nonprofit organizations, a topic that is also considered in Chapter 8. Chapter 9 discusses both the theory and the practice of human resource management in nonprofit organizations. One of the significant differences between many nonprofits and business or government is the substantial employment of volunteers to provide the organization's core services. Management of an unpaid workforce requires an understanding of human motivation and skill in managing effective relationships between an organization's volunteers and its paid professional staff. Chapter 10 considers the management of programs for communication and marketing, essential for organizations that are highly interactive with and dependent on the world around them. This section concludes with Chapter 11, which discusses advocacy and lobbying, important activities for many nonprofit organizations that seek to affect social change.

The next section of the book, encompassing four chapters, is concerned with the acquisition and management of resources. The securing of revenue and the management of financial resources are interrelated activities. Like many of the topics covered in this book, financial management is large, complex, and important. Chapter 12 provides a few basic concepts and directs students to additional sources from which they can obtain the more detailed understanding they may seek. Chapter 13 discusses principles of raising philanthropic funds from individual, corporate, and foundation donors. Chapter 14 explores the subject of nonprofits' earned income—that is, efforts to generate revenue through activities other than traditional philanthropy. That chapter explores the myriad and growing commercial partnerships between nonprofit organizations and corporations, including cause-related marketing, sponsorships, licensing agreements, joint ventures, and others. It also considers nonprofit business ventures, the development of revenue-generating activities that provide a stream of revenue to support mission programs. Chapter 15 considers principles involved in securing and managing grants and contracts from government, a significant source of revenue for many nonprofits.

The final section of the book includes two chapters that expand our perspective. Chapter 16 examines social entrepreneurship and social innovation. As discussed later in the text, this topic is not necessarily synonymous with the generation of earned income revenue or even with the adoption of business methods by nonprofit organizations. Nor is it always synonymous with the founding of new organizations. Rather, by the definition used in this book, it includes innovations that lead to "wide-scale change at the systemic level" (Leviner, Crutchfield, & Wells, 2006, p. 89). In other words, social entrepreneurship is related to social innovation, regardless of the specific methods or financial sources that may be involved. Chapter 17 looks beyond the United States to discuss the work of nonprofit organizations internationally. The Conclusion offers some of my final reflections and observations.

Students may observe that the book does not include a chapter on nonprofit law. Nonprofits are subject to a large and growing body of law at the local, state, and federal levels. However, I decided to discuss aspects of nonprofit law in the various chapters where they are most relevant rather than in a separate chapter. The book provides references to other resources for students who may want to know more. The book also does not include a separate chapter on ethics; rather, ethical issues are addressed at relevant points throughout the text, for example, in the discussion of Chapter 6 concerning accountability and in the ethical scenarios proposed for discussion at the end of Chapter 13 on philanthropic fundraising. At least one reviewer of the third edition suggested adding a chapter on risk management, an important topic in nonprofit management. Given the limitations of length, it was not practical to do so, but a discussion of risk management is included in relevant sections of other chapters.

Again, all the following chapters draw on the theoretical and academic literature as well as the writing of experienced practitioners and consultants. Key points are illustrated with actual cases, some drawn from the daily headlines. Students are encouraged to include the cases in their reading of each chapter, to consider the questions suggested for discussion of the cases, to consider the broader Questions for Discussion provided at the end of each chapter, and to think about the relevance of what they are reading to any nonprofit organizations with which they may have personal experience. Most also will find that the daily news within the span of almost any semester or academic year includes stories that relate to nonprofit organizations and provide real-time cases that illustrate points discussed in this book.

Ancillaries

Ancillary materials further support and enhance the learning goals of the fourth edition of *Nonprofit Management*. These ancillary materials include:

Instructor Resources

- Test banks with multiple choice, true/false and essay questions for each chapter
- Editable chapter-specific PowerPoint slides
- Sample course syllabi
- Chapter outlines
- Case activities
- Discussion questions for each chapter

Student Resources

- Video and multimedia links
- EXCLUSIVE! Access to certain full-text SAGE journal articles that have been carefully selected for each chapter

Visit study.sagepub.com/worth4e to access the support materials for *Nonprofit Management,* Fourth Edition.

Chapter Outline

Yale University became home to the first academic center devoted to the study of nonprofits. The Yale Program on Non-Profit Organizations (PONPO) was founded shortly thereafter in 1978.

Photo: © iStockPhoto.com/earntsen

Learning Objectives

After reading this chapter, students should be able to:

1. Describe the differences between management in the nonprofit sector and management in other sectors.

2. Explain various approaches to the study of nonprofit organizations.

3. Describe the growth of nonprofit management as a professional field and a field of study.

4. Explain forces that have led to the professionalization of nonprofit management.

5. Classify various authors in terms of their perspective on the nonprofit sector.

Nonprofit Management as a Profession and a Field of Study

1

This is a book about the management of nonprofit organizations. The topic begs two fundamental questions: Why do nonprofit organizations need to be managed? And, is management of a nonprofit organization really different from management of a business or government agency? In other words, is there really a need for a book like this, or is management a generic activity that could be learned as well from a textbook on business or public management?

Some may hold a perception of nonprofit organizations as primarily collections of well-intentioned people who struggle with minimal resources to meet human needs, without much attention to the bottom line, and with some disdain for management as an unwelcome distraction from the all-important work of delivering vital programs and services. However, there has been a management revolution in the nonprofit sector in recent decades, and this stereotype, if ever true, does not describe all nonprofit organizations today. Indeed, many nonprofits face management challenges no less complex than those faced by major corporations or large government agencies.

For most people, the term *nonprofit* conjures up the image of a small organization, perhaps run by a tiny band of volunteers more focused on delivering services to people in need than on building or managing an organization. Indeed, most nonprofit organizations are small, with perhaps few, if any, professional staff, but there are also others with activities that span the nation and the globe and that employ thousands of people.

Mention the word *business,* and people will likely think first of a large corporation such as Wal-Mart or Coca-Cola, although, in reality, most businesses are small. But it is large business enterprises that are the focus of most management texts and MBA case studies. That is because, as in the nonprofit sector, the need for management varies with the size and scope of activity. The corner dry cleaner needs few management skills beyond basic accounting and a rudimentary understanding of how to manage a few employees. The young technology entrepreneur starting a new business in his or her parents' garage is focused not on management but on development and delivery of a product, much as the directors of small nonprofits are often more concerned with delivering programs than with building or managing the organization. As a company grows, requiring outside investment and employing more people, its need for professional management increases. Founding entrepreneurs are often replaced by MBAs who have formal management training. So, too, as a nonprofit organization becomes larger, it faces more complex and interesting management challenges, especially if it comes to operate in more than one location across the United States or internationally. This book includes some examples drawn from small nonprofit organizations, but it is principally about organizations that have at least some full-time paid staff, and it includes examples and cases drawn from some of the nation's largest and best-known nonprofits.

services they will provide and to which customers. More sales translate into increased revenues, and activities that are not profitable can be discontinued. The same relationships do not always hold true for a nonprofit. Most nonprofits obtain resources from multiple sources and, like businesses, have considerable freedom to determine the activities in which they will engage. However, one important difference is that increased activity may strain resources rather than enhance them. That is because not all of a nonprofit's customers may pay the full cost of producing the good or service, and indeed, some may not pay at all. Judy Vredenburgh, a former executive of Big Brothers Big Sisters and the March of Dimes, describes the dilemma: "Every time we in nonprofits satisfy customers, we drain resources, and every time for-profits satisfy a customer, they get resources. That sounds very simple, but it has huge implications" (quoted in Silverman & Taliento, 2006, p. 41).

Thus, as Herman (2010) suggests, management of a nonprofit organization requires constant trade-offs among the mission, the acquisition of resources, and strategy. That distinguishes nonprofit management from the management function in the business or public sectors. Management in those sectors, while also complex, at least begins with some fixed points of clear goals and positive relationships between activities and revenues. Managing a nonprofit is more like swimming in the air, with everything variable and in constant motion.

Second, the complex relationships among a nonprofit organization's stakeholders require management that is especially skilled in negotiation and compromise, with a high tolerance for ambiguity. In corporations and in government agencies, the flow of authority from the top down is generally clear. But, as Helmut Anheier (2014) describes,

> nonprofit organizations consist of multiple components and complex, internal federations or coalitions among stakeholders . . . [therefore] the structure of nonprofit organizations may require a multi-faceted, flexible approach to management and not the use of singular, ready-made models carried over from the business world or from public management. (p. 328)

Jim Collins (2005) recounts a meeting between Frances Hesselbein, chief executive officer (CEO) of the Girl Scouts of the USA at the time, and a *New York Times* columnist, in which the CEO addressed this unique characteristic of nonprofit management:

> [The columnist] asked what it felt like to be on top of such a large organization. With patience, like a teacher pausing to impart an important lesson, Hesselbein proceeded to rearrange the lunch table, creating a set of concentric circles radiating outward—plates, cups, saucers—connected by knives, forks, spoons. Hesselbein pointed to a glass in the middle of the table. "I'm here," she said. Hesselbein may have had the title of Chief Executive Officer, but her message was clear: *I'm not on top of anything.* (p. 9)

Nonprofit management is unique because nonprofit organizations are different from businesses and governmental entities—often reliant on the support of donors and the work of volunteers, pursuing missions derived from values and principles about which there may be disagreement, and engendering a sense of ownership and a desire for influence among multiple constituencies both inside and outside the walls of the organization itself. In this environment, a nonprofit CEO must provide leadership as well as management, a distinction we will explore further in Chapter 5. Robert Higgins, who worked as both a nonprofit executive and a venture capitalist and thus was able to observe the differences between the sectors firsthand, explains,

> In most for-profit organizations . . . people arrive with common goals. The board of directors may have different viewpoints, but shareholder value as a fundamental goal is something shared by the board, by the CEO, and by senior management. You start off differently in the not-for-profit world,

with each board member arriving with a different set of goals and often different agendas. To manage that as a CEO is much more complex. (quoted in Silverman & Taliento, 2006, p. 38)

Third, managers of nonprofit organizations must measure their success by a *double bottom line*. A nonprofit exists to pursue a social mission, and success must be measured in terms of its ability to achieve that mission. That is one bottom line. But, in today's competitive environment, nonprofit managers also must pay close attention to the *financial* bottom line if their organizations are to survive and succeed. Ask a room of people, "What's the purpose of Apple?" and some may quickly reply, "To produce electronic devices," or perhaps some will joke, "To control the world!" But both responses miss the point because Apple, like all businesses, has one clear purpose: to increase the value of the business and thus the wealth of its owners. Producing products and controlling the world are but means to that end. To be sure, many corporations today are also guided by principles of social responsibility and ethics, but social progress is not their *purpose*. Indeed, social concerns are properly viewed as constraints on the pursuit of the purpose for which every business exists: to maximize profit in order to increase the value of the owners' equity. Managers may have their own personal social goals, but if they make them a central element of the company's purpose, they will not fulfill their principal responsibility to the owners of the firm.

In contrast, a nonprofit *exists* to serve a social purpose. But, as we have discussed, in today's competitive environment, financial results also require the executive's attention—he or she must manage the double bottom line of financial and social return. And the latter may be ambiguous in its definition, even a subject of disagreement and dissension among the organization's many stakeholders, or difficult to measure.

Fourth and finally, many of the problems that nonprofit managers address are exceptionally difficult and intractable. In other words, it may be more challenging to reduce poverty, prevent disease, or improve the global environment—especially when not everyone recognizes the problem or agrees on what the solutions might be—than it is to increase the sale of attractive products that people already desire to own. To say that managing a nonprofit is inherently more complex than managing a business of comparable size is not to demean the skills of business managers or to disparage their clear focus on profit. The creativity and problem-solving skills of business leaders have built great organizations and propelled economic progress. Moreover, it is the wealth created by the business sector that largely sustains nonprofits and makes social advancement possible. But the need to manage the double bottom line, to relate to disparate and competing constituencies, and often to work against the weight of deep-seated historical and cultural barriers adds complexity to the nonprofit CEO's challenge, a challenge that is too often underestimated by some who observe the nonprofit sector from a business perspective. William Novelli, a former businessman who built the public relations firm Porter Novelli and later served as the CEO of the nonprofit AARP, explains the challenge:

> It's harder to succeed in the nonprofit world. . . . It may be hard to compete in the field of consumer packaged goods or electronics or high finance . . . but it's harder to achieve goals in the nonprofit world because these goals tend to be behavioral. If you set out to do something about breast cancer in the country, or about Social Security solvency, it's a lot harder to pull that off. [And] it's also harder to measure. (quoted in Silverman & Taliento, 2006, p. 37)

This book is based on the premise that nonprofit management is a unique endeavor, distinguishable from management in business or government. It is necessary, however, to acknowledge that some see a convergence of management across the sectors in recent years, as both public managers and nonprofit managers are expected to be more businesslike and business managers are expected to demonstrate more responsibility toward the social and human impact of their actions (Salamon, 2012b). As we will discuss in the next section of this chapter, trends in nonprofit management education in universities have reflected this reality.

Nonprofit Management as a Field of Study

Students taking a course in nonprofit management today might reasonably assume that such courses have always existed. But they are a relatively recent addition to the curriculum at most colleges and universities, and scholarly research in the field, while growing, still does not approach the volume of study devoted to public or business management.

Indeed, recognition of *management* as an identifiable function—in any organizational setting—is relatively recent in the scope of history. While management-like functions have been performed throughout civilized history, the beginning of management as a field of study dates approximately to the development of an industrial economy in the late 19th century. Stephen Block (2001) credits an 1886 paper by the engineer Henry R. Towne as the first call for the development of management as an independent field of study with its own literature. The nation's first school of management, the Wharton School at the University of Pennsylvania, was established shortly thereafter, in 1898. The first two decades of the 20th century saw the growth of professional management societies, books, and university programs. The first doctoral dissertation in management was written in 1915. According to Block, interest in management was increased by the experience of American manufacturing during World War II, and the decades since have brought explosive growth in business management education and research, including the development of theories we will explore at relevant points in this book. But the early study of management was focused on business organizations, with attention to public management developing later. Mordecai Lee (2010) has identified some pioneering initiatives undertaken by the YMCA that may have represented the first efforts in nonprofit management education. They included the offering of a bachelor of association science degree by Chicago's Central YMCA College in 1911 and a 1935 textbook on the subject produced by the YMCA's publishing house. Notwithstanding those early efforts, interest in nonprofit management has emerged primarily within the past few decades.

As mentioned above, until about the 1960s, most management theorists advanced a "generic approach," arguing that their theories applied equally in all types of organizations, whether businesses, government agencies, or nonprofits. As Hal Rainey (2014), a public administration scholar, emphasizes, "With some clear exceptions . . . the theorists repeatedly implied or aggressively asserted that distinctions such as public and private, market and non-market, and governmental and nongovernmental offered little value for developing theory or understanding practice" (p. 45). However, by the 1960s, some authors began to challenge this approach and to call for more research focused specifically on the management of public agencies. This coincided with a period of growth in the federal government and the development of master of public administration (MPA) degree programs in universities, which for the first time emphasized management skills in government and differentiated the study of public management from the discipline of political science. The Network of Schools of Public Policy, Affairs, and Administration (NASPAA) was founded in 1970 and began to accredit such programs.

Attention was drawn to the nonprofit sector by an important national study conducted by the Commission on Private Philanthropy and Public Needs during the period 1973 to 1975. That commission, often called the "Filer Commission" in honor of its chair, business leader John H. Filer, issued a report titled *Giving in America* (Commission on Private Philanthropy and Public Needs, 1975), which was the most detailed study of philanthropy in the United States up to that time. The first academic center devoted to the study of nonprofits, the Yale Program on NonProfit Organizations (PONPO), was founded shortly thereafter, in 1978, and social scientists began to turn their attention to understanding the role of nonprofit organizations in economic and political life. The generic approach was beginning to yield to the view that nonprofit organizations might have unique characteristics that distinguish them from organizations in the other two sectors.

As previously discussed, the 1980s marked a turning point in public policy, with government outsourcing more of the delivery and management of social and human services to nonprofits. That development further increased the need for professional management in nonprofit organizations and captured the interest of some students previously aiming for careers in government. Public administration faculty members saw that a growing number of their students were interested in working in nonprofit organizations and responded by developing programs to teach nonprofit-specific skills (Joslyn, 2004). That decade also saw the establishment of new research centers and programs focused on the nonprofit sector, including Case Western Reserve University's Mandel Center for Nonprofit Organizations and the Center on Philanthropy at Indiana University.

Management scholars and writers turned significant attention to the nonprofit sector beginning in the 1990s. Writing in 1990, management guru Peter Drucker observed a "management boom" going on in nonprofit organizations, but he also noted the lack of recognition of nonprofit management as worthy of attention. "For most Americans," he wrote, "the word 'management' still means business management" (p. xiv). But as the nonprofit sector continued to grow throughout the 1990s and into the 2000s and 2010s, a burgeoning literature sought to adapt the theories and skills of business management to the planning, managing, and financing of nonprofits. Courses in the strategic management of nonprofits and on social entrepreneurship— a term we will discuss further later—began to proliferate in business schools, and new books applied the techniques used by companies and governments to the nonprofit sector (Oster, 1995; Steiss, 2003). The *Harvard Business Review* came to include occasional articles on the management of nonprofit organizations. The late 1990s brought an economic boom and a boom in the literature of venture philanthropy, social enterprise, entrepreneurial nonprofits, and business techniques applied to nonprofit organizations (Dees, 1998; Dees, Emerson, & Economy, 2001; Kearns, 2000; Letts, Ryan, & Grossman, 1999a; Oster, Massarsky, & Beinhacker, 2004). The Stanford University Graduate School of Business began publishing a journal, the *Stanford Social Innovation Review,* in 2003. New textbooks focused on nonprofit management began to appear, including the first edition of this text in 2009. Online journals, blogs, and other forums related to nonprofit management, social innovation, social entrepreneurship, and related topics continue to proliferate. In 2012, the Center for Philanthropy at Indiana University became the Lilly Family School of Philanthropy, the first such academic institution in the country ("School of Philanthropy to Be Named After Lilly Family," 2013).

The literature of nonprofit management is drawn from three principal areas: (1) the work of social scientists who study nonprofit organizations as social and economic institutions; (2) organizational theory, theories of organizational behavior, and management theory from the business and public sectors that have particular relevance for nonprofit organizations; and (3) a rich practitioner literature that offers important understandings. This book is based on the view that a balanced and integrated approach requires drawing on all three literatures, and that is reflected in the materials presented in the chapters that follow.

Nonprofit management, both as a profession and as an academic field of study, is still relatively young. Much of the nonprofit management literature is still written by or for practitioners and has a prescriptive, how-to-do-it approach. Consultants, including professionals working in for-profit consulting firms, also have made important contributions to the literature of nonprofit management. But there is a growing body of academic research, including the work of economists, sociologists, historians, and other social scientists who have developed taxonomies to identify and track the major components of the nonprofit sector; theories to explain the existence and behavior of the sector; theories describing its relationship to government and the business sector; examinations of its role and impact in the U.S. economy; and analyses of related public policy issues. The management of nonprofits also has been the focus of more applied studies drawn from the fields of public administration and business management.

Some scholars advocate defining a new academic field of "nonprofit studies" that would broaden the focus of nonprofit research beyond management (Mendel, 2014). Observing that "published scholarship on nonprofit organizations continues to cover primarily matters of interest to public management, business, social work, and other fields," Stuart Mendel (2014) argues that "nonprofit studies is approaching a tipping point [and is] ready to become an autonomous field of study" (p. 61). He also calls for a new approach to the training of nonprofit professionals that would go "beyond the management of transactional accountability" to include "the study of civil society; the dynamics of advocacy, community organizing, and public policy development; the political nature of the social sector; and the role that nonprofits play as places of employment" (p. 62).

This book is a textbook, not a manual for nonprofit executives. But neither is its purpose to offer an entirely theoretical examination of the nonprofit sector. Although it draws on a wide range of literature, it is intended to provide a background for nonprofit management rather than a foundation for nonprofit studies. It is intended to provide students who are considering or pursuing careers in nonprofit management with a broad overview, blending theoretical and practical topics relevant to the work they do or will do. This approach incurs the risk that some pragmatic individuals may find it too academic and that some academics may find it insufficiently grounded, but it is appropriate to provide a comprehensive and useful overview of a field that is still evolving.

Concomitant with the increase in literature, educational programs related to nonprofit management have grown rapidly since the 1990s. In a 2007 report, Mirabella revealed that the number of undergraduate programs related to nonprofit management grew by 30 percent between 1996 and 2002 and by an additional 36 percent between 2002 and 2006. By 2006, Mirabella identified a total of 426 programs in nonprofit management, offered at 238 colleges and universities. Indiana University was the first to offer a bachelor's degree in philanthropy and, as mentioned previously, in 2012 became the first university to establish a school of philanthropy. Recent years also have seen a virtual explosion in the availability of training for nonprofit managers and professional expertise directed toward the improvement of management practices in nonprofit organizations, including programs offered by educational institutions, regional associations of nonprofits, nonprofit infrastructure organizations, and for-profit consulting firms. Formal professional certification is available in some specialties of nonprofit management. For example, a professional specializing in fundraising can become a certified fundraising executive by successfully meeting criteria established by CFRE International, including an examination (see www.cfre.org for more information). And nonprofit professionals who manage volunteer programs can obtain certification from the Council for Certification in Volunteer Administration (see www.cvacert.org for more information).

Formalization of the nonprofit management curriculum in universities also has progressed. In 2001, NASPAA issued "Guidelines for Graduate Professional Education in Nonprofit Organizations, Management, and Leadership." The Nonprofit Academic Centers Council (NACC), a membership association of academic centers and programs that focus on nonprofit organizations, issued its first "Curricular Guidelines for Graduate Study in Philanthropy, the Nonprofit Sector, and Nonprofit Leadership" in 2004 and a second version in 2008. A third version was released in 2015. NACC undergraduate program guidelines were developed in 2007 and revised in 2015 (nonprofit-academic-centers-council.org).

There continues to be debate about whether nonprofit management should be taught in schools of business or management, in schools of public administration and public policy, or in other academic units. Some institutions have resolved the debate by establishing interdisciplinary centers, supported by more than one school. For example, at the University of Georgia, the Institute for Nonprofit Organizations operates as a component of the graduate school and offers coursework through departments of social work, political science, and management.

Many business school courses and programs relevant to the nonprofit sector are identified by the term *social entrepreneurship*. The term is used in different ways by various authors, and it is important to understand the distinctions. The literature reflects two schools of thought about the meaning of social entrepreneurship. J. Gregory Dees and Beth Anderson (2006) call these two perspectives the "social enterprise school" and the "social innovation school." Those in the social enterprise school think about social entrepreneurship as virtually synonymous with the application of business methods and the generation of earned income, that is, revenue that is received in exchange for goods and services provided, rather than as gifts. Those who hold this perspective propose market-based solutions to social problems and often emphasize the blurring of the sectors, advancing the idea of the double bottom line and applying it to both businesses and nonprofits. Earned income as a source of revenue for nonprofit organizations is discussed in Chapter 14 of this text.

On the other hand, those who belong to the social innovation school offer a broader definition of social entrepreneurship. In their view, a social entrepreneur is an innovator; a change agent; someone who identifies an opportunity, undertakes direct action to pursue it, and produces change that improves the condition of people and society. This may include the application of business principles and the pursuit of earned income, but not necessarily. Social entrepreneurs might access traditional philanthropy or government funds as well as earned income—whatever is needed and available—in order to implement their innovative ideas. In everyday conversation, we may think of an "entrepreneur" as someone who starts a new company or organization. Indeed, some social entrepreneurs may do so. But others may lead change within existing organizations, sometimes referred to as *intrapreneurs*. This latter definition of *social entrepreneur* is applied in Chapter 16 of this text, which discusses social entrepreneurship and social innovation in more detail.

Discussion and debate on the appropriate placement and content of programs to prepare nonprofit leaders is likely to continue. Many observers see a blurring of the nonprofit and business sectors, requiring that future nonprofit executives be trained in business skills. To some, that suggests that nonprofit management programs would be better located in business schools than in schools of public affairs and administration or in colleges of arts and sciences. But Michael O'Neill (2007), founder and former chair of the Institute for Nonprofit Organization Management at the University of San Francisco, notes that "[n]onprofits have different values, different financial systems, different laws to abide by, different people (like volunteers) to manage, and very different goals [than business organizations]" (p. 1715). He predicts that the future will see continued experimentation with regard to nonprofit programs but that business schools are unlikely to become the predominant hosts of nonprofit management programs. In addition, he predicts that despite the standards developed by NASPAA and NACC, nonprofit management curriculum is unlikely to become as standardized as the MBA curriculum in the next 20 years.

Roseanne Mirabella and Dennis Young (2012) observe the increase in the number of business school programs focusing on social entrepreneurship and speculate as to whether the future might see convergence of the content of such business school programs and "traditional" nonprofit management programs, meaning primarily those offered in schools of public policy and administration. One possibility that Mirabella and Young identify is that the traditional programs may come to incorporate more courses on social entrepreneurship, while business schools come to include more emphasis on such topics as philanthropic and political skills; in other words, the programs might become more alike. Another possibility is that the traditional and business school programs remain distinct. Echoing O'Neill (2007), the authors note that the respective academic units have different cultures and, in addition, that entrepreneurship more generally "has historically not been high in the pecking order of subjects valued within business schools" (Mirabella & Young, 2012, p. 55). The latter point is, of course, especially true if entrepreneurship is considered to be synonymous with the founding of new companies, which is an important but limited component of overall business activity.

In addition to the discussion about the relative desirability of business schools or other academic units as the home of nonprofit management, some call for more attention to nonprofits in the curriculum of all professional schools. There is an increasing number of collaborations and partnerships between nonprofits and government and between nonprofits and businesses—a topic that we will discuss in more detail in Chapter 8. This reality has contributed to some nonprofits becoming hybrids; that is, they include characteristics of businesses and government agencies as well as traditional nonprofit organizations. For that reason, some observers suggest that education about nonprofits should be integrated into the core curriculum of programs in business as well as public policy and administration and other professional fields (S. Smith, 2012).

Toward a Balanced Approach

The literature of nonprofit management reveals a variety of perspectives, not only on the questions and issues discussed previously, but indeed about the very nature and role of nonprofit organizations in society.

Generalization can, of course, sometimes lead to oversimplification; differences in perspective or approach are often nuanced. But students will likely observe that authors writing about nonprofit organizations and nonprofit management today reflect one of two perspectives on the purposes and role of nonprofits that are distinguishable, at least in tone and emphasis.

Some see nonprofit organizations primarily as social institutions. The services they provide are important, but nonprofits also are essential for creating civil society, pursuing social change, and sustaining the free expression of ideas and opinions in a democratic society—indeed, for preserving our most important values as a society. Process and involvement are valued nearly as much as the end results. In this view, involvement builds community and provides an important experience for the individuals involved, in addition to the benefits it may produce for other members of society. This is what Peter Frumkin (2002) calls the "expressive" purpose of nonprofits; that is, they provide an outlet for individuals to express their values and passions through their involvement with such organizations.

From this perspective, nonprofit managers often are portrayed as stewards of their organizations or servants of society. With regard to the education of nonprofit managers, those who hold this perspective usually emphasize the need to develop an appreciation of nonprofit values, an understanding of nonprofits' role in society, and a capacity for ethical decision making. In discussing charity and philanthropy, they tend to focus on their cultural and historical roots of giving and view giving as an expression of moral and religious values. They do not necessarily deny the usefulness of business methods in managing nonprofit organizations, but some do express skepticism about the possibility of measuring organizations' effectiveness against sometimes lofty missions. Some express concern that the application of business methods and business thinking holds the risk of undermining traditional nonprofit values and diminishing nonprofit organizations' unique contributions to society. They are often uncomfortable about nonprofits becoming too engaged in commercial activities or forming close relationships with business, fearing that nonprofit culture will be eroded and that organizations will lose sight of their social purposes in the pursuit of financial success. And, of course, depending on their social and political perspectives, some may even find it objectionable to see nonprofits associated with private businesses or government at all, perhaps viewing one or both of the latter as sources of problems that nonprofits are trying to correct.

From the other common perspective, nonprofit organizations are *social enterprises*, essentially businesses that have a social purpose. Those who hold this view do not dismiss the importance of nonprofits' social missions, nor do they necessarily deny the unique qualities and contributions of the nonprofit sector. Most give at least lip service to the idea that a business approach may not be appropriate for every nonprofit organization. However, they tend to emphasize the commonalities between nonprofit organizations and business firms and encourage the use of business principles and techniques in managing nonprofits.

Those who hold this perspective often discuss the education of nonprofit managers in terms of developing business skills. Their discussions often focus on building the capacity of nonprofits and the application of business methods, such as strategic planning, strategic management, performance management, and marketing. They often use the vocabulary of business, discussing a nonprofit organization's "competitive advantage" and "sustainability." Some criticize traditional charity and philanthropy and prefer that nonprofits rely more on earned income rather than on gifts. They emphasize what Frumkin (2002) calls the "instrumental" purposes of nonprofits, that is, the services that they provide and the needs they meet, rather than their role as vehicles for individuals' expression. They are concerned about results and the measurement of organizational performance against defined metrics. Some even support the idea of nonprofit capital markets that would allocate funds rationally to nonprofit organizations that show high performance, much as stock markets allocate investment dollars to the companies that produce the highest financial returns. Indeed, recent years have seen the initiation of new corporate forms and market-based approaches, which we will address at an appropriate point later in this book.

Again, the above characterizations of these two perspectives are oversimplified, and some writers take a moderate or blended stance between the two poles described. But it is usually not difficult to identify a particular book or article as leaning toward one perspective or the other. This text draws on literature from both approaches and strives to present a balanced and integrated understanding. Where disagreements may exist, it attempts to fairly summarize both sides of the argument. That is because this author believes that effective nonprofit management in today's environment indeed requires a balanced and integrated approach that draws upon diverse perspectives, skills, and tools.

That approach leads to the frequent use of the expression "on the one hand, but on the other hand" throughout this book. Some might prefer to know the "right answer" and learn what is the best way to lead a nonprofit organization. The philosophy reflected in this book is that there is often no one right answer and that the best way is often pragmatic and eclectic. It includes viewing a problem from multiple perspectives and drawing from various approaches selectively as situations may dictate. Students will find abundant other materials written by authors who come from one particular viewpoint or another that they may find to be especially attractive or persuasive.

Proceeding With Realism and Pride

This book is based on the view that while there is a need to improve the management of nonprofit organizations, it is a misperception to believe, as some do, that they are generically less well managed than businesses. This misperception is based in part on our society's bias toward defining success primarily in financial terms. The results of good business management are evident in bottom-line earnings, while the results of nonprofit management are reflected in progress toward a social mission, which may be less visible or easy to measure. In addition, the misperception is often reinforced when apples are compared with oranges, which may occur, for example, if someone's image of a nonprofit is as a small organization and that person's image of a business is that of a larger corporation. It may be accurate to observe that some small nonprofits are not well managed. But, it is important to note, the same is true of many small businesses, most of which fail in the first five years of their existence. It might be difficult to demonstrate that a family-run bed and breakfast is really better managed than the local homeless shelter, which would be more appropriate than comparing the shelter with a Marriott hotel.

When nonprofit organizations and companies are compared fairly, we find poor and excellent management in both. For example, the American Red Cross, one of the nation's largest nonprofits, confronted many management problems during the 2000s, which were widely publicized. In that decade, there were also highly visible scandals concerning executive compensation and expenses at American University and the Smithsonian Institution and allegations of conflict-of-interest problems at the Nature Conservancy, one of the nation's largest environmental nonprofits. In 2015, the Federal Trade Commission (FTC) alleged that James T. Reynolds Sr. had used nearly $200 million that had been given to cancer charities that he operated to pay for personal benefits for himself, friends, and family members. The FTC characterized it as one of the largest charity scandals in history (Ruiz, 2015). However, it is fair to ask, was the Red Cross less well managed than General Motors, which required a federal government bailout? Or were ethical failures at nonprofits more egregious than those at many financial institutions, which did as well? Were the allegations against Reynolds more shocking than those against Bernard Madoff, who was convicted of running a Ponzi scheme that cost investors millions of dollars? We might also ask, are Habitat for Humanity and Doctors Without Borders less innovative organizations than Microsoft or Google? Is the Mayo Clinic less capable of managing risk than BP? In a sequel to his best-selling book on business management, which focuses on the social (or nonprofit) sector, Jim Collins (2005) argues that the important difference is not between business management and nonprofit management, but between mediocrity and greatness:

Most businesses—like most of anything else in life—fall somewhere between mediocre and good. Few are great. Mediocre companies rarely display the relentless culture of discipline . . . that we find in truly great companies. [But] a culture of discipline is not a principle of business; it is a principle of greatness. (p. 1)

The author's purpose in making this point is to dispel any misperceptions that students may hold that nonprofit management is somehow second rate or, as implied by critical articles seen in the popular media, that incompetence and corruption are rampant in nonprofit organizations. Nonprofit managers are in general highly capable and dedicated individuals, worthy of the respect and regard of their counterparts in the other sectors of business and government. They work in organizations that are different from businesses or government, they have different purposes and goals, and they often work with fewer resources available to them, but they are not categorically less able or successful. Students pursuing education in nonprofit management should do so with a pride and confidence equal to that of their classmates who may be preparing for careers in business, government, or other distinguished professions.

At the same time, students should hold no illusions about the challenges of a nonprofit management career. Although salaries are improving, nonprofit managers are unlikely to achieve the wealth of their counterparts in business or the job security of their colleagues who hold civil service positions in the government. The pressures are significant. As Julie Rogers (2006), former president of the Eugene and Agnes Meyer Foundation, observes, nonprofit executives face a never-ending stream of advice from their boards, funders, clients, volunteers, and others: "Focus on finding dependable sources of income. Produce measurable results. Evaluate whether you are making a difference. Be strategic, not opportunistic. Build diverse boards. Spend more time on advocacy. Collaborate with other organizations" (pp. 45–46). And, too often, they are advised to do all this with smaller budgets, smaller staffs, less training, and less recognition than is provided to managers in business or government. Indeed, a 2011 study found that the complexity of the nonprofit manager's job and the multiple pressures he or she must handle frequently lead to frustration and burnout (*Daring to Lead* (Moyers, 2011)).

However, nonprofit managers also enjoy unique rewards, including the satisfaction of knowing that they are working to advance those aspects of human life that many consider to be the most important— the arts, education, the preservation of culture, the alleviation of poverty, and the development of young people. They experience the excitement of tackling some of society's most daunting problems and protecting society's most vulnerable members, making a difference in their lives and in the future of society. And they know the camaraderie and fellowship that comes from working alongside others who share their values, priorities, and commitments. For many who have dedicated their careers to working in nonprofit organizations, the value of such intangible rewards is beyond measure.

Chapter Summary

Through most of history, management scholars pursued a generic approach, believing that management in companies, government agencies, and nonprofits shared similar principles. But nonprofit management is a distinct profession because of the unique characteristics, missions, and cultures of nonprofits. Since the 1980s, this uniqueness has been recognized in the development of research centers and academic programs focused on the nonprofit sector and nonprofit management. By 2006, there were more than 400 programs in nonprofit management at colleges and universities. There continues to be discussion about whether such programs should be located in business schools, in schools of public policy and administration, or in other academic units.

Those who discuss social entrepreneurship reflect two schools of thought. Some people mean the pursuit of business income by nonprofits. Others define a social entrepreneur as someone who leads innovation and brings about systemic change, whether using business methods or some other strategy. Some think that business school programs in social entrepreneurship and traditional nonprofit management programs may converge. Others note the different cultures in various academic units and predict that such programs will remain distinct. Some advocate incorporating nonprofit management topics in the core curriculum in all professional degree programs. Some universities have established interdisciplinary centers for the study of nonprofits, which draw on faculty from various academic fields.

People hold two different perspectives on the purpose and role of nonprofits in society, which influences their views on how and where nonprofit leaders should be educated. Some consider nonprofits to be social institutions and emphasize their expressive purposes, that is, opportunities that they provide for people to express their values and passions through involvement. Others consider them to be social enterprises, essentially like business firms with a social purpose. They emphasize their instrumental purposes, that is, the services they provide and needs they meet. Many writers reflect a balanced understanding, but most tend to emphasize one or the other perspective. This book attempts to blend these perspectives and to provide a balanced overview of the field. This author believes that successful nonprofit management requires an eclectic approach, drawing concepts and tools from the work of scholars, practitioners, consultants, and others, as they are found to be useful in specific situations.

Although some people portray nonprofits as less well managed than businesses, that perception often is inaccurate. Small nonprofits should be compared to small businesses, which also often reveal mediocre management, and which often fail, rather than to large corporations. Many companies are innovative and well managed, and so are many nonprofit organizations. Students preparing for careers in nonprofit management should proceed with pride and confidence that their field is as distinguished as management in business or government. A nonprofit career brings challenges but also unique rewards.

KEY TERMS AND CONCEPTS

double bottom line

interdisciplinary field of study

intrapreneur

management

social entrepreneurship/social entrepreneur

QUESTIONS FOR DISCUSSION

1. Should preparation for a career in the nonprofit sector emphasize management skills or a broader understanding of civil society and the role of nonprofit organizations?

2. If nonprofit management challenges are as complex as those in business, should nonprofit managers be compensated at the same levels as managers at comparably large companies? Why or why not?

3. Should nonprofit organizations be viewed principally as businesses with a social purpose, or are they inherently different from for-profit companies?

SUGGESTIONS FOR FURTHER READING

Books/Journals

Ashcraft, R. F., & Stone, M. M. (Eds.). (2012, September). *Nonprofit management and leadership, 23*(1) [Special Issue: BenchMark 3.5 Conference on Nonprofit and Philanthropic Studies].

Frumkin, P. (2002). *On being nonprofit: A conceptual and policy primer.* Cambridge, MA: Harvard University Press.

FIGURE 2.1 ■ Overview of the Nonprofit Sector

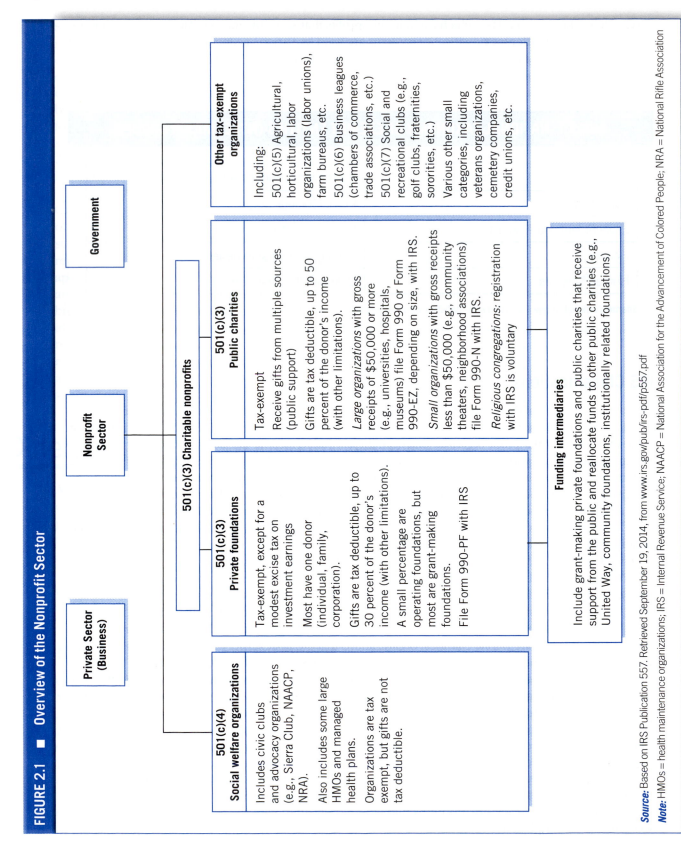

Private Sector (Business)

Nonprofit Sector

Government

501(c)(3) Charitable nonprofits

501(c)(4)
Social welfare organizations

Includes civic clubs and advocacy organizations (e.g., Sierra Club, NAACP, NRA).

Also includes some large HMOs and managed health plans.

Organizations are tax exempt, but gifts are not tax deductible.

501(c)(3)
Private foundations

Tax-exempt, except for a modest excise tax on investment earnings

Most have one donor (individual, family, corporation).

Gifts are tax deductible, up to 30 percent of the donor's income (with other limitations).

A small percentage are operating foundations, but most are grant-making foundations.

File Form 990-PF with IRS

501(c)(3)
Public charities

Tax-exempt

Receive gifts from multiple sources (public support)

Gifts are tax deductible, up to 50 percent of the donor's income (with other limitations).

Large organizations with gross receipts of $50,000 or more (e.g., universities, hospitals, museums) file Form 990 or Form 990-EZ, depending on size, with IRS.

Small organizations with gross receipts less than $50,000 (e.g., community theaters, neighborhood associations) file Form 990-N with IRS.

Religious congregations: registration with IRS is voluntary

Other tax-exempt organizations

Including:

501(c)(5) Agricultural, horticultural, labor organizations (labor unions), farm bureaus, etc.

501(c)(6) Business leagues (chambers of commerce, trade associations, etc.)

501(c)(7) Social and recreational clubs (e.g., golf clubs, fraternities, sororities, etc.)

Various other small categories, including veterans organizations, cemetery companies, credit unions, etc.

Funding intermediaries

Include grant-making private foundations and public charities that receive support from the public and reallocate funds to other public charities (e.g., United Way, community foundations, institutionally related foundations)

Source: Based on IRS Publication 557. Retrieved September 19, 2014, from www.irs.gov/pub/irs-pdf/p557.pdf

Note: HMOs = health maintenance organizations; IRS = Internal Revenue Service; NAACP = National Association for the Advancement of Colored People; NRA = National Rifle Association

Let's take a closer look at the 501(c)(3) and 501(c)(4) organizations that are the primary types discussed in this book. Although they are fewer in number than the charitable nonprofits, this chapter will first discuss the 501(c)(4) nonprofits, known to the IRS as *social welfare organizations*. Then let's return to discuss the charitable nonprofits that are the largest component of the sector.

Social Welfare Organizations

There are different types of organizations that are classified under Section 501(c)(4). A small number are HMOs and other medical and dental insurance plans, although they account for the major portion of the revenues in the 501(c)(4) category (Roeger, Blackwood, & Pettijohn, 2012). In this book, we generally ignore those organizations and focus on the vast majority of 501(c)(4)s that are considered advocacy organizations, because their purpose is to advance a cause or work for social change.

It is important at this point to distinguish between two concepts: the tax *exemption* of organizations themselves and the tax *deductibility* of gifts made to them. *All* organizations represented in Figure 2.1 are *tax-exempt*; that is, they are not required to pay federal taxes on their income. (As an exception, private foundations do pay a modest excise tax on their investment earnings.) As noted earlier in the chapter, organizations exempt from federal income tax are usually also granted exemption from state and local income taxes, which increases the benefits attached to this status. However, *only* those classified under Section 501(c)(3)—the charitable nonprofits—are tax-exempt themselves and *also* eligible to receive gifts that are tax deductible for the donors. Thus, the NAACP and the NRA, which are classified under 501(c)(4), are tax-exempt, but gifts made to them are not tax deductible for the donor because the NAACP and NRA are not classified as charitable organizations.

Advocacy organizations are tax-*exempt*—under Section 501(c)(4)—because they work, in the IRS's (n.d.b) words, "to further the common good and general welfare of the people of a community (such as bringing about civic betterment and social improvements)." But they cannot receive tax-*deductible* gifts. Why are advocacy organizations different from charitable nonprofits in the eyes of the tax code? One big difference between 501(c)(3) and 501(c)(4) organizations is that the latter do not face the same limitations on political activity that are imposed on the former. They can spend money on lobbying without limitation (IRS, n.d.-a). This is a point we will return to discussing in more detail in Chapter 11 of this text.

Because of the different advantages enjoyed and disadvantages experienced by 501(c)(3) and 501(c)(4) organizations, in terms of the tax treatment of gifts and the limitations on lobbying, some organizations have two arms—actually, two separately incorporated but related organizations. One organization is qualified under Section 501(c)(4) and is free to engage in lobbying without restriction. It cannot receive deductible gifts, but it can raise funds through member dues and others types of revenue. The other related organization is qualified under Section 501(c)(3) and is thus eligible to receive tax-deductible gifts. It pursues education, research, and other activities consistent with that classification.

Box 2.2 provides an example in the form of mission statements for the Sierra Club, an internationally known environmental organization based in the United States, and the related Sierra Club Foundation. The Sierra Club itself is a 501(c)(4) social welfare organization that works to preserve the environment, including lobbying for environmental protection legislation. The Sierra Club Foundation is a 501(c)(3) organization that supports certain activities of the Sierra Club and other environmental programs. As its description carefully explains, the foundation limits its support to "education, litigation, and training," activities that are consistent with the "charitable, scientific, literary, and educational purposes" allowed for 501(c)(3) organizations. Note the subtle differences in the mission statements of the two organizations. The Sierra Club's mission includes "enlisting" humanity, which suggests the possibility of building political coalitions and encouraging individuals to political action. The foundation supports projects that directly "preserve and restore" the environment and that "educate, inspire, and empower" the citizenry. The latter purposes are something that might be accomplished merely by providing individuals with information—that is, through education—without any call to political action. These may seem like subtle differences, but facing the possibility of an audit by the IRS and wishing to protect the tax status of both entities, most organizations are precise in monitoring their activities for consistency with tax law.

Charitable Nonprofits

Now let's turn to the two boxes shown in the middle of Figure 2.1—the charitable nonprofits that are public charities and the charitable nonprofits that are private foundations, both tax-exempt under Section 501(c)(3). These two groups have some characteristics in common, but in other ways, they are different.

All charitable nonprofits are not only tax-exempt but are eligible to receive tax-deductible contributions. The tax deductibility of gifts made to charitable nonprofits obviously provides a significant advantage to them in their fundraising efforts. Consider an individual donor who is in a 25 percent federal tax bracket and who makes a deductible gift of $100 to a charitable nonprofit organization. He or she can deduct that $100 from his or her income before calculating the income tax due. The donor's taxable income is reduced by $100, so the donor's tax bill is reduced by 25 percent of that amount, or $25. This is

---

BOX 2.2 COMPARISON OF CHARITABLE AND SOCIAL WELFARE (ADVOCACY) ORGANIZATIONS

Mission of the Sierra Club, a 501(c)(4) Organization

To explore, enjoy, and protect the wild places of the earth;

To practice and promote the responsible use of the earth's ecosystems and resources;

To educate and enlist humanity to protect and restore the quality of the natural and human environment; and to use all lawful means to carry out these objectives.

Source: Sierra Club website. Retrieved September 20, 2014, from www.sierraclub.org/policy.

Mission of the Sierra Club Foundation, a 501(c)(3) Organization

To help educate, inspire, and empower humanity to preserve the natural and human environment by

i. providing resources to the Sierra Club and, in appropriate circumstances, other nonprofit organizations, for charitable programs that protect and restore the environment;

ii. raising funds, donated for tax-exempt charitable purposes; and

iii. preserving, enhancing, and administering these funds.

Source: Sierra Club (2013).

Description of the Sierra Club Foundation

Founded in 1960, the Sierra Club Foundation is a 501(c)(3) tax-exempt public charity governed by an independent board of directors.

Our board and staff raise charitable funds, preserve and enhance these assets, and ensure they are used appropriately. As the fiscal sponsor of the charitable programs of the Sierra Club, we provide resources to it and other nonprofit organizations to support scientific, educational, literary, organizing, advocacy, and legal programs that further our charitable goals.

We work with individual and institutional donors to align financial resources with strategically focused campaigns, help build capacity in the environmental movement, and create partnerships with a broad spectrum of allied organizations that further our shared environmental goals.

We do this so that future generations will inherit a healthy planet with wild places left to explore.

Source: Sierra Club Foundation website. www.sierraclubfoundation.org/about-tscf.

considered a tax savings because, were it not for the gift, the donor would have paid that amount in additional federal income tax. The out-of-pocket cost of the $100 gift is thus reduced, from $100 to $75 ($100 minus the $25 tax savings). Some view the savings as a form of tax subsidy, or tax expenditure, in the form of foregone federal revenue. And, since many states also permit the deduction of charitable gifts, the donor often has an additional savings on taxes at the state level.

The tax deduction for gifts to charitable organizations is intended to encourage charitable giving and sustain the services provided by charitable organizations. It should not be viewed as a tax "loophole" because it is intentionally provided as an incentive to giving. Society has determined that the purposes nonprofits serve are to the public benefit and that if the nonprofits did not exist, those services might need to be provided by government. Being eligible to receive deductible gifts makes it easier for charitable nonprofits to raise funds, since the donors are, at least theoretically, able to give more because of the tax saving realized from the deductions.

To be recognized as tax-exempt under Section 501(c)(3), an organization must demonstrate three things; in other words, it must meet three tests. First, it must be *organized and operated* for one or more of eight purposes: charitable, religious, educational, scientific, literary, testing for public safety, fostering national or international amateur sports competitions, and prevention of cruelty to children and animals. (Curiously, the IRC does not specifically mention health care, although it is one of the largest components of the nonprofit sector.) The term *charitable* may seem somewhat imprecise, but the IRS (n.d.-a) defines it to include certain specific activities:

> relief of the poor, the distressed, or the underprivileged; advancement of religion; advancement of education or science; erection or maintenance of public buildings, monuments, or works; less-ening the burdens of government; lessening of neighborhood tensions; elimination of prejudice and discrimination; defense of human and civil rights secured by law; and combating community deterioration and juvenile delinquency.

In addition to demonstrating that its primary purposes include one or more of those discussed above, a 501(c)(3) nonprofit must meet two requirements. It must meet the nondistribution test, ensuring that its assets are not being used to benefit individual owners and that its managers are not being person-ally enriched through excessive compensation. And it must limit its political activities. A nonprofit that qualifies under Section 501(c)(3) cannot support candidates for public office, and again, it must limit its expenditures on lobbying—that is, efforts to influence legislation.

Charitable Subsectors. In this section, we will take a brief look at the major subsectors of the charitable non-profits, excluding religious congregations. Bear in mind that, as shown in Figure 2.1, religious congregations are charitable nonprofits under the tax code and they are tax-exempt under Section 501(c)(3). However, as we have noted before, religion is a unique component of the nonprofit sector. The U.S. Constitution guaran-tees the separation of church and state. Gifts to religious congregations are tax deductible, but congregations are not required to register with the IRS, although about half of them do so voluntarily (Giving USA, 2014). The principle of separation of church and state prevents government funds from going directly to religious congregations or to organizations that would use them for religious activities. However, congregations are to be distinguished from *faith-based organizations* that provide social services, which can receive government funds to support their secular programs. Federal legislation passed in 1996, 1998, and 2000 included *chari-table choice* provisions to allow faith-based organizations to receive grants under federally funded programs, and proposals to further increase the ability of faith-based nonprofits to obtain such funding generated controversy during the first term of President George W. Bush.[3] This book does not specifically discuss the management of religious congregations—for example, churches, synagogues, and mosques. Religious orga-nizations are the least professionalized of the subsectors. Although there has been some growth in the num-ber of church managers, the management of most congregations is still done by the clergy and volunteers.

As discussed below, the charitable subsectors differ significantly in their sources of revenue, the degree of commercialization they reflect, and the extent to which their management has been professionalized—that is, the extent to which they are run by paid staff rather than volunteers.

Arts, Culture, and Humanities. The arts and culture subsector includes museums, performing arts groups, art galleries, folk-life organizations, nonprofit radio and television stations, literary societies, arts education organizations, media and communications organizations, and arts councils and agencies. In 2012, this subsector accounted for almost 10 percent of charitable nonprofits, but only 1.8 percent of the sector's expenses (McKeever & Pettijohn, 2014, p. 6). This sector receives substantial earned income from admission fees, gift shops, and other sources and also receives gifts from individuals, corporations, and foundations. The management of arts institutions and that of museums are specialty areas within nonprofit management, and professionals often will have attended university programs focused on these fields.

Education. Education is perhaps the subsector best known to students. It includes colleges and universities, preschool, elementary and secondary schools, correspondence schools, libraries, parent–teacher groups, and education support organizations. Of course, most educational institutions are not nonprofits; they are entities controlled by state or local governments, including public schools and public universities and colleges.

It will not surprise students to learn that educational institutions receive a significant portion of their revenues from fees for service, including tuition. But anyone who has graduated from a college, university, or independent school knows that such institutions also actively seek gifts from alumni, parents, and other individuals who are affiliated. Educational institutions, and nonprofits with an educational mission, accounted for about 17 percent of the sector in 2012 and for more than 17 percent of all expenditures in the sector. College and university are among the largest organizations in the sector; while they account for just 0.7 percent of all nonprofits, their expenditures account for more than 11 percent of the total (McKeever & Pettijohn, 2014, p. 6).

Higher education, in particular, is a field in which professional management has increased in recent decades. While the senior executives of colleges and universities are still predominantly drawn from the academic ranks, on most campuses, there has been a proliferation of midlevel management in areas such as fundraising, student services, and financial administration. Middle management has grown as colleges and universities have faced increased competitive pressures, greater governmental regulation, and the need to expand revenues through intensified fundraising programs.

While for-profit education firms—for example, the University of Phoenix and Kaplan—have grown in recent decades, most schools, colleges, and universities remain either nonprofit or government controlled.

Environment and Animals. While the environment and the welfare of animals are important purposes, organizations working in these fields—including environmental preservation organizations, recycling programs, pollution abatement programs, animal protection organizations, wildlife preservation organizations, and zoos—constitute the smallest charitable subsector, representing only 4.5 percent of public charities and 0.9 percent of the nonprofit sector's expenses (McKeever & Pettijohn, 2014, p. 6). It is also a subsector that is highly dependent on charitable gifts, with relatively few opportunities to generate income from fees or sales. It is important to note that a number of organizations advocating for environmental issues and animal protection are 501(c)(4) organizations, rather than charitable nonprofits under 501(c)(3). The Sierra Club was mentioned earlier as one example. Such organizations are not included in the totals stated here for this charitable subsector.

Health. The health services subsector is the largest component of the overall nonprofit sector if measured by total revenue, expenditures, or the number of employees. It includes hospitals, home health agencies, outpatient clinics, hospice programs, nursing homes, some HMOs, dialysis centers, community health centers, residential treatment programs for emotionally disturbed youth, blood banks, public health organizations, and disease organizations such as the March of Dimes and American Cancer Society.

The health subsector is huge. While health organizations account for only 13.4 percent of public charities, they represent nearly 60 percent of the nonprofit sector's total expenses and more than 42 percent of the sector's total assets. The health subsector's revenues in 2012 accounted for 59 percent of all revenue in the sector, most of which came from fees for medical services and goods provided (McKeever & Pettijohn, 2014, p. 6).

Health services is the most commercialized of the nonprofit subsectors; in other words, many of the organizations are businesslike in deriving most of their revenue from fees charged for services provided. It also was one of the first subsectors to become professionalized in its management—that is, to develop large paid professional management staffs rather than depend on volunteers. There are many university programs in health care management and public health, and the salaries of many professional managers in the health subsector, especially in hospitals and large medical centers, are comparable to those in private industry. It is also a field in which nonprofits compete with for-profit firms to a significant extent. In some industries—for example, nursing homes—for-profits have captured the major portion of the market. The health services subsector also has seen the conversion of some nonprofits into for-profit entities, including insurance plans, hospitals, and nursing homes.

Human Services. Human service nonprofits account for more than one third of all public charities, making it the largest subsector if measured by the number of organizations (McKeever & Pettijohn, 2014). It includes what many people conventionally think about when the term *nonprofit* is used—organizations that provide job training, legal aid, housing, youth development, disaster assistance, and food distribution programs (Roeger et al., 2012). But many of these organizations are small; together they represent only 10.5 percent of the nonprofit sector's total assets and 12.8 percent of its total expenses (McKeever & Pettijohn, 2014, p. 6). Although many people might consider organizations in these fields as among the most charitable, they are in fact among the most reliant on government funds, a reality that is discussed in further detail in Chapter 14 (Roeger et al., 2012). That reflects the devolution and outsourcing of social programs over recent decades, as mentioned earlier in this text. This dependence on government funds also makes many human service organizations vulnerable when public policy shifts and government social spending declines. They are also vulnerable, of course, to declines in giving during economic recession, just when the need for their services may be increasing. For this reason, among others, many of the efforts to diversify revenues by developing alternative sources, including business enterprises, have occurred in this subsector. It is also the focus of much of the discussion regarding the need for improved management and accountability in the nonprofit sector as a whole. While there are certainly many volunteers working in human service organizations, there also has been a trend toward more professionalized management of such organizations in recent decades. In many instances, volunteers are managed by staff who have specialized training and skills in the management of volunteer programs.

International and Foreign Affairs. The subsector of international and foreign affairs includes over 6,100 organizations. They encompass those engaged with international exchange programs, international development and relief efforts, international peace and security, and human rights. It is a relatively small subsector, accounting for just 1.8 percent of expenditures by all public charities reporting to the IRS (McKeever & Pettijohn, 2014).

Public and Social Benefit. This subsector encompasses nonprofits involved in community improvement, the promotion of philanthropy and voluntarism, science and technology, and social science. In total, this group of diverse organizations accounts for 12 percent of all nonprofits and about 5 percent of the sector's expenditures (McKeever & Pettijohn, 2014, p. 6).

chapter 3

Chapter Outline

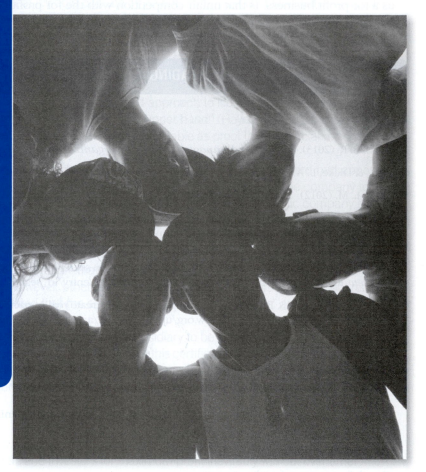

The freedoms of speech, religion, assembly, and petition, enshrined in the First Amendment to the U.S. Constitution, have supported voluntary action by nonprofit organizations on issues such as civil rights, women's rights, and the environment. Nonprofits often have focused public attention and helped create changes in social attitudes that paved the way for eventual legislative action.

Photo: Thinkstock/Comstock/Thinkstock

Learning Objectives

After reading this chapter, students should be able to:

1. Summarize key theories from various disciplines that explain the nonprofit sector.
2. Define public, private, and common goods and the role of nonprofit organizations in providing them.
3. Summarize key theories explaining the behavior of nonprofit organizations.
4. Explain factors influencing the organizational structure of organizations.
5. Analyze cases, applying concepts from the chapter.

Theories of the Nonprofit Sector and Nonprofit Organizations

3

In this chapter, we will discuss some theoretical views of the nonprofit sector and nonprofit organizations, as a foundation for consideration of more applied management topics in later chapters. We will first examine some macro theories advanced by scholars from various disciplines. These theories attempt to explain the nonprofit sector as a whole, addressing questions such as why the nonprofit sector exists at all in the United States; what role it plays in American society; and what relationship it has to the other two sectors, private business and government. In the second section of the chapter, we will consider some micro theories—that is, theories that attempt to explain nonprofit organizations as individual units. These will include concepts drawn from organizational theory that help explain why nonprofit organizations look and behave the way they do, how they make decisions, and how they are different from both public and for-profit organizations.

Explaining the Nonprofit Sector

Theories that seek to explain America's nonprofit sector have been developed by economists, sociologists, historians, political scientists, psychologists, social psychologists, anthropologists, and scholars in other disciplines. As we will discuss, some theories are at odds with others, and each theory has its advocates as well as critics. Some prominent theories are discussed in this chapter and are summarized in Box 3.1.

Nonprofit Theory Across the Disciplines

Historians explain the existence of America's nonprofit sector as largely a result of historical forces and events. As noted in Chapter 2, the growth of America's nonprofit sector closely parallels the development of the nation itself. The nation was founded in rebellion against the authority of the British monarch, and skepticism toward government is deeply embedded in American political attitudes. Moreover, many American towns and cities developed before local governments did, and vital services often were provided by voluntary associations, including volunteer fire departments, libraries, schools, and hospitals. In the small towns of early America, people came together to meet common needs and provide for the poor, their voluntarism often reflecting religious convictions. Religion played an important role in colonial

chapter 4

Chapter Outline

Working successfully with the board is critical to an executive's effectiveness. Since in most cases the CEO is appointed by and reports to the board, it is also essential to his or her professional survival.

Photo: Goodshoot/Goodshoot/Thinkstock

Learning Objectives

After reading this chapter, students should be able to:

1. Describe various types of boards.
2. Explain the advantages and disadvantages of various types of boards.
3. Explain the governing board's legal and functional responsibilities.
4. Summarize prominent models of the board–CEO relationship.
5. Summarize theories regarding board behavior.
6. Explain the roles of the board chair, governance committee, and board professionals.
7. Summarize board best practices.
8. Analyze cases, applying concepts from the chapter.

Nonprofit Governing Boards

4

The governing board of a nonprofit organization holds ultimate responsibility for ensuring that the organization serves its mission and for the overall welfare of the organization itself. In addition, as we discussed in Chapter 3, the board plays a critical boundary-spanning role in the open system of a nonprofit organization, connecting the nonprofit to its community and constituencies, often including important sources of financial support. Understanding the board's responsibilities and role and knowing how to work with the board is an essential skill of effective nonprofit managers, especially chief executive officers (CEOs). This chapter will discuss the nature and responsibilities of governing boards, some characteristics of effective boards, and some challenges faced by nonprofit boards today. It also will consider the important question of the relationship between the board and the organization's CEO. But before we get started, it is important to clarify some terminology.

The boards we are concerned with here are those that have a legal responsibility for governing their organizations—they are *governing boards*. Nonprofit organizations may have various groups that are called "boards" but that do not have such responsibilities—for example, advisory groups that may contribute their expertise to the organization and help raise funds but that do not hold any legal authority for its governance. We will discuss advisory boards and councils briefly later in this chapter, but it is important to recognize that while such boards may play an important role in the organization, they are not governing boards and they are not a principal focus of this chapter.

Nonprofit organizations may use different terms to identify their governing boards. Most nonprofits are chartered as corporations, and members of the governing board are directors of the corporation under the law. Thus, many organizations use the term *board of directors* to identify them. Educational, cultural, and medical institutions often use the term *board of trustees*. Other organizations may use the term *board of governors, governing council,* or something else to describe their governing boards. This book generally uses the generic term, *governing board,* except when discussing the board of a specific organization, in which case it maintains the name that organization uses.

In many cases, the person who heads the board is called the *president* of the organization, and the paid staff person who manages the organization is called the *director* or *executive director.* Some nonprofits—especially universities, hospitals, and major arts and cultural institutions—have adopted corporate terminology, calling the head of the board the *chair* and the paid executive the *president.* Others have adopted another corporate term, *chief executive officer,* or just *CEO,* to identify the top paid staff person. This chapter refers to the top board officer as the chair and the paid executive of the organization as the CEO.

One more point before we begin our discussion: The previous two chapters have drawn primarily from the academic literature, but this chapter also relies significantly on the practitioner literature. Although the body of academic research on nonprofit boards is growing, a substantial and influential literature on the topic has been developed by practicing nonprofit managers and consultants who work with boards and CEOs. Most of it *describes* what boards do or *prescribes* practices that boards should follow. This chapter draws on both academic and the practitioner literature, including the work of some authors who are academics but also provide applied advice to boards.

Types of Governing Boards

Nonprofit governing boards are not all the same. For one thing, they differ in the way their members are selected. This may have important implications for how they operate and what agendas, priorities, and pressures members may bring to their work on the board. Different types of boards also may interact differently with the organization's CEO. For anyone working in a nonprofit organization, especially as a CEO or other senior executive, understanding how individuals come to be sitting at the governing board table is essential to understanding and working successfully with the board. Working successfully with the board is not only critical to the executive's effectiveness, it is also essential to his or her success, since in most cases the CEO is appointed by and is evaluated by the board. Table 4.1 summarizes types of boards and some of the advantages and disadvantages of each, which are discussed in the following paragraphs.

Elected Boards

Some boards are *elected* by the membership of the organization. This is common in member-serving and advocacy organizations. The methods used to elect the governing board vary; for example, some elections are conducted by mail, and others are conducted at an annual meeting. Depending on the political and cultural environment within the organization, elections may be contested, and some individuals may, in effect, campaign for seats on the board. In other cases, a nominating committee of the existing board presents recommended candidates, who are often approved in a *pro forma* vote (that is, as a formality) by the membership.

Having an elected board may result in uncertainty about who will govern the organization from one year to the next—the outcome of elections is not always assured, and this may present a challenge to the CEO. What the board expects of the CEO may change; alliances and factions on the board may develop and shift; and the board's values and priorities may be dynamic, as political and philosophical crosscurrents among the membership find their way into the boardroom. The controversy that surrounded the election of the Sierra Club's board in 2004 provides an interesting illustration.

In 2004, anyone could join the Sierra Club with a $25 dues payment, and all members were eligible to vote in the election of the board. (That was an unusually low threshold for voting eligibility. Many organizations limit those eligible to vote to members who have been active for a certain period of time.) The Sierra Club's board included 15 members, and five seats were open for election that year. Individuals who were strong advocates for more restrictive U.S. immigration began to organize and encourage people sympathetic to their views to join the Sierra Club. Their goal was to have their sympathizers elect new board members who would change the Club's position on the immigration issue. Within three months, 30,000 people became new members of the Sierra Club, compared with only 22,000 the previous year. Some of these new members had been organized by the anti-immigration candidates who were, in effect, running for the board. The election became contentious. Some described the outsiders' efforts as a "hostile takeover" and accused them of pursuing "the greening of hate." Others portrayed their efforts as addressing needed reform in the Club's operation and claimed that their election would increase the Club's effectiveness (Greene, 2004).

The insurgents did not prevail, but the Sierra Club case illustrates the potentially tumultuous environment that may be created when governing boards are elected by an organization's membership. To be the CEO of such an organization requires a high tolerance for discussion, debate, and uncertainty. In addition, the membership terms of an elected board tend to be relatively brief, and turnover on the board may make it difficult to sustain its focus on long-range goals and plans. Doing so requires considerable repetition of presentations and discussions, to maintain consensus among the changing membership of the board. It may be difficult to motivate members of an elected board to make gifts or engage in fundraising, since the ability and inclination to do so have not been the criteria in their selection. The skills of board members may be uneven, since their personal popularity or their positions on certain issues may have been considerations in their election. However, elections do help ensure that the board will be representative of the constituency the organization serves and that the organization and its executive will be responsive to members' views and priorities. Elected boards are less likely than the next type, self-perpetuating boards, to become stale, uninvolved, or homogeneous in their membership.

Self-Perpetuating Boards

Most charitable nonprofits have *self-perpetuating boards*. New members of a self-perpetuating board are selected by the existing members of the board, who identify and enlist individuals according to criteria established by the board itself. When a new nonprofit organization receives a charter, it must identify the original, founding members of the governing board; many states mandate a minimum of three (Blackwood, Dietz, & Pollack, 2014). Those individuals then have the authority to develop bylaws, which specify the total number of members of the board. The original board members then may select others to join them, up to the maximum permitted under the bylaws (which, of course, the board retains the authority to change). As individuals leave the board or complete their terms of service, the remaining members select others to take their seats, and this cycle continues as long as the organization exists.

In contrast to a board elected by the membership, a self-perpetuating board creates a relatively stable situation for the organization and its CEO. Although the bylaws of many boards do limit the number of terms that members may serve, self-perpetuating boards tend to have longer terms than elected boards, and the board's membership changes more slowly. Thus, the board's policies and culture may reflect continuity, reinforced by the tendency of its members to select successors who generally share their values and views. Indeed, in some cases, strong or long-serving CEOs may gain significant influence in the selection of board members, in effect choosing their own bosses.

One advantage is that a self-perpetuating board can craft its own membership, selecting individuals specifically to bring needed skills or augment its strength in areas important to its work. Many boards maintain an inventory of the expertise and connections represented among their members and make a systematic effort to identify and recruit new members to fill any identifiable gaps. For example, if someone with financial expertise is needed, the board can seek out such an individual and recruit him or her to join the board in order to add those skills. A social service organization may try to find someone with professional social work experience who can help the board evaluate program recommendations from its staff. If the organization desires to increase the amount of support it receives from corporations, the board can identify and recruit corporate executives who may be helpful in that regard.

But these advantages of the self-perpetuating board are accompanied by some potential weaknesses as well. One is that the board may come to be unrepresentative of the constituency or community the organization serves. If the existing members of the board do not recognize the importance of diversity, they may continue to select new members who are just like them, drawing on their own business and social circles to fill board openings. Over time, the organization could become out of touch and be unable to adapt sufficiently to changes in its environment. Another risk is that a self-perpetuating board may become too stable in its membership and too complacent. There have been cases in which self-perpetuating boards, without the scrutiny that comes from the broader constituency of the organization, have been too lax in their oversight of their CEOs or even the behavior of their fellow board members, with disastrous results for the organization.

Appointed and Hybrid Boards

A third way in which board members may be selected is through appointment by some authority outside the organization. This is the typical model for public organizations; for example, the boards of state universities are usually appointed by the governor of the state. Few nonprofits have totally appointed boards, but some do have a number of appointed members. This is sometimes the case in nonprofit organizations that are affiliated with a religious congregation, which may have board members appointed by a church authority. Colleges and universities may have board members appointed by an alumni association. Organizations that work closely with government may have some board seats held by individuals who are appointed by a governmental authority. Boards also may have some seats that are held *ex officio*—that is, designated to be held by the individual who holds a certain office or position. For example, the head of the board of trustees of the Catholic University of America is the Archbishop of Baltimore, who serves ex officio. The vice president of the United States and the chief justice of the Supreme Court serve as ex-officio members on the Board of Regents of the Smithsonian Institution. The organization's CEO often holds a seat on the board in an ex officio capacity, which may come with or without a vote.

Other boards are hybrids, perhaps with some members being elected, some appointed, some self-perpetuating, and some serving ex officio. For example, a nonprofit that provides health services to under-served populations and that meets certain other requirements may become a Federally Qualified Health Center. That status brings certain benefits, including eligibility for enhanced reimbursements from Medicaid and Medicare for the medical care the organization provides. But this status also has an impact on the organization's governing board, since the law requires that a majority of board members be active, registered users of the health center and representative of the population served. Other members may be selected through another process and on the basis of other criteria, but the requirement regarding a majority of clients establishes a hybrid board and reduces flexibility in composing the board's overall membership (Rural Assistance Center, 2014).

Hybrid boards may represent the best of both worlds, encompassing an elected component that helps keep the organization responsive to its constituencies; a self-perpetuating component that provides stability, continuity, and perhaps financial support; and an appointed component that ensures the organization's accountability to a parent organization or government. However, hybrid boards also can present challenges. For example, if elected, appointed, and self-perpetuating members hold different views or agendas, stalemate may result. Ex officio members may not always feel a real commitment to the organization and its mission, having just landed on the board by virtue of some other position they hold. If this is the case, they may not fully participate in the work of the board or develop a full understanding of the organization and its work.

Advisory Boards and Councils

As mentioned earlier in this chapter, many nonprofit organizations and institutions have a variety of groups that may be called *boards* or *councils* but that do not have legal responsibility or authority for governance of the organization. Some authors suggest that such groups should be called councils rather than boards in order to keep this distinction clear, and the former term is used in this text (Worth, 2008).

There are various reasons why a nonprofit organization may create *advisory councils*, and the membership of a council will reflect its purpose. For example, it may be desirable to create a group of experts who can provide substantive advice on the organization's programs. A nonprofit providing human or social services may benefit from an advisory council of experts in the field, who can offer professional guidance and help to evaluate programs. Some may have advisory councils that include current or former clients, who provide feedback on the effectiveness of programs from that perspective. Professional schools in universities often have advisory councils that provide the dean and faculty of the school with advice regarding what skills are most needed by employers of their graduates, helping to shape the curriculum.

In other cases, advisory councils are established, at least in part, as a strategy for engaging more people who may become advocates or donors and who may assist in fundraising. Members of such a council augment the fundraising support that the governing board can provide. Sometimes, advisory councils also serve as a vehicle for engaging individuals who may eventually serve on the governing board, providing them with an opportunity to learn more about the organization and become better known to members of the governing board before they are invited to join it. Some individuals may prefer to serve on an advisory council rather than the governing board, desiring to make a contribution to the organization without assuming the formal responsibilities that come with service on a board of directors or board of trustees. Advisory councils also may be valuable as a sounding board for the CEO. Since the CEO does not report to the council and the council has no authority to formally evaluate the CEO, they may provide an opportunity to test new ideas and engage in brainstorming in an open manner before the CEO brings proposals directly to the governing board.

Some advisory councils may be formally established in an organization's bylaws, but others are informal, really just a group of individuals assembled by the CEO (or some other manager, for example, the director of a program or center) to bounce ideas and gain help with fundraising. However, even with advisory councils that are appointed by the CEO, it is often recommended that the council's role be formalized with guidelines that define its responsibilities, the limits of its activity, terms of service, and the manner

TABLE 4.1 ■ Types of Boards		
Type of Board	**Advantages**	**Disadvantages**
Elected governing boards	Help ensure that the organization and the CEO will be responsive to members' needs and priorities	Division among the membership may create disagreement on the board. Turnover on the board may make it difficult to sustain focus on long-term goals and plans. Skills of board members may be uneven, since personal popularity or positions on issues may influence election.
Self-perpetuating governing boards	Can maintain continuity of culture, priorities, goals Can craft the board membership to gain needed skills Can select members who are helpful in fundraising	May become unrepresentative of the community or constituency May become too stable to respond to changes in the environment May become too passive and yield too much authority to the CEO
Hybrid governing boards (often including appointed, self-perpetuating, ex officio)	May combine the responsiveness of elected boards, the stability of self-perpetuating boards, and accountability to an appointing authority—for example, a sponsoring church	Different interests and loyalties of board members may lead to a stalemate. Ex-officio members may not be fully committed to the organization.
Advisory boards or councils	May be a vehicle for gaining expert advice on technical matters and/or for engaging more people as advocates and donors	If roles and responsibilities are not clearly defined and understood, may intrude on areas in which only the governing board has authority.

of election or selection of members (Worth, 2008). Since advisory councils do not have a formal role in governance, most do not need to be mentioned in legal documents, such as bylaws. But a written statement of the council's role may help to prevent an evolution of its role that could come into conflict with the authority of the governing board. For example, during a search for a new CEO, an advisory council may meet with candidates and make recommendations to the governing board. In other instances, the council's advice may relate to the organization's programs, and its opinions may affect the thinking of the governing board. In such cases, the council may have *influence*, but it needs to be clear that the governing board is the only entity that has *authority* (Worth, 2008).

Our discussion in the balance of this chapter is focused on governing boards, that is, the boards that have legal responsibility for the organization and its programs.

The Governing Board's Responsibilities

Now that we understand different types of boards and how their members come to sit at the table, exactly what are their responsibilities? And to whom are they accountable for meeting those responsibilities? The answers are not always simple.

As Bruce Hopkins (2003) describes it, nonprofit governing board members are "fiduciaries of the organization's resources and guardians of its mission" (p. 1). The board is accountable, that is, answerable, "for everything the organization does and how those things are accomplished" (Howe, 2002, p. 30). In the corporate world, it is clear to whom the directors are accountable and for what. Members of the corporate board of directors are the agents of the owners (the principals), and their responsibility is to direct and monitor the activities of management in the interests of the owners. Those interests also are quite clear—the maximization of economic value, consistent with sustainability of the business and the values of the owners. There are, of course, boards in the public sector as well. Most of them also have an identifiable constituency whose interest they serve; for example, a city council is accountable to the citizens of the city who elected them. But with nonprofits in the private sector, it is not always so clear to which owners the governing board is accountable.

Perhaps the owners of a member-serving organization are the members—it is primarily their interests that the organization exists to serve. But suppose the organization is a professional association that also sets standards for practice and certifies members of the profession. It may be primarily a member-serving organization, but doesn't the public—especially individuals served by members of the profession—also have some interest at stake? Who owns a charitable nonprofit, chartered to pursue a mission in the public interest? Are the owners the donors who support the organization through their philanthropy, the clients served by the organization, or perhaps the general public? If it is the general public, how can the board serve its interests when there may not be consensus about what the public interest means? Lacking the simple measure of results that the bottom line provides to business, by what standards should a nonprofit's effectiveness be evaluated, and who should determine those standards? Without clarity or agreement about who owns the organization, it is difficult to answer those questions. This creates an environment in which the board's responsibilities and role may be the subject of discussion and debate.

The Governing Board's Legal Responsibilities

Some governing board responsibilities are unambiguous; they are defined by law. Most laws affecting nonprofit boards are state laws, enforced by state attorneys general and state courts. However, the federal government, and specifically the Internal Revenue Service (IRS), has gained increasing power in recent years.

A landmark case in 1974 is often cited as providing the most definitive statement of nonprofit board responsibility. In that case, *Stern v. Lucy Webb Hayes National Training School for Deaconesses and*

Missionaries (usually known as just "The Sibley Hospital Case"), parents of children who had been patients at the hospital alleged that members of the board of directors had mismanaged the hospital's assets and had placed hospital funds in accounts at banks in which they had personal financial interests. The parents claimed that hospital charges were unnecessarily high because of actions by the board. That claim provided their legal standing to bring the suit. Judge Gerhard Gessell found that the directors had not engaged in fraud or benefitted personally from their actions, but that they had breached their fiduciary responsibility to the hospital. He required that the board adopt a new policy and, in his decision, he articulated the standards of legal responsibilities of nonprofit boards that are still applied. Those responsibilities are summarized as the duties of *care, loyalty,* and *obedience.*

Care, Loyalty, Obedience

The *duty of care* in this context means paying attention and exercising due diligence in monitoring the organization's finances and supervising the actions of its management. Board members who do not attend meetings, who sleep through meetings, who do not read board materials, or who vote without understanding the issues are guilty of a lack of care. Included within the concept of care is the requirement that members of the board act in a prudent manner in managing the organization's finances—for example, by ensuring that any endowment assets are invested in a diversified portfolio to minimize risks. This does not mean that the board will necessarily have violated its responsibilities should it make the wrong investment decisions and the organization's assets decline, but merely that it should exercise common sense and not lose money as a result of recklessness, indifference, or failure to seek appropriate advice.

The *duty of loyalty* means that members of the board put the interests of the organization above their own personal financial interests or that of another organization with which they may also have a formal relationship. Individuals cannot use their position on a nonprofit board to enhance their own businesses or financial position. Closely related to the concept of loyalty is that of *conflict of interest.* A conflict of interest may arise, for example, when the board has to vote on whether to give a business contract to a company that may be wholly or partly owned by a member of the board itself or that perhaps may employ a board member's relative. Or a conflict could exist if the board is voting to enter some kind of partnership with another nonprofit, and one of the voting members serves on both boards. Conflicts of interest are not unusual, especially in smaller communities, where there may not be much choice about which suppliers or contractors the nonprofit can use and where prominent business leaders who own those businesses may serve on multiple nonprofit boards. Conflicts of interest are not illegal per se, but it is important how the board deals with them. Well-managed boards have formal conflict-of-interest policies that describe the procedures to be followed. Such policies usually require that potential conflicts be disclosed and that the board independently determine whether any business transaction that gives rise to the conflict is disadvantageous to the organization.

A legal concept related to conflict of interest is that of *private inurement.* Anyone who is an insider—generally any board member or officer of the organization—cannot unreasonably benefit from the organization's funds. This is related to the non-distribution constraint that was previously discussed. Nonprofits cannot use their profits to benefit owners, nor can they pay unreasonable amounts to board members or executives, which might have the same effect as sharing the profits with them—that is, giving them financial benefits as if they were owners. For example, a board can pay its CEO a salary and other compensation that is reasonable in exchange for his or her services, but anything exceeding a reasonable amount may be illegal private inurement. Likewise, an organization can do business with a company owned by a board member, but only if the payment is appropriate for the goods and services received.

The *duty of obedience* requires that the board make sure that the organization is complying with the law and, in addition, that any decisions or actions taken are consistent with the organization's mission and governing documents, including its charter. Following the law may seem a simple charge, but ensuring that the organization does not drift from its mission may require greater vigilance, especially if that drift may bring with it some unanticipated risks.

Intermediate Sanctions

In general, if a board member carries out his or her duties faithfully and prudently, he or she is unlikely to be found personally liable for any losses that the organization may incur. Just making a mistake, or even a bad decision, is not in itself a violation of the board's responsibilities, provided that one has met the standards of care, loyalty, and obedience in making it. However, the risks to individual board members are somewhat higher today than they were prior to 1996, when federal legislation was passed providing the IRS with the authority to impose *intermediate sanctions*—that is, financial penalties to punish individuals who engage in or permit improper transactions.

Prior to the passage of intermediate sanctions, virtually the only weapon available to the IRS in dealing with a nonprofit board that violated its fiduciary responsibilities was to drop the atom bomb by revoking the organization's tax-exempt status. Facing an all-or-nothing situation and reluctant to take a drastic step that might essentially impose a death sentence on the organization—and bring harm to its clients—the IRS had few options. Intermediate sanctions provided a fly swatter alternative to the atom bomb of revoking tax-exempt status by permitting the IRS to impose penalties on *individual* board members or officers who engage in an *excess benefit transaction,* meaning one in which "a person's level or type of compensation is deemed to be in excess of the value of the person's services" (Hopkins, 2005, p. 219). The intermediate sanctions legislation and the regulations that the IRS has issued pursuant to it are complex and beyond the scope of our discussion here, but in summary, the penalties can involve return of the excess benefits received as well as additional penalties. Because it made the possibility of IRS action more than a remote threat, the passage of intermediate sanctions was a wake-up call to nonprofit boards.

One of the first applications of intermediate sanctions involved the board of Hawaii's Bishop Estate, a charitable trust created through the will of Princess Bernice Pauahi Bishop, a descendant of King Kamehameha I, and has as its sole purpose supporting the Kamehameha Schools for children of native Hawaiian descent. It was reported in 1999 that the Bishop Estate was the largest landowner in Hawaii, and its assets were estimated at between $5 billion and $10 billion. According to the princess's will, the trust was to be governed by five trustees, who would be appointed by the justices of Hawaii's Supreme Court (Greene, 1999).

In the 1990s, the IRS began investigating the trust and expressed its concern about the activities of the trustees. Among other issues, the IRS said that the trustees were receiving excessive compensation for their services, reported to be more than $1 million annually to each (Greene, 1999). The IRS threatened to terminate the Bishop Estate's tax exemption, which would have required it to pay millions of dollars each year in federal taxes as well as state and county taxes, thus diminishing the benefit of its assets to the schools and the children. Reacting to the IRS criticism, in 1999, Judge Kevin Chang of the Hawaii probate court removed four of the five trustees and accepted the resignation of the fifth, saying that their "inaction and indifference" was "a breach of duty" (Greene, 1999, p. 30).

The IRS decided to pursue intermediate sanctions against the removed trustees. In 2001, the former trustees announced that they had settled with the IRS but did not disclose the details. The media reported that the State of Hawaii also had brought a case against the trustees. This, too, was settled, but the court records were sealed, so the final result could not be known (Schwinn, 2002).

Sarbanes-Oxley Act

Following corporate governance scandals in the early 2000s, including the demise of two major companies, Enron and WorldCom, Congress passed the *Sarbanes-Oxley Act* in 2002. Sarbanes-Oxley placed new requirements on the governance of publicly traded for-profit corporations. Only two provisions of Sarbanes-Oxley apply as well to nonprofit organizations: those regarding the destruction of documents and protection for whistle-blowers. However, Sarbanes-Oxley served as another wake-up call for nonprofit boards, and many nonprofits have voluntarily adopted some or all of its provisions (Williams, 2006). In addition, some state laws—for example, the California Nonprofit Integrity Act of 2004—have incorporated Sarbanes–Oxley-type requirements. Sarbanes-Oxley will be discussed again, in more detail, in Chapter 6 of this book, which discusses nonprofit accountability in a broader framework.

In 2004, the organization Independent Sector created a *Panel on the Nonprofit Sector* in the wake of several controversies involving nonprofit governance. The panel issued reports in 2005, 2006, and 2007, offering over 150 recommendations and 33 principles for good governance and ethical practice by nonprofits, many of which reflect Sarbanes–Oxley-like practices (Independent Sector, 2007). The Principles were revised in 2015 to include new points addressing the need for organizational codes of ethics; whistle-blower policies; risk tolerance and mitigation in response to technological advances; earned income ventures undertaken by nonprofits; transparency and privacy; executive compensation; overhead costs; and fundraising using online platforms, mobile giving, social media, and crowdsourcing (Independent Sector, 2015d). In addition to Independent Sector's principles, various state associations of nonprofits also have established standards and codes of best practices. Most encompass the practices of governing boards but also address practices in other areas. A fuller discussion of such standards can be found in Chapter 6 of this book.

Form 990

In 2009, the IRS introduced a revised version of *Form 990*, which nonprofits having at least $50,000 in annual revenues are required to file. The revised 990 included a number of changes, such as a new Part VI (see Figure 4.1), which requires "yes" or "no" answers to questions specifically addressing the practices of nonprofit boards. In effect, what had previously been a financial report was changed into a financial and *governance* report. To be clear, while all organizations that are required to file Form 990 must complete Part VI, the policies and practices described are generally *not required* by the Internal Revenue Code. That fact is even stated clearly in the heading for Section B of Part VI on the 990 form (IRS, 2013). And again, not all provisions of Sarbanes-Oxley apply to nonprofit organizations. But the questions included in Section B of Part VI of Form 990 inquire about practices that are strikingly consistent with its provisions. The IRS (2013) implies that providing the right answers may be well-advised:

> In general, the policies and practices described in Part VI are not required by the Internal Revenue Code. However, organizations are required by the Code to make publicly available some of the items described in Question 18 of Part VI. . . . The IRS will use the information reported in Part VI, along with other information reported on the form, to assess noncompliance and the risk of noncompliance with federal tax law for individual organizations and across the broader exempt sector.

The State of Governance

In light of the requirements of law and best practice we have discussed, what is the state of nonprofit governance today? In a 2010 study, Amy Blackwood et al. (2014) found that a majority of nonprofits are compliant with many, but not all, of the principles covered by Form 990 questions. More than 60 percent of organizations had an audit conducted by an independent accountant, a formal review process for executive compensation, and a written conflict of interest policy. However, less than half of the organizations they surveyed had whistleblower policies or document retention and destruction policies, ironically the only two provisions of Sarbanes-Oxley that do apply to nonprofit organizations. Not surprisingly, practices varied among organizations depending on certain characteristics. Larger organizations were more likely than smaller ones to follow all of the best governance practices. Health care institutions were the most likely to do so and arts institutions the least likely. Nonprofits that received government funds and older organizations were more likely to follow best practices than were others. In comparing their findings to some earlier studies, Blackwood et al. (2014) concluded that "The adoption of good governance practices certainly is on the rise" and speculated that IRS initiatives "may very well be creating a more effective culture of governance in the nonprofit sector" (p. 14).

The Governing Board's Functional Responsibilities

The law primarily dictates the things nonprofit boards *cannot* do—fail to exercise care, place its own members' individual interests above those of the organization, or lead the organization in directions inconsistent with its mission and the law. But what is it exactly that boards should *do*?

FIGURE 4.1 ■ IRS Form 990, Part VI

Part VI **Governance, Management, and Disclosure** *For each "Yes" response to lines 2 through 7b below, and for a "No" response to line 8a, 8b, or 10b below, describe the circumstances, processes, or changes in Schedule O. See instructions.*
Check if Schedule O contains a response or note to any line in this Part VI . . . . ☐

Section A. Governing Body and Management

			Yes	No
1a	Enter the number of voting members of the governing body at the end of the tax year . .	**1a**		
	If there are material differences in voting rights among members of the governing body, or if the governing body delegated broad authority to an executive committee or similar committee, explain in Schedule O.			
b	Enter the number of voting members included in line 1a, above, who are independent . .	**1b**		
2	Did any officer, director, trustee, or key employee have a family relationship or a business relationship with any other officer, director, trustee, or key employee?	**2**		
3	Did the organization delegate control over management duties customarily performed by or under the direct supervision of officers, directors, or trustees, or key employees to a management company or other person? .	**3**		
4	Did the organization make any significant changes to its governing documents since the prior Form 990 was filed?	**4**		
5	Did the organization become aware during the year of a significant diversion of the organization's assets? .	**5**		
6	Did the organization have members or stockholders?	**6**		
7a	Did the organization have members, stockholders, or other persons who had the power to elect or appoint one or more members of the governing body?	**7a**		
b	Are any governance decisions of the organization reserved to (or subject to approval by) members, stockholders, or persons other than the governing body?	**7b**		
8	Did the organization contemporaneously document the meetings held or written actions undertaken during the year by the following:			
a	The governing body?	**8a**		
b	Each committee with authority to act on behalf of the governing body?	**8b**		
9	Is there any officer, director, trustee, or key employee listed in Part VII, Section A, who cannot be reached at the organization's mailing address? *If "Yes," provide the names and addresses in Schedule O*	**9**		

Section B. Policies *(This Section B requests information about policies not required by the Internal Revenue Code.)*

			Yes	No
10a	Did the organization have local chapters, branches, or affiliates?	**10a**		
b	If "Yes," did the organization have written policies and procedures governing the activities of such chapters, affiliates, and branches to ensure their operations are consistent with the organization's exempt purposes?	**10b**		
11a	Has the organization provided a complete copy of this Form 990 to all members of its governing body before filing the form?	**11a**		
b	Describe in Schedule O the process, if any, used by the organization to review this Form 990.			
12a	Did the organization have a written conflict of interest policy? *If "No," go to line 13*	**12a**		
b	Were officers, directors, or trustees, and key employees required to disclose annually interests that could give rise to conflicts?	**12b**		
c	Did the organization regularly and consistently monitor and enforce compliance with the policy? *If "Yes," describe in Schedule O how this was done*	**12c**		
13	Did the organization have a written whistleblower policy?	**13**		
14	Did the organization have a written document retention and destruction policy?	**14**		
15	Did the process for determining compensation of the following persons include a review and approval by independent persons, comparability data, and contemporaneous substantiation of the deliberation and decision?			
a	The organization's CEO, Executive Director, or top management official	**15a**		
b	Other officers or key employees of the organization	**15b**		
	If "Yes" to line 15a or 15b, describe the process in Schedule O (see instructions).			
16a	Did the organization invest in, contribute assets to, or participate in a joint venture or similar arrangement with a taxable entity during the year?	**16a**		
b	If "Yes," did the organization follow a written policy or procedure requiring the organization to evaluate its participation in joint venture arrangements under applicable federal tax law, and take steps to safeguard the organization's exempt status with respect to such arrangements?	**16b**		

Section C. Disclosure

17 List the states with which a copy of this Form 990 is required to be filed ▶ ------------------------------------

18 Section 6104 requires an organization to make its Forms 1023 (or 1024 if applicable), 990, and 990-T (Section 501(c)(3)s only) available for public inspection. Indicate how you made these available. Check all that apply.

☐ Own website   ☐ Another's website   ☐ Upon request   ☐ Other *(explain in Schedule O)*

19 Describe in Schedule O whether (and if so, how) the organization made its governing documents, conflict of interest policy, and financial statements available to the public during the tax year.

20 State the name, physical address, and telephone number of the person who possesses the books and records of the organization: ▶

Source: IRS form 990 (http://www.irs.gov/pub/irs-pdf/f990.pdf).

A number of authors have offered lists of a board's functional responsibilities—that is, job descriptions listing the duties that boards should perform (see, e.g., BoardSource, 2010; Ingram, 2003). Most lists are similar on the principal activities in which the board should be engaged, although there are often differences among the experts with regard to the division of specific tasks between the board and the organization's CEO. The following responsibilities are common to most board job descriptions, although, as we will see later, some authors express contrary views.

Appoint, Support, and Evaluate the CEO

Although the CEO may serve as an ex officio member of the board, he or she is generally appointed by the board and serves at the pleasure of the board, subject, of course, to any contractual terms that may be negotiated at the time of appointment. However, having appointed the CEO, the board also has a responsibility to support that individual. This includes acting as a sounding board for the CEO to discuss ideas and problems and also coming to his or her defense when pressures may arise from within or outside the organization. If the board's response to every criticism of the CEO's actions is to challenge him or her or to take the side of the critic, the board will quickly undermine the CEO's ability to be effective, and it is unlikely to attract or retain a strong executive. But the board also is responsible for setting expectations for the CEO, monitoring his or her performance against those expectations, and providing the executive with performance evaluations. Of course, if expectations are regularly not met, the board also has the responsibility of dismissing the CEO and beginning a search for a successor.

The relationship between the governing board and the CEO is complex, and it is a topic that generates its own considerable literature. The subject is of such importance that we will return to a more thorough discussion of it shortly.

Establish a Clear Institutional Mission and Purpose

Establishing the organization's mission is the responsibility of the board. Although the organization's charter states its purposes in broad terms, the board can and should periodically review its mission; indeed, doing so is often the first step in the process of strategic planning.

Approve the Organization's Programs

Although experts advise boards to avoid becoming involved in the details of management, most think that the board should approve the programs undertaken by the organization to meet its responsibility for ensuring adherence to the mission and protecting the organization's financial viability. For example, the board of a liberal arts college would need to consider whether establishing a business school would be consistent with its mission, the implications for the college's financial resources, and the ability of the college to maintain its academic standards and reputation in light of such an expansion of its programs. The board of an organization serving dinners to the homeless would need to consider any extension of its activities to provide medical services or housing. Because such decisions relate directly to the mission, which is the responsibility of the board, they cannot be delegated to the CEO or the staff.

Ensure Sound Financial Management and the Organization's Financial Stability

Protecting the organization's assets is, of course, central to the board's legal responsibility as fiduciary. Most boards approve annual budgets and receive regular reports of the organization's financial status. Many boards also have separate audit committees that meet with outside auditors of the organization's finances (Williams, 2006). As mentioned previously, most engage outside auditors (Blackwood et al., 2014).

Some authors say that board members' responsibility to ensure the organization's fiscal soundness implies an obligation to provide their own financial gifts and actively engage in fundraising. Indeed, except perhaps for the debate about the appropriate relationship between the board and the CEO, no subject commands more ink, or more lung power, than the role of the board in giving and raising philanthropic funds. Of course, not all boards are expected to provide their personal financial support to the organizations they serve. Boards of member-serving organizations often have no significant responsibility for fundraising, since the largest portion of revenue may come from dues, subscriptions, or meeting fees. Organizations that are primarily or entirely dependent on revenue from government contracts and grants also may not place emphasis on the board's fundraising role. But in most charitable nonprofits, the board is expected to play a significant role in providing and soliciting philanthropic funds.

There are divergent views on whether board members should be required to give or raise a specific minimum amount, and the question raises some complicated issues. Some boards require a minimum personal gift from each board member. However, if this requirement is substantial, it may make it more difficult to achieve appropriate diversity among the board membership without making exceptions to the policy for those who may bring important skills and qualities but do not possess financial capacity. Then again, making such exceptions may introduce the perception that there are two classes of board members—those who give and those who don't. If that perception exists, those who cannot provide financial support may too readily defer to those who are known to be important sources of support to the organization. On the other hand, if the minimum is set so low that all board members can meet it, it can have the effect of converting an intended floor into a ceiling. In other words, some board members who have the financial ability to give more than the minimum may come to see the minimum as all that is expected of them, foreclosing the possibility of larger gifts. Such a situation may leave the organization with less total revenue than it might otherwise receive (Worth, 2005, p. 73).

Some boards do not set a minimum for personal giving by board members but adopt what is often called a *give-or-get policy,* requiring that each board member either give personally or solicit gifts from others to total the minimum amount. However, this may also establish a standard that some board members may find difficult to meet, especially if they are not involved in business or professional circles that provide access to wealth. Furthermore, it raises the risk that board members may solicit gifts without coordination with the organization's staff, creating a potentially chaotic situation that could alienate donors. An alternative to setting minimums for board giving and getting is to simply establish the expectation that each board member will give and participate in fundraising proportionate to his or her capacity to do so. If that standard is firmly embedded in the culture of the board, then conscience and the judgment of peers may motivate the board to its peak fundraising performance without the risks inherent in defining specific minimum amounts. Whatever approach is taken by individual boards, the subject of the board's responsibility for giving and fundraising is on the agenda for discussion at many nonprofit organizations today (Worth, 2005).

Establish Standards for Organizational Performance and Hold the Organization Accountable

The board should define the standards by which an organization's effectiveness in achieving its mission is to be evaluated. Establishing standards to judge whether the organization is effectively employing the resources entrusted to it in pursuit of its mission is a fundamental aspect of the board's responsibility to those who provide financial support, to the society that grants the organization exemption from taxation, and to those whose needs its programs serve.

Some authors see the role of nonprofit boards as especially important because many nonprofits do not face the same market discipline that business firms do. As John Carver (2006) explains, "Without a market to summarize consumer judgment, [a nonprofit] organization literally does not know what its product is worth . . . In the absence of a market test, *the board must perform that function* [italics original]" (p. 15). Christine W. Letts, William P. Ryan, and Allen Grossman (1999a) elaborate on this point:

Compared to their for-profit counterparts, nonprofit boards carry a much bigger burden in demanding and supporting performance . . . [In the for-profit world,] both boards and management can use market feedback to assess how well they are performing: customers, investors, and creditors all make evaluations that eventually show up in the bottom line . . . In contrast, the nonprofit board must often substitute for many of the feedback systems available in the marketplace. Nonprofit clients very often do not have a choice of providers, and are therefore unlikely to signal dissatisfaction by "voting with their feet." [Funders of nonprofits] may signal dissatisfaction by withdrawing their support, but are much less likely to play the affirmative role of a shareholder activist or institutional investor. (p. 133)

For these reasons, Letts et al. (1999a) argue that "nonprofit boards are more vital [than for-profit boards] in ensuring performance and accountability" (p. 132).

How do the activities of actual boards compare with the functional responsibilities identified by experts? In 2012, Grant Thornton conducted a survey of nonprofit boards and asked what activity or responsibility was the "most important focus" of the board in the preceding year. Of those responding, 27 percent identified strategic planning, 22 percent fundraising, 19 percent "ensuring effective programs," 9 percent "management performance," 5 percent protecting the organization's "reputation," 3 percent the "economy/recession," 3 percent "cash management," 2 percent "investment management," and 2 percent "enterprise risk management" (p. 4).

The Board and the CEO

Young, small nonprofit organizations often have a *working board*. In those situations, volunteer members of the board have a hands-on role and perform all of the organization's operations, from raising funds, to balancing its bank accounts, to making decisions about its programs. But as the organization grows and a professional is hired to serve as its executive officer, the division of responsibilities and functions between the board and that staff leader becomes a central consideration.

The relationship between the governing board and the organization's CEO is the subject of an extensive literature, reflecting divergent views. The questions addressed in this literature go well beyond who does what. They include fundamental assumptions about the nature of nonprofit governance and leadership.

At the heart of the matter is the question of who leads the nonprofit organization. In some organizations, the CEO may be dominant, with the board playing a passive role. The CEO proposes and the board disposes, often with little discussion or debate. As noted earlier, the CEO may even come to influence the selection of board members, in effect choosing his or her own bosses. This situation could arise in any organization, but it is especially common in organizations led by their founders, a special case we will discuss further in Chapter 5.

The realities of many organizations may enable CEOs to gain the upper hand. Boards are composed of "part-time amateurs," while the organization's staff, including the CEO, are "full-time professionals" (Chait, Holland, & Taylor, 1999, p. 3). In other words, the CEO may know more about the organization and its programs than do the lay trustees, especially if its programs involve highly technical services, and board members may be reluctant to show their ignorance by questioning. Large boards pose a special challenge in this regard. Individual board members may be unwilling to risk embarrassment by challenging a CEO's proposals in front of a large number of other board members, or they may assume that others on the board are well-informed and just go along with what appears to be a consensus. The CEO may control access to information about the organization, and indeed, the CEO may be the only one who knows what information actually exists. He or she may determine what information reaches the board and develop the agenda of matters that the board will even get to consider. In sum, it may be possible for a CEO to manipulate the board, orchestrate board meetings, and relegate the board to the role of a rubber stamp for his or her initiatives.

The danger in such a scenario is that the CEO could lead the board and the organization in directions that are inappropriate or risky and that the board may not be able to meet its responsibilities for ensuring adherence to mission, fiscal soundness, and optimum performance. For example, in 2002, the Washington, DC, community was shocked by allegations that the long-serving executive director of the United Way of the National Capital Area (UWNCA), Oral Suer, had received as much as $1.6 million in improper payments, including nonreimbursed cash advances, encashment of vacation and sick leave that he had in fact taken, and reimbursement for travel and entertainment that were personal rather than related to United Way business. Those improper payments were alleged to have occurred over the period of 27 years that Mr. Suer was employed at the UWNCA (Wolverton, 2003). The UWNCA's board had 45 members, and some observers attributed the abuses to the board's large size and the fact that the executive director had maintained tight control over communication with the board and among its members. One former employee of the organization told the *Chronicle of Philanthropy,* "This was definitely a 'clapper' board. They listened to staff members tell wonderful stories about how much money we were raising, and they applauded instead of asking tough questions" (Wolverton, 2003, p. 27). Others cited the organization's internal culture, which made it difficult for the board to meet its fiduciary responsibilities. One board member said that the board met only four times a year, a total of eight hours, and that the large board discouraged her from speaking. She said that she didn't have the phone numbers of the other board members, so she was unable to follow up with them after meetings. When she tried to obtain the numbers, a secretary at UWNCA told her that the numbers were confidential (Wolverton, 2003).

But an alternative scenario, in which the board micromanages the organization and usurps the authority of the CEO, is no better. Such a board is likely to find it difficult to attract or retain a strong chief executive and may find itself making decisions about details outside its expertise. What most experts recommend is neither of these extreme scenarios but rather a partnership between the board and the CEO in the leadership of the organization. There are, however, different views on exactly how this partnership should be constructed and should operate.

Various authors have addressed the subject of the board–CEO relationship, and a comprehensive review would be beyond the scope of this chapter. But let's compare the thinking of three authors who are widely cited and whose different approaches highlight the major issues. First, we will look at John Carver's "policy governance model," described in his 1990 book *Boards That Make a Difference* and in subsequent editions published in 1997 and 2006. Carver draws a clear line between the board's responsibility for *policy making* and the executive's responsibility for *implementation* and provides what he calls an "operating system" to ensure that the distinction is maintained. Next, we will review the concept of "governance as leadership," described by Richard Chait, William Ryan, and Barbara Taylor (2005) in their book of that title. The book was sponsored by BoardSource, an organization that provides research, education, and assistance to nonprofit organization boards. Chait et al. challenge Carver (2006), writing that "governing is too complicated to reduce to simple aphorisms, however seductive, like 'boards set policies which administrators implement'" (p. 5). Instead, they advocate a leadership role for the board that blurs the distinction between policy and implementation and focuses the attention of both boards and CEOs on "what matters most." And, finally, we will consider the research of Robert Herman and Dick Heimovics (2005), who argue that the most effective CEOs are those who accept the reality of their "psychological centrality" in the organization and provide "board-centered leadership," working to "develop, promote, and enable their boards' effective functioning" (p. 157).

Carver's Policy Governance Model

According to John Carver (2006), boards should be the leaders of the organization, "not by invading territory best left to management but by controlling the big picture, the long term, and the value laden" (p. 6). But his diagnosis of the prevailing reality is bleak. He observes boards mired in the trivial, largely reactive to staff initiatives, and absorbed in reviewing and rehashing actions the staff has already undertaken (pp. 19–20). Carver argues that board committees are often organized in a way that leads to this condition. Committee responsibilities often coincide with those of senior managers; for example, there may be committees on finance, fundraising, program evaluation, and other areas of the organization's operation overseen by professional staff. In many cases, the staff prepares materials for meetings of the relevant committee and influences what items the committee considers. This structure pulls the board's attention into the details of each of the management silos. Board members thus become either super managers or just advisors to the professional staff. This prevents them from staying focused on big-picture matters such as mission and goals. As Carver writes, "Our tradition of board work encourages boards to derive their agendas from staff-based divisions of work. This common board practice is tantamount to classifying a manager's functions on the basis of his or her secretary's job areas" (p. 46).

Carver (2006) calls for a clear distinction between the work of the board and that of the management staff, and he argues that the board should lead the organization, focusing its attention on establishing *policies*. But this does not mean the kinds of policies that boards often discuss, such as personnel policies, which really reflect the work of management and are related to implementation rather than leadership of the organization. The board should make policies that reflect the board's values and the interests of the "moral owners" of the organization. In Carver's (2006) model, boards lead by developing and maintaining policies in four areas:

1. *Ends to be achieved:* Ends policy statements describe what the organization is to achieve and "could be called results, impacts, goals, or outcomes as well as ends, each title having its own connotations" (p. 48). The broadest ends statement would be the organization's mission. More specific ends policies might address more detailed goals—for example, those related to products, consumers, and costs.

2. *Means to the ends:* In Carver's model, means statements are expressed in terms of "executive limitations"—that is, boundaries that the CEO may not cross in pursuing the ends established by the board. For example, the broadest statement of policy in this area might be that the CEO may not violate the law. More detailed limitations might address more specific constraints, perhaps levels of cost and debt that may not be exceeded. Carver argues that by stating executive limitations in negative terms—that is, by prescribing what executives may *not* do—the board preserves maximum flexibility for the CEO. Subject to the constraints that the board has explicitly stipulated, the CEO is free to determine the best methods for achieving the ends that the board has established, without the board's inappropriate involvement in operations.

3. *Board–staff relationship:* Policy statements in this area clearly delineate the responsibilities of the board and the CEO, defining what decisions are delegated to the CEO and which ones are retained by the board. This category of statement also includes specific criteria for monitoring and evaluating the CEO's performance. Carter argues that one benefit of such clarity is that it addresses the common concern about board members communicating directly with other staff within the organization or with other volunteers. "In a formal sense, the CEO role insulates the staff from the board and the board from the staff. However, the insulation does not rigidly prohibit contact between board and staff members. On the contrary, those very human connections are never problematic if the formal roles are clear" (p. 161).

4. *Process of governance:* This fourth category of policy addresses the board's own role and operation, clarifying which owners it represents and defining its own "job process and products"—for example, the procedure through which new board members are elected (p. 51).

A board practicing Carver's (2006) model would be driven in its meetings by the need to develop and maintain its policy manual. When issues arise, the first questions to be addressed would be to which category of policy the issue belongs, whose issue it is, and whether it is addressed by an existing policy—if not, a new policy needs to be adopted, eliciting discussion and debate. Carver argues that this approach steers boards away from the mundane, from show-and-tell presentations by staff, and from merely rubber-stamping the staff's recommendations. According to Carver, following the policy governance approach leads the board toward discussions that are focused on the long term and rooted in the board's values and perspectives (p. 129).

Chait, Ryan, and Taylor: Governance as Leadership

Now let's examine a different approach, the *governance-as-leadership* model proposed by Chait et al. (2005). Chait et al.'s 2005 book has gained wide visibility in the nonprofit sector, in part because of its sponsorship by BoardSource, which bases its board training programs largely on the model. A 2013 book by Cathy Trower provides a "practitioner's guide" that offers practical guidance to boards for implementing Chait et al.'s recommendations.

Chait et al. (2005) agree with many of Carver's criticisms of the way boards operate today. Boards are not leading their organizations. They are reactive to staff initiatives. They structure their work in a way that draws them into managerial details and routine technical work. Indeed, these authors argue, things are turned upside down. Boards are so mired in operational details that they are, in effect, *managing* [italics added] their organizations. Meanwhile, CEOs are articulating missions, beliefs, values, and cultures— in essence *leading* [italics added] their organizations and engaging in activities that "closely resemble conventional notions of *governing* [italics added]" (p. 3). As the authors explain,

> In theory, if not in practice, boards of trustees are supposed to be the ultimate guardians of institutional ethos and organizational values. Boards are charged with setting the organization's agenda and priorities . . . Boards are empowered to specify the most important problems and opportunities that management should pursue. If this logic holds, as we contend, then many nonprofit executives are not only leading their organizations, but . . . they are actually governing them as well. (p. 3)

> With sophisticated leaders at the helm of nonprofits, a substantial portion of the governance portfolio has moved to the executive suite. The residue remains in the boardroom. This surprise twist in the story line suggests that the real threat to nonprofit governance today may not be a board that micro*manages* but a board that micro*governs,* [italics original] while blind to governance as leadership. (pp. 4–5)

But while their diagnosis of board problems is similar to Carver's (1997, 2006), Chait and his colleagues (2005) offer a quite different prescription. Instead of drawing sharp lines between policy and implementation, clearly dividing the role of the board and that of the CEO, they call for breaking down the barriers and focusing the attention of both the board and the CEO on the critical issues facing the organization. In other words, the question should not be, "Is this an issue of policy or implementation?" Rather, the question should be, "Is the issue at hand important or unimportant, central or peripheral?" (Taylor, Chait, & Holland, 1999, p. 62).

In their book, Chait et al. (2005) define a new model, which they call "governance as leadership," based on three "modes" of governance in which a board may be operating at any given time:

1. *The fiduciary mode:* When the board is operating in this mode, it is concerned with the "bedrock of governance," that is, with matters such as stewardship of tangible assets, faithfulness to mission, performance accountability, and obedience to law—in other words, generally addressing its legal responsibilities.

2. *The strategic mode:* When operating in the strategic mode, boards go beyond their basic fiduciary responsibilities and "create a true strategic partnership with management," addressing matters such as the organization's long-term directions and goals (p. 69).

3. *The generative mode:* A board in generative mode is engaged in generative thinking—that is, the creative, out-of-the-box thinking in which visionary leaders often engage. It relates to values and judgments, encompasses "sense making" (essentially, coming to understand things in new ways), and may result in insights that lead to paradigm shifts. The authors say that generative thinking is a necessary foundation for setting direction and goals and thus an essential activity of leadership.

Chait et al. (2005) observe that most boards work only in the fiduciary and strategic modes and therefore are not participating in leadership of the organization. However, "when trustees work well in *all three* [italics added] of these modes, the board achieves governance as leadership" (p. 7). Thus, rather than maintaining a clear distinction between what is the board's territory and what is the CEO's, Chait et al. propose that boards and CEOs focus together on what matters most, moving together among the three modes as appropriate to address the issues at hand. Setting goals, and thus using generative thinking, cannot be a task for the CEO or the board alone but rather must be a *shared* activity.

> Because we resolutely regard this [generative thinking] as shared work, we cannot offer what the board-improvement field so often promises trustees and executives: a set of bright lights that neatly divide the board's work (policy, strategy, and governance) from the staff's (administration, implementation, and management). It simply makes no sense to reserve generative work for boards when leaders are vital to the process, or to reserve for leaders work that belongs at the heart of governance. Generative work demands a fusion of thinking, not a division of labor. (p. 95)

Simply stated, Carver (1990, 1997, 2006) envisions the board and the CEO on opposite sides of the table, one clearly labeled "policy" and the other "implementation." Chait and his coauthors (2005) envision a three-sided table, each representing one of the modes discussed previously. The board and the CEO sit together on one side but move around the table to the other sides, depending on the nature of the business to be considered at the time.

Which model is "right"? Does Carver's (1990, 1997, 2006) *policy governance model* improve board performance? Does the governance-as-leadership approach by Chait et al. (2005) improve performance? One 2003 study, by Patricia Nobbie and Jeffrey Brudney, compared organizations using the Carver model with others that had received training from BoardSource and suggested mixed results. There were few differences, and those were generally not significant. The job satisfaction of CEOs working under the Carver model measured somewhat higher than that of the others, but the researchers found the difference to be statistically insignificant. One important conclusion of the study was that boards that had received training tended to perform better than those that had not been trained, regardless of which model had been used. The study was, of course, prior to Chait et al.'s 2005 book, so it does not provide an evaluation of that specific model or a comparison of the Chait et al. model with Carver. Rather, it was intended to evaluate the relative effectiveness of Carver's model in comparison with other types of training practiced at that time. Carver, with characteristic confidence, responds to the Nobbie and Brudney study in the 2006 edition of his book, arguing that his model is superior and that the latter authors' choice of variables reflects an inaccurate understanding of its purpose.

Herman and Heimovics: Psychological Centrality and Board-Centered Leadership

In Carver's (1990, 1997, 2006) approach, boards lead their organizations. Chait et al. (2005) describe a model for leadership shared by the board and the chief executive. In 2005, Robert Herman and Dick Heimovics (2005) provided a third perspective, which Herman has reiterated in more recent writing (Herman, 2010). Based on their research concerning effective nonprofit CEOs, Herman and Heimovics offer a pragmatic approach, concluding that CEOs should lead but that their leadership needs to be *board centered* and designed to support the board in meeting its governing responsibilities.

The *purposive-rational model* of organizations, based on Max Weber's theory of the bureaucracy, conceives of the board as the top of a hierarchy and the CEO as merely its agent. Indeed, Herman and Heimovics's (2005) review of the normative literature on nonprofit boards finds that most research has been based on that model and thus "has advanced a heroic ideal for nonprofit boards" (p. 155). However, they apply the *social-constructionist model* and explain that "official or intended goals, structures, and procedures may exist only on paper. Actual goals, structures, and procedures emerge and change as participants interact and socially construct the meaning of ongoing events" (p. 156). Regardless of what the organizational chart or the conventional view of organizations may suggest, Herman and Heimovics find that the reality in most organizations is that of *executive psychological centrality*. In other words, it is the CEO who is actually *seen as* responsible for the organization's success or failure. They interviewed CEOs, board chairs, and other staff members and found that *all* of them saw the chief executive as "centrally responsible for what happens," including both successful and unsuccessful events (p. 156). This does not imply that the CEO holds more formal authority than the board or that the CEO *is* indeed the central figure in the life of the organization. "Psychological centrality" means that he or she is *perceived as* responsible, even by members of the board.

If this is the reality, then what do Herman and Heimovics (2005) recommend that CEOs should do? They do *not* recommend that CEOs become autocrats or demote their boards to rubber stamps, but rather that they take a leadership role to ensure "that boards fulfill their legal, organizational, and public roles" (p. 156). In exercising *board-centered leadership*, CEOs take responsibility for "supporting and facilitating the board's work." In doing so, they engage in six behaviors that Herman and Heimovics observed among the effective, board-centered executives they studied (p. 158):

1. Facilitating interaction in board relationships

2. Showing consideration and respect toward board members

3. Envisioning change and innovation for the organization with the board

4. Providing useful and helpful information to the board

5. Initiating and maintaining structure for the board

6. Promoting board accomplishments and productivity

Herman and Heimovics (2005) conclude that not only are the CEOs who have developed these board-centered leadership skills effective in their roles, but they also have hardworking, effective boards. "The board-centered executive is likely to be effective because he or she has grasped that the work of the board is critical in adapting to and affecting the constraints and opportunities in the environment" (p. 159). In a study of "high-impact nonprofits," Leslie Crutchfield and Heather Grant (2012) draw a similar conclusion, writing that while "many leaders try to minimize their interactions with their board, or they perpetually fight with them . . . great nonprofit leaders have a positive relationship with the board. They share leadership to advance the larger cause" (p. 201).

But, what is the reality? Do most nonprofit CEOs provide board-centered leadership as Herman and Heimovics (2005) and others recommend? The 2011 *Daring to Lead* study mentioned earlier (Moyers, 2011) suggests that many are not doing so. The majority of CEOs responding to the study reported spending less than ten hours per month on board-related activities. The author of the study report speculates that "perhaps executives fail to see the immediate benefit of spending more time with the board, since the activities on which the largest number of respondents said they need to spend more time—marketing and fundraising—produce tangible results" (p. 5). But, paradoxically, nonprofit CEOs who do spend more time on the board report more satisfaction with board performance, which is consistent with the conclusions of the earlier research by Herman and Heimovics (Moyers, p. 6).

Explaining Board Behavior

The recommendations of Chait et al. (2005), Carver (1990, 1997, 2006), and Herman and Heimovics (2005) suggest how things *should* be. But how do governing boards actually behave? Where do they focus their attention? And how do they define their relationship with the CEO? And what determines the patterns that we can observe? These questions have been the subject of research by various scholars, who have proposed contingency approaches; in other words, they argue that how boards behave *depends* on the internal and external conditions they face.

Patricia Bradshaw (2009) identified five "board configurations," determined in part by the external circumstances that the organization faces. For example, organizations facing an external environment that is simple and stable tend to follow something similar to Carver's policy governance model, in which the board is "more formalized, hierarchical, and bureaucratic" (p. 69). Boards that face an external environment of uncertainty and turbulence, but that also have a simple array of stakeholders, adopt an "entrepreneurial/corporate configuration." That is less formal and may include more overlap of board and staff roles (p. 70), perhaps something more like the environment implied by Chait et al. (2005). Those facing a stable environment but a complex constituency adopt a constituency/representative configuration, in which the board includes representatives of various groups or associated organizations (p. 69), perhaps something like the hybrid model discussed earlier in this chapter. Organizations that must address turbulence and uncertainty in their environments *as well as* complex, decentralized constituencies may exhibit what Bradshaw (2009) calls an "emergent cellular configuration." That includes a flatter structure that is dynamic and fluid, without clear roles and lines of authority, and with participants often demonstrating a commitment to alternative or "nonmainstream" ideologies (p. 70). And, of course, some boards illustrate variations on these four basic configurations. The existence of these models reflects the reality discussed in Chapter 3, that nonprofit organizations are open systems, highly influenced by the environment that surrounds them.

In 2010, Francie Ostrower and Melissa Stone studied boards and also took a contingency approach, looking at both internal and external variables. They found that boards at larger organizations are more focused on financial monitoring than on external roles (p. 912). Boards without a professional CEO are more likely to monitor programs and services than those that have a professional CEO in place (p. 912). Boards with women as members are more attuned to external roles and boards with members who also serve on corporate boards tend to focus more on financial oversight (p. 913). Larger boards are more involved in fundraising than are smaller boards, perhaps, as Ostrower and Stone (2010) speculate, because the board has been made larger in part as a fundraising strategy (p. 913). An interesting—and likely controversial—finding is that "having the CEO as a voting member of the board undermines the governance role of the board" (p. 913).

Managing Nonprofit Boards

In earlier times, an invitation to join a nonprofit board might have been construed as primarily a social opportunity. Although boards had legal responsibilities, in the days before Sarbanes-Oxley, Form 990, and charity watchdogs, many could operate informally and comfortably, without too much attention to their effectiveness, any expectation that their work would be scrutinized by outsiders, or perhaps any great understanding of the board's role. But developments discussed in this chapter have changed the environment, requiring that the board's activity and performance be actively monitored and managed.

Role of the Chair

The board chair is the individual responsible for leading the board. In addition, the chair is responsible for board process and board tasks. With regard to the former, it is the chair's responsibility to build the board into a team and to establish its culture. The chair also is primarily responsible for identifying the tasks that the board will undertake, that is, setting its agenda. In practice, identifying the board's tasks is often a responsibility shared with the CEO and committees of the board (BoardSource, 2010).

There sometimes can be tension arising from confusion about the respective roles of the board chair, the board, and the CEO (BoardSource, 2010). Carver (2006) emphasizes the point that only the full board can make decisions and take action; in other words, the chair leads the board but does not hold full authority for the organization. The CEO is appointed by the board, not by the chair, and the CEO reports to the board, not to its chair as an individual. In other words, as Carver (2006) explains, the board chair and the CEO are more like colleagues than supervisor and subordinate. Nevertheless, the board chair is often the board's principal liaison to the CEO, and it is important that the two individuals establish and maintain "a professional relationship with clear boundaries" (BoardSource, 2010, p. 88).

Governance Committee

In decades past, many boards—primarily those that were self-perpetuating—had a standing committee charged with identifying possible new board members and with recommending candidates for election by the full board. Usually called the *nominating committee* or committee on nominations, this group functioned essentially as the board's talent scout; its responsibility was primarily to assure that individuals selected to join the board would be compatible with the board's culture and, perhaps, bring the capacity to provide personal financial support and help with fundraising. In most well-managed boards today, the relatively simple task of the nominating committee has been expanded and the committee has been renamed as the *governance committee*, reflecting its larger role. As BoardSource (2010) explains:

> Rather than focusing on nominations for annual elections [like a nominating committee], the governance committee works year-round to guarantee that the board takes responsibility for its own development, learning, and behavior; sets and enforces its own expectations; and allots time, attention, and resources to understanding its stewardship role. The governance committee does not run the board, but it makes it possible for the board to be well-run (p. 63).

The responsibilities of the governance committee encompasses that of identifying potential new members, like the traditional nominating committee, but also a broader process of *board development*, which generally includes nine steps: identify the board's needs in terms of skills, knowledge, connections, and perspectives; identify and cultivate the interest of prospective board members to meet those needs; recruit new board members; provide new members with orientation, both to the board and the organization; involve board members in appropriate committee and task force assignments; educate the board, both with regard to the organization's mission and programs and best governance practice; evaluate the board as a whole and individual members; rotate members through term limits; and celebrate exemplary board performance (BoardSource, 2010, pp. 100–101).

Periodic self-evaluation is a best practice recommended by BoardSource (2010) and others. The governance committee initiates board evaluations, which typically use surveys, sometimes conducted by an outside consultant. Some boards also require the evaluation of individual members, which may include self-evaluation and/or evaluation by peers. This is commonly undertaken when an individual member is being considered for election to a new term (BoardSource, 2010, p. 269).

Board Professionals

Overall management of the board is a responsibility of the board chair, and perhaps a governance committee, working in cooperation with the CEO. Other members of the organization's staff also may be involved in supporting board committees; for example, the chief financial officer may work closely with a finance committee and the chief development officer with a development committee of the board. When such circumstances exist, most authors, notably Carver (2006), emphasize the importance of maintaining clarity with regard to reporting lines and the authority of individual board members. For example, the chief financial officer, chief development officer, and other senior staff members may provide staff support to their respective board committees and their chairs and develop close relationships with them, but those officers report to the CEO, not to the committee chairs. In addition, the committee chairs have no authority to direct staff of the organization. Their committees may develop recommendations to the full board, which the full board may adopt and transmit to the CEO, who may in turn delegate responsibility to other senior staff (Carver, 2006). Of course, in many cases personal relationships may lead to a situation in which not all communication and influence follow such formal lines. (Remember our earlier discussion about the informal hierarchies that exist in many nonprofit organizations.) But if the appropriate roles of the board, individual board members, and staff members are not respected, there is the potential for undermining the CEO and creating tension within the organization.

In some large organizations with large boards, a senior staff member is charged explicitly with supporting board development activities. This is a responsibility that is sometimes assigned to the chief development or advancement officer, since that individual often enjoys close relationships with board members. In other cases, the organization's general counsel may play this role, in light of his or her knowledge regarding the legal requirements of governance. The individual may also be titled *corporate secretary* and have responsibility for the maintenance of the organization's official documents and records. Some institutions, notably colleges and universities, have a senior staff officer for whom supporting the board is a full-time job. The Society of Corporate Secretaries and Governance Professionals was founded in 1946 and includes board professionals in the corporate and nonprofit sectors (www.governanceprofessionals. org/about/aboutus). Reflecting the growing prevalence of such positions in higher education institutions, the Association of Governing Boards of Universities and Colleges (AGB), maintains a program for board professionals and sponsors an online network and conferences for members (agb.org/agb-board-professionals). Governing board management is thus emerging as an identifiable subspecialty of nonprofit management.

Nonprofit Board Effectiveness

"So," students may be wondering at this point in the chapter, "what's the bottom line?" Are most nonprofit boards effective or not? What are the characteristics of effective boards? What is the right way to define the relationship between the board and the nonprofit CEO? What is indeed the best model for governance, and what are the best practices that boards should follow?

Critics of Board Performance

In answer to the question of how nonprofit boards are doing, there is no shortage of negative commentary extending over decades. For example, in 1999, Chait, Thomas Holland, and Taylor reported that "after 10 years of research and dozens of engagements as consultants to nonprofit boards, we have reached a rather stark conclusion: effective governance by a board of trustees is a relatively rare and unnatural act" (p. 1). Writing several years later, Carver (2006) essentially agrees, writing that "the problem is not that a group or an individual *occasionally* [italics original] slips into poor practice, but that intelligent, caring individuals regularly exhibit procedures of governance that are deeply flawed" (p. 18). Nearly a decade after Carver's observation, Ryan, Chait, and Taylor (2013) report continuing concerns, writing that "the board is widely regarded as a problematic institution. And it's not just the occasional nonprofit financial implosion or scandal that's troubling. All institutions, after all, have their failures. Perhaps more worrisome is the widespread sense that underperforming boards are the norm, not the exception."

Such criticisms cannot be ignored, but it may be prudent to question the evidence behind such sweeping statements. Some are based on experience rather than research. Some are reported by consultants who are called on to work with troubled boards and whose samples therefore may be somewhat self-selecting. Moreover, some assessments may reflect the values and views of the assessor about what nonprofit organizations and their boards should be like.

A 2011 study undertaken by CompassPoint and The Agnes and Eugene Meyer Foundation revealed the views of nonprofit chief executives regarding the performance of their governing boards, and the results were more nuanced. While 68 percent of the CEOs were at least somewhat satisfied with their board's performance, almost one third were either very unsatisfied or only a little satisfied (Moyers, 2011, p. 2). When asked whether their boards provide a significant amount of effort to support the organization, the majority of CEOs responded positively in three areas: financial oversight, community ambassadorship, and strategic decision making and planning. But less than a majority of CEOs were positive about their boards' efforts with regard to other technical management expertise, fund development (fundraising), supervision and guidance to the CEO, and policy advocacy (Moyers, 2011).

In sum, the evidence suggests that it is unreasonable to argue that board failure is the norm. However, it is reasonable to believe that the performance of boards and their members can be improved and to continue the search for best practices in nonprofit governance.

The Search for Best Practices

Various researchers have attempted to identify behaviors that are associated with effective nonprofit governing boards—that is, to identify those practices that, if followed, will lead to effective governance. In 2005, BoardSource assembled a panel of experts to address the question. Their consensus produced the following "twelve principles that power exceptional boards":

1. *Constructive partnership:* Exceptional boards govern in constructive partnership with the chief executive, recognizing that the effectiveness of the board and that of the chief executive are interdependent.

2. *Mission driven:* Exceptional boards shape and uphold the mission, articulate a compelling vision, and ensure the congruence between decisions and core values.

3. *Strategic thinking:* Exceptional boards allocate time to what matters most and continuously engage in strategic thinking to hone the organization's direction.

4. *Culture of inquiry:* Exceptional boards institutionalize a culture of inquiry, mutual respect, and constructive debate that leads to sound and shared decision making.

5. *Independent-mindedness:* Exceptional boards are independent-minded. When making decisions, board members put the interests of the organization above all else.

6. *Ethos of transparency:* Exceptional boards promote an ethos of transparency by ensuring that donors, stakeholders, and interested members of the public have access to appropriate and accurate information regarding finances, operations, and results.

7. *Compliance with integrity:* Exceptional boards promote strong ethical values and disciplined compliance by establishing appropriate mechanisms for active oversight.

8. *Sustaining resources:* Exceptional boards link bold visions and ambitious plans to financial support, expertise, and networks of influence.

9. *Results-oriented:* Exceptional boards are results-oriented. They measure the organization's advancement toward its mission and evaluate the performance of major programs and services.

10. *Intentional board practices:* Exceptional boards intentionally structure themselves to fulfill essential governance duties and to support organizational priorities.

11. *Continuous learning:* Exceptional boards embrace the qualities of a continuous learning organization, evaluating their own performance and assessing the value they add to the organization.

12. *Revitalization:* Exceptional boards energize themselves through planned turnover, thoughtful recruitment, and inclusiveness (n.p.).[1]

BoardSource's 12 principles of governance offer an attractive description of an exceptional board and reflect the consensus of a distinguished panel of experts assembled to develop them. But it is nevertheless primarily a compilation of practitioner wisdom rather than science. And there remains no single definition of board effectiveness. This is so in part because there is no single standard for defining the effectiveness of nonprofit organizations. As John Carver (2006) notes, the variables chosen for measurement in some research studies seem to imply

> that effectiveness in governance is to be judged by whether board members are more fulfilled, challenged, or involved; the CEO is happier or the board is less meddlesome; the board raises more funds; grant revenues are increased; committees are more active; or the board chair perceives the CEO to be meeting his or her objectives. (p. 337)

But the link between such variables and the effectiveness of boards—or organizations—remains elusive. In a 2002 review of the literature on nonprofit effectiveness, Robert Herman and David Renz conclude that "[board] effectiveness is whatever significant stakeholders think it is, and there is no single objective reality." Calling the concept of best practices "somewhat of a holy grail," they advise nonprofit boards and CEOs to take a skeptical view of "one right way" prescriptions:

> Many sources that claim to offer "best practices" for NPO [nonprofit organization] boards or management provide little or no basis for their assertions. *The evidence from our . . . study does not support the claim that particular board and management practices are automatically best or even good (that is, that using them leads to effective boards and organizations) [italics original].* We prefer to talk in terms of "promising practices" to describe those approaches that warrant consideration.

> Not only is there no "silver bullet" (i.e., one practice that ensures board effectiveness)—there is no "silver arsenal." In the context of other research, we support the assertion that boards (perhaps with facilitative leadership from their chief executives) need to identify those processes that are most useful to them. Boards should not use a practice just because other boards, experts, or consultants say it is useful. They should ask some key questions: Does the practice fit this board's circumstances? Does the practice actually help the board reach good decisions? Does the practice contribute to the organization's success? (pp. 6–7)

In a subsequent review, Herman and Renz (2008) reaffirm their previous expression of caution. They conclude that "recent research clearly adds further support for the conclusion that at least in some ways, board effectiveness is related to organizational effectiveness" (p. 403). But, with regard to specific best practices, they say "further research is needed" and add, "The evidence from our . . . study does not support the claim that any specific board . . . *practices* [italics added] are indeed best practices (assuming) that the purpose of 'best practice' is that of increasing effectiveness" (p. 405).

Herman and Renz's (2002, 2008) skepticism about best practices should not be interpreted as saying that boards are unimportant or that the literature on governance has nothing to offer and should be disregarded. Rather, their conclusions are consistent with the philosophy expressed in Chapter 1 of this text: There is often no right answer, and the best way is often pragmatic and eclectic. This includes viewing a problem from multiple perspectives and drawing from various approaches selectively as the situation may dictate.

The Challenge of Nonprofit Governance

Serving as a member of a nonprofit board today is an interesting and challenging assignment. Nonprofit boards are buffeted by strong crosscurrents emanating from virtually all their constituencies. The forces of law, media scrutiny, and more demanding funders are pushing them to do a better job of governance. At the same time, the financial pressures facing many nonprofits in light of diminished government support, increased competition for philanthropy, and the rising needs and expectations of their clients are leading to greater emphasis on their responsibilities to serve as the organization's advocates, protectors, and fundraisers. As the brief review in this chapter reveals, the literature of nonprofit governance includes an abundance of advice, but some of it is inconsistent, even contradictory. Today's boards are being exhorted not only to raise money and promote the organization, but also to be more aggressive in monitoring its performance. They are told to develop independent sources of information about the organization's operations but to stay focused on the big picture and not meddle in operations, to maintain a clear line between themselves and their CEO but not to forfeit their responsibility for leadership.

Nonprofit boards are expected to be Janus-like—that is, like the Roman god of doorways and arches, who was said to have two faces and be able to look outward and inward at the same time. Nonprofit organizations are open systems, with vaguely defined and often porous boundaries. The board is positioned on that boundary, between the organization and its external environment. From that position, the board is expected to look inward, fulfilling its fiduciary responsibilities on behalf of the membership or society. It is a kind of watchdog, responsible for ensuring that the organization is accountable for the resources entrusted to it, that those resources are used effectively in pursuit of its mission and for representing the interests and viewpoints of the owners, whoever they may be.

But board members are also expected to be looking outward in order to meet their responsibilities to the organization itself and advance its interests. This is especially true for boards of charitable nonprofits, which may depend at least in part on philanthropic support. Because they are often leading citizens themselves, board members bring credibility to the organization in the broader community and authenticate its worthiness to receive support. They serve as its ambassadors and advocates, increasing its visibility and reputation within their own social and business circles. They protect the organization against inappropriate intrusions on its autonomy by government, donors, or other external forces. Further, they have a responsibility to ensure the organization's financial strength and sustainability, which many accomplish in part through giving or helping secure financial resources. These dual responsibilities—to society and to the organization itself, looking inward at the same time as looking outward—can sometimes be complex and competing. As Chait et al. (1999) explain,

> Boards constantly wrestle with when to be "product champions" and when to be studied neutrals—whether to stand and cheer like rabid partisans when the President of the United States delivers the State of the Union address or to remain seated and stone-faced like the Supreme Court justices. (p. 3)

As Table 4.2 suggests, the complex responsibilities of boards may imply somewhat different ideal qualities in the individuals selected to serve, depending on which set of responsibilities is emphasized—a possible trade-off between what is often called "wisdom" (shorthand for the skills and judgment needed to govern well) and "wealth" (meaning the ability to give or obtain funds and other external resources). To fulfill their fiduciary responsibilities, boards must include individuals of integrity, and at least some will need to have specialized knowledge in finance and perhaps in professional fields related to the organization's programs and services.

But to advance its reputation, protect its interests, and secure funds, a nonprofit also needs board members who are individuals of stature in their communities, perhaps having influence with governmental officials or other regulators, and who have either the wealth to be significant donors or access to other individuals, foundations, or corporations that can provide financial support. Of course, there may be *individual* candidates for governing board service who are possessed both of wisdom and of wealth—that is, who are equally well suited to meet their responsibilities for governing the organization and for serving as its external advocates and fundraisers. But not all individuals may be strong in all the requisite qualities. Boards attempting to craft their membership and faced with selecting a new member to fill an open seat may indeed face a dilemma regarding which qualities should be emphasized (Worth, 2005).

Likewise, in deciding on which issues to focus its limited time and attention, a board may face either-or choices between the tasks associated with governing and those associated with advancing the organization, its interests, and its resources. Today's environment presents increasing pressures on boards to do all things better—to be better stewards and better fundraisers and to become more engaged with the organization's planning, programs, and effectiveness while also giving and raising more funds to support its work. The proper trade-offs between wealth and wisdom and how to balance the sometimes competing demands are questions prompting discussion—and some anxiety—in many nonprofit boardrooms today.

TABLE 4.2 ■ The Board's Sometimes Competing Responsibilities

To society:	To the organization:
Accountability for resources and results	Advocacy and authenticity
Adherence to mission and law	Protection of autonomy
Representation of community needs	Fiscal stability and sustainability
Indicated board member qualities:	**Indicated board member qualities:**
Integrity	Stature
Expertise on programs and finances	Influence
Knowledge of community/clients	Wealth or access to wealth

Chapter Summary

The governing board holds ultimate responsibility for the nonprofit organization. There are various types of boards, including those elected by the organization's membership; self-perpetuating boards; boards appointed by some outside authority; and hybrids, which may include elected, self-perpetuating, appointed, and ex officio members. Each of these types offers advantages but also introduces risks for the organization and the board.

The governing board's fiduciary responsibilities are defined in law and include the duty of care, the duty of loyalty, and the duty of obedience. Since the passage of intermediate sanctions in 1996 and the Sarbanes-Oxley Act in 2002, there has been increased scrutiny of nonprofit boards by the federal and state governments, the media, and other organizations. Under intermediate sanctions, nonprofit board members can face individual penalties for violating their fiduciary responsibilities, and many boards adopted new conflict-of-interest and disclosure policies in response to that legislation. Although Sarbanes-Oxley applies primarily to publicly traded corporations, many nonprofit organizations have voluntarily adopted some or all of its provisions, and some have been encompassed in legislation passed by states. Independent Sector's Panel on the Nonprofit Sector issued 33 principles for good governance in 2007 and a revised version was released in 2015. Some state associations of nonprofits also have established standards for best governance practice that are used as the basis for accreditation programs. Implementation by the IRS of a revised Form 990 in 2009 further focused the nation's attention on nonprofit accountability and the responsibilities of boards. Some questions on Form 990 reflect Sarbanes–Oxley-like principles, which will be considered further in Chapter 6 of this book.

Functional responsibilities of boards have been defined in the literature and include appointing, supporting, and evaluating the CEO; establishing a clear institutional mission and purpose; approving the organization's programs to ensure consistency with its mission and financial prudence; ensuring sound management and financial stability; and establishing standards by which the organization's performance will be evaluated. Some people view the board's responsibility to ensure the organization's financial stability and sustainability as implying an obligation on the part of board members to give from their personal resources and actively engage in fundraising. Some boards have policies requiring that members give or raise a minimum amount, but others rely on a culture that encourages members to participate as appropriate to their capacities. The relationship between the governing board and the CEO is the subject of a substantial literature. In some organizations, especially those managed by a founder, the CEO may be a dominant figure, and the board may be largely reactive to the executive's initiatives. Most experts call for a partnership between the board and the CEO but differ on how that partnership should be designed. Three experts discussed in this chapter include John Carver (2006), whose policy governance model suggests a clear separation of roles, defined in policies established by the board related to ends, means, board–staff relationships, and governance process. Chait et al. (2005) propose a model they call "governance-as-leadership," in which the lines between the responsibilities of the board and the CEO are broken down and both work together in focusing on the most critical issues and questions facing the organization. Leadership is shared, particularly when both engage in generative thinking. The research of Robert Herman and Dick Heimovics (2005) revealed that in reality both board members and the chief executive see the CEO as primarily responsible for the organization's success or failure, a condition they call "executive psychological centrality." They advise CEOs to accept that reality and practice board-centered leadership, not usurping the responsibilities of the board but rather supporting and facilitating its work.

The recommendations of Carver (2006), Chait et al. (2005), and Herman and Heimovics (2005) are prescriptive, but some scholars have sought to explain why boards are configured and operate the way they do. Some have taken a contingency approach, suggesting that boards are varied according to the internal and external realities that they face.

Responsibility for managing the governing board lies primarily with the chair, working cooperatively with the CEO. In recent years, more boards have established a governance committee, which has responsibility for the overall development of the board, including the enlistment of new members, board member orientation and education, and the evaluation of the board and individual members. Some large organizations with large boards have established a senior staff position to support board activity and the role of the board professional may be an emerging new subspecialty of nonprofit management. However, it is important to remain clear that staff members report to the CEO, not to the board or its officers, and that authority lies only in the full board rather than individual members.

In today's environment, there is considerable emphasis on the effectiveness of nonprofit governance. A 2011 study found that the majority of nonprofit CEOs were at least somewhat satisfied with their boards' performance, although the CEOs reported that boards expend more effort in some areas than others. BoardSource and others have identified best practices of effective boards, but research by Herman and Renz (2002, 2008) suggests that there may be no one right way that works for every organization.

Nonprofit boards today face conflicting pressures. They are expected to do a more effective job of governing but also become more active in generating financial support for the organizations they serve. The appropriate trade-offs between the wealth and wisdom needed to meet these sometimes competing priorities are a matter of current discussion and debate in many nonprofit boardrooms.

Note

1. Reprinted with permission from *Twelve Principles of Governance That Power Exceptional Boards,* a publication of BoardSource, formerly the National Center for Nonprofit Boards. BoardSource © 2013. For more information, call 1-877-892-6273 or e-mail learningcenter@boardsource.org. Available online at various URLs, including http://pipertrust.org/wp-content/uploads/2011/05/ExceptionalBoards.pdf.

KEY TERMS AND CONCEPTS

advisory councils	excess benefit transaction	Panel on the Nonprofit Sector
board-centered leadership	executive psychological centrality	policy governance model
board of directors	ex officio	private inurement
board of trustees	fiduciary mode	purposive-rational model
BoardSource	Form 990	Sarbanes-Oxley Act
conflict of interest	generative mode	self-perpetuating boards
corporate secretary	give-or-get policy	social-constructionist model
duty of care	governance as leadership	
duty of loyalty	governing boards	strategic mode
duty of obedience	intermediate sanctions	working board

CASE 4.1 The American University

The American University is an independent, coeducational institution of about 10,000 undergraduate, graduate, and professional students, chartered by the U.S. Congress and located in Washington, DC. In early 2005, Benjamin Ladner had been president for 11 years, during which the university campus had expanded, applications had increased, and the endowment had grown (Jaffee, 2006, p. 78). But then, in March of that year, the board of trustees received an anonymous letter alleging that Ladner had used university funds for extravagant personal expenses.

Ladner's employment contract allowed for the reimbursement of expenses for university-related activities and provided other specific benefits, such as a car and driver. It was reported that the contract had been signed only by Ladner and the chair of the board of trustees and that it was never approved by the full board. Some trustees had expressed concern about the president's high compensation, but the board's audit committee had never examined the president's expenses (Jaffee, 2006). One unhappy trustee said, "It began to feel like the board reported to [the president] rather than the reverse" (p. 118).

When the anonymous letter was received, one trustee suggested going after the whistle-blower, but the board decided to start an investigation of the president's expenses (Jaffee, 2006). The president was placed on leave, and a law firm and auditor were engaged to review his expenses. The president hired his own lawyers and maintained that he had not knowingly misspent university funds (Fain, 2005a). The board split into two camps. One supported the president and said the board was at fault for not having monitored his expenses. Another blamed the president for poor judgment and called for his permanent dismissal (Jaffee, 2006). Statements by the two factions reached the media, and acrimony among trustees became public. Four members of the board, including the chair, resigned (Fain, 2005b).

Upon completion of the audit, in October of 2005, the board voted to dismiss the president, although controversy remained over his severance compensation. Some members of the board maintained that his employment contract was not valid because it had not been presented to the full board (Fain, 2005c). Senator Charles Grassley, then chair of the U.S. Senate Finance Committee, began an investigation, and some people claimed that because the university was chartered by Congress, the Congress should replace the board (Jaffee, 2006). The controversy led, in part, to the IRS's closer examination of the compensation of university presidents and gave impetus to the efforts of Independent Sector to establish, in 2007, its first set of principles of good governance for the entire nonprofit sector.

By June of 2006, the university's board of trustees had developed and adopted recommendations to improve its inclusiveness, accountability, and oversight (Fain, 2006). Among other changes, the bylaws were amended to include a student and two faculty as nonvoting members. Other reforms included performance evaluations of trustees, procedures for greater board oversight of the president's contract and expenses, and provision for town hall meetings between the board and members of the university community (Fain, 2006).

Questions Related to Case 4.1

1. Which of the governing board's legal and functional responsibilities discussed in this chapter are relevant to the controversy at The American University?

2. Do you see any ways in which the recommendations of Carver (2006), Chait et al. (2005), and Herman and Heimovics (2005) might be relevant to The American University case?

3. If you had been the chair of The American University board of trustees, how would you have proceeded upon receiving the anonymous letter regarding the president's expenses?

CASE 4.2   The Hershey Trust

Milton Hershey was the founder of the Hershey Chocolate Company, which is now known as Hershey Foods, the maker of Hershey's Milk Chocolate, Hershey's Kisses, and other products with which all Americans are familiar.

Hershey and his wife, Catherine, did not have children of their own. In 1909, they founded a school to educate poor male orphans, created a charitable trust to support the school, and appointed nine trustees to manage the trust for the school's benefit. In 1918, after his wife's death, Hershey gave his entire personal fortune, consisting mostly of stock in the company, to the Hershey Trust to support the Milton S. Hershey School. The school today enrolls a diverse student body of about 1,200 low-income young men and women on a residential campus in central Pennsylvania. The students do not pay tuition or other fees, since the trust receives $80 million from its interest in the chocolate company each year to support the school's operation (McCracken, 2009).

By 2001, the Hershey Trust had grown to over $5 billion, most of which was stock in Hershey Foods. Indeed, the charitable trust owned a controlling interest in the company, and company stock was 56 percent of the trust's assets (Gadsden, 2002). As of 2009, as mentioned above, the trust's annual income from the chocolate company provided more than $80 million toward the school's operation. With 6,200 employees, the company was the largest employer in its hometown of Hershey, Pennsylvania (Scully, 2009).

However, in 2002, the trustees of the Hershey Trust were concerned by the lack of diversification in the trust's investments and by the increasing competition from other candy makers. Fearing that the chocolate company's decline could endanger the school's future, they proposed selling the trust's controlling interest. Wrigley, best known for its chewing gum, was prepared to pay $12.5 billion (McCracken, 2009).

The Hershey community strongly objected, fearing the loss of jobs and a negative impact on the local economy. Under Pennsylvania law, the state attorney general oversees charitable trusts. The attorney general at the time, Mike Fisher, sided with the community and petitioned the state court to block the sale, arguing that it "could have profoundly negative consequences" for the Hershey region. The court agreed, and the sale was stopped. The Pennsylvania legislature later passed a law affirming the court's decision (Larkin, 2002). Some argued that the attorney general and the court had overstepped their authority and had dangerously altered the law regarding the fiduciary responsibilities of charitable trustees. They might now be required to make their decisions not only in light of the interests of the trust's beneficiaries, but also in consideration of local political and economic pressures (Larkin, 2002).

The chocolate company's position continued to decline after 2002. By 2009, Hershey Foods had suffered years of stagnating revenue and a slumping stock price, which reduced the assets of the trust and thus the revenue of the school. In addition, a wave of mergers in the food industry was presenting increased competition from large multinational producers. Meanwhile, Hershey was finding it difficult to grow its business outside of the United States and derived only 10 percent of its revenue from overseas (Wachman, 2009).

Mars merged with Wrigley in 2008 and, in 2009, Kraft made a bid to take over the famous British candy brand, Cadbury (Scully, 2009). The trustees of the Hershey Trust were deeply concerned by this new challenge to Hershey Foods. They knew the law would not permit them to *sell* the company, but they considered making an offer to *buy* Cadbury. Kraft had offered $16.5 billion for Cadbury, and Hershey would need to offer more. Hershey was only half the size of Cadbury and a fraction of Kraft's size. Buying Cadbury would require borrowing massive amounts of money. It was reported that differences arose between the views of the company's board and management, on the one hand, and the board of the charitable trust on the other. The company's board and management were concerned that such borrowing would cause the company's credit ratings and stock price to decline, raise the cost of future borrowing, and hurt profits. The charitable trustees were concerned that failing to buy Cadbury would mean that Hershey would find it even more difficult to compete internationally in the future and that the long-term interests of the trust and the school would be jeopardized (Wachman, 2009).

Throughout January of 2010, there was daily speculation in the financial media about a possible Hershey

(Continued)

(Continued)

counteroffer for Cadbury. But, on January 22, Hershey announced that it would not proceed, and Kraft announced that Cadbury had accepted its revised offer of 11.9 billion British pounds ($19.4 billion). Kraft and Cadbury combined would become the largest candy company in the world (Gural, 2010).

Questions Related to Case 4.2

1. Why might the board of Hershey Foods and the trustees of the Milton S. Hershey Trust have held somewhat different views of the possible bid for Cadbury? To whom and for what are the respective boards accountable?

2. Should boards of nonprofits be concerned only with the intention of donors and the interests of those who benefit from the nonprofit's assets, or should they also consider the impact of their decisions on local communities, as the court directed in the case of the Hershey Trust?

3. What concerns might the trustees of the Milton S. Hershey Trust have held about their own legal responsibilities? In other words, which laws might have created liability for members of that board?

QUESTIONS FOR DISCUSSION

1. If you were a nonprofit CEO, how would you describe the ideal board for which to work?

2. If you were the chair of a nonprofit board, how would you describe the ideal relationship between the board and the CEO from your perspective?

3. Should boards be held responsible for the results achieved by the organizations they govern or is that primarily the responsibility of the CEO and staff?

SUGGESTIONS FOR FURTHER READING

Books

BoardSource. (2010). *The handbook of nonprofit governance.* San Francisco, CA: Jossey-Bass.

Carver, J. (2006). *Boards that make a difference: A new design for leadership in nonprofit and public organizations* (3rd ed.). San Francisco, CA: Jossey-Bass.

Gazley, B., & Kissman, K. (2015). *Transformational governance: How boards achieve extraordinary change.* San Francisco, CA: Jossey-Bass.

Trower, C. A. (2013). *The practitioner's guide to governance as leadership : Building high-performing nonprofit boards.* San Francisco, CA: Jossey-Bass.

Worth, M. J. (2008). *Sounding boards.* Washington, DC: Association of Governing Boards of Universities and Colleges.

Websites

Association of Governing Boards of Universities and Colleges: http://www.agb.org/

BoardSource: http://www.boardsource.org/

Daring to Lead: http://daringtolead.org/

Independent Sector: http://www.independentsector.org/

Companion Website

Visit study.sagepub.com/worth4e for access to certain full-text SAGE journal articles and links to relevant video and multimedia content.

chapter 5

The deep commitment of a leader, as evidenced by his or her willingness to sacrifice and suffer for the cause, confers a charismatic appeal. Clara Barton founded the American Red Cross and led the organization for 23 years.

Photo: wikimedia.org

Learning Objectives

After reading this chapter, students should be able to:

1. Describe the responsibilities of nonprofit CEOs.

2. Contrast leadership and management.

3. Summarize prominent leadership theories related to nonprofit organizations.

4. Describe the characteristic behaviors of successful nonprofit CEOs.

5. Explain founder syndrome.

6. Identify steps in the process of change.

7. Analyze cases, applying concepts from the chapter.

Executive Leadership

5

Chapter 1 of this text discussed why nonprofit management is a distinctive undertaking, different in important ways from management in the for-profit sector or in government. Among these differences were the need for nonprofits to integrate mission, the acquisition of resources, and strategy; the complex relationships among a nonprofit organization's stakeholders (including volunteers) that require negotiation and compromise and demand that executives possess a high tolerance for ambiguity; and the need to manage a double bottom line of financial results and social impact.

These differences may not directly affect the work of everyone employed at a nonprofit organization. For example, there is no particular nonprofit way of processing bills or payments, programming computers, or maintaining physical facilities. Many who work in the nonprofit sector are engaged in such technical work, and their skills may be readily transferable across the for-profit, nonprofit, and governmental sectors. Even those who provide the services of a nonprofit organization may not perform their functions in any unique way. For example, a doctor working in a nonprofit, for-profit, or government hospital will follow the same medical protocols; a counselor working with clients recovering from drug or alcohol addiction may use the same treatments whether working in a nonprofit organization or a state-managed entity; and teachers in private and public schools may teach a similar curriculum. Where the unique characteristics of nonprofit management come together with the greatest significance is in the position of the chief executive officer (CEO). The CEO is a position requiring unique skills in both management and leadership, which this chapter explores. In this examination, we will draw on the theoretical literature of leadership as well as the practitioner literature produced by consultants, other experts, and nonprofit CEOs themselves.

The CEO's Job

What do nonprofit chief executives actually do? In other words, what is the job description? Of course, because no two organizations are exactly the same, the CEO's job may vary widely from one to another. In some, fundraising may be an important expectation, while in others it is not. In organizations that have mostly paid professional staff, the skills required of a CEO may be different from those needed to lead an organization that relies on volunteers for a substantial portion of its workforce. Also, as discussed in Chapter 4, the type of governing board with which the chief executive works may greatly influence the types of challenges that he or she may face. While recognizing these inevitable differences, Richard Moyers identified ten basic responsibilities of the nonprofit chief executives in a 2013 publication for BoardSource:

1. *Commit to the mission:* The CEO must understand the mission, keep the mission prominently in mind when making decisions, and guard against mission drift.

2. *Lead the staff and manage the organization:* The CEO has direct responsibility for hiring, training, developing, and motivating the staff; developing an organizational structure that suits the organization's work; and ensuring that day-to-day operations and programs are effective and efficient.

3. *Exercise responsible financial stewardship:* While the governing board has overall responsibility for ensuring the organization's financial soundness, it is the chief executive who must manage its assets, revenues, and expenditures on a day-to-day basis and ensure that controls are in place to protect the organization against fraud or waste.

4. *Lead and manage fundraising:* The CEO's responsibility for fundraising will vary from one organization to another and is shared with the governing board. In charitable nonprofits, the CEO's direct engagement in fundraising, planning fundraising programs, and managing the fundraising staff may consume a substantial portion of his or her time and energy.

5. *Follow the highest ethical standards, ensure accountability, and comply with the law:* Again, the governing board may set policies (remember Carver's executive limitations discussed in Chapter 4) that establish standards and procedures to ensure legal and ethical behavior. However, it is the chief executive who needs to put these policies into practice in the organization's daily life and set an example through his or her own behavior.

6. *Engage the board in planning and lead implementation:* Planning for the organization's future is a shared responsibility of the board and the CEO, but the reality in many organizations requires that the chief executive take a significant role in initiating the planning effort, providing the resources for planning, and defining issues and questions for the board to deliberate.

7. *Develop future leadership:* In many organizations, the CEO plays a role in developing the leadership of the board, both informally and often as a member of the board's nominating committee. There is also an increasing emphasis on the importance of the CEO's preparing for possible staff departures by developing a bench of qualified successors and, indeed, for preparing the way for a smooth transition when he or she may leave the chief executive's position.

8. *Build external relationships and serve as an advocate:* Some research considered later in this chapter emphasizes that effective chief executives are those who are externally oriented—who are constantly alert to opportunities and threats in the external environment and engaged in building external partnerships for their organization.

9. *Ensure the quality and effectiveness of programs:* The board may set the standards by which the effectiveness of programs is to be evaluated, but the CEO must ensure that the right questions are asked and the right data collected so that a process of evaluation and continuous learning is a part of the organization's ongoing work.

10. *Support the board:* Just as the governing board has a responsibility to support its CEO, the CEO has a reciprocal responsibility to support the board. Moreover, as we discussed in Chapter 4, research suggests that effective CEOs are ones who practice board-centered leadership.[1]

Two realities are evident in Moyer's list of CEO responsibilities. One is the number of areas in which the chief executive shares responsibility with the governing board regarding mission, financial stewardship, fundraising, accountability, planning, performance standards, and the work of the board itself. This explains why the relationship between the CEO and the board is so complex and why so many experts have focused on delineating the CEO and board responsibilities in each area.

The second observation that emerges from a review of the CEO's responsibilities is that they involve both *managing* and *leading*. The CEO is responsible for ensuring that financial management systems are in place, for the hiring and evaluation of staff, and for monitoring the quality and effectiveness of programs. But chief executives are also expected to be external spokespersons for their organizations, able to articulate the mission and make a persuasive case for financial support; to be capable of motivating both paid staff and volunteers to high performance; and to hold a vision and strategy for the organization's future, which, working together with the board, they translate into a plan for the organization's advancement and growth. These latter tasks require something beyond management: They require that the CEO be a leader.

Management and Leadership

Although people may use the words interchangeably, leadership and management are not the same thing. *Management* is generally concerned with day-to-day operations, with making things work. It emphasizes policies, procedures, rules, and processes. Management is transactional; the manager provides rewards in exchange for the work contributions of others or imposes sanctions (punishments) on those who do not meet the requirements of their assignments. A manager is often concerned primarily with maintaining a smooth operation, that is, keeping the machine running and avoiding breakdowns, rather than with change.

Leadership is more about purpose, vision, and direction—that is, more about the "where" and the "why" rather than the "how." In a widely quoted statement, Warren Bennis and Burt Nanus (1985) suggest a moral element to leadership: "Managers are people who do things right and leaders are people who do the right thing" (p. 21). Leadership is interactive; that is, it is a *process,* and it involves a *relationship* between the leader and the people who are led. There can be no leaders without followers, and both play a part in the process of leadership. Leaders are focused on change, and that change is not directionless; leadership involves moving people toward the achievement of some defined *goals.* Some of the differences between leaders and managers are summarized in Table 5.1.

Sometimes, the roles of leader and manager are performed by different people; indeed, some argue that the two roles require different personal qualities or skills rarely found in the same individual. At other times, one person may have the responsibility both for leading the organization and for managing its affairs—for example, the CEO of a small nonprofit. But the functions of leadership and management are different, and such people need to be able to switch from one role to the other as the needs of the organization and the occasion may dictate. Indeed, there are those who assert that founders of nonprofit organizations often exhibit strong qualities of leadership but may be unable to provide the management the organization needs as it grows, sometimes leading to the problem known as founder syndrome, discussed later in this chapter.

In larger organizations, CEOs often play the leadership role and delegate management responsibilities to subordinates, such as a chief operating officer. It is possible for a CEO to delegate management to others, but only the CEO can provide leadership to the entire organization. Leadership of the organization is not a responsibility that can be delegated.

All organizations need both leadership and management to be successful in the long run. It is conceivable that an organization—whether a for-profit business, a government agency, or a nonprofit organization—can survive for a time with only good management. But to thrive and grow, an organization also needs leaders who define vision, articulate direction, set goals, and influence others to achieve these together.

Nonprofit organizations especially need leadership. The reasons are rooted in their characteristics, which we have discussed in earlier chapters. Corporations and government agencies generally have well-defined missions, straightforward measures of performance, and revenue that is derived from either appropriated funds or quid pro quo transactions with customers. In contrast, nonprofits are *values based* and *mission driven.* There is not always consensus about mission or about appropriate ways of measuring performance against the mission. Financial and other resources are often bestowed *voluntarily.* Leadership is essential to develop consensus about mission and performance and to articulate a vision that gains and holds the commitment of volunteer board members, service volunteers, donors, and others. This book includes the current chapter on executive leadership simply because leadership is so central to the role of a nonprofit CEO. A lack of leadership by the CEO of a nonprofit organization will eventually, and inevitably, lead to the organization's drift, decline, and failure.

TABLE 5.1 ■ Managers and Leaders Compared	
Managers	**Leaders**
Concerned with mastering routines	Concerned with vision and judgment
Adopt impersonal or passive attitudes toward goals	Active and visionary about the future
Excel in problem solving and work design	Seek out opportunities and take risks
Work with people in carefully controlled ways	Passionate about their work and likely to cause turbulence
See themselves as conservators or regulators	See themselves as agents of change

Source: Based on Denhardt, Denhardt, and Aristigueta (2013, pp. 203–204).

Overview of Leadership Theories

We have established that leadership is critical in nonprofit organizations. Now let's turn our attention to understanding it by looking at some fundamental questions. Are leaders born or made? If they are made, what specific knowledge or skills do individuals need to acquire in order to be strong leaders? What is it that successful leaders actually do—in other words, are there specific behaviors that are associated with effective leadership? These are questions that long have been asked, and there is a substantial body of research that has sought to provide answers.

It is important to remember two points as we review some of the well-known leadership theories. First, most of the theories are generic; that is, theorists intend them to apply to leadership in all types of organizations, not just nonprofits. And second, as in our earlier discussion of governing, there may be no one right theory of leadership that is applicable in every situation, at all times.

Leadership theory has evolved over the decades. Among the earliest theories were the *trait theories,* which explain leadership in terms of the innate characteristics of individuals who are leaders. They are essentially "great-man-or-woman theories," which hold the qualities of leadership to be fundamental aspects of an individual's personality. In the past, some have looked to physical characteristics to explain why certain people are leaders; for example, physical height and a resonant speaking voice—essentially male qualities—were once considered intrinsic to leadership, although they would not explain Golda Meir, Indira Gandhi, or Mother Teresa! Other trait theorists have pointed more to elements of personality, character, or psychology. For example, in 1948, Ralph Stodgill studied leaders and found them to be better than the average person in terms of intelligence, alertness, insight, responsibility, initiative, persistence, self-confidence, and sociability. Since it is difficult for individuals to change their intelligence or personalities, trait theories imply that leaders are born, not made; that is, leadership is not something that can be taught or learned (Northouse, 2013, p. 32).

The trait theories, however, do not seem to provide the whole answer. Thus, in about the middle of the twentieth century, theorists began to take a different approach, developing *skills theories* of leadership. Skills theories hold that it is not the innate qualities of individuals, such as physical appearance or even intelligence, that make them effective leaders. Rather, there are specific skills that effective leaders possess; in other words, effective leadership depends less on what the leaders are and more on what they are able to do. For example, in 1955, Daniel Katz suggested that effective leadership depends on the leader possessing skills in three areas: *technical* (knowledge of the job, profession, or task), *human* (the ability to work with people), and *conceptual* (the ability to understand ideas and principles). A skills theory is the assumption underlying most leadership training or development programs.

Beginning in the 1950s, leadership researchers started to move beyond studying the traits and skills of individual leaders toward looking at what it is that leaders actually *do*—that is, they considered whether it was possible to identify specific *behaviors* associated with effective leadership. Among the most famous of leadership studies that followed this approach were those conducted at Ohio State University. These studies identified two basic types of leader behaviors: *task behaviors* (actions that relate to the work to be done) and *relationship behaviors* (actions that focus on the feelings of subordinates). At about the same time, similar studies conducted at the University of Michigan identified essentially the same categories, which researchers there labeled *production orientation* and *employee orientation*. The ways in which leaders mix task and relationship behaviors can define a leadership style (Northouse, 2013, pp. 76–78).

Among the theorists who analyzed leadership styles are Robert Blake and Jane Mouton (1985) who developed the well-known *managerial grid*. This grid is based on different combinations of task and relationship behaviors and defines four styles. Organizations that are high on production (task) and low on relationships are said to have *authority-obedience management*. Essentially, they are dictatorships, although they may be productive. Those high on relationships and low on concern for production are described as having *country club management*. They may be great places to work, but they get little or nothing accomplished. Organizations that are low on both concern for people and production exhibit *impoverished management*. These would be dreadful places to work, and most people likely would not stay long in such an uninspiring environment. The ideal type, showing high concern for both people and production, is called *team management* (Rainey, 2014). It is likely that most readers can imagine situations, or perhaps have even experienced ones, in which each of these styles is practiced.

It might seem obvious that what may be an effective leadership style in one situation may not be so under different circumstances. But the idea that effective leadership behavior might depend on the situation was a new approach in the late 1960s and early 1970s. Building on the concept of leadership styles, the *situational theories* emphasized the fact that different styles might be more appropriate in certain situations than in others, that is, that leaders might need to adapt their styles to the environment in which they were working.

Contingency theories take situational theories one step further and provide a way of matching leader styles to defined situations. In other words, the most effective style of leadership is *contingent* on the situation. Different situations might call for different combinations of task-oriented and relationship-oriented behaviors. But what defines a "situation"? And exactly what differences between situations are relevant to determining the right leadership style (Northouse, 2013, p. 123)?

One of the best-known contingency theories is the one developed by Fiedler in 1967. According to Fiedler, the situation may be favorable or unfavorable to the leader, depending on three variables: *leader–member relations* (e.g., the degree of trust, cooperativeness, and friendliness between the leader and followers), the *task structure* (whether the job to be done is clear and specific or ambiguous and uncertain), and the *position power* of the leader (i.e., the formal position of authority the leader holds). The most favorable situation is when all three variables are high, and the least favorable is when all three are low, but there can be moderately favorable situations that show some combination of favorable and unfavorable conditions. According to Fiedler's findings, task-oriented leaders do best when conditions are very favorable or very unfavorable, while relationship-oriented leaders do best in the intermediate circumstances (Fiedler, 1967).

Contingency theories add a level of sophistication beyond the trait, skill, and behavior theories of leadership. They begin to explain why some styles of leadership may be successful in certain circumstances and not in others. Imagine, for example, a situation in which a nonprofit chief executive is facing the need to mobilize staff and volunteers to provide relief to victims of a natural disaster. The urgency of the situation makes everyone inclined to be cooperative. Let's also assume that the executive is trusted and well liked by the staff and volunteers. The task is clear and unambiguous: It is to provide food, clothing, and shelter to the victims as quickly as possible. These circumstances—cooperativeness, trust, a clear task, a leader with formal authority—would be a situation that Fiedler's model would define as favorable to the leader. A task-oriented style likely would be most effective. The important thing would be to get the job done, and there would be little need to concentrate on relationships among people, which are already good. But imagine a different situation, one in which an acting executive director has been on the job for just a few months while a search for a permanent director is proceeding. This person leads an environmental advocacy organization and is trying to mobilize volunteers to support critical environmental legislation by contacting their elected representatives. The task seems clear and specific. However, the person's position power is weak because of the acting status, and he or she may not have been in the role long enough to have gained the trust and friendship of the staff and volunteers. In Fiedler's theory, this situation is intermediate in its favorableness to the leader, who likely would need to devote considerable attention to nurturing his or her relationships with the volunteers and staff to mobilize them to action; in other words, the leader would need to emphasize relationship behaviors more than task behaviors.

Although not a theory per se, one approach to leadership that has gained a following and spawned a number of books is that of *servant leadership,* advanced by Robert Greenleaf (1977). Greenleaf argues that leadership begins with the leader's values and commitments and that moral leaders are more concerned with serving others than with meeting their own self-interest. Servant-leaders exhibit honesty, integrity, character, and spirit. Rather than trying to impose their will on others, they listen, empathize with others, and focus on relationships, approaching the position of leader as a type of stewardship of the organization, with the goal of social improvement (Denhardt, Denhardt, & Aristigueta, 2013, pp. 213–214).

Our discussion of leadership theories in this chapter is limited, but various scholars have taken approaches that depart from the theories discussed above. For example, *path-goal theories* emphasize how leaders can adapt their behaviors to motivate followers and enhance satisfaction and performance (Northouse, 2013, p. 137). *Leader-member exchange theories* view leadership in terms of interactions between leaders and followers (Northouse, 2013, p. 161). Students interested in knowing more about these approaches may wish to pursue additional reading suggested at the end of this chapter.

Transformational Leadership

A 1978 book by political scientist James MacGregor Burns, titled simply *Leadership,* had seminal influence on thinking about the topic and offers insights that may be of particular relevance to leadership in the nonprofit sector. First, Burns made a distinction between transactional leadership and transformational leadership. *Transactional leadership* is an exchange process, in which the leader exchanges rewards or punishments for the behaviors of others: If you come to work, you will get paid; if you don't, you won't. If you miss work too often, you will be fired. Thus, transactional leadership is essentially like management. In contrast, *transformational leadership,* as the name implies, is leadership that *changes* people. According to Burns, transformational leadership inspires and enables people to grow, both morally and in terms of their levels of motivation. It empowers individuals to go beyond self-interest and pursue goals that are in the common interest. Transformational leaders accomplish this by developing a relationship with followers and tapping into their personal values in a way that matches them to the values of the organization. They motivate followers not based on rewards and punishments, but by appealing to these shared values and ideals.

Let's consider a simple example that might illustrate transactional and transformational approaches. Tom is the CEO of a nonprofit organization that delivers meals to housebound older people. He is addressing a meeting of his staff, and he is concerned that some have been showing up late for work, delaying the delivery of meals to clients. One way to approach the issue would be for Tom to say something like,

I've noticed that I am the first one here in the morning. Some of you don't show up until an hour later. As a result, some meals are being delivered late. If this continues, I will need to consider docking the pay of staff who report late and firing people if it continues. I will expect to see you all here at 6 a.m. tomorrow morning.

However, taking a different approach, Tom might say something like,

I am concerned. I know that some of our clients wait for their meals to be delivered and that in fact their contact with our volunteers may be the high point of their days. When I see that we are late in getting the meals out the door in the morning, I cannot help but worry about a lonely older person, perhaps a little hungry, who is left waiting because maybe we had other things to do that morning. I know you share my concern about that. I know our clients appreciate everything you can do to make sure we are meeting their needs—and on time—because they count on us.

Which approach is more likely to result in staff arriving earlier? The first is purely transactional: You do (or do not do) this and I will do (or not do) that. The transactional approach may be effective in the short run; after all, staff members rely on their paychecks. But the effects of Tom's speech may wear off in a few days unless he repeats it and his threats are backed up. That will require his continuing intervention, possibly undermining his relationships with the staff over time. The second approach has tones of transformational leadership. It appeals to shared values rather than the promise or threat of consequences. It may move staff members to change their behaviors by affecting changes in their own heads and hearts. If accomplished, such change will likely be more lasting and powerful than the tools of a more transactional style.

Burns's book inspired work by other scholars, who adopted, expanded, and refined his ideas. One prominent leadership scholar, Bernard Bass (1985; Bass & Avolio, 1994), developed a more comprehensive model of transformational leadership. He differed slightly with Burns on some points. For one, Bass emphasized that transformational leaders also use transactional techniques in that they do provide goals and rewards for reaching them. This is not a problem as long as they do not overemphasize these techniques, especially those that are negative. Rewards may be more consistent with transformational leadership than are punishments. In other words, there may be times when the hypothetical CEO Tom may find that some staff members do not respond adequately to his values-based approach and will indeed need to be subject to "transactions" (Rainey, 2014, pp. 350–351).

Most of the leadership theories considered in this chapter describe a leader's relationship with *subordinates*. But what is significant about the concept of transformational leadership is that it also offers an approach to leading *organizations*—especially those that are values based and mission driven. A nonprofit chief executive must lead more than the members of his or her paid staff. Among others, the CEO must also at times lead donors, volunteers, and even members of the board.

Think back to the earlier example of Tom speaking to members of his staff. The transactional approach, using rewards and punishments to change behavior, might be effective with the staff, at least in the short run. But how could that approach be effective in motivating individuals to give or members of the board to increase their efforts in fundraising, or in inspiring volunteers to work longer and harder? Would not those goals be better accomplished by identifying how the values of those individuals coincide with those of the organization and appealing to those values in a way that the desired behavior is dictated from within their own hearts?

In *Good to Great and the Social Sectors*, a sequel to his best-selling book on companies, Jim Collins (2005) observes how nonprofit leadership is unique, and he describes two types (or styles) of leadership that have similarities to Burns's transactional and transformational approaches. *Executive leadership* exists when the leader has the power to simply make decisions. *Legislative leadership* is a style that "relies more upon persuasion, political currency, and shared interests to create the conditions for the right decisions to happen" (Collins, 2005, p. 11). Nonprofit executives often do not have the formal power of corporate CEOs. They generally do not have the financial resources with which to offer significant monetary incentives. Indeed, some of their workforce is not paid at all, and even those who are may be motivated as much by their commitment to the mission as they are by their financial needs. Rather than lead through rewards and punishments, nonprofit executives must use the less raw, but considerable, power of ideas, persuasion, inspiration, and relationships to lead others—and their organizations—in the directions they wish them to pursue. Collins (2005) also observes that effective nonprofit leaders are those who practice *Level 5 leadership*, the top level of a hierarchy he defines. Such leaders are "ambitious first and foremost for the cause, the movement, the mission, the work—*not themselves*—and they have the will to do whatever it takes *whatever* it takes to make good on that ambition" (p. 11) [italics original]. Collins (2005) argues that in the nonprofit sector, a leader's "compelling combination of personal humility and professional will is a key factor in creating legitimacy and influence" (p. 11).

Charismatic Leadership

The idea of charisma is one that is familiar to most people. When asked to name someone who is a leader, people often will mention the names of political figures, such as Ronald Reagan, Martin Luther King Jr., Barack Obama, or Eleanor Roosevelt. When asked what makes all these individuals unusual, some inevitably will use the term *charisma*.

The prominence of Burns's concept of transformational leadership has led to an increasing interest in *charismatic leadership,* which remains an active area of research today. Some debate whether transformational and charismatic leadership are the same, different, or overlapping concepts, but fine distinctions need not concern us here. The two types of leadership are, at the least, related.

There is debate about the nature of charisma. Is it based on personal characteristics of the leader—is it some kind of "right stuff" that some people just have and others do not? Or is charisma defined by behaviors that can be learned? Some argue that theories of charismatic leadership really represent a retreat to the earlier trait theories. But Bass and other scholars have identified specific behaviors that may cause followers to *attribute* the characteristics of charisma to the leader. In other words, a leader is someone who behaves in certain ways that cause others to see him or her as charismatic (Bryman, 1992).

What are some of the behaviors that may cause others to see the leader as charismatic? Here are some that researchers have identified (Rainey, 2014, p. 352):

- *The leader advocates a vision that is* different *from the status quo but still acceptable to followers.* Leadership is about change, but not change so radical as to alienate potential followers. Martin Luther King Jr. advocated an end to segregation and racial discrimination. This represented not only a change from the status quo in America in the 1960s, but also a change that King's followers, and eventually the nation, came to accept as morally compelling. Rather than call for violent revolution, King advocated nonviolent means, remaining within the boundaries of what his followers and sympathizers could find acceptable.
- *The leader acts in unconventional ways in pursuit of the vision.* King led boycotts and marches. Nelson Mandela spent 27 years in jail in protest against South Africa's inhumane system of apartheid. Neither brought about change merely by giving occasional speeches or by other more conventional means.
- *The leader engages in self-sacrifice and risk taking in pursuit of the vision.* Mandela sacrificed 27 years. Mother Teresa lived a life of poverty among the poor. King ultimately gave his life. The deep commitment of a leader, as evidenced by his or her willingness to sacrifice, even suffer, for the cause compels attention and confers a charismatic appeal. "By showing unswerving dedication to

the vision, making personal sacrifices, and engaging in unconventional behavior . . . [charismatic leaders] inspire their followers to transcend their self-interests for the sake of a collective goal" (Choi, 2006).

- *The leader displays confidence in his or her own ideas and proposals.* Perhaps the undoing of Jimmy Carter as president of the United States (he was not reelected to a second term) was a speech he gave to the nation in which he acknowledged his own shortcomings as president and described the nation's mood as discouraged. (This speech is often referred to as Carter's "malaise" speech, although he did not use that word.) In contrast, Ronald Reagan's optimistic vision of "morning in America" was an important factor in his election to the presidency in 1980, although many opinion polls showed that a majority of Americans disagreed with his specific positions on issues. Similarly, it was Barack Obama's optimistic assurance of "yes, we can" that inspired many of his supporters in 2008. Charismatic leaders command our following, partly because they appear so certain that their course is right.

- *The leader uses visioning and persuasive appeals to influence followers, rather than relying mainly on formal authority.* Martin Luther King Jr. never held public office. But the words "I have a dream" created a vision of a different America that inspired millions and changed the nation more dramatically than most presidents of the United States have ever been able to do.

- *The leader uses the capacity to assess context and locate opportunities for novel strategies.* Charismatic leaders read the moment; that is, they can take the temperature of their times and followers and create opportunities to demonstrate their cause in dramatic and novel ways. In 1987, Ronald Reagan stood yards from the Berlin Wall and addressed himself to the leader of the Soviet Union saying, "Mr. Gorbachev, tear down this wall!" It was a dramatic moment, which Reagan must have known would resonate with people on both sides of the wall at that point in history. Just over two years later, the wall was gone, not entirely as a result of Reagan's speech but rather as the culmination of historical forces that were gathering strength. However, Reagan understood the context and used the opportunity of his visit to the wall to dramatize the issue. Many years later, then-presidential candidate Barack Obama spoke to a large and enthusiastic gathering in Berlin, signifying in a visual way that he intended to pursue a policy approach to Europe that would represent change and improve U.S. international relationships.

To the above list of behaviors of charismatic leaders, James Fisher (1984), who writes about the use of charismatic leadership by college and university presidents, adds the idea of *social distance.* He suggests that to be perceived as charismatic, the leader cannot permit himself or herself to be too familiar. Consistent with the military's long-standing rule that officers are not to fraternize with enlisted personnel, leaders may be friendly, but not too much so. They can be congenial but never silly. They can socialize with subordinates (or board members or donors) but never stay too long or drink too much. If charisma is something attributed to leaders, as psychologists suggest, it seems that we may prefer just a bit of mystery and to believe that they are just a little different from us.

Although they play an important part in contemporary leadership theory and research, the ideas of transformational leadership and charismatic leadership have their critics. Some raise academic issues, saying that charisma is too ill defined to measure or analyze. Others say the idea of charismatic leadership is really just a newer version of the "great man/great woman" theory of leadership. (Remember the issue from our case in Chapter 3 about the Smithsonian's National Museum of American History and the Catherine B. Reynolds Foundation?) Still others raise substantive concerns about the risks of charismatic leadership to organizations: For example, the power of charismatic leadership may be abused, or an organization dependent on a charismatic leader may be vulnerable if that leader leaves, retires, or dies (Northouse, 2013, pp. 202–203).

TABLE 5.2 ■ Summary of Selected Leadership Theories

Theories	Representative Author(s)	Summary of Concepts
Trait theories	Stodgill (1948)	Leadership is explained in terms of inherent characteristic of individuals.
Skills theories	Katz (1955)	Leaders possess specific technical, human, and conceptual skills.
Leadership style (behaviors)	Blake and Mouton (1985)	Leaders engage in specific behaviors, including some that are task oriented and some that are human oriented. The mix of these behaviors defines a leadership style.
Situational theories	Hersey and Blanchard (1969)	Based on leadership styles; different situations call for a different leadership style, and the leader needs to adapt.
Contingency theories	Fiedler (1967)	Certain styles of leadership, including the mix of task-oriented and human-oriented behaviors, may be effective in some situations and not in others. Three important variables that define the situation are leader-member relations; the task structure; and position power of the leader. Contingency theories match leadership styles to particular situations.
Path-goal theory	Evans (1970)	Focuses on the motivations of employees and efforts to enhance performance and satisfaction
Leader-member exchange theory	Dansereau, Graen, and Haga (1975)	Emphasizes interactions between the leader and followers
Servant leadership	Greenleaf (1977)	Leadership is related to the leader's values and commitments; servant leaders see themselves as serving others.
Transformational leadership	Burns (1978)	Leaders develop a relationship with followers and tap into their values in order to enable them to grow, both morally and in terms of their levels of motivation.
Charismatic leadership	House (1976)	Leaders perceived as charismatic are those who engage in certain behaviors, including advocating a vision, sacrificing in pursuit of the vision, exhibiting confidence, and engaging in persuasive appeals rather than exercising formal authority.

The Effective Nonprofit CEO

If leadership is so vital to the success of the nonprofit organization, what do we know about what makes an effective nonprofit CEO? We have discussed some major theories of leadership, but what evidence do we have of what actually works best in the nonprofit sector?

As with the topic of governing boards, much of the literature on nonprofit executive leadership is prescriptive. In other words, "It tells more about how to lead and much less about how leaders actually go about their business" (Dym & Hutson, 2005, p. 6). And, as is the case with governing boards, a significant portion of the literature on nonprofit leadership has been written by consultants or reflective practitioners and is practitioner oriented in its approach.

Empirical research focused specifically on nonprofit leadership is growing. But research on effective nonprofit leadership faces challenges. One problem is how to define it; this is bound up with the larger issue of how to define an effective nonprofit organization. As in measuring the effectiveness of the nonprofit board, the idea of CEO effectiveness is also socially constructed, and the definition of what constitutes an effective nonprofit CEO may vary according to the perceptions of the organization's diverse constituencies.

Indeed, a common method that researchers have used for identifying effective nonprofit leaders is based on perceptions. Nonprofit executives or perhaps opinion leaders, such as foundation officers and academics, are asked to identify those CEOs whom they deem to be most successful or effective. The characteristics of these CEOs are then compared with those of another group of CEOs who were not named. But this method is problematic and raises the question of how the nominators are defining "effective." Those identified as effective may simply be the most visible or popular in their fields. Charismatic leaders may be favored over others of different styles because they are often highly visible and magnetic personalities. Or the executives identified by their colleagues as being effective might have been those who had been active as presenters at professional conferences or as authors, perhaps demonstrating their knowledge about nonprofit leadership, but not necessarily bearing any relationship to their performance as leaders of their own organizations. Furthermore, it is not always clear whether survey or interview respondents are describing how things are, how they believe they should be, or how they think they should respond.

Many studies based on surveys of perceptions reflect what seem to be trait or skills theories of leadership. For example, nonprofit CEOs interviewed by Mike Hudson (2005) identified openness and honesty as the most important qualities of effective nonprofit chief executives. In another study, nonprofit sector opinion leaders identified passion and commitment, vision, integrity, trust, and credibility (Light, 2002). Similar traits are also mentioned in the practitioner-oriented literature—integrity and trust (Pidgeon, 2004), vision, initiative, openness, and responsiveness (Howe, 2004).

Some research studies and the practitioner literature have also identified skills associated with effective nonprofit leadership. They commonly identify interpersonal skills, communication skills, delegation skills, staff management skills, the ability to articulate and write a message, and the ability to raise funds (Howe, 2004; Light, 2002; Pidgeon, 2004). Many of the skills identified are, of course, generic and would seem to be useful to leaders in any organization. The skills unique to nonprofits (e.g., fundraising) are essentially technical, and others mentioned are more related to management than to leadership.

Some authors do describe behaviors of effective nonprofit CEOs, but most of this literature is prescriptive. It tells us what CEOs should *do* to be effective, and it often emphasizes areas on which the chief executive should focus his or her time and attention. Five areas are frequently mentioned, and these are discussed below.

Focus on Mission

The importance of staying focused on the mission is emphasized by almost all authors on the topic of effective nonprofit CEOs. The mission is the nonprofit's reason for existence, and the CEO should use it as a guide for every decision. Many nonprofit boards include leaders from the business community, who may sometimes find it attractive to direct the organization toward activities that are financially lucrative but that may distract it from its primary mission. Staff may sometimes propose activities that would be "nice to do" but that may not advance the mission directly. The CEO can use the mission as a shield against such pressures from the staff or board, to explain, justify, and give coherence to his or her actions.

Focus on the Board

Many authors emphasize the importance of the CEO's relationship with the board. Chapter 4 discussed the research of Robert Herman and Dick Heimovics (1991, 2005), who identified board-centered leadership as the behavior distinguishing effective CEOs from others. As they report their research findings,

Analysis showed that executive leadership in relation to staff and in relation to the board are independent and distinct factors. Effective and comparison executives differed little in leadership with their staffs. The most important finding was that the effective executives provided significantly more leadership to their boards. (p. 157)

Focus on External Relationships

Effective nonprofit leaders are those who are not excessively focused on internal management. They are not obsessed with policies and procedures and the day-to-day activities of their subordinates. Rather, they "delegate much of the management of internal affairs and focus on the external" (Herman & Heimovics, 2005, p. 159). Practical strategies for enhancing external impact may involve developing an informal information network, including contacts in government, other nonprofits, foundations, and professional associations, to supplement hard data with soft information about emerging trends and practices in the field.

Fundraising is an important aspect of the external activity of many nonprofit CEOs, and indeed, its importance is growing as government support for many programs has been reduced. While the opinion leaders and nonprofit CEOs interviewed by Light (2002) mentioned fundraising as an important skill, it is surprising how seldom it is addressed in much of the nonprofit leadership literature.

Share Leadership and Empower Others

In their study of high-impact nonprofits, Leslie Crutchfield and Heather Grant (2008, 2012) determined that effective nonprofit CEOs share leadership with others. This sometimes includes having two people in top positions, with complementary skills—for example, someone who is good at outside relationships and another who specializes in internal operations. It also includes developing a team of leaders within the organization, that is, having bench strength and empowering members of the leadership team.

Focus on Key Roles and Priorities

In their well-known work on leadership, Nanus and Stephen Dobbs (1999) address the question of where the nonprofit CEO needs to direct his or her attention—their answer: almost everywhere. They define four quadrants in which the CEO may focus and operate at any given time—inside the organization, outside the organization, on present operations, and on future possibilities. They identify six roles defined by these four areas and argue that the effective CEO needs to be proficient in *all* of them. When the CEO combines an internal perspective with attention to present operations, he or she is acting in the role of "coach," guiding staff and others who are performing the organization's work. Looking inward but with a view to the future, the CEO is playing the role of "change agent." When CEOs are focused outside the organization but concerned with present operations, they are performing as "politicians" and as "fundraisers." And when CEOs are focused externally and looking to the future, they are performing as "visionaries" and "strategists."

Herman and Heimovics (2005) urge nonprofit CEOs to stay focused on key "goals or outcomes [that are] crucial"; that is, they advise nonprofit CEOs to "know your agenda" (p. 160). A well-managed organization may have goals derived from a formal process of strategic planning, but effective executives have their own short list of priorities—a few key things they wish to accomplish. Those priorities may be drawn from the plan or be supplemental to it. Rather than scatter their attention and efforts across a broad list of goals, CEOs will be more successful if they can limit their priorities to a few critical initiatives that will define their leadership of the organization and focus their own attention and that of others on those items. Mim Carlson and Margaret Donohoe (2003), both former nonprofit executives and now consultants, agree, advising, "Don't let a list of priorities exceed five items, and three is better" (p. 33).

Remembering that board members, donors, and even staff may not be thinking about organizational goals all the time and that they face innumerable distractions in their own personal and professional lives, it is important for the CEO to keep the short-listed goals constantly in front of them and to ensure that they have the same information and perspective as the CEO, so they will come to share his or her understanding of what the priorities are and why. Leaders also need to simplify the priorities and "lay a bread-crumb trail" to key decisions through communications and small actions that lead the way to larger changes, as a way of preparing the board and others, so that when changes need to be made, they will not seem to come out of the blue. The leaders will have prepared their constituents for change, one step at a time (Herman & Heimovics, 2005, pp. 160–161).

Use the "Political Frame"

In their insightful and practical research on nonprofit executives, Herman and Heimovics (2005) find that effective CEOs are distinguished from others by their use of a "political frame." Indeed, they say this is a finding of their research in which they have particular confidence.

The concept of frames was developed by Lee Bolman and Terrence Deal (2003). A *frame* is a perspective or a way of seeing and understanding things—like seeing the glass either half empty or half full. Bolman and Deal (2003) identified four frames that leaders may use. Some may view their organizations through a *structural frame*, focusing on structures and formal relationships. Or they may use the *human resources frame*, emphasizing interpersonal relationships and worker morale. A third frame is the *symbolic frame*, through which a leader may see events, rituals, and stories as central to his or her work.

When leaders use the *political frame*, that does not mean that they see things in terms of partisan or elective politics, but rather that they recognize the inevitable interplay among the organization's important constituencies. The political frame is a perspective through which the CEO sees and understands the environment in terms of the pressures brought by various constituencies that compete, bargain, and negotiate over the allocation of resources. Leaders using this frame will be sensitive to external forces that might affect the organization and, therefore, devote their time and effort to maintaining relationships and influencing various competing constituencies. All leaders may use all of the frames at particular times. What Herman and Heimovics (2005) found was that effective nonprofit CEOs use political frame substantially and more than others who were identified as less successful (p. 165).

Right Person, Right Place, Right Time

In a book focused on leadership in the nonprofit sector, but with more generic applications as well, Barry Dym and Harry Hutson (2005) argue that nonprofit executive effectiveness results from having the right person in the right job at the right time; in other words, it is necessary to have a good fit between the leader and the needs of the organization at the time.

They propose an *alignment model* that seeks to integrate the major leadership theories, that is, to provide "an overarching conceptual framework that brings the theories together, or at least describes how the theories relate to one another" (Dym & Hutson, 2005, p. 36). The leader's fit with the organization involves traits as well as skills, leadership style as well as situation. In other words, there is no one right theory, but all have relevance in the context of the right time and place. Invoking many of the major leadership theories in one paragraph to describe their concepts of fit and alignment, they write,

If one were to align a leader who is determined and communicates well and whose personality and behavior (style) fit well with the organizational culture, who understands how to structure the organization's future and light up the pathway to success, who communicates frequently with direct reports and makes staff followers feel supported and understood, and who holds high standards in a way that is sensitive to both individual and group psychological needs—if someone were to see such alignment, what would be witnessed is effective leadership. (p. 345)

TABLE 5.3 ■ Dym and Hutson's Alignment Map			
	Leader	**Organization**	**Community/Market**
Basic nature	Character and style	Organizational type	Patterns and norms
Underlying principles	Personal values	Organizational culture	Larger culture
Means available	Individual skills	Organizational resources	Economy and industry
Purpose and direction	Personal objectives	Mission and strategy	Community needs and market demands

Source: Dym and Hutson (2005, p. 93).

Dym and Hutson (2005) provide an *alignment map* (see Table 5.3), summarizing the components on which they say alignment must be achieved. It encompasses the characteristics of the individual as well as characteristics of the organization and of the community or market that the organization serves. All three must be aligned to produce a perfect fit. Thus, for example, a charismatic leader with an extroverted personality might be a good fit for an advocacy organization that is working to gain public awareness and change public policy, but such an individual might not be a good fit as a director of a museum, university, or think tank, where a more collegial, participative style might be more readily accepted. An executive director who does not speak Spanish and has little understanding of Hispanic/Latino culture would not be a good fit as the executive director of an organization that serves primarily Hispanic/Latino clients. A leader who comes from the business world—or even from a different type of nonprofit organization—might find it difficult to be effective in a nonprofit organization that has an established culture different from that with which he or she is familiar. An organization that encourages self-empowerment among its clients would not be aligned with its mission if its own leadership behaved in autocratic ways. In other words, for a CEO to be effective, his or her traits, styles, skills, and values need to be in sync with the organization and its constituencies. Too much dissonance may diminish the CEO's ability to lead or even, in the case of a bad fit, result in his or her eventual departure.

However, according to Dym and Hutson (2005), alignment is a two-way process. It may involve change by the leader and by the nonprofit itself: "Leaders must . . . align themselves to organizations by adapting themselves to the organization's structure, process, culture, and strategy—and by aligning the organization's to fit their style. Both processes are necessary for effective leadership" (p. 100). But, they advise, alignment should not be perfect and some tension is desirable. "A fit that is too perfect leads to stagnation. . . . Close but imperfect fit combines the smooth functioning we associate with efficiency and effectiveness with the flexible adjustment to change we associate with creativity" (p. 67).

Founder Syndrome

As Dym and Hutson (2005) discuss, one leadership style may be appropriate at one point in an organization's history and another at a different time. The idea that the organization's need for leadership might change over time derives from *life-cycle theories* of nonprofit organization development, which describe specific stages through which organizations naturally evolve.

For example, charismatic leaders are often seen leading an organization in its early stages, where the vision and inspiration of a committed founder drive volunteers and early generation staff members to exceptional effort. However, as the organization matures, it may require a different kind of leader—one "who feels comfortable in and supported enough by the stable organization to begin to implement long-term growth projects" (Dym & Hutson, 2005, p. 89). In other words, as the organization grows, adds staff, develops systems, and expands its programs, there will be an increased need for professional management, and the charisma of the founder may no longer suffice. (We will discuss organization life cycles in more detail in Chapter 8.)

There are many examples of nonprofit organizations founded by visionary and charismatic individuals who became the first executive directors. The founder attracts and inspires dedicated and loyal volunteers, donors, and staff. The board may consist of individuals recruited by the founder, who generally acquiesce to his or her authority and charisma (Block and Rosenberg, 2002). But at some point, as the organization grows and its needs for professional management, formal systems, and a more deliberate approach increase, the founder may not possess the required management skills or may be unable to adjust his or her vision of the organization to the new reality. He or she may prefer the entrepreneurial culture of the early organization.

The founder is likely to have a deep dedication to the organization and its cause—it may be the founder's life, and he or she may expect staff to make similar personal sacrifices. Founders often have task-oriented styles and are described as "difficult" and "demanding" by their subordinates. Like a controlling parent, the founder may have become accustomed to making all the decisions and may resist any initiative from the board or staff to be more independent. That style might work in the early days when the staff and board comprise a small number of loyal followers who share the founder's enthusiasm, but it may become less tolerated as the organization comes to require a larger staff of technical specialists and professional managers. Passion may no longer be an adequate substitute for rational decision making.

But the founder's psychological identification with the organization—after all, it's the founder's baby—may make it impossible for him or her to accept a more democratic, team approach. The situation becomes more stressful as staff turnover increases, management errors begin to mount, systems spin out of control, and the board feels increasingly torn between its loyalty to the founder and its responsibility to the organization. The board may begin to add more outsiders, people who are not personally selected by the founder and who bring more professional skills. These outsiders have less loyalty to the founder, and the balance begins to shift, increasing tension between the founder/executive director and the board: The organization is suffering from what is commonly called *founder syndrome.*

The arrival of founder syndrome in the life of the organization poses a challenge, even a crisis. Eventually, some crisis or event may trigger an explosion, resulting in the dismissal of the founder. Board members and staff loyal to the founder may leave amid bitterness, while others scramble to save the organization. Often the founder will be replaced by a professional manager, who then faces the challenge of rebuilding and developing new relationships. Or if the crisis is not resolved, the founder's departure may precipitate the organization's decline into turmoil and eventual death. Dym and Hutson (2005) portray the ugly scene:

> There is a declining certainty about the organization's original purpose. People wonder whether they were naïve to think they could accomplish so much in the first place. They question whether they can survive without being more realistic about their goals, their methods, and the people they trust. As doubt creeps in, people grow more conservative, more cautious. They see problems where before they mainly saw solutions. They begin to invest less of themselves—their hopes and dreams, their willingness to risk, and their time. Or they begin a somewhat frenzied and exhausting alternation of investing more and less. (p. 118)

If the transition from the founder to a professional manager is traumatic and risky for the organization, following the founder also can be a challenging assignment for the new CEO. It may be that the board, perhaps feeling guilty over its dismissal of the founder as executive director, has allowed him or her to remain as a member of the board—an unfortunate decision that may provide a platform for the founder to criticize and undermine the new executive. In other cases, the founder may be retained as a consultant or perhaps in an honorific position to engage in fundraising and other external tasks. But, under these arrangements, unless the founder has exceptional wisdom and grace and the new executive shows unusual understanding and sensitivity, the situation is likely to remain volatile for some time, continuing to burden the organization and distract it from pursuit of its mission.

Of course, there are enlightened and wise founders, who recognize their own limitations and their organization's changing needs. In this situation, founder syndrome really does not exist, since there are many options for providing both the leadership and management that the organization requires. For example, the founder may take on more of an external role, delegating much of the day-to-day management to others, perhaps an associate director, chief operating officer, or executive vice president. But, in such a scenario, it is also essential for the founder to avoid end runs around the new operating officer by staff who may have been hired by the founder, and to support and reinforce the operating officer's authority and control.

Executive Transitions

Every nonprofit will eventually face the need to replace its CEO. Indeed, the subjects of executive transition and *succession planning* have gained increased urgency as the nonprofit sector prepares for a significant transfer in leadership. The baby boomers, who have risen to the top ranks in many sectors, are reaching retirement age. A 2011 report, *Daring to Lead,* found that 67 percent of nonprofit CEOs expected to leave their positions within the next five years (Moyers, p. 2). For this reason, and others that are less anticipated, boards must be prepared to make one of the most important decisions they face—appointment of a new chief executive.

Sometimes the need for a change is first recognized by the board, and the current CEO needs to be persuaded—or forced—to step down. As we have discussed, this can be especially difficult when the chief executive is a charismatic founder of the organization, but the involuntary departure of any CEO is a difficult and potentially wrenching experience for an organization. In other situations, the CEO may initiate the change. This may occur for several reasons. The CEO may receive a better offer from another organization or perhaps just feel burned out and want a change of scene. For some CEOs, there comes a point when they feel that their major goals for the organization have been accomplished and that it is just time to move on to something new. This may occur at the completion of some major effort, for example, a successful fundraising campaign, or on reaching some milestone, such as ten years of service (Weisman & Goldbaum, 2004). There is a difference, of course, between an anticipated departure, such as retirement, and one that comes as a surprise, such as when the CEO receives an unanticipated job offer that is just too good to turn down. In the first instance, the board has time to prepare for the transition; in the second, some boards may be caught unprepared to make one of the most critical decisions they will ever face.

In business corporations, it is not unusual for chief executives to come up through the ranks. They are often individuals who have worked in the company for a long time, are steeped in its culture, and are knowledgeable about its products and markets. Indeed, as a corporate executive approaches retirement, it is not unusual for there to be an heir apparent who has been groomed for the top position for years. For example, Apple CEO Steve Jobs had selected Tim Cook, then Apple's chief operating officer, to be his successor as CEO when his own health began in decline, and he knew that a transition eventually would need to occur. Nonprofit boards work in the same way with regard to their own membership;

bylaws often include limits on how long the board chair can serve, and thus, the transition in leadership is predictable and planned. There is often a vice chair of the board or even a chair elect, who is well prepared to take over the job in a smooth transition. But nonprofit CEOs are more often than not recruited from outside the organization. This is frequently because the organization is thinly staffed and tightly budgeted and cannot afford the luxury of a number-two executive with the capability to be the CEO (Froelich, McKee, and Rathge, 2011). The lack of an internal candidate for the chief executive position might also exist if the organization is still led by a founder who may not have provided others with the opportunity to learn and grow sufficiently to be prepared for leadership. Thus, nonprofits may be faced with the need to appoint as CEO an individual who is a virtual stranger—not someone whom they have known or have had the opportunity to get to know in more junior positions before advancing him or her to the top office. In these circumstances, the selection of a new CEO may carry some risk that the wrong person will be selected, with potentially serious consequences for the effectiveness and stability of the organization.

There is a growing literature concerning executive succession planning, and an increasing number of nonprofits are preparing for the eventuality even before the CEO's departure is foreseen or imminent. Internal preparation is a shared responsibility of the board and the CEO. If the organization is large enough to have staff members capable of eventually filling the CEO position, the CEO can intentionally prepare those individuals by including them in important meetings and decisions, providing them with opportunities for additional professional training, giving them assignments with responsibility that can help develop their leadership skills, and exposing them to the board so that they will know the board and the board will know them (Weisman & Goldbaum, 2004). This requires, of course, a confident CEO with a participative style of leadership and a genuine commitment to the organization even beyond his or her own tenure as its leader.

In small organizations, there may be no internal candidate believed capable of rising to the CEO position within any reasonable period of time. But the CEO can still prepare for the possibility of a transition whether planned or unexpected, by developing systems, documenting policies and procedures, and sharing responsibility with others in a way that will make it possible for a successor, or perhaps an interim director, to maintain the organization's activities with minimum disruption. Boards are advised to ensure that such internal planning is occurring and also to remain aware of leaders in other similar organizations whom they might try to recruit should the need arise (Weisman & Goldbaum, 2004).

The need for *transition planning* goes well below the level of the CEO. Other staff members, for example, program directors or even key volunteers, may need to be replaced and there may not always be advance warning. Again, communication, documentation, and cross-training of staff in the responsibilities of each other's jobs can minimize disruption during the period of transition after someone leaves the organization.

Most nonprofits continue to appoint their chief executives from outside and conduct searches to identify and select their new executive leaders (Froelich et al., 2011). But not all do it well. Some boards fail to prepare for the eventuality that a new CEO will be required. Some underestimate the risks and cost of making the wrong decision about whom to hire. And boards sometimes focus more on the problems of hiring a new CEO, rather than the opportunity that it presents (Allison, 2002). A full discussion of the search process is beyond the scope of this text, but there is a growing literature on the subject and many excellent resources are available, through BoardSource, CompassPoint (www.compasspoint.org), and other organizations. As competition for management talent has intensified, professional executive search firms also have come to play a larger role.

The search for a new CEO must be rooted in the organization's own understanding of itself—its mission, its values, its vision, and its goals. The process cannot be rushed, and it is often about far more than just finding someone qualified for the job. To define who may be the right person in the right place at the right time, the organization must have a clear understanding of its past, its purpose, its constituencies, and its aspirations.

Leading Change

Leadership often involves change. Indeed, James Kee and Kathryn Newcomer (2008) observe that "some . . . argue that leadership is inherently change-oriented—that the function of management is to protect and nurture the status quo, while the function of leadership is to continually examine better ways of doing things" (p. 23).

There are a number of prominent *change theories* and models. Kee and Newcomer (2008) propose a taxonomy of change models, placing some well-known theories into the categories of *leader-centered, follower-centered,* and *change-centered* leadership, each of which have advantages and disadvantages (p. 23). While arguing for "a model of change leadership that engages other stakeholders in a 'whole systems' approach to the change process," Newcomer and Kee acknowledge that "the dominant advice in the literature on change management is that . . . leaders . . . must overcome resistance to change through a variety of top-down approaches" (p. 32).

Indeed, one of the best-known authors on change, John Kotter (1996), describes a top-down approach. Kotter's model is based on business corporations, which is why some scholars fund it less than ideal for nonprofit organizations. However, elements of it may be adapted to the nonprofit setting. One hallmark of the model is its emphasis on the importance of organizational culture—the shared values, attitudes, feelings, beliefs, rituals, habits, codes of conduct, and other such characteristics of an organization—invisible rules that may support or hinder an initiative for change.

Kotter (1996) describes eight common mistakes that leaders trying to implement change are prone to make and proposes a parallel eight-step change process to avoid them. According to Kotter, efforts at transformational change in an organization often fail because leaders allow too much *complacency;* that is, they do not engender a sufficient sense of urgency about the need for change. For example, in a mature organization, decline may be gradual, and future threats may not be visible to most people. As long as the operating budget is balanced, there is no negative publicity or scandal, and staff positions seem secure, most people may be content to continue with business as usual and not be receptive to changes that would disrupt their worldviews or routines.

Leaders often fail to develop what Kotter (1996) calls a "powerful guiding coalition" in support of change. In other words, they too often try to drive the change alone without first developing a critical mass of allies—perhaps including key staff members, members of the board, and others—who share their commitment to the need for change. Leaders sometimes underestimate the power of *vision.* They try to bring about change through a series of actions—incremental changes, perhaps small modifications to procedures, reorganizations of staff, or modest enhancements to fundraising or communications programs. These are steps along the way that may appear unconnected to those who do not see or understand the larger vision toward which they are intended to lead. Leaders may try to operate behind the scenes, without adequately painting the picture of what the future will be like. In that case, they are unlikely to build the steam necessary to propel real and lasting change in the organization. The inertia of current culture and practice may be just too strong to overcome with an incremental approach.

Too often, change leaders *undercommunicate* the vision, perhaps relying on routine communication vehicles such as newsletters, annual reports, and other publications. They may assume that everyone in the organization carefully reads and considers such publications—or takes them seriously—and is thus sufficiently aware of the plan for change and shares the leader's commitment to it, when in fact this may not be true.

Kotter (1996) says that leaders may fail because they do not create "short-term wins"—that is, set intermediate goals that can be achieved and reassure followers that the ultimate longer term changes can be successfully reached. Setting some achievable short-term goals and celebrating their attainment can be an essential tactic to retain the commitment of staff and volunteers to a long-term change process and prevent frustration and inertia from bringing it to a halt midstream.

But there is also the risk of *declaring victory too soon.* Change may have occurred on the surface, but leaders err when they do not stay with the program long enough for the changes to "sink down deeply into the [organization's] culture" (Kotter, 1996, p. 13). Only by *anchoring the changes* in the organization's culture can the leader pursuing change ensure that the board and successive generations of management will also adhere to new ways of doing things. As Kotter explains,

> Smart people miss the mark here when they are insensitive to cultural issues. Economically oriented finance people and analytically oriented engineers can find the topic of social norms and values too soft for their tastes. So, they ignore culture—at their peril. (p. 15)

Kotter (1996) offers an eight-step change process that avoids each of the potential mistakes (p. 21). To ensure that the momentum for change is not overwhelmed by the inertia of existing culture and practices and to make certain that the change is real and permanent, the leader should follow the steps sequentially, not moving on to the next until the previous has been solidly accomplished:

1. Establish a sense of urgency
2. Create a guiding coalition
3. Develop a vision and strategy
4. Communicate the change vision
5. Empower broad-based action
6. Generate short-term wins
7. Consolidate gains and produce more change
8. Anchor new approaches in the culture

What is the essential ingredient of successful change? Kotter (1996) argues that it requires 70% to 90% leadership and just 10% to 30% the skills of management. "Leadership defines what the future should look like, aligns people with that vision, and inspires them to make it happen despite the obstacles" (p. 26). But leadership may be in short supply when an organization needs it to drive essential change. Kotter describes a life-cycle theory of business firms that is reminiscent of the nonprofit life cycles we discussed earlier. Companies start as entrepreneurial businesses, then grow and achieve a position of market dominance. As size and dominance increase, control becomes most important, and management predominates over leadership. However, that can produce a bureaucratic, inward orientation that causes managers to become complacent about performance. The situation requires change, but the forces of complacency and inertia make change difficult, requiring "sacrifice, dedication, and creativity." These cannot be engendered through coercion but instead require "leadership, leadership, and more leadership" (p. 31).

Chapter Summary

The position of CEO in a nonprofit organization is different from similar positions in government or the business sector, for reasons that relate to the distinctive nature of nonprofit organizations themselves. While every organization, regardless of sector, requires capable management in order to be effective, nonprofits especially need CEOs who can exercise strong leadership. This is true because they are organizations based on values and driven by their missions, which mobilize commitment and support by appealing to a shared vision.

Theorists have defined leadership in terms of individual qualities, skills that leaders possess, behaviors that successful leaders exhibit, and interactions between leaders and followers. Most contemporary theories recognize that effective leadership may be contingent; that is, it may depend on the circumstances, including human relationships, the nature of the task, and the formal position of the executive.

James MacGregor Burns offered a definition of transactional leadership that sounds very much like management. The transactional leader rewards or punishes others in exchange for the work that they perform and emphasizes rules, policies, and procedures to ensure that things are done right. Burns introduced the concept of transformational leadership, in which the leader enables individuals to experience their own moral and motivational growth by appealing to values that they share with the organization. This text suggests that transformational leadership may be especially appropriate in organizations that often attract the participation of people motivated by commitment to their values-based missions. The concept of charismatic leadership is frequently observed in the founders of nonprofit organizations. They are individuals who inspire others to extraordinary effort through the model of their own commitment and their articulation of a vision, among other behaviors.

Various scholars and practitioners have tried to define the effective nonprofit CEO. Some reflect trait theories or skills theories of leadership, while others have described the behaviors of effective chief executives. The behaviors most often identified involve the CEO focusing his or her attention on the mission, the board, external relationships, and a few key priorities while understanding the political reality of competition among constituencies for the organization's resources. A framework offered by Dym and Hutson (2005) seeks to integrate various leadership theories and describe how effective leadership arises when the individual, the organization, and its community or market are aligned—in other words, when the right person serves in the right place at the right time.

Some organizations will face a significant challenge when a founding CEO leaves the organization, either voluntarily or through a forced transition. Chief executive transitions in general have received greater attention in the recent literature of nonprofit management. Organizations and their boards are encouraged to prepare and plan for changes in executive leadership and to base the search for a new CEO firmly in the organization's mission, values, vision, goals, and aspirations.

Leadership often involves change, and some authors argue that this is inherently so. There are various theories of change leadership, including those that are leader centered, those that are follower centered, and those that are change centered. Each has its advantages and disadvantages, and the model selected should be appropriate to the organization. One common principle is the importance of anchoring changes in the organization's culture.

Note

1. Reprinted with permission from *The Nonprofit Chief Executive's Ten Basic Responsibilities* (2nd ed.) by Richard L. Moyers, a publication of BoardSource. For more information about BoardSource, call 800-883-6262 or visit www.boardsource.org. BoardSource © 2013. Content may not be reproduced or used for any purpose other than that which is specifically requested without written permission from BoardSource.

KEY TERMS AND CONCEPTS

alignment map	executive leadership	leadership
charismatic leadership	follower-centered	legislative leadership
change-centered	founder syndrome	management
contingency theories	leader-centered	managerial grid
employee orientation	leader–member exchange theories	path-goal theory

production orientation   *succession planning*   *transformational leadership*

relationship behaviors   *task behaviors*   *transition planning*

skills theories   *trait theories*

situational theories   *transactional leadership*

CASE 5.1   A Change in Leadership at Habitat for Humanity

Habitat for Humanity International is an ecumenical, faith-based nonprofit dedicated to eliminating substandard housing and homelessness. Habitat constructs houses with the assistance of volunteers and partner families, who then purchase the homes with affordable loans. It has built or repaired more than 800,000 homes, serving more than 4,000,000 people worldwide (Habitat for Humanity International, 2015). Habitat has been hailed as one of the most successful nonprofits of the past 30 years and "one of the most dramatic examples of social entrepreneurship . . . that blends commercial and social methods to generate much of the cash, labor, and materials needed to construct its programs" (Dees, Emerson, & Economy, 2001, p. 12).

Habitat was founded in 1976 by Millard Fuller, who led the organization as its CEO for many years. Fuller had acquired wealth before the age of 30 and then dedicated himself to a life of service. While he was the CEO of Habitat, Fuller accepted an annual salary of only $15,000, declined raises, and lived for 23 years in a modest house without air-conditioning (Bixler, 2005). Fuller was widely praised as a visionary, and his commitment attracted volunteers and donors to Habitat, including former president Jimmy Carter, who became one of the organization's most prominent advocates.

But by the early 2000s, issues began to arise between Mr. Fuller and Habitat's board. As Fuller approached the age of 70 in 2004, he sought to extend his service as CEO until 2005, when Habitat would complete its 200,000th house. But the board began to plan for transition and appointed a former board chairman as managing director. Although Fuller retained the title of president and chief executive officer, he was said to have complained that the board's decision forced him into a figurehead role (Pierce, 2004).

The board had received a specific complaint about an incident involving Fuller and a Habitat employee and conducted an investigation. Although the board found insufficient proof of wrongdoing, the process brought to the surface other issues that had been developing over a period of years (Jensen, 2005). One board member observed that a gradual change had occurred in the composition of the board, saying, "There was a movement to start engaging board members who had some 'juice'—people who were powerful in different fields and were well connected." The changing board became critical of Fuller for undertaking some projects without its approval (Pierce, 2004), and Fuller became critical of the board, saying, "I've always seen Habitat for Humanity as a movement. . . . There's a certain mentality on the board now that wants to change it into an organizational bureaucracy" (Jensen, 2005).

In January of 2005, the board fired Fuller and his wife, who also had held a position at Habitat, and appointed an interim CEO. The interim CEO explained the situation saying, "The strength of vision and ego that was so important for the beginning and initial growth of Habitat are not what we need today to provide the structure for what has become a large, far-flung operation" (Jewell, 2005, p. 24). Fuller spoke out against the board's action, saying trustees were not committed to the faith-based nature of Habitat and just wanted to replace him with a "high paid bean counter" (Jewell, 2005, p. 24).

Some Habitat for Humanity affiliates, volunteers, and donors spoke out in opposition to the board's action and in support of Fuller. Fuller created a new organization, which he called Building Habitat, but he later changed its name to the Fuller Center for Housing after Habitat for Humanity filed suit, alleging infringement of its trademark (Wilhelm, 2005b). Habitat for Humanity undertook a search for a new CEO and eventually

(Continued)

(Continued)

hired Jonathon Reckford, a former businessman with Goldman Sachs and Best Buy. Reckford met with Fuller. Afterward, Fuller said, "I was not prepared to like the guy, but I did" (Wilhelm, 2005b).

Reckford committed the organization to continued growth but said that it needed to "build the platform" for that growth and determine the right organizational structure and ways of maximizing effectiveness (Wilhelm, 2005b). Fuller continued to voice opinions about Habitat's directions.

Reflecting on the controversy that had surrounded the transition in leadership from Habitat's founder, one nonprofit scholar observed, "Habitat for Humanity is much bigger than one man, and that speaks of Mr. Fuller's success" (Minor, 2005). Mr. Fuller passed away in 2009 at age 74.

Questions Related to Case 5.1

1. Which theory or theories seem to best describe the career of Millard Fuller at Habitat for Humanity?

2. In what ways is the story of his departure an example of founder syndrome?

3. If this case is indeed a case of founder syndrome, do you think Fuller could have avoided it, or had the organization evolved in a way that was just inconsistent with his values and experience? (This question obviously calls for some speculation.)

Case 5.2   Challenge and Change at United Way

In 1887, Denver became the first city to establish a united organization to raise funds in order to meet community needs. Other cities adopted the idea, creating organizations that were commonly called the Community Chest, later becoming known as United Way (www.unitedway.org). By 2003, there were more than 1,400 local United Ways, raising almost $4 billion to support a broad range of nonprofits in their communities (Wolverton, 2003). Local United Ways are independent nonprofit organizations. The national office provides support and assistance to local United Ways, and the local organizations are required to meet certain standards in order to use the name.

In 1995, the president of the United Way of America, then the national umbrella organization, was convicted of stealing funds for personal use, eroding public confidence. Another blow came in 2001, when the CEO of the United Way of the National Capital Area, the local chapter serving the Washington, DC, region, was charged with similar abuses. But larger forces also were at work, presenting challenges to the United Way and its model. By 2003, the amount of gifts to United Way that were designated for specific nonprofit organizations had risen 13 years in a row (Ogden, 2008). That approach to giving denied the United Way the ability to select recipient nonprofits, reducing its influence. More donors were bypassing the United Way altogether to make gifts directly to nonprofits that interested them. Some were questioning the continued relevance of the United Way model, which raised funds through workplace fundraising campaigns and provided support to a wide variety of nonprofit organizations. Both individual and corporate donors were becoming more interested in the impact of their gifts and less interested in giving to a fund that would benefit any nonprofit organization that qualified (Philanthropy News Digest, 2007). In addition, a national economic recession in 2003 had led to a significant decline in workplace giving by employees, which accounted for 66 percent of United Way revenues, and support for United Way from corporations, which comprised the balance (Wolverton, 2003). Brian Gallagher, who had worked in local United Way chapters for 20 years, had been appointed as the new President and CEO of the United Way of America in 2002. He recognized the urgent need for change.

Gallagher raised a basic question about the mission of United Way: was it to raise funds or to have an impact on communities? "We are in the business of changing people's lives," he concluded, "Fundraising is a strategy." He explained, "We had forgotten to connect with donors as customers and to combine community interests and corporate interests because we were so focused on raising money in the workplace using a monopoly position" (Boston Consulting Group, 2011).

Gallagher committed to undertaking a significant transformation. Although the idea had preceded Gallagher's presidency, he began to promote a plan in which United Way would move from being just a fundraising organization to one that would focus its resources and be measured by its impact on communities. But it would not be easy to accomplish such change in an organization with so many decentralized and independent components, each of which supported a wide range of local nonprofits that depended on the funds. Supported organizations would be worried about the possible loss of United Way support, and local United Way organizations might remain committed to the old model

Gallagher brought together local United Way leaders from across the country to discuss the new model. About half were receptive to the proposed new approach, but the other half wanted to remain primarily fundraising organizations (Wolverton, 2004). Gallagher focused the discussion on the question about the mission, helping to build greater consensus (Boston Consulting Group, 2011). He also hired new people for the national staff who were less committed to the old way of thinking. He surveyed United Way professionals in various communities to learn what issues concerned them and consulted experts from think tanks, foundations, and government to identify the most pressing social problems facing the country (Ogden, 2008). Gallagher created new channels to increase communication among local United Ways, including webinars and other online tools, so that they could exchange ideas on best practices (Philanthropy News Digest, 2007).

"United Way has a theory about how to create changes of this magnitude," Gallagher wrote. "It begins with declaring *bold goals* [italics original]. When the stakes are high, Americans will rise to the occasion" (United Way of America, n.d.). But some resisted the new vision, including some employees both at local United Ways and the United Way of America (Wolverton, 2004). Gallagher knew that change would take time and require a shift in his organization's culture. "Your field of vision has to be really wide," he explained, "and you have to be willing to take risks. You have to be flexible and adjust as you go" (Boston Consulting Group, 2011).

Six years later, in 2008, United Way or America adopted a ten-year plan reflecting the new approach. It would emphasize the health, education, and finances of working families and be focused on achieving three "Goals for the Common Good" by 2018: cut in half high-school dropout rates across the United States, cut in half the number of families with working parents who don't earn enough to cover the family's basic expenses, and increase by one third the number of Americans who are healthy and avoid risky behaviors (Schwinn, 2008).

Rather than distributing funds widely, United Way would focus on organizations that were achieving progress toward the three goals and would hold them accountable for specific performance metrics (Schwinn, 2008). Gallagher recognized that United Way could not do it alone and sought to establish partnerships with other national nonprofits, including the YMCA and Boys and Girls Clubs of America. United Way also would increase its advocacy efforts to encourage government to spend money on the three priorities (Schwinn, 2008).

Charities that had traditionally received United Way support continued to be concerned that they would be shut out of the new program. Gallagher stated that many could still qualify for United Way support, but they would need to adopt a different approach as well: "Activity is not going to be enough anymore, [for example,] saying we served 200,000 seniors last year. The question is, what are we doing to increase the financial stability of seniors?" (Schwinn, 2008) A tracking system would be established for local United Ways, which would report data to United Way of America so that progress toward the goals could be measured at a community level (Ogden, 2008).

In 2009, United Way of America merged with United Way International to form United Way Worldwide. Brian Gallagher became CEO of the new organization and turned his attention to promoting the impact model internationally. In 2012, Stacy Stewart became the new president of United Way USA, the national organization in the United States. There remained work to be done. Stewart identified her challenges to include

(Continued)

(Continued)

the need to continue building the United Way culture; to achieve cooperation among the many local United Ways, while maintaining local flexibility; and to encourage donors to designate their gifts for one of the three community impact priorities (Donovan, 2012).

Questions Related to Case 5.2

1. Which leadership theory or theories seem to best describe the leadership of Brian Gallagher at United Way?

2. In what ways does the process for change at United Way reflect Kotter's model?

3. If you had been the CEO of a nonprofit organization that had been receiving United Way funds, how would you have prepared for the changes that Brian Gallagher led?

4. What advice would you give to Gallagher's successor about how to keep the change process moving forward?

QUESTIONS FOR DISCUSSION

1. Are leaders born or made? Can anyone learn to be a leader or does it require some innate qualities or characteristics of the individual?

2. Could one individual be a great leader in government, a corporation, or a nonprofit? Why or why not?

3. Is leadership necessarily moral? Was Hitler a leader even though he was evil? Why or why not?

4. Who are some contemporary leaders that you would identify as charismatic? How do they exhibit the behaviors of charismatic leaders identified in this chapter?

SUGGESTIONS FOR FURTHER READING

Books

Collins, J. (2005). *Good to Great and the social sectors: A monograph to accompany Good to Great.* New York, NY: Harper.

Dym, B., Egmont, S., & Watkins, L. (2011). *Managing leadership transition for nonprofits: Passing the torch to sustain organizational excellence.* Upper Saddle River, NJ: FT Press.

Kee, J. E., & Newcomer, K. E. (2008). *Transforming public and nonprofit organizations: Stewardship for leading change.* Vienna, VA: Management Concepts.

Northouse, P. G. (2013). *Leadership: Theory and practice* (6th ed.). Thousand Oaks, CA: Sage.

Perry, James L. (Ed.). (2010). *The Jossey-Bass reader on nonprofit and public leadership.* San Francisco, CA: Jossey-Bass.

Article

Froelich, K., McKee, G., & Rathge, R. (2011). Succession planning in nonprofit organizations. *Nonprofit Management & Leadership, 22*(1), 3–20.

Websites

Center for Creative Leadership: http://www.ccl.org/leadership/index.aspx

Daring to Lead: http://www.daringtolead.org

Frances Hesselbein Leadership Institute: http://www.hesselbeininstitute.org

Companion Website

Visit study.sagepub.com/worth4e for access to certain full-text SAGE journal articles and links to relevant video and multimedia content.

PART III

Managing the Nonprofit Organization

Chapter Outline

chapter 6

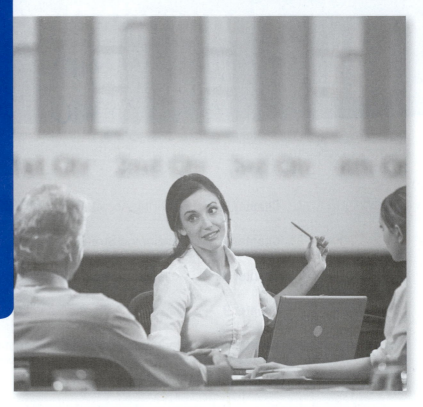

Accountability requires not only that the resources entrusted to the nonprofit not be misused but also that they be used to maximum benefit in pursuing the organization's mission. However, this component of accountability turns out to be the most complex, since there is not always consensus on how results should be measured.

Photo: © iStockphoto.com/Sportstock

Learning Objectives

After reading this chapter, students should be able to:

1. Define the concepts of accountability, effectiveness, and performance.

2. Explain current mechanisms for ensuring the accountability of nonprofit organizations.

3. Summarize the major points included in prominent standards for nonprofit accountability.

4. Describe various approaches to measuring organizational performance.

5. Explain the pros and cons of various approaches to measuring organizational performance.

6. Create a basic logic model for a program.

7. Identify appropriate performance metrics related to an organization's mission.

8. Analyze cases, applying concepts from the chapter.

Ensuring Accountability and Measuring Performance

6

Nonprofit organizations enjoy considerable autonomy in defining their missions, setting their own goals, and crafting their own strategies for achieving those goals. They are private organizations, but they are granted charters to serve purposes that society has deemed to be of public benefit. The organizations are exempt from taxation, and donors are permitted deductions for gifts made to charitable nonprofits to further those purposes. Tax exemption and the tax deductibility of gifts represent foregone government revenue and therefore are regarded by many as a form of tax subsidy; in other words, to some extent, nonprofits are working with the public's money. That gives society an interest in ensuring that they are *accountable* for their use of the resources entrusted to them and that those resources are indeed being directed toward the pursuit of their social missions. But what exactly is society entitled to expect?

The question is a little like asking, "What is a good student?" Does one qualify just by attending all classes, turning in papers on time, and showing up for exams—that is, by not breaking any of the rules of the course? Or is a good student someone who studies hard and seeks help from the professor when something is not clear—in other words, someone who shows exemplary student behavior? Does being a good student require earning good grades? Do grades accurately reflect what a student may have learned in a course, or is it possible that a better measure would be to compare what he or she knew or could do at the beginning of a course with what he or she knew or could do at the end, maybe basing the label of *good student* on some measure of value added? As we will see in this chapter, similar questions arise when we consider ideas such as the accountability, effectiveness, and performance of nonprofit organizations.

Defining and Ensuring Accountability

To be *accountable* essentially means being required to answer, to take responsibility, for one's actions. Perhaps the narrowest concept of *accountability* for a nonprofit would require merely following the law—for example, obeying the non-distribution requirement, avoiding conflicts of interest, treating staff without discrimination, and filing IRS reports as required. But that might seem to be a minimal standard to expect. Perhaps we might look for something more, not just following the law but also going beyond the requirements of law to follow best practices in governing and managing the organization—in other words, doing the right things as well as not doing things that are wrong.

But does even a definition of accountability that expects nonprofits to do the right things really go far enough? For example, the board may meet regularly, the budget may be invariably balanced, the staff may be happy and motivated, and there may be a written strategic plan, but that does not ensure that clients are recovering, the symphony is achieving artistic excellence, or public attitudes on the environment are being changed. Thus, perhaps, accountability needs to include more than just avoiding transgressions and exhibiting model behavior. It may need to encompass demonstrated effectiveness in achieving the purposes for which the nonprofit exists. That requires not only that the resources entrusted to the nonprofit not be misused, but also that they be used to maximum benefit in pursuing the organization's mission. As we will see, however, this component of accountability turns out to be the most complex, since there is not always consensus on how results should be measured, or even on how they should be defined.

The question of to whom nonprofits must account has long been asked—to clients, to donors, to the larger community, and/or to other stakeholders? It has gained more precise answers in recent years, as governments have increased their reporting requirements and a variety of other entities have cast the light of transparency on nonprofit behavior.

Concern about the accountability of nonprofit organizations has a long history. As early as 1918, the National Charities Information Bureau was created to educate the public about nonprofit organization behavior in order to reduce the incidence of charity fraud. But concern about accountability became heightened in the 1990s and 2000s. In 1992, the widely publicized misuse of United Way funds by the man who was then president, William Aramony, for which he was convicted and served jail time, shocked the nation. Again after September 11, 2001, accusations that some charity fundraising appeals were misleading and questions about the use of the funds given to help victims of the terrorist attacks further undermined the public's confidence in the integrity of the sector. Controversies at the Nature Conservancy, American University, and other organizations in the mid-2000s captured the attention of the media as well as the U.S. Congress and further heightened concern about accountability in the nonprofit sector. Members of the U.S. Congress held hearings, and there was discussion of passing new legislation to regulate the nonprofit sector. The sector responded by developing voluntary principles for accountability, including the Independent Sector principles, first issued in 2007 and revised in 2015 (Independent Sector, 2007, 2015d). Some states also responded by passing new legislation regulating nonprofits chartered within their jurisdictions and various state associations of nonprofits adopted codes and standards that have been implemented by some organizations.

The broader definition of accountability, including the requirement to produce results, also has become more pronounced with the growing impact of donors who view their giving as social investment and demand specific evidence of the impact of their support. For these reasons, the topics of accountability and *performance* are intrinsically linked today, and both are explored in this chapter.

Mechanisms for Accountability

There are three principal mechanisms by which nonprofits are held accountable: the *rule of law, self-regulation,* and *transparency*—that is, holding nonprofit behavior up in clear view for donors, the media, and others to see. Table 6.1 summarizes these mechanisms and provides some examples. Let's take a closer look at some of them.

Requirements of Law

Chapters 3 and 4 covered some of the legal requirements facing nonprofits, so we need only review a few key points here. Nonprofits must comply with laws at both state and federal levels. State governments grant nonprofits their charters, and state attorneys general and state courts have the authority to take action against law-breaking nonprofits. This can include the removal of board members who violate their fiduciary responsibilities and possibly even revoking of the organization's charter. Most states also have laws regulating the behavior of nonprofits in specific areas—for example, requiring that they be registered in order to solicit gifts from the general public.

At the federal level, regulation of nonprofits is carried out primarily by the IRS's Division on Tax-Exempt and Government Entities. The IRS has the authority to impose intermediate sanctions or to revoke an organization's tax exemption, eliminating its ability to raise tax-deductible gifts and subjecting it to the requirement to pay income taxes itself. Nonprofits that receive federal funds above certain amounts are also subject to additional rules with regard to their use of the federal dollars. Organizations with revenues greater than $50,000 (except religious congregations) are required to file an annual *Form 990*, 990-EZ, or 990-PF with the IRS. Organizations with revenue of less than $50,000 are required to file a postcard (Form 990-N), which provides very basic information. As discussed in Chapter 4, beginning in 2009 (with filing of the Form 990 covering 2008), the IRS introduced a revised form that greatly expanded the information required. The revised 990 includes questions related to governance as well as finances and programs. (See Figure 4.1 for the Form 990, Part VI questions related to governance.) Since 2008, even small nonprofits that are not required to file Form 990 are required to electronically file Form 990-N, also known as the *e-Postcard*. It includes minimal information that essentially reflects the organization's existence, without the data encompassed by Form 990.

In 2002, as noted in Chapter 4, Congress passed the Sarbanes-Oxley Act, responding to corporate governance scandals. While Sarbanes-Oxley (or "SOX," as it is commonly called) pertains primarily to publicly traded corporations, two of its provisions—those regarding protection for whistle-blowers and destruction of documents—also apply to nonprofit organizations. Some states, including California, have passed legislation directed at nonprofits that essentially incorporates Sarbanes–Oxley-type requirements (Nonprofit Integrity Act, 2004). Many nonprofits have voluntarily adopted Sarbanes-Oxley provisions as a way to assure their donors that they are operating with high integrity, transparency, and sound governance. In addition, questions included in Part VI of Form 990 imply that nonprofits should comply with some Sarbanes-Oxley practices, even if not required to do so by law.

Principles of good governance and ethical practice, such as those established by the Panel on the Nonprofit Sector, also include many points consistent with Sarbanes-Oxley. These developments clearly have pushed the definition of accountability beyond just "do no wrong"; it now includes adherence to best practices in governance and ethical behavior. Using the "good student" we discussed at the beginning of the chapter as a metaphor, nonprofits are now expected to do more than just not be absent from class and miss paper deadlines; they are also expected to demonstrate that they have done their homework, have studied, and have engaged in other activities defined as good-student behaviors.

The federal *Pension Protection Act of 2006*, as its title implies, is principally focused on the reform of pensions, but it also contains a variety of provisions that affect the nonprofit sector. They include, among others, changes in the law regarding charitable giving, tighter regulation of certain types of nonprofit organizations, greater communication between the IRS and state authorities regarding action taken against nonprofits, and the requirement that nonprofits with unrelated business income make public their Form 990-T (Johnson, 2006).

This text does not include a complete discussion of laws affecting nonprofit organizations. Moreover, regulations change frequently and the law may change at any time. The suggested readings at the end of this chapter include books that provide detailed discussion of the nonprofit legal framework, and students will find the website of Independent Sector (www.independentsector.org) to be an excellent source of up-to-date information on new or pending legislation.

TABLE 6.1 ■ Mechanisms for Accountability and Examples	
Mechanism	**Examples**
Requirements of law	Sarbanes-Oxley Act Pension Protection Act of 2006 State laws IRS regulations
Self-regulation	Independent Sector Principles for Good Governance and Ethical Practice (2007, 2015) Accreditation bodies in education and health care State nonprofit association standards and voluntary accreditation programs
Transparency	Form 990, available on GuideStar and other websites News media scrutiny Charity watchdogs and raters (*U.S. News & World Report* rankings, Better Business Bureau Wise Alliance, Charity Navigator) GreatNonprofits (www.greatnonprofits.org)

Self-Regulation: Standards and Accreditation

If the nonprofit sector would prefer not to be burdened by increased government regulation, then the alternative is to develop more effective mechanisms for self-regulation. In 2004, concern about nonprofit accountability prompted the Finance Committee of the U.S. Senate to hold hearings and consider proposals for significantly increased regulation of the nonprofit sector at the national level. At the committee's request, Independent Sector convened a Panel on the Nonprofit Sector to develop recommendations. The panel's report was presented to the Congress in June 2005; it suggested increased enforcement of existing state and federal law, increased reporting by nonprofits, and some additional legislation. But its emphasis was on the importance of maintaining the sector's independence and on its capacity for self-regulation (Independent Sector, 2005; Panel on the Nonprofit Sector, 2005). The Panel on the Nonprofit Sector's recommendations and 33 principles for good governance and ethical conduct were published in 2007 and revised in 2015. They are organized into four broad areas: legal compliance and public disclosure, effective governance, strong financial oversight, and responsible fundraising (Independent Sector, 2015d).

There are a number of well-known standards of practice in addition to the Independent Sector principles, some of which are the basis for *accreditation* of nonprofits by various authorities. There is a long history of accreditation of educational and health care institutions. For example, schools and colleges are accredited through regional associations. Individual institutions engage in self-studies according to a process defined by the accrediting body and are evaluated through intensive visits by teams from peer institutions. Professional schools within universities have separate accrediting mechanisms; for example, law schools are accredited by the American Bar Association and business schools by the Association to Advance Collegiate Schools of Business. Health care organizations, including hospitals, nursing homes, health care networks, and other service providers, are accredited by the Joint Commission on Accreditation of Healthcare Organizations, itself a nonprofit organization.

Although educational accreditation is voluntary, accrediting bodies are recognized by the U.S. Department of Education, and accreditation is required in order to be eligible for certain government funds. Likewise, accreditation of health care organizations is voluntary, but the power of government creates a significant incentive, since status as an accredited health care provider is required in order to be eligible to receive certain government reimbursements, an essential source of revenue for many organizations.

In the broader nonprofit sector, the accreditation of organizations is a relatively recent concept, having its origins in the development of accountability standards and definitions of best practices by state associations of nonprofits and others. As one example, Maryland Nonprofits (previously known as the Maryland Association of Nonprofits; 2014) developed Standards for Excellence in nonprofit management that are well regarded and have become a model for other state associations across the country. The Maryland standards are summarized in Table 6.2. These standards essentially describe recommended best practices—that is, a set of guides for behavior that reflect a consensus about how well-managed and accountable nonprofits should operate.

Like other state associations, Maryland's offers a voluntary accreditation program to organizations that wish to demonstrate their adherence to its standards. The program is available to nonprofit organizations nationwide through the Standards for Excellence Institute, an initiative of Maryland Nonprofits (Standards for Excellence Institute, 2014). Similar to the accreditation process in educational and health care institutions, the process requires that the organization complete a lengthy application, pay a fee, and be approved by a team of trained peer reviewers. Organizations that successfully complete the process are entitled to use of a Standards for Excellence Seal, a kind of "Good Housekeeping Seal" of approval, in their solicitations and other materials (Standards for Excellence Institute, 2014).

TABLE 6.2 ■ Maryland NONPROFITS Standards for Excellence®: An Ethics and Accountability Code for the Nonprofit Sector (2nd edition, 2014)

PREAMBLE

America's nonprofit sector serves the public interest and plays an essential role in our society and economy. Hard at work strengthening communities across the nation, nonprofits enrich our lives in a variety of ways by creating a broad array of benefits to society in fields such as charitable, religious, scientific, economic, health, cultural, civil rights, environment, and education.

Public investment and confidence drive the success of nonprofit organizations. Individuals, corporations, foundations, and federal, state, and local governments add value to the services that nonprofits provide by investing time, resources, and funds.

The Standards for Excellence Institute aims to raise the level of accountability, transparency, and effectiveness of all nonprofit organizations to foster excellence and inspire trust. The Standards for Excellence code (Standards, or code) provides a framework and step-by-step guidelines to achieve a well-managed and responsibly governed organization.

The code builds upon the legal foundations of nonprofit management, governance, and operations to embrace fundamental values such as honesty, integrity, fairness, respect, trust, compassion, responsibility, and transparency. The code consists of six Guiding Principles in 27 topic areas with specific performance benchmarks that characterize effective, ethical, and accountable organizations. The Institute helps the nonprofit sector operate in accordance with the Standards for Excellence code by providing educational resources, assistance, and a voluntary accreditation process.

The Standards for Excellence Institute encourages all nonprofit organizations to adopt the Guiding Principles of the Standards for Excellence code. By implementing the performance benchmarks in the code, nonprofit organizations will meet the highest ethical standards for effective service in the public interest.

MISSION, STRATEGY, AND EVALUATION

Guiding Principle:

Nonprofits are founded for the public good and operate to accomplish a stated purpose through specific program activities. A nonprofit should have a well-defined mission, and its programs should effectively and efficiently work toward achieving that mission. Nonprofits have an obligation to ensure program effectiveness and to devote the resources of the organization to achieving its stated purpose.

A. Mission and Impact

1. A nonprofit should have a mission statement that is a clear and formal statement of the organization's purpose as defined and approved by the board of directors. The organization's activities should be consistent with its stated purpose.

(Continued)

TABLE 6.2 ■ (Continued)

4. Managing Employees and Volunteers
   - Staff and volunteers should be recruited, screened (including required background checks), selected, trained, supervised, evaluated, and recognized appropriately. Staff and volunteers should be oriented to their positions, the organization, and the Standards for Excellence code, and should be provided with appropriate professional development opportunities.

C. Cultural Competency
   1. A nonprofit's leadership should ensure that the organization has a policy, plan, or strategies in place that enables the organization to effectively serve and interact with people equitably across different cultures and backgrounds.

LEGAL COMPLIANCE AND ETHICS

Guiding Principle:

Nonprofits enjoy the public's trust, and therefore must comply with a diverse array of legal and regulatory requirements. Organizations should conduct periodic reviews to address regulatory and fiduciary concerns. One of leadership's fundamental responsibilities is to ensure that the organization governs and operates in an ethical and legal manner. Fostering exemplary conduct is one of the most effective means of developing internal and external trust as well as preventing misconduct. Moreover, to honor the trust that the public has given them, nonprofits have an obligation to go beyond legal requirements and embrace the highest ethical practices. Nonprofit board, staff, and volunteers must act in the best interest of the organization, rather than in furtherance of personal interests or the interests of third parties. A nonprofit should have policies in place, and should routinely and systematically implement those policies, to prevent actual, potential, or perceived conflicts of interest. In this way, ethics and compliance reinforce each other.

A. Maintaining Legal Compliance
   1. Nonprofits must be aware of and comply with all applicable federal, state, and local laws. This may include, but is not limited to complying with laws and regulations related to IRS filing requirements, governance, human resources, licensing, financial accountability, taxation, valuation of in-kind gifts, unrelated business income, document retention and destruction, related entities, data security, accessibility, fundraising, lobbying, and advocacy.
   2. Nonprofits should periodically conduct an internal review of the organization's compliance with known existing legal, regulatory, and financial reporting requirements, and should provide a summary of the results to the board of directors.

B. Required Public Disclosures
   1. Nonprofits should have at least one designated representative who is responsible for ensuring that the organization is complying with both the letter and the spirit of federal and state laws that require disclosure of information to the public.

C. Reporting Misconduct and Whistleblower Protection
   1. Organizations must provide employees, board members, and volunteers a confidential means to report suspected impropriety or misuse of organizational resources. Organizations should have in place a policy prohibiting retaliation against persons reporting improprieties.

D. Conflicts of Interest
   1. Nonprofits should have a written conflict of interest policy and statement. These should be applicable to board members and staff, as well as volunteers who have significant, independent decision-making authority regarding the resources of the organization. The policy and statement should be executed by covered individuals, both at the time of the individual's initial affiliation with the organization and at least annually thereafter.

   The conflict of interest policy should identify the types of conduct or transactions that raise conflict of interest concerns, should set forth procedures for disclosure of actual or potential conflicts, and should provide for review of individual transactions by the uninvolved members of the board of directors. The conflict of interest statement should provide space for the board member, employee or volunteer to disclose any known interests that the individual, or a member of the individual's immediate family, has in any business entity which transacts business with the organization.

E. Ethics

1. Nonprofits should ensure that they have an explicit and clear set of ethical principles and, as appropriate, operational or program standards that have been discussed by their board and staff and that are transparently clear to all stakeholders.
2. In rendering its programs or services, a nonprofit should act with the utmost professionalism and treat persons served with respect.
3. Nonprofits should provide an effective procedure for problem solving or reporting grievances, including but not limited to, legal or ethical misconduct by the organization's employees and volunteers. The procedure should include actions for addressing and resolving complaints effectively.
4. Nonprofits should have policies in place that protect the confidentiality and privacy of personal information.

FINANCE AND OPERATIONS

Guiding Principle:

Nonprofits should have sound financial and operational systems in place and should ensure that accurate records are kept. The organization's financial and non-financial resources must be used in furtherance of tax-exempt purposes. Organizations should conduct periodic reviews to address accuracy and transparency of financial and operational reporting, and safeguards to protect the integrity of the reporting systems.

A. Financial Budgeting, Reporting, And Monitoring

1. The board should annually approve the organization's budget and the organization should be operated in accordance with this budget.
2. The organization should periodically assess the organization's financial performance in relation to the budget. A nonprofit should create and maintain reports on a timely basis that accurately reflect the financial activity of the organization. Internal financial statements should be prepared at least quarterly, should be provided to the board of directors, and should identify and explain any material variation between actual and budgeted revenues and expenses.
3. The board should annually review the percentages of the organization's resources spent on program, administration, and fundraising.
4. For nonprofits with annual revenue in excess of $500,000, the annual financial statements should be subject to audit by a Certified Public Accountant. The board should hire the auditor. The full board should approve the audited financial statements and receive a copy of the management letter (if any). The board should monitor the implementation of the recommendations of the management letter, if applicable.

B. Internal Controls And Financial Policies

1. Nonprofits should have written financial policies that are adequate for the size and complexity of the organization. These policies should address investment of the assets of the organization, internal controls, purchasing, and unrestricted current net assets.

C. Personnel Policies

1. A nonprofit should have written, board-approved personnel policies and procedures that govern the work, actions, and safety of all employees and volunteers of the organization. The policies should cover the basic elements of the relationship (e.g., working conditions, telecommuting (if applicable), employee benefits, vacation, and sick leave). The policies should address orientation to the organization, employee evaluation, supervision, hiring and firing, grievance procedures, employee growth and development, and confidentiality of employee, client, and organization records and information.

D. Administrative Policies

1. A nonprofit should have written, board-approved administrative policies that are periodically reviewed by the board. At a minimum, these policies should address issues such as crisis and disaster planning, information technology, communications, and social media.

(Continued)

TABLE 6.2 ■ (Continued)

E. Risk Management And Insurance

   1. Organizations should make every effort to manage risk and periodically assess the need for insurance coverage in light of the organization's activities and its financial capacity. A decision to forego general liability insurance coverage or Directors and Officers liability insurance coverage should be made only by the board of directors. The decision should be reflected in the minutes for the meeting at which the decision was made.

RESOURCE DEVELOPMENT

Guiding Principle:

The responsibility for resource development is shared by the board and staff. Nonprofit organizations depend on an array of sources of financial support. An organization's resource development program should be maintained on a foundation of truthfulness and responsible stewardship. Its resource development policies should be consistent with its mission, compatible with its organizational capacity, and respectful of the interests of donors, prospective donors, and others providing resources to the organization.

A. Resource Plan

   1. Nonprofits should have a resource development plan in place. This plan should outline a framework for ensuring appropriate financial resources for the organization, and a reasonable process to evaluate cost effectiveness of all resource development activities. Ideally, the resource plan should include diversified income sources to avoid dependence on a single source. The resource development plan should be board approved, regularly reviewed, and in accordance with the organization's budget.
   2. A nonprofit's fundraising costs should be reasonable over time. On average, over a five year period, a nonprofit should realize revenues from fundraising that are at least three times the amount spent on conducting them. Organizations whose fundraising ratio is less than 3:1 should demonstrate that they are making steady progress toward achieving this goal, or should be able to justify why a 3:1 ratio is not appropriate for their organization.

B. Sources of Income

   1. When determining what types of income sources are pursued by a nonprofit to meet its mission, the organization should carefully consider the income source's impact on the population served, its demographics, and overall mission alignment. The organization should also assess these sources of income for feasibility and any associated risk.

C. Fundraising Activities

   1. Solicitation and promotional materials should be accurate and truthful and should correctly identify the organization, its mission, and the intended use of the solicited funds.
   2. All statements made by the nonprofit in its fundraising appeals about the use of a contribution should be honored.
   3. Solicitations should be free from undue influence or excessive pressure, and should be respectful of the needs and interests of the donor or potential donor.

D. Donor Relationships and Privacy

   1. Nonprofits should respect the donor's right to determine how their name and contact information is used, including providing opportunities to remain anonymous, request that the organization curtail repeated mailings or telephone solicitations from in-house lists, and have their names removed from any mailing lists which are sold, rented, or exchanged.
   2. Nonprofits must honor the known intentions of a donor regarding the use of donated funds.

E. Acceptance of Gifts

   1. An organization should have policies in place to govern the acceptance and disposition of charitable or in-kind gifts that are received in the course of its regular fundraising activities. These policies should include procedures to determine any limits on individuals or entities from which the organization will accept

a gift, the purposes for which donations will be accepted, the type of property which will be accepted, and whether to accept an unusual or unanticipated gift in light of the organization's mission and organizational capacity.

F. Fundraising on Behalf of the Organization

1. Resource development personnel, including both employees and independent consultants, should not be compensated based on a percentage of the amount raised or other commission formula.
2. When using the services of a paid professional fundraising consultant, organizations should only use the services of professional solicitors and fundraising consultants who are properly registered with the appropriate state authorities.
3. Organizations should exercise control over any staff, volunteers, consultants, contractors, other organizations, or businesses that are known to be soliciting contributions on behalf of the organization.

PUBLIC AWARENESS, ENGAGEMENT, AND ADVOCACY

Guiding Principle:

Nonprofits should represent the interests of the people they serve through public education and public policy advocacy, as well as by encouraging board members, staff, volunteers, and stakeholders to participate in the public affairs of the community. When appropriate to advance the organization's mission, nonprofits should engage in promoting public participation in community affairs and elections. As such, they should communicate in an effective manner to educate, inform, and engage the public.

A. Educating and Engaging the Public

1. Information about the organization's mission, program activities, finances, board members, and staff should be easily accessible, accurate, and timely (i.e., updated at least annually).
2. Nonprofits should provide a meaningful opportunity for the public to communicate with a representative of the organization.
3. Nonprofits should assure that any educational or advocacy information provided to the media and policymakers, or distributed broadly, is factually accurate and provides sufficient contextual information to be understood.

B. Advancing the Mission through Public Policy and Advocacy

1. Nonprofits should have a written, board-approved policy on advocacy defining the process by which the organization determines positions on specific issues.
2. Working independently and in partnership, nonprofits should strive to influence public policies that affect the organization's ability to achieve its mission.

C. ENGAGING IN LOBBYING AND POLITICAL ACTIVITY

1. In promoting public participation in community affairs, charitable nonprofits must be diligent in assuring they do not participate or intervene in any political campaign on behalf of or in opposition to any candidate for public office.

Source: Reprinted with permission of the Standards for Excellence Institute, a project of Maryland Nonprofits, 2015.

The Standards for Excellence®: An Ethics and Accountability Code for the Nonprofit Sector identifies 6 major areas of nonprofit governance and management which contain 27 different topic areas. Each topic area includes specific benchmarks and measures that provide a structured approach to building capacity, accountability, and sustainability in nonprofit organizations. In addition to the code, the Standards for Excellence Institute® has developed a series of educational resources that include information on implementing specific standards, justification for the standards, best practices associated with the issue, model procedures and sample policies. These resources are available to members of the Institute and collectively cover each of the benchmarks in the Standards for Excellence code. Nonprofits that adhere to these benchmarks can become formally recognized or accredited by the Standards for Excellence Institute. The Standards for Excellence Institute also licenses individual consultants and regional and affiliate associations to offer various resources and trainings to nonprofits interested in implementing the Standards for Excellence code throughout their organization.

Learn more about the Standards for Excellence Institute and its signature programs at standardsforexcellence.org.

Transparency

In addition to the force of law and the desire to comply with voluntary guidelines, nonprofits also may be motivated to accountability by public scrutiny. As discussed earlier, Form 990 provides information that may be considered by donors, the news media, and others and that may reveal an organization's divergence from accepted best practices. Donors have online platforms on which they can provide their own reviews of organizations (greatnonprofits.org/). In addition, there is an increasingly influential array of charity watchdog organizations that proactively examine nonprofit organizations, applying their own standards. They are not really examples of self-regulation because some undertake their evaluations with or without the cooperation of the organizations on which they focus. They are an important force in creating increased transparency, and they have influence because of the visibility they enjoy, but they are also often controversial.

For example, among the best known may be the ratings of colleges and universities and hospitals by popular magazines, notably *U.S. News & World Report,* which have been shown to influence students' choices about where to attend college and patients' decisions about where to receive medical care. Such ratings surely do not have the force of law, but they are powerful. A negative ranking poses a significant potential threat to an organization, since publicity may deter potential customers, chill giving, or even invite scrutiny from government. And yet, many educators and hospital administrators do not agree that the standards by which *U.S. News* determines its rankings are appropriate or indicative of quality.

One well-known charity watchdog that operates at the national level is the Better Business Bureau (BBB) Wise Giving Alliance. Formed in 2001 through a merger of the National Charities Information Bureau and the Better Business Bureau's Philanthropic Advisory Service, the Wise Giving Alliance (hereafter, the Alliance) focuses its attention on the largest nonprofits in the United States. Since the BBB has a long history and an established reputation as an organization that acts to protect consumers against unethical business practices, the Alliance standards for nonprofits are among the best known and most widely cited in the news media.

The BBB undertakes investigations of an organization based on complaints or inquiries from the public (in the long-established tradition of consumers reporting businesses to the BBB). Nationally soliciting charities also may request a review in order to ensure compliance and may be eligible to use a "BBB national charity seal" in their promotional and solicitation materials. While the Alliance does not rate organizations, it does report whether they meet or do not meet its various standards, which are available on its website (www.bbb.org/us/Wise-Giving).

The BBB Standards for Charity Accountability are based on best practices; that is, they prescribe what accountable nonprofits should *do* in the areas of governance and oversight, measuring effectiveness, finances, fundraising, and informational material. They require that organizations have a mechanism for measuring results that involves the governing board, but it is important to note that they do not prescribe the *specific* standards that organizations must apply. The BBB standards require that organizations "have a board policy of assessing, no less than every two years, the organization's performance and effectiveness and of determining future actions required to achieve its mission." And the organization must submit "to [its] governing body, for its approval, a written report that outlines the results of the aforementioned performance and effectiveness assessment and recommendations for future actions" (BBB Wise Giving Alliance, 2003). In other words, the BBB standards emphasize process and accountability, but they are not about setting specific standards of effectiveness or performance, aside from a couple of key financial ratios, which we will discuss soon.

Many nonprofit organizations have accepted the idea of best practices, adhere to one or another of the recommended standards, and have sought some type of accreditation or certification. It may be that in addition to the potential threat of negative publicity, the widespread acceptance of voluntary standards reflects, as Light (2000) suggests, institutional theory at work. Enunciated standards become a part of the conventional wisdom of what constitutes ethical or sound practice and are increasingly adopted by organizations that seek recognition for being consistent with the norms of the subsector or profession within which they operate.

But the questions remain: Does doing the right things ensure that the organization is effective in accomplishing its mission? Or that it can be described as a high-performing organization? Is there some mechanism that automatically leads from best practices in governance and management to a successful nonprofit organization? Robert Herman and David Renz (2008) advise caution on this question:

> The popularity of "best practices" attests to the hope of finding a pot of gold at the end of the search. One key assumption of the best practices approach is that a particular technique or process that works well in one setting can and should be incorporated into other different settings. This may be true for certain rather common administrative functions, particularly those that must comply with externally mandated standards such as the adoption of procedures to ensure adequate internal controls. However, in many instances a practice that enhances effectiveness in one organization may be a poor choice for another. (p. 411)

In a 2015 study, Kellie Liket and Karen Maas surveyed both the academic literature and nonprofit managers and found that they agreed on 26 practices that they believed to be related to organizational effectiveness, including some related to transparency; to the focus, strategy, and board of the organization; and to the organization's programs. But in reflecting on their findings, they also sound a note of caution, writing, "due to the absence of consensus on the concept and measurement of [organizational effectiveness], it is not possible to empirically validate the recommended set of practices." In other words, it is difficult to determine what leads to effective when there is not agreement on how effectiveness should be defined or measured. Let's take a look at some approaches to doing so.

Measuring Performance

If doing the right things does not guarantee that the organization is effective in achieving its mission, then we need some standards by which to evaluate results. But how should results be defined, and how should they be measured? The subject has been the focus of national conversation in recent years, but there are still differences in view and a somewhat inconsistent vocabulary in the field. Distinctions among terms and concepts are important.

For example, there may be a difference between the performance of a nonprofit's *programs* and the performance of the *organization* as a whole. Let's first consider the performance of programs.

Performance management is "the process of defining, monitoring, and using objective indicators of the performance of organizations and programs to inform management and decision making *on a regular basis* . . . [italics added]" (Poister, Aristigueta, & Hall, 2015, p. 1). In other words, it is an *ongoing*, internal process used to collect and analyze data in order to track the effectiveness of programs *continuously*. There are a growing number of tools available to help nonprofits develop performance management systems. For example, in 2012, the Urban Institute, Child Trends, and Social Solutions collaborated to develop tools for measuring the performance of programs against data drawn from research. The resources are available on the PerformWell website (www.performwell.org). In addition, the volume and sophistication of available data have increased in the first decades of this century through the development of data analytics, data visualization, and "big data" (Hatry, 2014).

Program evaluation is another method that many nonprofits use to determine whether specific programs are effective in achieving results. As one prominent text explains, a program "is a set of resources and activities directed toward one or more common goals, typically under the direction of a single manager or management team" and program evaluation is "the application of systematic methods to address questions about program operations and results." (Newcomer, Hatry, & Wholey, 2010, pp. 5–6). Program evaluation may include "ongoing monitoring of a program as well as one-shot studies of program processes or program impact" (p. 6). But performance management and program evaluation are different in practice:

> People external to the program usually collect and analyze all information in an evaluation, and the evaluation is primarily used for research purposes or to inform large scale decision making. With performance management, program staff collect and analyze information themselves, and use this information to make programmatic or organizational decisions while the program is operating and immediately upon the conclusion of the program. (PerformWell, n.d.)

But is a nonprofit with high-performing programs automatically a high-performing organization? Or should the latter determination include such questions as whether the organization as a whole is effective in achieving its mission, is financially sound (recall the double bottom line concept discussed in Chapter 1), and is capable of learning and adapting to change, among other considerations? Of course, for a small nonprofit with a single program, the distinction may not be very meaningful. For larger, more complex organizations with broad missions, however, the difference may be significant. For example, a university might have a very effective basketball team, one that frequently wins championships, but it may not be a very effective university overall. Or it might be academically sound but suffer from financial challenges that threaten its long-term existence.

Again, the vocabulary is unsettled. For example, some use the terms *organizational effectiveness* and *organizational performance* synonymously. Others define an organization's performance as broader than effectiveness, with the latter measuring achievement against mission and the former encompassing "other concepts such as efficiency, productivity, or quality" (Baruch & Ramalho, 2006, p. 41). For example, let's consider a nonprofit that meets the needs of clients. That could define an effective organization. But if the organization loses money every year, the staff are miserable, and management is always just skirting the law, it would be hard to say it is high performing as an organization. Being effective may be necessary to be high performing, but it is not necessarily sufficient.

It is also important to distinguish between *effectiveness* and *efficiency*. As Kathleen Kelly (1998) explains it, efficiency is "a measure of the proportion of resources used to produce outputs or attain inputs–cost ratios," whereas effectiveness "is measured by comparing the results achieved with the results sought." As Kelly further observes, "Although efficiency may help an organization be more effective, the two concepts are not interchangeable" (p. 428). Indeed, some argue that an emphasis on efficiency may in fact work against the effectiveness of organizations by discouraging investment in capacity, a topic that will be discussed in greater detail in Chapter 7.

Financial Ratios

In the business world, financial data and ratios are the principal ways to measure a company's performance and strength. A company's earnings, earnings per share, stock price, and the ratio of stock price to earnings (the P:E ratio) are important variables that investors consider. Some have applied a similar approach to nonprofit organizations. The advantages of using financial indicators are that the data are objective, readily available, and easily compared, across either the nonprofit sector or particular subsectors. For nonprofits, these data are available on Form 990, and they are easy to access and compare.

What are some of the financial ratios that a nonprofit might produce? A 2004 study by the Urban Institute and Harvard's Hauser Institute (Fremont-Smith & Cordes, 2004) looked at 10 monitoring organizations that use financial ratios and found a variety of measures being applied, including variations of the following:

- The ratio of program expenses to contributed income
- The ratio of fundraising expenditures to private support received—that is, the cost of raising a dollar

- The percentage of total expenditures (or income received from contributions) applied to charitable programs or activities
- The percentage of total expenditures applied to fundraising and administrative (overhead)
- Accumulated cash and asset reserves in relation to operating budget

Until 2011, one of the prominent charity raters, Charity Navigator, based its ratings exclusively on financial ratios. In response to widespread commentary on the limitations of such ratios, Charity Navigator expanded its methodology to consider accountability and transparency in addition to financial ratios. The latter are assessed based on data from Form 990 and organizations' websites. A mathematical formula is used to calculate an overall score, which is then compared with the scores of other organizations.

Unlike the BBB Wise Giving Alliance, which rates nonprofits according to whether they meet or do not meet its standards, Charity Navigator ranks nonprofits using a system of "stars," like those used by Morningstar to rank mutual fund performance (Charity Navigator, 2014). By 2015, Charity Navigator was working to add a third component to its methodology: results. Development of what was labeled "C.N. 3.0" was in process at the time of this writing, with the intention of implementation in 2016. Students should consult the Charity Navigator website to check on the progress of this initiative (www.charitynavigator.org).

Despite their limitations as indicators, two of the variables most emphasized by those who use financial ratios to assess charities are the cost of fundraising and the percentage of expenditures that go for overhead rather than for programs and services. These ratios are so well known and easy to calculate that they have become popular shorthand for some donors, who may prefer to support low-overhead nonprofits that do not appear to spend too much on fundraising. As mentioned above, while the BBB standards do not in general emphasize financial ratios, they require that an organization's spending on fundraising be no more than 35 percent of the funds raised. However, the BBB also permits an organization to offer a justification for higher ratios. Charity Navigator does not set an absolute limit, but fundraising costs are one element in the formula by which it ranks organizations. As shown in Table 6.2, the Maryland Standards establish a 3:1 ratio for fundraising costs (i.e., expenditures should be no more than about 33 percent of gift revenue), but they also permit some flexibility, suggesting that organizations not meeting that standard may provide a justification (Maryland Nonprofits, 2014).

The percentage of total expenditures directed toward program-related activities, rather than overhead or fundraising, is viewed by some as a measure of an organization's efficiency in delivering its services. Too low a percentage may even be seen as a potential red flag, suggesting that management is deriving excessive compensation or other benefits from the organization or that fundraising has replaced mission as the organization's highest priority. For example, the BBB standards require that at least 65 percent of expenditures be devoted to programs but, again, they allow that organizations not meeting that standard may provide an explanation.

Indeed, organizations that spend too much on overhead or fundraising may be making inefficient use of donor funds or perhaps may be spending too lavishly on salaries and other overhead costs. Very high fundraising costs may suggest the possibility of inefficiency, or even unethical or fraudulent behavior. But, critics argue, rating organizations based on their overhead and fundraising costs may create perverse incentives. For example, this approach could simply encourage organizations to engage in creative accounting to allocate costs to programs rather than administration. Insisting on low fundraising costs also may place young organizations at a disadvantage. They often need to invest substantial amounts in developing a database of regular donors that will ultimately produce continuing revenue at lower costs. Moreover, low fundraising costs may not be realistic for an organization that advocates unpopular causes or lacks a constituency of major donors (Fremont-Smith & Cordes, 2004).

Other critics argue that "the fundraising efficiency standard is not a measure of efficiency at all. [Rather,] it documents the sunk costs associated with cultivating donors" (Hager & Flack, 2004, p. 3). In other words, looking at just this year's fundraising costs ignores the substantial amounts that the organization may have spent in earlier years to develop relationships with donors who now make larger gifts, lowering the per-dollar cost of fundraising today.

Still others argue that program-spending ratios are not a measure of organizational effectiveness at all, and indeed, that emphasizing low administrative cost may even work against building effective organizations by encouraging them to "value thrift over excellence." Trying to maintain a low ratio may cause an organization to invest too little in "good governance, planning, compliance and risk management, collection of data for service performance evaluations, and staff training" (Hager & Flack, 2004, p. 4).

Financial ratios do provide one perspective on the operations of an organization. If they are widely divergent from accepted practice, they may indeed reflect mismanagement or even fraud. And, as a practical matter, high fundraising costs may be viewed suspiciously by some donors. However, despite their ease of use, these ratios may not present the complete picture. Indeed, the shortcomings of such ratios have become part of the national dialogue concerning the nonprofit sector. In a 2010 book, Dan Pallotta, founder of fundraising firm Pallotta TeamWorks, argues against the use of the overhead ratio for evaluating organization and their fundraising efforts (Pallotta, 2010). Pallotta's 2013 TED talk, arguing the same point, gained millions of views on YouTube and focused further attention on the topic (Pallotta, 2013). In December 2013, the leaders of GuideStar, Charity Navigator, and the Better Business Bureau Wise Giving Alliance issued a joint "Letter to the Donors of America," urging that overhead ratios be kept in appropriate perspective. The authors note that, "At the extremes the overhead ratio can offer insight: it can be a valid data point for rooting out fraud and poor financial management." But, they add, "In most cases . . . focusing on overhead without considering other critical dimensions of a charity's financial and organizational performance can do more damage than good" (Overhead Myth, 2013).

Other observers agree that an exclusive focus on financial ratios can have negative consequences. As Mark Hager and Ted Flack (2004, p. 4) caution, "the undue emphasis on financial ratios diverts attention and resources from the development of more meaningful measures that address performance against mission and program objectives." For this reason, there has been an increasing emphasis on outcomes measurement, which many consider a source of more meaningful data related to achievement of the nonprofit's mission. This is an approach that will be discussed further later in this chapter.

Benchmarking

If simple financial measures applied to all nonprofit organizations are potentially misleading, perhaps a more accurate picture may be obtained from comparing data from organizations that are similar in their mission, size, location, and other characteristics. Comparing similar organizations is at the heart of benchmarking.

As Theodore Poister et al. (2015) note, the term *benchmarking* is often misused. Some organizations set goals for future years in their strategic plans and then measure their progress by looking at targets, which they call "benchmarks." But in its proper definition, benchmarking involves *comparisons* among organizations, either at the macro (whole organization) or at the micro (program or function) level. Benchmarking involves collecting data from multiple organizations in order to "gauge [an organization's] performance against other similar organizations . . . to see how its performance stacks up against counterpart programs elsewhere" (p. 382). For example, an organization might look at statistics on client outcomes across a group of organizations providing services to individuals with similar problems or compare its patterns of gift revenues with those of similar organizations. This macro approach, called *statistical benchmarking,* or *comparative performance measurement*, may be a useful technique in strategic planning and may help highlight strengths or weaknesses of the organization that require further analysis. It is not really a tool for evaluating the whole organization, although some assume that "a thorough program of benchmarking will 'roll up' to provide a good indicator of how well the organization is doing overall" (Murray, 2010, p. 447).

Another approach to benchmarking, what Poister and colleagues (2015) call *corporate-style benchmarking,* "focuses directly on so-called best practices or [organizations] that are high performing (p. 386)." The purpose of this type of benchmarking is to identify the most effective or efficient methods of performing specific functions and seeing how the subject organization compares with the best. The organization conducting the benchmarking then would intend to adopt those practices in order to increase its own performance.

Christine Letts, William Ryan, and Allen Grossman (1999a), advocates of benchmarking, argue that it "bridges the gap between great ideas and great performance" (p. 86) and that the nonprofit culture of openness and sharing may make it a more feasible approach for them than for competitive businesses. However, like the use of financial ratios, benchmarking also has its shortcomings and critics. For one, it requires a larger investment of time and effort than comparing financial ratios, which are readily available from Form 990. Second, there is no way to really know whether the practice being studied is related to an organization's overall effectiveness. For example, how does the amount of time required to process the payroll relate to whether it is an effective organization? In addition, it is often difficult to identify the specific indicators on which the best practice is to be compared. For instance, what number best indicates how many clients have "recovered" from an illness or addiction? Should recovery be declared shortly after the client completes a treatment program or only after some period of time has passed? It is also often tricky to identify which organizations can really be considered alike. For example, nonprofits in different cities may face very different funding environments and more or less favorable markets for volunteers and staff. There also may be methodological issues, for example, concerning the availability and reliability of comparative data (Poister et al., 2015).

Benchmarking is a useful tool, but perhaps more for examining specific program or administrative functions than for evaluating the effectiveness or performance of an organization. Moreover, since the selection of peer organizations is often complicated by local factors, benchmarking may be better used as a tool for learning than for evaluating. If used (or perceived) as a technique for evaluating the performance of specific departments or staff, it also may come to be manipulated; that is, individuals may try to game the system by selecting peer organizations with which they think they may have the most favorable comparisons.

Outcomes

Financial ratios and benchmark data may provide some insights into a nonprofit's performance, but mission is the heart of the matter. It is the very purpose for which a nonprofit exists. Thus, the most important indicators of effectiveness should be related to its success in accomplishing that mission. As Brian Gallagher, president of the United Way of America, expressed it in 2005,

> Financial accountability is just table stakes. You *have* [italics original] to get that right first. But, ultimately, the American public should hold our sector accountable for delivering on our missions. . . . We should be asked to report concrete results that are tied directly to our missions, not just the level of activity we produce. (n.p.)

The outcomes approach to measuring program effectiveness has gained wide acceptance, in part through the early efforts of the United Way of America during the 1990s. It also has been adopted by many foundations and government agencies for measuring their grantees' effectiveness. Venture philanthropy funds and foundations that have adopted concepts from venture philanthropy also have placed an emphasis on the measurement of outcomes.

TABLE 6.3 ■ Basic Definitions Related to Outcomes

Theory of Change—how we effect change

The overarching set of formal relationships presumed to exist for a defined population, the intended outcomes that are the focus of the organization's work, and the logic model for producing the intended outcomes. A theory of change should be meaningful to stakeholders, plausible in that it conforms to common sense, doable with available resources, and measurable.

Logic Model—what we do and how

The logically related parts of a program, showing the links between program objectives, program activities (efforts applied coherently and reliably over a sustained time), and expected program outcomes. A logic model makes clear who will be served, what should be accomplished, and specifically how it will be done (i.e., written cause-and-effect statements for a given program design).

Inputs—what resources are committed

The resources—money, time, staff, expertise, methods, and facilities—that an organization commits to a program to produce the intended outputs, outcomes, and impact.

Outputs—what we count

The volume of a program's actions, such as products created or delivered, number of people served, and activities and services carried out.

Outcomes—what we wish to achieve

Socially meaningful changes for those served by a program, generally defined in terms of expected changes in knowledge, skills, attitudes, behavior, condition, or status. These changes should be measured, be monitored as part of an organization's work, link directly to the efforts of the program, and serve as the basis for accountability.

Indicators—what we use to stay on course

Specific, observable, and measurable characteristics, actions, or conditions that demonstrate whether a desired change has happened toward the intended outcome. Also called "outcome indicators" or "predictive indicators."

Impact—what we aim to effect

To slightly oversimplify, the results that can be directly attributed to the outcomes of a given program or collective of programs, as determined by evaluations that are capable of factoring out (at a high level of statistical probability) other explanations for how these results came to be.

Editorial Note: These definitions were adapted from the *Glossary of Terms* of the Shaping Outcomes Initiative of the Institute of Museum and Library Services, Indiana University and Purdue University Indianapolis; *The Nonprofit Outcomes Toolbox: A Complete Guide to Program Effectiveness, Performance Measurement, and Results* by Robert Penna; and the *Framework for Managing Programme Performance Information* of the South African government. The definitions were informed by distinguished reviewers who provided valuable insights.

Source: Morino (2011, p. 9).

Again, it is important to define terms and concepts. Table 6.3 summarizes some of the important definitions that many authors use when discussing outcomes.

The United Way outcomes model is illustrated in Table 6.4, which highlights the key variables: inputs, activities, outputs, and outcomes. *Inputs* are the resources dedicated to the program, including money, staff, volunteers, facilities, equipment, and supplies, as well as the constraints imposed by the external environment. *Activities* are what the program does—for example, tutoring children, feeding the homeless, or providing job training. *Outputs* are the direct products of the activities and are often relatively easy things to

TABLE 6.4 ■ United Way Program Outcome Model			
Inputs	**Activities**	**Outputs**	**Outcomes**
Resources dedicated to or consumed by the program, e.g., money, staff and staff time, volunteers and volunteer time, facilities, equipment, and supplies Constraints on the program, e.g., laws, regulations, funders' requirements	What the program does with the inputs to fulfill its mission, e.g., feed and shelter homeless families, provide job training, educate the public about signs of child abuse, counsel pregnant women, create mentoring relationships for youth	The direct products of program activities, e.g., number of classes taught, number of counseling sessions conducted, number of educational materials distributed, number of hours of service delivered, number of participants served	Benefits for participants during and after program activities, e.g., new knowledge, increased skills, changed attitudes or values, modified behavior, improved condition, altered status

Source: United Way of America (1996).

measure—for example, the number of children tutored, the number of homeless fed, and the number of individuals trained in employment skills. But measuring outputs does not make the connection to the program's goals, which are generally to change in some way the individuals it serves and to make a lasting difference in their lives. *Outcomes* are the changes that occur in the individuals as a result of their participation in the program—for example, new knowledge, expanded job skills, or a better position in life.

Outcomes may be measured immediately after the individual completes the program (initial outcomes); after a longer period has elapsed, say a few years (intermediate outcomes); and after an even longer period of time (long-term outcomes). Thus, it may be found that students who participate in an after-school tutoring program improve their grades, but are they still succeeding academically two years later? Do they go on to complete college in larger numbers than students who do not participate in the program? Are they more likely to be employed a decade after their participation in the program? Obviously, measuring outcomes over the longer term can require considerable effort and expense, perhaps involving the tracking of former clients and follow-up surveys. That can be difficult for organizations that serve clients who are highly mobile and difficult to reach—for example, homeless people.

But measuring outcomes is not quite the same as evaluating programs. In other words, it is one thing to establish that outcomes have occurred, but evaluating the program requires determining that these outcomes were in some way related to the program. That requires developing a sound and plausible *logic model*—that is, a theoretical explanation of the links all the way through the process from inputs to outcomes. As John McLaughlin and Gretchen Jordan (2010; p. 56) explain, "A logic model is a plausible and sensible model of how a program will work under certain environmental conditions to solve identified problems." The logic model is related to a *theory of change,* which is "a more detailed description of the theoretical basis for a program and the assumed causal mechanisms that are needed to produce desired ends. The logic model is a condensed version of theories of change" (Hatry, 2014, p. 12).

Figure 6.1 depicts the logic model of a program offering tutoring to at-risk teens. It shows how the organization believes the process works. To justify using school graduation rates as an outcome measure for its program, the organization would need to explain how the mentoring experience *causes* students to complete their homework and attend school more regularly and how homework and attendance affect graduation rates. Otherwise, the rate of students' graduation from high school cannot be a useful indicator of the tutoring program's outcome. One obvious problem in developing such logic models is how to identify the external influences that can cause the outcome in addition to the activities associated with the program. This becomes more of an issue the higher up in the model one ascends. For example, students' grades and graduation rates may be positively affected by the tutoring program, but they also could be affected—either positively or negatively—by students' experiences at home or in the

It must be emphasized again that the outcomes model does not necessarily incorporate other important aspects of organizational performance. For example, it is possible to conceive of an organization that is delivering effective programs but whose sustainability as an organization over the long run is imperiled by financial imbalances. It could also be possible to achieve positive program outcomes, but at a very high cost; in other words, the organization could be very inefficient. Moreover, measuring program outcomes does not tell us anything about the organization's ability to learn and adapt to change.

Focusing on outcomes provides a different understanding of "efficiency" than the simple version encompassed in the emphasis on low "overhead," discussed earlier. As Harry Hatry (2014) explains:

> Performance measurement of efficiency has traditionally used indicators of the form: "average cost (or number of FTEs) per unit of output." However, "true" efficiency is reducing costs without sacrificing service quality. A more important indicator is to relate cost to the amount of outcome achieved. The performance measurement is then "average cost per unit of outcome." (p. 21)

How are nonprofit CEOs actually choosing between overhead and outcomes in measuring the effectiveness of their organizations? In a survey of CEOs of international nonprofits, George Mitchell (2012) found that most defined the effectiveness of their organizations in terms of outcomes, while a minority thought about it in terms of maintaining low overhead. But, like Hatry, Mitchell (2012) argues that the two perspectives are related, since the definition of efficiency would need to include outcomes as well as the costs incurred to produce them. In other words, considering outcomes gives efficiency a different, and more appropriate, meaning than if we are looking at overhead alone.

Common Indicators

As mentioned above, measuring the performance of nonprofit organizations has gained more attention, but the proliferation of approaches has proved frustrating to many. Some have cited the complexity of academic approaches and the demands on staff time and attention to compile and analyze data. Some have questioned to what extent the data compiled are actually used in the operation of many organizations. And some scholars have even concluded that systemically measuring impact in the nonprofit sector is impossible (Lampkin et al., 2006). And yet, demands for performance data are unlikely to abate.

To address this need, in 2004, the Urban Institute and the Center for What Works undertook a project to identify a common set of outcomes and outcomes indicators that nonprofits could use to inform practice and that could be practical to implement. The project's team identified 14 separate program areas regarding their missions, the outcomes they sought, and potential outcomes indicators for tracking progress toward those program areas' missions.

The first step was development of an outcome sequencing chart, essentially a logic model, to explain how outcomes would ultimately lead organizations in each area to fulfill their missions. The chart was then applied to 14 program areas: adult education and family literacy, advocacy, affordable housing, assisted living, business assistance, community organizing, emergency shelter, employment training, health risk reduction, performing arts, prisoner reentry, transitional housing, youth mentoring, and youth tutoring. In addition, the project's 2006 report included a generic "nonprofit taxonomy of outcomes" as a guide for organizations in program areas in which specific indicators had not yet been developed.

The 2006 report issued by the Urban Institute and its partner, the Center for What Works, included several caveats, including acknowledgment that further research would be needed to test and revise the core indicators for the 14 areas, add indicators for additional program areas, and develop a common framework for general guidance. Students should consult the website of the Urban Institute for more information on the project (www.urban.org/center/cnp/projects/outcomeindicators.cfm).

Balanced Scorecard

Financial ratios may be an indication of organizational performance, but they do not measure whether the organization's mission has been achieved. Outcomes measure effectiveness against mission, but may not provide insight on broader organizational performance. Benchmarking may be useful as a learning tool, but it has shortcomings as a method of evaluating performance, as discussed above. The *balanced scorecard,* and variations on the concept, has been adopted by some nonprofit organizations as a tool for monitoring indicators across various dimensions. Like other models, it has its strengths and weaknesses.

The balanced scorecard is a concept developed by Robert Kaplan and David Norton (1992) as a way for businesses to obtain, as the term suggests, a balanced perspective on performance by combining financial data with other considerations. It has since been adopted by many nonprofit organizations and government agencies as a way to combine financial ratios and other data in measuring organizational performance. The balanced scorecard looks at an organization from four perspectives:

1. *The financial perspective,* including financial performance indicators

2. *The customer or client perspective,* including measures of customer satisfaction

3. *The internal business perspective,* including measures of operational efficiency and quality

4. *The innovation and learning perspective,* including measures of the organization's ability to adapt to changes in the environment (Murray, 2010, p. 446)

Rob Paton (2003) offers a variation of the balanced scorecard designed specifically for nonprofits, which he calls the *dashboard.* The terms *balanced scorecard* and *dashboard* are often used interchangeably (Poister et al., 2015). Paton's model seeks to answer two fundamental questions: Does it work? In other words, "do the different activities, services, and programs achieve broadly the results intended?" (pp. 139–140). And is the organization well-run? Paton notes that there may be a relationship between how well-run an organization is and the effectiveness of the programs it delivers, but that the two are separate matters and both need to be measured in order to obtain a complete picture of the organization's performance:

A valuable and innovative service may be provided by an organization that is inefficiently administered, or even by one whose funds are being discretely embezzled; and a well-administered organization with excellent morale may be delivering high-quality programs to clients whose needs are slight compared to those of the client group originally envisaged. (p. 140)

Paton's (2003) dashboard thus looks at the organization from five perspectives, encompassing short-term, medium-term, and long-term measures:

1. *Current results:* Monthly checking against key targets—for example, a summary of achievements, a finance report, and a marketing report

2. *Underlying performance:* Annual reviews of the appropriateness and cost-effectiveness of programs and support functions—for example, service outcomes, business outcomes, and external comparisons

3. *Risks:* Monitoring of the ways the organization may be put in jeopardy—for example, by a liquidity crisis, legal or procedural noncompliance, or a breakdown in key relationships

4. *Assets and capabilities:* Annual reviews of capacity to deliver future performance—for example, physical and financial assets, external reputation and relationships, and expertise and process knowledge

5. *Change projects:* Regular reports on projects intended to bring about improvements in the organization that the board and the CEO are supervising directly (p. 142)

Many nonprofit organizations have developed some version of a dashboard to provide an overview of performance to executives and the governing board. It often includes key variables and graphics displays on a single page that provides a comprehensive snapshot of the organization at a point in time, change compared to previous periods, and progress toward goals. The dashboard often summarizes key indicators with regard to both program outcomes and financials.

In recent years, there has been an increase in the availability of tools to help nonprofits track and report their performance in a consistent manner. For example, in 2012, the BBB Wise Giving Alliance, GuideStar USA, and Independent Sector launched Charting Impact, an online tool that is provided through GuideStar and offers a common report format for nonprofits to use (Guidestar, 2015). The report is organized around five key questions:

1. What is your organization aiming to accomplish?

2. What are your strategies for making this happen?

3. What are your organization's capabilities for doing this?

4. How will your organization know if you are making progress?

5. What have and haven't you accomplished so far?

There are also various commercially available software products that nonprofits use to monitor their activities and outcomes.

The balanced scorecard and similar approaches have critics, too. For example, Marshall Meyer (2002) notes that the balanced scorecard really measures very different things—for example, financial results and customer satisfaction, numbers that must be looked at alongside each other rather than combined. It does not provide a single measure of an organization's performance. He suggests instead the idea of identifying correlations between measures. For example, do good financial results always go along with customer satisfaction? If so, there is no need to measure customer satisfaction directly, since it can be assumed from the financial results.

Social Return on Investment

The concept of the double bottom line has been mentioned earlier in this text. It refers to the need for nonprofit managers to look to both their organization's financial performance as well as the social impact of its programs. In 1996, the Roberts Enterprise Development Foundation (now known simply as REDF), a venture philanthropy fund based in San Francisco, pioneered the concept of *social return on investment* (SROI) as a way to put a dollar figure on—that is, to monetize—the social value created by an organization. The idea was to add social return to financial return in order to generate a single number—in dollars—that could be used as an indicator of the organization's performance and value.

As a venture philanthropy fund, REDF approaches giving as a form of investing in a select group of social enterprises that have a social mission. And, like other investors, REDF seeks to measure the return on its investments. Financial return is easy to understand: If you invest $100,000 and receive $200,000 back, that's a 100 percent return on your investment. But how do we measure the less tangible social benefits created by a nonprofit's programs? SROI provides a method for measuring those social benefits in dollar terms so that they can be compared with expenditures to produce a single number as simple to understand as the rate of return on a philanthropic investment.

REDF's SROI methodology evolved from *benefit–cost analysis (also called cost–benefit analysis),* a technique drawn from applied economics and most often used to evaluate government programs. As Stephanie Cellini and James Kee (2010, p. 494) define it, "cost-benefit analysis . . . identifies and places *dollar values* on the costs of programs [and weighs] those costs against the *dollar value* of program benefits" [italics added]. The advantage of this approach is that it produces a ratio that can be used to compare programs against programs. But putting a dollar value on social benefits—that is, monetizing them—can be a challenge. As an example, let's consider a program that offers job training, helping people move from welfare to work. The benefits may include the new income taxes paid by the people who become employed, savings through lower welfare costs, less need for homeless shelters, and perhaps savings in the cost of policing as fewer people are on the streets. These benefits can be given a dollar value and summed to find the SROI in the nonprofit's job-training programs. But that does not include, for example, the very real benefits of reduced fear and social tension resulting from the decrease in crime. Though real, they are hard to measure, especially in dollar terms. Moreover, costs are incurred to support the program today, but many of the benefits may not be realized until far into the future. For example, one benefit of an after-school tutoring program that helps young people complete high school may be their higher wages after graduation. That is, at least theoretically, easily stated in dollar terms. But increased education also may lead to healthier and happier lives through their lifetimes, although this is hard to capture and harder to monetize. In addition, SROI and similar approaches face what Alnoor Ebrahim and V. Kasturi Rangan (2010, p. 8) call the "thorny issue of causality." That is, benefits may reflect the influence of other variables beyond the program that is being evaluated.

SROI has been adopted by a number of organizations, especially social enterprises that worked with REDF and other venture philanthropy funds. However, REDF no longer uses SROI exclusively as its measure of an organization's social performance. A 2008 report by Carla Javits acknowledges the shortcomings of the approach:

- The SROI analysis process is resource intensive;
- Engaging the practitioner is essential and time consuming;
- Metrics are important, but metrics aren't everything;
- SROI is a good tool, but SROI isn't everything. (p. 2)

Javits goes on to say,

One of the primary flaws was that the model was built on, and had the tendency to focus attention upon, cost savings to society, while it did not adequately incorporate many of the ways that social enterprise employment improved peoples' lives. For example, while social return could and did measure the dollar value of reduced time in prison or jail, we were not able to incorporate factors that we were unable to quantify, such as improved family relationships or mental health status. (p. 2)

Blended Value

The concept of *blended value*, defined by Jed Emerson (Blended Value, 2004.), builds on the idea of social return on investment by adding a third component—impact on the environment. With the increasing focus by nonprofits on financial results and the growing corporate concern about social responsibility, many observers note a blurring of the nonprofit and for-profit sectors; in other words, they argue that nonprofits and business firms are becoming more alike and that it should therefore be possible to define some common measures of performance that could be applied to *all* organizations *across the sectors,* including nonprofit, for-profit, and hybrid enterprises. Blended value is advanced as the answer. Simply defined,

Value is what gets created when investors invest and organizations act to pursue their mission. Traditionally, we have thought of value as being either economic (and created by for-profit companies) or social (and created by nonprofit or non-governmental organizations). What the Blended

(Continued)

FIGURE 6.2 ■ Youth Villages Dashboard

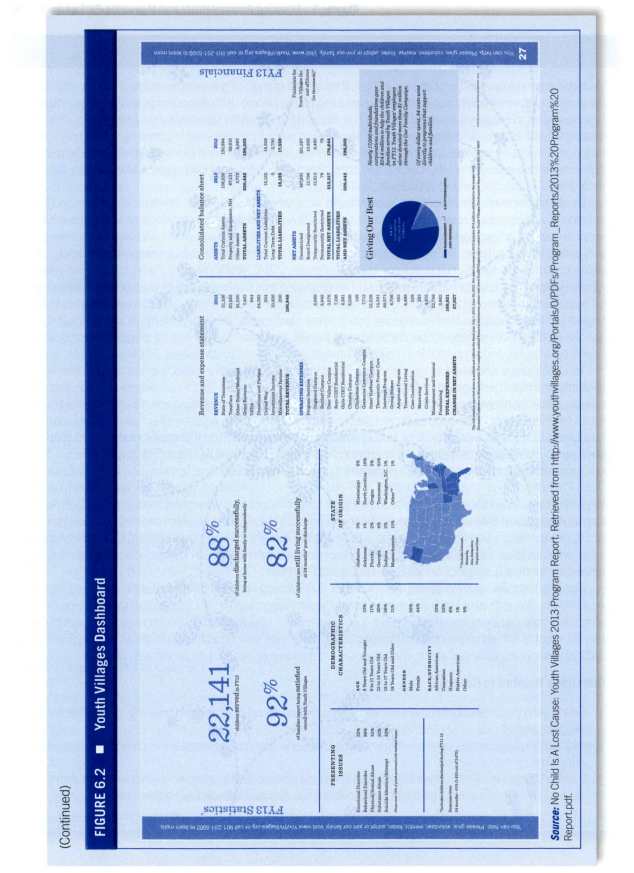

Source: No Child Is A Lost Cause: Youth Villages 2013 Program Report. Retrieved from http://www.youthvillages.org/Portals/0/PDFs/Program_Reports/2013%20Program%20 Report.pdf.

QUESTIONS FOR DISCUSSION

Below are statements excerpted from three organizations' websites, describing their purposes. Based on these statements,

1. How are their missions different?

2. What metrics would you use to measure their effectiveness?

3. Could some or all use common indicators, or would the indicators need to be varied in light of their distinctive missions?

- The SEED Foundation is a national nonprofit that partners with urban communities to provide innovative educational opportunities that prepare underserved students for success in college and beyond. (http://www.seedfoundation.com/)

- [The District of Columbia College Success Foundation] provide[s] a unique integrated system of supports and scholarships for underserved, low-income students to finish high school, graduate college and succeed in life. (http://www.dccollegesuccessfoundation.org/dc/meet-csf)

- College Summit is the nation's largest nonprofit dedicated to transforming the lives of low-income youth by connecting them to college and career. College Summit uses peer leadership, custom curricula, real-time student performance data and technology to help get these high school students from low-income communities to and through college. (http://www.collegesummit.org/about-us/)

SUGGESTIONS FOR FURTHER READING

Books

Clark, C., & Emerson, J. (2014). *The impact investor: Lessons in leadership and strategy for collaborative capitalism.* San Francisco, CA: Jossey-Bass.

Morino, M. (2011). *Leap of reason: Managing to outcomes in an era of scarcity.* Washington, DC: Venture Philanthropy Partners. [Full text available for download at http://www.vppartners.org/]

Newcomer, K. E., Hatry, H. P., & Wholey, J. S. (2015). *Handbook of practical program evaluation* (4th ed.). San Francisco, CA: Jossey-Bass.

Niven, P. R. (2008). *Balanced scorecard step-by-step for government and nonprofit agencies.* Hoboken, NJ: Wiley.

Pallotta, D. (2010). *Uncharitable: How restraints on nonprofits undermine their potential.* Lebanon, NH: Tufts University Press.

Penna, R. M. (2011). *The nonprofit outcomes toolbox: A complete guide to program effectiveness, performance measurement, and results.* Hoboken, NJ: Wiley.

Poister, T. H., Aristigueta, M. P., & Hall, J. L. (2015). Managing and measuring performance in public and nonprofit organizations (2nd ed.). San Francisco, CA: Jossey-Bass.

Articles/Report

Brest, P. (2010, Spring). The power of theories of change. *Stanford Social Innovation Review.* Retrieved from http://www.ssireview.org/articles/entry/the_power_of_theories_of_change

Hatry, H. P. (2014). *Transforming performance measurement for the 21st century.* Washington, DC : Urban Institute.

Kania, J., & Kramer, M. (2011, Winter). Collective impact. *Stanford Social Innovation Review*, 36–41. Retrieved from http://www.ssireview.org/pdf/2011_WI_Feature_Kania.pdf

Websites

Balanced Scorecard Institute: http://www.balancedscorecard.org/

BBB Wise Giving Alliance: http://www.give.org/

Blended Value: http://www.blendedvalue.org/

Charting Impact: http://www.chartingimpact.org/

GuideStar: http://www.guidestar.org/

Independent Sector (Principles): https://www.independentsector.org/principles

PerformWell: http://www.performwell.org/

REDF: http://www.redf.org/Standards for Excellence Institute, http://www.standardsforexcellenceinstitute .org/dnn/

Urban Institute: http://www.urbaninstitute.org/

Venture Philanthropy Partners (Leap of Reason): http://www.vppartners.org/leapofreason/overview

Companion Website

Visit study.sagepub.com/worth4e for access to certain full-text SAGE journal articles and links to relevant video and multimedia content.

c h a p t e r   7

Strategic planning begins with where the organization is, defines some new place where it wants to be, and develops a plan to get there, all in the context of its mission and values and the realities of the environment in which its operates.

Photo: BananaStock/BananaStock/Thinkstock

Learning Objectives

After reading this chapter, students should be able to:

1. Define *strategy*, *strategic planning*, and *strategic management*.
2. Describe the key steps in the strategic planning process.
3. Explain the pros and cons of strategic planning.
4. Explain various approaches to developing an organization's strategy.
5. Define *organizational capacity*.
6. Describe models for capacity building.
7. Identify capacity building appropriate to an organization's point in its life cycle.
8. Analyze cases, applying concepts from the chapter.

Developing Strategy and Building Capacity

7

Nonprofit organizations are driven by their *missions,* and those who work in them, as staff or volunteers, are often motivated primarily by their passion for the social purpose that the organization serves. But, as discussed in Chapter 6, society increasingly demands that nonprofits be accountable for the use of the resources entrusted to them. While passion for the cause is essential, nonprofit organizations also must apply tools of rational management. This chapter discusses some tools that a nonprofit can use to develop a strategy for achieving its *goals,* create a strategic plan, and build the organizational *capacity* needed to deliver its mission.

Understanding Strategy

Some people may hear the term *strategy* and think it is synonymous with strategic planning. But there is a difference; let's consider an example. In 1989, Robert Egger was managing nightclubs in Washington, DC. His fiancée persuaded him to join her in a volunteer program that passed out food to the city's homeless from trucks that toured the streets and parks. This gave him an understanding of the prevalence of hunger and a new idea. Egger began to think about how homeless people were trapped in their situation because they lacked the ability to gain employment. And he thought about the tons of food that were wasted every day by restaurants, hotels, and caterers throughout Washington. He put these two realities together, which led him to found DC Central Kitchen. The Kitchen collects surplus food, processes and repackages it, and today provides more than 5,000 meals a day to shelters and other facilities throughout the area, while also providing job training to homeless people who work in the kitchen and eventually move on to jobs in the food service industry (www.dccentralkitchen.org). Egger (2002) didn't start out with a strategic *plan.* He didn't have a written document that described the details of how he would proceed. But he had a winning *strategy.*

Management scholars and consultants have offered many definitions of strategy, and there is not agreement on exactly what it is or how to develop it. It may be articulated in a plan, that is, a written document, or it may be more intangible, perhaps no more than an idea or an approach to reaching a goal. Strategy is focused on the long term, not on the day-to-day, or as Michael Allison and Jude Kaye (2015) write, "It is concerned with the longer-term course that the ship is steering, not with the waves" (p. 7). Developing strategy does not necessarily require any particular process or result in any written document at all. It does require creativity and a different way of seeing reality. In this chapter, we will look at the process of *strategic planning,* but it is important to keep in mind that "strategic thinking,

TABLE 7.1 ■ Summary of Strategic Planning Terms

Term	Meaning	Other terms commonly used
Mission	The reason the organization exists; the starting point for strategic planning	Purpose
Vision	Description of an ideal future, either for the organization (internal vision statement) or of society (external vision statement)	Vision of success
Values	Principles the organization holds as the most important	Guiding principles
SWOT analysis	An inventory and analysis of the organization's strengths and weaknesses and of opportunities and threats (SWOT) posed to the organization by the external environment	Environmental scan
Strategic issues	"The fundamental policy questions or critical challenges facing the organization's mandates, mission and values, product or service level and mix, clients, users or payers, cost, financing, structure, processes, and management" (Bryson, 2011, p. 42)	Strategic questions
Goals	Directions that the organization will pursue with respect to the strategic issues	Strategic goals Strategic directions Objectives Strategic objectives
Strategies	Actions that the organization intends to take to achieve its goals	
Objectives	Specific, quantified targets that represent steps toward accomplishing the goals	Goals

of various approaches, which is appropriate because the planning process needs to be tailored to fit each specific situation. A basic, generic strategic planning model is depicted in Figure 7.1 and includes the steps common to many models:

- Plan to plan—that is, determine the process, the players, and their roles.
- Clarify the organization's *mission, values*, and *vision*.
- Assess the situation—that is, scan the external environment and the organization's internal realities.
- Identify the strategic issues or strategic questions that need to be addressed.
- Develop goals, strategies, and objectives.
- Write and communicate the plan.
- Develop operational and implementation plans.
- Execute the plan.
- Evaluate results.

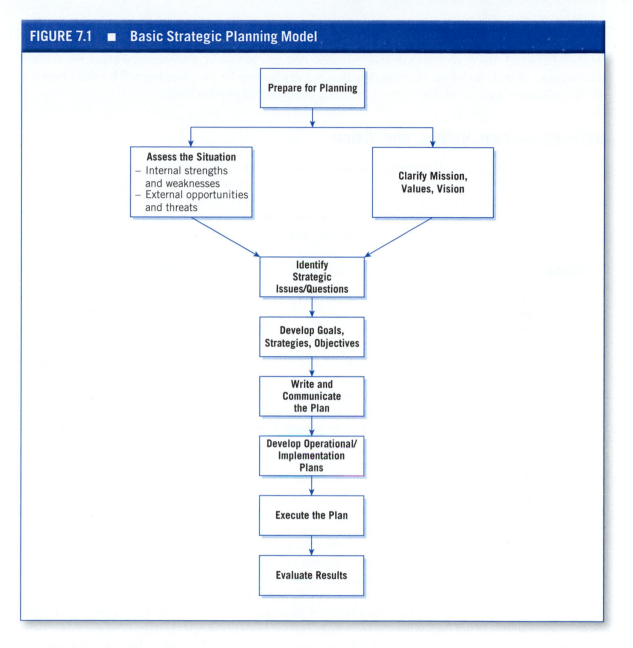

FIGURE 7.1 ■ Basic Strategic Planning Model

Planning to Plan

It is important to have a plan for planning, that is, to identify what process will be used, who will participate, and what information will be needed to inform the planning. There needs to be agreement among the participants on points such as the purpose of the effort; the steps in the process; the form and timing of reports that will be issued; the role, functions, and membership of any group or committee empowered to oversee the effort; the role, functions, and membership of the strategic planning team; the commitment of the resources necessary for proceeding with the effort; and any important limitations or boundaries for the effort (Bryson, 2011, pp. 47–48).

Some organizations use an outside consultant to guide their strategic planning process; others prefer to manage it themselves. Some plan an off-site retreat at some point in the process—perhaps a day or weekend in which the participants devote extensive time to discussion of strategies without the normal interruptions of daily business. Up-front time devoted to planning for the planning will be well spent if it avoids misunderstandings or wasted motion during the planning process itself.

Defining Mission, Values, and Vision

Effective planning begins with consensus about basics—mission, vision, and values. Discussion on these basics often can take considerable time, and some pragmatic individuals, eager to jump into identifying issues and goals, may find the exercise frustrating. But experience has shown that neglecting to create a solid foundation for planning by achieving consensus on the basics of mission, vision, and values will likely lead to a breakdown in planning at some later stage.

Mission

As we have discussed before, mission is everything to a nonprofit organization—it is the reason the organization exists, and it must be the starting point for its planning. James Phills (2005) speaks eloquently to this point:

> Mission is the psychological and emotional logic that drives an organization. It is the reason why people get up in the morning and go to work in a nonprofit . . . Mission [defines] the social value that the organization creates. The key feature of social value—whether it is spiritual, moral, societal, aesthetic, intellectual, or environmental—is that it transcends economic value. Thus, it is inextricably linked to fundamental human values, which are the basis for intrinsic worth or importance. (p. 22)

It is important to distinguish mission from mandates. *Mandates* are functions that the organization is *required* to perform, perhaps by its charter or law. For example, a college may have a charter that requires it to enroll only women students. The American Red Cross has mandated services that it is required to provide to the government under its congressional charter. If the organization faces mandates, they will need to be clarified at the outset and incorporated in the plan. They are "givens." But, in general, nonprofit organizations have fewer mandates than do public agencies and thus have considerable freedom to design their own futures; this may include redefining their missions.

There are different philosophies about mission statements. Some prefer fairly simple statements that are almost like a slogan—they capture the essence of the organization's purpose in a sentence. But many mission statements say not only what the organization does, but also, at least briefly, how it does it. Some organizations develop separate statements of their vision and values, while others include some components of vision and values in their mission statements, either explicitly or implicitly. Box 7.1 provides a sampling of three mission statements that reflect somewhat varied approaches.

We might think that an organization's mission should be relatively unchanging. Indeed, a performing arts organization is not likely to one day alter its mission statement to address environmental issues or the welfare of animals. But there are often changes that require a rethinking, or at least a restatement of the mission. For example, you may recall Miriam's Kitchen, the Washington-based organization serving homeless people, which we passed in our hypothetical walking tour back in Chapter 2. Miriam's began as a breakfast program, and its mission was once simply to provide a healthy meal each day to homeless men and women. But as its programs evolved, it began to offer case management services to its clients and expanded medical services and other programs. Its work came to include more advocacy, and it focused its efforts on securing more supportive permanent housing. Over time, the scope of its purposes and

BOX 7.1 MISSION STATEMENTS

Big Brothers Big Sisters

Provide children facing adversity with strong and enduring, professionally supported one-to-one relationships that change their lives for the better, forever. (www.bbbs.org)

City Year

City Year's mission is to build democracy through citizen service, civic leadership and social entrepreneurship. It is through service that we can demonstrate the power and idealism of young people, engage citizens to benefit the common good, and develop young leaders of the next generation. (www.guidestar.org/organizations/22-2882549/city-year.aspx#mission)

Special Olympics

The mission of Special Olympics is to provide year-round sports training and athletic competition in a variety of Olympic-type sports for children and adults with intellectual disabilities, giving them continuing opportunities to develop physical fitness, demonstrate courage, experience joy and participate in a sharing of gifts, skills and friendship with their families, other Special Olympics athletes and the community. (www.specialolympics.org)

activities had changed, and it became essential to consider a broader mission statement that enveloped all the organization's activities: "Our mission is to provide individualized services that address the causes and consequences of homelessness in an atmosphere of dignity and respect, both directly and through facilitating connections in the Washington, DC community." (Miriam's Kitchen, n.d.). This broader statement of mission encompassed what Miriam's was actually doing but did not represent a complete departure from its original purposes.

Saying that the mission can change is not to suggest that organizations should simply expand their programs and then change their mission statements to fit. But, inevitably, programs and missions often will evolve as the organization grows and expands its capabilities. Revisiting the mission is really asking the questions, "What business are we in?" and "What are we really trying to accomplish?" Getting to the right answer sometimes requires adopting a new perspective. There is always a trade-off between keeping the mission sufficiently broad and keeping it sufficiently focused. There is a risk in going to extremes in either direction. Too narrow a mission statement may be too constraining, making it impossible for the organization to grow or expand. But a statement that is too broad may become meaningless and open the door to *mission creep*—a gradual evolution away from the organization's purposes into ancillary activities that may eventually result in an organization that is very unfocused.

Vision and Values

Most organizations clarify their *vision* and *values* in the first phase of strategic planning. The vision statement is a description of an ideal future. Some vision statements describe the future of the organization itself; these are *internal vision statements*. For example, the Boy Scouts of America envisions the future of its impact as an organization: "The Boys Scout of America will prepare every eligible youth in America to become a responsible, participating citizen and leader who is guided by the Scout Oath and Law" (Boy Scouts of America, 2014). Other vision statements paint a picture of the ideal world that the organization

Scenario	Competitive Position	Program Attractiveness	Alternative Coverage	Suggested Strategy (MacMillan)	The Situation in Ordinary Language
					TABLE 7.3　■　(Continued)
5	Strong	Low	High	Build up best competitor	We're the best at doing this, but it is just not attractive to us to do it any longer. We don't want to let people down who rely on this program, but there are other organizations that do the same thing. Let's talk to the next-best organization and help them take this over from us.
6	Strong	Low	Low	Soul of the agency	We are the best and almost the only organization doing this. We're really known for it. It's not that attractive to us in many ways—for one thing, we lose money on it. But a lot of people depend on us and have nowhere else to go. We just have to find a way to keep it going.
7	Weak	Low	High	Orderly divestment	This is just not an attractive program for us, and we're not that good at it either. A lot of other organizations offer the same thing. No rush, but let's gradually direct people elsewhere and phase this program out.
8	Weak	Low	Low	Joint venture	We're not very good at this, and we really don't want to do it. Some people need the program, but not that many. We're stuck with it for now, but let's see if we can find another organization that's willing to partner with us in this area, so we can focus on our higher priorities.

Setting Objectives

Objectives are *specific*, *quantified* targets that represent steps toward accomplishing the goals. (Again, remember that in some models, these objectives statements are called *goals*.) Objectives are often stated in the form of "Increase (something) from (some number) to (another number) by (deadline)." The statement could, of course, also use *decrease, reduce*, or some other verb that implies a change in the value used to define the objective. This form is useful in communicating not only what the objective is, but also how ambitious it is—it enables any reader of the plan to see exactly what rate of change is anticipated and the date by which it is to be achieved.

Let's pick up with the example of the urban theater that we have been discussing. Given the goals and strategies that its plans have identified, one objective might be: "Increase the number of major donors from one to ten within three years." Another might be, "Double the number of visits to our website from x to y within the next year." For new activities, objectives need to be stated differently, and in some cases, a numeric objective may not be appropriate—just accomplishing something may constitute achievement of the goal, although a deadline should be included. For example, the theater might establish objectives such as "Retain an architect by June 1 to begin planning for renovation of our facility," "Appoint a marketing director within three months," "Appoint a director of development within six months," "Establish promotional partnerships with six neighborhood restaurants by the beginning of the next season," "Create a Facebook page within three months," and "Obtain five positive media reviews in the next season."

There need not be a one-to-one correspondence between objectives and goals—that is, achievement of an objective might well address more than one goal. Quantifiable objectives create the bridge from strategy to implementation by setting specific targets to be achieved. Operational plans then can be developed to spell out in detail exactly what will be done, when, and by whom in order to achieve the objectives in the strategic plan.

Writing the Strategic Plan

Strategic plans are, almost by definition, written documents. The written plan records the decisions reached and the goals, strategies, and objectives to be pursued. Usually, it is best if one or two people do the actual writing, but the draft is often used to stimulate wider discussion throughout the organization and its constituencies. Eventually, the governing board should take formal action to adopt the plan as the organization's policy.

The length of the written plan varies. Some plans may be no more than a few pages, summarizing mission, vision, values, and core strategies, and including a list of programs and objectives. Others may run 50 pages or more and include appendices with supporting data.

Once the written plan has been completed, it is important to use it as a tool for communication throughout the organization. The audience may include board members, staff, volunteers, clients, funders, other organizations, the news media, and the public (Allison and Kaye, 2015, p. 188). One of the benefits of strategic planning is that it helps build wide consensus and common understanding about mission, vision, values, goals, and strategies. That benefit is sacrificed if it remains a document available only to a select few in management or so voluminous that few are likely to read it. As Allison and Kaye emphasize, "The more concise and ordered the document, the greater the likelihood that it will be used and be helpful in guiding the organization's operations (p. 188)."

Developing an Operational Plan

Once the strategic plan is in place, there remains the job of developing a detailed operational plan—that is, a plan for implementation. This will include identifying specific tasks to be completed, establishing a timeline for their completion, assigning responsibility for each task, identifying the resources that will be needed—human and financial—determining the right organizational structure, identifying what information systems will be required, defining measures by which the completion or success will be determined, and other operational details. As explained earlier, some organizations combine the strategic and operational plans in one document, but developing them requires separate processes, usually with different individuals involved. Whereas board members and representatives of other constituencies may be involved in developing the strategic plan, the detailed work of producing an operational plan generally needs to be done primarily by the staff.

Benefits and Limitations of Strategic Planning

Strategic planning in some form is practiced by most nonprofit organizations today. However, it is important to recognize that strategic planning has its critics. One criticism was mentioned briefly earlier in this chapter: Strategic planning is not synonymous with and does not inevitably produce strategy. The risk is that traditional strategic planning may produce a list of goals, but not anything bigger (La Piana, 2008). Richard Chait, William Ryan, and Barbara Taylor (2005) reinforce this point, writing that "disillusionment with strategic planning has escalated." They observe that in too many plans, "dreams trump reality," that is, they include "blue sky" goals without addressing existing barriers to their achievement (p. 57).

Others point to the amount of time and effort that is required by the traditional strategic planning model, arguing that it may prove frustrating to the organization's staff and distract them from management of current programs. Indeed, when strategic planning is mentioned, some people will resist, or perhaps groan, based on previous negative experiences—the long meetings spent debating every word in the mission statement, the weekend retreats filled with team-building exercises. Strategic planning should not become the purpose of the organization, which is to say, it should not become an all-consuming activity. Bryson (2011) suggests that it should take no more than 10 percent of any key decision-maker's time during the year, and even that may be more than most organizations will require (p. 397).

Planning cannot just be about putting a report on the shelf. It needs to be a continuous part of the organization's way of operating, and the plan itself needs to be a living document that is revisited and adjusted in light of experience and the changing environment. La Piana (2008) argues that a process requiring perhaps 6 to 12 months to complete may put the organization "on hold" for too long, causing it to defer decisions, miss emerging opportunities, and fail to respond to pressing current needs while awaiting the outcome of the planning process. In addition, strategic planning usually occurs on a fixed cycle, perhaps every three years, which may be too infrequent for the fast-changing environment that most nonprofits face. La Piana (2008), who is a consultant to nonprofit organizations, proposes a continuous, "real-time" strategy development model that he characterizes as a "planning-doing cycle" (p. 19). In other words, instead of undertaking planning in a process that is "long, discrete, and separated from the external environment," La Piana recommends that nonprofits engage in "ongoing strategic thinking and acting in the context of the environment on a much shorter cycle" (p. 19).

Strategic planning is not a panacea for every organization's problems at every point in its existence or under all circumstances. As mentioned earlier, it may not be a useful thing to undertake in a new organization, especially one guided by a charismatic, visionary leader. Likewise, strategic planning may not make sense for an organization that is in a state of crisis. What's the point of taking time to debate the mission or scan the environment when the roof is caving in, the creditors are at the door, or the executive director has just resigned and the staff are scrambling to keep things afloat until a new CEO can be found?

Strategic planning is not a substitute for leadership. Unfortunately, some organizations may try to make it so. Perhaps confused and out of ideas, board members or managers may say, "What we need is a strategic plan." They hire a consultant, go through a series of meetings and retreats, and end up with a document that is as lifeless and unimaginative as the paper it is printed on. Planning may provide a road map for implementing a vision, but it is not the vision, and it can only succeed if it is used as a tool of leadership.

Despite its critics and its limitations, strategic planning offers many benefits. It forces the organization to think about its mission and to confront basic questions about where it stands, what it does, and where it wants to go. It requires that the organization look beyond itself to the environment around it and see itself in the context of broader trends and forces, including the society, economy, and other organizations. It provides a basis for rational decision making, rather than relying on guesswork or intuition. It may help to build consensus and understanding about mission, vision, values, and goals throughout the organization. And, when properly executed, it may produce strategies that can help guide a nonprofit toward achievement of its mission. And it may provide a foundation for building the organization's capacity to achieve its mission.

Building Organizational Capacity

As discussed in Chapter 2, interest in building the capacity of nonprofit organizations increased partly as a result of several books and articles that received wide attention in the late 1990s. They noted the problem of inadequate nonprofit capacity and laid the blame on traditional models of grant making, which emphasized short-term support for programs and required that organizations maintain low overhead expenses, preventing investment in their own capacity (e.g., Letts, Ryan, & Grossman, 1997; Shore, 1999). These authors advocated shifting the focus to building strong organizations that could support, sustain, and expand effective programs to a scale that could have meaningful impact (Shore, 1999).

Such critiques influenced the thinking of some funders, who began to shift some of their focus from program grants to providing support for capacity-building initiatives. That was central to the approach of some *venture philanthropy* funds that originated in the 1990s, which adopted the methods of venture capitalists in business, who emphasize building a company for sustainability. *Capacity building* became a movement in the first half of the 2000s, with an explosion of articles, books, and conferences dedicated to the subject. Much of the literature in the field dates from that period. But by 2004, foundation funding to support nonprofit capacity-building efforts began to decline (Jensen, 2006b). In addition, the recession that began in late 2007 shifted the priorities of many nonprofits—and funders—toward sustaining essential programs, further reducing funds available for capacity building. However, in 2009, capacity building received a new boost when the U.S. Congress passed the Edward M. Kennedy Serve America Act, which included a Nonprofit Capacity Building program to provide grants for organizational development to small and mid-size nonprofits. By 2012, interest in capacity building was growing again and 30 percent of funders had increased their support for such activities within the previous two years (Raynor, 2014). Grantmakers for Effective Organizations, an organization that has foundations as its members, stated in 2014 that "capacity building support [is] here to stay" (Raynor, 2014). However, the availability of external funds to support capacity building always has been and remains modest compared with the total of philanthropic giving, and most capacity-building efforts are undertaken by nonprofit organizations using their own internal resources.

Defining and Understanding Capacity

Exactly what is an organization's "capacity"? Paul Light (2004b) offers a succinct, but expansive, definition: Capacity is "everything an organization uses to achieve its mission, from desks and chairs to programs and people" (p. 15). What is *capacity building*? Christine Letts, William Ryan, and Allen Grossman (1999a) call it simply a process to "develop, sustain, and improve the delivery of a [nonprofit's] mission" (p. 4). But these brief definitions are like saying that life encompasses everything that happens and that eating sustains it. They do not really offer enough for us to have a clear understanding of either term. That requires that we go inside the black box of capacity to look at its component parts and observe some specific activities that it comprises.

It is no more meaningful to think about an organization's capacity as an indivisible quality than it is to think about a person's capacity in that way. For example, your capacity for study may be different from your capacity for athletics or for singing, so we would need to think about your capacities in the plural—that is, break capacity down into different categories or elements. Having done so, we could then consider what activities you might need to undertake in order to increase your capacity in areas that need improvement—perhaps some tutoring to improve your study skills, weight training to enhance your athletic prowess, and singing lessons. Fortunately, various authors have identified components of nonprofit organization capacity in much the same way, in categories.

Although they offer somewhat different lists, there are many similarities in the elements they include. Mike Hudson (2005) divides capacity into internal and external elements, writing that building organization capacity is about systematically investing in developing an organization's internal systems (e.g., its people, processes, and infrastructure) and its external relationships (e.g., with funders, partners, and volunteers) so that it can better realize its mission and achieve greater impact (p. 1). When the term *capacity* is used, many people first think primarily about the internal elements. That is understandable. For example, if we think about individuals' capacities—like studying, swimming, or singing—we are really talking about the skills or talents they possess. We are perhaps less inclined to think about their relationships with others as elements of their capacity as individuals. But, as discussed before, nonprofit organizations are open systems and are resource dependent. Their relationships with the external world—including other nonprofits, the media, government, and donors and other funders—are critical to their survival. Establishing and strengthening these relationships may thus be important aspects of capacity building, equal in importance to developing their internal structures, systems, and skills.

Internal and external are still two very broad categories. Paul Connolly and Carol Lukas (2002) offer a more comprehensive framework that helps deepen our understanding. The elements of capacity they identify include (1) the organization's mission, vision, and strategy; (2) its governance and leadership; (3) its ability to deliver programs and ensure the impact of its programs; (4) its strategic relationships—that is, the important external relationships that are critical sources of revenue or that may present constraints on the nonprofit's activities; and (5) its internal systems and management—its human resources; financial management systems; technology and information systems; facilities; plans for managing risk; programs for volunteer recruitment and management; and working relationships among its managers, staff, and volunteers. Connolly and Lukas's list reminds us again that capacity encompasses almost everything a nonprofit organization has or does.

Letts et al. (1999a) break down the concept of capacity in a different way, describing three types of capacity an organization may possess: program delivery capacity, *program expansion capacity*, and *adaptive capacity*. They say that most nonprofit organizations are familiar with the first two, but it is "adaptive capacity that makes an organization not only efficient but also effective" (p. 20). As the term implies, *program delivery capacity* grows out of the organization's knowledge of a specific field—for example, education, the environment, or public health. Its capacities include the skills of its staff, who are recruited for their professional expertise. If this is the only capacity the organization possesses, "the organization is little more than a convenient venue where programs are implemented" (p. 20). As an organization expands its program, possibly to multiple sites, it needs to develop additional capacities, including payroll and financial systems, fundraising, and staff with supervisory skills. But, Letts and her coauthors argue, it is the third capacity—adaptive capacity—"that an organization needs to be sure it is delivering on its mission" (p. 21). This includes the ability to learn as an organization and identify ways to improve, to change in response to client needs, to create new and innovative programs, and to create an environment that is motivating to staff and volunteers (p. 23). Letts et al. draw on models developed in the business sector that they say can be adapted to build the capacity of nonprofits, and they emphasize the need to develop a "culture of performance."

As the discussion in this section demonstrates, the definition of capacity is so broad that it may seem difficult to distinguish capacity building from simply managing the organization. It may help for us to look at some specific processes and activities that nonprofits actually undertake when they say they are engaged in building capacity, which we will do in the next section.

Capacity Building in Action

An organization beginning a capacity-building initiative might use one of a number of tools that are available to evaluate its various capacities and identify areas of weakness that might need to be addressed. For example, in 2001, the consulting firm McKinsey & Company (2001) developed a guide for assessing organizational capacity and a capacity assessment tool (OCAT), which was revised in 2013 (McKinsey & Company, 2013). The tool is available on an open-access basis to any nonprofit organization (mckinseyonsociety.com/ocat/). Nonprofit managers, staff, board members, and others can use it to rate the organization's current status on each element of capacity, assigning a score of 1 where there is a clear need for increased capacity, a 2 when there is a basic level of capacity in place, a 3 if there is a moderate level of capacity, and a 4 if there is a high level of capacity on the element being evaluated. When the instrument is completed by various people within the organization, the combined scores help identify areas in which there is consensus about the need for improvement. The tool could be used as a part of the SWOT analysis described earlier in this chapter as a part of the strategic planning process, since it would help to identify organizational strengths and weaknesses.

Having identified areas of its capacity that need to be strengthened, exactly what actions might an organization undertake? There is a large toolbox available, with tools designed to address almost any need. Capacity building often includes efforts to strengthen the organization's leadership, including the governing board and the CEO. As discussed in Chapters 4 and 5, there are a variety of tools for assessing and improving the skills of boards and CEOs and for developing policies designed to improve their performance. Board development activities might include, for example, board self-assessments, retreats, and establishing a governance committee of the board to focus on the board's own responsibilities, structure, and operation. There are a number of ways in which organizations invest in their executive leadership. Participation in professional associations and activities enables CEOs to learn from the experiences of their peers. There are a wide variety of formal leadership training programs available. Some organizations support their CEOs by retaining an executive coach, a practitioner of a field that has grown into a distinguishable profession in recent years. Having a plan for executive transition is a recommended practice for well-managed nonprofit organizations, and the existence of such a plan is indeed an element of capacity (Kibbe, 2004; Light, 2004b).

Establishing a system for performance management, as described in Chapter 6, would add to an organization's program delivery capacity. Strengthening fundraising and partnerships, perhaps developing strategies for increasing earned income, improving facilities and systems, and enhancing staff and volunteer skills are all important purposes of capacity building. Undertaking a campaign, which will be discussed in Chapter 12, may be an important capacity-building activity that will provide the funds needed for improving physical facilities and strengthening the organization's financial base. Strengthening internal management systems and functions, including human resource management, volunteer programs, financial systems, and operating procedures and policies, is commonly included in capacity-building initiatives.

A Model for Capacity Building

We now have an understanding of the various elements of capacity and the broad array of activities that can be undertaken to enhance capacity in each area. But where do we start? How do the elements fit together, and where should an organization begin to address its capacity in a holistic way?

In its work for Venture Philanthropy Partners in 2001, McKinsey & Company developed a comprehensive capacity framework that helps answer these questions. That framework was revised in 2013 (McKinsey & Company, 2013). The 2013 version is depicted in Figure 7.2. McKinsey defines nonprofit capacity in a pyramid of 10 essential elements. These elements include some of the items identified earlier in this chapter, but their depiction in the framework of a pyramid implies relationships among them and suggests a process for capacity building. McKinsey & Company's pyramid also highlights the importance of an intangible but powerful force that affects every aspect of capacity and efforts to strengthen it—the organization's culture and values.

In McKinsey & Company's (2013) model, capacity building is a process, in which the 10 elements are addressed sequentially, beginning at the top of the pyramid. Like strategic planning, it begins with "aspirations," which encompass mission, vision, and values. At the next level of detail are the organization's strategies, and then its leadership and funding—in other words, the questions descend from purposes to

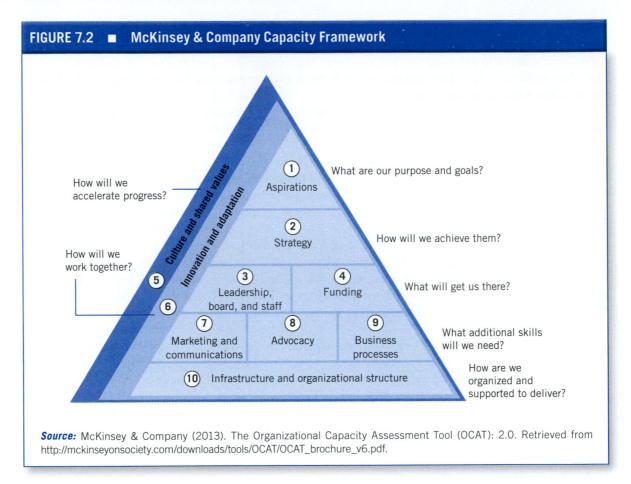

FIGURE 7.2 ■ McKinsey & Company Capacity Framework

Source: McKinsey & Company (2013). The Organizational Capacity Assessment Tool (OCAT): 2.0. Retrieved from http://mckinseyonsociety.com/downloads/tools/OCAT/OCAT_brochure_v6.pdf.

how they will be achieved, to the resources that will be needed to get there. The organization's skills and organizational structure come further down in the pyramid and thus would be considered only after the high-level elements had been addressed.

In the McKinsey (2013) framework, all 10 elements are surrounded by, or embedded within, the shell called *culture and shared values.* Culture affects all the elements and provides the overall environment in which capacity-building efforts may be undertaken. McKinsey & Company (2001) calls it the "invisible thread that runs throughout the entire subject of capacity building" (p. 63).

It may be tempting to initiate capacity building near the bottom of the McKinsey pyramid, perhaps by looking at business processes, staff resources, and organizational structure. Indeed, that may be what many people think about first when capacity is mentioned. These are areas in which many organizations have some deficiencies, and they often affect the daily work of its staff, so there is a high awareness of them. They are concrete and specific and thus easy for people to get their heads around. But McKinsey & Company (2001) emphasize the importance of following a process that begins at the top of the pyramid and works down, stating that its capacity-building work with nonprofits has been most successful when larger questions of mission, vision, and values are addressed before the work proceeds to the elements farther down in the pyramid (p. 15).

Thus, capacity building may mean more than making modest enhancements to staff skills or management systems. Like strategic planning, capacity building also may require disruptive transformational change that goes to the basic values and purposes of the organization.

Capacity and Organizational Life Cycles

Let's look at two examples of capacity building in action, undertaken in two different organizations under very different circumstances. Wendy Kopp founded Teach for America in 1989, recruiting recent graduates from top colleges and universities to spend two years teaching in schools serving low-income students before beginning other careers. She attracted hundreds of talented young men and women to her cause, and her organization grew rapidly. But five years later, Teach for America was "on the verge of collapse" (Hauser, 2003). While Kopp's energy and charisma were sufficient to keep the organization running and growing for a time, its lack of organizational structure, management systems, and comprehensive fund-raising strategies eventually left it in debt and struggling with problems of communications and morale (Hauser, 2003). After considering the possibility of closing, in 1995, the organization launched an effort to achieve stability. "They . . . implemented a plan to build a diverse and sustainable funding base, to concentrate on core activities, to introduce much-needed management processes, and to strengthen the [organization's] culture" (Hauser, 2003, n.p.). It worked. By 2013–2014, Teach for America had grown to include 11,000 corps members engaged in teaching more than 750,000 students (www.teachforamerica.org).

Rubicon Programs, a California-based organization that helps low income people gain independence and self-sufficiency, did not face a crisis like Teach for America. Rather, its goal in 1994 was to further develop its already successful programs and increase their impact. With support from the Roberts Enterprise Development Fund (now REDF), Rubicon built a measurement system to track client outcomes. The new system made it possible not only to serve more clients and better match programs to their needs but also to accurately report outcomes to funders, and it "fundamentally reshaped the organization's performance culture" by making management and staff focus on social impact. By 2000, Rubicon had quadrupled its staff, achieved financial self-sufficiency, and increased the number of people served from 800 to 4,000 (McKinsey & Company, 2001, pp. 55–56). Since 2000, Rubicon has continued to refine its system and to expand its impact. In 2013, it served more than 4,000 people and placed more than 670 people in jobs (www.rubiconprograms.org/index.html).

Teach for America and Rubicon programs offer examples of nonprofit organizations at different places in their histories, one struggling to survive and the other aspiring to greater scale and effectiveness. But both represent examples of capacity-building efforts that helped lead to stability, growth, and recognition for performance.

A number of authors have advanced *life cycle* models describing how organizations grow, mature, and may eventually decline. Many are similar and include the same basic stages, identified by different terms (see, e.g., Adizes, 1999; Carlson & Donohoe, 2003; Stevens, 2001). Let's look at one life cycle model of nonprofit organizations, developed by Judith Sharken Simon (2001) and summarized in Table 7.4.

As Table 7.4 suggests, an organization begins as an idea, a dream, often in the mind of its founder. Once chartered as a formal organization, it still resonates with the enthusiasm of the founder and a small group of founding board or staff members, who work to frame its programs, establish some structure, and chart its direction for future growth. Like an adolescent, it may sometimes seem to be in chaos, but raw energy and commitment drive it forward. Once a foundation has been established, the organization may grow as rapidly as an adolescent. It adds new programs, raises more funds, hires more staff, and becomes more systematic in its approach. It will place greater emphasis on measuring results and ensuring accountability as it approaches maturity. Just as with individuals, organizational maturity has its risks. The organization may be stable, its programs churning along in an effective way, its systems operating so well that it runs almost on autopilot. But there is the risk of complacency, bureaucracy, stagnation, and decline.

Simon's (2001) concept of *life stages* is a more optimistic one than some models depict. For example, in Susan Steven's (2001) model, the final stage is "terminal!" In Simon's model, the organization proceeds from an idea to existence as a mature organization and then has the capacity to renew itself and return to an earlier stage of growth. But there are threats at every stage. A new organization may not have sufficient

TABLE 7.4 ■ Life Stages of Nonprofits

Organizational Life Stage	Description of Organization
Stage I: Imagine and inspire	The organization has not yet been founded; it is still an idea or a dream. This stage is characterized by enthusiasm, energy, and creativity.
Stage II: Found and frame	The organization is created and begins to frame its program. There is still great enthusiasm and energy.
Stage III: Ground and grow	The organization is building its foundation and growing. There is an emphasis on accountability, but rapid growth can be challenging to management.
Stage IV: Produce and sustain	The organization is mature and stable. It may be on autopilot. There is the risk of becoming stale, and maintaining momentum is a concern.
Stage V: Review and renew	The organization revisits its mission and programs and undertakes change. Minor changes may take it back to Stage IV. Major changes may take it back to Stage II. Returning to one of the earlier stages then may lead to renewed and continued growth.

Source: Based on Simon (2001).

resources or skills to survive past its childhood. It may be unable to raise enough funds; attract enough volunteers or staff; or keep pace with the competition offered by older, more established organizations in its field. The organization's leadership may not be able to manage the period of rapid growth. For example, Chapter 5 discussed the risk of founder syndrome, in which a founding CEO is unable or unwilling to step aside while the organization's growth demands a different set of management skills. Systems and skills may lag behind the demands placed on them by expanding programs, and quality may deteriorate. Chaos may reign, and the organization may collapse during this period.

John Brothers and Anne Sherman (2012) describe nonprofit life cycles in terms of an *arc*, depicting a rise and then a decline. Some high-arc organizations may proceed through the life stages rapidly, perhaps growing too quickly in the early stages and then facing a precipitous decline. Others are low arc, that is, their rise is slower and more deliberate; the conditions for potential decline arise more slowly, providing more time to adjust and avoid the worst case (p. 9).

If the organization survives to the stage of maturity, it may be in danger of losing its edge. A mature organization might not have the energy and innovativeness of its early years. It may become a lumbering bureaucracy. Its staff could just be going through the motions. It might not confront the need for change. It may be unprepared to respond to changes in its environment, to the loss of a key source of support, or to shifting patterns of community needs. If it does not move to the stage of "review and renew," it may stagnate, decline, and eventually expire (Simon, 2001).

This suggests that a focus on capacity is important at every stage of an organization's life but that the elements of capacity that are most relevant may be different in each stage. A young organization may need to be concerned primarily with honing its mission, developing its core program, securing funds, and ensuring accountability (Brothers & Sherman, 2012, p. 7). A growing organization may need to devote attention to its infrastructure, for example, its human resources and IT systems (p. 7). A mature organization may be primarily concerned with its "impact expansion," focusing capacity building on its external capacities, such as fundraising and advocacy (p. 7). A mature organization facing potential decline may need to return to its aspirations in order to renew the enthusiasm and energy of its earlier years, revive growth, and ensure its continued relevance and survival (Simons, 2001).

In a study of 318 nonprofits, Light (2004b) discovered that the types of capacity-building activities undertaken do vary according to the organization's size and age. He found that younger organizations are more likely than older ones to develop collaborations with other organizations and undertake organizational assessments but are less likely to focus their capacity building on media relations, reorganization, team building, leadership development, or the implementation of new information or personnel systems (p. 60). Older and larger organizations in Light's (2004b) study were more likely to "behave like weight-conscious organizations: They adopt capacity-building approaches designed to counter bureaucratic encrustation," including reorganization, team building, leadership development, changes in their personnel systems, staff training, and program evaluation (p. 60). Strategic planning also is more likely to be used by older and larger nonprofits than by younger and smaller ones and is an approach that may enable them to break out from a stage of maturity and potential stagnation to a period of renewed growth.

Capacity Building Evaluated

Like strategic planning, capacity building offers many benefits, but it is also important to note its limitations. Does it work? In a 2013 study of nonprofits that received support under the federal government's Compassion Capital Fund Demonstration Program in 2006, Amy Minzner, Jacob Klerman, Carrie Markovitz, and Barbara Fink (2014) found that capacity building efforts had indeed increased the *capacity* of the organizations that participated. But some people raise a more fundamental question: Does capacity building really affect an organization's effectiveness or impact? A positive answer may seem intuitive. How could improved governance, strengthened leadership, better systems and facilities, more highly trained staff, and an adaptive culture *not* lead to the more effective delivery of programs and a better performing organization? Indeed, some scholars have proposed theories for examining the link between capacity and outcomes. But Minzer et al. concluded in 2014 that there had been "virtually no work" on finding evidence of such a link (p. 550). Light (2004b) concludes that greater capacity does lead to increased effectiveness. He acknowledges that it may be difficult to measure effectiveness directly but argues that increased effectiveness will be reflected in perceptions, trust, and confidence in the organization. However, his evidence of the link between capacity and effectiveness is based on the perceptions of nonprofit employees who participated in his study. He acknowledges that "perceptions are always affected by self-interest" but nevertheless concludes that "given the lack of objective data for measuring nonprofit capacity and effectiveness, perceptions will have to do for now" (p. 15).

Others remain somewhat skeptical with regard to the importance of some elements of capacity. For example, in their study of high-impact nonprofits, Leslie Crutchfield and Heather Grant (2012) suggest that while "textbook strategies like relentless fundraising, well-connected boards, and effective management are necessary . . . they are hardly sufficient" (pp. 35–36). They explain that some of the organizations they identified in their study as those with high impact are, indeed, not especially well managed or focused on internal capacity. Rather, they are "satisfied with building a 'good enough' organization and then spending their time and energy focused externally on catalyzing large-scale systemic change." The authors conclude that "Great organizations work *with and through others* [italics original] to create more impact than they ever could achieve alone" (p. 36). We will look more closely at nonprofits' collaboration and partnerships with others in the next chapter.

Chapter Summary

Strategy is an abstract concept that may simply mean a direction or a new, innovative approach to getting from one place to another. It may arise from a leader's vision, incrementally from smaller decisions the organization makes one at a time, or from a formal analytical approach such as strategic planning.

Strategic planning is a process that many nonprofit organizations have adopted from the business world. It is a useful tool for organizations in designing their futures but may not be appropriate in every situation. Strategic management is a broader concept that links the goals of the strategic plan to decisions on managerial matters such as program design, budgeting, organizational structure, human resources development, and evaluation.

There are many different models for strategic planning, and most organizations practice a hybrid of different approaches. One well-known version is the Harvard policy model, on which many alternative models are based. Most start with clarification of the organization's mandates, mission, vision, and values. The opportunities and threats presented by the external environment are compared with the organization's internal strengths and weaknesses (the SWOT analysis) in order to identify strategic issues or questions on which the planners need to focus. Broad goals are then established, and strategies, programs, and objectives are developed to achieve them. Operational plans are written to set specific timetables and accountability for the achievement of the objectives according to the plan.

With appropriate modifications in vocabulary, tools that businesses use to analyze their competitive environment may be adapted to help nonprofits identify strategies. A portfolio analysis model developed by MacMillan suggests generic strategies under scenarios defined by the organization's strengths or competitive position, the desirability of various programs, and the extent to which other organizations are providing similar coverage.

Some critics of strategic planning argue that it may lead to setting goals but not strategy, that it is time consuming and may distract the organization from current opportunities and problems, and that its periodic nature does not permit an organization to be responsive and flexible in real time in a fast-changing environment. Strategic planning is not a panacea for all problems. It may not be appropriate for some organizations at some points in their history, and it cannot substitute for vision or leadership. But, properly executed, strategic planning can bring many benefits.

A nonprofit organization's capacity includes all of the resources it uses to pursue its mission. An organization's capacity is not an indivisible quality; rather, there are various elements of capacity—or capacities—that it might concentrate on strengthening. These elements include internal systems as well as external relationships and more abstract qualities of the organization, such as its culture and capacity for innovation. There are tools for identifying components of capacity that need to be strengthened and models for undertaking such activity. One such model, provided by McKinsey & Company, emphasizes the importance of beginning with "aspirations" (mission, vision, and values) before proceeding to examine such elements as strategies, financial resources, business processes, and organizational structure. The McKinsey framework also emphasizes that capacity building occurs in the overall context of an organizations culture.

Some theorists describe life cycles of nonprofit organizations. The type of capacity building that is needed differs at various stages. Whether capacity building increases organizational effectiveness remains a debated question and some researchers advocate spending more time and energy on catalyzing large-scale systemic change by working with others.

KEY TERMS AND CONCEPTS

adaptive capacity	*internal vision statement*	*organizational strategies*
capacity	*life cycle*	*portfolio analysis*
capacity building	*life stages*	*program delivery capacity*
core competencies	*mission*	*program expansion capacity*
distinctive competencies	*mission creep*	*programmatic strategies*
external vision statement	*objectives*	*stakeholder analysis*
goals	*operational planning*	*strategic issues/questions*
Harvard policy model	*operational strategies*	*strategic management*

strategic objectives   *SWOT analysis*   *vision*

strategic planning   *values*

strategy   *venture philanthropy*

CASE 7.1   New Hope Housing Strategic Plan 2011–2016

The following is a summary of the 2011–2016 strategic plan of New Hope Housing, a nonprofit organization in Northern Virginia, founded in 1977, that provides shelter, transitional, and permanent housing for homeless families and single adults.

Introduction

New Hope Housing has demonstrated over 33 years of innovative and award-winning programs and services assisting homeless families and individuals in our northern Virginia community. Our founders saw a need and responded, opening the first homeless shelter in Fairfax County, Mondloch House, in 1978. Since that beginning, New Hope Housing has added programs and services, always in response to needs in the community.

New Hope Housing continuously assesses its programs and services, evaluating how best to focus its future work for greatest impact. In recent years, New Hope Housing has been deeply involved in collaborative efforts across northern Virginia jurisdictions striving to end and prevent homelessness. As these efforts are underway, new approaches are developed, and greater emphasis placed on prevention, rapid re-housing and housing first approaches, New Hope Housing has re-evaluated the priorities for its future work. These priority areas, outlined here, will guide the work of the agency over the next four to six year period. The Strategic Plan 2011–2016 presents the principles that ground the agency's work, the assumptions that underlie the plan, and the strategic directions going forward.

Grounding Principles

Vision: The vision we work for is a home and bright future for every man, woman and child in our community.
Mission: New Hope Housing provides homeless families and individuals shelter and the tools to build a better life.

Our Core Values:

We are a community-based organization.
We welcome all, including the un-welcome.
We treat each person with dignity and respect.
We are effective stewards of the human and financial resources entrusted to us.
A competent and dedicated staff is critical to our mission.

Planning Assumptions

We will remain focused on serving the needs of persons who are homeless, or who are rebuilding their lives from previous homelessness, while expanding to serve those who are at high risk for becoming homeless.

We will continue to serve populations that are difficult to serve—persons with extremely low income, persons with disabling conditions, persons with violent criminal records, and others who are therefore less likely to receive services as readily through other agencies.

(Continued)

(Continued)

We will continue to serve both single adults and families.

We will focus any new program development primarily within the footprint of existing programs and services—southeastern Fairfax County, the City of Alexandria, the City of Falls Church, and Arlington County—to maintain a geographically cohesive service area.

We will focus on assisting persons at imminent risk of homelessness to remain housed, on reducing time spent in shelter, on "rapid re-housing" of persons who are homeless, on the "housing first" approach in serving chronically homeless persons, and on providing ongoing services to these individuals and families once they are housed.

These approaches are consistent with current national, state, and local public policy directions to prevent and end homelessness.

Government sources of funding for homeless programs, supportive and affordable housing, and support services will be under pressure for reductions as a result of the economic downturn and governments struggling with accumulated debt. Public funding of new directions in programs and services will likely come from redirecting funds from current programs and services. Long term planning for major new activities must consider how new revenue can be secured, including increased private support.

Strategic Directions

Strategic Direction A: New Hope Housing will demonstrate leadership in developing and implementing effective approaches in prevention, shelter and transitional housing to move homeless persons quickly to housing, and provide ongoing support services until housing stability is achieved.

At New Hope Housing we have been successful in developing and implementing effective service strategies—using engagement, building trust relationships, responding to needs as expressed by those we serve, providing low barrier entry to programs, and fostering access to services over time as the individual is ready to engage in services. Our approaches are grounded in the agency philosophy that emphasizes treating each person with dignity and respect, and welcoming all including those often unwelcome in other settings. These service delivery strategies are appropriate and effective whether working in homelessness prevention, or shelter services, or post-shelter housing programs. We believe it is our approach and philosophy that sets New Hope Housing apart, and we will continue to demonstrate them across the continuum of programs we operate.

Strategic Direction B: New Hope Housing will work collaboratively to increase permanent supportive housing for underserved populations on the verge of homelessness or moving out of homelessness. New Hope Housing's primary role will be that of service provider.

Lack of availability of appropriate housing is a major impediment for many persons the agency serves to be able to attain permanent housing. Of special need is more permanent supportive housing. Permanent supportive housing (PSH) is a specific model of housing designed to serve individuals and families with very low income and disabling conditions, providing ongoing supportive services, such as case management, assistance with daily living skills, and help in accessing services in the community. New Hope Housing will continue to be active and direct in fostering new supportive housing development, both larger developments and small scale programs. While the agency will primarily seek to work in the role of service provider, not housing developer, particularly for larger developments, New Hope Housing may continue to add to its own stock of PSH units if opportunities arise.

Strategic Direction C: New Hope Housing will focus on organizational development to optimize its effectiveness and viability.

New Hope Housing has worked to strengthen its staff professional and leadership development and to build an effective management structure. Such efforts have been recognized, for example, in receiving the 2008

Helios HR Hercules Award for an outstanding employee development program, and in being named a finalist in the 2009 *Washington Post* Excellence in Nonprofit Management Award program.

At the same time areas of challenge are present—a lean infrastructure is stressed by growth in number, complexity, and geography of programs; continued success in attracting support will require effective marketing, clarity in demonstrating program outcomes, and enhanced private fund raising; continued emphasis on staff development is essential for effective program delivery and fulfilling agency values; and thoughtful planning is needed to address the potential for significant changes within senior leadership over the next 5+ years, along with a flat organization structure that limits internal succession and continuity.

As the field of homeless services and related public policy change, and as New Hope Housing's direct service programs respond, New Hope Housing must look comprehensively at its structure, operational and support systems, key personnel, resource streams, and other aspects of the agency to ensure that it is aligned with the environment in which it works, and strengthens effectiveness and viability.

Strategic Direction D: New Hope Housing, as an agency, as well as its staff and board, will bring awareness to the issue of homelessness and serve as advocates for policies to prevent and end homelessness in the communities we serve.

In recent years much progress has been made in local jurisdictions in building and implementing plans to seriously address homelessness. From both an economic and moral values perspective, homelessness affects the quality and health of our entire community. However, in the arena of many competing demands and desires for support, it is important that the issue of homelessness, and the need for programs and services to assist those who are most vulnerable in our community, not be pushed aside in the debate regarding use of resources. New Hope Housing, its staff and its board members must serve as vocal advocates to maintain and expand resources and policies to address homelessness. This includes monitoring human services issues affecting persons who are homeless or at risk of homelessness; educating the community about these issues; and participating in communication and advocacy networks in our area.

Approved by the New Hope Housing Board of Directors
March 21, 2011

Source: New Hope Housing website, retrieved from http://www.newhopehousing.org/about/strategic-plan.

Questions Related to Case 7.1

1. What might have been the strengths, weaknesses, opportunities, and threats identified in the process that developed the plan for New Hope Housing; in other words, can you work backward from the plan summary to determine what the SWOT analysis might have revealed?
2. What are the strategic issues or questions identified by the planners for New Hope Housing?
3. What are the goals and strategies in this plan, consistent with the vocabulary used in this chapter?
4. How are New Hope's assumptions about the environment reflected in its strategic priorities? Are there any strategic directions you might add, based on the assumptions?
5. Which elements of capacity described in the McKinsey & Company capacity building framework are reflected in the strategic plan of New Hope Housing?

QUESTIONS FOR DISCUSSION

1. One organization that all students will have some knowledge about is their own college or university. What are the strengths, weaknesses, opportunities, and threats that you see facing your college or university? What strategic issues do you suggest for your institution?

2. Suppose a nonprofit organization's strategy requires that it phase out a program on which few people rely, but those people are vulnerable and no good substitute exists. How might the organization proceed with its plan in an ethical and humane manner?

3. Select an organization that you know well—maybe you work there, have been a volunteer, or just follow it on Twitter. What do you think is the organization's *strategy*, as that term is discussed in this chapter?

SUGGESTIONS FOR FURTHER READING

Books/Brochure

Allison, M., & Kaye, J. (2015). *Strategic planning for nonprofit organizations: A practical guide for dynamic times* (3rd ed.). Hoboken, NJ: Wiley.

Brothers, J., & Sherman, A. (2012). *Building nonprofit capacity: A guide to managing change through organizational life cycles.* San Francisco, CA: Jossey-Bass.

Bryson, J. M. (2011). *Strategic planning for public and nonprofit organizations* (4th ed.). San Francisco, CA: Jossey-Bass.

Crutchfield, L. R., & Grant, H. M. (2012). *Forces for good: The six practices of high-impact nonprofits* (Rev. ed.). San Francisco, CA: Jossey-Bass.

La Piana, D. (2008). *The nonprofit strategy revolution: Real-time strategic planning in a rapid-response world.* Saint Paul, MN: Fieldstone Alliance.

McKinsey & Company (2013). The Organizational Capacity Assessment Tool (OCAT): 2.0 (Available at https://mckinseyonsociety.com/downloads/tools/OCAT/OCAT_brochure_v6.pdf)

Websites

Alliance for Nonprofit Management: http://www.allianceonline.org/

The Bridgespan Group: http://www.bridgespan.org/

Grantmakers for Effective Organizations: http://www.geofunders.org/

LaPiana Consulting: http://www.lapiana.org/

McKinsey on Society: https://mckinseyonsociety.com/ocat/

Venture Philanthropy Partners: http://venturephilanthropypartners.org/

Companion Website

Visit study.sagepub.com/worth4e for access to certain full-text SAGE journal articles and links to relevant video and multimedia content.

Pressures for nonprofits to collaborate and merge are not likely to abate. Continued encouragement from funders, increased competition for resources, and the nation's focus on performance and accountability are likely to make complete independence less tenable for smaller and decentralized organizations and to increase the potential benefits to be gained through collaboration. However, as cases discussed in this chapter illustrate, there is also a need to ensure that relationships between and among organizations are well considered and that mission remains paramount. Those driven *exclusively* by financial considerations may find that the human and financial costs ultimately exceed the gains and that missions may be diluted or lost, to the detriment of the organizations and society.

Cross-Sector Collaboration

As Forrer et al. (2014) observe, "Nothing is simple. No aspect of modern society is the domain of any single sector. None" (p. xi). The complexity of problems, interconnectedness of communities in a wired global community, and limited resources have combined to increase interest in collaboration across the public, for-profit, and nonprofit sectors in order to address social needs and issues.

A Continuum of Cross-Sector Collaboration

Forrer et al. (2014) define *cross-sector collaborations (CSCs)* as "the interaction of two or more of the three organizational sectors" and depict a range of possible relationships along a continuum. Writing from the perspective of public administrators, the authors define positions along that continuum in terms of the degree of government control over the goods and service provided. Of course, from the nonprofit perspective, the continuum reflects the extent to which organizations maintain their autonomy or share responsibilities and risks with partners in other sectors.

As depicted in Figure 8.2, on the left side of the continuum, goods and services are provided totally by government. They are likely to be public goods, as we discussed in Chapter 3. On the right side, goods and services are provided entirely by the business and nonprofit sectors, perhaps subject only to government regulation. Again reflecting on our discussion in Chapter 3, they are probably private or common goods. In the middle are a variety of arrangements defined by varying degrees of government control and the autonomy of the private and nonprofit actors involved. As we move from left to right, the private and nonprofit collaborators "are [increasingly] not treated as agents of the government but as principals deserving of a voice in production decisions" (Forrer et al., 2014, p. 16).

As mentioned earlier in this chapter, when one entity *contracts* with another, that is not necessarily a collaboration, since the issuer of the contract may be a principal that is simply hiring an agent to perform some specific function. That might be the case, for example, if a government agency contracts with Goodwill Industries to provide janitorial services in its office building. The relationship is pretty simple, the service provided is rather straightforward, and the government can easily determine whether it is receiving the service for which it paid. But, Forrer et al. (2014) argue that some contracts are "relational"—they are *collaborative contracts*—since they require the ongoing interaction of the parties (p. 59). This is especially true when the solutions to a problem cannot be easily specified in advance and the principal and agent must communicate about adjustments to the services as the needs of the people being served are identified and understood. This is often the case, for example, when the purpose of the relationship is to address social issues, such as public health, poverty, or homelessness. Government contracts and grants and the implications for nonprofits that receive them are discussed further in Chapter 14.

Moving farther right on Forrer et al.'s (2014) continuum, government may engage in *ad-hoc collaborations* with nonprofits or for-profit firms. As the term *ad hoc* implies, these relationships are short term. One might occur, for example, in response to a natural disaster, in which government agencies might

FIGURE 8.2 ■ Cross-Sector Collaborative Arrangements

More government control

Less government control

Public provision of goods and services · Contracting · Ad-hoc collaborations · Partnerships (PPPs) · Networks · Independent public-service providers · Private provision of goods and services

Source: Adapted from Forrer et al. (2014), p. 15.

collaborate with the nonprofit Red Cross as well as corporations such as Federal Express and Home Depot, which have the means to supply the stricken areas with urgently needed supplies. These relationships are collaborations rather than purely contractual relationships, since the parties involved are likely to maintain considerable independence to decide their own activities. There may or may not be contracts involved, and if there are, they are likely to be of the collaborative nature that Forrer et al. (2014) describe. Indeed, research undertaken by Beth Gazley (2008) found that "government agencies and nonprofit organizations interact in myriad ways, both formally and informally" (p. 142).

In the middle of the continuum are *partnerships*, commonly referred to as *public-private partnerships (PPPs)* (Forrer et al., 2014). As explained earlier in this chapter, the term *partnership* implies a formalized relationship that is not ad hoc, with the parties sharing power as well as risks (p. 86). A partnership between government and a for-profit or non-profit entity is undertaken differently from a traditional contractual relationship. In contracting, the government usually conducts a competitive process, in which the low-cost provider is advantaged. However, the government is likely to choose a *partner* because of its unique *capabilities* rather than just cost. One example is the federal government's partnership with the United Way of New York City (UWNYC) to distribute assistance following the terrorist attacks of September 11, 2001. The UWNYC was not in competition with other potential partners; it was judged by the government to be the only organization capable of providing the needed service (Forrer et al., p. 86).

Forrer et al. (2014) describe *networks* as "collaborative, not bureaucratic, structures that involve autonomous organizations, often responsive to a broad range of nongovernmental stakeholders, while also working independently with both government and other network participants" (p. 113). In other, words, members of networks may work collaboratively in some ways and independently in other ways, with a common focus on the same issues but with none exerting control over the other members. And, finally, near the right side of the continuum are *independent public service providers*—nonprofit organizations that may provide public services and sometimes work with government, but that determine their own priorities and operate with autonomy outside of government control (Forrer et al., p. 140). They include, for example, quasi-governmental organizations such as federally funded research laboratories and fundraising entities that work with government agencies, such as the National Park Foundation.

Advantages and Disadvantages of CSCs

Forrer et al. (2014) identify a number of advantages and disadvantages of various CSCs, writing from the perspective of public administrators. Some of the same advantages and disadvantages are also relevant from the perspective of nonprofit managers. As relationships move from left to right across the continuum (depicted in Figure 8.2), public managers are likely to be concerned about their decreasing ability to control the services provided or to assure outcomes. But the tradeoffs may include "greater efficiency, more innovation, greater targeted service, and the growth of the private sector" (p. 21). Nonprofit managers may hold their own concerns about their increasing entanglement with government and possibly corporate partners. Collaborating with government and/or the for-profit sector entails a sacrifice of autonomy, the potential for mission drift, and possible negative reactions from donors and other established funders. But the tradeoffs may include enhanced resources and capacity with which to increase mission impact. Business managers also may have concerns about collaborating with government or nonprofits, but find such relationships helpful in enhancing their company's image and advancing their own definition of *corporate social responsibility* (p. 34).

There may be increased risks to all parties resulting from the reduction of autonomy and control. Public administrators may face less certainty in being able to account to their principals (elected officials and the public). For-profit managers may face similar concerns in accounting to their shareholders and nonprofit managers to their boards and other constituents (p. 22). But the risks of collaboration may be accompanied by strategic benefits to leaders in all three sectors, including the following:

1. Deliverables and outcomes: This might include enhancing operations, attaining goals, or achieving better overall results.

2. Increased capacity and competence: This might result in greater capacity for individuals, the organization, or the community.

3. New resources and opportunities: This might lead to new funding, opportunities for new markets or program areas, and the potential for further cross-sector collaboration (Forrer et al., 2014, p. 41).

Obstacles and Conditions for Success

The obstacles to successful cross-sector collaboration and the conditions for success are quite similar to those discussed earlier in this chapter with regard to collaborations between and among nonprofit organizations.

Nonprofits, businesses, and government agencies have different incentives, motivations, legal constraints, and cultures. Nonprofit managers think about benefits for their clients; public administrators think about the public interest; and the first responsibility of corporate managers is to their shareholders. Leaders in the three sectors may use different vocabularies and even suspect the values of those in other sectors. Individual egos and organizational identities can be equally powerful in all three sectors and may impede the sacrifice of control and identity that collaboration requires. Relationships between government and nonprofit organizations may raise political issues, with the potential to become visible in the media. And collaborations may involve costs, requiring the investment of resources that are diverted from other activities that the collaborators might otherwise devote to their individual efforts. All of these realities can present obstacles.

What conditions may lead to success? Again, positive conditions are similar to those discussed earlier with regard to collaboration among nonprofits. Forrer et al. (2014) identify trust among the collaborators as a fundamental requirement, but also note the need for governance and accountability structures to measure respective contributions. As with collaborations between or among nonprofits, the chances for success may be enhanced by following a careful process in exploring and implementing the relationship. And, finally, successful collaborations require an approach to leadership by individuals in all sectors that goes beyond traditional notions of hierarchy and control and that is characterized by "systems thinking." It requires a perspective that goes beyond a job description and includes "viewing one's role within a wider structure of collaboration" (Forrer et al., p. 241).

Achieving Collective Impact

Now let's take a look at an example cross-sector collaboration that has gained considerable attention and discussion. The concept is called *collective impact.*

In 2006, community leaders in Cincinnati became alarmed by the disappointing statistics on the school failures of students in Ohio and Kentucky. Ohio ranked 42nd out of 50 states on the number of young people earning a bachelor's degree, and Kentucky ranked next to last, at 49th place (Bridgespan Group, 2012). Conversations about how to address the situation began among the former president of the University of Cincinnati, the former CEO of KnowledgeWorks (an education foundation), and the superintendent of Cincinnati's schools (Bridgespan Group, 2012). Eventually, more than 300 leaders, including individuals from the public sector, private business sector, and nonprofit sector, joined the dialogue (Kania & Kramer, 2011). This cross-sector collaboration eventually became known as the Strive Partnership.

The leaders recognized that just addressing one point on the education continuum, for example, early childhood education or college access, would not be enough to solve the overall problem. It would require a comprehensive and coordinated approach and would require that various organizations put aside their individual agendas to focus on shared objectives. While individual organizations had missions and expertise related to one aspect of education, greater impact could be achieved by collaborating to provide young people with support "from cradle to career" (Bornstein, 2011). This approach encompasses five critical life stages: early childhood, adolescence, early adulthood, and transition from high school or postsecondary training to the workforce (Bridgespan Group, 2012).

An influential 2011 article in the *Stanford Social Innovation Review* by John Kania and Mark Kramer gained attention for the term that describes Strive's approach: *collective impact.* Kania and Kramer (2011) are affiliated with the consulting firm Foundation Strategy Group (www.fsg.org), which advises some collective impact initiatives. The authors argue that even a high-performing nonprofit can have only "isolated impact" and that no one organization—or sector—can meet the challenges presented by complex, entrenched social problems by working alone. Moreover, such problems have no predetermined solutions and can only be addressed by multiple organizations developing consensus about possible strategies and acting in a coordinated manner. Collective impact is different from *routine cross sector collaboration*, since it "envisions an even higher standard of collaboration that requires long-term commitment and consensus from all" (Carson, 2012a).

As summarized in Box 8.1, Kania and Kramer (2013) identify five conditions essential to successful collective impact partnerships, including participation by all sectors within a community; measurement of results by common, agreed-upon indicators; mutually reinforcing activities; continuous communication among the partners; and a centralized coordinating infrastructure with dedicated staff providing support to the entire initiative. The creation of a dedicated backbone organization is a hallmark of collective impact that distinguishes the approach from other cross-sector collaborations. In addition to these five conditions, collective impact requires shifts in mindset, including the inclusion of people who have directly experienced the social problem, recognition that relationships are as important as data, accepting that structure is as important as strategy, and understanding that sharing credit is as important as taking credit (Kania, Hanleybrown, & Juster, 2014). In other words, the experts on collective impact reinforce a point mentioned earlier in this chapter with regard to collaboration more generally: Successful collaboration requires that nonprofit leaders adopt a perspective that goes beyond their own job descriptions.

Initially, the Strive Partnership was managed by a steering committee but appointed an executive director and other full-time staff, who manage collaborative work, engage in advocacy, and maintain communication among the partner organizations (Bridgespan Group, 2012). Strive publishes an annual report card on the partnership's efforts. By 2011, kindergarten readiness in the Cincinnati schools had increased by 9 percent; fourth-grade reading and math scores had increased by 7 and 14 percent, respectively; and graduation rates for students from local urban schools had increased at both the University of Cincinnati and Northern

BOX 8.1 THE FIVE CONDITIONS OF COLLECTIVE IMPACT

Common Agenda	All participants have a shared vision for change including a common understanding of the problem and a joint approach to solving it through agreed upon actions.
Shared Measurement	Collecting data and measuring results consistently across all participants ensures efforts remain aligned and participants hold each other accountable.
Mutually Reinforcing Activities	Participant activities must be differentiated while still being coordinated through a mutually reinforcing plan of action.
Continuous Communication	Consistent and open communication is needed across the many players to build trust, assure mutual objectives, and create common motivation.
Backbone Support	Creating and managing collective impact requires a separate organization(s) with staff and a specific set of skills to serve as the backbone for the entire initiative and coordinate participating organizations and agencies.

Source: Kania and Kramer (2013).

Kentucky University (Bornstein, 2011). Based on such results, similar partnerships were created in other U.S. communities as well as in Canada, Australia, Israel, and South Korea (Kania et al., 2014). In 2010, Strive's experience gained the attention of the White House Council for Community Solutions, which created tools to help additional communities pursue the approach (Nee & Jolin, 2012). By 2014, the initial partnership in Cincinnati had evolved into a national network of 53 similar initiatives in 28 states and the District of Columbia, involving more than 8,000 organizations (StriveTogether, 2014).

Collective impact does face skeptics. For example, Emmett Carson (2012a), CEO of the Silicon Valley Community Foundation, argues that collective impact may be difficult to achieve even under ideal conditions and "in some cases, may undermine key values of the nonprofit sector." Carson further observes that solutions to complex problems will require a long-term approach and questions whether all parties in a collective impact partnership will be able to persist. He asks, "Can a mayor afford to be engaged in an effort that will take years to reach consensus? Will her successor be equally committed to the initiative? Will business leaders believe that a multiple-year process just to develop the strategy is a productive use of their time?" Moreover, Carson (2012a) asks whether it is realistic to think that nonprofits with distinctive values can readily sign on to consensus solutions without sacrificing their purposes and offending their donors; for example, if the issue is family planning, there are likely to be nonprofits that advocate very different approaches. Carson sees a downside if foundations focus their support on nonprofits participating in collective impact: that could prevent other organizations from exploring innovative approaches that do not coincide with the consensus of the collective impact partners (Carson, 2012b). And, finally, Carson argues, the idea of collective impact is still relatively new and has not generated strong evidence to prove its long-term effectiveness (Carson, 2012b).

However, Carson (2012b) reaches a nuanced conclusion regarding collective impact, which may apply as well to collaborations more broadly:

The job of every nonprofit and foundation is to make difficult decisions based on vision, mission and values. If other entities share those perspectives, collaboration—and perhaps some form of collective impact—is possible and desirable. But to come together on any other basis undermines the very reason for the nonprofit sector's existence. Sometimes, the hardest thing to do is to say no to the crowd, especially when they are your friends and colleagues.

That view is generally consistent with the philosophy of this book—that nonprofit managers should maintain a balanced approach, remaining open to new ideas and innovation, but also keeping their organizations' distinctive missions central and exercising caution with regard to any proposed one-right-way solutions.

Chapter Summary

With the growth in the number of nonprofits in recent decades, there has been an increased emphasis on collaboration and mergers among nonprofits, in order to reduce inefficiencies and increase the capacity and impact of the sector overall. Funders, including government bodies and foundations, have been visible among those calling for such consolidation. However, some observers argue that funders have contributed to the problem and that small nonprofits may better provide more personal attention to clients.

It is not unusual to see the terms *collaboration* and *partnership* used interchangeably to describe any relationship in which two or more entities are working together in some way. But others make finer distinctions, and the vocabulary in the field is not consistent. Partnerships generally involve more formal relationships than collaboration, which may be ad hoc. Nonprofits have relationships with government and with corporations. Relationships with corporations include philanthropic collaborations, strategic collaborations, commercial collaborations, political collaborations, and operational relationships. Contracts are a type of relationship that nonprofits may have with corporations or with government. Traditional contracts are not collaborations; they are principal–agent relationships. Some may be considered collaborative contracts, if decision making is shared between the two parties. Collaboration between and among nonprofits occurs along a continuum; it may include informal collaboration or more formal relationships, in which the organizations are legally committed to each other. Some organizations create additional corporations to provide services or to pursue new ventures, yielding some of their autonomy to these new entities. A *merger* is a combining of two or more organizations that includes a change in legal control. There are *intermergers,* combinations of previously independent organizations, and *intramergers,* which are consolidations of chapters or units within a single legal entity, usually a large, national nonprofit. Obstacles to collaboration and merger include the distinctive motivations of nonprofit entities; organizational cultures that may be resistant to change; the egos of the individuals involved, especially founders; concerns about brand identity; community or political concerns; and the costs, in time and money, of the study, planning, and negotiations required. Successful collaborations and mergers are driven primarily by mission, rather than just financial benefits. Other conditions needed for success include support from the board and CEO, an appropriate process, trust, and relatedness. Relatedness means that there is a logic to the relationship based on mission, constituency, organization or structure, or geography.

Pressures to collaborate and merge are unlikely to abate as nonprofits face an increasingly competitive environment and there is a nationwide focus on performance and accountability. It is important that mission remain paramount and that such relationships not be based entirely on potential financial gains.

Cross-sector collaborations involve organizations from two or more of the three sectors— government, business, and nonprofit. Such relationships also lie along a continuum. From the perspective of public administrators, points on the continuum are defined by the degree to which the government relinquishes control. Nonprofit managers may view various relationships in terms of the degree to which they relinquish autonomy. Cross-sector collaboration may bring benefits to all parties, but leaders in all three sectors may have concerns about risks and performance. For nonprofits, collaborating with business or government may increase resources and capacity, but also bring challenges of accountability to stakeholders and possible mission drift. Obstacles to successful cross-sector collaborations and the conditions necessary for success are similar to those related to collaboration between and among nonprofit organizations. Such relationships require leaders to think beyond their own jobs and view the wider structure of society.

One approach to cross-sector collaboration that has gained wide attention is known as collective impact. It includes participation by all sectors within a community: focus on common goals, measurement of results by common indicators, decision making based on data, a centralized coordinating infrastructure with dedicated staff, and continuous communication among the partners. As with other aspects of nonprofit management, there is continuing debate about the effectiveness of such initiatives.

KEY TERMS AND CONCEPTS

ad-hoc collaborations

administrative consolidations

affiliations

agent

alliances

collaboration

collaborative contracts

collective impact

commercial collaborations

constituency relatedness

corporate integrations

corporate social responsibility

cross-sector collaborations (CSCs)

drivers

external drivers

independent public service providers

integration

intermerger

internal drivers

intramerger

joint programming

joint venture corporations

management service organizations (MSOs)

merger

networks

operational relationships

parent–subsidiary structures

philanthropic collaborations

political collaborations

principal

public–private partnerships (PPPs)

strategic alliances

strategic collaborations

strategic restructuring

Case 8.1 N Street Village and Miriam's House

Like many American cities during the 1960s and 1970s, Washington, DC, experienced declining population, economic challenges, and growing social problems, as many middle class families and businesses moved to the suburbs. In addition, in 1963, Congress passed the Community Mental Health Center Act, leading to the deinstitutionalization of people who were mentally ill, but for whom inadequate services were available, which then led to an increase in the number of homeless people on urban streets. Riots followed the assassination of Martin Luther King Jr. in 1968, leaving burned-out stores on streets that had been commercial corridors, accelerating economic decline and the flight of middle-class families. By 1970, the area near 14th and N Streets, Northwest, in the Logan Circle neighborhood of Washington, was a dystopian scene, known primarily for prostitution, drug dealing, and the visibility of homeless people.

In 1970, Pastor John Steinbruck and his wife Erna arrived at Luther Place Memorial Church, in the midst of the troubled neighborhood. By 1972, an interfaith organization called ProJeCt (standing for Protestant, Jewish, and Catholic) began distributing food and clothing in the area and, in 1973, Deborah's Place opened on N Street as the city's first residence for homeless women. Led by John and Erna Steinbruck, N Street Village (NSV) was incorporated as a 501(c)3 organization in 1973, with the mission of "[empowering] homeless and low-income women to claim their highest quality of life by offering a broad spectrum of services and advocacy in an atmosphere of dignity and respect" (N Street Village, n.d.).

Services expanded in the decades that followed, and by 2014, what had begun with housing provided with sleeping mats on the floor of the church and food served in a parking lot had evolved into an organization providing a comprehensive continuum of care for homeless and low-income women, including a day center, health and wellness programs, and shelter and housing. Based in a 150,000-square-foot facility on N Street, NSV was serving more than 1,400 women each year, with an operating budget of nearly $6 million (N Street Village, n.d.).

From its founding in 1973, NSV experienced periods of growth as well as periods of crisis. Mary Funke, who had a background in counseling and education, was appointed as executive director in 2004 and immediately faced a financial crisis. She recognized that urgent action would be needed, but also that the current crisis was deeply rooted in long-term problems, which would require more complex planning and change. Funke implemented emergency measures, including budget cuts, staff reductions, and intensified fundraising. She also put in place new policies and practices intended to provide long-term stability, including performance measurement, strategic planning, strengthened governance, and a leadership succession plan (N Street Village, 2011). She also worked with the board and staff to create a culture of accountability and performance. By 2006, N Street Village was meeting its goals and its financial situation had been stabilized. It applied for the Washington Post Award for Excellence in Nonprofit Management. The staff benchmarked other organizations, developed the application as a team, and succeeded in winning the competition.[i]

Despite N Street's improved management and financial position, it could not escape the impact of the serious economic downturn that began in 2007, which some labeled the Great Recession. Overall philanthropy declined and foundation giving in the Washington region dropped 8 percent just from 2008 to 2009. Meanwhile, the recession was increasing the need for NSV's services. Funders were encouraging grant recipients to do more with less and to seek partnerships with other nonprofits (Tomassoni, 2011).

In 2010, Mary Funke was followed as executive director by Schroeder Stribling, in a planned succession. Stribling was a social worker with a background in mental health programs, who had served as director of programs at NSV since 2003 and deputy executive director since 2008. Faced with the economic crisis, Stribling implemented a hiring freeze, reduced some employee benefits, and was forced to use some funds from the organization's reserves. She warned the board that if the financial environment did not improve, NSV might be forced to cut programs, despite the growing need for services. As she reports, "The stress was really tremendous during those times" (Small, 2012). The board approved a strategic plan to deal with the continuing economic downturn, including the pursuit of partnerships with other nonprofits serving low-income women (Small, 2012; FitzGerald, 2013).

Meanwhile, the recession also was having an impact at Miriam's House.[ii] Miriam's House had been founded in 1996 to provide transitional housing for women living with HIV and AIDS. The founder, Carol Marsh, had retired as executive director in 2010 and was followed by Sam Collins. Like Stribling, Collins walked right into the economic maelstrom. Just prior to his arrival, Miriam's revenue had declined from $800,000 to $600,000 in only a year. A fifth of the staff had been laid off. Despite reductions in costs, Miriam's reserves had been exhausted in just three years. "We were trying to carve pieces off of our budget until in 2010, there was nothing left to shave off," said Miriam's executive director Tim Fretz (Small, 2012). In addition to the economic downturn, Miriam's House was adjusting to changes in the need for its services. Miriam's hospice model was becoming outdated, as medical advances were extending the lives of people with HIV and increasing the need for HIV treatment programs (Small, 2012). Given the environment, Miriam's House, like NSV, began looking for a partner.

The partnership began with NSV offering mental health and employment services at Miriam's House, which Miriam's would have been unable to provide with its strained resources (Tomassoni, 2011). But talk soon turned to the possibility of merger. As Stribling recalls, "Given the very strong mission-fit and positive chemistry between our two organizations, it occurred to me right away that we could make a successful

(Continued)

McGregor's perspective places the responsibility for performance on managers as well as subordinates. If people are by nature capable and responsible, then a manager holding that theory of human behavior would likely give individuals more autonomy, decentralize responsibility, and seek to unleash human potential. If workers are not motivated, then the manager needs to examine ways to make the job more satisfying, so as to unleash the innate positive qualities of people. This is obviously a very different way of seeing the work environment from that reflected in Taylor's scientific management.

McClelland: Three Needs Theory

David McClelland, also writing in the 1960s, placed the focus even more on managers themselves. He explained that it is not only workers who have needs that affect their behavior in the workplace. Managers have their own psychological needs, too, which influence how they behave with regard to their subordinates. McClelland's (1961) theory is called the *three needs theory* because he identified three principal needs that people have: the need for achievement, the need for power over others, and the need for affiliation or good relationships with others. McClelland's theories stimulated a large body of follow-up research and the development of instruments to measure managers' needs. The standing of his theories today is mixed, with some still supporting them and others criticizing them harshly (Rainey, 2014, p. 275). But, like Maslow, McClelland helped us recognize that managers, like all human beings, do not come to the workplace as empty canisters; they come with their own psychological needs and may behave at work in a way that helps address them.

Myers and Briggs: Personality Types

Katharine Cook Briggs and her daughter Isabel Briggs Myers made an important contribution to management by developing a tool known as the *Myers–Briggs-type indicator,* which is widely used in the workplace today. Myers-Briggs and other similar instruments are used to reveal *personality style,* which "refers to the manner in which individuals gather and process information" (Denhardt et al., 2013, pp. 30–31). Based on the theories of the psychologist Carl Jung, personality tests like Myers-Briggs are used to provide individuals with insights about their own perspectives and preferences, which may help them understand their own behavior and that of others with whom they work. Perhaps the best-known distinction made by Myers-Briggs is that between introverts and extroverts, although it measures personality in many additional dimensions.

Herzberg: Motivators and Dissatisifers

Like most theories, those of Frederick Herzberg, first described in the late 1960s, have been challenged by other researchers. However, his findings are still widely cited. Herzberg claimed to identify two sets of factors that influence *motivation.* He called them *motivators* and *hygiene factors,* but they are also sometimes called *satisfiers* and *dissatisfiers.* Table 9.2 shows both sets of factors. The motivators also are called *intrinsic motivational factors,* because they relate to individuals' feelings and the nature of *the job itself.* The dissatisfiers relate to what are called *extrinsic motivational factors,* since they come from the environment and are external to the work itself (Lee & Wilkins, 2011; Leonard, 2013). *Hygiene* is a term we usually associate with health and, indeed, we might think of the hygiene factors as determining whether the work environment is healthy or not. According to Herzberg (1968), there is a big difference in how these two sets of factors affect people. Hygiene factors can lead to dissatisfaction, but they cannot be used in a positive way to *motivate* people. Only the motivators can do that. This implies that managers should design work to reduce any hygiene factors that are creating dissatisfaction and increase motivators related to the work experience.

To understand Herzberg's (1968) theory, students may find it useful to think about their own work or volunteer experience and what they find to be satisfying or intolerable in specific cases. Looking at the right-hand column of Table 9.2, dissatisfaction with a job can be caused by the frustrations that derive from company policy or administration—for example, the mindless bureaucracy reflected in Dilbert cartoons. Dissatisfaction may arise from poor interpersonal relationships with a supervisor or peer or from physical working conditions that do not provide safety and security. (Remember Maslow's [1954] hierarchy!) A tyrannical or incompetent boss, petty colleagues, or an unclean and unsafe work environment are reasons that might cause most people to go home discouraged and start looking for alternative employment. Students will note that compensation—that is, salary, benefits, and other financial rewards—appears on the list of potential dissatisfiers and not as a motivator! Let's return to that interesting point in a moment.

TABLE 9.2 ■ Herzberg's Motivators (Satisfiers) and Hygiene Factors (Dissatisfiers)

Motivators (Satisfiers) (Related to the job and to motivation)	Hygiene Factors (Dissatisfiers) (Related to the environment)
Achievement	Company policies and administration
Recognition	Relations with supervisor
The work itself	Interpersonal relations with coworkers
Advancement	Working conditions
Growth	Compensation
Responsibility	Status and security

Source: Adapted from Herzberg (1968).

Take a look at the left-hand side of Table 9.2, a list of Herzberg's (1968) motivators. People who participated in his studies described the factors that motivated them at work as including achievement and recognition, opportunities for advancement, opportunities for greater responsibility and personal growth, and the inherent rewards of certain types of work. For example, tutoring children might be an intrinsically rewarding activity, as opposed to, let's say, slaughtering pigs. If that work is also carried out in an environment that provides the other motivators, the job may prove very satisfying, unless some dissatisfiers from the right-hand column get in the way. If the dissatisfiers are present at significant levels, even rewarding work may not be enough to compensate for the aggravation, and people may become unmotivated and perhaps inclined to look for other places to spend their working hours.

What about money? It may seem counterintuitive to many people that salary appears in Herzberg's (1968) theory not as a motivator but rather as a potential dissatisfier. After all, do not many companies, and an increasing number of nonprofits, offer financial incentives to encourage higher performance? That practice suggests an underlying theory that people are motivated in a positive way by the opportunity to make a greater income. But then, how do we explain the fact that many nonprofit staff members—and, indeed, people in other sectors—work for less income than they could earn elsewhere? Or that volunteers work for no financial compensation at all? And, we might wonder, how many people would be inclined to leave a job they love for a job they hate only because it pays more money, assuming that their current pay is sufficient to meet their needs? Surely, if the wage is so low that it isn't livable, or if employees feel that they are not paid what their effort is worth, that may be a source of dissatisfaction. If the employee believes that others, within the organization or elsewhere, are being paid more for the same work, that sense of unfairness may be dissatisfying. If Herzberg (1968) is right, sufficient and fair may be enough to remove money as a cause of dissatisfaction. As long as those standards are met, more money may not produce greater motivation. According to Herzberg, motivation comes from the factors on the left-hand side of Table 9.2.

Motivations of Nonprofit Staff

It is important to understand that Herzberg's theory was not focused on nonprofit organizations. So it is useful to consider how Herzberg's concepts may apply in the nonprofit sector. Is motivation in the nonprofit sector somehow different than in the public sector or in the for-profit sector?

First, let's consider how nonprofit staff members compare to individuals working in government. A number of studies concerning *public service motivation* have established that employees working in government hold values that are distinguishable from those working in the private sector and some studies suggest that that the motivations of nonprofit employees may be similar to those of individuals who work in government (Word & Carpenter, 2013). Others find that despite a similar commitment to public service government and nonprofit employees also demonstrate some differences. For example, employees in the public sector may be motivated by good benefit programs, job security, and opportunities for advancement, while nonprofit employees may be motivated more by family-friendly environments and opportunities to take on more responsibility. Nonprofit employees are also more likely to have served as volunteers, perhaps providing a clue as to their motivations (Lee & Wilkins, 2011). Thus, some research suggests that in both government and the nonprofit sector, intrinsic motivational factors may be more important than extrinsic factors, like financial compensation (Lee & Wilkins, 2011; Leonard, 2013). In addition, a study by Shuyang Peng, Sanjay Pandey, and Sheela Pandey (2015) found that nonprofits have an advantage over public agencies in fostering congruence between individual and organizational values.

How do nonprofit staff compare to those who work in business? A number of studies find that nonprofit staff have stronger intrinsic motivation than those working in for-profits, more commitment to "mission, activism, and social growth" (Chen, 2014, p. 740). These findings suggest that even though nonprofit staff often are paid less than their counterparts in the for-profit world and volunteers are, by definition, unpaid in financial terms, many may find their work very rewarding if Herzberg's motivators are present. Since they do not expect to receive the same salaries that are paid in some for-profit companies, perhaps they are not necessarily dissatisfied by their nonprofit incomes so long as they are at least adequate and perceived as fair. This perspective has many implications for nonprofit management practice. If managers can design jobs and create working environments in a way that provides their staff and volunteers with opportunities for achievement, recognition, advancement, and growth, and if the nature of the work is inherently rewarding, staff and volunteers may be highly motivated even within the limits of nonprofits' financial constraints. It could even be argued that nonprofits have an advantage over for-profit companies in motivating their workforces. Their sometimes limited financial resources do not prevent them from eliminating most of the potential dissatisfiers or increasing most of the Herzberg (1968) motivators. In addition, many offer work that is inherently rewarding because it is tied to a social purpose and the improvement or enrichment of human lives, something that only some, but not all, for-profit companies can offer. If nonprofit managers keep their staff and volunteers focused on the nonprofit's mission, they may keep them highly motivated. (Remember transformational leadership, discussed in Chapter 5.) Nonprofits may even have an advantage over government agencies, which also provide public service, since nonprofits may have the flexibility to offer some lifestyle advantages that would be more difficult for government employers to provide.

However, the reality of motivation in the nonprofit sector may be somewhat more complex and nuanced than some studies suggest. As Chung-An Chen (2014) explains, some of the research findings are based on comparing nonprofit staff with their counterparts in the for-profit sector. However, when scholars look *just* at nonprofit employees without comparing them to people in business, they find that extrinsic rewards, including salary, are also quite important to them (p. 740). Chen concludes that the research has "disproportionately emphasized" the importance of intrinsic over extrinsic factors in the nonprofit workplace, since people are most likely motivated by both. Interestingly, in one study, Jasmine McGinnis (2011) found that Generation Y (millennials) may place a higher emphasis on financial compensation than did previous generations of nonprofit staff members.

So, it cannot not be assumed that nonprofit staff members are *unconcerned* about their financial compensation. Indeed, financial incentives to reward performance have become more common in the nonprofit sector, especially for CEOs and fundraising professionals. Financial incentives for nonprofit employees are not illegal or unethical, provided they are properly defined—for example, compensating fundraisers with a commission based on amounts raised is almost universally considered inappropriate, while paying them a bonus for having increased their number of visits to prospective donors is generally within accepted practice.

But introducing such financial incentives may entail certain risks for nonprofit organizations. Gerhard Speckbacher (2013) notes three presumed advantages that incentive compensation provides: motivation for increased effort, signals that lead to self-selection of high-performing people to the workplace, and channelling employee attention to desired outcomes (p. 1007). But, he finds, incentive compensation also may have an impact on a nonprofit's relationship with its employees. Introducing explicit incentives (i.e., money) changes the relationship from social to contractual—in other words, it becomes a market relationship. "Trust and the feeling of obligation may disappear" (p. 1021). Moreover, it is difficult to mix social incentives with financial incentives; the entire relationship is likely to become based on the latter. And if such incentives are introduced for some staff members (e.g., fundraisers), it is likely that there will be "spillover effects" on other staff members of the organization (p. 1021), who may come to see their relationship with their employer more in market terms. Speckbacher's analysis suggests that the debate about incentive compensation may have significant implications that the nonprofit sector must carefully consider.

Perhaps the most realistic understanding of motivation in the nonprofit sector is that employees choose their jobs based on a mix of motivating factors, including both mission and money, both intrinsic and extrinsic considerations. But the balance of intrinsic and extrinsic rewards offered requires care and judgment and must be considered in the context of each organization. As Gazley (2015) advises, "Nonprofits should begin by understanding the intrinsic motivations of prospective employees [and also] communicate the extrinsic rewards of a position in terms of both monetary and non-monetary benefits" (p. 97).

Life Cycles and Generations

Another category of theories relates to the changing needs of people as they advance through the various stages of their lives. *Life-cycle theories* of motivation have critics but also have received some attention in the scholarly literature in recent decades (Denhardt et al., 2013, p. 176). Some theorists argue that both the skills and needs of workers change over their lifetimes. For example, young people may have "fluid intellectual abilities" and excel at abstract thinking (p. 176). By middle age, these abilities may diminish somewhat, but middle-age individuals will bring the benefits of greater experience. Similarly, motivations may change as people age. Young workers may be looking for opportunities to learn and be promoted, while middle-age and older workers may value job security and salary more (p. 176). This could imply that managers need to provide younger staff and volunteers with experiences that utilize their skills and meet their needs, while providing a somewhat different experience to those who are older. But, as some critics of life cycle theories point out, this could also lead to ageism in the workplace, and managers need to be sure that they are not making erroneous assumptions about the skills or interests of individuals based exclusively on their stage in life (p. 176).

Life cycle differences are, of course, distinct from generational differences. All people will advance through a cycle from young to middle age to older, and their needs and priorities may evolve in similar patterns. But the time period in which an individual was born and the significant events that marked the emergence of a generational cohort also may create differences that managers need to understand. There are three generations that predominate among nonprofit staff and volunteers today. The values and worldviews of each generation have been shaped in part by the economic conditions that prevailed during their formative years and by critical historical events that have occurred within their lifetimes. The baby boomers (born between 1946 and the mid-1960s) were shaped by the pressures of the Cold War and events such as Watergate and the Vietnam War. Many members of Generation X (born in the 1970s and early 1980s) were the first to grow up in families with both parents employed outside the home and witnessed such powerful events as the Challenger disaster and the fall of the Berlin Wall. The *millennials* (born after 1980) came of age with the development of the Internet, and some were shaped by events that included the terrorist attacks of September 11, 2001. Because of the advance of worldwide communication and increased opportunities for travel, many millennials have developed a greater international awareness than previous generations held. Although generalizations about individuals based on their generation can be as insidious as those based on age, sex, or other characteristics, a number of scholars have found some commonalities among members of particular generations. For example, some argue that baby boomers are committed to institutions and organizations and are most likely to be motivated by praise, money, and position. Members of Generation X may be distrustful of large organizations and are motivated by independence and involvement. Millennials (also called *Generation Y*) seek work that provides meaning and makes a difference. Focused on meaning and purpose, "they want to know why before what" (Denhardt et al., 2013, p. 177). As Robert Denhardt, Janet Denhardt, and Maria Aristigueta explain, "[Millennials] arrive at the workplace at the top levels of Maslow's hierarchy of needs" (p. 177). And, as mentioned in our previous discussion about motivation, it may be that millennials place a greater emphasis on financial compensation than previous generations did (McGinnis, 2011).

Again, it is essential to recognize that, as with life cycle stages, individual differences may outweigh generational patterns. But it also may be useful for managers to recognize that individuals who are of generations different from their own may be motivated in different ways and that it may be a mistake to assume that one's own values and worldview are fully shared by others.

Again, there are many additional theories of motivation that this chapter does not discuss in detail, some of which are reflected in Table 9.1 and discussed in suggested readings listed at the end of this chapter. Much recent work has been devoted to attempts to integrate earlier theories. Most theories offer some useful insights that may help guide managers and increase their understanding of staff and volunteers. But, as Hal Rainey (2014, p. 259) states, "the basic research and theory provide no conclusive science of motivation. Leaders have to draw on the ideas and apply the available techniques pragmatically, blending the experience and judgment with the insights the literature provides." This nuanced advice is consistent with the philosophy expressed throughout this text.

Applying Theories to Managing the Nonprofit Workforce

As noted at various points earlier in this book, the literature of nonprofit management includes both theory and the prescriptions of practitioner-oriented authors. This book attempts to integrate both perspectives. Now that we have reviewed some of the theoretical literature on human motivation, let's look at one attempt to translate that theory into specific recommended practices in managing the nonprofit workforce.

In the third edition of their book, *Managing Human Behavior in Public and Nonprofit Organizations*, Denhardt et al. (2013, pp. 182–185) review the motivation literature and offer nine suggested "ways of acting" for nonprofit and public sector managers, which they found to reflect commonalities of the various theoretical approaches. The following paragraphs discuss each of their recommendations and how they may relate to the various theories discussed earlier.

1. *Managers should be reflective and proactive about their own motivation.* McClelland (1961) and other theorists have suggested that the manager's own psychological needs and motivations affect how he or she interacts with and communicates with colleagues and subordinates. This is a point

that is also reflected in McGregor's (1960) description of Theory X and Theory Y. The manager's values and worldview, perhaps shaped by his or her generational experience or stage of life, also may affect his or her behavior with regard to the people supervised. This would imply that self-knowledge and understanding are essential for any individual who aspires to be an effective manager of others.

2. *Managers should be aware that what motivates them is not necessarily what will motivate others.* This advice is supported by several theories and reflects the simple but important understanding that people are not all alike. As Maslow (1954) and other theorists suggest, they bring their own needs to the workplace, which may reflect circumstances in their personal lives, their cultural backgrounds, or other characteristics. Or they may have different preferred ways of communicating, perhaps reflecting their personality styles or comfort with various media. Again, generational and life-stage differences may be relevant.

3. *Managers should have realistic expectations about the extent to which they can influence the motivation of others.* Again, as Maslow (1954) and other theorists explain, people come to the workplace already motivated. They are motivated to meet whatever psychological needs they may already have. The manager may not be able to influence those motivations very much. It may be more productive to assign people to jobs that enable them to meet their existing needs or perhaps redesign jobs to make them a better fit with the natural inclinations of those who hold them. Of course, if individuals' needs and motivations simply do not align with the goals of the organization, it may be best to suggest that they find employment in a more suitable environment. Too much effort to change the individuals may prove frustrating and fruitless.

4. *Managers should participate in setting clear and challenging goals.* As Herzberg (1968) discovered, the opportunity for achievement is a motivator for most individuals. But achievement requires that there be clear goals by which it is defined. Otherwise, effort yields no emotional reward, or a situation may evolve in which individuals feel that even "enough" is not sufficient to please their supervisors. And, as Rensis Likert (1967) and others have proposed, participation in goal setting may itself be an important source of motivation. The manager thus should establish goals in a participative manner so that the staff member accepts them as his or her own, provide regular feedback on progress, and grant recognition when the goals are reached. As Christine Letts, William Ryan, and Allen Grossman (1999a) observe, managers often face two challenges: getting the job done and keeping the staff satisfied. But they state, "Organizing jobs so employees can achieve and see results does both: It advances the organization's mission and motivates people in the process" (p. 108).

5. *Managers should think about the salience of various rewards.* Again, individuals are motivated differently. They have different values. And what they will find rewarding may be different in each case. A manager needs to listen, determine what each member of the staff finds important, and provide rewards consistent with that insight. Some may thrive on recognition—for example, being named "staff member of the week." Others may value the opportunity for flexible hours or to earn additional free time through outstanding performance. Some may need to have a clear understanding of the social impact of their efforts. And some may have financial needs that make salary a priority. As Denhardt and colleagues (2013) emphasize, and as the Hawthorne experiments suggested so many years ago, the interest and attention of the manager may itself be a reward that will reinforce high performance for some members of the staff. And, as discussed previously, some staff may consider their financial compensation to be highly important.

6. *Managers should be honest with people about what rewards are possible and what rewards are not.* As *expectancy theory* (Vroom, 1964) describes, individuals may be motivated not only by the value of rewards but also by the probability that they can be obtained. A manager who is unrealistic

in promising increased compensation, increased responsibility, community recognition, or some other reward for achievement of goals may buy some short-term motivation. But over time, such a manager will lose credibility and the power to influence the behavior of his or her staff.

7. *Managers should treat people equitably and fairly.* People in a workplace have a sense of what is equitable, in terms of effort, compensation, status, and other matters. As Herzberg's (1968) theory suggests, inequities in salary paid to individuals who perform similar work or put forth comparable effort may create more dissatisfaction than fair compensation that is modest in absolute terms. Similar points are made by the equity theorists (Adams, 1965). Of course, no person should be treated unfairly for reasons of his or her race, nationality, religion, sex, sexual orientation, gender identity, disability, political perspective, or other personal characteristics. To do so is morally wrong and generally illegal. And it is just poor management, likely to result in a dysfunctional, dissatisfied, and unproductive workforce that will not build a high-performing organization. Effective nonprofit organizations today go beyond the requirements of law and embrace diversity as an organizational value, seeking to draw the strength that comes from bringing together people of different perspectives, experiences, cultures, and backgrounds. In our complex society, any organization that does not incorporate such diversity will quickly lose touch with its community and constituency and, by excluding important talent, weaken its ability to serve its mission and achieve its goals.

8. *Managers should make the work satisfying and meaningful.* Motivation arises not only from the characteristics of people but also from the nature of the work they are given to perform. As Herzberg (1968) observed, some work is intrinsically motivating. But routine tasks may become monotonous and dissatisfying. Even interesting work may become less interesting if it is unchanging over time. Good managers provide their staff members with opportunities to grow personally and professionally, to take on new challenges, and to develop new skills in a variety of areas. This may be accomplished by rotating assignments or redesigning jobs, by providing training, and by offering opportunities for advancement from within the organization. Those who are employed in nonprofits are usually motivated by the impact of their work on the lives of clients. It is good practice to provide staff with as much exposure to clients as possible, enabling them to see firsthand the outcomes of their efforts.

9. *Managers should think about the life stages of the people they work with and offer appropriate support.* The life stage theories describe the needs and motivations of people in various periods. Such theories do have many critics, but they suggest that understanding the issues facing individuals in their personal lives may provide the manager with a useful perspective that is of benefit both to the individual and to the organization. It is also an approach that creates a humane environment consistent with the values of most nonprofit organizations. In addition, as discussed above, there may be differences among generations in what workplace culture or management style may be preferred and most effective. A manager needs to understand these differences and adjust the work experience in order to gain the maximum contribution from each individual.

Managing Volunteers

The discussion in the previous section of this chapter was focused primarily on the management of nonprofit staff members. Let's now shift our discussion to look at some principles that apply specifically to managing service volunteers. Effective management of volunteers is an important topic because volunteers are a major component of the workforce of many nonprofits. *Volunteering and Civic Life in America,* a report published by the Corporation for National and Community Service, estimates that 63 million Americans engaged in volunteer service in 2013, providing almost 8 billion hours of service

(Corporation for National and Community Service, 2014b). However, of some concern was the decline in volunteering in 2013, by over 1 percent, to the lowest level since 2002 (Bureau of Labor Statistics, 2014). Adults ages 35 to 44 are the most likely to volunteer, with almost 31 percent doing so in 2013, compared with only 19 percent of people in their early 20s. In general, women are more likely to be volunteers than men, and this is true across all age groups, educational levels, and other characteristics (Bureau of Labor Statistics, 2014).

The service of volunteers is of enormous economic importance to nonprofit organizations and to society. Independent Sector (2014) estimates that each hour of volunteer time contributed to nonprofits in 2013 was worth $22.55; that is an average of what organizations would have needed to pay to obtain similar services from paid staff—not an inconsequential sum. It is important to note, however, that individuals cannot claim a tax deduction for the value of their volunteered time. A nonprofit organization can cite the value of volunteer services in its communications, to demonstrate wide community support or for purposes of recognizing volunteers like donors. However, there are limitations on how that value can be used on nonprofit financial statements. According to rules established by the Financial Accounting Standards Board (1993), the value of volunteer work can be used on financial statements, in grant proposals, and in other formal ways only if the volunteers are providing specialized services for which the nonprofit would otherwise have paid. That might include, for example, services of accountants, architects, doctors, and similar professionals.

As Michael O'Neill (2002) observes, "Nonprofits differ greatly with regard to the role of volunteers." Many nonprofits are small, all-volunteer efforts. Many nonprofits with paid staff also rely heavily on volunteers. Others, such as research institutes, universities, and private foundations, use few volunteers (p. 31). Recent decades have seen the increased professionalization of nonprofit management, with paid staff replacing volunteers in some organizations, especially the largest and most commercialized. Today, volunteers often work alongside paid staff, and *volunteer management* has itself become a specialty of professional nonprofit management.

Types of Volunteers

There are different types of volunteers, characterized by the pattern of their participation, the extent of their commitment, and their motivations. There is not a consensus about the definitions of the various types (Brudney, 2010, p. 771).

Sunney Shin and Brian Kleiner (2003) identify one type as what they call the *spot volunteer,* whose participation is casual. For example, an individual may respond to a call for volunteers to help clean up a park or a hiking trail—it is a one-day commitment, and there is likely enough work to occupy as many people as show up. The effort may not need to be repeated again, at least for some period of time, and there is no special skill required to participate.

Other volunteers may participate more than once, but only for a short period of time or during a certain time of the year, for example during the holiday season or in the summer. Some authors refer to them as *episodic volunteers*, although, again, there is not a universally accepted terminology. Some use the term *episodic volunteer* to describe *both* someone who volunteers just once (same as a spot volunteer) *or* who volunteers from time to time, that is, episodically (Brudney, 2010, p. 771).

Another type defined by Shin and Kleiner (2003) is the *regular volunteer,* who makes a commitment to the activity and gains a sense of gratification and accomplishment from the work. Such volunteer assignments may have the formality of regular paid jobs; there may be job descriptions, clear statements of responsibilities, and specific skills required to perform the work. Continuity may be important; for example, those who participate in tutoring programs need to be present in every session in order to develop relationships and gain the trust of the children. In other situations, dependability is essential; for example, volunteer fire departments or disaster relief organizations cannot rely on whoever may choose to show up on a given occasion.

An additional type of volunteer is one who is pressured (or perhaps just strongly encouraged) to engage in service. Robert Stebbins (2009) refers to this type as the "marginal volunteer," but that term might have unfair negative connotations, so we refer to them simply as *encouraged or mandated volunteers* in this chapter. For example, a significant number of corporations encourage their employees to engage in community service activities, as a strategy both for gaining goodwill for the company and for building camaraderie among the workforce. Some employees may find this encouragement almost impossible to resist if they desire to gain advancement in their company. In other cases, someone may volunteer because they are asked to do so by friends, for example, in an activity such as a walk or run. They may enjoy the experience but participate primarily because of peer pressure; without a personal commitment to the organization, they may be unlikely to become regular volunteers. Many states require (or mandate) that high school students complete a volunteer experience as a graduation requirement. In addition, some professional education programs require that students complete an internship as a requirement of graduation. (Although whether an intern is truly a "volunteer" and whether interns should always be compensated is an issue of debate.) And of course, courts often assign first-time offenders of minor crimes to community service as a form of restitution. Although some may regard mandatory voluntarism, or even that performed under pressure, as an oxymoron, others speculate that the requirement of service for young people may be helpful in introducing them to the concept, perhaps beginning a commitment that they will continue throughout their lives. Of course, volunteers who are encouraged or even required to participate may also be motivated by other reasons and may find their service rewarding.

A relatively new type of volunteer, which has become more important in recent years, is the *virtual volunteer*, someone who works from a distance using electronic technology, perhaps serving the nonprofit via e-mail, the Web, or postings on Twitter, Facebook, and other social media. For example, Kiva Microfunds is a nonprofit that provides funds to borrowers throughout the world. Potential entrepreneurs can develop proposals that then are matched with lenders on Kiva's website (www.kiva.org). Some volunteers work at Kiva's headquarters in San Francisco, but over 300 individuals work as *virtual volunteers*, editing loan profiles and translating them into English. Kiva volunteers commit a minimum of two hours per week for a minimum of six months to "review and edit Kiva loans on their personal computers from their homes, offices, local coffee shops, the beach, etc., using Kiva's web interface" (www.kiva.org).

Jayne Cravens and Susan Ellis (2014) emphasize that principles of sound volunteer management, which we will discuss further later in this chapter, apply to virtual volunteers as well as those who serve onsite. Those principles encompass recruitment, supervision, and support. Special efforts are required to build and maintain a sense of community among virtual volunteers in order to retain their interest and commitment. That includes frequent communication, both online and through regular mail, and recognition of success (pp. 70–71).

In recent years, there has been growth in international volunteering, perhaps reflecting the increased international awareness created by global communications and the visibility of philanthropic organizations such as the Gates Foundation, which focuses on global problems. Volunteers, mostly from the United States and other western nations, travel to other parts of the world to work on conservation, educational, and humanitarian projects, usually for a brief period of time. In the vocabulary discussed above, they are generally spot or episodic volunteers, rather than a distinctive type.

Some international volunteer experiences fall under the rubric of *voluntourism*, also called *volunteer vacations*. Some are structured to place the primary emphasis on the volunteer project, with some period of vacation attached. Others are primarily vacations with work on a volunteer project incorporated for some portion of the trip. Individuals who participate in such programs often have mixed motives; some are undoubtedly motivated at least in part by altruism, but some may be seeking primarily an opportunity for adventure and self-development (Chen & Chen, 2011). Some authors have questioned the impact of such short-term projects and whether voluntourism really represents "an effective [economic] development strategy or feel-good tourism" (West, 2011).

TABLE 9.3 ■ Types of Volunteers	
Spot volunteers	Participate casually, usually on one occasion, for example, in a one-day effort to clean up the park
Episodic volunteers	May participate on only one occasion or on multiple occasions or for brief periods of time, for example, distributing food during the holiday season
Regular volunteers	Serve essentially as unpaid staff, performing duties specified in job descriptions and requiring specialized skills, for example, tutoring children one or two days per week on an ongoing basis or standing prepared to provide disaster-relief services to a community
Encouraged or mandated volunteers	Participate primarily because service is encouraged or required, often by an employer, educational program, or court, but may also find their volunteer activity to be rewarding
Virtual volunteers	Serve an organization from afar, usually via electronic technology

Motivations of Volunteers

We need to consider the motivations of volunteers in two ways: first, in terms of what motivates people to become volunteers in the first place, and second, what factors motivate them to perform at a high level and continue in their volunteer roles.

Research provides us with insights on *who* volunteers. People who volunteer tend to have more diversity in their friendships, more education, and greater intensity of religious belief. They also are more likely to engage in religious activities, social networking, and social groups (Forbes & Zampelli, 2014). But *why* do people volunteer? Some may be motivated by the mission of the organization, the desire to advance a cause, or perhaps the desire to repay for some benefit that the individual received. These are altruistic reasons; that is, the individual's motivation for volunteering is based on the public good accomplished, not by any benefits that may accrue to the volunteer himself or herself. On the other hand, some people may volunteer because of benefits that they receive from doing so. This may include the intangible warm feeling of emotional satisfaction or more tangible benefits, such as gaining increased job skills, building an enhanced resume, or making social contacts. As Jeffrey Brudney (2010) observes, research on the motivations of volunteers has been "voluminous" and the basic conclusion it reaches is that motivations are "complex and multi-faceted" (p. 773). In other words, most volunteers may be motivated by a combination of reasons; as Femida Handy and Laurie Mook (2010) describe, they are "impure altruists." The fact that people may be motivated by a combination of altruism and personal needs does not diminish the value of their efforts or make them less admirable. However, it is essential for the nonprofit manager to understand these sometimes mixed and complex motivations in order to create an experience that will attract and retain the volunteer workforce.

A considerable body of research on volunteers suggests that the factors leading to their motivation and satisfaction are very similar to those for paid staff. For example, studies have found that volunteers are motivated by a desire to serve the mission, that volunteers who remain with the organization are those who experience positive relationships with other volunteers, that those who continue to serve are those who find the nature of the work itself rewarding, and that volunteers value opportunities to learn new skills through their voluntary service. Volunteers who have participated in studies assign importance to factors such as clearly defined responsibilities, a reasonable work schedule, and competent supervision, all consistent with the motivation theories we have previously discussed. Although not all experts agree (Brudney, 2010, p. 759), research suggests that a list of recommended practices for managing volunteers should include many points similar to those outlined above for the management of staff (McCurley, 2005). Some studies suggest that nonprofits desiring to maintain relationships with volunteers over the long term should avoid subjecting them to pressure, deadlines for completing work, or external controls; in other words, volunteers may highly value autonomy in completing their assignments (Oostlander, Güntert, van Schie, & Wehner, 2014).

Volunteer Program Practices

There is much information available on the design of volunteer programs and on the management of volunteers. The list of suggested readings at the end of this chapter provides a small sample of the many publications and websites that offer access to additional materials. Although there are varied opinions on many points, there is also much commonality among the recommendations of experts on recommended practices in developing and managing an effective volunteer program. Most authors offer some or all of the following points (see, e.g., McCurley & Lynch, 2006; Brudney, 2010).

Assess the need for volunteers. Before an organization launches a program for the use of volunteers, it needs to determine why volunteers are needed and desired. If the need is for *spot volunteers* to complete an essentially simple one-time project, that is obviously a different matter from establishing a program that will engage *regular volunteers* in delivering ongoing services to clients. Some may assume that regular volunteers offer a cost-effective way to provide services, but that may not always be the case. The costs related to recruiting, supporting, and managing volunteers—possibly requiring the appointment of additional paid staff—must be taken into consideration. Moreover, volunteers who are inadequately supported may well become dissatisfied, and high turnover could affect the quality of programs. Although regular volunteers are unpaid, they are not free, since they can only be effective in the context of an organized and managed effort.

Nonprofits may have reasons for desiring the involvement of volunteers that go beyond the economics of needed labor. The involvement of volunteers may increase connections with the community or clients, inject passion and energy into the organization's culture, and even open doors to new sources of funding (Brudney, 2010). These are all among the good reasons for maintaining a volunteer program, but again, the organization should be clear and explicit about what it expects to gain and clear eyed about the costs of making the program successful. Recruiting volunteers exclusively for the sake of community engagement or fundraising and without a clear understanding of how they will make substantive contributions toward achieving the organization's mission is likely to be a counterproductive approach.

One fundamental decision to be made is which jobs or functions may best be performed by volunteers and which require the full-time attention of paid staff. Lack of clarity on this question may lead to unrealistic expectations, tensions between staff and volunteers, or a mismatch of volunteers' skills to their responsibilities. The HandsOn Network (2010, pp. 1–2), an organization that supports volunteerism, emphasizes that volunteers should supplement and not supplant staff members, suggesting that the jobs most appropriate for assignment to volunteers might include the following:

- Work currently done by employees that does not require special skills but would allow paid staff to increase the services they provide—[for example,] a child welfare worker could have volunteers drive children to their clinic appointments
- Work that requires specialized skills that paid staff do not have—[for example,] an older adult service center could ask volunteers with accounting and tax backgrounds to assist clients in completing and filing their taxes

- Work that would not be done if volunteers did not do it—[for example,] volunteers could visit home-bound clients or mentor children
- Work that must be completed by a certain time each week or month but does not have to be done daily—[for example,] volunteers can update the organizational or program database
- Work that can be done off site or after hours—[for example,] volunteers can work on public relations projects, such as newsletters and mass mailings
- Work that requires extra attention—[for example,] volunteers can administer and analyze program evaluations

Determine the structure of the volunteer program. A successful volunteer program requires that the relative roles of volunteers and staff be clearly defined and that the responsibility for supervision of volunteers be explicit. Again, engaging spot volunteers for a one-time effort may not require that much thought be devoted to organization, but the regular involvement of volunteers raises questions of how they will be integrated within the operations of the organization.

One alternative may be to take a decentralized approach, with volunteers based in specific programs and supervised by the leaders of those programs, whether staff or other volunteers. This approach offers the advantage of being able to match volunteer interests and skills to specific activities. But it also may lead to uneven experiences and limit the organization's flexibility to reassign volunteers as needs may change across its departments. An alternative is to develop a centralized program, with management of all volunteers assigned to a single department or office, perhaps led by a paid professional volunteer manager. This may facilitate training, evaluation, and coordination of effort across the organization. It also provides some protection against risk, since potential volunteers can be screened by the same criteria and a single manager can monitor their performance to assure both the quality of programs and the safety of volunteers and clients. But there also may be potential downsides to a centralized model if support for the volunteer program is not broadly present in all departments (Brudney, 2010).

The manner in which the volunteer program is organized should be consistent with the overall structure of the organization. Thus, a highly decentralized organization, in which many decisions are delegated to program directors or local offices, may best engage and manage volunteers in a decentralized manner. But an organization that is highly centralized in other aspects of its operation most likely will take a more centralized approach to volunteers. The size of the organization is an obvious consideration in selecting the organizational model, but the overall management culture also needs to be considered.

Develop volunteer job descriptions. If volunteers are to serve episodically (e.g., a group is going to the woods for one day to clean up trash and repair hiking trails), there may not be a need for much formality in defining volunteer jobs—a supervisor can just assign those who show up to the tasks that need to be done. But if the organization needs volunteers to play an ongoing role as a part of its workforce, then volunteer jobs need to be designed and defined with some precision in order to establish clear expectations and ensure that the volunteer's work is related to program needs. Having formal job descriptions also helps communicate to volunteers that they are accepting a significant responsibility and that their assignment involves doing real work that is central to the program of the nonprofit.

Job descriptions do not need to be complex or extensive but should carefully state the type of work, skills needed, and expectations of volunteers. For example, the job description for a volunteer at the Harry S. Truman Library in Independence, Missouri, shown in Box 9.1, lists the specific tasks that the volunteer will perform and the qualifications required for the position, as well as the organization's commitment to provide training and compensation in the form of nonfinancial benefits.

BOX 9.1 VOLUNTEER JOB DESCRIPTION

Harry S. Truman Library

TITLE OF POSITION: Archives Assistant

SUPERVISED BY: Archives Staff

PURPOSE OF JOB: Assist archives staff with basic archival functions such as processing, preservation, reference, etc. Objective is to assist in increasing availability of research material.

DUTIES MAY INCLUDE BUT ARE NOT LIMITED TO:

1. Photocopying and filing
2. Maintain proper care and maintenance of all documents handled.
3. Create finding aids (indexes, catalogs, etc.).
4. Data entry.
5. Stamping of documents.
6. Prepare material for preservation work.
7. Attend orientation sessions and complete training readings.
8. Communicate regularly with assigned supervisor as to concerns, issues, or ideas arising from the current project.
9. Participate in reviews within archives of assignments prior to extension, reassignment, or completion.
10. Ensure the goals and policies of the archives and library are promoted and adhered to.

COMMITMENT REQUIRED:

A minimum commitment of 4–5 hours per week for a 3-month period is required. Volunteer opportunities will be available Monday–Friday, 9:00 a.m.–4:30 p.m. There are no weekend or evening opportunities for this position.

QUALIFICATIONS NEEDED:

- Must be age 16 or older
- Basic computer skills and/or good handwriting helpful
- Flexible to changing situation
- Reliable, responsible
- Able to work independently as well as in a group environment
- Able to accept supervision
- Interest in history
- Ability to perform repetitive tasks and detail oriented
- Good organizational skills

TRAINING/ORIENTATION PROVIDED:

Since the duties performed by the Archives Assistants are varied, training and work assignments are both designed to meet the individual requirements of the task to be accomplished. Training is provided on-the-job by the Truman Library's archives staff.

Basic reading material on the Truman presidency and archives work is additionally provided.

LOCATION OF JOB:

The Harry S. Truman Library, Independence, Missouri

VOLUNTEER BENEFITS:

Knowledge about Harry S. Truman, the Library and Museum, and the educational aspects offered to visitors through a variety of programs/exhibits; discount prices in the museum gift shop; invitations to special events; volunteer appreciation programs; free parking; free subscription to *Whistle-Stop*, the quarterly newsletter of the Harry S. Truman Library Institute; free admission to the museum for you and your immediate family; work with original and unique historical documents.

Source: Harry S. Truman Library website (http://www.trumanlibrary.org/voluntee/archivjd.htm).

Develop formal volunteer policies. Volunteers may be unpaid, but they are a part of the organization's workforce. Indeed, they often work alongside of paid staff in delivering its services. There should be formal policies that spell out the expectations, rules, and standards by which volunteers will be evaluated and, if necessary, terminated. The policies should describe the relationship between volunteers and any paid staff by whom they are supervised or whom they may supervise. Organizations have personnel policies to govern their relationship with paid staff; not having such policies for volunteers might imply that they are not as essential as staff and may set the stage for misunderstandings, conflict between volunteers and staff members, or even legal problems.

Having formal volunteer policies is also an important element of risk management for the organization. This is especially important in settings where volunteers will have direct contact with clients or access to confidential client information, or in which clients are particularly vulnerable or potentially volatile. For example, Box 9.2 includes sample volunteer policies suggested by the Indiana Nonprofit Resource Network for health care organizations, which may present an especially sensitive environment. New volunteers should be given a copy of the policies and should sign a statement acknowledging that they have read them. In addition, most organizations should carry liability insurance, to protect both organizational assets and volunteers.

BOX 9.2 SAMPLE ORGANIZATIONAL VOLUNTEERING POLICY (HEALTH CARE)

This is a sample policy geared toward a hospital volunteer program. However, many of the aspects included in the policy are items that are considered best practice to have in any organization volunteering policy. In most areas, you may be able to replace the word *hospital* or *health care* with your organization's specialty: hospice, senior center, after-school program, etc.

PURPOSE

1. To establish the Director of Volunteer Services as responsible for recruitment, utilization, and supervision of volunteers throughout [the organization]

2. To provide [the organization's] customers the benefit of an organized and consistent volunteer program

(Continued)

(Continued)

3. To recruit, train, and retain community members for an effective hospital system volunteer program, thereby creating good public relations between [the organization] and the community it serves

4. To provide volunteers from all segments of the community a means of meeting the need to provide service to others

5. To provide community members 14 years of age and older an opportunity to become acquainted with the health care field and to encourage their interest in health careers as student volunteers, or special case volunteers

DEFINITIONS

Volunteer: Anyone who, without compensation or expectation of compensation beyond reimbursement, performs a task at the direction of and on behalf of [the organization]. A "volunteer" must be officially accepted and enrolled by [the organization] prior to performance of the task. Volunteers must be at least 14 years of age to be officially accepted and enrolled by [the organization's] Volunteer Services department.

Special Case Volunteers: [The organization] also accepts as volunteers those participating in student intern projects, corporate volunteer programs, and other volunteer referral programs. In each of these cases, however, a special agreement must be in effect with the organization, school, or program from which the special case volunteers originate and must identify responsibility for management and care of the volunteers.

[The organization] does not accept volunteers who must complete community service hours related to a court order.

GENERAL INFORMATION

1. Volunteers will be encouraged, but not required, to become members of [the organization].

2. New volunteer opportunities shall be proposed to various hospital system departments. All qualified volunteers will have the opportunity to staff the service. The Director of Volunteer Services will work cooperatively with the designated staff person to implement the service. All new programs are the responsibility of the Director of Volunteer Services or his/her designee.

3. Volunteers will not replace paid employees but serve to supplement and enhance existing services to patients, their families, and hospital system programs.

4. Volunteer service will be an important, honored role at [the organization], including Hospice and the Community Health Center with every effort made to integrate and coordinate volunteer talents and needs with the hospital system's program.

5. Volunteer programs and activities will be monitored and evaluated on an on-going basis by the Director of Volunteer Services or his/her designee in conjunction with other involved staff members.

PROCEDURE

1. Potential volunteers will complete an application and submit to the Director of Volunteer Services or his/her designee. Volunteers 18 years of age and older will complete and submit a Release of Information, which will be reviewed by the County Sheriff's Department for history. Volunteers assisting in secured hospital departments will also complete a criminal background application for the State of Indiana.

2. Reference checks will be completed on all volunteers.

3. Volunteers will be interviewed by the Director of Volunteer Services, his/her designee and/or department manager to assure placement is in accordance with skills of the volunteer.

4. All volunteers will receive a TB test or a chest x-ray and a photo ID badge before volunteerism begins. Departmental training will be done by department staff or trained volunteer.

5. Volunteers are required to attend volunteer orientation session provided by Volunteer Services Department.

6. Hospital system managers wanting volunteer assistance will complete a volunteer service requisition and submit it to Volunteer Services. After the Director of Volunteer Services or his/her designee has selected a volunteer, the requesting department will be notified.

7. A record of individual hours of service by all volunteers will be maintained by the Volunteer Services Department.

8. The Director of Volunteer Services will maintain a . . . database record and a personnel file on each volunteer, to include

   - Application
   - Background check(s)
   - Reference checks
   - Medical clearance (sick leaves)
   - Orientation record
   - Attendance at educational in-services
   - Evaluations

9. Volunteers will be honored each year for the hours they have volunteered in the previous year for [organization]. Activities to honor the [organization's] volunteers are held during National Volunteer Week.

Source: Indiana Nonprofit Resource Network, retrieved from http://www.inrn.org/resources/staff-volunteer/organizational-volunteering-policy.pdf.

Indiana Nonprofit Resource Network (INRN) is a regionally based service delivered on behalf of Indiana United Ways. Used with permission.

Provide a sufficient budget and personnel to manage the volunteer program. Without adequate resources, such as books, computers, tools, transportation, supervision, or whatever their work may require, volunteers are no more likely than staff to be successful. Depending on the scope of the volunteer program, it may be important to have a full-time member of the paid staff to manage the organization's overall relationship with volunteers. This does not imply that volunteers necessarily report to the volunteer manager with regard to their specific assignments but that the manager maintains an overall view of volunteers' involvement and performance. It is also important that all members of the paid staff who work with volunteers, including perhaps program or unit directors, are provided with training on the special considerations in managing them.

Recruit and hire volunteers as if they were employees. Some organizations may be in such need of volunteers that they may be tempted to accept anyone who may indicate an interest. This is what Stephen McCurley (2005, p. 595) calls *warm body recruitment*, the implication being that if the person is breathing and willing, they are signed on as a volunteer. But taking this approach may produce only a short-run gain and, indeed, it is likely to neither meet the organization's needs nor provide a satisfying experience for the volunteers.

In contrast to the warm-body approach, *targeted recruitment* of volunteers "is designed to attract fewer, select volunteers for jobs that require particular skills or interests or are appropriate for specific age or cultural groups" (McCurley, 2005, p. 595). A well-managed program is likely to attract, at least over time, sufficient interest to permit selectivity in the hiring of volunteers. A selective volunteer program requires that prospective volunteers complete an application and undergo an interview process. Background checks may also be required by law or be advisable in consideration of risk management.

Gaining the ability to be targeted and selective in choosing volunteers offers the organization at least two advantages: First, it can select people with the right skills to meet its needs and those who are likely to remain committed to their volunteer responsibilities. Second, the organization may be able to craft its volunteer program in order to include groups from prospective donor companies, religious congregations, or other groups with which it wishes to establish closer relationships. A volunteer program thus can become not only a vehicle for delivering the organization's programs but also an instrument of its fundraising, communications, and community relations efforts. However, as stated previously, it is important not to permit the latter considerations to predominate. Engaging volunteers simply as a fundraising strategy but failing to provide them with a structured and meaningful experience is likely to lead to their frustration and undermine, rather than enhance, their perception of and affiliation with the organization.

Provide orientation and training to volunteers. Volunteer orientation should include an introduction to the organization that covers not only practical operational matters but also a discussion of its mission, values, and culture. It should clarify the relationship between volunteers and paid staff and the expectations of each. Depending on the nature of the volunteer's work, training may include working with another, more experienced volunteer for a period or a more formal program designed to develop specific skills.

Set clear goals, evaluate performance, and recognize achievement. As discussed previously, people are motivated by clear goals, the explication of a clear path to their achievement, and recognition for having succeeded in reaching them. Since volunteers are not compensated financially, their achievement of goals and recognition may be their primary rewards. This suggests that volunteer job performance should be evaluated, which of course implies that volunteers could be terminated when appropriate as well, the same as paid staff. Some organizations may find that a difficult decision to reach because they are in need of volunteers and feel they cannot afford to let one go. Or perhaps the culture of the organization may not encompass individual performance standards, at least not for volunteers. It also can be problematic if volunteers are also donors—even board members, whose termination might bring additional consequences. However, such concerns should be balanced against the need to maintain the overall quality and reputation of the program, the importance of achieving quality in service delivery, and the negative consequences for the morale of both staff and other volunteers of retaining someone whose work or attitude does not make a positive contribution. Of course, evaluation should be a two-way street. Volunteers should be given opportunities to provide feedback on the quality of their experience, including the conditions, supervision, and resources with which they work.

In summary, many experts suggest that, in most respects, volunteers should be managed with many of the same practices that apply to paid staff. To be sure, volunteers are entitled to respect and gratitude. Their impact is much the same as that of donors of financial gifts, and they are a precious asset that nonprofits need to nurture and cultivate. However, for all these reasons, they also deserve a structured and professional approach that maintains high expectations and stays focused on achievement of the organization's mission and goals.

Volunteer Management as a Career Field

As mentioned before, volunteer management has become a distinct specialty in nonprofit management. In a 2004 study conducted by the Urban Institute, 3 out of 5 nonprofits had a paid professional position for management of volunteers (Idealist, 2014a). Many positions in the study were part-time, but full-time positions are increasing in number. Titles of such positions are varied, including for example, volunteer manager, volunteer coordinator, director of volunteers, director of volunteer services, and vice president of volunteers/volunteer resources (Idealist, 2014b). Obviously, the higher the title, the greater the role and the more the individual in the position is a part of the senior management team of the organization. There is a multitude of training programs for volunteer managers, including university-based and online courses and various organizations offer professional certification (Idealist, 2014b). Box 9.3 provides an example of a job description for a volunteer management position and shows many of the responsibilities and expectations that are commonly included.

BOX 9.3 POSITION DESCRIPTION FOR VOLUNTEER COORDINATOR: WINDY CITY HABITAT FOR HUMANITY

LOCATION:

Chicago, IL

GENERAL DESCRIPTION:

The Volunteer Coordinator is responsible for all aspects of the volunteer program. This includes the recruitment, processing, education, retention, and coordination of all Habitat volunteers, including construction, committee, and office volunteers. The Volunteer Coordinator works closely with Habitat's home sponsors to coordinate sponsor volunteers and coordinates home dedications. The position works closely with all staff members and volunteers to create a positive and productive atmosphere for volunteers.

CORE RESPONSIBILITIES:

Volunteer Program

- Produce written informational and educational materials for volunteer outreach
- Respond to all individual volunteer inquiries
- Effectively schedule volunteers to meet the volunteer needs of construction staff
- Meet with construction staff weekly
- Interview and place volunteers for specific needs such as committee, office, ReStore, and special events
- Coordinating the scheduling of groups and skilled volunteers

(Continued)

(Continued)

- Maintain volunteer records and statistics in the database
- Develop and implement formal and informal volunteer appreciation program
- Develop, maintain and evaluate "regular" construction volunteer programs to retain ongoing volunteers
- Conduct monthly orientations for volunteers
- Monitor and assess the need for volunteer services and suggest program improvements
- Prepare job descriptions for volunteer positions
- Monitor volunteer satisfaction
- Ensure that volunteer liability waivers are signed and filed
- Work with staff to handle any volunteer concerns or issues
- Manage community service volunteers from local jurisdictions
- Coordinate activities for youth volunteers (Boy/Girl Scouts, etc.)
- Recruit, train, and schedule site hosts

Sponsors

- Meet with home sponsors to develop volunteer coordination plan
- Coordinate the scheduling of sponsor volunteers during home construction process
- Plan and coordinate home dedication ceremonies with Family Support Committee

Committees

- Provide training materials, procedures, and current information to all Habitat committees
- Maintain communication and provide support to committee chairs
- Hold annual committee chair meeting and provide training as needed
- Work with staff liaisons to ensure productive committees that provide a meaningful experience for volunteers

Other

- Work closely with sponsors, HFHI and other organizations on special projects and builds
- Represent Habitat to the community through community presentations
- Establish and maintain effective relationships with sponsors, HFHI, and the community
- Supervise volunteers in the office who assist with data entry, thank yous and other tasks to support the volunteer department
- Promote teamwork and foster motivation and understanding
- Contribute to newsletter for volunteer related articles
- Assist staff members in appreciation efforts for office volunteers
- Coordinate volunteers for booths and fairs
- Other responsibilities as assigned by Executive Director

KNOWLEDGE, SKILLS, ABILITIES:

- Enthusiasm, teamwork focused and strong customer service orientation
- Well organized and detail oriented
- Effective leadership and team building skills
- Self-motivated, able to work independently with minimal supervision
- Possess tact, diplomacy, and flexibility

- Good supervisory skills
- Excellent written and verbal communication skills
- Project management skills
- Ability to multitask
- Computer skills required including database experience, MS Office, and Internet

EDUCATION, EXPERIENCE:

- BA/BS Degree
- Personal volunteer experience

PHYSICAL REQUIREMENTS NECESSARY TO PERFORM THIS JOB:

This position is primarily performed at a desk in the office. Outside meetings and presentations are frequently required. Some evening and weekend meetings required in locations and times when public transportation is unavailable. Occasional special projects require spending multiple consecutive days at the construction site overseeing volunteer logistics.

WORK ENVIRONMENT AND CONDITIONS:

- Most of work is performed at a desk, sometimes for long periods of time
- Must work at a computer for periods at a time

Windy City Habitat for Humanity is an Equal Opportunity Employer. This organization does not and will not discriminate in employment and personnel practices on the basis of race, sex, age, handicap, religion, national origin, or any other basis prohibited by applicable law.

Source: Adapted from Windy City Habitat for Humanity website, retrieved from https://www.windycityhabitat.org/uploads/Volunteer_Coordinator_Job_Description.pdf.

The Future of Volunteerism

Scholars who have studied volunteerism in the United States have identified trends that offer opportunities for nonprofit organizations but that may also present challenges to nonprofit managers who rely on volunteers for delivery of important programs and services. The long-term trend in volunteering has been positive. One study, conducted by the Corporation for National and Community Service in 2005, examined rates of volunteer participation all the way back to 1974. While there were periods of decline, participation in volunteer activities had generally increased and reached an all-time high by 2005 (Corporation for National and Community Service, 2006). But participation in volunteering has been generally stagnant since 2005 and, as mention earlier, it declined in 2013 (Bureau of Labor Statistics, 2014). Some have speculated that the reason for this downturn may have been lingering effects of the economic recession of 2007–2009 or a lack of nonprofits' capacity to recruit and train volunteers. Some have called for more foundation funding to increase the ability of nonprofits to manage volunteer programs. Others argue that the data miss the growing numbers of virtual volunteers (Perry, 2014).

But some scholars have discerned deeper social changes. Based on a 2005 study, Walter Rehberg makes a distinction between "old volunteering" and "new volunteering." He argues that old volunteering was based on a connection to religious or political communities and was motivated by a sense of membership, altruism, and concern for the collective good. In new volunteering, "volunteers are not particularly loyal to organizations, tend to be choosy about what they do, and expect some personal benefit from their [volunteer experience]" (2005, p. 109). According to Rehberg, this shift is more than a statistical trend; it reflects more profound social changes in which individuals are less inclined to find inspiration in commitment to a local community, traditional institution, or set ideology and who are more inclined to see volunteering as a way to combine "self-directed or instrumental motives with a sense of compassion or duty" (p. 110). In other words, as discussed earlier in this chapter, volunteers may be motivated both by altruism and the personal benefits derived from their voluntary activities. But, as Rehberg suggests, the sense of connection and duty to communities and traditional institutions may be less than in the past. People may have become more concerned with personal growth and identify. If so, then the latter set of motives may continue to grow in importance.

Both demographic and social changes may have significant implications for how nonprofit organizations enlist and manage volunteers. First, in the years ahead, older people may be the most promising source of regular volunteers; that will require that volunteer managers understand and address their particular interests and needs. Second, with regard to volunteers of all ages and generations, the sense of duty and obligation may not be sufficient to compensate for a poor volunteer experience. This is not to suggest that altruism and the desire to help others will not continue to be an important motivation for volunteering; it is to suggest that volunteers may be unwilling to participate for long in an experience that is unrewarding and offers little opportunity for personal growth. Nonprofits will need to become even more mindful of principles discussed in this chapter, in order to assure that volunteer efforts are well defined, well managed, and meaningful to those who participate.

Chapter Summary

Human resources management (HRM) involves formal systems and activities related to recruitment, selection, training and development, compensation and benefits, retention, evaluation, promotion, and labor–management relationships. One important aspect of human resources management is assuring compliance with the law. Some laws affect only employees, but others also apply to volunteers.

Early management theories were often developed in industrial settings and portrayed human beings as part of a production machine, whose performance could be increased by focusing on procedures and rules. Since at least the Hawthorne experiments of the 1920s, theorists have focused on human psychology and motivation, emphasizing the influence of human needs and feelings on behavior in the workplace. Theories are often advanced, gain wide acceptance, and are subsequently discredited through further research. But most offer some principles that are adopted in new approaches or that gain continued acceptance by practitioners.

One theory, advanced by Frederick Herzberg, suggests that there are two sets of factors present in the workplace. One set of factors, which includes rewarding work and opportunities for achievement, recognition, and advancement, serves to motivate workers. Another set of factors, related to the work environment and including supervision, working conditions, and compensation, may be dissatisfiers but are not in themselves motivating. Managers should try to reduce or eliminate dissatisfiers and increase motivators. These principles may apply to the motivation of volunteers as well as paid staff members. Other theories, including those of Maslow, McClelland, and Myers and Briggs, suggest that individuals bring their own personal needs and styles into the workplace. This may require that managers design jobs to reflect the existing motivations of their staff and volunteers. Some research suggests that employees in nonprofit organizations have unique motivations, including commitment to the mission, but other research suggests that extrinsic variables, including salary, also may be important to people who work in the nonprofit sector. Some nonprofits provide financial incentives to reward performance and some scholars warn that doing so may change employees' relationship with the organization from social to contractual. Nonprofits should understand the intrinsic motivations of prospective employees but also communicate about extrinsic rewards, including financial and non-monetary benefits.

Based on motivation theory, some recommended practices for managers of paid staff include being reflective about their own needs and motivations, being aware that what motivates the manager may not necessarily be what will motivate others, holding realistic expectations about the extent to which a manager can influence the motivation of others, participating in setting clear and challenging goals, thinking about the salience of various rewards to individuals who have different needs, being honest with people about what rewards are possible and what rewards are not, treating people equitably and fairly, making the work satisfying and meaningful, and considering the implications of life stages and of personal life events for the individuals they manage. Fostering workplace diversity, encompassing characteristics such as race, gender, nationality, religion, sexual orientation, and others, is not only the right thing to do but also is an essential element of sound management. Effective nonprofits embrace diversity as a strength, recognizing that combining individuals of different backgrounds, perspectives, values, and views adds to the organization's capacity for high performance.

Volunteers are the only workforce for some organizations and constitute an important component of the workforce for many others, including those that employ paid staff. Individuals may be motivated to volunteer by altruism and concern for others, by their own needs, or by some combination of factors. In the workplace, they are usually affected by many of the same principles of motivation as paid staff. Some recommended practices for managing volunteers include assessing the need for volunteers; determining the organizational structure for the management of volunteers; developing volunteer job descriptions; developing formal volunteer policies; providing a sufficient budget and personnel to manage the volunteer program; recruiting and hiring volunteers as if they were employees; providing orientation and training; and setting clear goals, evaluating performance, and recognizing achievement.

Following these practices may be especially important if volunteers provide regular service in the organization's programs, but it may be less essential with regard to episodic volunteers who just participate occasionally. The number of virtual volunteers, who work from a distance using the Internet, is growing. Experts suggest that principles of managing such volunteers are similar to those applied to volunteers who work on site, including frequent communication and recognition of achievements. Volunteer management has become an identified subspecialty of nonprofit management, and its practitioners have access to professional associations, publications, and training to improve their skills.

The number of volunteers has increased long term but has leveled off or even declined in recent years, for reasons that may be complex. Demographic trends suggest that older people may be a primary source of regular volunteers in the future. In addition, research indicates that younger volunteers have become more selective and may not be as strongly motivated by a traditional sense of duty, requiring that volunteer assignments are rewarding and provide opportunities for growth and learning. Nonprofits that hope to attract and retain them will need to ensure that volunteer programs are well organized, well managed, and provide meaningful experiences.

KEY TERMS AND CONCEPTS

disparate impact	*expectancy theory*	*human resources management (HRM)*
dissatisfiers	*extrinsic motivational factors*	
encouraged or mandated volunteers		*hygiene factors*
	Hawthorne experiments	*intrinsic motivational factors*
episodic volunteers	*hierarchy of needs*	*life-cycle theory*

millennials	*public service motivation*	*Theory X and Theory Y*
motivation	*regular volunteers*	*three needs theory*
motivators	*satisfiers*	*virtual volunteers*
Myers–Briggs-type indicator	*scientific management*	*volunteer management*
personality style	*spot volunteers*	*voluntourism*

CASE 9.1 Getta Grant

Getta Grant is director of development at a medium-size nonprofit that provides a range of services to adolescents from disadvantaged urban communities. She reports to the executive director. The organization receives some government funding but is also reliant on foundations and individual donors. Getta's responsibilities include staying informed about foundation interests and giving patterns and working with the organization's three program directors to identify foundations that may be prospects for support of their programs and projects. She drafts letters of inquiry and, where appropriate, meets with foundation officers and writes proposals. Getta has been with the organization for five years and was hired by the previous executive director, who always gave her "excellent" (the highest rating) on her annual performance reviews. The current executive director has been in her job less than a year. She inherited Getta from her predecessor. When she had just arrived, it was already time for Getta's annual evaluation. The new executive director read a couple of proposals Getta had written, thought they were good, and continued her "excellent" rating without much further thought. Getta seemed pleased to have her high rating continued.

When Getta writes something, it is generally of high quality. But over the past year, the executive director has become unhappy with the amount of work Getta produces and with her inability to meet deadlines. Since her last review, Getta has produced only a handful of letters and two proposals. The executive director gave her positive feedback on that work, which was indeed good, thinking that would motivate her to work harder and faster. But Getta has continued to produce relatively few proposals, and in some cases, they have taken so long that she missed foundation deadlines. She is coming up soon for her second evaluation with the executive director, who is now quite frustrated with her performance.

The executive director met with Getta recently and explained that she is unhappy. She warned Getta that her next performance evaluation may not be so positive this year. Getta seemed shocked. "But you said my proposals are good," she protested, "and you gave me an 'excellent' rating last year!" Since that meeting, Getta has missed several of days of work, calling in sick or saying she was "working at home." And the executive director has seen almost no additional work.

CASE 9.2 Rita Writer

Rita Writer is a member of the communications and marketing staff at a large environmental nonprofit. She has various responsibilities, including writing press releases, articles for the quarterly magazine, copy for brochures that are produced for fundraising and other purposes, and material for the organization's website. Rita had previously worked as a marketing specialist in the alumni relations office of a local college and came with outstanding references. When she accepted her new job, she said she wanted to make the change so that she would have more opportunity to write, since her job in alumni relations also included responsibility for attending events and required considerable travel.

Rita now has been in her current job for about three months. She produces an adequate volume of writing, but it is consistently full of glaring errors. Her manager, the vice president for communications and marketing, sometimes sends the work back to Rita for revisions. But most times the vice president just edits the work himself, not wanting to confront Rita and thinking that it is faster for him to take on the task. He has not said anything to Rita, but he is becoming increasingly unhappy with her performance. He is concerned that firing her would make him unpopular among the other staff, so he is reluctant to do so. But he is wondering what he can do to increase Rita's contribution to the organization.

One of Rita's colleagues mentioned to the vice president that Rita spends a lot of time on the phone talking to people in chapter offices around the country. In addition, the organization sponsors a number of public events, including lectures on environmental issues that are followed by receptions. Although she is not required to do so, Rita attends many of them on her work time and always stays for the reception, mingling with the guests. One of her colleagues said sarcastically to the vice president, "Rita just seems to prefer socializing to doing her job."

CASE 9.3   Bob the Builder

Bob is a volunteer at an organization that provides services to older people in the community, enabling them to continue living in their own homes. Older clients are matched with volunteers, who agree to visit with them at least once a week to assist them with matters such as paying bills, performing light housework or yard work, and similar tasks. When their homes need modest upkeep or repairs, such as painting, volunteers with appropriate skills are assigned as a team to complete the job. The organization's director of volunteers recruits volunteers with needed skills, assigning them to clients and projects and ensuring quality in the work they perform.

Bob was a building contractor and has recently retired. He has been a long-time but occasional volunteer. His wife, Mary, is a member of the board of directors, and Bob and Mary have been regular contributors to the annual fundraising campaign. A few months ago, Bob approached the director of volunteers and said that he now will have more time and would like to do more work with the organization. Delighted at the offer, especially in light of his professional skills, the director assigned him to supervise several home repair project teams.

Recently, however, she became concerned when she heard from another volunteer that Bob was going way beyond the scope of the projects assigned. In one case, the project team was sent to do some painting for a homeowner, but Bob had performed some electrical wiring in the woman's house. In another case, he replaced some plumbing. The director became concerned about the risks in that type of work and the potential liability to the organization should something go wrong. In addition, she is now receiving complaints from other volunteers who have worked with Bob. One volunteer has told her that Bob treats other volunteers as if they were members of the crew of his former construction company. And he doesn't treat them well. He assigns them work and then criticizes them for not doing it fast enough or well enough. Some of the volunteers have said that they will not work with him again.

The director of volunteers met with the executive director and discussed her concerns about Bob. The executive director was somewhat dismissive, saying she thinks Bob is a great asset to the organization. "After all," she said, "He's a professional builder. We are fortunate to have someone with his skills involved." She then added, "Anyway, it's difficult to do anything about it with Mary serving on the board."

One professor immediately came to his feet, saying, "Wait a minute. Are you saying we are going to market the college like a brand of soda? We have a good reputation now and that will just tarnish it by making us look desperate." Another added,

> I agree. We attract students now because of the quality of our academic programs. If we want more and better students to apply, the money should be spent on academic resources, like the library, science labs, and computer technology. Those are the things that will attract the kind of students we want.

A third member of the faculty joined the conversation, saying,

> It concerns me that we are going for the hard sell. We don't need Madison Avenue types out representing us, exaggerating and misleading students into coming to Siwash. That wouldn't be fair to the students and could cause people to question our integrity.

While the concerns of the Siwash College faculty may not be completely unfounded, they may also reflect an incomplete understanding of *marketing*. Although marketing principles are widely applied in many nonprofit organizations, misunderstanding of the concept is still common, and some individuals have a viscerally negative reaction to the use of marketing's vocabulary in organizations that are based on values and driven by missions. In part, the comments and concerns of the Siwash College faculty may reflect the shadows of earlier approaches to marketing in the business sector that remain prominent in some people's understanding of the concept.

When marketing first came on the business scene around the beginning of the 20th century, it reflected a *product mind-set*. In other words, the prevailing view was "that to be an effective marketer, you simply had to 'build a better mousetrap,' and, in effect, customers would beat a pathway to your door" (Andreasen & Kotler, 2008, p. 37). That was essentially what Henry Ford did by inventing the Model T, and it may be the view of the Siwash faculty, who think it sufficient to improve the college's educational programs, assuming that prospective students will inevitably discover them and apply in greater numbers.

But the product mind-set became obsolete in business in about the mid-20th century. It became increasingly clear that simply making a better product would not provide assurance that customers would buy it. An increasingly competitive economic environment led to a new approach to marketing in the business world, one reflecting a *sales mind-set* (Andreasen & Kotler, 2008). The goal for a company or an organization with a sales mind-set is to *convince* customers that they should buy the company's product rather than buy nothing or buy what a competitor is offering. With the adoption of this marketing perspective by American business in the middle part of the 20th century, advertising became a major industry, and the "hard sell" became the preferred tactic of businesses trying to survive in a competitive environment. For many people, marketing is still synonymous with sales, and like some members of the Siwash faculty, they see it as something possibly inconsistent with the values and the culture of the nonprofit sector.

Both the product and sales mind-sets lead an organization to begin the marketing process *inside* its own walls, with the goal it wishes to achieve—more sales of the product or service, resulting in more revenue for the organization. When the sales mind-set is predominant, messages are pushed out through advertising and other channels of communication with the hope that they will fall on receptive ears—the goal is to "change the . . . audiences to fit what the organization [has] to offer" (Andreasen & Kotler, 2008, p. 38). Both the product and the sales mind-sets still exist and are reflected in the practices of some for-profit and nonprofit organizations today (Andreasen & Kotler, 2008), but modern marketing reflects a *target-audience mind-set*. It is outside in, not inside out. As Alan Andreasen (2006) explains, "The key to marketing is to focus on our audiences and not ourselves" (p. 12).

Following this outside-in approach requires that

the organization systematically study target audiences' needs, wants, perceptions, preferences, and satisfaction, using surveys, focus groups, and other means . . . [and that] *the organization . . . constantly act* on *this information to improve its offerings to meet its customers' needs better* [italics added]. (Andreasen & Kotler, 2008, p. 39)

Understood in this way, then, marketing seems not so contrary to nonprofit values, as the Siwash faculty may have initially believed. For nonprofits, marketing is focused on the needs of constituents or consumers; it is not about pushing something that those individuals do not want, nor does it require misrepresentation or exaggeration.

Unlike the sales model, which tries to persuade the customer that he or she wants what the organization has to offer, target-audience marketing implies that the organization develops its product to be responsive to what the *customer* needs and wants.[1] Of course, businesses do so readily. If consumers want larger cars, the automakers will produce them. If consumers shift their priorities to saving oil and preserving the environment, automakers will respond to that change by producing more fuel-efficient vehicles. If the product or service is well matched with what people really want, it will still be necessary to let potential customers know of its existence and the benefits it provides—there is still a need for advertising and communication—but there will be little need to persuade individuals or sell them on the desirability of purchasing it. The situation is, of course, more complicated if the goal of marketing requires the customer to sacrifice—for example, to quit smoking or change his or her dietary habits—but the purpose is nevertheless to improve individuals' situations, through better health or in some other aspect of life. In those instances, the sale requires communicating a *value proposition* in which members of the target audience see benefit in the exchange.

Marketing Serves the Mission

Of course, even the more up-to-date, target-market mind-set may still give some pause to the faculty of Siwash College and to others who work in nonprofit organizations. How responsive should a nonprofit be to the expressed desires of its clients or customers? Should a college's curriculum be designed to encompass only what students say they wish to know, or should it reflect what the faculty believe to be the essential elements of a sound education? If a performing arts center is not attracting symphony audiences of sufficient size, should it abandon Beethoven in favor of rock concerts? If patients express displeasure about having their blood tested, should hospitals skip that procedure in order to gain more customer satisfaction? If church attendance is declining, should the pastor yield on fundamental principles? Should a museum abandon its mission to preserve antiquities and educate museum patrons in order to provide entertainment along the lines of Disney World? Stated at the extreme, all these ideas are obviously inappropriate, indeed ridiculous. A nonprofit organization cannot abandon its mission or act in a way that is contrary to its values merely to increase sales of its product or service. To do so would be inconsistent with the essence of its nonprofit character and status. Marketing must serve the mission and not become the driver of the nonprofit organization's program.

However, nonprofits cannot ignore the reality that they operate in a competitive environment, even if they do not compete directly against each other. A homeless shelter may not compete with another for clients, but two such organizations may compete for gifts from local corporations, foundations, and individuals. Organizations that advocate a cause or social goal may compete against others that advocate opposing positions; they compete in a marketplace of ideas, attitudes, and beliefs. Even those that may advocate relatively noncontroversial ideas like wearing seat belts and avoiding addictive drugs still compete against complacency and habit, and they compete for attention amidst the distraction of all the other messages with which people are bombarded every day, what communication theory calls *noise*.

Of course, many nonprofits do offer products and services for a fee, and they may compete against each other as well as against for-profit companies and public organizations engaged in similar activities. For example, two colleges may compete for students, and two theaters may compete for audiences. Even without such direct competition, organizations face *generic competition* from alternative uses of individuals' time and money. People can only be in one place at a time. Attending the museum, especially if it charges an admission fee, competes with attending a theater performance, going to the movies, or staying home on the couch watching TV. The museum must offer something that will motivate people to spend their time, and perhaps their money, to visit the museum rather than engage in such alternative activities. Marketing is a strategy for competition, whether for resources, convictions, or customers, and thus marketing principles may prove useful for every nonprofit, regardless of its mission.

Marketing Means Action

Marketing and *communications* are terms often combined in the titles of individuals or offices—for example, the Director of Communications and Marketing or the Office of Marketing and Communications. The concepts are related but also distinguishable.

Communication, in the simplest of definitions, is the transmission or exchange of information. As a discipline, *communications* is more complex, encompassing an understanding of the principles by which information is transmitted and received—that is, "how messages are encoded, transmitted, screened, decoded, stored, retrieved, and acted on" (Gainer & Moyer, 2005, p. 303), as well as the various technologies employed, for example, print and electronic media. We will discuss more about communications theory later in this chapter. *Strategic communications*, as the term implies, is undertaken in the context of a master plan and in pursuit of specific organizational goals ("What is strategic communications?", 2011). But communications is not synonymous with marketing; it may be undertaken with multiple goals.

Marketing also is different from *public relations*. The Public Relations Society of America (PRSA), the professional association of individuals working in the field, defines public relations as "a strategic communication process that builds mutually beneficial relationships between organizations and their publics" (Public Relations Society of America, n.d.). Every organization has *internal publics*, including, for example, employees, volunteers, suppliers, customers, and neighbors, and *external publics*, including news media, educators, government officials, and others. One important component of public relations involves relationships with news media. As John Burnett (2007, p. 228) observes, communication channeled through news media places a third party between the organization and the intended recipients of the communication, sometimes complicating the task of evaluating the impact of the public relations program. The same complication arises with social media, in which the communications may be filtered by various individuals over whom the public relations professional has no control.

As Burnett (2007) notes, "the ultimate objective of [public relations] is to retain, as well as create, goodwill" (p. 226). It thus "deals with [an] intangible—creating a positive image of the organization" (p. 224). In other words, public relations is primarily concerned with advancing and protecting the reputation of the organization. It may help to establish the environment in which marketing occurs, but it is not the same function.

Marketing is a process that uses communication, but with a very specific purpose: to influence the behavior of someone else. Marketing focuses on exchanges. For example, you buy a ticket and hear the symphony in exchange for your payment. Or you change your behavior, say by eating fewer sweets, and realize the benefit of greater fitness in return. An exchange does not occur until the individual—a member of the target audience—takes *action*. As Andreasen and Philip Kotler (2008) explain,

Marketing's objectives are not *ultimately* [italics original] either to educate or to change values or attitudes. It may seek to do so as a *means* [italics original] of influencing behavior . . . If someone has a final goal of imparting information or knowledge, that person is in the education profession, not marketing. Further, if someone has a final goal of changing attitudes or values, that person may be described as a propagandist or lobbyist, or perhaps an artist, but not a marketer. While marketing may use the tools of the educator or the propagandist, its critical distinguishing feature is that its ultimate goal is to influence behavior (either changing it or keeping it the same in the face of other pressures). (p. 36)

Marketing as a Process

As Figure 10.1 depicts, marketing is a process. Consistent with our discussion above, it begins with defining the *target audience* and gaining understanding of its members' values, needs, and wants; it acknowledges the environment, including the presence of direct and generic competition; it focuses on defining an exchange, honing and delivering the message (communication); and it ends with action by members of the target audience. Communication (i.e., honing and delivering the message) is a part of the marketing process but does not encompass it or substitute for it. Moreover, the ultimate goal is not persuasion in and of itself, but rather *action* by members of the target audience. Evaluation of a marketing program thus must be based on measuring what actions have been taken. As Andreasen (2006) emphasizes, that requires thinking "beyond our far-off mission (like helping people overcome poverty, increasing consumer access to affordable health care, or strengthening schools) and zero[ing] in on specific audience actions that are tangible, achievable, and measureable" (p. 14).

The Marketing Mix

Marketing implies an interaction between the customer and the organization. As discussed earlier, it begins with research to identify the needs and wants of potential customers or clients, which informs the development of the products or services to be offered. A simple description of the marketing process that is often stated says, "Find a need and fill it." That implies a malleable marketer, one who will create almost any product or service for which there is a demand. This simple understanding of course may raise difficult issues for nonprofit organizations that are driven by the missions and values that are at the heart of their existence.

However, any organization hoping to exchange its services for payment cannot be oblivious to the desires of its potential consumers. A college with great programs but no students eventually will close, and one that does not introduce new programs to address emerging new fields and industries will not keep pace with others that are more innovative. It is necessary and appropriate that nonprofits sometimes push back against the market to preserve their core values in pursuit of their missions, but tailoring the product to address the target market is also essential to survival. Fortunately, there is a middle choice between rigidity and complete capitulation to the market: A nonprofit can change its *marketing mix* in response to information about what customers, clients, or donors need and want, while remaining faithful to its core purposes. By doing so, it can *differentiate* its product from that offered by others, *position* itself in a unique *market niche,* and gain a *competitive advantage* over others.

To illustrate the ideas of the marketing mix, differentiation, and market niche, let's start with a familiar example from the for-profit world—Starbucks. The campus on which this author works is in an urban setting; there are many places to buy coffee, including the student union, street vendors, and other restaurants and delis in the neighborhood. For many years, there was a large study room located in the front of the university library that was accessible through a door directly from the street—24 hours a day. It was rarely used at any time of the day or night. Then the university decided to lease the space to Starbucks, which converted it to one of its ubiquitous coffee stores. The Starbucks is always busy; indeed, students, faculty, and staff sometimes stand in lines extending out the door to pay a higher price for Starbucks coffee than they would need to pay for coffee at other nearby locations. And, in the space formerly occupied by an underused study room, students now spend time studying—at Starbucks! How has Starbucks differentiated itself from the other coffee sellers in the neighborhood? What is it that people receive in exchange for their money when they patronize Starbucks, and how is that different from what others are offering? Obviously, it's the coffee, which is pretty good, but it's also the atmosphere of the store, the convenience of its location, the comfortable chairs and laid-back atmosphere—the fact that Starbucks lets you stay for a long time and offers wireless Internet access for those who wish to use their laptops or tablets. It's also the familiarity and instant recognition of the Starbucks logo, which lets you know exactly what to expect inside, and something that's indescribably just cool about buying coffee with complex-sounding names in sizes other than "small, medium, and large." In other words, there are more variables involved than just the core product, or service, that is being sold by any business. The four key variables—*product, place, promotion,* and *price*—are called the *Four P*s of marketing. Various combinations of these variables are called the marketing mix.

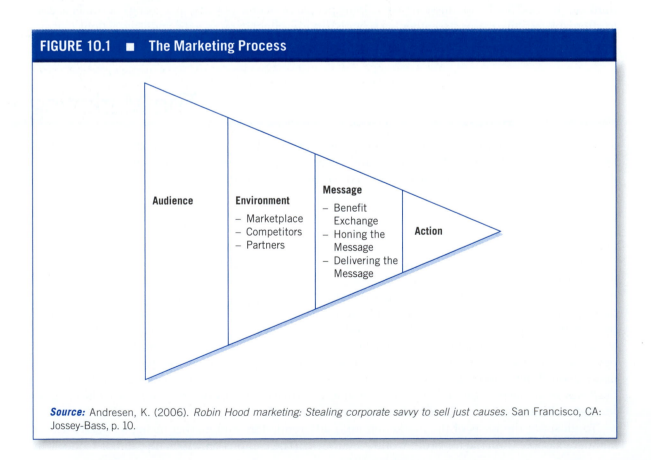

FIGURE 10.1 ■ The Marketing Process

Audience

Environment
– Marketplace
– Competitors
– Partners

Message
– Benefit Exchange
– Honing the Message
– Delivering the Message

Action

Source: Andresen, K. (2006). *Robin Hood marketing: Stealing corporate savvy to sell just causes.* San Francisco, CA: Jossey-Bass, p. 10.

Product

The product, generally the good or service being offered, seems like the simplest variable to understand. In the nonprofit sector, it's education, health care, counseling, tutoring, food, or whatever programs the organization may operate. Products have both tangible and intangible qualities, like the consumption of Starbucks coffee. Education offers a clear example. There is little basis on which to conclude that an Ivy League education is always superior to that offered at other colleges and universities across the country, and indeed, other institutions may be stronger than any of the Ivy League schools in some fields. Why would a student be willing to pay more at an Ivy League university than perhaps at a local college or state university that may provide an equally good education? Because the prestige of holding an Ivy League degree is itself an intangible quality of the product. An Ivy League degree may instantly convey intellectual distinction because those universities are known to be selective in admissions. Membership in the alumni association of such a university may bring influential contacts and open important doors throughout life. Furthermore, it happens that most Ivy League campuses are also attractive ones that provide an intellectually stimulating environment outside as well as inside the classroom. In other words, the product is not just the education itself; it's also the experiences and intangible benefits that may go along with it.

Intangibles may also be a part of the product in health care. For example, a hospital that provides a pleasant, modern environment may be preferred to one with a rundown facility that nevertheless provides excellent medical treatment. If the doctors and the nurses are nice and take the time to explain medical conditions to their patients, they are offering a different product from another hospital that follows exactly the same medical protocols but in which the staff are more distant or abrupt. A nonprofit that provides services to homeless individuals without significant barriers—that is, helps anyone without preconditions to receiving service—is offering a different product than one that is more difficult to access, although both may offer food, counseling, and housing of basically the same quality.

Think back on the meeting of the Siwash College faculty earlier in this chapter. Their concern that the academic program be centered on educational values and not be shaped entirely to suit the expressed desires of high school students is understandable. But the college's product is not just its curriculum. The product also includes the quality of its facilities, the teaching skill of its professors, the closeness of relationships that professors form with their students, the quality of student activities offered, and many other aspects of the student experience that go beyond the classroom. These are qualities of the product that can be enhanced in response to student wants and needs without compromising the college's commitment to its educational mission or values.

Place

The location at which the product or service is available is an important variable in the marketing mix. A program operated in a location that is convenient for clients is a different product from the same program offered in a remote place beyond easy reach. A college located in a small rural town offers a different experience from one located in the suburbs of a big city, although it may offer an identical curriculum. A concert hall located on a bus line offers something different from one located in the distant suburbs accessible only by car. Some programs need to be taken to where the clients are. For example, many colleges offer off-campus courses for working adults and online courses for those who cannot (or prefer not to) attend classes on a campus, symphony orchestras located in cities periodically bring their concerts to smaller towns in their regions, major museums place exhibits on tour across the country, and hospitals send vans offering mammograms into neighborhoods in which many women do not have easy access to health care. The decision about place involves consideration of both the physical and the virtual worlds. An attractive and interactive website and a presence on Facebook and Twitter may be as much a part of the overall product as services provided in a physical location.

Promotion

In the minds of some, marketing may be virtually synonymous with *promotion,* which is the visible activity that everybody can see—the announcements, advertisements, brochures, and other efforts undertaken to gain visibility and notice for the organization's products. Marketing is not synonymous with promotion, but promotion is part of the marketing mix. Clients and customers cannot partake in products or services if they do not know of their existence or what they comprise. But to whom should the nonprofit's programs and services be promoted? A simple answer might be "to the public," but that would require a foolishly expensive effort, since most of the public is likely to have no interest in or need for the organization's offerings. The need to keep promotion cost-effective requires focusing communication on segments of the public most likely to respond—that is, on the target market. This *segmentation* is based on research and may employ sophisticated tools developed in the business sector and increasingly adopted by many nonprofits as well.

Market Segmentation

For an organization's promotion to be cost effective, it needs to identify its *target market* or *target audience.* As Figure 10.1 suggests, this is the initial step in thinking about a marketing program. The target market is a subset of the larger general population. Some of this may seem intuitive. For example, a college likely will focus its promotion of undergraduate programs on high school students and their parents. A symphony orchestra might limit its mailing of concert announcements to people who live in higher income areas, who can afford the cost of the tickets. A medical clinic that provides screenings for HIV might target its communication to neighborhoods with low-income or younger single people rather than areas with primarily families and older residents. But variables used for segmentation are often more sophisticated than these somewhat obvious examples suggest.

Objective measures include *demographic variables,* for example, age, gender, race or ethnicity, income, and *geography,* that is, where people may live, work, or travel. The examples described previously reflect simple segmentation along these lines. Markets also may be segmented according to *behavioral measures*—in other words, patterns of past behavior that divide people into identifiable groups. For example, people who have never attended the theater constitute a segment different from those who attend occasionally, which is, in turn, different from the group of people who are season ticket holders. A theater would design its strategy to communicate with these different segments of its market in different ways, perhaps offering varied prices or emphasizing unique aspects of the theatergoing experience to each.

Some of the most sophisticated methods of segmentation involve *psychographics.* Psychographic measures combine demographic data with knowledge about individuals' *lifestyles,* defined by their activities, interests, and opinions (AIOs) (Andreasen & Kotler, 2008; Sargeant, 2005). Market researchers group individuals according to various lifestyles that are associated with certain behaviors, attitudes, or likes and dislikes. For example, we might assume that a young single person who lives with roommates, rides a motorcycle, and holds politically radical views may have different tastes in music than a couple with two young children and an SUV who live in the suburbs and have liberal views or a retired couple with a politically conservative orientation who live in a condo and travel only by public transportation. Individuals' lifestyles often predict not only the type of music they prefer but also the political and social causes they may favor, the kinds of artistic events they may attend, and the types of nonprofits they may support. Their patterns of behavior can help identify them as part of the target market for a particular product or service.

For example, in one study undertaken in selected cities, Andreasen and Russell Belk were able to identify six lifestyle groups, which they labeled *Passive Homebodies, Active Sports Enthusiasts, Inner-Directed Self-Sufficients, Active Homebodies, Culture Patrons,* and *Social Actives.* People in the Culture Patron lifestyle were more likely than others to attend the theater or the symphony, while those in the Social Active lifestyle were more likely to attend only the symphony (Andreasen & Kotler, 2008, p. 148).

That kind of insight would be useful to a performing arts center in selecting those segments to which it would promote specific performances, ensuring that marketing dollars were used most efficiently. In other words, segmentation enables the nonprofit to target its promotion like a rifle shot, rather than scattering it like buckshot at greater total expense and with the result that much of it is wasted on those who are unlikely to attend its programs or feel a need to use its services.

The smallest conceivable market segment is, of course, the individual, and the most sophisticated for-profit marketers have become adept at targeting their messages to one person at a time. Think, for example, about experience you may have had with Amazon.com. Amazon remembers what you purchased before and suggests new titles and other products that may be in line with your demonstrated interests—it segments based on your past behavior. Knowing your interests in reading and in music, it lets you know what products are being purchased by other people who are reading the same books or listening to the same music as you; this reflects the company's assumptions about your lifestyle. Facebook knows what you like and what your friends like. Your interests and preferences are also revealed through your use of Google searches and the websites that you visit, which may be tracked by cookies placed on your computer's hard drive. Online advertising then is targeted to match the profile you have provided of yourself through your past behavior, defining the characteristics of a very precise market segment that includes just you! Among nonprofits, segmentation at this level is increasingly applied in Internet fundraising.

Our discussion above has focused on identifying market segments for the commercial marketing of nonprofits' programs and services. Of course, in the case of social marketing, segmentation is equally important. Target audiences will include those who engage in behaviors that the marketing is intended to change, but there is still a need for differentiation. For example, if the goal is to prevent texting while driving, different strategies may be required to address adolescents, parents, businesspeople, and other segments.

Price

The *price* of a product or service is a straightforward concept for most people. It's what we pay to obtain what we want in the marketplace. Let's first consider how nonprofits that charge fees for their services might go about establishing those prices and then return to the idea of marketing as an exchange—an approach to thinking about price that may be a better fit than our usual understanding of the term for nonprofits engaged in social marketing.

Pricing can be an especially sensitive issue for nonprofit organizations. Some provide their services to clients without charge; others have missions suggesting that prices should be kept as low as possible to encourage participation.

There are essentially four methods for establishing the price at which a product or service will be offered. One approach is *cost-oriented pricing,* in which the price charged to the customer or client is set to cover what it costs the organization to produce or provide it. A popular method is to set prices to produce a break-even situation for the organization overall. This method may seem the most appropriate for a nonprofit organization, which does not have the purpose of maximizing its profits. But it is important to ensure that the price reflects the direct costs of providing the service as well as the overhead needed to run the organization. Indeed, as we discussed in Chapter 7, earned income, including fees for service, may be a principal source of funds for capacity building, and a price set to break even might need to encompass the costs of such efforts.

Cost-oriented pricing is popular in the nonprofit sector for a variety of reasons. First, it is simple. Second, since costs are likely to be similar for different organizations, this method often will mean that different organizations charge about the same, eliminating competition based on price and perhaps reorienting competition to the quality of programs. Third, some people see it as socially fair: "Sellers do not take advantage of buyers when the demand becomes acute, yet sellers earn a fair return on their investment" (Andreasen & Kotler, 2008, p. 244).

Another way to establish prices is by using *competition-oriented pricing*. The nonprofit might look at its competitors, perhaps in order to charge a bit less or provide a somewhat better product than others are offering at the same price. As discussed before, even if a nonprofit does not compete directly with another, it must take generic competition into account in establishing its prices. For example, a theater needs to consider how its ticket price compares not only with that of other theaters, but also with the cost of going to the movies instead. The price and the product interact. What does the theater experience offer to justify spending the price of a ticket rather than just staying home and watching TV? Does the product need to be more than just a play? For example, can a higher ticket price be justified and obtained if the experience includes a backstage reception attended by the cast of the play?

A third way of establishing prices is *value-based pricing* (Andreasen & Kotler, 2008). This approach takes into consideration the perceived value of the product or service to the customer, which may not be closely related to the costs of production. Indeed, some consumers may equate higher price with quality, for example, in buying wine or automobiles. A $30 bottle of wine may not be demonstrably better than a $10 bottle of wine, and it likely did not require three times as many grapes to make it. But buyers who are not wine experts might prefer to pay more, believing that the price will equate to quality—or at least that their dinner guests will believe so. Is a Lexus a much better car than a Civic? Possibly it is, although both will go about the same speed and arrive at a destination with equal dependability. But there is some psychological value to the buyer in owning a car that comes with more prestige, based at least in part on its higher price. A controversial example of value-based pricing involves the tuition policies of many colleges and universities. Critics have charged that some higher education institutions have intentionally increased their tuitions to create the image that they are elite, since that will be attractive to some students and their families.

Price Discrimination

Price discrimination sounds like something unethical, immoral, or even illegal, but it is an essential element of marketing strategy. It does not mean charging people different prices based on their race or ethnicity, sex, religion, or other personal characteristics. Rather, it means charging people different prices based on the market segment to which they belong, determined by objective variables.

Nonprofits may undertake price discrimination to cover the actual higher costs of serving a particular segment. For example, a college may charge more for on-campus courses than those offered off-campus, to cover the additional costs of providing library support and other services to students who come onto the campus. Price discrimination may also be used as a way to match the price to the perceived value of the experience. For example, concert halls charge more for seats close to the stage than for seats in the balcony, although the music may sound much the same from either location. A third reason to charge different prices might be to shift utilization. Theaters often charge less for matinees than for evening performances as a way to fill the hall at a time when it might otherwise be empty. Price discrimination also can help maximize a nonprofit's revenues by pricing the most desirable products or services at a high point that some may be willing and able to pay. An interesting example of that is provided by the Bolshoi Theater in Moscow.

One of the world's most renowned ballet companies, the Bolshoi was heavily subsidized by the government of the former USSR. But with the fall of communism, it faced two challenges. One was to pay its artists at competitive rates, since they were now free to perform elsewhere in the world for potentially higher compensation. The other challenge was to replace reduced government support with other sources of revenue.

Under the communist system, the Bolshoi's best seats always had been reserved for artists, high-ranking government officials, and other VIPs, but, in fact, they often had not been used by those people. Instead, the tickets were sold to scalpers, who became known as "pillar people" because they often waited for possible customers while lurking behind the pillars in the lobby. Because the seats for which they had tickets were desirable, the scalpers could sell them for a profit and had done so for many years. Facing a new need to generate revenue on the introduction of a market economy, and freed from the constraints of the previous system, the Bolshoi revised its pricing policies to capture the higher value of those better seats for itself and put the pillar people out of business. It introduced price discrimination, charging varied prices for seats depending on their perceived desirability. The result was an increase in its ticket revenue of 82 percent in the first month. At the same time, it lowered the prices for less desirable seats, making them more accessible for students and others without wealth (Klintsov & von Löhneysen, 2001, p. 6).

Defining the Exchange

In the examples mentioned above, the concept of price is what most of us would understand from the term; it's what a client or customer pays to receive a good or a service. Theaters charge for admission, colleges charge tuition, and hospitals charge for medical procedures, although some may be provided free for those who cannot pay. But what about nonprofits engaged in social marketing, with the goal of bringing about changed behavior believed to be of benefit to individuals who are part of the target market? How can we understand the concept of price in these situations?

Setting a price is defining a *benefit exchange* (Andresen, 2006, p. 131). In a commercial transaction, you give something up (money) in exchange for a reward that you receive, whether an education, a concert, or medical care. Social marketing similarly requires that an individual pay some price in the form of changed behavior—for example, by stopping smoking, eating healthier foods, or using seat belts. That change will only occur if the marketer can offer a reward that equals or exceeds the perceived sacrifice involved in making the change.

As Katya Andresen (2006) explains, the most effective rewards are those that are immediate, personal, reflective of audience values, better than competing rewards, and credible. And positive rewards are more effective than threats (p. 131). "The Truth" antismoking campaign offers a good example of an effective strategy. For some teenagers, smoking is rewarding because it is a form of rebellion and coolness. An appeal to quit in order to avoid getting cancer years later may not be effective, because the reward of changed behavior is not sufficiently immediate. An appeal to quit because smoking annoys their parents may not be competitive with the reward of continuing to smoke because pleasing their parents is not as highly valued as rebellion. "The Truth" campaign took a different approach. It engaged teen spokespeople to encourage their peers to picket tobacco companies' headquarters, crank-call the companies, and speak out about their manipulation by the tobacco industry. This approach offered the reward of rebellion and was, of course, inconsistent with continuing to be a smoker (Andresen, p. 143). In other words, the price paid in giving up (or avoiding) one behavior was justified by a reward that *exceeded* the reward of the alternative. The reward was offered based on what was known about the inherent motivations of the target market.

Building the Brand

Remember that competition requires an organization, nonprofit or for-profit, to differentiate its products or services from those of others. One strategy for doing so is building a recognizable *brand* and a positive image for that brand. When we think about a brand, what most readily comes to mind are commercial products, such as soda, cars, or clothing, and names like Coke or Pepsi, Honda or Toyota, Gap or Benetton. But nonprofits have brands as well.

Burnett (2007) and other authors define *brand* in a narrow sense as "a name, term, sign, symbol, design, or a combination of these that is intended to identify the goods and services of one seller or group of sellers and differentiate them from those of competitors" (p. 179). Thus, some brands may be names, some may be brand marks (or logos), and others may be trademarks—brand marks that have legal protection (p. 179). Many brands are instantly recognizable, for example, the Nike swoosh and Apple's apple. They do not even require a word for people to identify them with the companies and their products. Some nonprofit logos are equally well-known worldwide—for example, the Red Cross's red cross and WWF's (formerly the World Wildlife Fund's) panda. But some authors offer a more encompassing definition of brand. For example, according to Nathalie Kylander and Christopher Stone (2012), "A brand is more than a visual identity: the name, logo, and graphic design used by an organization. A brand is a psychological construct held in the minds of all those aware of the branded product, person, organization, or movement."

In other words, a name or logo is shorthand for a collection of perceived qualities of the organization or its products, known as *brand attributes*. A brand may evoke feelings, attitudes, memories, and other intangibles that we associate with the name or symbol. *Coke* may bring to mind a refreshing break on a summer day. *Disney* may evoke memories of a childhood trip with one's family. And, depending on one's age, either *Chevy* or *Honda* may evoke a sense of confidence, quality, and durability. *Greenpeace* or *Doctors Without Borders* likely stimulate very different images—and feelings—from *Harvard* or *MoMA* (the Museum of Modern Art in New York City).

An individual's reaction to a brand may, of course, be quite different from that of others, depending upon his or her own values and perception of the values of the organization. A brand is a promise, and the term *brand promise* describes the expectations that you have about what you will receive when you buy a specific product or service. For example, as discussed previously, when you walk into Starbucks, you expect the coffee to be good and the atmosphere to be comfortable and welcoming; those are experiences that Starbucks has promised you by placing its logo over the door (Sargeant, 2005). When you make a gift to Doctors Without Borders, you expect it to be used effectively because such responsible behavior is an attribute of the organization's brand.

Establishing a strong and positive image for a brand brings many benefits to an organization. Examples are provided by responses to natural disasters, for example Hurricane Katrina in 2005, the Haitian earthquake in 2010, Hurricane Sandy in 2012, and the 2015 earthquake in Nepal. Horrified by the scenes unfolding on their television screens, many Americans went to their computers or used text messaging to make a gift to help those displaced by the disaster. They were most likely to go to organizations with known brands—the Red Cross, the Salvation Army, and Habitat for Humanity—both because their brands were familiar and because donors attributed to them the qualities of competence and trust. Of course, a brand image can be fragile, and if an organization fails to deliver on the implied promise of its brand, the negative effect on its support can be both immediate and long lasting. The brand *Toyota*, once synonymous with quality for many car buyers, was damaged when persistent safety problems with its cars were revealed in 2010, especially since the news stories implied that the company may not have taken sufficient action when it first learned of the risks. When, in 2002, the CEO of the United Way of the National Capital Area, serving the Washington, DC, region, was forced to resign amid allegations of his misuse of donor funds, ripples battered the United Way brand across the country. The national office and local United Ways in other cities rushed to reassure their donors that the problems were limited to the National Capital chapter and to institute additional controls and safeguards so as to reestablish the credibility of the United Way brand. The CEO of United Way of America, the national umbrella organization at that time, expressed the problem in this way:

> To a United Way—to a nonprofit—trust is everything. [The National Capital Chapter] need[s] to do everything that has to be done to address the issues, create aggressive long-term resolutions to them, do it transparently, do it quickly—and that's the way you build trust back. (Lipman & Williams, 2002, p. 30)

A positive brand image has value—monetary value, called *brand equity*. For example, if another company were to buy Nike, a part of the purchase price would reflect the value of the swoosh logo, which the buyer would expect to continue, stimulating sales and thereby increasing future revenue. When, in the 1990s, Nike was criticized for allegedly employing people in sweatshop conditions, the value of the brand, and thus the company, was at least temporarily suppressed. In 2012, Apple also responded quickly when working conditions at Chinese factories making Apple products were questioned, eager to prevent the controversy from tarnishing the company's brand. A company that finds its brand degraded can be expected to undertake aggressive action, not necessarily to change its products or services but to resuscitate the value of its brand. Although nonprofit organizations are not bought or sold like corporations, their brands also have value. Its brand value is among the assets that a nonprofit brings to the table when it negotiates a partnership with a for-profit company, which will be discussed further in Chapter 12.

How does an organization build its brand? In her book *Brandraising*, Sarah Durham (2010) provides a model, depicted in Figure 10.2, which is in some aspects reminiscent of McKinsey's capacity-building model that we saw in Chapter 7.

The process begins at the top of the pyramid, at the *organizational level*, with decisions about fundamental purposes of the organization, including its vision, mission, values, and goals—concepts that will be familiar to students from our earlier discussion on strategic planning. Next, the organization must identify its audiences, which Dunham places in three categories: fundraising audiences (i.e., donors and prospects); program audiences (i.e., clients, patrons, members); and advocacy audiences (i.e., community leaders, media, policymakers, and other influential people). As discussed above, the organization must decide how it will be positioned in order to differentiate itself from others—in other words, as Durham explains, it must determine "the single idea [it] hopes[s] to own in the minds of [its] target audience" (p. 59). An organization's *personality* is defined by the attributes it hopes will become attached to its brand. Only after these steps have been addressed does the brandraising process move down to the next level of the pyramid, the *identity level*.

The identity level involves the organization's *visual identity*—the logo, color palette, typography, imagery, and use of graphics (Durham, 2010, p. 73). In addition, it encompasses the *message platform*, also called the *written brand*. The message platform includes such elements as the organization's name;

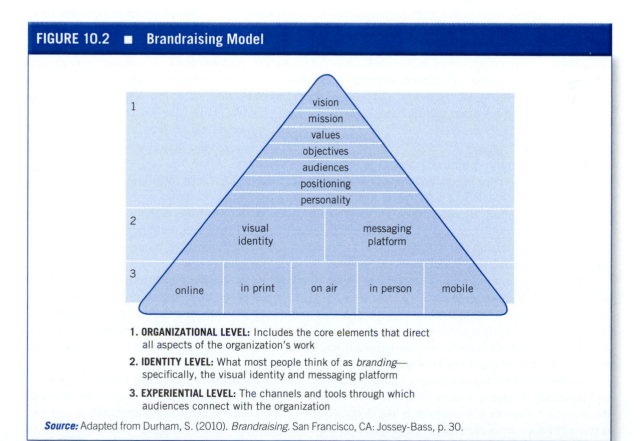

FIGURE 10.2 ■ Brandraising Model

1. **ORGANIZATIONAL LEVEL:** Includes the core elements that direct all aspects of the organization's work

2. **IDENTITY LEVEL:** What most people think of as *branding*—specifically, the visual identity and messaging platform

3. **EXPERIENTIAL LEVEL:** The channels and tools through which audiences connect with the organization

Source: Adapted from Durham, S. (2010). *Brandraising.* San Francisco, CA: Jossey-Bass, p. 30.

taglines; mission, vision, and values statements written for external presentation; key messages (ideas that the organization will weave throughout its statements in order to establish its position in the minds of its audiences); boilerplate copy (an "about us", of sorts) that will be used in various publications and media; an elevator pitch (brief statement of the organization's positioning); and a recommended lexicon (p. 89). Embedding the lexicon in the culture of the organization can help to communicate values. For example, referring to "children experiencing poverty" may be less degrading than "children at risk."

Finally, in Durham's model, the brandraising process moves to the *experiential level*, where audiences are matched with communications media and a communications strategy is developed.

Integrated Marketing Communication (IMC)

Building a positive and consistent brand image requires that an organization integrate its marketing and communication efforts—in other words, that it ensures "that all the communications [it] generates represent a coherent whole" (Sargeant, 2005, p. 140). This is known as *integrated marketing communication,* or IMC.

An integrated approach requires that the messages and the values that they reflect permeate every aspect of the organization's work. If, for example, the organization desires to create an image of itself as "caring," its logo may include fuzzy small animals. However, its staff also must treat clients in a caring manner, answer the phone in a responsive tone, and create an internal culture consistent with the external image the organization seeks to build. As Adrian Sargeant (2005) expresses it, the organization needs to "live the brand" in everything it does (p. 140). The brand and its image are unlikely to settle too far from the reality of what the organization actually does or what it really is.

In an integrated approach, communications with various constituencies and stakeholders, both internally and externally, must be coordinated and consistent. As illustrated in Figure 10.3, internal audiences may include staff, board members, volunteers, and perhaps regional chapters or offices of a national or international organization. External audiences may include clients or customers; partners (such as sponsors, donors, and other organizations that are collaborators); other nonprofits (both competitors and otherwise); and various publics, such as government, the media, and professional or industry associations of which the nonprofit may be a member. There is also a need to achieve integration—that is, consistent messages—across communication channels. That includes printed materials, online presence, and personal (one-on-one) communication.

The need for integration is perhaps greater in a nonprofit organization than in any other type. This reality is rooted in the essential nature of nonprofits. As mentioned before, the constituencies of a nonprofit are often overlapping and interlaced. Remember the idea of open systems from back in Chapter 3? Staff members talk to clients and to volunteers, who may also be donors, who may communicate the staff's attitudes to their family, friends, and neighbors in the broader community. Although the organization may have high-quality publications and may skillfully manage its communications with the news media, these are unlikely to outweigh the word-of-mouth information and impressions communicated by those who have firsthand knowledge about the organization.

The *source* of information is a critical variable in its credibility. People are more inclined to believe what they hear from other individuals than what they read in the newspaper or hear on television. This is especially the case if the individual who provides the information is someone close to them, whom they trust, or close to the organization and thus presumed to know the real truth. This is one of the reasons why members of nonprofit boards, who are generally respected citizens in their communities, are so important as advocates for the organization's goals.

The sources of information people find to be most credible are family members, closely followed by friends and associates. This may include verbal communication or postings that known people may make on social media such as Facebook. Professionals like clergy, doctors, and counselors rank right after friends as credible sources of information. Newspapers, direct mail, and the Internet come next. Although positive publicity from a mass media source is often highly prized by organizations that wish to improve their image, the mass media,

FIGURE 10.3 ■ Integrated Marketing Communication

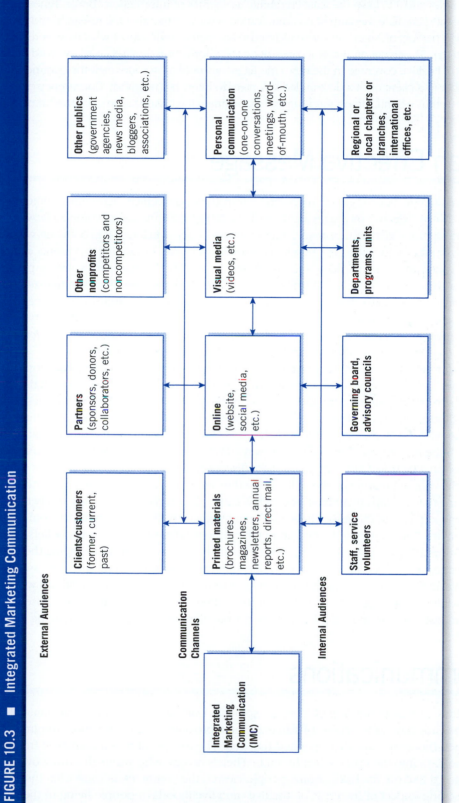

External Audiences

Clients/customers (former, current, past)

Partners (sponsors, donors, collaborators, etc.)

Other nonprofits (competitors and noncompetitors)

Other publics (government agencies, news media, bloggers, associations, etc.)

Communication Channels

Printed materials (brochures, magazines, newsletters, annual reports, direct mail, etc.)

Online (website, social media, etc.)

Visual media (videos, etc.)

Personal communication (one-on-one conversations, meetings, word-of-mouth, etc.)

Internal Audiences

Staff, service volunteers

Governing board, advisory councils

Departments, programs, units

Regional or local chapters or branches, international offices, etc.

Integrated Marketing Communication (IMC)

including radio and TV, have the least credibility as sources of information (Bonk, Tynes, Griggs, & Sparks, 2008). The most credible medium of communication is word of mouth. One research study, reported in 2006, found that 53 percent of Americans were inclined to accept the credibility of what they were told by friends and family and that 51 percent are likely to pass along the information they received by word of mouth to others (Hall, 2006). Positive coverage in the news media is thus unlikely to outweigh the comments of an unhappy staff member to a client or of a disgruntled volunteer to his or her neighbor. Consistency of message—and of behavior—is thus essential to establishing and maintaining the organization's positive brand image.

Crafting an Effective Message

What makes an effective message? Andresen (2006) offers a convenient acronym to remember the essential elements: CRAM. Effective messages are those that establish a Connection, promise a Reward, inspire Action, and stick in Memory (p. 163). Communicating a message requires tailoring it to both one-way communication and two-way communication, and brevity is essential. A slogan or tag line represents a shorthand for the message in one-way communication, such as advertising (p. 172). For example, "Share the power of a wish" is a clear call to action from the Make-a-Wish Foundation. The Nature Conservancy summarizes its mission and its programs in just four words: "Protecting nature. Preserving life" (www.nature.org). The central message also needs to be communicated in conversation—in two-way communication, and brevity is again essential. The story must be capable of summary in the course of an elevator ride, called an *elevator pitch*. Clarity, brevity, and consistency are the essential elements of effective communication.

It is important to bear in mind a reality that has been established in communications theory: The way a message is received has as much to do with the predilections of the receiver as with the intentions of the sender. The receiver will interpret the message in the context of his or her own values, culture, and pre-formed attitudes about the organization. And established views may be difficult to change. For example, if a woman who has been a loyal donor to the local Humane Society hears rumors that animals are being mistreated, she may respond in one of four ways: (1) She may practice denial—persuade herself that the rumors just can't be true; (2) she may search for disconfirmation of the rumors, perhaps calling the director of the shelter hoping that he or she will tell her they are not correct; (3) she may minimize the problem, rationalizing that perhaps there have been a few cases of mistreatment, but that surely they are not part of a consistent pattern and the stories have just been exaggerated by people who, for some reason, have it in for the Humane Society; or (4) she may accept the rumors as true and change her beliefs, discontinuing her financial support (Andreasen & Kotler, 2008). Human beings tend to resist changing their beliefs, whether positive or negative; thus, a minimum goal of communication is to communicate messages that reinforce the positive attitudes that your friends may hold, positively affect those of individuals who have been previously indifferent, and do nothing to further strengthen the negative attitudes of those who may already hold them. Just as for an individual, a tarnished reputation for an organization may be difficult to repair.

Crisis Communications

In 2010, BP's oil well in the Gulf of Mexico exploded, leading to the worst environmental disaster in history. In the early days of the crisis, BPs' management provided little information, minimized the problem, and blamed the contractor that operated the well. The low point was a comment from the company's CEO some days into the crisis, when he said, "There's no one who wants this thing over more than I do. You know, I'd like my life back." Some people viewed the comment as somewhat insensitive in light of the devastating impact of the crisis on the lives and livelihoods of people living in the Gulf region. BP's response was called "a textbook example of how not to do crisis management" (Shogren, 2011). The crisis also affected The Nature Conservancy (TNC), which was criticized for the financial support it had received from BP. TNC responded by posting a blog on its website, explaining its relationship with BP. The blog elicited many comments, to which TNC staff responded. The Conservancy's CEO and director of external affairs also participated in an online discussion, responding to questions from many critics (Wallace, 2010b). The incident demonstrated alternative approaches to communicating with an organization's various publics in the face of a crisis or controversy.

A *crisis* is "a significant threat to operations that can have negative consequences if not properly handled" (Coombs, 2011). The crisis may involve public safety, financial loss, or a loss of reputation (Coombs, 2011). As mentioned previously in our discussion of brands, for a nonprofit organization, a loss of reputation or trust can be especially devastating.

There is, of course, a distinction between crisis management and *crisis communications*, with the former encompassing all actions taken to address the situation and the latter, as the term implies, related to how the organization communicates information about the situation to its various constituents. Nonprofits should maintain a *risk management plan*, to minimize the potential for a crisis occurring in the first place and to define the process for responding to such an event if and when it occurs. Depending on the nature of the crisis, the overall response likely will involve various individuals and departments, including, for example, public relations, legal, security, finance, human resources, and others (Coombs, 2011). Our focus in this chapter is on the communications response, that is, crisis communications.

The literature on crisis management and crisis communications is extensive. Much of it consists of principles or rules prescribed by public relations practitioners based on cases, but theories also have been developed. One of the best-known theories is W. Timothy Coombs's (2007) Situational Crisis Communication Theory (SCCT). Coombs's theory states that how much of a threat a crisis may present to an organization's reputation depends on three variables: the extent to which it is responsible for the crisis, rather than a victim itself; its crisis history; and its reputation prior to the crisis (Sisco, 2012). Managers can identify the appropriate strategies for responding to a crisis by considering these three variables. Research studies testing this theory and others have involved corporations, but some suggest that similar principles of crisis communications can be applied in nonprofit organizations (Sisco, 2012).

Organizations facing a crisis are advised to respond quickly, accurately, and consistently (Coombs, 2011). Failure to speak out quickly may leave an information vacuum, which the news media or others (for example, bloggers) may try to fill, possibly with information that is not accurate. In addition, by responding quickly, even if it does not have much information to provide, the organization positions itself as a resource and thus takes control of the story, rather than permitting it to be driven by others (Coombs, 2011). It is essential that information provided by the organization be accurate, even if it is limited, since later inconsistencies will diminish credibility. Maintaining consistency does not necessarily require that the organization have only one spokesperson, but "spokespersons should be briefed on the same information and the key points the organization is trying to convey in [its] messages" (Coombs, 2011). If people have been harmed by the crisis, then the organization's spokespersons should express sympathy and concern for the victims. Research suggests that reputational harm is reduced when such feelings are voiced, rather than expressions that may seem indifferent or self-focused, such as the statement by the BP executive mentioned in the earlier example (Coombs, 2011).

Much of the advice that experts offer on crisis communications relates to working with the news media. Communicating through the news media may be an effective way of reaching a large number of people quickly and is especially appropriate to get the message out if there is some threat to public safety (Coombs, 2011). But microsites, intranets, systems to send alerts to mobile phones, and social media have added communications channels that also can be used to provide a quick response. Some of these channels enable an organization to bypass the news media and engage in direct communication with constituents and the public, as exemplified by the example of The Nature Conservancy during the Gulf oil crisis. That can be advantageous, since it enables the organization to control its message and tell its side of the story without filtering or interpretation by the news media. But such media also empower others over whom the organization has no control, including bloggers and individuals who post online comments, not all of whom may be totally accurate or respectful. The growth of online media thus has changed the rules, not only for crisis communications but for all communications programs. Let's take a closer look at the implications in the next section of this chapter.

Online Media

Development of *Web 2.0* in the 2000s has introduced a revolution in communication to which nonprofits, as well as organizations in other sectors, are continuing to adapt. By late 2011, 9 in 10 nonprofits had a Facebook account, and many were also using other platforms (Fine, 2011). As discussed further in Chapter 13, the use of the Internet for fundraising is rapidly growing, but it still presents some challenges and limitations. But for communication between nonprofits and their various constituencies, new media have had a powerful impact.

Many nonprofit organizations have maintained websites and sent e-mail newsletters since the late 1990s or early 2000s. In many ways, static websites are merely brochures on a screen. That is, their content is produced and controlled by the organization. With the exception of registering to make a gift or receive additional information, the viewer of the site has limited ability to interact. *Social networks* and *social media* such as Facebook, Twitter, LinkedIn, and YouTube, have enabled users to create their own content and engage in dialogue. The organization's clients, donors, and volunteers—including critics—have the ability to interact and to add their own comments and viewpoints to the well-considered messages originated by the organization itself. Previously, communications theory and practice, including many of the principles discussed above in this chapter, were based on the notion that organizations could determine their own messages, ensure consistency in their expression, and thereby shape their own brands. Today, anybody can begin or join a discussion about a nonprofit organization and have a powerful impact on the brand. Cameras are ubiquitous (a standard feature on smartphones), and photos or video can be instantly uploaded and available to millions of viewers. This has increased transparency and enabled individuals to become reporters—or citizen journalists—who can draw attention to an organization in a positive or negative light.

The growth of online media offers nonprofits positive opportunities but also presents new challenges. In 2011, there were two widely publicized examples of the power of online media and the potential impact on nonprofit brands. One was disruptive of the organization; the other provided an example of how a savvy communications strategy can avert potential damage. In the first case, an officer of National Public Radio (NPR) was recorded in what he believed to be a private conversation with two individuals whom he believed to be potential donors. The individuals were indeed political activists who recorded the NPR executive making controversial, political remarks and uploaded them to the Internet, from which it was picked up by traditional news organizations. The incident ultimately led to his resignation and that of NPR's CEO (Memmott, 2012). On February 15, 2011, a social media specialist at the American Red Cross posted a tweet, believing she was using her personal account but instead using the Red Cross account. The result was that she informed thousands of Red Cross followers (and those who received their retweets) that she was in the process of "getting slizzerd" (inebriated). Illustrating a creative approach to crisis communications, her supervisor reacted quickly, posting, "We've deleted the rogue tweet but rest assured the Red Cross is sober and we've confiscated the keys." The response to this humorous tone was positive and, indeed, resulted in additional gifts to the Red Cross, as well as increased sales of the brand of beer referenced in the original tweet. In a follow-up, the Red Cross posted, "While we're a 130-year-old humanitarian organization, we're also made up of human beings. Thanks for not only getting that but for turning our faux pas into something good" (McCambridge, 2011).

The new communications environment raises a variety of management questions for nonprofit organizations. One is the need to determine the appropriate level and allocation of resources to electronic communication. Although the cost of establishing an online presence, for example a Facebook page, may be minimal, there is a continuing cost to maintaining it. Indeed, as interaction increases, so too may the need for resources devoted to online communication, possibly requiring a trade-off with resources dedicated to traditional communication programs. This reality requires that organizations identify their goals for online media and tools to evaluate its impact on their performance. As discussed in Chapter 6, measuring outputs may be relatively easy, but determining the impact on outcomes related to mission and goals requires development of a logic model. As Christine Durand and Kristen Cici (2011) write,

> Counting the number of fans, followers, visits, or likes is the norm. Knowing that you have 1,378 followers on Twitter is great, but what does that actually mean? Nonprofits need to ask themselves: "Why are we using social media?" The answer probably isn't to have a thousand likes on Facebook. . . . What does it mean to have a thousand likes? Is that translating into more volunteers, more donations, more education about your mission or your issues?

Another management question, especially relevant in larger organizations, is whether the online presence should be managed centrally by social media staff or be dispersed throughout the organization. Allison Fine (2011) makes the case that having "social media plans or departments to live separate and distinct from the rest of an organization is a mistake." Rather, she recommends, social media tools should be "integrated into every department and every function of the organization." If various staff members may be active in social media, then there is a need for a social media policy that defines standards regarding appropriate messages to be conveyed. There is also a need for ongoing training of staff throughout the organization. For example, the National Wildlife Federation has trained more than 90 staff members to use Twitter, "to share their work with the world, using their own voice, using their own identities" (Fine, 2011).

The technologies of online media likely will continue to evolve, requiring continuing analysis and learning. But maintaining an active presence online has become an essential component of communications and marketing for nonprofit organizations and is certain to grow in importance in the years ahead. Fortunately, a substantial number of books, articles, training programs, and consultancies exist to guide organizations in addressing key issues in developing their online media strategy. Some resources are listed as suggested reading at the end of this chapter.

Evaluating Marketing and Communication

As in other aspects of nonprofit management, the important question about any marketing or communication plan is a simple one: Does it work? In other words, what impact does adoption of a marketing approach have on the performance of a nonprofit organization? By now, readers who have progressed through this book from the beginning will recognize the issues associated with the question—the complexity of defining what constitutes nonprofit organizational performance and how to measure it once defined.

It is, of course, relatively easy to establish the link between marketing and performance in a for-profit company. Indeed, most research on the link between marketing and performance has been focused on the business sector, and a number of studies have identified a relationship between market orientation and financial outcomes, such as return on investment (Gainer & Moyer, 2005; Shoham, Ruvio, Vigoda-Gadot, & Schwabsky, 2006). Similar methods may be suitable to studying marketing by nonprofits that also provide services in a competitive environment, such as health care. For many nonprofits, however, assessing the benefits of marketing and communication efforts also requires measuring the effects on donors, clients, and the advancement of causes or ideas, outcomes that may be less easily quantified.

The findings of several studies suggest that nonprofit organizations that hold a market orientation, perhaps better defined as a *social orientation*, do attain greater financial support and client satisfaction than those that do not (Gainer & Moyer, 2005). In an exploratory study published in 2012, Helisse Levine and Anne Zahradnik (2012) looked specifically at nonprofits' use of online media and focused on financial impact. They tracked nonprofits' website content over time and compared it with financial indicators for those organizations at corresponding points in time. They found a "positive relationship between higher market orientation via online media presence and improved financial viability" (p. 26). Their article reporting on the study also provided a tool for nonprofits to use in assessing their online media. As the authors acknowledge, an expansion of the research would be useful to determine how the findings may apply to various types of nonprofits and to explore the cause-and-effect question— whether financially viable nonprofits maintain a more active online presence or whether having a robust online presence indeed produces financial benefits. In addition, there is a need for additional research that goes beyond financial indicators to further explore the impact of online media in advancing nonprofit missions.

Chapter Summary

Marketing, communications, and public relations are related fields, but are also have specific definitions that distinguish them. Communications is the transmission or exchange of information; public relations is "a strategic communication process that builds mutually beneficial relationships between organizations and their publics" (Public Relations Society of America, n.d.). Marketing is a process distinguished by its objective: to influence the behavior of someone else. Marketing focuses on exchanges.

Marketing principles have been widely adopted in the nonprofit sector. Some nonprofits engage in commercial marketing to attract customers to the goods and services that they provide. Others use social marketing to change behavior in order to benefit people and society. Some remain concerned that commercial marketing may not be appropriate to nonprofit values and cultures. This may reflect, in part, an understanding of marketing that is a throwback to earlier mind-sets about the concept, especially the idea that marketing is equivalent to sales.

Contemporary marketing follows a customer mind-set that requires that "the organization systematically study customers' needs, wants, perceptions, preferences, and satisfaction . . . and act on this information to improve its offerings to meet its customers' needs better" (Andreasen & Kotler, 2008, p. 39). This implies that the organization's programs and services need to be adapted to meet identified customer desires; but this should not be taken as a reason for a nonprofit to abandon its mission or central values. Rather, marketing should be used as a tool for pursuing the mission and achieving mission-related goals.

The marketing mix includes four variables (called the *Four P*s of marketing): product, place, price, and promotion. Organizations can adjust the marketing mix to differentiate themselves from others and position themselves in a unique market niche, gaining an advantage over other organizations or alternative activities with which they may compete. Nonprofits may compete directly with other organizations, nonprofit or for-profit, but they also face generic competition from all alternative uses for individuals' time and money.

Products have tangible and intangible qualities, including the prestige associated with a degree from a well-known university or the environment in which coffee is consumed. Place, or location, determines access to a program or service and is a critical variable in the marketing mix. Some products and services need to be taken to where the customers are—for example, vans that provide mobile medical care. Prices for products and services may be set to provide a break-even result for the nonprofit, to compete with what others are charging, or to reflect the perceived value of the product or service to the customer. Sophisticated marketers practice price discrimination, charging different prices to different segments of their target market. Price discrimination may be intended to match differences in product value, for example, seats closer to or farther from the theater stage; to shift utilization from peak to nonpeak periods; or to maximize revenue by charging the highest prices that some consumers are willing to pay.

Brand is commonly defined as "a name, term, design, symbol, or any other feature that identifies one seller's good or service as distinct from those of other sellers" (Burnett, 2007, p. 179), but some offer a broader definition that includes intangible perceptions as a part of a brand. Individuals attribute qualities to a brand, and organizations work to establish a positive brand image, which may help attract both clients and donors. A positive brand has a monetary value, called brand equity, which may form the basis of some partnerships between nonprofits and for-profit companies. Building an organization's brand requires initiatives at the organizational level, the identity level, and the experiential level (Durham, 2010).

Communications and marketing must be integrated; that is, their goals must permeate all aspects of the organization with consistent messages being delivered to various constituencies. This approach is known as integrated marketing communication, or IMC. It is especially important in nonprofits because their borders are porous, and members of various constituencies, including staff, volunteers, and donors, may communicate with each other. Individuals attribute greater credibility to information they receive through word of mouth than to what they read or see in the public media, especially if the source is someone close to them or with inside knowledge of the organization. This requires that messages delivered both internally and externally be consistent.

Nonprofit organizations should have a plan for risk management that includes both prevention of crises and preparation for communicating, should a crisis occur. Principles of crisis communications include the need to respond quickly, accurately, and consistently, and with expressions of empathy and concern for any individuals who may have suffered as a result of whatever incident occurred.

The development of Web 2.0, including social networks and social media that permit users to create content and join conversations regarding an organization, requires new communications strategies and presents nonprofit organizations with critical decisions about the resources and staffing needed to adapt. Some have adopted social media policies to guide the way in which volunteers and staff members communicate about the organization and provide training to staff members on the use of online media.

Research suggests that nonprofits that adopt a market orientation or a societal orientation do achieve greater financial support and client satisfaction. Research also has found a relationship between an organization's online presence and financial viability. However, additional research is needed to assess the broader impact on the achievement of nonprofits' missions.

Note

1. If a product or service is provided for a fee, then the relevant variable is what the customer *wants,* not what he or she may need. For example, a person may need more exercise, and his or her doctor may even recommend it. That person should join a health club. But unless the person also *wants* more exercise, personal need is irrelevant from a marketing perspective because he or she will not be willing to spend money on health club dues.

KEY TERMS AND CONCEPTS

brand

brand attributes

brand equity

communication

communications

competitive advantage

cost-oriented pricing

crisis communications

demographic variables

differentiate (the market)

external publics

four Ps of marketing

integrated marketing communications (IMC)

internal publics

market niche

marketing

marketing mix

place

position

price

price discrimination

product

product mind-set

promotion

psychographics

public relations

sales mind-set

segmentation

social media

social networks

strategic communications

target-audience mind-set

target market/target audience

Web 2.0

CASE 10.1   AARP

AARP is one of the United States's largest nonprofit organizations, with more than 37 million members, all of whom are over the age of 50 years. Its founding purposes, to which it still adheres, include promoting "independence, dignity and purpose for older persons," enhancing "the quality of life for older persons," and encouraging older people "to serve, not to be served" (www.aarp.org/about-aarp/info-2009/History.html). With its emphasis on the interests of older people, AARP advocates on issues such as Social Security, health care, and supportive housing; it provides information on services such as caregiving and driver safety training; and it offers a wide range of special products and services to its members, including insurance plans and discounts on travel and various other products (www.aarp.org).

What is today known as AARP was founded in 1958 by Dr. Ethel Percy Andrus and, for most of its history, was known as the "American Association of Retired Persons." For most of that time, the name accurately reflected the status of most of its members. But in 1998, it needed to respond to powerful demographic trends. The baby boomer generation, with some 78 million people, was aging, with its oldest members entering their fifties. They were the future market for the association's programs, but their lives were different from those of earlier generations. People were living longer and working longer. The baby boomers were in apparent denial about their own aging—remember, this was the generation that in the 1960s had invented the phrase, "Don't trust anybody over 30." If the association was going to continue growing, it would need to attract this rising and somewhat different generation of Americans.

Beginning in 1998, AARP undertook extensive research into the attitudes of baby boomers toward the organization, and the findings were reason for concern. Many baby boomers were attracted to AARP's products and services, but as the organization's president summarized the situation, "Boomers right now think of AARP as more for their parents [than for them]" (Lipke, 2000, p. 37). Armed with the insights of market research, the organization went about changing itself to become more attractive to the growing hoard of aging baby boomer Americans.

For one thing, the "American Association of Retired Persons" became just AARP, much as Kentucky Fried Chicken had become KFC and the American Telephone and Telegraph Company had changed to simply AT&T. In other words, the word *retired* was retired, since it no longer applied to the actual working status of most of the organization's prospective members. But the name change was not all. AARP introduced a new magazine targeting baby boomers and divided its existing magazine into two editions—one for people who are retired and one for people who are still working (Lipke, 2000). It launched a $100 million advertising campaign to announce its rebranding and to promote its various products and services. It developed new online resources focused on issues facing baby boomers. In 2006, it was developing additional new products aimed at the baby boom generation, including podcasts and an "audio logo" like the well-known sound of "Intel inside" (Elliott, 2006). In 2009, a small group of AARP staff began planning for AARP's entry into social media. By 2014, the effort had expanded to include AARP Studios, charged with developing AARP content to be shared on social media (O'Neil, 2014).

The stakes were high, and AARP set ambitious goals for increasing its membership by capturing a larger share of the baby boomers who were reaching the age of eligibility. By 2012, only 47 percent of AARP members were retired, and one third of its members were less than 60 years old. Each issue of its publication *AARP The Magazine,* reached 22.4 million people, the largest of any magazine. In addition to advertising hearing aids, it also included ads for Bose Wave music systems (Newman, 2012)! By 2014, AARP had a social media audience of two million on Facebook, Twitter, YouTube, Pinterest, GooglePlus, and Tumblr, with content being generated from 250 to 300 social media accounts throughout the organization (O'Neil, 2014).

Questions Related to Case 10.1

1. Which principles from this chapter are illustrated by the case of AARP?

2. In your opinion, is rebranding that involves adopting an abbreviation for the previous name (e.g., AARP instead of American Association of Retired Persons) an effective strategy? Can you think of examples where you think this approach was successful and others where it was not?

3. Think back on (or read again) the discussion of strategic planning in Chapter 7. What strengths, weaknesses, opportunities, and threats do you think AARP might have identified, leading to the changes discussed in this case?

CASE 10.2 Susan G. Komen Foundation

In 2012, the Susan G. Komen Foundation, one of the nation's leading breast cancer research organizations, announced that it was discontinuing funding to Planned Parenthood, one of the nation's largest providers and advocates in the field of reproductive health care. Komen had provided funds to Planned Parenthood to support breast cancer screenings. The announcement that it would no longer fund Planned Parenthood created a national controversy that eventually led Komen to reverse its decision. The reaction, much of it expressed on social media, reflected the nation's divided views regarding abortion, but it also provided a case study of nonprofit communication strategies and the power of social media.

Planned Parenthood responded quickly to Komen's announcement, immediately posting information on its Facebook page and on Twitter, attracting more than 1,000 comments during its first 24 hours online. In contrast, Komen waited two days to mention the controversy on its Facebook page and then offered a less-than-detailed explanation: "Grant-making decisions are not about politics—our priority is and always will be the women we serve" (Panepento, 2012). By that time, Planned Parenthood's posting had received more than 2,000 comments, and the extensive online discussion had captured the attention of traditional news media. The story came to dominate national news, with Planned Parenthood largely framing the dialogue.

(Continued)

(Continued)

In subsequent days, Komen's founder and CEO, Nancy Brinker, responded in more detail. But she offered inconsistent explanations for the termination of funding to Planned Parenthood. At first, she stated that Komen's policy prohibited funding for organizations that were under investigation. Some noted that while a Congressional committee was investigating the question of whether Planned Parenthood had used federal funds to provide abortions, there was no criminal investigation of the organization underway. Brinker then explained that Planned Parenthood did not conduct breast cancer screenings directly, but rather referred women to other providers, offering that as a reason for defunding by Komen (Condon, 2012). In another interview, Brinker suggested that the reasons for ending support were related to Komen's "new standards of criteria for how we can measure our results and effectiveness in communities," but she did not explain how Planned Parenthood had failed to meet those standards ("Andrea Mitchell," 2012).

Within three days of its announcement that it would cease funding Planned Parenthood, Komen reversed its position and offered an apology. Komen's board chair and other officials resigned. Contributions to Komen declined by 22 percent in the year following the controversy, while gifts to Planned Parenthood increased ("Komen Gifts Plunged", 2014). In 2014, Komen's CEO, Judith Salerno, said that the organization had "moved past" the controversy ("Komen Has 'Moved Past,'" 2014). But a new phrase to describe the potential impact of social media criticism on a nonprofit had entered the vocabulary: "getting Komened" (Peregrine, 2012).

Although differing political and social views surely were one explanation of the controversy, some authors who analyzed the events objectively viewed it as a case study in crisis management and communications, drawing lessons for nonprofit organizations generally. Some cited Komen's delayed and inconsistent response as critical mistakes. As one author wrote, "YouTube, Facebook, and mass e-mail contributed mightily to the uproar by quickly informing and galvanizing hundreds of thousands of concerned individuals. Cyberspace proved to be a tenuous place, even for the dedicated. The need for charities to be media savvy was never more evident, never more on display" (Grunfeld & Lash, 2012).

Questions Related to Case 10.2

1. Is the case of Planned Parenthood and the Susan G. Komen Foundation primarily related to the concepts of marketing, communications, or public relations? Explain.

2. How does Coombs's Situational Crisis Communication Theory (SCCT) apply to the case of Planned Parenthood and the Susan G. Komen Foundation?

3. Leaving aside your personal views on the issues that were involved, how do you think the controversy between the Susan G. Komen Foundation and Planned Parenthood may have affected the brand of each organization?

QUESTIONS FOR DISCUSSION

1. Below is a list of some well-known nonprofit organizations and a list of attributes. Look at each nonprofit and identify up to three attributes that you would use to describe your impression of the organization. Don't think too long; just write down the first three words that come to mind when you read the organization's name. (If you've never heard of the organization, just leave it blank.) When you are done, consider these questions:

   1. How do your results compare with those of your classmates?

   2. What do the results suggest about attributes of the brand in each case?

   3. Why do you think each organization has the image that it does, either positive or negative?

American Red Cross	___,___,___	(a) innovative
Salvation Army	___,___,___	(b) well-managed
Nature Conservancy	___,___,___	(c) caring
Greenpeace	___,___,___	(d) greedy
Boy Scouts	___,___,___	(e) unresponsive
Teach for America	___,___,___	(f) dependable
National Geographic Society	___,___,___	(g) high quality
City Year	___,___,___	(h) patriotic
United Way of America	___,___,___	(i) responsive
Boys and Girls Clubs	___,___,___	(j) untrustworthy
Doctors Without Borders	___,___,___	(k) cold-hearted
Habitat for Humanity	___,___,___	(l) friendly
Children's Defense Fund	___,___,___	(m) radical
Boston Symphony Orchestra	___,___,___	(n) exciting
Yale University	___,___,___	(o) prestigious
YMCA	___,___,___	(p) traditional

SUGGESTIONS FOR FURTHER READING

Books/Journals

Andreasen, A. R. (2006). *Social marketing for the twenty-first century*. Thousand Oaks, CA: Sage.

Andreasen, A. R., & Kotler, P. (2008). *Strategic marketing for nonprofit organizations* (7th ed.). Upper Saddle River, NJ: Prentice Hall.

Bonk, K., Tynes, E., Griggs, H., & Sparks, P. (2008). *Strategic communications for nonprofits* (2nd ed.). San Francisco, CA: Jossey-Bass.

Coombs, W. T. (2014). *Ongoing crisis communication: Planning, managing, and responding* (4th ed.). Thousand Oaks, CA: Sage.

Durham, S. (2010). *Brandraising: How nonprofits raise visibility and money through smart communications.* San Francisco, CA: Jossey-Bass.

International Journal of Nonprofit and Voluntary Sector Marketing. Hoboken, NJ: Wiley. (Available at http://onlinelibrary .wiley.com/journal/10.1002/(ISSN)1479-103X)

Mathos, M., & Norman, C. (2012). *Social media tactics for nonprofits.* Hoboken, NJ: Wiley.

Websites

American Marketing Association: http://www.marketingpower.com

Public Relations Society of America: http://www.prsa.org

Network for Good: http://www.networkforgood.org

Companion Website

Visit study.sagepub.com/worth4e for access to certain full-text SAGE journal articles and links to relevant video and multimedia content.

chapter 11

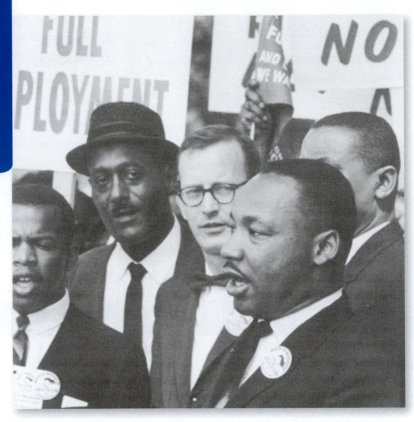

Nonprofit organizations have played an essential role in shaping our country by bringing issues to the public's attention, influencing attitudes, and lobbying for new laws.

Photo: US National Archives.

Learning Objectives

After reading this chapter, students should be able to:

1. Describe the life cycle of a social change issue.

2. Define *advocacy*, *lobbying*, and *political activity*.

3. Summarize federal law related to nonprofit lobbying.

4. Describe the points that need to be considered when implementing an advocacy program.

5. Explain current policy issues related to nonprofit advocacy, lobbying, and political activity.

6. Analyze cases, applying concepts from the chapter.

Advocacy and Lobbying 11

Within the lifetime of many people alive today, African American children were taught in schools segregated by law. Women could legally be denied jobs, barred from entire professions, and paid less than men simply because of their gender. Gay people were regularly fired from their jobs if their sexual orientation became known. People with physical disabilities were unable to access many public buildings, limiting their opportunities for employment and life experiences. Companies dumped raw sewage and industrial wastes into rivers with impunity. Highways were lined with ugly billboards and trash thrown from cars by un-seat-belted motorists. People could smoke in offices and other public places, and driving while drunk often was punishable by no more than a minor fine, even if it resulted in the death of another person. There remain many injustices, threats to the environment, diseases to be cured, and other problems to be solved, but over decades, new laws have been enacted to correct many of the intolerable situations mentioned above.

As explained in Box 11.1, social issues often follow a life cycle. In the beginning, there may be inattention to the problem, although it exists. Some event may cause the problem to be discovered by individuals and the news media. Advocates, usually including nonprofit organizations, then drive the issue to higher visibility and courses of possible action are identified and evaluated. Initial interventions may include efforts by government and social marketing by nonprofits, as discussed in Chapter 10. Progress may be uneven as time goes by, but the problem ultimately is either resolved or found to be intractable. It may drop off the public's radar until some new event causes it to gain attention again (Andreasen, 2006).

In most instances, nonprofit organizations have played an essential role by bringing the issue to the public's attention, influencing attitudes and building support for change, and lobbying for new laws. Indeed, nonprofits have been at the forefront of every important social change in the United States from the beginning of the nation. They have been the principal advocates for people who are disadvantaged or disenfranchised and for causes that initially concern only a minority of people. Nonprofits often have identified and given visibility to emerging issues and problems that ultimately became the focus of national attention and action.

BOX 11.1 STAGES IN THE LIFE CYCLE OF A SOCIAL CHANGE ISSUE

Stage 1: Inattention to the problem	The social problem exists, as evidenced by concrete data or dramatic anecdotes, but it has not yet become anyone's concern.
Stage 2: Discovery of the problem	The problem comes to the attention of individuals or groups (including the media) who think it needs to be addressed. At this stage, initial baseline analyses or measurements will be undertaken. Nuances of the problem will begin to emerge—for example, learning who is most affected by the problem.
Stage 3: Climbing the agenda	Activists, advocacy groups, individual politicians, investigative reporters, and nonfiction writers raise the volume on the issue. They marshal even more evidence, produce real victims, and potentially raise the guilt level of those not affected. At this stage, funders and potential interveners begin to find the issue sufficiently important for attention and possible action.
Stage 4: Outlining the choices	Analysts and advocates look at the data and consider how the problem might be addressed. Evidence about causal linkages will be important, as will scenarios for possible intervention.
Stage 5: Choosing courses of action	This is where debate takes place over the benefits and costs that action and inaction will have on society, victims, and those who have to take action (e.g., donate money, pass laws) if there is to be a solution. Attention will be paid to the efficacy of various solutions. Opposing forces emerge and solidify their positions.
Stage 6: Launching initial interventions	Foundations or government agencies put money into programs. Organizations mount pioneering efforts and test alternative strategies and tactics. These will involve both downstream and upstream interventions, in which social marketing can play a major role.
Stage 7: Reassessing and redirecting efforts	With most difficult changes, progress is slow, and there are periods of acceleration, deceleration, progression, and regression. At some point, key figures will feel that it is time to take stock of where the problem stands. The outcome may be a reorientation and resurgence of interventions—or it may not.
Stage 8: Achieving success, failure, or neglect	After a number of years, the problem will have found some major solutions or will have proven basically intractable and, in the absence of dramatic progress or new data, will "drop off the radar screen." The latter may also be the result of new competition from the latest social problem that captures the public's imagination and drives the "old" problem into the "dustbin of history" (Cohen, 2000, cited by Andreasen, 2006).

Source: Andreasen, A. R. (2006). *Social Marketing in the 21st Century.* Thousand Oaks, CA: Sage, p. 42.

Nonprofits may be found on every side of any issue, and they reflect all shades of opinion. There are organizations that advocate pro-life positions and others that are pro-choice. There are nonprofits that work to advance religious values and others that strive to protect the separation of church and state. There are those whose mission is to promote sound government and those who seek to limit government's size and power. There are nonprofits that work toward economic growth and others with a mission to preserve and protect the environment, historic structures, animals, and communities from the effects of commercial development. The public interest that is served by such diversity is the preservation of an uninhibited marketplace of ideas, allowing the free exchange of information and discussion that is believed to lead ultimately to sound public policy. Nonprofit advocacy and lobbying is thus a fundamental pillar of a democratic society.

However, various authors observe that most nonprofits do not engage in advocacy or lobbying. For example, Pablo Eisenberg observed in 2007 that "fewer than two percent of nonprofit organizations choose to exercise their legal right to influence legislation or lobby" (p. 53), and Smucker, writing in 2005, lamented that "many charities view lobbying as irrelevant to their mission, inappropriate, or even illegal" (p. 231). Research by Curtis Child and Kirsten Grønbjerg (2007) also found that many nonprofits are ambivalent about advocacy and that only a relatively small number devote substantial resources to such efforts.

There are various reasons why relatively few nonprofits have engaged in advocacy. One obvious reason is that many lack the staff or resources, especially given the many demands of managing core service programs. Not surprisingly, larger national nonprofits are more likely to be directly involved in advocacy and lobbying than are smaller, local organizations, and such activity is more common among organizations in fields that are significantly regulated, such as health care (Child & Grønbjerg, 2007). Although small nonprofits might not conduct much lobbying on their own, they may belong to an association or coalition that represents their interests and issues at the state or national level. Such coalitions exist to serve specific groups of nonprofits, for example, higher education institutions, health care providers, and organizations concerned with homelessness.

Concern about alienating government foundation funders may be a barrier for some, and nonprofits that are dependent on gifts from individuals also may be reluctant to take a position on issues that affect the organization but on which their donors hold different opinions. But a common conclusion about why nonprofits do not lobby more is that many nonprofit executives are simply unclear about what the law allows. They may decide to err on the side of caution by keeping their distance from the legislative process. As Jeffrey Berry, the director of a 2003 study, concluded, "Nonprofit organizations are excessively worried about losing their charity status. And that reflects a mis-understanding of how the law is enforced" (p. 33).

Basic Distinctions

Before we go further into this topic, let's clarify three basic concepts and terms: advocacy, lobbying, and political campaign activity. *Advocacy* includes action taken in support of a cause or an idea. As Robert Pekkanen and Steven Smith (2014) observe, advocacy may encompass a wide range of activities, "from organizing a massive demonstration to encouraging board members to write letters to the editor of the local paper (p. 1). And it may occur at the local, state, federal, or international level (p. 1). Advocacy is a basic right of every individual and organization in the United States and may be practiced without limit; it is an exercise of free speech protected by the U.S. Constitution. *Lobbying* is action taken to support or oppose *specific* legislation at the national, state, or local level. This could include, for example, contacting a member of Congress, a state legislator, or a city councilperson to request his or her sponsorship or vote in favor of or against a specific bill. It does not include contacting members of the executive branch, unless that individual is in a position to influence legislation.

Organizing includes identifying people you think will share your positions and enlisting them to be a part of your base of support, which may enhance the effectiveness of your advocacy and lobbying (Avner, 2010).

Political campaign activity is action taken in support of or opposition to specific candidates for office, including the publication or distribution of statements or printed materials. It does not include, however, conducting nonpartisan activities such as get-out-the-vote efforts or sponsoring a candidate debate or forum (Halloran, 2013). But the line sometimes has seemed fuzzy, and there have been some controversial cases in recent years surrounding the involvement of nonprofits in political campaigns. Some current issues are discussed further at a later point in this chapter.

There is sometimes understandable confusion between what is advocacy and what is lobbying. Indeed, the former encompasses the latter. For example, the marches, protests, and sit-ins of the civil rights movement were advocacy for equal rights, but they were not lobbying since they were not actions undertaken with the purpose of supporting or opposing any specific item of legislation. Once the Civil Rights Act of 1964 was up for consideration in Congress, many individuals and organizations contacted their elected representatives to urge a favorable vote. That activity was lobbying. The law defines lobbying quite precisely, including the identification of specific activities it does and does not include.

Overview of Lobbying Law

The law on lobbying is complex and may change from time to time. The following discussion thus simplifies some concepts and definitions and it should not be relied upon as legal advice. Students should check various Web resources to see if there have been changes since this chapter was written and, of course, nonprofit organizations always should consult legal counsel about what activities are permissible in this area.

Our discussion throughout the text has emphasized the charitable nonprofits, tax-exempt under Section 501(c)(3) of the Internal Revenue (IRS) Code, and the social welfare or advocacy organizations, also called advocacy organizations, that are tax exempt under Section 501(c)(4). Students will recall from Chapter 2 that there also are other types of tax-exempt organizations that fall under other sections of the tax code. They include, for example, labor unions, exempt under Section 501(c)(5); business associations, exempt under Section 501(c)(6); and political action committees (called PACs), most of which are classified under Section 527. These various types of organizations are subject to differing requirements with regard to their activities.

Charitable nonprofits, exempt under Section 501(c)(3), must comply with legal restrictions on their lobbying activity, which are discussed in more detail soon. Social welfare organizations, exempt under Section 501(c)(4) are permitted to engage in lobbying essentially without limit (Hopkins, 2005). They are also permitted to engage in political activities, including the endorsement of candidates, so long as it is not their primary purpose. But they are not allowed to contribute directly to a candidate's campaign (Independent Sector, 2015b). As discussed in Chapter 2, some 501(c)(3) organizations work with related 501(c)(4) organizations. The relationship between the Sierra Club and the Sierra Club Foundation was presented as an example in that earlier discussion.

The 501(c)(5) and 501(c)(6) organizations are treated similarly to 501(c)(4) organizations under lobbying laws. Political action committees, mostly exempt under Section 527, are permitted to engage in partisan political activity—indeed, it is their primary purpose—but face some limitations on their lobbying. Table 11.1 summarizes permissible activities and limitations that apply to various types of tax-exempt organizations, but our discussion in this chapter focuses on charitable nonprofits and social welfare organizations.

The reason that charitable nonprofits face restrictions on lobbying is directly related to the tax deductibility of gifts, which is viewed as a form of public subsidy given to the organization. Donors to 501(c)(4) organizations do not receive the benefit of such deductions; the tradeoff is the ability of those organizations to engage in unlimited lobbying. In other words, the foregone tax revenue attributable to the deduction of gifts to charitable nonprofits is regarded as public money. The purpose of the subsidy is to support an organization's charitable activities, and the law requires that its resources be used to

TABLE 11.1 ■ Summary of Allowable Activities				
	Tax Exempt	**Deductible Gifts**	**Engage in Lobbying**	**Engage in partisan political activity**
501 (c) 3 Public Charities	Yes	Yes (up to 50% of donor's income)	Yes, but limited, using either "no substantial part" test or 501 (h) expenditure limits	No
501 (c) 3 Private Foundations	Yes, but pay nominal excise tax on investment earnings	Yes (up to 30% of donor's income)	No	No
501 (c) 4 Social Welfare (Advocacy) Organizations [also 501 (c) 5 and 501 (c) 6 organizations]	Yes	No	Yes (without limit)	Yes, but cannot contribute directly to campaign and political activity cannot be the organization's "primary purpose." Not required to disclose donors to the public.
527 organizations (political action committees)	Yes	No	Limited (insubstantial) lobbying is permitted. May be subject to tax if not furthering political purposes.	Yes, but expenditures are subject to state and federal limitations on campaign contributions. Must disclose donors to the public.

Source: Based on Koulish, 2013; Bolder Advocacy, 2015; Independent Sector, 2015e.

pursue those purposes as its primary activity. Any lobbying it conducts must be limited. But what is the limit?

Prior to 1976, the answer was unclear. Nonprofits were instructed that their lobbying needed to be "insubstantial" in relationship to overall activities. What is the meaning of *insubstantial?* The IRS never defined it precisely and looked at each situation on a case-by-case basis. One of the problems was that the *substantial part test,* which determined whether lobbying was a "substantial part" of an organization's activities, looked not only at how much a nonprofit spent on lobbying activity, but also at how much time and effort was devoted to the activity. Some courts held that nonprofits were safe if they spent less than 5 percent on lobbying, but other courts said such an arbitrary standard was not appropriate. Thus, like a child whose parents just say, "Don't wander too far," many nonprofits were unsure exactly how far they could safely go, that is, how much lobbying the IRS might find to be a substantial part of their activities. Some were inhibited from engaging in lobbying at all for fear of losing their tax-exempt status by crossing the fuzzy line.

In 1976, Congress passed Public Law 94-455 (the 1976 Lobby Law), which sought to clarify the situation. Since then, nonprofits have two options, as follows.

Option I: Substantial Part Test

The first option is to continue to be covered by the substantial part test, essentially the same imprecise standard that applied before 1976. This may be a reasonable option for an organization that does not engage in lobbying or that does very little. If it is careful to differentiate lobbying from advocacy, it may find that it spends too little time or money on actual lobbying to be concerned about it. This might be the simplest approach for the majority of nonprofit organizations.

Option II: 501(h) Expenditure Test

The second option, provided by the 1976 Lobby Law and subsequent IRS regulations, is for the nonprofit to file Form 5768 with the IRS, electing to be covered by the specific expenditure guidelines under *Section 501(h)* of the Internal Revenue Code. Selecting this option offers a number of advantages. First, the limits do not consider the amount of time or effort devoted to lobbying—they are based entirely on how much the organization *spends* on lobbying activity, as a percentage of its total budget.[1] The standard is thus exact, and an organization can easily determine whether it is within or is approaching the limit. Second, it means that lobbying that does not involve expenditure is not limited at all. For example, if a volunteer calls on a congressperson or a local legislator, that effort does not count unless the organization spends money to support it. If the organization reimburses the volunteer for his or her cab ride to the meeting, that expense would need to be included in its lobbying expense, but the volunteer's time would not. The *501(h) option* also presents fewer risks for nonprofits and their staff than does the substantial part test. Nonprofits that exceed the spending limits will not lose their tax exemption unless they exceed them by at least 150 percent averaged over a four-year period. Moreover, there are no penalties imposed on individual managers of an organization that exceeds the limit (Independent Sector, 2015a).

The spending limits are stated as a percentage of the nonprofit's total expenditures (on exempt activities), on a sliding scale depending on the size of the organization. There is an important distinction between the limit for direct lobbying and for grassroots lobbying. *Direct lobbying* includes any communication the organization has "with legislators or government officials who participate in the formulation of legislation or with its own members with regard to specific legislation and that expresses a view on it" (Smucker, 2005, p. 240). Thus, it does not include communication with officials of the executive branch of government or communication that just provides information without expressing an opinion for or against the legislation.

Grassroots lobbying "refers to attempts to influence legislation by [trying] to affect the opinion of the public with respect to the legislation *and encouraging the audience to take action with respect to the legislation* [italics added] (Internal Revenue Service, 2015). Thus, if a communication does not include a call to action, that is, does not ask people to do something to support or oppose the legislation, then it is not lobbying. The "public" means the *general public,* which includes any individuals who are not *members* of the organization. But "members" is broadly defined. It includes donors to the organization as well as those who may be members in the formal sense of someone who pays dues in order to belong. Thus, if a nonprofit sends an e-mail to its donors urging them to contact their elected representatives to support or oppose a bill, that expenditure comes under the limit for direct lobbying. But if it takes out an ad in the newspaper or hands out flyers on the corner urging members of the general public to do the same, that is grassroots lobbying, and any money expended in such an effort comes under a different, lower limit. (Again, if the communication does not specifically ask individuals to take action, it does not count as lobbying at all.)

There are other activities that also do not count as lobbying. For example, if the legislature asks the nonprofit for advice on a bill, responding to that request does not count. *Self-defense activity* also does not count as lobbying. For instance, if the city council is about to pass an ordinance that would adversely affect the nonprofit, it may contact council members to oppose the legislation without having any expense involved count against its lobbying limit. Policy research organizations, such as the Brookings Institution or the American Enterprise Institute, may prepare reports that are nonpartisan and objective, and they will not count as lobbying efforts even if they recommend a specific course of action. In sum, the 1976 Lobby Law is quite generous in permitting nonprofit organizations to engage in lobbying. This is especially true if the distinction between what is lobbying and what is advocacy is carefully maintained, since expenditures on the latter do not count against the limits at all.

Table 11.2 summarizes the expenditure limits on direct and grassroots lobbying for nonprofits of various sizes. An organization may spend only one fourth as much on grassroots lobbying as on direct lobbying, and there is an overall cap of $1 million. For example, if a nonprofit spent the maximum of $1 million on all of its lobbying and $250,000 of that was spent on grassroots efforts, it could spend the remaining $750,000 on direct lobbying (Independent Sector, 2015a). Keep in mind that for organizations that selected the 501(h) option, lobbying activity does not count against the limit if it does not involve the expenditure of money by the nonprofit. The limit is thus not that restrictive in terms of the amount of activity it allows.

Charitable nonprofits must report their lobbying expenses on Form 990. In addition, organizations that employ professional lobbyists and spend more than $12,500 on lobbying during a quarter at the federal level must meet the requirements of the Lobbying Disclosure Act. This requires that they register and report their lobbying expenditures to Congress on a quarterly basis (Independent Sector, 2015a).

The rules discussed so far apply to nonprofits that are public charities. Private foundations face stricter limitations. They may not endorse or oppose legislation in communications with legislators or the general public if the communication includes a call to action. However, like public charities, they may provide technical advice to a legislature if asked to do so, provide nonpartisan analyses and studies, and lobby in self-defense. Like public charities, foundations are barred from participating in political campaigns. They can support nonpartisan activities such as candidate forums and get-out-the-vote drives, but they face strict regulation of their participation in voter registration drives (Independent Sector, 2015e). What if a private foundation makes grants to a nonprofit that comes under the more generous rules applied to public charities? Well, to start with, in general, the foundation would not be permitted to *designate* a grant to support lobbying. That would be just an obvious end-run around the restrictions on its activity. But if the foundation provides unrestricted operating support to a public charity, there is nothing to prevent that organization from spending the money on lobbying activity. If a foundation makes a grant to support a nonprofit's program that has lobbying as one component of it, the lobbying is acceptable, but it must be paid for using funds from some other source, not with the foundation's grant funds and the grant amount may not exceed the budgeted non-lobbying expenses of the program (Independent Sector, 2015e).

In addition to the basic provisions we have discussed in this chapter, nonprofits also must comply with various laws related to lobbying practice, which include restrictions on the participation of elected officials in charity events and on the way in which lobbyists can interact with legislators and their staff. In January of 2007, the 100th Congress amended House Rule 25 (called the *gift rule*), placing stricter limits on what gifts or privately supported travel members of the House of Representatives can accept from lobbyists. However, the law is always in a state of flux, and students with an interest in more details should check contemporary sources. The website of Independent Sector (www.independent-sector.org) provides timely updates on recent legislation and policy actions and should be consulted for the latest information. Other websites listed as resources at the end of this chapter also track and report on recent changes in law with regard to lobbying, campaign finance, and other relevant activities. And, of course, nonprofits should consult their legal counsel and not rely on publications, including this text.

TABLE 11.2 ■ Limits on Lobbying Expenditures for Charitable Nonprofits		
Total Expenditures on Exempt Purposes	**Total Limit on Lobbying Expenditures**	**Limit on Expenditures for Grassroots Lobbying**
Up to $500,000	20% of exempt-purpose expenditures ($100,000)	Up to $25,000
$500,000 to $1 million	$100,000 plus 15% of excess over $500,000	$25,000 plus 3.75% of excess over $500,000
$1 million to $1.5 million	$175,000 plus 10% of excess over $1 million	$43,750 plus 2.5% of excess over $1 million
Over $1.5 million	$225,000 plus 5% of excess over $1.5 million (Overall maximum of $1 million in lobbying expenditures)	$56,250 plus 1.25% of excess over $1.5 million (Overall maximum of 25% of total lobbying expenditure)

Source: Internal Revenue Service (www.irs.gov/Charities-&-Non-Profits/Measuring-Lobbying-Activity:-Expenditure-Test).

Political Campaign Activity

As discussed earlier, charitable nonprofits—including public charities and private foundations—are prohibited from engaging in campaigns and from endorsing candidates, either implicitly or explicitly. They may not coordinate their activities with those of a candidate or a campaign, contribute money or time to working for a candidate, or contribute the use of their facilities for a candidate or campaign (Halloran, 2013). But some types of nonprofit face fewer restrictions on such activity, and the rules were changed by a Supreme Court decision in 2010.

The Supreme Court's decision in the case of *Citizens United v. FEC* was focused on corporations. Previous law prohibited corporate contributions in support of political candidates. Corporations still cannot make monetary or in-kind contributions directly to candidates for federal office or coordinate their communication with candidates' campaigns. However, after Citizen's United, they now can make independent expenditures from their general treasury to expressly support or oppose candidates for the U.S. House, Senate, and president. This ruling also affected certain nonprofits, including the social welfare organizations (exempt under Section 501(c)(4)) and organizations exempt under Sections 501(c)(5) and 501(c)(6), which include labor unions and business associations. They now can engage in political activities, so long as political activities are not their primary purpose. But, to emphasize, the 2010 Supreme Court ruling does not change the law for charitable nonprofits, which remain prohibited from supporting or opposing candidates or making expenditures on communications that may suggest who is the "better" candidate (Halloran, 2013).

The Supreme Court's decision prompted some to suggest that the rules should be changed for charitable nonprofits as well, arguing that the principle of free speech that was the basis for the court's position should apply to all nonprofits as well as corporations. However, some legal experts noted that the prohibition on campaign activity is a trade-off for the deductibility of gifts and thought it unlikely that the law would change (Perry, 2010).

There have been some controversial cases that have highlighted the fine line between what is permissible advocacy and what is illegal involvement in electoral politics by charitable nonprofits. In the federal elections of 2004, 2006, and 2008, there were accusations that some organizations had crossed the line. In 2006, the Internal Revenue Service investigated activity by churches that allegedly had held events featuring a political candidate, distributed voter education guides that were favorable to a particular candidate, or engaged in other such activities (Schwinn, 2006a, 2006b). In one celebrated case, the IRS investigated the National Association for the Advancement of Colored People (NAACP) based on allegations that its president's remarks opposing the war in Iraq implied opposition to President George W. Bush's reelection and thus violated the prohibition on political activity. Following a two-year investigation, it concluded that no violation had occurred (Jensen, 2006a). Some expressed concern that the IRS's enforcement activity was inhibiting nonprofits, including churches, from legitimate advocacy activity, and others charged that the investigations were politically motivated (Jensen, 2006a). In June of 2007, the IRS released a Revenue Ruling (2007-41) to clarify the criteria by which it would determine what is and is not illegal campaign involvement. The ruling included 21 hypothetical examples of activity and a discussion of why each does or does not constitute a violation of the law. But the area remains one of some uncertainty and controversy. By the time of the 2012 election campaign, nonprofits' growing use of Facebook and Twitter had raised the new concern that even off-hand comments made online might unintentionally cross the line and subject the nonprofit to the charge that it had engaged in political commentary (West, 2012d). And by 2013, the topic of permissible political activity had again become a topic of considerable debate; we will consider some of the issues again later in this chapter.

Implementing an Advocacy Program

Now that we have explored basic concepts and reviewed the law governing nonprofit advocacy, let's turn our attention to the practice of advocacy and lobbying. There is an extensive practitioner literature on lobbying. Various authors have developed manuals that offer guidance specifically to nonprofit organizations and take into consideration the unique requirements that apply to them. Some are listed as suggested additional reading at the end of this chapter. In addition, websites listed in this chapter provide practical suggestions and guides, as well as links to other resources. Since the law changes from time to time, the websites are usually the best sources of legal information. However, the techniques or tactics of lobbying are more consistent over time, and even some relatively dated but classic sources provide guidance that is still sound.

Various sources that advise nonprofits on developing an advocacy and lobbying effort offer many common points, including the following:

- *Determine the reason for lobbying and how it advances the nonprofit's mission.* For a social welfare organization that exists for the purpose of changing public policy, the connection to the mission is obvious. A charitable nonprofit will need to consider how lobbying may advance its programs or the welfare of the constituents it serves and make strategic decisions about the emphasis to be given to lobbying in relationship to its service programs.
- *Understand the legislative process.* To lobby effectively, the organization needs to understand how legislation is considered at the local, state, or national level—wherever its lobbying efforts will be focused. This includes knowledge of which committees play important roles and the stages in the process at which a lobbyist's intervention may be most helpful or persuasive.
- *Identify the sources of funds to be used for lobbying.* As discussed above, there are restrictions on the use of government or foundation funds, but unrestricted revenues from gifts, grants, or earned income may be used to fund a lobbying effort.
- *Undertake research to develop an understanding of the public policy issues related to the organization's mission and to obtain data needed to make the case with legislators.* Such information is available from, among others, policy research organizations, national charitable organizations with established public policy programs, and coalitions concerned with issues in particular areas. Approaching a legislator with facts is not only important to persuasion but may indeed be providing

a real service to the legislator, whose time and staff may not be sufficient to undertake the depth of research that an interested nonprofit may offer.

- *Develop an infrastructure to support the lobbying program.* For an ongoing effort, this may require hiring staff or working with a professional lobbying firm, but smaller efforts may be managed by an existing staff member as a part-time assignment. An information system may be needed to track the progress of legislation and calls or visits with legislators. Managing a lobbying program has many of the same requirements as fundraising management since it involves developing and maintaining relationships, and undertaking contacts, in a systematic manner.
- *Inventory existing relationships and identify decision makers.* A nonprofit may have many existing relationships in its community, through staff, members of the board, or other friends who may in turn know key decision makers in the relevant legislature. They may be effective ambassadors who can be armed with information to deliver the nonprofit's messages to those decision makers, or they may help open the door to communications and visits by the nonprofit's CEO.
- *Use a strategic mix of tactics.* Direct lobbying with legislators may be the centerpiece of a lobbying program, but such efforts are more effective if they are used in conjunction with grassroots lobbying to influence and mobilize the community's opinions and with a media relations program to gain wider visibility for the issues. The latter might include developing relationships with reporters who may have an interest in writing articles about the issue as well as paid advertising, op-eds, and letters to the editor written by the nonprofit's CEO or volunteers. Walks, runs, marches, and demonstrations also are available tactics for drawing attention to a cause (Hessenius, 2007).
- *Form a Coalition.* Forming a coalition with other organizations may be an important part of the strategy and "the broadest possible array of stakeholders [may help] to show that it is more than the 'usual suspects' that are affiliated [with the cause]" (Libby & Associates, 2012, p. 104).

The tools used for lobbying vary depending on whether the effort is grassroots or direct lobbying. Grassroots lobbying engages many of the principles and techniques of marketing that were discussed in Chapter 10. Direct lobbying also may use those tools as well as personal visits with legislators and their staff members. Both approaches use various communications vehicles, including letters, phone calls, faxes, petitions, and e-mails. The Internet offers great advantages to nonprofits in developing coalitions and constituencies as well as for contacting legislators. However, because e-mails are so easy to send and thus can arrive in volume, some legislative staff have come to ignore them or to prevail on organizations to cease such efforts. Ironically, because e-mail has become so common and voluminous, the old technology of regular mail sometimes may be more effective. A letter, especially if written by a constituent of the legislator, signifies that the individual cares enough to have taken the time to write, rather than tap out a quick e-mail or text message. Letters from clients of a nonprofit also may have an impact on the legislator and even gain the attention of the news media. However, form letters that make it obvious they have been solicited by the nonprofit or a professional lobbyist have less credibility than those that appear to genuinely express the views of an individual (Hessenius, 2007). As in fundraising, there is no tool more powerful than the personal visit by an individual or group of individuals to a legislator or a member of his or her staff who is in a position to influence what information and data the legislator receives.

Social media and social networks have become increasingly important tools for nonprofit advocacy. Consider the impact of one example:

In March, 2012, Invisible Children, a San Diego-based nonprofit advocacy organization dedicated to bringing awareness to the activities of indicted Uganda war criminal Joseph Kony, started an Internet video campaign called *Kony 2012*. The goal was to make Kony internationally known in order that he be arrested by year's end. Within three days, the *Kony 2012* video quickly became one of the greatest viral successes in the short history of social media, drawing millions of viewers on YouTube. Within three weeks, it spurred action on Capitol Hill: Over a third of U.S. senators introduced a bipartisan resolution condemning Kony and his troops for "unconscionable crimes against humanity." (Guo & Saxton, 2014)

Facebook, Twitter, and other social networking sites have provided nonprofits with an important mechanism for educating and engaging people who share their interests (Held, 2014). Illustrating the growing importance of the Internet as a tool for advocacy, Change.org, an online platform enabling individuals to start and sign petitions related to issues, had 70 million users in 196 countries in 2015 (www .change.org/about). OurTime.org, dedicated to issues of concern specifically to millennials, reported 2015 membership of one million people (www.ourtime.org/about-us). In 2011, the White House launched its We the People website, which enables users to start petitions on policy issues. Petitions that receive a minimum number of signatures require a formal response from government officials.

Continuing Issues and Debate

For nonprofits that are social welfare organizations, advocacy and lobbying are, of course, the essence of the mission. With regard to charitable nonprofits, some take a larger role in advocacy while others remain cautious. In *Forces for Good,* Leslie Crutchfield and Heather Grant (2012) urge nonprofits that provide programs to expand their advocacy activity. The authors identify twelve organizations that have high impact, that is, that are "catalytic agents of change" (p. 18). One defining characteristic is their involvement in advocacy and lobbying as well as program delivery. Some began by offering programs and later expanded into advocacy roles. Others went the other way, having begun as advocacy organizations and later added direct service programs. "And," the authors state, "the more they advocate *and* [italics original] serve, the greater the impact they achieve" (p. 38).

One consequence of shifting a nonprofit's activities from direct service to advocacy may be that it becomes more challenging to measure impact. As Pekkanen and Smith (2014) observe, this is true for three principal reasons. First, the definition of what constitutes advocacy is blurry and it may involve different levels of effort: "dashing off a quick letter is one thing, but spending hours or days crafting a thoughtful and substantive epistle is a substantially different endeavor" (p. 1). Second, causality is difficult to determine; a new public policy may be approved, but it may not be possible to attribute that to the efforts of nonprofits overall or one nonprofit in particular. And, third, "advocacy is fungible" (p. 2). A nonprofit may delegate advocacy to a separate, related organization or to a trade association, or to a chapter or national headquarters (Pekkanen & Smith, 2014). Thus, a shift toward advocacy may make it more difficult for some organizations to measure their results at a time when the importance of such measurement is being emphasized.

Political activity by tax-exempt organizations remains controversial. A contentious debate emerged in 2013, subsequent to the Citizen's United case discussed earlier. The IRS was accused of having inappropriately identified some organizations that had applied for tax exemption under 501(c)4 and subjected them to additional scrutiny based on their political affiliations (Independent Sector, 2015c). Some called on the IRS to develop more specific definitions of what constitutes "political activity" and more precise standards than the somewhat vague requirement that political activity not be the "primary purpose" of such organizations. But when IRS proposed new guidelines later in 2013, negative responses ensued, emanating from organizations on both sides of the political spectrum. Concerns went beyond the limitations placed on 501(c)4 organizations, with some critics claiming that the proposed regulations could affect even 501(c)3 charitable nonprofits by defining some nonpartisan activities, such as voter-registration drives, to be political activity (Aviv & Bass, 2013). Nonprofit sector organizations, including Independent Sector, advanced alternatives to the initial IRS proposal and IRS promised to release new rules (Independent Sector, 2015c). Students should consult Web resources to see what changes may have been made since this chapter was written.

In a period of debate about issues with which some nonprofits engage, it is likely that there will be continuing calls for all nonprofits to increase their advocacy and lobbying efforts. At the same time, there may also be risks to be considered in an environment of political polarization and scrutiny of nonprofits by elected officials and the media. Nonprofits of all types will need to be informed of the law and careful to follow best practices in this area of activity.

Chapter Summary

Advocacy by nonprofits has played an important role in the most significant social changes throughout U.S. history, including the civil rights movement, the expansion of women's rights, and environmental protections. Issues often move through stages of public awareness and action, and nonprofits play an important role in that process (see Box 11.1). Nonprofits may advocate on any side of any issue, and their advocacy and lobbying is thus a fundamental pillar of a democratic society. However, various studies have found that only a small percentage of charitable nonprofits engage in advocacy or lobbying. Some are hesitant to do so for various reasons, including lack of staff and resources, concern about alienating private or government funders, and misunderstanding of what the law permits them to do without jeopardizing their nonprofit status.

Advocacy includes action taken in support of a cause or an idea. It may include, for example, providing education, distributing information, or holding events to dramatize an issue or the effects of a problem on people or a community. Advocacy is a basic right of every individual and organization in the United States and may be practiced without limit—it is an exercise of free speech protected by the U.S. Constitution. Lobbying goes beyond advocacy—it is action taken to support or oppose specific legislation at the national, state, or local level. Advocacy is the larger concept, which encompasses lobbying.

Some nonprofits—for example, 501(c)(4) social welfare organizations—are permitted to lobby without limitation but are not eligible to receive tax-deductible gifts. Because they can receive such gifts, which are a form of public subsidy, charitable nonprofits exempt under Section 501(c)(3) face limitations on their lobbying activity. There are two standards under which a charitable nonprofit can determine the amount of permissible lobbying. The substantial part test was the standard that existed prior to the 1976 Lobby Law, and organizations can still choose to be subject to it. However, *substantial part* applies to both time and expenditures, and it is not precisely defined.

The other option is to elect the expenditure test provided under Section 501(h) of the Internal Revenue Code. That section establishes a specific percentage of total qualified expenditures that nonprofits of various sizes can spend on lobbying, with an overall cap of $1 million. This option also distinguishes between direct lobbying and grassroots. A lower limit applies to grassroots activities that attempt to influence the public's attitudes and that include a call to action in support of or opposition to specific legislation. It also identifies specific activities—for example, self-defense—that do not count as lobbying. The expenditure test does not consider activities of volunteers or other efforts that do not involve expenditures. It is thus relatively generous in the amount of lobbying that it permits nonprofits to undertake.

Private foundations are not permitted to lobby or to make grants to other nonprofits designated for support of lobbying. Foundation grants to public charities that are unrestricted operating support may be used for lobbying by the charity within its allowable limit.

Charitable nonprofits may not participate in political campaigns or endorse candidates. The 2010 Supreme Court decision in the case of *Citizens United v. FEC* changed the law to permit corporations and nonprofits exempt under sections 501(c)(4), 501(c)(5), and 501(c)(6) to endorse candidates, subject to the requirement that political activity not be the organization's primary purpose, but the prohibition on campaign activity by charitable nonprofits remains, as the trade-off for the tax deductibility of gifts made to them. There have been recent cases in which the IRS investigated reports that churches and other nonprofits may have violated this prohibition, and some violators were punished by having their tax-exempt status revoked. In 2014, the IRS promised to develop new guidelines on political activity by 501(c)(4) organizations in order to reduce uncertainty. It had not done so by mid-2015. Students should check Web sources to learn if these new guidelines have been issued subsequent to the writing of this chapter.

There are many guides to the practice of lobbying. Most practitioner guides emphasize linking the activity to the nonprofit's mission, understanding the legislative process, identifying sources of permissible funds to support lobbying, developing an infrastructure of staff and systems to support the lobbying effort, conducting research to identify public policy issues and gathering facts needed to make the organization's case, conducting an inventory of friends and identifying their relationships with key legislators, and developing a strategic mix of tactics to be employed. Some tools include letters, e-mails, media coverage, events, and personal visits with legislators and their staff members.

Although nonprofits have considerable freedom to engage in advocacy and lobbying, there have been attempts in recent years to impose more restrictions. It can be challenging to measure the results of nonprofit advocacy, since it is not always possible to establish causation between such activity and changes in public policy. Some call for a greater role for nonprofits in advocacy and electoral politics, but others voice caution and concern. There has been controversy regarding IRS rules for 501(c)4 organizations, and some issues may have relevance for charitable nonprofits as well. Debate is likely to continue, and nonprofits should remain informed as to the latest requirements.

Note

1. Specifically, this means its expenditures on exempt activity, which excludes fundraising and certain administrative expenses.

KEY TERMS AND CONCEPTS

501(h) option	*gift rule*	*Section 501(h)*
advocacy	*grassroots lobbying*	*self-defense activity*
Citizens United v. FEC	*lobbying*	*substantial part test*
direct lobbying	*political campaign activity*	

CASE 11.1 Mothers Against Drunk Driving (MADD)

As MADD Executive Director Chuck Hurley describes it, "Before the 1980s, drunk driving was how people got home. It was normal behavior." In May of that year, Candy Lightner's 13-year-old daughter was killed by a hit-and-run driver while walking to a church carnival. As her mother was soon to learn, drunk driving was just not on society's radar as an issue. Although 60 percent of automobile deaths were alcohol related, drunk driving was a low priority for law enforcement and the courts. Congress had spent $35 million on Alcohol Safety Action Programs, with little effect. After her daughter's death, Candy Lightner established Mothers Against Drunk Driving (MADD), determined to change society's attitude and behavior as well as the law.

She found other victims' families through classified ads and mailings, learned about California laws and lobbied the governor for new legislation, made speeches, and raised money. In October of 1980, MADD held a news conference on Capitol Hill that captured the nation's attention. Other mothers began establishing chapters in their hometowns and the organization grew rapidly, with 100 chapters in place by 1982.

(Continued)

contracts, but it has not yet received payment. Using the accrual basis of accounting, the anticipated payment shows up as *revenue* on its financial reports. But it may not have cash on hand in the bank to meet this month's rent or payroll. For these reasons, organizations—and individuals—also need to track cash flow. We will see more about how they do so in the next section of this chapter.

Nonprofit Financial Statements

Again, accounting is about following the rules. For nonprofit organizations, rules are established by the *Financial Accounting Standards Board* (FASB), which people often pronounce as "Faz-bee," which defines *generally accepted accounting principles* (called GAAP). The standards especially relevant to nonprofit organizations are No. 93 ("Accounting for Depreciation"), No. 95 ("Statement of Cash Flows"), No. 116 ("Accounting for Contributions Received and Contributions Made"), No. 117 ("Financial Statements of Not-for-Profit Organizations"), and No. 124 ("Accounting for Certain Investments Held by Not-for-Profit Organizations") (Anthony & Young, 2005, p. 469). We will not go into detail on all these in this discussion, but there will be occasions to refer in particular to the Statement of Financial Accounting Standards (SFAS) No. 116 and SFAS No. 117. These standards have ramifications not only for how nonprofits keep track of their finances, but also for their relationships with donors. FASB regularly reviews its standards, and students are encouraged to check its website (www.fasb.org) to see if any changes have been made subsequent to the writing of this text.

Tables 12.2, 12.3, 12.4, and 12.5, respectively, provide examples of four financial statements that nonprofit organizations prepare: (1) *statement of financial position* (sometimes called the *balance sheet*), (2) *statement of activities* (sometimes called the *income statement*), (3) *statement of cash flows,* and (4) *statement of functional expenses.* All of the data in these statements, which are often included in organizations' annual reports and websites, also are reported on Form 990, in a somewhat different format. Space does not permit a line-by-line discussion of the statements, so let's just look at a few key items, especially those that illustrate unique features of nonprofit accounting.

The examples in this chapter are the fiscal year 2014 financial statements of Big Brothers Big Sisters of Massachusetts Bay (BBBSMB), which serves the Boston area. Its financial statements have been taken directly from its audit report, which is posted on its website (www.bbbsmb.org). Like many organizations, BBBSMB does its accounting on a fiscal year basis—in its case, the year runs from July 1 to June 30—rather than a calendar year ending on December 31. The federal government ends its fiscal year on September 30, and some nonprofits that receive significant government support also use that date, making it easier to reconcile their accounting with required government reports. Much of the same data shown on official financial statements are also provided in an organization's Form 990, which is filed with the Internal Revenue Service and is easily accessed through services such as GuideStar. For purposes of space and simplicity, the examples shown in this chapter do not include the *Notes to the Financial Statements,* the notes that follow financial statements and provide supplemental information. But the notes are an integral part of an organization's overall financial statements and often illuminate some important details. Anyone wishing to have a complete understanding of the financial position of BBBSMB, or any nonprofit, should read the full audit report, including the auditor's comments and the notes. But let's look at just a few key points in BBBSMB's financial statements that relate to some of the principles we discussed above.

Statement of Financial Position

The *statement of financial position* (sometimes called the *balance sheet*) provides a snapshot of the organization at a point in time, usually the end of a fiscal year. It summarizes its *assets,* that is, "the items that the organization possesses, with which it carries out its programs and service," and its *liabilities,* the "amounts of borrowed money, or debt, that the organization has used to finance some of those assets"

TABLE 12.2 ■ Statement of Financial Position

BIG BROTHERS BIG SISTERS OF MASSACHUSETTS BAY, INC.
Statements of Financial Position
June 30, 2014 and 2013

ASSETS		
	2014	2013
CURRENT ASSETS:		
Cash and cash equivalents	**$ 3,286,153**	$ 2,878,320
Current portion of contributions receivable	**1,986,716**	755,043
Grants receivable	**70,000**	86,458
Investments	**1,078,711**	1,079,187
Prepaid expenses and other current assets	**246,197**	175,201
Total current assets	**6,667,777**	4,974,209
PROPERTY AND EQUIPMENT, NET	**208,746**	211,480
OTHER ASSETS:		
Contributions receivable, net of current portion	**2,935,976**	5,011,041
Investments	**3,945,796**	3,452,575
Total other assets	**6,881,772**	8,463,616
Total assets	**$13,758,295**	$13,649,305
LIABILITIES AND NET ASSETS		
	2014	2013
CURRENT LIABILITIES:		
Current portion of long term debt	**$ 3,466**	$ 3,249
Current portion of capital lease obligation	**7,789**	1,381
Accounts payable	**100,065**	117,741
Accrued expenses	**458,066**	258,823
Deferred revenue	**68,450**	-
Deferred lease incentive	**29,566**	-
Total current liabilities	**667,402**	381,194
LONG-TERM LIABILITIES:		
Long term debt, net of current portion	**36,181**	39,756
Capital lease obligation, net of current portion	**21,759**	2,596
Total liabilities	**725,342**	423,546
NET ASSETS:		
Unrestricted:		
Operations	**3,837,025**	3,294,155
Board designated	**1,164,355**	991,365
Total unrestricted net assets	**5,001,380**	4,285,520
Temporarily restricted	**6,283,812**	1,747,761
Permanently restricted	**7,207,478**	1,732,761
Total net assets	**13,032,953**	13,225,759
Total liabilities and net assets	**$13,758,295**	$13,649,305
See notes to financial statements.		

Source: Big Brothers and Big Sisters of Massachusetts Bay, Inc. Retrieved January 21, 2015, from http://www.bbbsmb.org/site/c.9gKMJZMxF7LUG/b.8453153/apps/s/content.asp?ct=12489953

TABLE 12.3 ■ Statement of Activities

BIG BROTHERS BIG SISTERS OF MASSACHUSETTS BAY, INC.
Statements of Activities
Year Ended June 30, 2014, with Comparative Totals for the Year Ended June 30, 2013

	Unrestricted	Temporarily Restricted	Permanently Restricted	2014 Total	2013 Comparative Total
REVENUES AND OTHER SUPPORT:					
Special events	$ 3,421,877	$ 94,281	$ -	$ 3,516,158	$ 3,866,951
Less cost of special events	(1,385,548)	-	-	(1,385,548)	(1,260,968)
Net revenues from special events	2,036,329	94,281	-	2,130,610	2,605,983
Individuals	943,776	588,616	15,000	1,547,392	3,692,785
Corporations, foundations, government and United Way	693,746	94,100	-	787,846	916,247
BBBS Foundation and other revenue	423,866	-	-	423,866	172,448
	4,097,717	776,997	15,000	4,889,714	7,387,463
Net assets released from restrictions Endowment appropriation	2,020,587	(2,020,587)	-	-	-
	90,000		-	90,000	52,000
Total revenues and other support	6,208,304	(1,243,590)	15,000	4,979,714	7,439,463
EXPENSES:					
Program sendees	4,289,454	-	-	4,289,454	3,603,936
General and administrative	380,142	-	-	380,142	381,834
Fundraising and development	995,838	-	-	995,838	1,041,554
Total expenses	5,665,434	-	-	5,665,434	5,027,324
CHANGE IN NET ASSETS FROM OPERATING ACTIVITIES	542,870	(1,243,590)	15,000	(685,720)	2,412,139
NON-OPERATING ACTIVITY:					
Income from investments, net of fees	16,129	41,607	-	57,736	63,452
Net realized and unrealized gains on investments	156,861	368,317	-	525,178	203,628
Endowment appropriation	-	(90,000)	-	(90,000)	(52,000)
Total non-operating activity	172,990	319,924	-	492,914	215,080
CHANGE IN NET ASSETS	715,860	(923,666)	15,000	(192,806)	2,627,219
NET ASSETS. BEGINNING OF YEAR	4,285,520	7,207,478	1,732,761	13,225,759	10,598,540
NET ASSETS. END OF YEAR	$5,001,380	$6,283,812	$1,747,761	$13,032,953	$13,225,759

See notes to financial statements.

Source: Big Brothers Big Sisters of Massachusetts Bay, Inc. Retrieved January 21, 2015, from http://www.bbbsmb.org/site/c.9gKMJZMxF7LUG/b.8453153/apps/s/content.asp?ct=12489953

TABLE 12.4 ■ Statement of Cash Flows

BIG BROTHERS BIG SISTERS OF MASSACHUSETTS BAY, INC.
Statements of Cash Flows
Years Ended June 30, 2014 and 2013

	2014	2013
CASH FLOWS FROM OPERATING ACTIVITIES:		
Changes in net assets	**$ (192,806)**	$ 2,627,219
Adjustments to reconcile changes in net assets to net cash provided by operating activities:		
Depreciation	**46,117**	44,314
Unrealized and realized gains on investments	**(525,178)**	(203,628)
Change in assets and liabilities:		
(Increase) decrease in:		
Contributions receivable	**843,392**	(1,669,747)
Grants receivable	**16,458**	96,042
Prepaid expenses and other current assets	**(70,996)**	(1,777)
Increase (decrease) in:		
Accounts payable	**(17,676)**	25,373
Accrued expenses	**199,243**	10,889
Deferred revenue	**68,450**	(39,050)
Deferred lease incentive	**29,566**	-
Net cash provided by operating activities	**396,570**	889,635
CASH FLOWS FROM INVESTING ACTIVITIES:		
Purchase of properly and equipment	**(13,366)**	(20,469)
Proceeds from sale of investments	**4,257,096**	2,358,301
Purchase of investments	**(4,224,663)**	(2,321,677)
Net cash provided by investing activities	**19,067**	16,155
CASH FLOWS FROM FINANCING ACTIVITIES:		
Principal payments on long-term debt	**(3,358)**	(4,263)
Principal payments on capital lease obligations	**(4,446)**	-
Net cash used by financing activities	**(7,804)**	(4,263)
NET INCREASE IN CASH AND CASH EQUIVALENTS	**407,833**	901,527
CASH AND CASH EQUIVALENTS, BEGINNING OF YEAR	**2,878,320**	1,976,793
CASH AND CASH EQUIVALENTS, END OF YEAR	**$3,286,153**	$2,878,320
SUPPLEMENTAL DISCLOSURES OF CASH FLOWS INFORMATION:		
Cash paid during the year for:		
Interest	**$ 2,742**	$ 3,735
Assets acquired under capital lease	**$ 30,017**	$ -
See notes to financial statements.		

Source: Big Brothers Big Sisters of Massachusetts Bay, Inc. Retrieved January 21, 2015, from http://www.bbbsmb.org/site/c.9gKMJZMxF7LUG/b.8453153/apps/s/content.asp?ct=12489953

TABLE 12.5 ■ Statement of Functional Expenses

BIG BROTHERS BIG SISTERS OF MASSACHUSETTS BAY, INC.
Statements of Functional Expenses
Year Ended June 30, 2014, with Comparative Totals for the Year Ended June 30, 2013

	Program Services	General and Administrative	Fundraising and Development	2014 Total	2013 Comparative Totals
OPERATING EXPENSES:					
Payroll	$ 2,479,540	$214,287	$ 735,761	$3,429,588	$3,091,401
Benefits	513,817	45,469	115,879	675,165	654,153
Professional fees	375,968	25,581	13,246	414,795	189,070
Occupancy	302,731	10,802	34,388	347,921	335,993
Advertising and promotion	94,465	-	-	94,465	71,290
In-kind expense	88,226	-	-	88,226	141,656
Insurance	70,284	2,809	9,136	82,229	76,698
Activity fee	48,686	-	-	48,686	23,106
Depreciation and amortization	39,311	1,600	5,206	46,117	44,314
Bad debt	-	45,958	-	45,958	-
Business meetings	28,231	757	9,790	38,778	29,707
Travel	26,639	306	10,668	37,613	36,793
Telephone	32,504	1,062	3,455	37,021	38,269
Equipment rental and maintenance	22,843	760	13,211	36,814	40,796
Printing	19,433	163	16,323	35,919	44,345
Postage	17,489	257	15,761	33,507	29,330
Volunteer stewardship	23,615	2,746	6,119	32,480	25,795
BBBSA dues	30,347	-	-	30,347	21,989
Office supplies	23,349	688	3,202	27,239	31,742
Charge card fees	-	24,755	120	24,875	21,486
Membership/research	19,403	234	2,581	22,218	40,125
Scholarships and camperships	20,151	-	-	20,151	28,122
Conferences/training	6,879	1,794	621	9,294	7,409
Interest	5,543	114	371	6,028	3,735
Total expenses	$4,289,454	$380,142	$995,838	$5,665,434	$5,027,324

See notes to financial statements.

Source: Big Brothers Big Sisters of Massachusetts Bay, Inc. Retrieved January 21, 2015, from http://www.bbbsmb.org/site/c.9gKMJZMxF7LUG/b.8453153/apps/s/content.asp?ct=12489953

(Zietlow et al., 2007, p. 172). To put it in personal terms again, your personal assets may include your bank accounts, the book value of your car, and the market value of your house. They need to be offset by your liabilities, for example, the balances on your car loan, mortgage, and credit cards. The difference is equal to your personal *net worth*. In a for-profit company, the difference is called *equity;* it represents the value of the owners' interest in the firm. For a nonprofit, there is no ownership interest, so the difference between assets and liabilities is simply defined as *net assets*. The way balance sheets are constructed, assets always equal the sum of liabilities and net assets; if these totals do not agree, there is something wrong with the numbers.

The BBBSMB balance sheet reflects some of the accounting principles discussed before. For example, notice that net assets (down toward the bottom of the statement) are divided into those that are unrestricted, those that are temporarily restricted, and those that are permanently restricted. The temporarily restricted assets are funds that donors intended to be used for specific activities that have not yet been carried out. (A breakdown of these intended purposes is provided in Notes to the Financial Statements, which are not shown in this simplified example.) Permanently restricted assets usually represent endowment.

Under "current assets," BBBSMB's balance sheet shows an asset called "contributions receivable" and another called "grants receivable." That reflects the accrual basis of accounting; these are gifts and grants that have been promised but not yet received. The total shown for contributions receivable usually includes an adjustment for what are called "doubtful accounts," which means gifts and grants that may end up not being paid for some reason. That amount is estimated based on past experience. SFAS 116, which was mentioned earlier, requires that under certain circumstances nonprofits show pledges ("contributions receivable") as assets, even if they have not received payment of the gift. It was a controversial requirement when introduced in the 1990s, which caused some organizations to reconsider how pledges were written and documented. It was one of the factors that have led to more formal relationships between nonprofits and their donors over the past decade.

Under "current liabilities" on BBBSMB's statement of financial position, we see another example of the accrual basis, *accounts payable*, which represent commitments that BBBSMB has made, but which have not yet been paid. The obligations are liabilities that must be shown on the balance sheet.

Statement of Activities

Now, let's go to Table 12.3, BBBSMB's statement of activities. The balance sheet, or statement of financial position (shown in Table 12.2), is a *snapshot* of the organization's finances taken at a point in time. But the *statement of activities* shown in Table 12.3 is more like a *video* that shows the flow of revenues and expenses of the organization, and the resulting changes in net assets, *over a period of time,* generally a fiscal year. Accordingly, some nonprofit organizations call this the "statement of revenues, expenses, and changes in net assets." For a business, this statement would be the same as its "profit and loss," or "P&L" statement (Zietlow et al., 2007, p. 179).

BBBSMB's statement of activities shows various sources of revenue, including the net revenue from events (after expenses related to the events), contributions from private donors, and government funds. These all would be considered "public support" in determining that BBBSMB is a public charity rather than a private foundation. (The difference was discussed in Chapter 2.) All revenues are divided into the categories of "unrestricted," "temporarily restricted," and "permanently restricted." In 2014, BBBSMB received $4,097,717 in unrestricted revenue, which could be used to meet its general operating expenses or for any legitimate purpose determined by its leadership. BBBSMB received $776,997 in revenue that was temporarily restricted. That means the donor or grantor has specified that the funds be used for some specific purpose or program and they cannot be expended until those activities occur; perhaps the work is scheduled for some time in the next year. At the same time, there were "net assets released from restrictions," totaling $2,020,587, either because a time restriction expired or because the organization provided the services that the funds were intended to cover. This point can be a little difficult to understand, but Bowman (2011) provides a helpful example:

Assume that a not-for-profit theater sells season subscriptions for a series of five plays [and the buyers pay cash]. Before the season begins, none of the cash can be recognized as revenue because the theater has not yet earned it. Subscription sales go on the statement of financial position [the balance sheet] as cash, and the theater's accountants balance it by creating an equal amount of deferred revenue as an offsetting liability. Since net assets do not change, there is no revenue recognized at this time. It should be easy to see why cash received before being earned is a liability: If the theater cancels the season, it must refund the cash to its patrons. After each performance, deferred revenue is reduced by one-fifth, which increases net assets, causing recognition of one-fifth of the cash as revenue. (p. 22)

Gifts that are permanently restricted are generally for endowment; BBBSMB received $15,000 that was permanently restricted in 2014. And it received a $90,000 appropriation from endowment funds to be applied to its 2014 operating budget. (Management of endowment funds is discussed further in a later section of this chapter.)

Statement of Cash Flows

Table 12.4 shows BBBSMB's statement of cash flows for 2014. As discussed previously, the statement of activities does not give the whole picture because of the accrual basis of accounting it reflects. (Remember your friend who never had any cash but thought himself wealthy because of his anticipation of future funds from his aunt.) For that reason, SFAS 117 requires that nonprofits also produce a *statement of cash flows* to show cash inflows and outflows over the year, enabling us to see how the cash amount changed from one year to the next. There are two methods of presenting cash flow, direct and indirect, but this chapter does not go into detail about them (McMillan, 2003a).

Look again at BBBSMB's statement of financial position in Table 12.2 and the first line under "current assets" as of June 30, 2014— it shows cash and cash equivalents totaling $3,286,153. Now look at the line near the bottom of the statement of cash flows in Table 12.4—the line labeled "cash and cash equivalents, end of year"—it's the same number ($3,286,153). What the statement of cash flows does is walk us through exactly how the cash changed from the beginning to the end of BBBSMB's fiscal year, which began July 1, 2013, and ended June 30, 2014. Cash flow may occur through operating activities, investing activities, or financing activities. Think again about your own checking account. Cash might flow in from your paycheck. You may have sold your car, a physical asset, and placed the proceeds in the same account. Or you may have borrowed money from the bank and then deposited the amount of the loan directly into your checking account. All those transactions comprise your cash flow, but again, tracking just the flow of cash into and out of your checking account would not provide a complete picture of your financial position; that requires looking at the cash flow in relationship to the other financial statements discussed above.

Statement of Functional Expenses

The last financial statement we will consider is shown in Table 12.5—the *statement of functional expenses*. This statement shows how every category of expense was allocated among the uses of program services, general and administrative activities, and fundraising. It is from this data that charity watchdogs, certain donors, and others calculate the ratios that some use to evaluate the efficiency of an organization's management and fundraising efforts. Let's come back to that point shortly.

Before leaving the discussion of financial statements, there is one additional concept that is important to understand—*depreciation.* The concept of depreciation, and the way it is handled in financial accounting, is sometimes difficult for individuals to quite grasp in terms of their personal financial life. The most familiar experience that most of us have with depreciation is the decline in the book value of our cars. Your new car may lose much of its value as soon as it is driven off the dealer's lot, and it will continue to decline every year that you own it. If you keep it long enough, it will continue to decline until it is ready for the junkyard and is worth next to zero. You may not feel that decline as an expense as it occurs, since it is not coming out of your pocket or checking account each day, but clearly your personal net worth is less when the car gets old than it was when the car was new. Thus, the car's depreciation is a real expense in terms of its effect on your total net worth, even though it may not affect your cash flow.

Let's say a nonprofit organization owns physical assets, including cars, buildings, and equipment. Those assets have a value, and that value is reflected on its balance sheet. But they are assets that will be used up or wear out over some period of time, so their value declines with every passing month or year. That decline must be accounted for as an *expense,* even though it does not involve an actual outlay of money. Take a look at BBBSMB's statement of functional expenses in Table 12.5; the amount of depreciation of its assets in 2014 is reflected in about the middle (included in "depreciation and amortization"), totaling $46,117. But it is an accounting expense rather than a real outlay of cash, so an adjustment needs to be made to provide a clear picture of BBBSMB's cash flow. Take another look at Table 12.4, the statement of cash flows. The $46,117 has been added back in on the first line under "adjustments to reconcile changes in net assets to net cash provided by operating activities." Without this adjustment, the statement of cash flows would understate the amount of cash generated by operations during the year (Zietlow et al., 2007, p. 182). Although depreciation is an accounting item rather than a cash outlay, some organizations fund depreciation, that is, they set aside money for future maintenance or replacement of their capital assets. This is not a cash expenditure in the given year because the funds are, in effect, placed in a savings account to be used when needed at a later time; they remain an asset of the organization. Failure to fund depreciation can present a problem for a nonprofit when its facilities or other capital assets do become inadequate. *Deferred maintenance* can make the financial picture look brighter than it really is, a fact that becomes clear when the organization is faced with the need for a major expense, say for a new roof or vehicle, without having put funds aside to cover it (Mattocks, 2008, p. 91).

Using Financial Ratios

Now that we have examined some basic accounting principles and looked at the financial statements that nonprofits produce, what do we make of the data? How can we interpret the financial data and use it to make decisions about the financial management of the organization?

The concept of financial ratios was introduced back in Chapter 6, which discussed some ratios that external observers use to evaluate the performance of nonprofit organizations. Readers may recall from that chapter that a 2004 study by the Urban Institute and Harvard's Hauser Institute (Fremont-Smith & Cordes, 2004) looked at 10 charity watchdog organizations that use financial ratios and found a variety of measures being applied, including variations of the following:

- The ratio of program expenses to contributed income
- The ratio of fundraising expenditures and private support received—that is, the cost of raising a dollar
- The percentage of total expenses (or income received from contributions) spent on charitable programs or activities
- The percentage of total expenses spent on fundraising and administration (overhead)
- Accumulated cash and asset reserves in relation to operating budget

These ratios measure an organization's efficiency rather than its effectiveness. They might be of interest to the organization's board and management, but taken alone, they may not provide an appropriate way to rate or rank nonprofits. Indeed, some argue that a misplaced emphasis on efficiency has prevented many nonprofits from building capacity and achieving impact (Pallotta, 2010).

There are a number of ratios that can be calculated from the data provided on an organization's financial statements or similar data obtained from the Form 990. The ratios that are most commonly tracked by managers are those that measure *profitability, liquidity, asset management,* and *long-term solvency* (Anthony & Young, 2005, p. 488). This chapter does not go into detail on the calculation of ratios but rather will focus on explaining the concepts that they are intended to measure and their significance to assessing the financial health of a nonprofit organization.

Although the term *profitability* may seem out of place in the nonprofit setting, it is just describing the change in net assets on the statement of activities; in other words, it considers whether the organization had an operating surplus, broke even, or operated at a loss. Liquidity relates to the organization's use of cash.

Remember from the earlier discussion the example of the friend who thinks himself wealthy because he anticipates an inheritance but who lacks the cash to pay for dinner. To avoid being in a similar bind, an organization needs to manage its cash flows effectively in order to be sufficiently *liquid,* that is, possessed of sufficient cash at the right times to meet its obligations as they come due. An analysis of cash management would address areas such as accounts receivable, accounts payable, and inventory maintained. For example, if clients are slow to pay bills for service, the organization will need to keep more cash on hand to pay its own bills as they come due. If the collection process could be made more efficient, it would need to maintain less of a cash balance and that money then could be put to work in other productive ways. Vendors need to be paid on time, but effective management of the process could reduce the amount of unproductive cash needing to be kept on hand. To use another example from personal financial life, there may not be a need to keep money sitting in your checking account on the 15th of the month if the rent is not due until the 1st, and you know you will be receiving a paycheck in the meantime. Tracking when revenues come in and when bill payments are due is a way to stretch dollars further and gain more leverage from your personal cash flow.

Another issue for organizations is management of inventories. If too much money is tied up in inventories, it may leave too little liquidity to meet cash obligations as they arise. For example, if a food program spends all its cash to fill up its freezers with a six-month supply of food, then it may be in a bind to pay its staff or other expenses. Developing a more efficient system for food purchases that could reduce the amount of inventory kept in the freezer could provide for more liquidity to meet other obligations or to be put toward more effective purposes.

Management of fixed assets requires looking at how efficiently they are being used; for example, how much revenue is being generated through the use of buildings and equipment? The condition of assets needs to be tracked and adequate funds earmarked for replacement or repairs. That is a way to avoid unexpected expenses for which there may not be funds readily at hand from current revenue.

Assessing *long-term solvency,* that is, evaluating whether the organization is financially strong or in jeopardy, requires looking at the right-hand side of the statement of financial position, the liabilities, as well as the revenue and expenses shown on the statement of activities. One big issue is the amount of debt, specifically the relationship between assets and liabilities. Borrowing funds may be a good thing; it provides the organization with a way to leverage its assets and support a larger program of services than it could just with current revenue. But obviously, debt also increases risk and requires careful management of cash flow to ensure that debt payments can be made when due (Anthony & Young, 2005).

Ron Mattocks (2008) describes a "zone of insolvency," a "period of . . . financial distress during which prudent people could at least foresee the possibility of insolvency" (p. 87). Insolvency means a situation in which the organization can no longer continue in business and may need to either declare bankruptcy or close down. This condition can be detected by monitoring indicators and ratios that may sound an alarm bell. Most boards will be alert to the alarm, since the law imposes especially demanding requirements on the governing board in such a situation (Mattocks, 2008). What are the alarms that may signify the *zone of insolvency*? Liabilities exceeding assets is one, although that may occur temporarily without too much concern, for example, if the organization has recently borrowed money to expand its programs and anticipates increased revenue soon. One warning sign is inadequate cash flow, especially if it is inadequate in comparison to the organization's debt. Another test is whether the organization would be able to pay all of its creditors should it cease operations tomorrow; if not, then it may be in financially unhealthy territory (Mattocks, 2008).

Which are the most important financial ratios to watch and manage? Zietlow et al. (2007) make the case that for most nonprofit organizations, liquidity—"the ability of the organization to augment its future cash flows" (p. 23)—is the biggest potential problem. Many nonprofits depend on contributions, but giving may fluctuate from year to year. An unforeseen event, such as the loss of a key donor or perhaps a decline in allocations from United Way, can leave a nonprofit in a cash crunch, stretched to meet its own obligations. Some pledges, which are reflected on the financial statements as assets, may in fact not be paid, and estimates of how much may be uncollectible may not be based on reliable information. If the organization depends on earned income, it faces business risks; if a college's enrollment turns down, a concert attracts fewer than expected attendees, or a blizzard reduces attendance at a major fundraising event, revenue may turn out to be much different from what the budget anticipated.

Nonprofits that rely on contracts may face similar problems; for example, costs may exceed what was projected and exceed the revenue that the contract provides. Some clients may be slow to pay. The only options might then include obtaining short-term financing from banks or other lenders, making emergency appeals to donors, tapping into reserves or even quasi endowment, delaying payments to vendors, and reducing costs by cutting staff or their compensation. Zietlow and colleagues (2007) argue that such problems are "endemic to the nonprofit sector [and that liquidity] is one of the most important yet least studied areas in the management of nonprofits" (p. 23). Zietlow et al. criticize the charity watchdogs, such as the BBB Wise Giving Alliance and others, who set a maximum that organizations should keep in reserves. The view of the charity raters is that excess funds held in reserve should instead be used to support current programs and services. But Zietlow and colleagues argue, "[While] these policy guidelines may be appropriate for commercial nonprofits, [they] will severely limit the management style of small donative . . . organizations" (p. 24). Drawing on data from a study that Zietlow conducted in 2002 to 2004, these authors suggest a model that nonprofits can use to determine the appropriate level of liquidity to maintain (pp. 28–43).

Managing Endowment Funds

As noted previously, most nonprofit organizations do not have significant endowments; most are held by large institutions such as colleges and universities, health organizations and medical institutions, museums, and major arts centers. The largest is the endowment of Harvard University, which totaled almost $33 billion in 2013. Other institutions with substantial endowments in 2013 included the Salvation Army ($2.2 billion), United Way Worldwide ($1.5 billion), the Art Institute of Chicago ($870 million), WWF (World Wildlife Fund) ($208 million), and Save the Children ($141 million) (Explore Endowment Data, 2014).

Of course, the stock market decline in 2008 and early 2009 hit many nonprofit endowments hard. Many nonprofits were forced to make adjustments in their operating budgets to reflect the lower income available from endowment, and others postponed new projects or programs. But remember our discussion in the early part of this chapter; unlike individuals, many substantial organizations and institutions intend to exist forever. They make adjustments to accommodate to economic cycles but also expect to recover their endowments as the economy turns around in years ahead. Indeed, by the fall of 2012, U.S. stock markets had almost doubled from the bottom reached in March of 2009, and, by 2015, market indexes had reached historic highs.

As discussed earlier, some endowment may be created by the nonprofit's board from internal resources, perhaps from excess operating surpluses accumulated over several years. Although board-designated endowment could be expended at the board's discretion, it is intended for long-term use and would generally be managed according to the same policies applied to permanent endowment created through donor-designated gifts. *Term endowments,* which are established for a period of years, after which the funds may be spent, might be invested and managed differently, depending on the date of their anticipated termination. The discussion of endowment management here applies to funds that the organization intends, or must, hold for investment in perpetuity, using only the annual income earned from investments to support its operating needs. There are two key concepts related to the management of endowment funds. One is the *total return* approach to investing endowment assets, and the other is the *spending limit* that determines how much will be available from endowment for expenditure each year.

In earlier decades, a large portion of endowment assets was invested in relatively secure, interest-paying instruments, such as bonds and bank certificates of deposit. The drawbacks of this approach became evident in the high-inflation economy of the 1970s, since the fixed amount of interest income became increasingly inadequate to support the activities for which the endowment was intended. Over the long term, investments in stocks produce higher overall returns and keep pace with inflation, but stocks often pay dividends that provide less current income than bonds. Institutions found a way around this dilemma by adopting the total return approach to investing endowments, combined with a spending limit to determine how much could be used each year.

The approach is to invest in a portfolio that includes stocks, cash, bonds, real estate, and other classes of assets, providing for the *long-term* growth of the principal. The investment strategy is to maximize total return—that is, the total of interest, dividends, and appreciation in the value of stocks and other assets—consistent with a level of risk that the organization's board has determined to be acceptable. Each year, some percentage of the total market value of the endowment is withdrawn from the endowment fund and transferred to operating funds for expenditure that year. Any additional investment returns are reinvested in the principal, enabling it to grow. The amount withdrawn and spent is determined by the spending limit (or payout rate) established by the board. It can be varied from year to year as economic conditions change. The goal is to provide enough payout each year to meet the needs of current programs, while also allowing the value of the endowment principal to grow to keep pace with inflation and provide more income to sustain programs in future years. The latter is not only important to maintain the benefit of the endowment to the organization; it is also essential in order to keep faith with the intention of a donor who wished to support some activity in perpetuity.

Let's take a look at a simple example in Table 12.6 to see how this approach might work over a period of five years. It is important to emphasize that Table 12.6 shows a simplified example and that most organizations do not spend a percentage of the market value of their endowments based on its value at the end of a given year. For example, many calculate a multiyear average of the endowment's market value, and the spending policy is then applied to that average. That is a way to ensure that the amount available for spending each year does not fluctuate wildly with changes in the value of stocks and other assets—using the average will smooth out the ups and downs. Many foundations also use a similar methodology, which accounts for why their grant-making may be affected only a few years after a significant downturn or upturn in the financial markets. Some endowments are managed using a somewhat more complicated approach, but that is beyond the scope of this discussion.

Again, in order to simplify our discussion here, Table 12.6 does not reflect the averaging approach; it just assumes that the nonprofit has a spending policy that permits spending the following year equivalent to a fixed percentage of the endowment fund's value at the end of the previous year.

In looking at Table 12.6, assume a donor has made a gift of $500,000 for the purpose of endowing "full-tuition scholarships" to students in perpetuity. Tuition is now $25,000, but the assumption in this example is that it will increase by an average of five percent each year. Assume also that the original gift is invested in a portfolio of securities that will earn an average of 10 percent each year, in some combination of interest, dividends, and appreciation. That would be high in terms of actual experience, but the round number will simplify our example.

Based on the assumptions, in the first year, the $500,000 endowment earns $50,000. The college could spend $50,000 to award two full-tuition scholarships that year. But the problem with that approach would start to become obvious in the second year. The endowment would still be just $500,000; it would again earn $50,000, which would no longer be enough for two full-tuition scholarships at the higher tuition rate. Instead, if the college awards one $25,000 scholarship the first year (equivalent to the five percent

TABLE 12.6 ■ Hypothetical Endowment Fund					
Year	Return Tuition ($)	Endowment Spendable 10% ($)	Reinvest 5% ($)	Endowment 5% ($)	Principal ($)
Gift					500,000
1	25,000	50,000	25,000	25,000	525,000
2	26,250	52,500	26,250	26,250	551,250
3	27,563	55,125	27,563	27,563	578,813
4	28,941	57,881	28,941	28,941	607,754
5	30,388	60,775	30,388	30,388	638,142

payout rate that the board has established), and reinvests the additional $25,000 back into the endowment, the principal of the endowment now becomes $525,000. If it follows that practice every year—spend five percent and reinvest five percent—look what happens as we go down the table to Year 5. Because the endowment principal has been increased, the five percent available for spending also has increased sufficiently to cover the ever-higher cost of tuition.

Following this approach and continuing out forever into the future, if all the assumptions hold, there will always be sufficient income from this endowment to provide a "full-tuition scholarship," which was the intention of the donor. Now, if the market has a bad year, it may not earn 10 percent, but in some years it may do *better* than 10 percent, averaging out over the long haul. Tuition may increase more than expected, or less. The board can adjust the spending limit as well as the investment portfolio to accommodate these trends as they emerge. Properly executed, this approach enables the organization to count on ever-increasing income from its endowment and to keep faith *in real terms* with the intention of its endowment donors.

Endowment management is governed by state law. A model act, called the *Uniform Prudent Management of Institutional Funds Act* (UPMIFA), was introduced in 2006 and by 2012 had been adopted by most states. It requires that in making investment decisions, boards exercise "the care an ordinary prudent person in a like position would exercise under similar circumstances" (Griswold & Jarvis, 2009). The law thus provides flexibility but places responsibility on boards for preserving the purchasing power of endowment funds and assuring that the intent of endowment donors is carried out to the extent possible.

Developing and Managing the Budget

A nonprofit organization's financial statements are important documents to individuals both inside and outside the organization. But on a month-to-month or day-to-day basis, for most people working in the organization, the budget and reports related to the budget are the guides to action. A full discussion of budgeting is beyond the scope of this text, but this section will summarize some of the more important principles and concepts.

Most nonprofit organizations have three separate budgets: an *operating budget,* a *capital budget,* and a *cash budget.* As their names suggest, the first tracks all revenues and expenditures; the second concerns the purchase or disposal of long-term physical assets, such as buildings and equipment; and the third tracks the flow of cash during the year, whether related to operating or capital activities. As David Maddox (1999) correctly observes, "Most people think of the operating budget when they think of a budget (if they do at all)" (p. 60). Our discussion in this section focuses generally on principles that relate to developing and managing the operating budget, although some are relevant to the others as well.

A budget is a political as well as financial document. Some say that the budget reveals an organization's "real strategy," despite what may be written in the strategic plan or other documents (Maddox, 1999, p. 12), because the budget is a tangible expression of what the organization's real priorities are. It reflects not only considered plans but also the push and pull of political forces within the leadership of the organization. Readers may recall the idea of nonprofit leaders' political frame, an idea described by Robert Herman and Richard Heimovics (2005) and discussed in Chapter 5. Managers may be guided by a strategic plan, but various departments, programs, or purposes are in competition for the organization's limited resources, and the outcome of that competition may be important in determining where funds are actually allocated.

Budgets invariably create incentives and disincentives that will affect the behavior of managers and staff. For example, some organizations have a use-it-or-lose-it approach to annual budgets. If a department has not expended its budgeted funds by the end of the fiscal year, the remaining funds do not carry over to be available to the department the following year. The organization's top budget managers may be counting on unexpended funds in some department budgets to cover overspending by others or as a reserve of sorts to cover unanticipated expenses of the general organization. But savvy managers often work to ensure that no unspent money remains, rushing to place orders for supplies and new computers before the fiscal year ends. The use-it-or-lose-it policy thus may turn out to create a perverse incentive that results in needless spending.

The way in which budgets are structured, whether on an organizational or center basis, also affects incentives. For example, a university may develop a budget that treats tuition from all students as revenue to the institution as a whole. Individual colleges, schools, and programs then are given an expense budget on which they need to operate, and the dean or director of each is responsible for not exceeding the budgeted amount. The individual units thus are viewed as *cost centers,* and their managers may have little incentive beyond controlling costs. Or the university may budget on a center basis, that is, the university regards each unit as a *profit center.* In this model, the school or college keeps the revenue it generates, from which it meets its own direct costs and makes some contribution to cover general institutional costs and services provided to the unit by the overall organization, for example, its share of expenses related to utilities and information systems technology. This approach may create considerable incentive for unit heads to be entrepreneurial and undertake new efforts to increase revenue. However, the trade-off may be that the central administration has less control and a reduced ability to reallocate funds across units, either to address institutional priorities or to cross-subsidize less profitable programs through the surpluses of others.

Another consideration is whether budgets are developed incrementally or allow for redistribution. A common and simple way to develop next year's budget is just to add some percentage to last year's budget or to the amounts actually expended, maybe one percentage for salary increases and another for other expenses. If the allocation is based on funds expended, then it will, of course, exacerbate the tendency of units to make sure they spend all of last year's budgeted amount before the year ends. If they do not, they take, in effect, a double hit: They lose the unexpended funds at the end of the year and also receive a reduced allocation for the year that follows. Other budgeting systems allow for considerable redistribution from one year to the next. One benefit of having a strategic plan with specific goals and objectives is that it can serve to justify such redistribution over time in order for the organization or department to pursue strategic priorities. If the plan has been developed in a participative process, with buy-in from all parts of the organization, it may help mitigate the inevitable political pressures that come to bear on annual budgeting.

Another process, perhaps at the extreme of the redistribution spectrum, is the zero-based approach. All programs and departments start at zero at the beginning of each year's budget process and need to justify their budgets from the ground up. But this approach has a number of disadvantages, including the amount of time and effort required to prepare justifications and the potential for management competition and negative staff morale (McMillan, 2003b).

A fundamental idea in budgeting is to recognize the difference between controllable and uncontrollable expenses and to hold managers accountable accordingly. Individual departments or programs may be credited with or charged with revenues and expenditures attributable to them, but a manager can only be held responsible for line items under his or her control. For example, a manager may be able to control salaries, travel, and the use of outside consultants, but he or she may not be able to control, at the department or program level, items such as fringe benefits, rent, heat, or electricity. Monthly budget reports typically show—for each line item—the amount budgeted for the year, the amount and percentage of the annual budget for that item expended year-to-date, and a comparison with the amount spent the previous year to the same date. Such reports enable managers to note significant variations from the budget and make midyear corrections as needed.

Sample nonprofit budgets are difficult to find in public sources, such as on the Web, because they are typically specific to each organization. The operating budget for the organization is an internal document that it is not required to be made publicly available. There are, however, a variety of online resources available that do provide templates and other guides to budget development.

Risk Management, Financial Policies, and Controls

As discussed in Chapter 6, recent years have included increased demands for accountability throughout American society. In this environment, it is essential for well-managed nonprofits to identify potential risks to the organizations and to develop strategies for preventing or minimizing the impact of those that could adversely affect achievement of the mission.

Although we discuss risk management in this chapter on financial management, it is important to understand that not all risks are strictly financial, although many have financial implications. A risk is "any uncertainty about a future event" and usually falls into one of four categories:

- People: Board members, volunteers, employees, clients, donors, and the general public
- Property: Buildings, facilities, equipment, materials, copyrights, and trademarks
- Income: Sales, grants, and contributions
- Goodwill: Reputation, stature in the community, and the ability to raise funds and appeal to prospective volunteers ("A primer on risk management," 2007)

Risk management requires identifying scenarios that could negatively impact the organization and then devising policies and controls to either prevent those events from occurring or to provide financial protection to the organization if one does occur. Some risks are related primarily to finance. For example, a major donor or sponsor could withdraw support, precipitating a budget crisis or that costs of a program might exceed projections for some unforeseen reason. An organization dependent on government funding might be impacted by budget cuts, or earned income revenues might decline if the economy goes into a recession. A decline in the overall economy and the stock market also could adversely affect gift revenue and the value of endowment. And, unfortunately, there is always the risk of financial fraud and abuse by a volunteer or executive. Other risks are not primarily financial but have financial implications. For example, a volunteer, client, or staff member may be treated unfairly or unethically. That could have negative consequences for the organization's reputation and, in addition, that person might bring legal action that would result in a financial payment. Someone could slip and fall on the sidewalk or be injured in the nonprofit's facility due to conditions that would create liability. There could be damage to the organization's facilities, vehicles, or other physical assets as a result of an accident catastrophe. An organization must establish policies to minimize the chances of such negative events and maintain insurance and reserves to provide financial protection if one does occur.

liquidity. If key ratios are not within acceptable limits, an organization may be flirting with bankruptcy, that is, it has entered the zone of insolvency. This condition places increased responsibilities on governing boards.

The largest endowment funds are held by major institutions, such as universities, but in recent years, many types of nonprofits have worked to establish or build endowments. Most endowments are invested under the total return concept. The board of the organization sets a spending limit, which is a percentage of the endowment's market value each year (or, commonly, of an average over a period of months or years). That amount is spent to support programs, and any additional investment gain is reinvested in the principal of the endowment. The payout may come from interest, dividends, or the appreciation in value of equities. That approach enables the principal and the income to grow over the years to match the higher future costs of activities that the endowment is intended to support.

Most nonprofits have three budgets: an operating budget, a capital budget, and a cash budget. The operating budget usually commands the most attention. The budget is a political document that reflects not only plans but also the competition for resources within the organization. How budgets are constructed creates important incentives and disincentives that affect managers' behavior. One important consideration is whether budgets are maintained on an organizational or center basis and whether departments and programs are treated as cost centers or profit centers. Some budgeting methods simply add a percentage increment to previous years' budgeted or expended amounts, while others provide greater opportunity for the redistribution of funds across programs or units. Some expenses, such as salaries, are controllable. Others, such as fringe benefits, are less so. Unit managers should be accountable for expenses that are within their control.

Accountability in the current environment requires that nonprofits have explicit policies in three areas: accountability and regulatory compliance policies, financial and financial management policies, and data integrity policies. Internal controls are established to prevent financial fraud or abuse. They should be applied within an environment of control and include processes related to risk areas. One essential principal is that financial transactions involve more than one person. Audits and other compliance reports can be used to monitor the effectiveness of the control system. Ensuring that appropriate policies and controls are in place is a fundamental aspect of the governing board's responsibility.

Notes

1. There are some endowments called *term endowments* that can be spent after a period of time passes. They are temporarily restricted. We do not consider them in this discussion.
2. Because the board does have the power to withdraw money from a quasi endowment, accounting rules require that such funds be treated as unrestricted in financial statements.
3. Some property owned by a nonprofit may also be considered permanently restricted, like endowment. For example, this would be true of a work of art that a donor gave with the condition that the nonprofit not sell it.

KEY TERMS AND CONCEPTS

accountability and regulatory compliance policies

accounting

accounts payable

accounts receivable

accrual basis of accounting

asset management

bookkeeping

capital budget

cash basis of accounting

cash budget

cash flow

cost center

data integrity policies

endowment (board-designated and permanent)

financial accounting

Financial Accounting Standards Board (FASB)

financial management

generally accepted accounting principles (GAAP)

in perpetuity

internal controls

liquidity

managerial accounting

operating budget

operating reserves

permanently restricted

prescriptive policies

profit center

profitability

pure endowment

quasi endowment

restrictive policies

risk management

spending limit

statement of activities

statement of cash flows

statement of financial position

temporarily restricted

total return

Uniform Prudent Management of Institutional Funds Act (UPMIFA)

unrestricted

zone of insolvency

CASE 12.1   Hull House

Hull House was founded in Chicago in 1889 by Jane Addams and Ellen Gates Starr, with the purpose of serving Chicago's immigrants and helping the city's poorest citizens improve their lives. Hull House was the flagship of what became known as the "settlement house movement," including nearly 500 facilities by 1920. Hull House was pioneering and established a model for many nonprofits founded in following years. In 1931, Addams received the Nobel Peace Prize for her work (Wade, 2005; West, 2012b).

Hull House and other settlement houses provided residential facilities and a range of social services. In addition, Addams and house residents became advocates who worked for many social reforms of the early 20th century, including public recreational facilities, child labor laws, juvenile courts, and women's suffrage. By the 21st century, the Hull House Association had become a federation of neighborhood centers and programs, including job training, homeless services, foster care, child care, domestic violence, and small business development, serving 60,000 people a year in various locations throughout Chicago. In 2012, after 120 years, it was forced to close and dismiss its 300 staff members. Many of its programs were taken over by another nonprofit, Metropolitan Family Services (Wade, 2005; Weber, 2012; West, 2012b).

In its early years, Hull House was supported primarily by private funds raised by Addams. That pattern began to change in the 1960s, when the Great Society programs of President Lyndon Johnson expanded funding for social programs, much of it channeled through nonprofit organizations (West, 2012b). By 2012, Hull House depended on government funds for 85 percent of its budget (West, 2012b). With the economy entering recession in the late 2000s, the demand for services greatly increased, while government support did not keep pace. Hull House reduced its budget from $40 million to $23 million and cut programs, but its debt continued to grow. When it filed for bankruptcy in 2012, it reported liabilities of $10 to 50 million against assets of just $1 to 10 million (Yerak, 2012).

There was disagreement about the causes of Hull House's demise. The board chair blamed the economic climate, although Hull House had financial problems in 2007, before the recession that began that year (Moyers, 2012). "We should have narrowed our focus even more," the board chair acknowledged. But he also claimed that the staff had sugarcoated the situation, providing financial statements that were late and failed to reveal the seriousness of the situation, although a former chief executive disagreed with that

(Continued)

Where does the money go? Next to religion, the largest recipient of philanthropy is education, accounting for 16 percent in 2013, followed by human services (12 percent). Giving to create or enlarge foundations accounts for another 11 percent of the total, followed by gifts to health (10 percent), and public benefit organizations (7 percent). The latter include organizations such as United Way and Jewish federations, among others. Although they are important causes for many people, the environment and animals and the arts, culture, and humanities receive relatively small shares of the philanthropic pie, together accounting for 8 percent of total giving in 2013. An important and growing component of philanthropy is *bequests*—that is, gifts made by individuals through their wills or other estate-planning vehicles. Bequests accounted for 8 percent of total giving in 2013. With the aging of the population and the growing wealth of older people, giving through bequests is expected to grow substantially in the coming decades (Lilly School of Philanthropy at Indiana University, 2014).

Definitions and Distinctions

When the planes hit the World Trade Center towers on September 11, 2001, millions of Americans went to their computers or reached for their checkbooks to give more than $2 billion to help the victims and their families. Four years later, when Hurricane Katrina hit the Gulf Coast, the response was again immediate and overwhelming, totaling more than $3.3 billion in gifts to organizations providing relief and support for rebuilding (Lipman, 2006). When tragedy struck again in 2012 with Hurricane Sandy devastating sections of the U.S. east coast, millions of donors again responded generously. That same year, Facebook founder Mark Zuckerberg and his wife, Priscilla Chan, gave nearly $500 million to the Silicon Valley Community Foundation, to be used for education and health ("Facebook's Mark Zuckerberg gives $500 million," 2012). And in 2013, Zuckerberg and Chan gave another $1 billion to the community foundation, becoming the largest donors under age 30 in history (Bermudez, Daniels, & Wallace, 2013). In 2014, individuals gave over $100 million to the ALS Association in response to its ice bucket challenge, a crowdfunding initiative that attracted participation from many celebrities, as well as average people (Wolfman-Arent & Switzer, 2014). These examples demonstrate the scale and impact of giving in the United States, but they also illustrate two different *approaches* to giving—one focused on immediate needs and the other taking a more long-term, strategic perspective.

In Chapter 2, this text made a distinction between charity and philanthropy as two types of voluntary giving. *Charity* includes gifts to meet immediate human needs, for example, to provide food to those who are starving or shelter to those dislocated as a result of natural disaster—such as the post-September 11 and post-Sandy outpouring of generosity. It is often impulsive and always driven by human compassion. *Philanthropy* is giving to strengthen the infrastructure of society, that is, to develop institutions that serve human needs or enhance human development over the long run. The objects of philanthropy often include hospitals, universities, museums, and arts organizations—institutions with missions that are perpetually relevant across generations, but which do not have the same urgency as immediate human suffering. Some philanthropic gifts, such as Zuckerberg and Chan's, go to create or expand foundations, most of which are established to last forever or a very long time, tackling long-term problems and issues. Philanthropic gifts are made carefully and thoughtfully, often as the culmination of a long-standing relationship with an institution. Emotion plays an important role in the decision to make philanthropic gifts— certainly for individual donors, but many also reflect a highly rational analysis that makes giving a form of investing in society and its important institutions. In practice, many people use the terms *charity* and *philanthropy* as if they were synonymous or use philanthropy as the broader concept, encompassing all voluntary giving. But the distinction is important, and it is useful for nonprofit organizations to be mindful of how their donors may think about their giving in these different ways.

The past 15 years have seen the rise of new concepts of giving, including *venture philanthropy, strategic philanthropy, catalytic philanthropy,* and *outcome-oriented philanthropy*. Each has a somewhat different definition—and various authors define them differently—but the common element is encompassed by the latter term; it refers to philanthropy in which "donors seek to achieve clearly defined goals; where they and [the organizations they support] pursue evidence-based strategies for achieving those goals; and where both parties monitor progress toward outcomes and assess their success in achieving them . . ." (Brest, 2012). These are styles of philanthropy that emphasize the impact of gifts, and donors who follow them usually intend to bring about change to address social problems—for example, poverty and unemployment. These approaches may fall somewhere between charity and philanthropy as those terms have been defined above. Unlike charity, this type of giving is not intended to alleviate immediate human needs, for example, displacement by a natural disaster. Rather, like philanthropy, it is long term in its perspective and is intended to build organizations that can effectively address social needs. However, gifts from venture philanthropists are generally not intended to sustain traditional institutions, such as universities and hospitals, but rather to build the capacity of nonprofit organizations that work for social change and improvement of educational and economic opportunity.

Before proceeding further, it is important also to clarify some other common terms that have somewhat different meanings but are sometimes used interchangeably in everyday conversation. *Fundraising* is an activity undertaken with the goal of eliciting charitable or philanthropic giving. Fundraising is related to philanthropy as teaching is to learning; that is, one is intended to accomplish the other, with no guarantee of success because the response lies significantly within the power of the respondent to determine. In the simplest understanding, fundraising means "asking for a gift," although, as we will soon discuss, it is really a process in which asking for, or *soliciting,* a gift is but one step in a more complicated process.

Many organizations have what's known as a *development office.* Staff who work in that office may be called development officers and have titles such as director of development. If asked what they do, they are likely to respond that they are engaged in fundraising. The two terms, fundraising and development, represent somewhat different concepts, although the difference is not always maintained in common usage. *Development* is a term that originated in the 1920s at Northwestern University (Worth, 1993, p. 6). The university had completed a fundraising *campaign* to build a new campus. When the campaign was completed, they determined that fundraising should be an ongoing, organized effort to continually improve and *develop* the institution, rather than a sporadic activity undertaken now and then to meet a specific need. The university created a new department to manage this ongoing effort and called it the office of "development," meaning "institutional development." Although fundraising and development became interchangeable over time, the latter is properly understood as a more comprehensive approach to the long-term growth of an organization or institution. As I explain in an earlier work,

> Fund raising is but one aspect of a complex process involving the institution, its hopes and goals, and the aspirations of its benefactors. Fund raising is episodic; development is continuous. Fund raising is focused on a particular objective or set of goals; development is a generic and long-term commitment to the financial and physical growth of the institution. Successful fund raising requires a specific set of interpersonal and communication skills; development requires a broader understanding of the institution and its mission as well as patience, judgment, and sensitivity in building relationships over the long haul. A "fund raiser" is an individual skillful in soliciting gifts; a "development officer" may be a fund raiser, but he or she is also a strategist and manager of the entire development process. (Worth, 1993, pp. 7–8)

By the mid-1970s, however, the terms *fundraising* and *development* had become so interchangeable in use that when the Council for Advancement and Support of Education (CASE) was established in 1974, it adopted the new term *institutional advancement* to describe the activities performed by its members. Institutional advancement, or just advancement, encompasses not only fundraising or development but also the related activities of communications, marketing, and other programs for constituent relations. In other words, institutional advancement has a meaning similar to the original concept of development—a long-term and broad-based program to build an organization or institution. In the decades since CASE's founding, "advancement" has been widely adopted by colleges and universities and also has gained currency in nonprofit organizations more broadly. Ironically, it also has come to be used synonymously with fundraising by many people.

Motivations for Giving

The question of what motivates donors is of obvious practical interest to nonprofit managers in determining which of their needs may be met through philanthropy and in designing their fundraising programs. But donor motivation is also a topic that has generated a substantial body of research. Let's look at motivation from the perspective of the three principal sources of giving—corporations, foundations, and individuals. Although they are the largest source of gifts, we discuss individuals last because their motivation is the most complex of these three types of donors.

Understanding Corporate Philanthropy

Corporations make philanthropic gifts both directly and through foundations that some have established as separate nonprofit entities. Using a foundation offers advantages over direct giving by the corporation, including the ability to add resources to the foundation in highly profitable years and then sustain a relatively even level of giving in years when the business may not be as profitable. Corporations make cash gifts and also gifts of products, known as *gifts-in-kind*. But corporations also support nonprofits through a variety of *partnerships*, which, as the term implies, offer benefits to both the nonprofit and the business. These partnerships are sometimes complex and represent a growing component of nonprofit revenue. Although they provide financial benefit to many nonprofit organizations, they are not "philanthropy," since the company expects a financial return as well as a benefit to the nonprofit partner.

Corporate philanthropy is a relatively recent phenomenon. Indeed, prior to the case of *A.P. Smith Mfg. Co. v. Barlow* in 1953, the courts imposed restrictions on corporate giving that did not directly benefit the interests of shareholders or employees of the firm. This landmark case opened the door to the concept of *enlightened self-interest,* that is, the idea that companies could make gifts that might not have a direct or immediate benefit to the bottom line, but that would generally help maintain a healthy society in which to do business.

Corporate giving generally increased during the decades of the 1960s, 1970s, and 1980s, and its purposes often reflected the interests and affiliations of the senior executives and directors of the company. However, during the 1980s and with increasing momentum in the 1990s and 2000s, corporate giving became professionalized. Many companies created committees to make decisions about where to direct the corporation's giving or created separate foundations to undertake philanthropy in the company's name.

Since the mid-1980s, corporate giving has increasingly reflected an approach known as *strategic philanthropy*—that is, giving according to a plan that relates the corporation's philanthropy to its overall strategic and business goals. Giving is viewed as an investment and is subject to evaluation based on how much return it produces—the extent to which it enhances the corporation's competitiveness. For example, a corporation might target its giving in communities where it plans to develop new facilities or to specific groups of people who are likely to be customers of its products. The various corporate–nonprofit partnerships, which will be discussed in Chapter 14, have evolved from the strategic philanthropy approach. Today, the line between corporate philanthropy and marketing has become blurred, as has the line between fundraising and negotiating business relationships. Indeed, in 2004, the *Association of Fundraising Professionals* (AFP) amended its code of professional ethics, which had long required that fundraisers not accept compensation based on a percentage of gifts, to include a similar prohibition with regard to the solicitation of corporate partnership arrangements (Hall, 2005).

To understand the motivation for corporate giving, a nonprofit needs to understand the company's business plans and goals on which its program of philanthropy is likely to be based. This is not to imply that corporations give in a way that is detrimental to the interests of nonprofits or society or that their motivations should be viewed as invidious. And many companies have principles of social responsibility to which they faithfully adhere. Nevertheless, the realities do suggest that nonprofits begin their search for corporate dollars not in terms of their own needs but rather with a view to how there can be a mutual benefit to the nonprofit's welfare and the interests of the corporation from which it seeks support.

Foundation Giving

It is not difficult to understand the motivations for giving by foundations. Very simply, that is what they exist to do; indeed, it is what they are *required* to do as a condition of their tax-exempt status. Foundations are required to expend a minimum of an amount equivalent to 5 percent of the value of their invested assets each year, either for grants or operating expenses.

Foundations are created by corporations, individuals, or families and their activities generally reflect the interests of the founders. *Family foundations* are a type of *independent foundation* in which the board is dominated by members of the donors' family. They often evolve as they grow, expanding their boards beyond family members, employing professional staff, and developing formal programs and guidelines that make explicit their interests and priorities. Many foundations have geographic and other restrictions on their giving and have well-defined areas of interest and grant programs through which they provide support, as illustrated by the example of the Kellogg Foundation, shown in Box 13.1. It is usually fruitless for an organization to approach a foundation for support if it does not operate programs related to the organization's activities or has policies and priorities that exclude the organization from consideration. Foundation priorities may change from time to time; for that reason, Box 13.1 should be considered an example obtained at the time this book was written, but not relied upon as current policies of the Kellogg Foundation at the time it is being read.

Because foundations are rational donors, obtaining foundation support often requires preparation of a written proposal. The art of doing so is often called *grantwriting*, although the seeker is indeed writing a proposal, not a grant—the grant is made by the foundation, and if the grant is "written," the writing would be done by a foundation official. *Proposal writing* thus is a more accurate description of what a nonprofit organization or a member of its staff does. This text does not go into detail on the techniques of foundation proposal writing, but many good guides are available, and organizations such as AFP and the Foundation Center offer training on the topic. Box 13.2 provides an outline of a typical foundation proposal, although each must be tailored to the guidelines and requirements of the specific foundation to which the proposal is being directed.

Other types of foundations include *operating foundations* that support their own programs and generally do not make grants to other organizations. And, as discussed earlier in this book, some public charities use the term *foundation* in their names, although they both raise money and distribute it, usually to a single organization or a defined community. Operating foundations usually are not good fundraising *prospects* for other nonprofits, nor are most foundations that are public charities, although some community foundations have discretionary funds that may be available to nonprofit organizations in their areas.

BOX 13.1 KELLOGG FOUNDATION PRIORITIES

Kellogg Foundation Priorities

The W. K. Kellogg Foundation (WKKF) places the optimal development of children at the center of all we do and calls for healing the profound racial gaps and inequities that exist in our communities. We believe in supporting and building upon the mindsets, methods and modes of change that hold promise to advance children's best interests generally, and those of vulnerable children in particular.

Concentrating our resources on early childhood (prenatal to age 8), within the context of families and communities, offers the best opportunity to dramatically reduce the vulnerability caused by poverty and racial inequity over time.

There is strong evidence that optimal child development means providing children with the stimulus, tools and support necessary for their emotional, intellectual, physical and cultural growth. To achieve this, we organize our work and investments toward attaining three strategic goals:

- Educated Kids: Increase the number of children who are reading-and-math proficient by third grade.
- Healthy Kids: Increase the number of children born at a healthy birth weight and who receive the care and healthy food they need for optimal development.
- Secure Families: Increase the number of children and families living at least 200 percent above the poverty level.

Within and around each goal are commitments to Community & Civic Engagement and Racial Equity – because both are necessary for communities to create the conditions under which all children can thrive.

We take a place-based approach to our work, concentrating as much as two-thirds of our grantmaking in a limited number of specific places where we believe we can have maximum impact.

Source: W. K. Kellogg Foundation website (www.wkkf.org/what-we-do/overview).

BOX 13.2 SECTIONS OF A STANDARD GRANT PROPOSAL

- Title page and table of contents
- Executive summary—1 page
- Narrative

  Statement of need—2 pages
  Project description—3 pages
  Organization information—1 page
  Conclusion—2 paragraphs

- Budget
- Appendices and supporting materials

Source: Foundation Center (www.cohhio.org/files/pdf/08conference/Conf08pdf/09_Proposal_Writing.pdf).

Motivations of Individual Donors

As illustrated by the spontaneous response to 9/11, Hurricanes Katrina and Sandy, and the ice bucket challenge, the motivations of individual donors are often more complex and less calculated than those of corporations or foundations. Individual donors have been the focus of a substantial number of research studies. In a 2011 review, René Bekkers and Pamala Wiepking provide a comprehensive overview of the academic research on the topic to that time (Bekkers & Wiepking, 2011). Most studies have examined characteristics that distinguish donors from non-donors and have identified statistical relationships between giving and certain characteristics, for example, age, gender, income level, and geographic location. Fewer have explored the more complex question of donor motivation, to answer the question of *why* they give.

Traditionally, the literature has been divided between those who attribute giving to altruism—those who say that individuals are driven by their nature to help others and improve the human condition, and those who say that individuals give to obtain some benefit for themselves, perhaps recognition, social position, or control. A 1994 study by Russ Prince and Karen File identified seven motivational types that some fundraising practitioners find to be intuitively attractive. According to these authors, the largest group of donors (26 percent) are "communitarians," motivated by the belief that giving makes good sense in terms of a better community for their businesses and lives. Another 21 percent are the "devout," who give because of their religious beliefs. The third-largest group is the 15 percent that Prince and File call "investors." These are donors who are particularly concerned with the tax and estate benefits of giving and will be interested to know exactly what result will be accomplished with their support. "Socialites," 10.8 percent of donors, give because it provides opportunities for social interactions; they are often people who will attend charity events. The "altruists," the selfless donors who may give without any desire for recognition, comprise another nine percent. "Repayers," who give based on gratitude for benefits they have received, make up 10.2 percent. The final category, the "dynasts," are people who give because it is a family tradition; they constitute another 8 percent of donors (pp. 14–16). Different types of donors gravitate toward various nonprofit subsectors; for example, the devout tend to support religion, the socialites give to arts organizations, and repayers often direct their support to universities and hospitals that may have influenced their own or their family members' lives.

In the early 2000s, Paul Schervish and John Havens of the Social Welfare Research Institute at Boston College studied social-psychological factors influencing the giving of wealthy individuals and identified several "dispositions" or "inclinations" that motivate individuals to engage in significant philanthropy. These inclinations include "hyperagency," the ability to make history and affect the conditions under which people live; "identification," the unity of self-regard and regard for others; and consideration of income and estate tax benefits. The authors de-emphasize the impact of tax incentives, arguing that their data suggest that as wealth increases, individuals gain a preference for leaving their estates to charity rather than to heirs. They speculate that removal of estate taxes thus would result in more money becoming available for bequests to nonprofit organizations (Schervish & Havens, 2001).

The influence of tax incentives on giving is controversial. In self-reports by donors, the importance of the charitable deduction is often minimized. For example, in a 2011 study conducted by the Center on Philanthropy at Indiana University (now the Lilly Family School of Philanthropy) and Bank of America, 50 percent of survey respondents indicated that their giving would stay the same even if they received no tax deduction. Fewer than 10 percent indicated that their giving would decrease dramatically if the deduction were eliminated (Center on Philanthropy at Indiana University, 2012). But research tells a somewhat different story. Based on a meta-analysis of studies over 40 years, John Peloza and Piers Steel (2005) acknowledge a lack of consensus, but conclude that "changes in tax deductibility indeed appear to have a marked effect on charitable giving" (p. 269). Some studies addressing this topic may be flawed because they ask people to say what they would do under certain hypothetical circumstances rather than analyzing data reflecting actual past behavior. People are often inclined to give what they think to be the right or appropriate answer, which may or may not predict what their behavior would actually be under the hypothetical circumstances described. For example, when asked if we would wait for a red light in the middle of the night when the police are not in sight, most of us probably would answer yes. But what some might actually do could differ from this appropriate response to the question. In other cases, the survey question may relate to a public policy issue, for example, tax rates. People responding to the question may view it as an opportunity to influence the policy debate and their answers thus may reflect their opinions more than they predict what their actual behavior might be under different conditions.

The mathematics of giving and taxes suggests that tax rates may influence the amount that individuals are *able* to give, regardless of what their *desire* to give might be. For example, assume that an individual in a 35 percent income tax bracket makes a gift of $1,000 that is tax deductible. Because of the deduction, the donor's income is reduced by $1,000, which reduces his or her income tax bill by $350 below what it would otherwise have been (35 percent of $1,000). That makes the out-of-pocket or actual cost of the $1,000 gift $650, since there is a *tax savings* of $350. Now, assume that the donor's tax rate has been reduced to 10 percent. The $1,000 gift now saves $100 in taxes, making its *out-of-pocket cost* $900. Although it may seem counterintuitive, a lower tax rate increases the cost of a gift. Depending on donors' overall financial position, this could have the effect of making it more difficult for them to give as much as they otherwise might have been able to, regardless of how highly motivated they might be to give.

The preponderance of research suggests that the motivations of most individual donors are mixed, including some combination of altruism and self-interest, and that tax policies have an impact on the amount that individuals are able to give, whether during their lifetimes or through their estates on their death. But both questions are likely to remain controversial and the focus of future research.

With the increasing diversity of the American population, a number of studies in recent years have examined the particular giving traditions and patterns of various groups, including women, African Americans, and Hispanics/Latinos. The topic is of increasing interest to many nonprofits, as greater wealth is being accumulated by women and members of minority groups. Students will find additional reading on this topic suggested at the end of this chapter.

The Fundraising Process

Some people may think of fundraising as synonymous with asking for money, but it is indeed a process with identifiable stages and steps. Without following the process, fundraising is random and not really very different from standing on a corner with a tin cup, hoping that some passerby will drop in a few coins. That is not an approach that is likely to generate the substantial and continuing support needed to sustain an organization.

The fundraising process is depicted in Figure 13.1 and includes six basic steps. Once an organization has (1) identified its priorities for financial support and developed a case to justify its goals, it must (2) identify the prospects most likely to give. (3) A process of *cultivation* develops a relationship between the organization and the prospect and, at the appropriate point in the relationship, (4) the prospect is asked for a gift. (5) The gift is acknowledged and the donor is recognized. (6) The organization then works to properly *steward* the gift, keeping the donor engaged and informed of what it has accomplished with the support provided. The process is usually described as a cycle because effective fundraising programs seek to develop a base of donors who continue to give on a regular basis. *Stewardship* is really part of the process of continued cultivation of donors who may provide additional, and it is hoped increased, support in the future. Let's walk through each step in the process in greater detail.

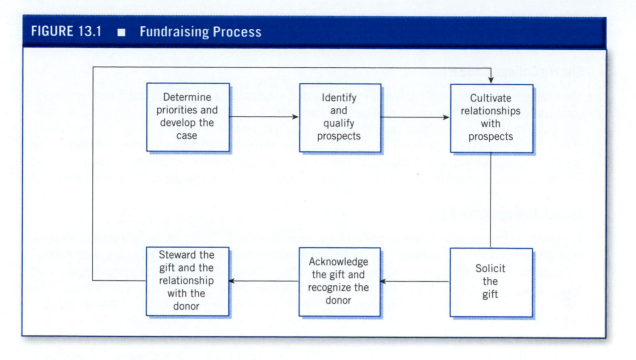

FIGURE 13.1 ■ **Fundraising Process**

Identifying Priorities and Developing the Case

Fundraising without a purpose is unlikely to elicit support. As Thomas Broce (1986) writes in his classic book, "Donors give gifts to meet objectives, not simply to give money away" (p. 19). This reality requires that an organization base its fundraising on identified priority needs related to achievement of its mission and rooted in a plan for its future growth and improvement. Strategic planning is often the first step in setting the organization's vision and goals for the future, which then can be translated into specific fundraising objectives with a rationale for why the support will enhance its ability to achieve its social mission.

The organization must develop a *case for support,* or a rationale for giving, that goes beyond its own needs and links its goals to broader social and human purposes. An organization's leaders may be convinced of its worthiness and the importance of its financial needs. But in a competitive philanthropic marketplace, they must make the case for how support for its purposes will bring a greater benefit than a gift to another organization or cause. For example, Box 13.3 shows a summary of the case for the hypothetical Siwash College that is based entirely on what its faculty and students perceive to be important to them and on the institution's self-interest. The needs may be real, but this statement is unlikely to inspire many donors to sacrifice in order to address them. In contrast, the second case explains Siwash's need for philanthropy in relation to social justice and economic prosperity, helping place its needs in a broader context and appeal to the values and emotions of potential donors.

The case for support is the reason the organization seeks support, derived from its mission and values—it is the answer to the questions, "Why should I give to this organization?" and "Why is this cause more important than others that also ask for my support?" It is often expressed in a *case statement*, a document that may include a comprehensive discussion of the organization's fundraising objectives and the justification for each. Case statements may be developed to provide a resource within the organization (an *internal case statement*) or as a printed brochure or electronic document for use in communicating with donor prospects (an *external case statement*). It is also common to produce a video, which expressed the

---

BOX 13.3 THE CASE FOR SUPPORT

Siwash College Case #1

The College's enrollment has increased in the past decade, resulting in crowded classrooms and inadequate office space for the faculty. Colleges are competing for the best students with offers of scholarship support. We now have fallen behind our competitors in the quality of our facilities and the amount of financial aid that we can provide. We are losing many of the best students to other institutions. For this reason, we are seeking $10 million in funds for new campus construction and scholarships that we will offer to the students from our region who have the highest SAT (Scholastic Aptitude Test) scores.

Siwash College Case #2

The United States always has been a nation of economic opportunity. Today, as we face great challenges from global economic competition, the talents of too many young men and women are undeveloped because they lack the financial means to attend college. College tuition has risen dramatically, and financial aid has not kept pace. This is unjust and threatens America's future economic prosperity. Educational opportunity always has been fundamental to the mission and values of Siwash College. The Board of Trustees has established a plan to maintain our tradition by expanding enrollment and providing additional scholarship support for worthy young men and women of our region. To that end, we seek $10 million in support to expand our facilities and increase scholarship support to promising and worthy students.

---

case statement in a visual format. But the product known as the case statement should not be confused with the *idea* of the case. An organization that rushes to produce a glossy brochure or website without careful thought about the essence of its case is unlikely to successfully address the motivations of donors, whether corporations, foundations, or individuals.

Identifying and Qualifying Prospects

Just as an individual seeking a marriage partner likely would not do well by calling people at random or by proposing to strangers on the street, an organization seeking gift support needs to focus on *prospects* who offer a better-than-average chance of giving. Otherwise, its time and fundraising resources will be allocated inefficiently and ineffectively. The *identification of prospects* begins by limiting the search to those who have the financial *ability* or *capacity* to give. Obviously, an individual or company in bankruptcy or a foundation that has already allocated all its resources would not be worthy of further attention. They might have a keen interest in the nonprofit, but their financial inability would preclude considering them as prospects. However, making a list of successful companies and wealthy individuals still does not provide likely prospects for a particular nonprofit; it would be a large list and include many who are remote or already deeply committed to other causes. It would be like making a list of marriage prospects that included every single person in the world; they might have the ability to consider marriage, but it would still be a fruitless task to send proposals to all of them. The list would need to be culled by some additional criteria. For example, it might help to limit the search to people with whom the marriage seeker already has some connection—maybe schoolmates, individuals who attend the same church, or friends of friends. And, being single does not automatically imply a desire to be married, so it would be wise to limit the list of prospects to those who may have indicated some interest in getting married. (It is instructive to observe that online dating sites do provide tools for screening a large pool of people in order to identify those with the ability and desire to marry and who have some interests in common with the searcher—the matching is not random.)

Like marriage prospects, the most likely prospects for charitable gifts will be those who have not only the *ability* to give but also some *linkage* to and *interest* in the organization or the area of activity in which it is engaged (Seiler, 2011, p. 15). A prospect is described as "qualified" only when both financial capacity and potential interest have been determined. Identifying individuals, foundations, and corporations who are prospects is a task often performed by professionals engaged in *prospect research,* a specialty increasingly in demand by nonprofit organizations with sophisticated fundraising programs. Prospect researchers have a variety of tools and techniques, including a growing array of electronic databases, to help narrow the list to those with the greatest likelihood of making a gift to their organizations. Financial ability may be easily determined for foundations, on which information is readily available in published sources. Corporations may be somewhat less easily assessed, but some indication of ability to give may be assumed from revenue and profits. Individuals present more of a challenge. Although public information can help determine levels of income and wealth—for example, real estate values—much of the wealth will be less visible.

Linkage to the organization may occur in a variety of ways. Volunteers, graduates, and former patients or their families have obvious connections to the organization that have served them. But other types of nonprofits may need to build their network of prospects in a pattern similar to concentric circles, beginning with those who are already part of the organization's inner circle of friends and donors, then moving outward to less connected members of the community. The organization's governing board is its principal link to the outside world and, absent an easily identifiable constituency of potential donors with direct linkage, board members' efforts in identifying and engaging prospects among their own business and social contacts may be important.

Interest may be relatively easy to determine for a foundation, if it provides a clear statement of its priorities. Some corporations that have formal giving programs offer similar clarity about their interests, while in other cases, interest may be presumed because the company's business activities bear a close relationship to the work of the nonprofit. For example, a home builder or a mortgage lender may have an interest in the issues of homelessness and affordable housing; similarly, companies that manufacture products for use by women are often among the most prominent contributors to nonprofits that address women's issues or diseases. For individual prospects, interest may be revealed by past gifts to the organization or perhaps gifts to another organization addressing similar issues or needs, but often an individual's interest can be determined with confidence only through personal contact and discussion.

Cultivating Prospects

To invoke again the metaphor of courtship, most people would not consider proposing marriage on the first date. The odds of such a proposal gaining a positive response are increased if some time and effort have been devoted to cultivating a relationship, perhaps involving smaller steps such as having dinner and going to the movies. A nonprofit cultivating a prospective donor likewise will increase the chances of gaining support if it devotes some time and attention to *cultivating* a relationship before moving to solicit a gift. The larger the amount of the gift to be solicited, the greater the investment that will need to be made in cultivation of the relationship in advance of asking.

In fundraising for small gifts, solicitation may not require significant cultivation; for example, very little cultivation precedes broad-based solicitations by mail, phone, or the Internet. However, fundraising for *major gifts* involves developing and executing a series of planned initiatives expected to *move* an individual toward a closer relationship with the organization, leading to support. Major-gift fundraisers manage and track such activity through what are known as *moves management* systems. A moves management system includes electronic systems but also manual methods and processes for tracking contacts with prospective donors to ensure that cultivation of relationships occurs in a planned and strategic manner.

Soliciting the Gift

Nonprofit fundraisers have an array of techniques available for soliciting gifts, and a full discussion is beyond the scope of this chapter. Box 13.4 provides a summary of some commonly used methods and the advantages and disadvantages of each. In general, the more personal the contact, the more effective it is. Personal solicitations and mail, e-mail, or phone solicitations that include a message tailored to the individual being asked are more effective than communications that are very impersonal, such as broad-based mailings and telemarketing calls. On the other hand, direct mail remains a popular method of soliciting gifts and provides something tangible—a letter and/or a brochure—that an individual may retain and reread sometime after its receipt. This may be an advantage over e-mail, which many people skim and delete. The selection of methods employed by a nonprofit depends on several considerations. First, the method used must be appropriate to the level and type of support that the organization needs. Soliciting by direct mail, by phone, or through e-mail may be appropriate to secure a large number of relatively

BOX 13.4 COMMON SOLICITATION METHODS: ADVANTAGES AND DISADVANTAGES

Method	Advantages	Disadvantages
Personal solicitation	• Focused attention of prospect • Includes nonverbal cues • Builds relationship	• Expensive • Low volume
Direct mail	• Inexpensive • Creates a visual image • Long life (may be kept and read again later) • Can communicate complex message	• Easily ignored, lost in clutter • Requires donor initiative to make gift • Limited ability to personalize
Telemarketing	• Two-way communication • Can negotiate gift • Can tailor message to individual • Immediate gift (credit/debit card)	• More expensive than mail • Barriers (caller ID, mobile phones) • Intrusive
Events	• Visibility/involvement • May provide first contact with potential new donors	• Not usually cost-effective (hidden costs) • Often the event makes no connection to the cause
E-mail	• Inexpensive • Can personalize/segment message • Interactive/relationship building • Immediate gift	• E-mail list maintenance • Barriers (e.g., spam filters, overload)
Crowdfunding/social media and networks	• Inexpensive • Generates interest • Mobilizes networks	• Useful for one-time projects rather than ongoing support • Requires exciting cause that will go viral
Text	• Inexpensive • Immediate response	• Limited content • Intrusive • Barriers to follow up with donor

small gifts on a recurring basis to support the current operating budget. But major gifts to address capital or endowment needs will require personal contact and time for a full discussion of the organization's plans and the purpose that will be achieved through the gift. If the gift being solicited is for the organization's endowment, the personal contact with the prospective donor may need to be prolonged, in order to fully explore the individual's desires about his or her legacy to society beyond his or her lifetime. The use of social media and crowdfunding may be effective in raising funds for one-time projects that generate excitement, but are not assured to produce the ongoing support on which many organizations rely. Most gifts made in response to a challenge from friends or celebrities are likely to be relatively modest, not major gifts.

A second, related consideration is the costs and benefits of the method selected. Personal solicitation, by fundraising staff or volunteers, is generally more effective than solicitation by phone, mail, or e-mail, but it may also require a substantial commitment of time by the CEO, a development officer, and perhaps a volunteer; it may also involve costs for travel. Personal visits are to be reserved for the most promising prospects for the largest gifts. Personalized letters are generally more effective than impersonal, "Dear Friend" letters, but they also require more labor or more sophisticated technology to produce. The expected better returns always need to be balanced against the costs of a particular method. Third, an organization needs to consider what resources are available to it at particular points in its organizational life cycle. For example, a nonprofit that has little visibility, no clear donor constituency, and a fundraising program that is just beginning, may find special events to be a useful method for engaging new people, increasing its visibility in the community, and raising some funds. Fundraising or benefit events are not an especially effective way of raising money, and the costs of producing them may in fact consume much or all of the gross revenues. But if they can be used as a strategy for developing a new group of interested friends who may later be solicited for gifts through more effective methods, including mail, phone, and personal contact, then they may play a useful role in a comprehensive fundraising strategy.

Fourth, the nonprofit organization should adopt the solicitation method that is most likely to reach its target audience. For example, direct mail is effective with older donors, who have time to read letters and may be uncomfortable with providing credit card information on the telephone or over the Internet. Events or the Internet may be a better way if the organization is hoping to reach younger donors, who may not respond to direct mail or have land lines that make it easy to obtain their phone numbers for telemarketing calls.

Again, the organization's position in its life cycle is important to consider and will determine the type of philanthropy that can be attracted. For example, a young organization, perhaps with a somewhat uncertain future, would be unlikely to attract significant bequests for its endowment. Many people would question whether it would use such gifts effectively or whether it provides a lasting purpose for their philanthropy. However, a well-established nonprofit that continues to raise funds through events and e-mail and does not solicit larger gifts is not maximizing its long-term revenue potential. In other words, the methods used to raise funds, and the purpose for which they are raised, must match the realities of an organization's financial needs and philanthropic market—or, as architects say, form should follow function.

The Web, E-mail, Social Media, and Social Networking

Direct mail remains the primary source of gifts and of new donors. But giving online is growing at a rapid pace. The most common method of online solicitation is e-mail. The purpose of the e-mail is to drive donors to the organization's donation page. This page may be maintained by the organization itself or it may be operated by an outside vendor, such as Network for Good (www.networkforgood.org), which provides back-office support for processing online gifts. Soliciting gifts through e-mail follows many principles that are similar to those for direct mail. It starts with list development and requires continuing attention to list maintenance. The list can be grown by including every contact with the organization. As in direct mail, e-mail lists can be segmented to deliver personalized messages and costs can be very low. However, as with all methods, there are disadvantages, as well, including the use of spam filters and the ease with which prospective donors can delete a message from their crowded inbox without opening it. Many organizations make effective use of e-mail to stay in touch with current and past donors and even to discuss or negotiate the terms of a major gift. But such gifts will generally require some other form of contact, usually in person, with e-mail being used as a device to continue an ongoing discussion (Network for Good, 2014).

A growing number of nonprofit organizations are using social media and networks as tools for communicating, building a constituency, and advocating a cause. Some are also benefitting from fundraising events organized on social networking sites and the capabilities of social networking sites are expanding, suggesting that they are likely to become more important tools for fundraising in the future. Social networking is especially effective in peer-to-peer fundraising, in which friends invite friends to participate in such activities as walks and runs. But for most nonprofits, social networking remains more important for communication and building a constituency than for fundraising (Held, 2014). In 2014, it was reported that only 1 percent of all funds raised online was attributable to social media, including Facebook (Held, 2014). But this is not to suggest that organizations can minimize the importance of having a presence on social networking sites, including Facebook, Twitter, and others. As Julie Dixon and Denise Keyes (2013) emphasize, social networks enable individuals to become advocates, or "cause champions" for organizations and causes, bringing value beyond their own giving. And, again, fundraising through social networks is likely to grow as the capabilities of those networks are expanded.

Crowdfunding sites have received increasing attention. They include sites such as Kickstarter (www.kickstarter.com), which enables individuals to support creative projects, and Donors Choose (www.donorschoose.org), through which individuals can support specific needs of classroom teachers. Other well-known sites include CauseVox (www.causevox.com), Fundly (fundly.com), Razoo (www.razoo .com), and indiegogo (www.indiegogo.com); all have unique features. These sites have proven effective in raising funds for projects, but may be less useful for developing ongoing support. For example, a campaign on indiegogo in 2012 raised almost $1.4 million to build a museum in honor of electricity pioneer Nikola Tesla (Bray, 2013, p. 104). Crowdfunding also may be a less effective method for soliciting major gifts.

In order to be successful, a crowdfunding appeal needs to go viral. That may only occur if it is something especially exciting or urgent. If the organization intends to raise the funds from its established constituency, then other strategies may be more effective in reaching them. According to Ilona Bray (2013), crowdfunding may be an effective strategy only under specific circumstance, including the following:

- [The organization] has a particular, tangible goal in mind, such as a new piece of equipment; a trip to project site; medical care for an individual; production of a film; or a time-delineated concept around which to fundraise, such as a matching grant . . .
- [The organization] can confidently predict that the goal is sufficiently exciting, moving, or fun that [its] existing supporters and social media contacts will tell their friends about it and they, despite knowing little to nothing about [the] organization, will be moved to pitch in.
- [The organization] has the skills to present the idea in an attractive way, preferably complete with photos, graphics, and videos.
- [The organization] has supporters who will create tangential pages connected to [the] nonprofit's master page (as is allowed on some sites), on which they ask friends and connections to give. (Bray, 2013, pp. 104–105)

Some nonprofits also have used mobile communication as a method for soliciting and receiving gifts. For example, texting was a significant component of giving to the Red Cross following the earthquake in Haiti in 2010. Until recently, gifts made through text messaging were limited by the service carriers to relatively small amounts, usually $10 to $25. That has limited the potential in all but the most visible causes, for example, disasters that received worldwide attention. However, some charities have used mobile giving as a method in connection with events and have devised methods for permitting donors to text pledges of major gifts, to be charged to their credit or debit cards (Flandez, 2012a).

The technology of fundraising is in transition. It seems likely that an increasing proportion of dollars will come through online and mobile giving in the years ahead, but the traditional methods of direct mail and phone calls remain important; indeed, these methods remain the backbone of fundraising for many organizations. The continuing effectiveness of direct mail, along with the growing importance of online giving, suggests that nonprofit organizations need to pursue a multichannel strategy, combining new technologies with traditional methods. For some, the costs of doing so may be daunting, but there may be little choice except to invest in growing new technologies while also maintaining traditional programs in order to meet current fundraising goals. It is essential that the use of various channels be integrated, as illustrated in the sample fundraising plan in Box 13.5.

BOX 13.5 SAMPLE ONLINE FUNDRAISING PLAN

This is a sample plan for an imaginary local animal rescue organization called Save the Animals (STA), which is trying to take their outreach efforts online to become well known in the community. While the specifics of your online fundraising plan will be unique for your organization, the overarching themes will likely be similar. This intensive plan calls for a relatively high budget, but you will likely want or need to dedicate much less.

The goals of this online fundraising plan are to

- Open an online channel of communication with direct mail donors who want it
- Acquire new online donors
- Cultivate and resolicit existing and new online donors

The key to acquiring new online donors will be developing partnerships to drive traffic to our site, building a large e-mail list for prospecting, and making our site even more successful in converting visitors into donors. In addition, we'll expand the opportunities for raising money elsewhere online. At the same time, we will use our direct mail (and telephone) program to offer online communications to those donors and to integrate online communication with other fundraising communications.

1. Website

Our site should be a major tool in engaging and interacting with new and existing donors, while still meeting the needs of our various other constituencies—people seeking to adopt, kids, animal lovers, etc. Some of our donors also probably visit our site now and then, so it needs to demonstrate to them that they've invested wisely. They should see offline fundraising themes reflected on the site, new content, things to do, compelling features, etc. Many new people will also visit our site simply to look at the animals, without any intention of adopting. We'll need online mechanisms to engage those people and to turn them into donors. Here's what we'll do to make that happen:

- We'll redevelop our site to improve its look and feel and increase its functionality.
- We'll focus on finding vendors and/or application service providers (ASPs) who offer easy-maintenance solutions to reduce the burden on staff. Then, we'll work to make our site more appealing to our various constituencies with interactivity (surveys, contests), news, compelling appeals, easy event sign-ups, and new features such as e-cards.
- We'll maximize our giving opportunities on the site and give them high visibility on our homepage and other pages, especially our most visited pages and those pages that tend to evoke strong emotions (animal pages).
- On an ongoing basis, we'll monitor opportunities for promoting STA's work online in the context of animal-related news and our many events.

(Continued)

(Continued)

2. **E-mail marketing**
   - We'll develop an e-mail outreach program for communicating regularly with donors and prospects. The program will initially include a monthly e-newsletter with donor and non-donor versions and occasional action or event alerts. Eventually, we'll build in targeted e-mail messages for people with expressed interests in certain subjects such as no-kill policy, dogs, feral cat care, etc., and deliver e-mail renewals for existing online donors; and solicitations and special appeals for both existing donors and prospects.
   - We'll develop and implement strategies for building our e-mail list. In addition to offering simple e-mail sign-ups on our site, we'll design creative ways to build our prospect e-mail list through incentives, such as offering a chance to win a gift certificate to a local pet store for people who subscribe to our e-newsletter.

3. **Increasing site traffic**

With a compelling website and technology in place to manage content and donor relationships, we'll develop campaigns to drive traffic to our site. We'll work to improve our search engine and directory rankings and links, create and run campaigns on our site and elsewhere, and develop corporate partnerships and sponsorships to drive traffic to our site. Strategies will include:

   - Finding an appealing, easy-to-remember URL
   - Increasing our visibility on our . . . corporate partners' websites through links, banners, and special campaigns
   - Promoting our site as a no-kill information center by disseminating (free) content, tips, facts, and interactive devices to other sites with links back to our site
   - Promoting our fundraising campaigns on media sites. We'll develop graphics and try to place them free on national, regional, and local media sites.
   - Promoting our events online through event listing services such as CitySearch.com, local media listings, and others
   - Maximizing our search engine rankings by improving our meta tags, utilizing keywords, and paying for increased rankings at some sites

4. **Special Campaigns**

We'll run a few targeted online campaigns throughout the year: one in December, and one in the spring.

   - The December campaign will have a holiday focus with special holiday giving opportunities (gift memberships, with the calendar as one of its features) and also drive traffic to our store.
   - The spring appeal will be combined with a no-kill (or other issue) awareness campaign with special Web pages and a strong tell-a-friend element. While it will have a fundraising element, the focus of this campaign will be to build our online reputation and our e-mail list.

5. **Integration with Direct Mail**
   - We'll use traditional communications channels to build our donor e-mail list and promote our website.
   - We'll send a cultivation mailer to our lapsed donors inviting them to visit our website. We can direct them to a special page on our website that makes an appeal for why they should make another gift.
   - As our e-mail list grows, we'll test ways to use e-mail to boost response to direct mail, such as
     - Sending a pre-mail e-mail that tells people that they'll be receiving an important letter in the mail or invite people to respond
     - Sending a post-mail e-mail that says, "We hope you received our recent letter. If you haven't had a chance to give yet, please give online today. It's fast, easy, and efficient."

- We'll promote some online services in our direct mail—especially our store during the holidays.
- We will develop a persistent program for gradually gathering the e-mail addresses of direct mail donors who want to add e-mail to their communications with us. We will test asks in the direct mail (P.S., buckslip, reply device, etc.) and track response to find the most effective and least expensive ways to gather e-mail addresses without depressing gift response. We'll send test and track communications and resolicitations to these donors.

6. **Tracking, benchmarking, reporting**
   - We'll evaluate the e-mail messaging program by tracking the number of recipients that are converted into new donors and the number of gifts and renewals received from existing donors in direct response to an e-mail solicitation. We'll also carefully monitor the overall giving levels of donors receiving the e-news versus donors not receiving the e-news to evaluate the e-news as a cultivation tool.
   - We'll evaluate our site traffic to determine which content is most appealing and increase the visibility of that content, as well as tie in giving opportunities.

Source: Adapted from Network for Good. Retrieved from www.fundraising123.org/print/182. Used with permission of Network for Good. Network for Good provides nonprofits with fundraising tools and training to help organizations raise more money online.

Acknowledging and Recognizing Donors

Well-managed development offices acknowledge gifts promptly, and most tailor the acknowledgment to the level of the gift or status of the donor. For example, donors of gifts above a certain level may receive a letter or e-mail from the CEO, while others may receive a letter or e-mail from the director of development, and small gifts may be acknowledged only with a preprinted paper or online receipt. Nonprofits are required by law to provide and donors are required to have a formal receipt in order to deduct cash gifts of $250 or more from their taxes. Additional rules apply to the substantiation of the value of gifts-in-kind.

Recognition of donors may include listing their names in an annual report or on the website, including them in special recognition societies according to the level of the gift, and displaying their names on plaques or wall displays. Larger gifts may be recognized through the naming of facilities or endowment funds. While some donors may request anonymity, most appreciate tasteful and appropriate recognition, which itself becomes a part of the process of cultivation for the next gift.

Stewarding the Gift and the Relationship

The stewardship of past donors is an activity that has received more attention in most development offices in recent years. Experience suggests that past donors are the best prospects for future gifts, and it is therefore important to continue building their relationship with the organization after a gift has been made. The concept of stewardship can have two meanings. The most common usage encompasses the activities that the organization undertakes to keep the donor informed and engaged. These may include recognition, sending reports about the impact of the gift, and developing events to strengthen donors' involvement and knowledge about the organization's activities. It is essentially the cultivation of current and past donors with an eye toward future support. The second meaning of stewardship is more substantial, relating to the organization's responsibility to manage the gift according to the donor's intention, that is, to keep faith with the donor. This is especially important with gifts made to endowment, which are invested in perpetuity to produce income supporting current programs. Many organizations have developed regular written reports to endowment donors, informing them of the fund's financial performance as well

Another criticism of the fundraising pyramid is that it describes a situation most applicable to large nonprofit institutions, such as universities, and that it is less relevant for smaller nonprofits. Colleges and universities have natural lifelong relationships with their graduates, and most have sufficient financial stability that they can patiently nurture relationships leading to ultimate gifts. For many nonprofits in urgent need of increased support to balance current budgets, the distant promise of an ultimate gift may seem unworthy of too much time and effort today. But as Dunlop (1993) emphasizes, most organizations have at least a few close friends and donors with whom they should be cultivating long-term relationships with the hope that they will eventually produce the level of giving that can be transformative.

Planned Giving

A rapidly growing component of philanthropy includes gifts that are made in connection with individuals' financial or estate planning, known as *planned gifts*. Many major gifts today do involve the use of sophisticated financial instruments, and *planned giving* has become a major subfield within the fundraising profession. Experienced planned giving officers, or *gift planners* as some are called, are highly sought after by all types of nonprofit organizations. The aging of the U.S. population and the increasing wealth held by older people suggests that this form of giving will grow in importance in coming decades.

As shown in Table 13.2, there are three types of planned gifts: *outright planned gifts, expectancies*, and *deferred gifts*. Some outright gifts are planned gifts because they involve complex assets, such as stocks or real estate, and may require the assistance of financial experts to complete. An expectancy is a promise that a donor makes to provide a gift to the organization at some future time, generally at death, through a bequest, life insurance, or a retirement plan. These are also commonly known as *testamentary gifts*. Deferred gifts are gifts that the donor makes now, but which are not available to the organization until some future time, generally after the death of the donor or some other individual (Regenovich, 2011, pp. 146–150). Table 13.1 provides a brief summary of vehicles available for planned gifts; this chapter discusses only a few of the most common.

One of the simplest forms of a planned gift is a *bequest,* which is merely a statement in an individual's will or living trust dictating that on his or her death, some amount or portion of his or her estate is to be given to a charitable organization. Other planned gifts, for example, those using *charitable remainder trusts* and *charitable gift annuities,* are arrangements that provide for the donor or another beneficiary to receive lifetime income, with the charitable organization not gaining full use of the donated assets until after the death of the donor or the last income recipient. Such gifts provide a tax deduction for some portion of the gift, but not for the full amount, since the donor has a retained life income interest attributable to the noncharitable portion of the payment. In addition to qualifying for income tax deductions, donors may avoid or defer capital gains taxes on appreciated assets used to make a planned gift and, since the donated assets are removed from the donor's estate, there may be an estate tax saving, as well. As in our earlier example, these tax benefits reduce the out-of-pocket cost of the gift, which can make the rate of income received by the donor an attractive feature.

Other planned giving vehicles include lead trusts and life estates. A donor may place an asset in a *lead trust* for a period of years, with the income being paid to the nonprofit organization. At the termination of the trust, the asset is returned to the donor or the donor's heirs. A donor who gives his or her personal residence to a nonprofit organization may retain the right to continue living in the property for the balance of his or her life, an arrangement that is known as a *life estate. Donor advised funds*, maintained by community foundations and other managers of charitable funds, permit individuals to make a gift and earn a tax deduction currently, while reserving the right to make future recommendations on how the funds are to be distributed. It is important to recognize, however, that the donor does not have the right to direct gifts and can only make recommendations to the trustee of the fund.

The future of planned giving could be affected by changes in the federal estate tax. Assets that a donor gives during life or at death are removed from the individual's estate, and thus, there is a tax saving, similar to the saving produced by the income tax deduction for gifts, as discussed above. If tax rates change, the value of that tax deduction changes and affects the amount that an individual may be able or motivated to give. In 2015, estates valued at $5,430,000 or more (double that for a couple) are subject to a federal estate tax on amounts above those levels. However, the estate tax is an ongoing topic of debate, so the exemption amount

TABLE 13.1 ■ Common Planned Giving Vehicles

Name	Description	Most attractive to . . .
OUTRIGHT GIFTS		
Gift of appreciated property	Individual gives an asset, for example, stock or real estate, which has a value greater than what was paid to acquire it (cost basis).	Individuals who wish to receive an income tax deduction for the full value of the asset and avoid paying a capital gains tax on its sale.
Donor advised fund	An individual irrevocably transfers assets to a fund, maintained by a community foundation or other charitable entity. The donor (or other designated individual/s) retains the right to recommend recipients of gifts to be made from the fund but cannot direct or require the distributions.	Individuals who wish to earn an immediate income tax deduction for their gifts to the donor advised fund but to have the funds paid to one or more nonprofit organizations in the future. This may be the case with individuals who have a year in which they receive unusually high income, for example, upon sale of an asset or a business.
Lead trust	An individual places assets in a trust, which is managed by a trustee. The trustee pays income earned by investments of the trust to a nonprofit organization for a specified period of years. At the end of that period, the trust ends and the assets are returned to the donor, the donor's heirs, or to other named beneficiaries.	Individuals who own income-producing assets do not need the income they produce and wish to make gifts to a nonprofit organization. There are also potential estate tax savings if the assets are ultimately returned to the donor's heirs.
EXPECTANCIES (TESTAMENTARY GIFTS)		
Bequest	A statement in an individual's will or revocable trust that designates a specific asset, amount, or percentage of the estate to be paid as a gift to a nonprofit organization upon the individual's death.	Individuals who wish to retain control of their assets during their lifetimes and who seek a simple method of making a charitable gift at death.
Retirement plan or IRA	An individual names a nonprofit organization as the beneficiary of assets remaining in a retirement plan or IRA at the individual's death.	Individuals who wish to retain access to their retirement funds while living and who seek a simple method of making a charitable gift at death.
Life insurance	A nonprofit organization is named as the owner and beneficiary of a life insurance policy that will pay a benefit to the organization upon the individual's death.	Individuals who can afford premium payments but wish to make a larger gift at death than their assets may permit.

(Continued)

TABLE 13.1 ■ (Continued)		
Name	**Description**	**Most attractive to . . .**
DEFERRED GIFTS		
Charitable gift annuity	A contract between an individual and a nonprofit organization in which the organization agrees to pay a fixed lifetime income to the individual (or to another designated individual/s) in exchange for the gift. The income payments are secured by the full faith and credit of the organization. Some charitable gift annuities are immediate (the income starts as soon as the gift is made) and others are deferred (the income begins at some designated future date). There are other variations.	Individuals who wish to receive an immediate income tax deduction (for a portion of the gift) and receive a relatively secure but fixed lifetime income. A fixed income may be more attractive to older donors, who are less concerned with the effects of inflation over their remaining lives.
Charitable remainder trust	An individual gives assets to a trust. The trustee manages the trust and pays income to the individual (or to one or more other designated individual/s) for life. Upon the death of the last surviving income recipient, the trustee pays the trust's principal to a designated nonprofit organization. There are two basic types. Charitable remainder annuity trusts pay a fixed income. Charitable remainder unitrusts pay a variable income that is a fixed percentage of the trust's assets each year. Income payments would cease if the trust's assets became depleted. There are other variations.	Individuals who own appreciated assets and wish to avoid or defer capital gains taxes that would be payable if the assets were sold outside of the trust. Individuals who seek an immediate income tax deduction (for a portion of the gift.) The unitrust may be attractive to individuals who want the possibility of increasing income payments over their lifetimes and are willing to accept the risk of an income that may vary from year to year.
Life estate	An individual gives his or her personal residence to a nonprofit organization, retaining the right to continue living there for his or her lifetime.	Individuals who desire to use their homes as an asset to make a gift but also desire to continue living there.

Source: Developed by the author using various sources.

or tax rates may change in the years ahead. Similarly, the law regarding donor advised funds is a topic of recurring debates and changes could affect the attractiveness of these vehicles to some donors (Daniels, 2015). Students are encouraged to check with websites such as Independent Sector (www.independentsector.org) or AFP (www.afpnet.org) for up-to-date information on the law.

Planned giving is a complex topic, and a full discussion is beyond the scope of this text, but additional reading is recommended at the end of this chapter for those who wish to pursue a more in-depth understanding. The *Partnership for Philanthropic Planning* (www.pppnet.org) is a professional organization of gift planners that offers important education and materials. There are also websites that provide cases, resources, and tools for planned giving professionals, and some are listed at the conclusion of this chapter.

Campaigns

Fundraising campaigns have been a part of the nonprofit landscape since the early years of the 20th century, when the campaign method was developed by fundraisers for the YMCA. The model was later adopted by higher education institutions and subsequently by most other nonprofit organizations. Historically, campaigns were known as *capital campaigns* and were usually undertaken specifically to construct new physical facilities. Over the past three decades, however, many campaigns have become comprehensive, including within their goals not only funds for facilities but also endowment, operating funds, and support for programs. At any given time in most communities today, there will be highly publicized campaigns underway by multiple organizations, seeking funds for all these purposes. The dollar goals are often substantial and to be achieved typically in five to eight years.

What distinguishes a campaign from just ordinary fundraising? First, a campaign is intensive, ranking among the highest priorities of the organization and usually commanding a significant amount of time and energy from the CEO, board members, fundraising staff, and others. This intensity is created by two essential characteristics of a campaign—an announced dollar goal and a deadline. A campaign has defined objectives, that is, specific purposes for which the funds are being raised that are spelled out in campaign literature. The solicitation of gifts to a campaign follows the principle of *sequential fundraising,* in which prospects are solicited in a planned sequence beginning with those closest to the organization and the most promising prospects, proceeding later to those who are less related or who are deemed to have less financial potential. This process helps raise the sights of prospective donors by offering the example of those who have already made impressive financial commitments. Finally, solicitations in a campaign request a specific amount that has been deemed realistic for the particular donor. Donors are rated according to their capacity to give and are solicited, in the appropriate order, for a gift at that level. Without meeting these essential conditions, a fundraising effort is not really a campaign. Thus, fundraising that aims to raise "as much as possible" or "as soon as possible" is, by definition, not a campaign, because it does not proceed against a specific goal that it intends to reach within a defined period of time. Solicitations that ask people to give as much as they can represent a "collection," but not a campaign, which seeks specific gifts from donors deemed capable of making them (Worth, 2010).

Campaigns proceed in phases, as depicted in Figure 13.3. They are rooted in the organization's strategic planning, which defines goals and directions and financial needs. Planning for a campaign itself is a

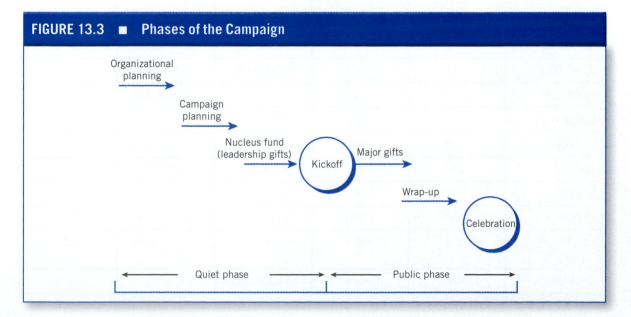

FIGURE 13.3 ■ Phases of the Campaign

process that may encompass months or years and includes the identification of prospects, enlistment of volunteer leaders, and the hiring of fundraising staff. In order to maximize the solicitation of significant early gifts, and their impact on the sights of donors in later phases, a campaign is not announced to the public until a significant portion of its total goal has been raised as part of a *nucleus fund* during what is known as the campaign's *quiet period* or *quiet phase* (sometimes called the *silent phase*). A formal *kickoff* of the campaign usually includes announcement of the overall goal, celebration of the amount already raised toward it as part of the nucleus fund, and recognition of nucleus fund donors. The kickoff is intended to establish momentum, generate good feelings, demonstrate that the campaign is likely to be successful, and inspire prospects who have not yet given to set their sights in relationship to what the nucleus fund donors already have done.

Following the kickoff, the campaign is in its *public phase.* Efforts to bring visibility to the campaign and its goals often become a significant component of the organization's communication efforts for the duration of the campaign. Planning for today's campaigns includes marketing and communication goals that are nearly as important to the organization as the financial goals addressed by the campaign. They have become tools for positioning organizations and, indeed, some campaign goals, especially in higher education, are often set at least in part to make a statement about the institution's relative rank and prestige, rather than reflecting exclusively its considered financial needs.

An important tool in planning and managing a campaign is the *gift chart,* also known as the *gift standards chart* (although the format might more appropriately be called a *table.*). An example, based on a campaign goal of $250 million, is provided in Table 13.2. The chart reflects the proportional giving necessary to achieve the campaign's overall goal, starting with a lead gift that is at least 10 percent of the goal, and then doubling the number of gifts needed at each successively lower dollar level. The ratios used to

TABLE 13.2 ■ **Gift Range Chart for Campaign With Goal of $250 Million**

Gift Range (in $)	Number of Gifts Required	Number of Prospects Required	Total of Gifts in This Range (in $)	Cumulative Total (in $)	Cumulative Percentage of Goal
25,000,000	1	4	25,000,000	25,000,000	10
10,000,000	3	12	30,000,000	55,000,000	22
5,000,000	6	24	30,000,000	85,000,000	34
2,500,000	12	48	30,000,000	115,000,000	46
1,000,000	27	108	27,000,000	142,000,000	57
500,000	52	208	26,000,000	168,000,000	68
250,000	100	400	25,000,000	193,000,000	77
100,000	180	720	18,000,000	211,000,000	84
50,000	300	1,200	15,000,000	226,000,000	90
25,000	560	2,240	14,000,000	240,000,000	96
Less than 25,000	Many	Many	10,000,000	250,000,000	100
Totals	1,241+	4,964+	250,000,000	—	—

construct the table have been developed through experience in many campaigns over the past century and often reflect the pattern of giving to a campaign when studied retrospectively. In recent years, however, some campaigns have diverged from these historic patterns, with an increasingly large percentage of the total coming from a decreasing number of very large gifts at the top of the chart—in other words, from fewer major donors but larger gifts. That change reflected the economic booms of the late 1990s and mid-2000s as well as the increasing concentration of wealth in the United States and other economic and demographic changes. The gift-range chart is useful in projecting how many gifts will be needed to obtain a specified goal. Using the industry standard, that about four prospects are required to produce every closed gift, it also provides a way to assess if the organization has developed a donor constituency sufficient to support a proposed campaign goal. It may also be useful in demonstrating to the early donors, often including board members, why their gifts need to be exceptional, in order to meet the requirements at the upper ranges of the chart and set the standards for others who will ultimately be asked to support the campaign.

Managing Fundraising Programs

Fundraising programs today are sophisticated undertakings, even at modestly sized nonprofit organizations. In larger institutions, the staff of a development office may include dozens or even hundreds of professionals in various specialties, including annual giving, corporate and foundation relations, major gifts, and *advancement services*.

Advancement Services

Advancement services has emerged as an important subspecialty in the field, encompassing all the back-office operations such as gift recording and acknowledgment, prospect research, and information systems management.[1] Most nonprofit organizations use one of the commercially available software packages that are comprehensive in their capabilities to maintain donor information and gift records as well as track cultivation and solicitation activity and evaluate the productivity and effectiveness of specific initiatives or fundraising staff.

As mentioned earlier, the growing availability of information on the Web has revolutionized the field of prospect research. Databases of corporate and foundation giving programs enable researchers to identify promising prospects quickly. The giving capacity of individual prospects can be evaluated using a number of sophisticated electronic screening tools that will also identify known relationships of prospects, for example, to members of the organization's board. However, the costs of such screening can be high for many small nonprofits, and there is still much insight and information to be obtained through the more traditional method of having prospects screened by peers. Individuals in the same business community, the same church, or in the same graduating class may have a good sense of the financial capability and interests of their peers and are often willing to rate their capacity in a setting that provides confidentiality.

Prospect Management

In sophisticated fundraising programs, relationships with donors and prospects are not developed casually or randomly. Contacts are planned, scheduled, and tracked, and a member of the development office staff is assigned as the *prospect manager* with responsibility for moving the relationship forward. A strategy is developed for each major prospect, and *contact reports* entered into the fundraising information system document every interaction and make it possible for a fundraising manager to monitor the movement of prospects through the fundraising cycle.

In large organizations, especially those with multiple units and decentralized fundraising, policies requiring prior clearance of contacts with donors are essential. For example, this situation is common in universities, where alumni may hold degrees from more than one school and be viewed as prospects for giving to all of them. Multiple contacts by different units of the organization may be irritating to donors and create the impression that the organization is poorly managed or inept. In addition, there is always the risk of a preemptive smaller gift that disrupts a careful plan that might have led to a more significant commitment.

Fundraising Efficiency and Effectiveness

The costs of fundraising are a topic that receives considerable discussion and that has been the focus of various studies. As discussed in Chapter 6, some charity watchdog organizations have established guidelines suggesting that fundraising costs should not exceed about one third of the total funds contributed. The Supreme Court has held that government may not set a maximum level of fundraising expenditure because doing so would be an abridgement of free speech rights under the U.S. Constitution, but the public availability of Form 990 and other financial information has made organizations sensitive to the appearance of high costs in the eyes of their donors as well as the watchdog raters.

Some people say that setting limits on fundraising costs is unfair to organizations that are new or controversial and, therefore, must expend more effort and more money in order to meet their needs for gift support. In addition, it can sometimes be difficult to determine the true total costs of fundraising by an organization. Some portion of the time and effort of a CEO may be devoted to cultivating and soliciting gifts, but it is not always easy to identify that portion exactly, since some activities may involve donors but may also have other purposes. For example, is the CEO's time spent with a board member who is also a donor to be considered fundraising activity, or is it related to broader governance of the organization? Printed materials and mail solicitations may include a solicitation as well as other information, which may be considered educational or informative and thus an activity related to the organization's mission rather than fundraising. Accounting rules describe how the costs of such mailings and materials are to be allocated between fundraising and mission-related purposes, but some nonprofits may not be clear about exactly how such costs should be apportioned.

Historically, the ratio most commonly used to evaluate the efficiency of fundraising was *cost-per-dollar-raised,* that is, the amount of expenditure on fundraising divided by the total gifts received—it is a cost–benefit ratio stated in dollar terms. For example, if an organization spends $50,000 on fundraising and receives $500,000 in gifts as a result, its cost would be 10-cents-per-dollar-raised. If the same expenditure brought in $1,000,000, its relative cost would be half as much, just five-cents-per-dollar-raised. However, most now argue, this ratio is an inappropriate measure for at least two reasons. First, it is a negative way of looking at fundraising—as an expense rather than as an investment. For example, if an organization spends as much as 50 cents to raise a dollar, which would be considered a relatively high cost, that would still represent a 100 percent return on its original investment. There are few investments in which it is possible to double one's money, and a 100 percent return would be considered very good performance by a manager of an investment portfolio.

The second related objection is that cost-per-dollar-raised measures fundraising efficiency, but it says nothing about fundraising effectiveness. For example, if one organization spends $50,000 to raise $500,000, its cost is just 10-cents-per-dollar and its net revenue is $450,000. Suppose another organization spends twice as much, $100,000, and its efforts result in gifts totaling $600,000. Its relative cost is much higher than the first organization—almost 17-cents-per-dollar. Its fundraising is less *efficient,* but its net revenue of $500,000 is higher than that of the first organization and its fundraising is thus more *effective.* For these reasons, most organizations today consider the *return-on-investment* in fundraising and look at what is spent in relation to what is raised over a time frame of years.

Attention to the costs—and results—of fundraising is commanding more attention by nonprofit managers as well as charity watchdogs and donors. Despite the argument that fundraising costs and returns should be viewed on a long-term basis, it is also the reality that organizations spending a high percentage of gift revenue on fundraising activities may be subject to criticism. The negative impact of controversy may more than offset whatever financial gains their fundraising plan anticipates.

Staff Performance and Accountability

An important question, especially in larger development offices with staff members who are specialized in the area of major gift fundraising, is how to evaluate the performance of individual fundraising professionals.

Perhaps the simplest measure would be the amount of money each staff member raises, but that approach creates a number of issues. First, most major gifts do not result from the efforts of a single individual. As we have discussed, a donor's relationship with an organization may develop over a long period of time, perhaps exceeding the tenure of any single member of the staff. There are many key players in building such relationships, including perhaps the CEO and volunteers, as well as members of the board. It is usually not easy to identify exactly who is responsible for the receipt of a major gift; indeed, the individual who solicits the gift may have played a relatively minor role.

A second problem with using dollars raised to evaluate the performance of a development staff member is that it might create incentives that would lead to inappropriate behavior. That is not to suggest that the fundraiser would necessarily engage in unethical or immoral behavior with regard to a donor, but it is possible that a development staff member who knows he or she will be evaluated on the basis of gifts secured will, even if unconsciously, short-circuit the process in a way that is disadvantageous to the organization. For example, a fundraiser with such an incentive might direct his or her efforts toward soliciting gifts from prospects who are known to be ready to give, rather than cultivation of prospects who may not be ready yet but whose long-term capacity to give is much higher. The staff person might neglect stewardship of past donors who are still making payments on long-term pledges and who have a high likelihood of giving again, while pursuing new donors to hit some dollar target on which his or her own performance will be evaluated. And, of course, there could be instances in which a development staff member under pressure to maximize gift revenue misleads a donor or exaggerates the benefits of a gift under a reward system that values only gifts completed. For these reasons, some organizations evaluate the performance of fundraising staff primarily on the activity they undertake, for example, the number of visits made and the number of proposals submitted, rather than the dollars they raise in the short run. Others use formulas that combine credit for such activity with the value of gifts closed.

Again, while it is an issue mostly in larger fundraising operations, the best method for evaluating and rewarding professional staff is a topic of current discussion and debate. Some development staff are paid incentive-based compensation, including bonuses, which may reward activity (e.g., the number of donor visits completed) exceeding some predefined objectives. Such programs need to be carefully designed to ensure that the fundraising staff is not being paid a commission—that is, a percentage of the gifts they raise. Basing staff compensation on a percentage of gifts raised is unethical behavior, explicitly prohibited by the ethical codes of the Association of Fundraising Professionals and other professional organizations in the field. The practice would not only raise concerns about the possibility of incentivizing misbehavior by fundraisers, but it also goes to the heart of the philanthropic relationships and the assumption of trust and mutual commitment to a cause or organization that donors assume to be present when they discuss a gift with the organization's representative.

Ethics and Professional Standards

The question of compensation for fundraising staff is just one area of potential ethical challenge always present in the complex relationships among organizations, their donors, and the individuals who solicit funds on the organization's behalf. Most ethical questions that arise in fundraising can be placed into one of four principal categories.

First, some issues involve the behavior of the staff person who is interacting with the donor. They would include making misleading or dishonest representations, for example, exaggerating the organization's effectiveness, lying about how the gift will be used, or making unreasonable or unrealistic promises to the donor about recognition or the financial benefits of giving. It is also unethical for a nonprofit staff member who is managing a relationship with a donor to attempt to use that relationship for his or her personal benefit or gain or to engage in behavior toward the donor that would be morally repugnant, for example, sexual harassment.

A second category of ethical issues that may confront nonprofit organizations relates to the donor rather than the staff member. For example, what if the organization has reason to believe that the donated funds were illegally obtained? Should a nonprofit accept gifts from a company that makes products it knows to be harmful? What about the question of accepting a gift from a donor who has been convicted of a white-collar crime or who simply has an unsavory reputation that might reflect badly on the organization, were the gift to receive publicity? There have been a number of examples of such dilemmas posed by gifts from businesspeople who were later involved in corporate corruption scandals, after a building or program had been named to recognize a past gift. Should the organization remove the name? By whose judgment should such decisions be made, and what are the limits of the organization's responsibility—and right—to investigate and judge the character of donors who may offer them support?

A third, and sometimes less obvious ethical, question is presented by restricted gifts: Under what circumstances should an organization refuse to accept a gift that may require it to undertake new programs and perhaps incur additional expenses that it had not anticipated? What if the new program is not entirely consistent with the organization's mission or would require a redefinition of its mission? For example, if an organization concerned with young children were offered a gift to begin a new program to help prevent high school students from dropping out, it would need to consider whether expanding its mission in that way would jeopardize its focus on its primary mission, what additional costs the new efforts might create in the future, and whether such expansion might endanger the organization's overall health and other sources of support. It might not be an easy decision to make if the offered gift were very substantial and, especially, if the donor were an important local businessperson or even a member of the organization's board. The risk to the relationship in turning down the gift would need to be weighed against the potential risk to the organization if it were accepted with the conditions that accompany it.

Another subcategory of questions arises with gifts that come with conditions that might give the donor inappropriate control. For example, most colleges will accept scholarship gifts that require recipients to be enrolled in certain academic programs; that raises few problems unless, for example, the college thinks it unlikely will be able to recruit many students meeting the conditions. But there are limits to how much influence a donor can be allowed to have in the process of selecting specific scholarship recipients. Allowing the donor to select the recipient of the scholarships would not only present an ethical concern but, indeed, it could also invalidate the tax deductibility of the donor's gift, making it legally a gift to the scholarship recipient *individually* rather than to the college, university, or school.

A fourth category of ethical concern that has increased with the growing sophistication of prospect research involves maintaining appropriate safeguards to protect the privacy of donors and prospects. The development offices of many organizations may possess information obtained from public sources about individuals' financial wealth and income, real estate holdings, and even family situations. It is legal to obtain such data. But some would argue, when it is assembled to create a donor profile, its wide distribution may be an inappropriate invasion of privacy. In addition, development office files may include information gained from reports written by staff members who have visited the donor over the years or heard secondhand from others who know the donor. Maintaining such information in the files of the fundraising office runs the risk that the donor, and the organization, could be embarrassed if it were inappropriately or inadvertently disclosed to another person.

The Association of Fundraising Professionals "Code of Ethical Principles" and "Principles of Professional Practice" cover many of the major issues that nonprofits and members of their staff may encounter in raising philanthropic funds. But possible situations are so varied that no code can substitute for continuing ethical awareness and the application of good judgment by nonprofit managers who value the interests of their organizations and their missions above all else (see Box 13.6).

BOX 13.6 AFP CODE OF ETHICAL PRINCIPLES AND STANDARDS

(Ethical principles adopted 1964; amended September 2007)

The Association of Fundraising Professionals (AFP) . . . exists to foster the development and growth of fundraising professionals and the profession, to promote high ethical behavior in the fund-raising profession and to preserve and enhance philanthropy and volunteerism. Members of AFP are motivated by an inner drive to improve the quality of life through the causes they serve. They serve the ideal of philanthropy, are committed to the preservation and enhancement of volunteerism; and hold stewardship of these concepts as the overriding direction of their professional life. They recognize their responsibility to ensure that needed resources are vigorously and ethically sought and that the intent of the donor is honestly fulfilled. To these ends, AFP members, both individual and business, embrace certain values that they strive to uphold in performing their responsibilities for generating philanthropic support. AFP business members strive to promote and protect the work and mission of their client organizations.

AFP members [both individual and business] aspire to:

- practice their profession with integrity, honesty, truthfulness, and adherence to the absolute obligation to safeguard the public trust;
- act according to the highest goals and visions of their organizations, professions, clients and consciences;
- put philanthropic mission above personal gain;
- inspire others through their own sense of dedication and high purpose;
- improve their professional knowledge and skills, so that their performance will better serve others;
- demonstrate concern for the interests and well-being of individuals affected by their actions;
- value the privacy, freedom of choice and interests of all those affected by their actions;
- foster cultural diversity and pluralistic values and treat all people with dignity and respect;
- affirm, through personal giving, a commitment to philanthropy and its role in society;
- adhere to the spirit as well as the letter of all applicable laws and regulations;
- advocate within their organizations adherence to all applicable laws and regulations;
- avoid even the appearance of any criminal offense or professional misconduct;
- bring credit to the fundraising profession by their public demeanor;
- encourage colleagues to embrace and practice these ethical principles and standards;
- be aware of the codes of ethics promulgated by other professional organizations that serve philanthropy.

Ethical Standards

Furthermore, while striving to act according to the above values, AFP members, both individual and business, agree to abide (and to ensure, to the best of their ability, that all members of their staff abide) by the AFP standards. Violation of the standards may subject the member to disciplinary sanctions, including expulsion, as provided in the AFP Ethics Enforcement Procedures.

(Continued)

(Continued)

Member Obligations

1. Members shall not engage in activities that harm the members' organizations, clients, or profession.

2. Members shall not engage in activities that conflict with their fiduciary, ethical, and legal obligations to their organizations, clients or profession.

3. Members shall effectively disclose all potential and actual conflicts of interest; such disclosure does not preclude or imply ethical impropriety.

4. Members shall not exploit any relationship with a donor, prospect, volunteer, client, or employee for the benefit of the members or the members' organizations.

5. Members shall comply with all applicable local, state, provincial, and federal civil and criminal laws.

6. Members recognize their individual boundaries of competence and are forthcoming and truthful about their professional experience and qualifications and will represent their achievements accurately and without exaggeration.

7. Members shall present and supply products and/or services honestly and without misrepresentation and will clearly identify the details of those products, such as availability of the products and/or services and other factors that may affect the suitability of the products and/or services for donors, clients, or nonprofit organizations.

8. Members shall establish the nature and purpose of any contractual relationship at the outset and will be responsive and available to organizations and their employing organizations before, during, and after any sale of materials and/or services. Members will comply with all fair and reasonable obligations created by the contract.

9. Members shall refrain from knowingly infringing [on] the intellectual property rights of other parties at all times. Members shall address and rectify any inadvertent infringement that may occur.

10. Members shall protect the confidentiality of all privileged information relating to the provider/client relationships.

11. Members shall refrain from any activity designed to disparage competitors untruthfully.

Solicitation and Use of Philanthropic Funds

12. Members shall take care to ensure that all solicitation and communication materials are accurate and correctly reflect their organizations' mission and use of solicited funds.

13. Members shall take care to ensure that donors receive informed, accurate, and ethical advice about the value and tax implications of contributions.

14. Members shall take care to ensure that contributions are used in accordance with donors' intentions.

15. Members shall take care to ensure proper stewardship of all revenue sources, including timely reports on the use and management of such funds.

16. Members shall obtain explicit consent by donors before altering the conditions of financial transactions.

Presentation of Information

17. Members shall not disclose privileged or confidential information to unauthorized parties.

18. Members shall adhere to the principle that all donor and prospect information created by, or on behalf of, an organization or a client is the property of that organization or client and shall not be transferred or utilized except on behalf of that organization or client.

19. Members shall give donors and clients the opportunity to have their names removed from lists that are sold to, rented to, or exchanged with other organizations.

20. Members shall, when stating fundraising results, use accurate and consistent accounting methods that conform to the appropriate guidelines adopted by the American Institute of Certified Public Accountants (AICPA)* for the type of organization involved. (*In countries outside of the United States, comparable authority should be utilized.)

Compensation and Contracts

21. Members shall not accept compensation or enter into a contract that is based on a percentage of contributions; nor shall members accept finder's fees or contingent fees. Business members must refrain from receiving compensation from third parties derived from products or services for a client without disclosing that third-party compensation to the client (for example, volume rebates from vendors to business members).

22. Members may accept performance-based compensation, such as bonuses, provided such bonuses are in accord with prevailing practices within the members' own organizations and are not based on a percentage of contributions.

23. Members shall neither offer nor accept payments or special considerations for the purpose of influencing the selection of products or services.

24. Members shall not pay finder's fees, commissions, or percentage compensation based on contributions, and shall take care to discourage their organizations from making such payments.

25. Any member receiving funds on behalf of a donor or client must meet the legal requirements for the disbursement of those funds. Any interest or income earned on the funds should be fully disclosed.

Source: Used with permission of the Association of Fundraising Professionals.

Chapter Summary

Gifts are a significant component of revenue for many nonprofit organizations, although patterns vary widely among subsectors. Gifts comprise a small percentage of revenue for health care institutions, which derive most of their revenue from fees for service. At the other end of the spectrum, gifts are almost the only source of income for religious congregations and many human services nonprofits. Organized fundraising is rapidly becoming more common across the world, but it is still most highly developed in the United States. The term *fundraising* is often used synonymously with the term *development* or *advancement*, but the latter two terms are properly understood to encompass a more comprehensive approach to institution building that includes other external relations functions.

It is important to distinguish between charity, that is, giving to address current human needs, and philanthropy, which seeks to establish or strengthen institutions that address society's needs on a long-term basis. Charity is sometimes impulsive and is emotionally driven; philanthropy is often more thoughtful and deliberate.

The motivation to give is quite different among corporations, foundations, and individual donors. Corporate philanthropy generally seeks to advance the corporation's business interests while also accomplishing some social benefit. Corporate support of nonprofits encompasses philanthropy and also various partnerships, which will be discussed in the next chapter. Foundations exist to make gifts and are required by law to do so. There are various types of foundations, some of which may be prospects for support of nonprofit organizations and others that operate their own programs and generally do not provide grants to others.

Most individual donors are likely to be less organized and rational in their giving than are corporations or foundations. A considerable body of research exists on the motivations of individual donors. Findings generally suggest that individuals are motivated by altruism, a desire to pay back for benefits that they have received, desires for social advancement and recognition, as well as other reasons. The influence of tax incentives on giving by individuals is a subject of debate among economists and other experts.

Fundraising is a process that begins with the organization identifying its own priorities and developing a case for support and progresses to identifying prospects who have linkage, interest, and the ability to give; cultivation of relationships with those prospects; solicitation of the gift; acknowledgment and recognition of the gift and donor; and stewardship to continue the relationship and prepare for continued support from past donors. Development of the case, or the rationale for why the organization deserves support, is a critical step. A strong case is larger than the organization—it starts with the social needs that the organization's programs address and then becomes more specific in describing how needed funds will enhance the organization's ability to address those broader needs.

The solicitation of gifts may use various media, including mail, phone, personal meeting, and—increasingly—electronic communication, such as the Internet, e-mail, texting, and social media. Each of these approaches offers advantages and disadvantages. Social media are generally of more value to nonprofit organizations as a way to build and maintain relationships than as a fundraising method, but their importance for fundraising is likely to increase.

The fundraising pyramid depicts how many donors evolve in their giving relationship with an organization, beginning as regular annual donors and possibly advancing to become major donors and eventually donors of ultimate gifts. Organizations often build their fundraising programs in accordance with the pyramid, beginning with solicitations for annual gifts and then developing major gift and planned gift programs as their constituency is ready.

Planned giving is a growing area of fundraising and philanthropy. There are three basic types of planned gifts—outright planned gifts, expectancies, and deferred gifts. Each offers various advantages to the donor, and the vehicle selected will reflect the individual's financial and estate considerations. Campaigns are intensive fundraising efforts that seek to raise a given amount by a specified deadline for specific purposes or campaign objectives. Campaigns proceed in phases, and it is important that the model be followed to ensure success in achieving the goal. The gift-range chart depicts the pattern of giving necessary to achieve a dollar goal and is a useful tool in planning and managing a campaign.

Advancement services, encompassing the back-office operations of fundraising, has become an important subspecialty of the field. This area includes prospect research, gift accounting, and the maintenance of fundraising information systems and records.

Questions about the efficiency and effectiveness of fundraising are often discussed and debated. Evaluating the ratio of fundraising cost to dollars raised may be unfair to younger, smaller organizations and does not reveal the effectiveness of a fundraising program in maximizing net revenue. The *return on investment* in fundraising is a more appropriate measure of effectiveness, but some still emphasize the ratio of costs to revenue and prefer to see fundraising expenditures at a minimum. Fundraising costs that are high may attract the attention of the media, donors, and government officials and result in negative publicity. Discussion also surrounds the compensation of fundraising staff, some of whom receive financial incentives for performance. Compensation based on a percentage of gifts secured is considered unethical in the field.

Fundraising often raises ethical issues, including, among others, those related to the behavior of fundraisers themselves, the reputation of the donor or the source of that individual's wealth, the impact of restricted gifts on the mission of the organization, and concerns about donor privacy and the use of information resulting from prospect research. AFP and other organizations have established ethics codes that are widely followed by practitioners.

Note

1. In an office that engages only in fundraising, this function might be called "development services" or "development operations." But in some organizations, the back office supports not only fundraising but also marketing and communications programs—for example, by maintaining mailing lists for newsletters and records for special events—and is thus known as "advancement services," reflecting the broader concept of institutional advancement, as discussed earlier.

KEY TERMS AND CONCEPTS

ability, linkage, interest

advancement

advancement services

Association of Fundraising Professionals

bequest

campaign

case for support

case statement

catalytic philanthropy

charitable gift annuity

charitable remainder trust

charity

contact reports

cost-per-dollar-raised

crowdfunding

cultivation

deferred gifts

development

donor advised fund

enlightened self-interest

expectancies

external case statement

family foundations

fundraising

fundraising pyramid

gift chart/gift standards chart

gifts-in-kind

identification of prospects

institutional advancement

internal case statement

kickoff

lead trust

life estate

major gift

nucleus fund

outcome-oriented philanthropy

out-of-pocket cost

outright planned gifts

Partnership for Philanthropic Planning

philanthropy

planned giving

prospect

prospect management

prospect research

quiet phase

regular gifts

return on investment

soliciting

special gifts

stewardship

strategic philanthropy

testamentary gifts

venture philanthropy

CASES 13.1a-g Fundraising Ethics

Case 13.1a

A generous gift is offered to your organization by a donor whose company was involved in the mortgage crisis of the late 2000s. His gift would be recognized through naming of a major wing on the new building that the gift would help to fund. Although he was not personally accused of legal wrongdoing, members of your governing board express concern that identifying his name with the organization could harm its image and reputation. One board member also raises the possibility that the donor might become involved in questionable business practices in the future and suggests that you negotiate a gift agreement that specifically permits the organization to remove the donor's name from the facility should he ever be criminally indicted or otherwise become an embarrassment to the organization. Do you accept the gift? How do you approach the donor about the proposed terms of the gift agreement?

Case 13.1b

A donor wants to give an art collection to the art gallery at which you are employed. Her requirement is that the gallery be set up just like her home and that she be able to use it for private events on request. Do you accept? What are the ethical issues and what are some possible legal concerns?

Case 13.1c

In private conversation, a fundraiser is told that a prospect's husband is terminally ill and the family has financial problems, despite appearances. Do you record that in the database? A volunteer is about to solicit that prospect for a major gift. Do you reveal this information to the volunteer?

Case 13.1d

A donor is considering a major gift to a center on competitiveness at your institution, a public policy "think tank." He is a corporate executive, and you know that he is a strong proponent of tariff protection for U.S. companies. A leading proponent of free trade is about to be appointed as a senior fellow in your research center and you know this, but it hasn't been publicly announced. Do you tell the donor about the impending appointment or just stay quiet?

Case 13.1e

A donor you had cultivated on behalf of your nonprofit employer dies. In her will, she leaves you a watch you had once admired as a personal gift. (Assume that your employer does not have a formal policy prohibiting this.) Do you accept it? Why or why not? What if she leaves you $5,000? What if it's $5 million? Does the amount make a difference?

Case 13.1f

A donor pledges $1 million payable over five years to name a room in a new building. Another donor pledges $1 million to name the identical room next door but says he can only pay it over 10 years. Do you accept the second gift and name the room? If so, are you obligated to tell the first donor about the difference in terms? If you think you are not, then how would you handle questions from the first donor were he or she to learn of the arrangements through a conversation with the second donor?

Case 13.1g

An older donor says that she wants to change her will, leaving everything to your organization. This will cut out her daughter from whom she is estranged. The daughter, whom you know personally, is disabled.

Do you encourage the donor? Do you tell the daughter what is going on? Do you tell anyone else or just let this woman make her own decision? What if you personally have doubts about the donor's mental ability to make financial decisions?

Questions Related to Cases 13.1a-g

1. In the cases above, do the ethical issues involve behavior of a fundraiser, conditions placed on the gift or the impact of the gift on the organization's mission and resources, characteristics or personal reputation of the donor, or concerns about privacy?
2. How would you handle the issues raised by each case?

QUESTIONS FOR DISCUSSION

1. Do you think that people give primarily for altruistic reasons or in order to receive benefits for themselves, including warm feelings, recognition, and social approval? Might the motivations differ among various types of gifts? Explain your answer and provide examples.

2. Some people argue that donors should receive a more generous tax deduction for gifts to organizations that serve the poor, such as homeless shelters, than they receive for gifts to institutions that primarily serve the affluent, such as symphony orchestras. Do you agree or disagree? Why?

3. If a friend asks you to sponsor his or her participation in a charity event, such as a run or walk, do you usually give a positive response or not? Why? Would your response be different if that friend asked you to do something similar the next month? Why?

SUGGESTIONS FOR FURTHER READING

Books

Arrillaga-Andreessen, L. (2012). *Giving 2.0: Transform your giving and our world.* San Francisco, CA: Jossey-Bass.

Crutchfield, L. R., Kania, J. V., & Kramer, M. R. (2011). *Do more than give: The six practices of donors who change the world.* San Francisco, CA: Jossey-Bass.

Davis, E. (2012). *Fundraising and the next generation: Tools for engaging the next generation of philanthropists.* San Francisco, CA: Jossey-Bass.

Salamon, L. (2014). *The new frontiers of philanthropy.* New York, NY: Oxford University Press.

Worth, M. J. (2016). *Fundraising: Principles and practice.* Thousand Oaks, CA: Sage.

Articles

Bekkers, R., & Wiepking, P. (2011, October). A literature review of empirical studies of philanthropy: Eight mechanisms that drive charitable giving. *Nonprofit and Voluntary Sector Quarterly, 40*(5), 924–973.

Mesch, D. J., Brown, M. S., Moore, Z. I., & Hayat, A. D. (2011, November). Gender differences in charitable giving. *International Journal of Nonprofit and Voluntary Sector Marketing, 16,* 342–355.

Websites

Association for Healthcare Philanthropy: http://www.ahp.org/

Association of Fundraising Professionals: http://www.afpnet.org/

Lilly School of Philanthropy at Indiana University: http://www.philanthropy.iupui.edu

Council for Advancement and Support of Education: http://www.case.org/

Foundation Center: http://foundationcenter.org/

Network for Good: http:www.networkforgood.org/

Partnership for Philanthropic Planning: http://www.pppnet.org/

Planned Giving Design Center: http://www.pgdc.com

Companion Website

Visit study.sagepub.com/worth4e for access to certain full-text SAGE journal articles and links to relevant video and multimedia content.

events. We are all familiar with corporate sponsorships; they would be hard to miss. They are represented by the corporate logos on the scoreboards in many university stadiums and arenas, on the T-shirts worn by participants in events like the Race for the Cure, and almost everywhere at the Olympic Games.

It is important to note that some authors (e.g., Galaskiewicz & Colman, 2006) define sponsorships as a form of strategic philanthropy, rather than a commercial partnership. For one thing, unlike licensing agreements and cause-related marketing (which we will discuss in a following section) sponsorships do not tie the nonprofit's revenues directly to the company's products. In addition, sponsorship is not the same as advertising. Advertising communicates more information and describes the virtues of the company's products—it is intended to increase sales of those products. Sponsorship is limited to exposure of the company's name or logo. It is intended to enhance the company's overall visibility and image. But in this chapter, as in much other writing about the topic, sponsorships are included as a type of commercial relationship rather than philanthropy because they do involve an exchange: the nonprofit receives a payment in exchange for permitting the corporation to associate its name with the nonprofit's cause, in a specific format and location that is negotiated as a condition of the payment, and in a manner than is more visible than just the company's name on a donor list. It is, in effect, a method for the nonprofit to leverage its brand or cause in order to create a stream of income.

Corporations sponsor events such as charity walks, runs, and rides, or athletic competitions. Some also sponsor organizations, entitling them to visibility and recognition across a broad range of programs, products, and communications. Others sponsor facilities, such as athletic arenas and concert halls, which may be named for the corporation. The facility may be named in perpetuity to recognize a corporate gift, but many are named only for the term of a sponsorship contract under which the company makes annual payments to the organization or institution operating the facility. Again, sponsorship does not include detailed descriptions of the company's products, and the payment to the nonprofit is tied to opportunities for visibility and exposure, not directly to sales.

Like licensing of a nonprofit's own name and logo, corporate sponsorships offer nonprofits the benefits of added revenue and increased visibility through the company's promotion of the relationship. Since they do not imply as strongly the nonprofit's endorsement of the company's products, the risk to the nonprofit's reputation may be somewhat less. But there are still reasons for caution. One consideration, of course, is the consistency of the corporation and its products with the mission and values of the nonprofit organization. It would be unlikely for an athletic event to accept sponsorship from a tobacco company or an organization serving children to be visibly associated with a company that sells alcohol. But some cases are closer calls, and it is wise to review sponsorship opportunities against a predetermined list of criteria reflecting the judgment of the organization's board.

Cause Marketing

Some writers use the term *cause marketing* (or *cause-related marketing*) broadly to encompass virtually all relationships in which a nonprofit's and a corporation's identities are combined, including licensing and sponsorships. This text uses the term in a more specific way to mean an arrangement under which the company contributes either a fixed amount for each sale of a product or a specified percentage of its sales of a product to the nonprofit, usually in connection with a short-term promotion. Cause marketing is different from social marketing, which we discussed in Chapter 10. The purpose of social marketing is to influence behavior in order to bring a benefit to the individual or society. Social marketing has no direct impact on revenue of the nonprofit, although it may create greater visibility for the cause and possibly bring additional gifts to the organization promoting it. The purpose of cause marketing is to sell more of the corporate partner's products, with a financial benefit to the nonprofit. There may be, of course, the additional benefit of visibility, which can increase awareness of the cause it advances, with an indirect impact on social behavior.

Unlike sponsorships and licensing arrangements, the nonprofit's revenue from a cause-marketing relationship is *transaction based;* that is, it is directly related to the volume or amount of sales of the company's products. Let's look at a few examples:

- Yoplait promised to give 10 cents to Susan G. Komen, Bright Pink, or Living Beyond Breast Cancer (based on the customer's choice) for every pink yogurt lid mailed in between October 1, 2014, and March 31, 2015, up to a maximum of $350,000 in total (friendsinthefight.yoplait.com/#enter-your-codes).
- Every September since 2008, over 9,000 restaurants, representing 373 brands, participate in Dine Out for No Kid Hungry, a program of nonprofit Share Our Strength. As a part of this overall effort, Denny's, one of the nation's largest restaurant chains, and the America's Egg Farmers donated one egg to local food banks for every "Build Your Own Omelette" purchased at a Denny's restaurant from September 9 to September 15, 2013 (Hessekiel, 2013).
- In 2010, Nestlé, a food company, encouraged consumers to participate in a drawing for a $5,000 prize by entering a code found on specially marked bags of candy. Nestlé promised to give 10 cents to Reading Is Fundamental, a literacy organization, for every submission and $2 for every instant winner, with a minimum donation of $100,000 (www.rif.org/us/donate/supporters/nestle.htm).

Again, cause marketing ties the nonprofit's income directly to the number or amount of total sales made by the corporate partner and thus represents a true partnership in which the interests of both parties are aligned. The corporation may find the relationship beneficial both as a strategy for increasing sales and as a way to improve its image and attract a new customer base, perhaps among the members of a specific market segment. In a number of studies, consumers have indicated that they would be more inclined to buy products when they know that the sale benefits a charitable organization. For example, a 2013 study conducted by Cone Communications, a company that works with businesses on nonprofit partnerships, found that 93 percent of consumers have a more positive image of a company that supports a cause; 82 percent reported that the extent to which a company supports a cause influences their decisions about where to shop or what to buy (Cone Communications, n.d.). Of course, such studies may be subject to positivity bias; in other words, people are inclined to give the "right" answer to questions about what their hypothetical behavior might be, and that does not ensure that they will actually behave in that manner.

For the nonprofit, the marketing relationship may generate not only additional revenue but also increased visibility. Promotions of the relationship often feature the logos of both the nonprofit and the corporate partner, and a comprehensive campaign may include advertising, in-store displays, and exposure in other media.

Cause-marketing relationships are governed by a contract between the nonprofit and the corporate partner. Among other matters, the contract usually spells out how much is to be paid (e.g., a fixed amount per sale or a percentage); the length of time for which the promotion will be in effect; the maximum sum (if any) that the corporate partner will give; and rights of approval that each partner retains with regard to ad copy, use of its logo, and related concerns. One important question is whether and how the terms of the contract will be clearly disclosed to consumers. Promotions that include statements such as "a portion of your purchase will be given to charity" are inadequate, since they do not disclose what portion, whether the promotion covers only certain dates, or whether the total contribution by the company is capped at some maximum amount, as many are. In sum, such a statement does not assure an individual consumer that his or her own purchase will result in a payment to the nonprofit.

Standard 19 of the Better Business Bureau (BBB) Wise Giving Alliance (2003) Standards of Excellence addresses these potential issues, requiring that nonprofit organizations clearly disclose how the charity benefits from the sale of products or services and the terms and conditions of its agreement with the corporate partner. It reads as follows:

19. Clearly disclose how the charity benefits from the sale of products or services (i.e., cause-related marketing) that state or imply that a charity will benefit from a consumer sale or transaction. Such promotions should disclose, at the point of solicitation:

a. the actual or anticipated portion of the purchase price that will benefit the charity (e.g., 5 cents will be contributed to *abc* charity for every *xyz* company product sold),

b. the duration of the campaign (e.g., the month of October),

c. any maximum or guaranteed minimum contribution amount (e.g., up to a maximum of $200,000). (n.p.)

Standard 19 applies to the conduct of the nonprofit organization. It requires that when a nonprofit enters a cause-related marketing contract, the contract it negotiates with the corporation should include the disclosure requirements as a provision binding on both parties. In addition, laws in 22 states (as of December 2014) require registration by *commercial co-venturers*, that is, corporations that are engaged in cause marketing. Some require specific provisions in the contract between the nonprofit and the corporation and registration with a state agency (Copilevitz & Canter, 2014).

In addition to traditional cause-marketing relationships, recent years have brought a number of variations, including the proud supporter method; the donation with label or coupon redemption; the corporate donation with consumer action; the dual incentive method; consumer pledge drives; the consumer-directed corporate donation; and the buy-one, give-one method. Given limitations of space, this chapter does not provide a description of these variations; more details are provided by Cone Communications (2010) and other sources.

Many nonprofit relationships with corporations are now comprehensive and integrated. They may include sponsorship, cause marketing, corporate philanthropy, employee volunteering, and additional interactions. Some are also long-term relationships that result in a close identification of the corporate brand with the nonprofit organization or cause. Another trend has been the development of products branded with a cause. For example, Product Red is a brand licensed by the Global Fund to Fight AIDS, Tuberculosis, and Malaria to a variety of corporate partners, including American Express, Apple, Dell, Starbucks, and others (see the website www.joinred.com). Pink products, intended to raise awareness of breast cancer and provide support for breast cancer research, also have become ubiquitous. Such programs have attracted critics, who express concern about a lack of transparency regarding the use of funds generated. Some fear that consumers will believe the problem has been sufficiently addressed through their shopping habits and will divert their attention and charitable giving elsewhere (Raymond, 2009).

Operational Relationships

The relationships we have been considering so far all involve the blending of nonprofit and corporate identities in some manner. The nonprofit's principal contribution to the partnership is its name, recognition, and reputation, for which the corporation is willing to pay in order to enhance its own visibility, image, and sales. Such relationships are largely an exchange of intangibles. But some nonprofit–corporate relationships bring the nonprofit into the heart of the company's business operations by "acting as a supplier, improving training or recruitment services, offering benefits for employees, or serving as a test site for new products" (Sagawa & Segal, 2000, p. 23). For example, Pioneer Human Services in Seattle is a nonprofit that provides rehabilitation and employment services for individuals who are ex-offenders or in recovery from alcohol or drug addiction. Pioneer has a long-standing relationship with Boeing, under which it manufactures parts for Boeing aircraft (Pioneer Human Services, 2015). Goodwill Industries International, Inc., through its independent local chapters, provides training for individuals who are disadvantaged or have disabilities. The nonprofit has contracts with businesses to provide temporary workers in document management, assembly, mailing, custodial work, grounds keeping, and other fields (www .goodwill.org).

As discussed in Chapter 8, such relationships are not collaborations and usually do not meet the strict definition of a *partnership*, although that term is sometimes used to describe them. Operational relationships between nonprofits and corporations are business relationships, but a corporation may be motivated to undertake them in part by social responsibility as well as business interests.

As in the Pioneer and Goodwill examples, a number of operational relationships involve nonprofits that provide employment or training programs. The nonprofits provide services and resources that corporations need for their business operations, but they also provide opportunities for companies to achieve a social benefit with resources that are outside their philanthropic or marketing budgets. By directing some portion of their payroll or purchasing dollars to a nonprofit serving people with needs, companies gain a kind of double impact: They advance a social purpose while also meeting their own core operational needs.

Joint ventures are another type of operational relationship between nonprofits and for-profit companies. As the term suggests, they are new initiatives undertaken jointly by the two entities. A joint venture may involve a specific activity or the creation of a new entity jointly owned by the two partners. Joint ventures between nonprofit hospitals and for-profit health care companies have been especially common, reflecting the high capital needs of such institutions. Entering a joint venture with a for-profit company can provide a nonprofit access to capital that it might find otherwise impossible to raise and access to management and technical skills that it does not possess. But there are risks, including possible distraction from the nonprofit's mission, potential financial losses, damage to the nonprofit's image and reputation through actions of the for-profit partner or the joint venture, and a multitude of legal hurdles. The IRS requires that the joint venture serve a charitable purpose and that the nonprofit be free to act exclusively to pursue its own purposes without benefit to the for-profit co-venturers (Simon, Dale, & Chisolm, 2006). The law regarding joint ventures is complex and beyond the scope of this text.

Putting Partnerships Together

Successful partnerships have a logic to them, and a nonprofit seeking a corporate sponsor needs to think in terms of the company's interests and goals. For example, it makes sense for The Home Depot to help nonprofit KaBOOM! build playgrounds. It sells building materials, its employees know something about construction, and it has stores in many locations and an interest in maintaining good relationships with the communities from which it attracts both employees and customers. Home Depot also supports the American Red Cross with disaster relief, which also makes sense, since recovery from a disaster often includes repairing buildings. These relationships are good fits. It sounds right for Denny's to work with the No Kid Hungry campaign, since it is in the business of providing food. It is logical that Yoplait would support the fight against breast cancer, since many of its customers are women. These relationships make sense; the nonprofits and causes that are supported are important to individuals who are part of the company's target market, and there is an obvious relationship between what the company does, where it does it, and the work of the nonprofit partner. But it would not be logical, or even appropriate, for a tobacco company or a brewer to partner with an organization serving children, nor would it make obvious sense for a company that manufactures entertainment products to be a partner with a nonprofit concerned with homelessness. For a nonprofit seeking a corporate partner, it therefore is essential to identify potential

FIGURE 14.3 ■ Leverageable Assets

Source: From Community Wealth Ventures (now Community Wealth Partners) (2001, p. 14).

Figure 14.3 illustrates some types of assets that a nonprofit might possess and that could have value in the marketplace. Some assets may seem obvious—for example, space. Many museums rent their attractive spaces for special events, and some have opened restaurants. Underutilized space might be leased to a commercial retailer, like Starbucks on a university campus, or perhaps unused offices could be rented for use by other nonprofits. But relationships and access to a constituency may be assets that can be leveraged, too. In the example mentioned above, First Book leveraged its relationships with networks of other nonprofits, assets that made it possible to negotiate favorable financial arrangements with for-profit suppliers whose access to those markets was not as well established. DC Central Kitchen used what it knew how to do (prepare food) and what it had (a kitchen) as the basis of new business ventures.

Feasibility Analysis and Business Planning

Having completed the process described in the previous section and identified some assets that might be leveraged into business ventures, a nonprofit may proceed to analyze the feasibility of a selected set of ideas. A *feasibility analysis* uses many of the tools we have described previously in this text; it looks both to the market and to the organization's own capacities (Community Wealth Ventures, 2004). The external variables that need to be considered include

- the overall size of the market for the product or service that the nonprofit plans to provide;
- the outlook for the industry in which it will be engaged—for example, whether it is expanding or contracting;
- competitive factors, including the study of others offering the same or competing goods and services, as well as generic competition for the same consumer dollars;
- the ease of entry—that is, how much investment will be required to break in; for example, starting a coffee shop may be relatively easy to do, but setting up a factory to manufacture complicated electronics would be a more daunting challenge; and

- profitability—whether this is a business in which it is possible to make money or whether it is, like many restaurants and retail stores, an enterprise that is likely to have a very small profit margin if any at all.

Looking at itself, the organization needs to ask whether

- the venture fits with its mission;
- the organization possesses the skills and expertise, or capacity, to undertake it;
- its facilities and other material resources are adequate to the challenge; and
- it is prepared to undertake and manage the risk associated with the new activity.

Of the few business opportunities studied in detail, one may be selected for development of a full *business plan*. Some nonprofits develop business plans to guide the overall operation of the organization. Such plans encompass strategy and may be an alternative to traditional strategic planning, discussed in Chapter 7. This might be the approach taken by an organization that defines itself as a social enterprise, for which the business model is integral to the overall strategy. More commonly, business plans are developed with regard to a specific initiative, an earned income business venture, rather than the organization as a whole. Developing such a plan is a time-consuming endeavor, and it would not be practical to make such an investment of effort unless the feasibility analysis has produced an encouraging result. A business plan is a detailed, comprehensive document that encompasses elements of strategic, marketing, business, and operational plans. It is an essential tool both internally, to guide development of the business, and externally, as a sales document for enlisting donors or investors.

Business plans may follow somewhat different formats, but most include the same essential components. Box 14.1 provides a typical outline for a business plan and its major sections. Most plans begin with an executive summary that gives a thorough but succinct overview of the major points made in the following sections of the plan. A potential investor or donor should be able to read the executive summary and have a basic understanding of what the venture entails. Another section of the plan describes the nature of the business and the products or services it intends to offer, provides an overview of the industry in which it plans to operate, and summarizes the strategic plan. A section on management and organization includes the organizational structure and the backgrounds of key staff and board members.

BOX 14.1 ELEMENTS OF A TYPICAL BUSINESS PLAN

1. Executive summary
2. Description of the business
3. Management, organizational structure, key personnel
4. Market analysis and marketing plan
5. Description of products and services
6. Operational plan
7. Financial assumptions
8. Detailed financial plan
9. Uncertainties and risks
10. Plan for growth or exit

the organization's mission. Perceptions do, of course, matter, especially if they might erode confidence in the nonprofit or create the impression that it no longer needs other sources of support, such as philanthropic giving. But the issues are often separable, and it is those that relate to the mission that require the most thoughtful and careful consideration.

Another issue that some have raised is the need for better evaluation of the benefits to nonprofits from partnerships with corporations. For example, Alan Andreasen (2009) cites a study of a partnership between Toyota and the Sierra Club in which the benefits to both sides were monetized, that is, assigned a value in dollars. The total value of the partnership was calculated to be $12 million, but 83 percent of that value went to Toyota and only 17 percent went to the Sierra Club. As Andreasen notes, there is a need to improve the metrics by which partnerships are evaluated so that nonprofits can use the data in negotiating equitable relationships with their corporate partners (p. 184).

Evaluating Opportunities Against Mission

Leaving aside for the moment the view of those who do not favor the involvement of nonprofits in commercial activities at all, opinions on the appropriate relationship of the activity to the mission fall at two poles. Some argue that nonprofits should consider only ventures that are aligned with their missions and should not undertake activities intended solely to produce additional revenue. In other words, some say nonprofits should confine their businesses to the top half of Figure 14.1. For example,

> those who hold this view would consider it suitable for a nonprofit group that trains its clients in culinary skills to start a restaurant business to provide a quality work experience for its graduates, but would look askance at an environmental organization that opened a restaurant. (Hochberg, 2002, p. 35)

Others take a different view, arguing that nonprofits should look almost exclusively at whether a business venture is financially profitable. Since the profits are plowed back to support mission-related programs, maximizing revenue from the business ultimately helps deliver more and better services to clients, thus serving the mission. In addition, some say, even successful business ventures that are not related to the mission may create a halo effect that brings other benefits to the nonprofit, including greater visibility and the ability to attract and retain capable staff (Hochberg, 2002). But the question may involve more shades of gray than these two positions encompass.

The economist Dennis Young (2006b) provides a useful framework for decision making, which is illustrated by Table 14.1. Young's model helps in thinking through the risks and rewards of possible partnerships or business ventures. As the table suggests, a profitable opportunity is worth exploring if it also supports the mission or if its impact on the mission is neutral. The former would seem to offer the best of all possible worlds. In the latter case, nothing really is lost, and additional revenue may be gained. However, an activity that could be profitable but that threatens the mission surely would require the most exacting of scrutiny. If it offered the possibility of a huge gain in revenue that would make it possible to greatly expand mission-related programs, with considerable benefit to the organization's clients, then a nonprofit might consider it, making adjustments to manage the mission risk.

What about a partnership or business venture that would just break even financially? If it enhances the mission, then it makes sense to explore it. It may be an opportunity to expand mission programs and services, totally supported by new revenue. If the new venture would just break even while having no impact on the mission, it might seem to be nothing more than a potential distraction that has little to offer. It would best be avoided unless it could be tweaked in some way to either produce more profit or better serve the mission. A break-even business that threatens the mission offers nothing, except for those who may be feeling masochistic. Undertaking a business that loses money while either having no

TABLE 14.1 ■ Evaluating Earned Income Opportunities			
	Mission-enhancing	**Mission-neutral**	**Mission-threatening**
Profitable	**undertake** (fine-tune)	**undertake** (fine-tune)	**scrutinize** (adjust)
Break-even	**undertake** (fine-tune)	**avoid** (or redesign)	**avoid** (or redesign)
Loss-creating	**consider** (adjust)	**avoid** (or redesign)	**avoid** (or redesign)

Source: Young (2006b).

impact on the mission or actually threatening it may appeal only to nonprofit managers who are, indeed, professionally suicidal. Unless such possibilities can be redesigned to overcome their shortcomings, they are most certainly best avoided.

Finally, there is the possibility of a partnership or business venture that actually generates a financial loss but contributes in some way to advancing the mission. A nonprofit might consider engaging in that activity, but it would need to be thought about carefully. The benefits and costs of the proposed venture would need to be weighed against those of alternative activities that might SERVE the mission equally or better, at the same or a lower cost.

A Continuing Debate

There is a continuing debate regarding commercialization in the nonprofit sector and the relative value of earned income and philanthropy as sources of nonprofit revenue. For example, an article in the *Harvard Business Review* (Foster & Bradach, 2005) argued against encouraging nonprofits to pursue "the holy grail of earned income," saying that "sending social service agencies down that path jeopardizes those who benefit from their programs—and it harms society itself, which depends for its well-being on a vibrant and mission-driven nonprofit sector" (p. 100). Just months before, the economist Burton Weisbrod (2004) had argued in the *Stanford Social Innovation Review* that Congress should discourage nonprofits from undertaking business ventures and instead should increase the tax incentives to donors for philanthropy. Angela Eikenberry and Jodie Kluver (2004), in the *Public Administration Review,* made the case that,

> though marketization may be beneficial for the short-term survival needs of nonprofit organizations, it may have negative long-term consequences. Marketization may harm democracy and citizenship because of its impact on nonprofit organizations' ability to create and maintain a strong civil society. (p. 132)

Others argue that earned income is preferable to nonprofits' dependence on philanthropy and government support and that shifting to an earned-income model makes an organization more sustainable and effective. Thomas Lyons and colleagues (2010) write that "philanthropy, alone, is not sustainable" and the executive director of the Global Good Fund argues that moving toward reliance on earned income makes an organization more nimble and adaptable, attracts talented people to the staff, opens doors to corporate partnerships, and permits the organization's "growth and impact [to] become accelerated and exponential" (Rich, 2014). But such authors sometimes minimize the fact that running a business can be no less demanding of effort and attention than traditional fundraising or grantsmanship and that sustainability of a business enterprise itself is far from guaranteed. In addition, there are examples of nonprofit organizations that have developed a base of donors that has sustained them well for many years.

(Continued)

Meanwhile, the economy was about to sink into a major recession that would make philanthropic fundraising more difficult. Kales started to think about earned income as a possible source of increased revenue and perhaps also a strategy to create jobs for people with disabilities. With a grant from the UPS Foundation, he and his staff started exploring possibilities. In a meeting one morning, they were all drinking coffee and the idea hit: how about coffee? They began researching the coffee market, studying both low-priced and upscale coffee brands, analyzing trends in coffee price, and looking for a niche that Aspire might be able to fill (Frechette, 2011).

Just a few years earlier, Tony Dreyfuss had launched a new business in Chicago. He had worked at a coffee shop while a graduate student and had learned the business, working his way up to a management position. In 2003, with his father as a partner, he established Metropolis Coffee Company. The company operates a café, roasts coffee in small batches to fit customers' preferences, and sells coffee retail to grocery stores. The company features coffee that is hand-roasted, organic, and purchased according to fair-trade principles (www.metropoliscoffee.com).

Kales's market research led him to discover Metropolis and he called Tony Dreyfuss to propose a partnership. Dreyfuss's response was positive. "Where have you guys been?" he asked, adding "We've been looking for an opportunity like this!" After some further discussion, Aspire CoffeeWorks was launched in 2009 (Frechette, 2011).

Aspire CoffeeWorks is not a separate company; it is a partnership of Aspire and Metropolis that generates profits that go entirely to support Aspire's program serving people with disabilities (www.aspirecoffeeworks.com/learn/company). The coffee is produced by Metropolis under the Aspire brand. Aspire-branded coffee is sold in store like Whole Foods at a modestly higher price than the Metropolis-branded coffee, providing additional revenue to Aspire and also a choice for socially conscious consumers who wish to provide support for people with disabilities (Frechette, 2011).

Aspire clients work side by side with Metropolis staff, grinding the coffee, weighing it, packing it, calculating inventory, and shipping it (Frechette, 2011). But there is more to Aspire's strategy than providing these jobs; it also advances the goal of bring people with disabilities out of a sheltered work environment into the real world, where they learn to develop skills that they may be able to take to other employers. Aspire provides additional training as a part of the CoffeeWorks program and, indeed, some Aspire workers have been hired in full-time jobs with Metropolis (Frechette, 2011).

In 2013, Aspire's total revenue was over $11 million. Program service revenue (earned income) accounted for $9.3 million, including $112,396 from Aspire CoffeeWorks. Government grants totaled $391,000; gifts and other grants accounted for another $680,000 (Aspire of Illinois, 2013 Form 990).

Aspire has continued to develop partnerships with businesses, including Groupon and Office Max, which sells Aspire coffee for use in commercial settings. Aspire advises other nonprofits to see companies not just as donors, but as potential business partners, and emphasizes the importance of approaching potential partners with a proposal that brings benefits to their bottom lines as well as serving the nonprofit's cause (Ronquillo, n.d.).

Questions Related To Case 14.2

1. What was the asset that Aspire of Illinois leveraged to create a source of earned income from Aspire CoffeeWorks? Was that asset something it had, something it did, something it knew, or some combination of these?

2. How important is it that Aspire CoffeeWorks helps to advance Aspire's mission? Would it have made sense to undertake if it only provided a source of revenue not directly related to the mission?

3. Why do you think Metropolis was interested in the partnership with Aspire? What does it stand to gain?

4. What might be some risks of the partnership to Aspire and to Metropolis?

QUESTIONS FOR DISCUSSION

1. Some well-known nonprofit–corporate partnerships are listed below. In each case, what do you think is the logic behind the relationship; in other words, why does this relationship make sense? What may be the principal benefits that each party receives as a result of the partnership? Do you see any possible issues or problems related to each of these relationships?

   o Neutrogena sells sunscreen with the American Cancer Society logo.

   o The Sierra Club endorsed a new line of environmentally friendly cleaning products from Clorox, called "Green Works," in exchange for a fee (Jensen, 2008).

   o Microsoft created technology centers at Boys & Girls Club locations.

   o Christmas in April is a nonprofit that renovates homes for the elderly and disabled. The Home Depot has provided the organization with training for its volunteers, assistance from The Home Depot employees, and lines of credit for merchandise at its stores, as well as cash gifts.

   o In 2010, Susan G. Komen for the Cure, a nonprofit organization that works to fight breast cancer through research, community health outreach, and advocacy, and restaurant chain KFC (formerly Kentucky Fried Chicken) initiated a promotion called "Buckets for the Cure." KFC agreed to give Komen 50 cents for every special pink bucket of chicken purchased by the operators of their restaurants from April 5, 2010, through May 9, 2010 (Huget, 2010).

2. Some well-attended exhibits at art museums have included collections of automobiles, motorcycles, and photographs of rock stars. Are these appropriate subjects for exhibition in a nonprofit art museum? Why or why not? Do they put the museum's mission at risk—in the short term or long term? Why or why not?

3. The Cystic Fibrosis Foundation invested $150 million in a small biotechnology company to support development of new drugs to treat the deadly lung disease with which the Foundation is concerned. In 2014, the Foundation announced that it would receive $3.3 billion from selling the right to royalties related to the new drugs that were developed, an amount twenty times its annual budget. Some people said the investment helped produce needed new drugs and also fund future research. They said it should be a model for other disease-fighting nonprofits. Other people noted that use of one new drug would cost a patient $300,000 per year and said that the Foundation should have done more to push for lower prices. Critics argued that charities should support academic research but that it is a conflict of interest for an organization like the Cystic Fibrosis Foundation to invest in research by a company when it stands to gain financially. What is your opinion? (Source: Pollack, 2014)

SUGGESTIONS FOR FURTHER READING

Books

Lane, M. J. (2015). *Mission-driven venture: Business solutions to the world's most vexing problems*. Hoboken, NJ: Wiley.

La Piana, D., Gowdy, H., Olmstead, R., & Copen, B. (2012). *The nonprofit business plan: A leader's guide*. Nashville, TN: Turner Publishing.

Social Enterprise Alliance. (2010). *Succeeding at social enterprise: Hard-won lessons for nonprofits and social entrepreneurs.* San Francisco, CA: Jossey-Bass.

Yunus, M. (2010). *Building social business: The new kind of capitalism that serves humanity's most pressing needs.* Philadelphia, PA: PublicAffairs.

Websites

Duke University Center for the Advancement of Social Entrepreneurship: http://www.caseatduke.org/

Social Enterprise Alliance: https://www.se-alliance.org/

Also see suggested readings on social entrepreneurship at the end of Chapter 16 of this book.

Companion Website

Visit study.sagepub.com/worth4e for access to certain full-text SAGE journal articles and links to relevant video and multimedia content.

chapter 15

Chapter Outline

Learning Objectives

- In some cases, the terms of contracts can be changed unilaterally by the government agency after they have been approved.
- The costs of administering the grant or contract itself, including the development of proposals, recordkeeping, and reporting are seldom covered by the award.
- Contracts are increasingly *performance based*, meaning that payment and renewal are contingent on meeting outcomes goals. This raises the risk that a contract will be terminated or that payment will be less than the nonprofit anticipated (Smith, 2010).

Research studies, including those conducted by the federal Government Accountability Office, have found that these realities are not the exception, but rather are common across agencies and states, especially with regard to nonprofits that provide human services (Boris et al., 2010). In light of these problems, scholars at the Urban Institute have offered the following recommendations to government and nonprofits on how to improve their relationships: Government should standardize and simplify applications, financial reporting formats, and outcome reporting requirements across agencies with input from nonprofits; implement prompt payment processing standards; create feedback mechanisms to learn how practices are working; collect and report data on contracting practices and assess their impact on nonprofits; and work with nonprofits to agree on mutually beneficial accountability processes. Nonprofit organizations should help create feedback mechanisms regarding contracting processes; participate in efforts to simplify and standardize; encourage foundations and other private funders to accept the standard formats and standards in their reporting requirements; build the capacity to obtain and manage government contracts, including the ability to track staff time and allocate its costs and the capability to track outcomes; and educate the public about the importance of government grants and contracts in providing community services (Boris et al., 2010, p. 23). Whether these reforms are fully implemented will, of course, depend on the political and policy environment as well as the resources that may be available to both governments and nonprofits in future years.

The current realities of government funding discussed above favor larger organizations over smaller ones, since larger nonprofits have the diversified revenues, endowments, and philanthropic giving to offset shortfalls or delays in government payments and a scale of administrative operations that can absorb the complex record keeping and reporting. The administrative requirements of managing public funds have driven increased investment in information systems and professional managers, resources that larger organizations can more easily obtain. These considerations also have played a role in some nonprofit mergers and may force smaller organizations to collaborate with others, in ways discussed in Chapter 8, in order to gain necessary scale. Performance-based contracts have increased competition among nonprofits as well as competition between nonprofits and for-profits. That may have implications for the culture of nonprofit organizations and the sector. For example, some researchers have found that where government contracts are a substantial portion of a nonprofit's revenue, the power of the CEO may be enhanced and the role of the board diminished, with implications for governance (Smith, 2010). Finally, becoming primarily or exclusively a government contractor reduces a nonprofit organization's autonomy and may lead to mission drift. As Jeremy Hall (2010) describes, "The great paradox of grant seeking is that those organizations . . . with the least resources (i.e., the greatest need) find grant funding to be very appealing, often valuing production of something over doing nothing and thus allowing grantor priorities to overwhelm local values and priorities. This is a significant burden to bear" (p. 5).

None of this discussion is intended to imply that nonprofit organizations should always avoid accepting government funds, but rather that managers must be prepared for the various contingencies that doing so may create and clearly understand the risks as well as the potential benefits. It is also important to recognize the impact that public funding may have on nonprofit organizations and on the nonprofit sector overall. Faced with the uncertainties and complexities of public funding, the fact that many grants and contracts do not cover full costs, and a desire to preserve autonomy and focus on mission, many nonprofit executives have intensified efforts to diversify revenues by increasing philanthropic support and earned income, as discussed in Chapters 13 and 14.

Seeking Government Support

The pursuit of support from government (or foundations) is commonly called *grantwriting* (e.g., the NIH website at grants.nih.gov/grants/grant_tips.htm), but that is not an accurate term. More correctly, the process of pursuing a grant is *grant seeking* and the specific activity of preparing a proposal is *proposal writing*. Grant seeking is a broader process than proposal writing, since it includes the identification and investigation of funding opportunities as well as planning and preparation that precedes the preparation of an application or proposal. This is analogous to defining fundraising as something that encompasses more than the act of soliciting a gift.

Identifying Grant Opportunities

The first step in pursuing government support is to identify available programs. In some instances, this task may be relatively easy, since the funding agency may issue a *request for proposals (RFP)*. The RFP invites applications and generally is quite specific about the purposes and terms of the grants or contract that will be awarded. The RFP also usually defines the specific format and content for a proposal and the process for submitting it; nevertheless, the organization may be well advised to seek further information and insight though communication with officials in the agency before preparing the written proposal (Hall, 2010, p. 53).

Unless an RFP has been issued, nonprofits can identify grant opportunities through their own research. This is similar to engaging in prospect research with regard to philanthropic fundraising as discussed in Chapter 11. For grants at the federal level, one resource is the Catalog of Federal Domestic Assistance (CFDA), which provides an exhaustive list of programs and is available online at www.cfda.gov. The CFDA lists all programs that have been authorized; the availability of funding that has been appropriated can be found in the *Federal Register* (www.federalregister.gov), the federal government's daily newspaper, where Notices of Funding Availability (NOFAs) are published. Another essential federal resource is Grants.gov (www.grants.gov), a centralized resource that provides access to over 1,000 grant programs of the federal government and through which proposals may be prepared and submitted. The websites of individual federal agencies also include descriptions of grant opportunities. There is no comprehensive source of grant opportunities at the state or local levels, and a search usually requires reviewing the documents or websites of relevant agencies (Hall, 2010, p. 57). There are also a variety of additional government and commercial databases and guides that can be useful tools in the search for grant programs, a full catalog of which is beyond the scope of this chapter.

Evaluating Grant Opportunities

In Chapter 13, we discussed the fact that not every individual, corporation, or foundation is a prospective donor to every organization. Similarly, not every government grant program is a realistic opportunity for a given nonprofit organization. Hall (2010) suggests six criteria by which organizations should evaluate grant opportunities and decide which may be appropriate to pursue: *eligibility, conditions, match requirements, allowable costs, program purpose*, and *the funding amount* (p. 33).

Eligibility to receive a grant under a government program may be defined by four variables: the type of organization, the activities that the organization wishes to undertake, geographic location, and characteristics of the organization or a geographic area. For example, some research grants offered by National Institutes of Health and the National Science Foundation can only be awarded to universities or research institutes, so it would be a wasted effort for any other type of nonprofit to apply. Grant programs also may require, prohibit, or limit the expenditure funds on certain activities, for example, construction, outreach, or research. It would be useless to consider such a program if it simply does not include the activities for which the organization seeks support. Some grant programs may be limited to certain geographic areas (e.g., rural or urban) or to areas or organizations with certain characteristics, for example, communities with high rates of poverty or organizations with demonstrable experience in treating certain diseases (Hall, 2010, pp. 33–39). If an organization is not eligible for a grant from a particular agency or program, that is an obvious reason to look elsewhere. But even if the nonprofit and its activities are eligible for a grant, a careful review of grant conditions may screen out some programs from consideration. For example, if the grant would impose administrative burdens that the organization cannot support or matching funds that it cannot obtain, it would be inadvisable to pursue it.

Grant awards usually define what specific costs may be covered by the grant and which may not. For example, some may permit grant funds to be used for equipment or salaries—or not. A nonprofit must consider what expenditures it wishes to cover through grant support and alternative sources of support to meet expenses that are excluded. However, as Hall (2010, pp. 46–47) points out, some dollars may be *fungible*. That means that if a grant covers some expense that the organization is currently incurring, that may free up other money to be spent for things that the grant cannot directly support. For example, the CEO may contribute a portion of his or her time toward the grant-funded project, and thus a portion of the CEO's compensation may be eligible for reimbursement under the grant. In that circumstance, it is both ethical and legal to reallocate that portion of the CEO's compensation, which would have been paid in any event from other revenues, to accomplishing something that the grant itself cannot support, for example, a facility renovation, purchase of equipment, or the salary of a position unrelated to the grant (pp. 46–47).

It is important to understand the purpose of the grant program and consider whether that purpose is consistent with the organization's mission and values. For example, if a grant program's purpose is to advance medical approaches to addiction treatment and the organization's values favor a faith-based approach to the same end, there might not be a good fit. And, finally, the range of grants available under certain programs may exclude them from consideration by a nonprofit organization with an identified need. It may make no sense to apply under a program that makes average grants of $10,000 if the need is to fund a program requiring $100,000 per year or to apply under a program that awards multimillion-dollar grants when the nonprofit is small and does not have the capacity to manage activities at that scale (Hall, 2010, p. 48).

Preparing and Submitting an Application or Proposal

There are extensive resources available on proposal writing and on the management of contract and grant funds, including books, manuals, and websites. The management of grants is often complex and involves technical elements, such as performance management systems, cost allocation, and procedures for purchasing. This book does not include a detailed discussion of these specific topics, but suggested readings listed at the end of this chapter may be useful for students who may wish greater depth. Chapter 13 provides a basic outline of a proposal in the section discussing foundation support. But proposals submitted under government grant programs are often more complex than those required by private funders, especially in their inclusion of detailed budgets and timelines. Again, many RFPs or program guidelines will include specific guidelines on the format and content of proposals and often will differ, so no one template is applicable.

Preparing to submit a grant proposal does not begin with the drafting of a document. There is a need for advance planning and discussion of important questions. For example, in some cases the chances of obtaining a grant may be enhanced if a nonprofit works collaboratively with other nonprofit partners. Some grant programs are designed to encourage collaboration. Collaboration may be necessary to support the infrastructure needed to manage programs at a larger scale and provide the administrative support needed for grant management. Collaboration also may enable organizations to share the risk of new programs and the uncertainties that come with accepting public funds, as discussed earlier in this chapter. But, of course, as discussed in Chapter 8, collaboration involves additional considerations, including the organization's autonomy and the potential for disagreement, even conflict. There are pros and cons and larger questions that an organization needs to consider before adopting this approach for the purpose of securing a grant (Hall, 2010).

Whether an organization decides to proceed in collaboration with others or alone, it is often important to secure broad support for the proposal. Government officials at any level of government are ultimately accountable to elected officials, who are in turn accountable to their constituents. Most will be reluctant to award funding to an organization that is viewed as risky or disconnected from its community. In preparing to apply for a grant or contract award, some nonprofits solicit letters of endorsement from community leaders, create an advisory board or council to signify community engagement, or engage "symbolic partners" (Hall, 2010, p. 83) that is, community organizations that have an interest in the program for which the grant is sought but who will not actively participate in its activities.

Before developing a proposal, or even before beginning the grant-seeking process, a nonprofit organization may need to address fundamental questions with regard to the possibility of government support. In the terminology of Richard Chait, William, Ryan, and Barbara Taylor (2005), discussed in Chapter 4 of this text, some questions may be fiduciary in nature. For example, will the resources and attention devoted to the funded program distract from other important activities? Do we have sufficient resources to accept the potential risks of becoming a government contractor? Will our organizational culture permit us to accept the accountability that comes with public funds? Others are similar to generative questions of Chait et al. (2005). For example, is our purpose in seeking the grant primarily financial, that is, to bolster our revenues, or to enhance our impact? And, most fundamentally, will the purpose, terms, and conditions of the grant be consistent with our organization's mission and values?

Nonprofits in the Policy Arena

Although some nonprofits managers may be focused on the mechanics of grant seeking and grant management, nonprofits hoping to secure and continue government funding cannot ignore the public policy process or the importance of maintaining relationships with individuals in government. As Steven Smith (2010, pp. 568–569) observes, the political process can have a significant impact not only on the availability of funds, but also on the regulations, terms, rules, and procedures under which contracts and grants are awarded. To be successful as recipients of government funds, nonprofits need to maintain ongoing engagement with their communities, constituencies, and public agencies and officials. This would include, for example, agency and program directors, state legislators, city councilpersons, and school boards through which their programs may be funded or administered. As in any type of fundraising, relationships do matter, and the insights and understandings that may be obtained through personal contacts and conversations are as useful as the information that may be conveyed in documents. Larger organizations may find that they are able to effectively advocate on their own behalf, while smaller organizations may find it more effective to participate as members of an association representing the interests of multiple nonprofits offering programs in a given community or subsector (Smith, pp. 568–570). But with government funding representing a significant component of nonprofit revenue, neither nonprofit organizations nor the sector can stand totally apart from the larger policy arena.

Chapter Summary

Government support is a significant component of revenue for the nonprofit sector, especially for organizations in certain subsectors, including health care, education, and human services. There has been change over the past 30 years in the patterns and mechanisms through which government funds are delivered, with many federal programs devolved to states and by states to local governments. Many nonprofits receive support from all three levels of government and need to have an understanding of complex policies and procedures.

Public funds may be awarded to nonprofit organizations directly as grants, which may permit some flexibility to the recipient or payments under contracts. Or funds may be paid under contracts, in exchange for the delivery of specific goods and services and with defined performance requirements. The distinction between a grant and a contract are defined in federal law and the government applies specific questions in deciding which route to follow to address a particular need or project. Some government benefits are provided to individuals in the form of vouchers or under *voucher-type programs*; the funds come to the nonprofit organization in the form of payments for services delivered to the individual. The government nevertheless will impose requirements on nonprofit or for-profit organizations that serve clients receiving public support. There are various types of contracts that will be used by the federal government, depending on the circumstances under which the award is made. The types involve varying levels of government oversight and risk for the contractor.

Nonprofits benefit from public funding, which they may not be able to obtain at comparable levels from other sources. Government benefits from the impact of services provided by nonprofits, which it may not be able to provide effectively or efficiently on its own. Nonprofits may have a competitive advantage over for-profit firms in competing for government contracts, since they may be viewed by government officials as more worthy of trust. However, the receipt of government support may present challenges to nonprofits, and some research has found that these challenges are common. They may include matching requirements, delayed payments, complex administration and reporting, changed conditions, and performance requirements that may lead to termination of support. Government funding also may affect the culture and the distribution of power within a nonprofit organization. Nonprofits that seek and accept public funds need to prepare to address any such challenges that may occur.

The administrative requirements that come with public funds favor larger over smaller organizations and encourage collaborations or mergers among organizations, intended to gain the scale and depth of management capacity that is needed. Experts have offered recommendations to government and nonprofits on how to improve their relationships, including the simplification and standardization of processes and requirements and increased nonprofit capacity to manage contracts and grants.

Grant opportunities may be identified through various resources, including the Catalog of Federal Domestic Assistance (CFDA), the *Federal Register*, the website Grant.gov, or through individual agencies of the federal, state, and local governments. Nonprofits should evaluate grant opportunities and decide which may be appropriate to pursue based on six criteria: eligibility, conditions, match requirements, allowable costs, program purpose, and the funding amount.

The process of pursuing government support is correctly called *grant seeking.* A part of that process usually involves proposal writing. Proposal writing and grant management are not topics covered in detail in this text, but many resources are available—as books, on websites, and in other media. Writing a proposal is not the first step in grant seeking. Rather, nonprofit organizations need to engage in planning, address the advantages and disadvantages of collaboration with other organizations, consider ways of developing and demonstrating broad community support, and address fundamental questions regarding the purpose of seeking grant support and the consistency of grants or contracts with the organization's mission and values.

KEY TERMS AND CONCEPTS

allowable costs

block grants

Catalog of Federal Domestic Assistance (CFDA)

conditions (of a grant)

contracts

cost-reimbursement contract

eligibility (for a grant)

Federal Register

firm-fixed-price contract

fungible

grant

grant seeking

incentive contract

indefinite-delivery contract

indirect costs

labor-hour contract

matching funds (requirement)

proposal writing

public–private partnership

request for proposals (RFP)

time and materials contract

vouchers

voucher-type programs

CASE 15.1   SEED Foundation

Founded in 1997 in Washington, DC, by social entrepreneurs Rajiv Vinnakota and Eric Adler, the SEED Foundation operates urban, college-preparatory, public boarding schools in Washington, DC, Maryland, and South Florida, with plans to expand nationwide. SEED schools serve young people from low-income backgrounds with a rigorous academic program, provided in a 24-hour nurturing environment. SEED's program is comprehensive, including life skills, health and medical and social components. As of 2011, 91 percent of SEED students who entered the ninth grade graduated from high school, and 94 percent of graduates were accepted in college (SEED Foundation, 2014a, 2014b).

A 2012 study by economists at Harvard and Stanford found that SEED's impact on student achievement was significant and, indeed, greater than that of the average charter school (Curto & Fryer, 2012).

SEED has gained national attention. In 2009, President Obama visited the Washington, DC, SEED school to sign the Edward M. Kennedy Serve America Act. In 2010, SEED was featured on CBS's *60 Minutes* and in the documentary film *Waiting for Superman* (SEED Foundation, 2014a).

SEED's funding model is a mix of private and government funds. The costs of developing a school's facilities and its start-up costs are provided by philanthropists. Once opened, the school's operating costs are covered by public funds (www.seedfoundation.com). But the patterns and mechanisms of public funding vary.

In opening the Washington, DC, school in 1998, SEED lobbied the U.S. Congress and the District of Columbia City Council to amend the education budget to fund a boarding school and then obtained a charter from the District of Columbia Public Charter School Board. Charter schools are public schools, but they are given more autonomy than traditional public schools, in exchange for their agreement to produce specific results, as identified in their charters. Charter schools receive payment on a per-pupil basis, generally equivalent to the per-pupil expenditure for traditional public schools (www.dcpubliccharter.com). The Washington SEED school receives operating funds equivalent to other charter schools, but special legislation was needed in order to add extra payments to cover the boarding component (Bruce, 2010).

SEED's approach in Maryland was somewhat different. Rather than operating as a charter school, SEED's Maryland program is funded under an act of the Maryland legislature, H.B. 1432, passed and signed by the Governor in 2006 (SEED Foundation, 2014a). Students come from all parts of the state of Maryland; the state provides the school with a payment equivalent to 85 percent of the per-pupil amount that would have been spent if the student had remained in his or her home school district, plus additional payments for transportation and school administration (McCausland, 2008).

In 2011, the SEED Foundation was awarded a $3.5 million grant from the Edna McConnell Clark Foundation and the federal government's Social Innovation Fund, to help expand its programs nationwide (SEED Foundation, 2014a). The Social Innovation Fund was created in 2009 and provides federal grants to funding intermediaries, such as the Clark Foundation, which then select high-impact organizations to receive support. The grants require that the intermediaries and the subgrantees match federal money with other funds raised from private sources (Corporation for National and Community Service, 2014a).

SEED's model for funding of new schools may vary according to the environment in each state. For example, in 2012, Ohio passed legislation for a SEED school in Cincinnati, with the possibility of additional schools elsewhere in Ohio. The Cincinnati school's development would be supported by a philanthropist, but its operation would be supported by public money. Unlike the schools in Washington, DC, and Maryland, the Cincinnati school would be operated in partnership with the local Cincinnati public school system. It would

(Continued)

(Continued)

be neither a traditional public school nor a charter school, but rather a "brand new model of education" (NPR State Impact, 2012). In early 2012, SEED obtained approval for a charter school from the Miami-Dade public school board in Florida. The SEED School of Miami opened in 2014 on the campus of Florida Memorial University (www.seedfoundation.com/index.php/seed-schools/south-florida).

Questions Related to Case 15.1

1. Based on the information provided in the case of the SEED Foundation, are public funds contractual payments, grants, voucher-type benefits, or some combination?

2. Do the SEED schools meet the definition of a public–private partnership, as discussed in Chapter 8? Why or why not?

QUESTIONS FOR DISCUSSION

1. If you were a government official, would you prefer to contract with a small community-based non-profit organization or with a for-profit company that might have greater resources? What could be the advantages and disadvantages of each?

2. If you were a nonprofit CEO, how would you summarize the advantages and disadvantages of the three primary sources of nonprofit revenue: philanthropy, earned income, and government?

SUGGESTIONS FOR FURTHER READING

Books/Reports

Boris, E. T, deLeon, E., Roeger, K. L., & Nikolova, M. (2010). *Human service nonprofits and government collaboration: Findings from the 2010 national survey of nonprofit government contracting and grants*. Washington, DC: Urban Institute. Retrieved from http://www.urban.org/uploadedpdf/412228-nonprofit-government-contracting.pdf

Boris, E. T., & Steuerle, C. E. (Eds.). (2006). *Nonprofit and government: Collaboration and conflict*. Washington, DC: Urban Institute.

O'Neal-McElrath, T. (2013). *Winning grants step by step* (4th ed.). San Francisco, CA: Jossey-Bass.

Hall, J. L. (2010). *Grant management: Funding for public and nonprofit programs*. Sudbury, MA: Jones & Bartlett.

Websites

Catalog of Federal Domestic Assistance: https://www.cfda.gov/

Grants.gov: http://www.grants.gov

Companion Website

Visit study.sagepub.com/worth4e for access to certain full-text SAGE journal articles and links to relevant video and multimedia content.

PART V Special Topics

pursue it; and ultimately upsets the status quo and makes previous products, services, and approaches obsolete. This can be seen, for example, in how the personal computer eliminated the typewriter and the Internet is challenging the survival of traditional newspapers. Companies and organizations adhering to old ways decline and disappear, while new companies and industries grow to replace them, a process that Schumpeter calls *creative destruction* (cited in Martin & Osberg, 2007, p. 31). The process is similar to a forest fire—nature's way of clearing out old and dying trees and making way for new growth. It may be ugly and disruptive, but it ultimately leads to a healthier and more vibrant forest. Entrepreneurs thus are central to competition in free market economies and play an essential role in economic progress; without them, we would live in a stagnant world without economic growth or rising prosperity.

So, we now understand what an entrepreneur is in the context of the economy, but what is a *social entrepreneur*? Like many other concepts discussed in this text, it has no universally accepted definition. For some, a social entrepreneur is someone who uses business concepts and methods in pursuing a social purpose. Some think of a social entrepreneur as someone who starts a new organization. Others use the term almost synonymously with *leadership*. But the literature reflects two principal schools of thought about social entrepreneurship that offer more specific definitions. J. Gregory Dees (Dees & Anderson, 2006) calls them the *social enterprise school* and the *social innovation school*.

Social Enterprise School

Those in the *social enterprise school* think about social entrepreneurship as the creation of earned-income ventures by nonprofits, like those we discussed in Chapter 14, or with for-profit companies that serve a social purpose. Their straightforward definition generally coincides with common usage—an entrepreneur is someone who starts a new business and, in the case of a social entrepreneur, a business with a social purpose. For example, this is the perspective of the Social Enterprise Alliance and many business school academic programs. Those who come from the social enterprise school emphasize the importance of nonprofits freeing themselves from reliance on government and philanthropic support and achieving sustainability through revenue-producing business activities. They propose market-based solutions to social problems and often emphasize the blurring of the sectors, advancing the idea of the double bottom line, which we have discussed previously in this text, or even a triple bottom line, which considers environmental impact as well as financial and social value. For example, Steve Case, former chair of America Online, reflects this point of view when he says,

> Too many people act as if the private sector and the social sector should operate on different axes, where one is all about making money and the other is all about serving society. A better approach is to integrate these missions, with businesses that are "not-only-for-profit" and social service groups with their own earned income. (quoted in Dees & Anderson, 2006, p. 44)

Social Innovation School

On the other hand, those who belong to the *social innovation school* offer a broader definition of social entrepreneurship. In their view, social entrepreneurs play a role in society similar to that of the business entrepreneur in the economy, as described by Say and Schumpeter. They are "distinguished from other leaders in the citizen sector [nonprofit sector] by their long-term focus on creating wide-scale change at the systemic level" (Leviner, Crutchfield, & Wells, 2006). In this view, the social entrepreneur is an innovator; a change agent; someone who identifies an opportunity, undertakes direct action to pursue it, and produces change that improves the condition of people and society. This may include the application of business principles and the pursuit of earned income, but not necessarily. The emphasis is on innovation and transformational approaches to combining resources in order to achieve social outcomes, not on the sources of funds applied to doing so. Thus, social entrepreneurs might access traditional philanthropy or government funds as well as earned income—whatever is needed and available—in order to implement their innovative ideas.

As Dees and Beth Anderson (2006) explain this perspective,

social entrepreneurship is not about generating earned income or even about incremental innovation in the social sector. It is about innovations that have the potential for major societal *impact* [italics added] by, for instance, addressing the root causes of a social problem, reducing particular social needs, and preventing undesirable outcomes. (p. 46)

Thus, in this view of social entrepreneurship, one defining characteristic is impact or systemic change. In other words, not all founders may be social entrepreneurs and not all social entrepreneurs need to

TABLE 16.1 ■ Definitions of Social Entrepreneurs/Social Entrepreneurship

Definitions Consistent With the Social Enterprise School	
"A social entrepreneur is any person, in any sector, who uses earned income strategies to pursue a social objective."	Boschee, J. and McClurg, J. (2003). Toward a better understanding of social entrepreneurship: Some important distinctions. Retrieved from http://toolbelt.se-alliance.org/resources/180
"SOCIAL ENTREPRENEURSHIP: The art of simultaneously pursuing both a financial and a social return on investment (the double bottom line)."	Institute for Social Entrepreneurs website. Retrieved from http://www.socialent.org/Social_Enterprise_Terminology.htm
Definitions Consistent With the Social Innovation School	
Social entrepreneurs are "transformative forces: people with new ideas to address major problems who are relentless in the pursuit of their visions, people who simply will not take 'no' for an answer, who will not give up until they have spread their ideas as far as they possibly can."	Bornstein, D. (2007). *How to change the world: Social entrepreneurs and the power of new ideas*. New York, NY: Oxford University Press, p. 1.
"A social entrepreneur is an individual, group, network, organization, or alliance that seeks sustainable, large-scale change through pattern-breaking ideas in what governments, nonprofits, and businesses do to address significant social problems."	Light, P. (2006). Searching for social entrepreneurs: Who they might be, where they might be found, what they do. In R. Mosher-Williams (Ed.), *Research on social entrepreneurship: Understanding and contributing to an emerging field*. Indianapolis, IN: Association for Research on Nonprofit Organizations and Voluntary Service.
"We believe that social entrepreneurs are those exceptional individuals who dream up and take responsibility for an innovative and untested idea for positive social change, and usher that idea from dream to reality."	What is social entrepreneurship? (n.d.). Echoing Green website. Retrieved from http://www.echoinggreen.org/about/what-is-social-entrepreneurship
"Social entrepreneurship is a very broad idea. As it is generally defined, any innovative initiative to help people may be described as social entrepreneurship. The initiative may be economic or non-economic, for-profit or not-for-profit. Distributing free medicine to the sick can be an example of social entrepreneurship. So can setting up a for-profit health care center in a village where no health facility exists. And so can launching a social business. In other words, social business is a subset of social entrepreneurship. All those who design and run social businesses are social entrepreneurs. But not all social entrepreneurs are engaged in social businesses."	Yunus, M. (2007). *Creating a world without poverty: Social business and the future of capitalism. Philadelphia*, PA: Perseus Books, p. 32.

be founders. For example, someone who establishes a new nonprofit that increases or extends services offered in a community may make a great contribution but might not be considered a social entrepreneur if the person uses established models and methods that are not innovative and do not drive fundamental change (Martin & Osberg, 2007). Moreover, entrepreneurs may not be founders of new organizations at all; they may be individuals who lead innovation and change within an established company or nonprofit. Indeed, some companies and nonprofits include individuals whose title is *intrapreneur* and whose job is to drive creativity and innovation within the organization. In this broader conception of the term, social entrepreneurs may be identified working in nonprofits, business, or government.

There are points of intersection among academic and practitioner authors from both perspectives, and indeed, Dees and Anderson (2006) suggest that academic study of the field should focus on a blend of the schools, that is, on what Dees calls "enterprising social innovation" by entrepreneurs "who carry out innovations that blend methods from the worlds of business and philanthropy to create social value that is sustainable and has the potential for long-term impact" (p. 50). Again, *impact* is a key term in this blended definition. This text adopts the social innovation conception of social entrepreneurship, but indeed, the use of business methods and market mechanisms characterize many of the innovative approaches that we will discuss.

Table 16.1 includes a sampling of definitions of social entrepreneurship that reflect the two schools we have discussed here. However, it is useful to note one interesting finding of a study by the Duke Center for the Advancement of Social Entrepreneurship (2008). Many social entrepreneurs who were surveyed do not identify themselves with the term *at all* and some think that "the seemingly endless definitional disputes are 'getting in the way' of [actually] doing the work" (p. 4).

History of Social Entrepreneurship as a Field

Examples of what we today call social entrepreneurs can be found throughout history. For example, David Bornstein (2007) includes as an example St. Francis of Assisi, founder of the Franciscan Order, who "built multiple organizations that advanced pattern changes in his field" (p. 3). Others might include important historical figures such as Clara Barton, founder of the Red Cross, and Robert Baden-Powell, founder of the Boy Scouts movement, and others. Antecedents of social entrepreneurship as a defined field include the "scientific charity" movement in the United Kingdom in the late 19th century and the emergence of "professionalized philanthropy" in the United States in the early 20th century. But use of the term *social entrepreneurship* has become common only since the 1980s (Duke Center for the Advancement of Social Entrepreneurship, 2008).

Some writers cite the work of Bill Drayton, founder of Ashoka, as having been particularly influential in establishing social entrepreneurship as a field (Duke Center for the Advancement of Social Entrepreneurship, 2008). Drayton was a U.S. Environmental Protection Agency official in 1978 when he became interested in the potential of social entrepreneurs to bring about social change. He founded Ashoka: Innovators for the Public, taking the name from the Sanskrit word meaning "active absence of sorrow" (Bornstein, 2007, p. 15). He and his colleague set out on a global search to identify the most promising social entrepreneurs and to raise funds with which to support their efforts. Ashoka Fellows are selected through a rigorous process, which includes evaluation of their proposed work as well of their personal qualities (Bornstein, 2007, p. 125).

The first Ashoka Fellow, Gloria de Souza, was selected in 1981. De Souza was an elementary school teacher in Bombay who had developed new educational methods and was convinced that their application could revolutionize education in India. With a four-year living stipend from Ashoka, totaling $10,000, she dedicated herself full-time to advancing her ideas. In 1982, she founded an organization called Parisar Asha and began building a team to implement her ideas. By the end of the 1980s, she had proven her methods and they were formally adopted by the Indian government as part of its national curriculum for

Grades 1 through 3 (Bornstein, 2007, pp. 17–20). By 2015, Ashoka was supporting 3,000 fellows in more than 70 counties (Ashoka, n.d.-a), providing them with funding, professional assistance, contacts with companies, and other types of support (Bornstein, 2007, p. 11).

Ashoka was a pioneer, but soon other organizations adopted some of its concepts and methods. In 1987, the private equity firm General Atlantic founded Echoing Green, which follows a venture philanthropy approach to providing start-up funding and other support to social entrepreneurs in the United States and across the globe. The first entrepreneur supported by Echoing Green was Diana Propper de Callejon, who created an economic base and livelihood for residents of the Amazon region, as an alternative to deforestation (Echoing Green, n.d.-a). By 2015, Echoing Green had invested over $36 million in the work of more than 600 social entrepreneurs and counted among its fellows the founders of such well-known organizations as Teach For America, City Year, College Summit, Citizen Schools, One Acre Fund, and SKS Microfinance (Echoing Green, n.d.-a).

Interest in social entrepreneurship exploded in the 1990s and the years since, generating numerous books, articles, journals, and conferences and academic programs dedicated to its study, including the Center for the Advancement of Social Entrepreneurship at Duke University, the Center for Social Innovation at the Stanford University Graduate School of Business, and similar entities at many other colleges and universities. As discussed in Chapter 1 of this text, programs in social entrepreneurship have become common in business schools and some courses on the topic also have been developed in nonprofit management programs in schools of public policy and public administration. As mentioned in that earlier chapter, there is continuing discussion and debate about the relationship between these two educational approaches and how they may evolve in the years ahead (Mirabella & Young, 2012).

Theories of Social Entrepreneurship

Scholars in various disciplines have studied entrepreneurship, usually in the business sector, and have developed theories to explain it. Theories of entrepreneurship are analogous to the theories of leadership that we discussed in Chapter 5 in that some of the theories emphasize the characteristics or traits of individuals who become entrepreneurs. Other theories emphasize behaviors, things that entrepreneurs (and social entrepreneurs in particular) do. Still others stress the environment in which entrepreneurship occurs and take a situational approach, arguing that entrepreneurship occurs when an individual with the right characteristics coincides with circumstances in the environment that are conducive to entrepreneurial activity. And, of course, there is some debate about whether entrepreneurs are born or made, that is, whether some innate qualities are essential or whether training can make it possible for almost anyone to become an entrepreneur.

Scholars have identified demographic characteristics of entrepreneurs, finding, for example, that such activity is more likely among immigrants, first-born children, and individuals who have suffered some trauma earlier in their lives. They also often undertake entrepreneurial endeavors around milestone ages, i.e., turning 30, 40, or 50 (A. Brooks, 2009, p. 12). Other research has focused on the psychological characteristics of entrepreneurs, finding that they exhibit innovativeness, an achievement orientation, independence, a sense of control over their destiny, low risk aversion, a tolerance for ambiguity, and—in the case of social entrepreneurs—a high community awareness and social concern (pp. 12–13). Some have studied the motivations of entrepreneurs. For entrepreneurs in business, making money is usually the principal motivation, whereas social entrepreneurs are motivated mostly by a desire to create social change. But entrepreneurs in both sectors may also share some common motivations, what Schumpeter described as the "desire to found a private dynasty, the will to conquer in a competitive battle, and the joy of creating" (quoted in Bornstein, 2007, p. 24). Many writers describe entrepreneurs in heroic terms; for example, Roger Martin and Sally Osberg (2007) include "courage" and "fortitude" among the characteristics that they exhibit (p. 33).

Other writers emphasize the behaviors in which social entrepreneurs engage, although some also imply certain traits or characteristics. For example, Dees, Jed Emerson, and Peter Economy (2001) write that social entrepreneurs behave in the following ways:

- *Adopting a mission to create and sustain social value.* For social entrepreneurs, the mission of social improvement is critical, and it takes priority over generating profits. Instead of going for the quick fix, social entrepreneurs look for ways to create lasting improvements.
- *Recognizing and relentlessly pursuing new opportunities to serve that mission.* Where others see problems, entrepreneurs see opportunities! Social entrepreneurs have a vision of how to achieve their goals, and they are determined to make their vision work.
- *Engaging in a process of continuous innovation, adaptation, and learning.* Social entrepreneurs look for innovative ways to ensure that their ventures create social value and obtain needed resources and funding as long as they are creating value.
- *Acting boldly without being limited to resources currently in hand.* Social entrepreneurs are skilled at doing more with less and attracting resources from others. They explore all resource options, from pure philanthropy to the commercial methods of the business sector, but they are not bound by norms or traditions.
- *Exhibiting a heightened sense of accountability to the constituencies served and for the outcomes created.* Social entrepreneurs take steps to ensure that they are creating value. They seek to provide real social improvements to their beneficiaries and the communities, as well as an attractive social and/or financial return to their investors. (p. 5)

Other theorists emphasize the environment or context in which entrepreneurship occurs. Some argue that entrepreneurial behavior is stimulated when there is some *perturbation,* that is, when "people are displaced from their regular business routines by political, cultural, or economic factors" (A. Brooks, 2009, p. 9). Thus, for example, the seeds of new business ventures may be planted in economic recessions, when people lose their jobs and pursue new ventures as an alternative. The later decades of the 20th century and the first decade of the 21st saw significant changes in the world, including the fall of repressive governments around the world, increasing levels of education, the advancement of women in most regions, increased communication and awareness of global conditions, and a shift in attitudes that favored private or government action to solve social problems. These changes were often disruptive and provided new opportunities for business and social entrepreneurship across the globe (Bornstein, 2007).

Students will recall from Chapter 5 that some scholars have proposed models that integrate various approaches to leadership theory. (See Dym and Hutson's alignment map in Table 5.3.) Similarly, Arthur Brooks (2009) describes a kind of "perfect storm" for entrepreneurship, where external conditions and the internal characteristics of individuals converge to provide the opportunity for the entrepreneurial process to unfold. According to Brooks (2009), entrepreneurship is possible when social, economic, and political conditions are conducive. But even in an environment favorable to entrepreneurship, there must be individuals with the right characteristics and the right education and experience in order for the entrepreneurial process to begin. In other words, change may occur when the right person is in the right place at the right time with the right skills.

Jane Wei-Skillern, James Austin, Herman Leonard, and Howard Stevenson (2007) describe a similar model of entrepreneurship, involving the fit among four variables: the People, the Context, the Deal, and the Opportunity. In business, the "deal" refers to the "bargain that defines who in a venture gives what and who gets what and when those deliveries and receipts will take place" (p. 11). In the case of social entrepreneurship, "the deal" translates to the *social value proposition* (pp. 21–22). Similar to Arthur Brooks, Wei-Skillern et al. (2007) emphasize that "because these [four components] are interdependent and situationally determined, the entrepreneur must manage the fit among them and adapt continuously to new circumstances over time" (p. 10).

Social Entrepreneurship Across Fields and Around the World

Now that we have defined social entrepreneurship and considered some theories that explain it, let's look at a few examples of social entrepreneurs at work. Ashoka categorizes the work of its Fellows into six fields: Civic Engagement, Economic Development, Environment, Health, Human Rights, and Learning/ Education. A few examples based on the work of Ashoka Fellows illustrate a wide array of innovation across these fields.

Civic Engagement. As a recent college graduate, Gerald Chertavian was introduced to then 10-year-old David Heredia. As Chertavian recalls, "I thought it was so wrong that the opportunities he had access to in life could be limited due to things like his zip code, the color of his skin, the bank balance of his mother, or the school system he attended. We are wasting so much talent in a country where we have no one to waste" (Year Up, n.d.). The relationship that developed between them eventually led them to found Year Up in Boston in 2000 (Year Up, n.d.). Year Up provides young people from low-income backgrounds with an intensive one-year training program that includes hands-on skill development, college credits, and corporate internships (Year Up, n.d.). Since its founding, Year Up has served over 10,000 young adults, 85 percent of whom are employed or attending college within four months of completing the program (Year Up, n.d.).

Economic Development. Most Ghanaians live in rural areas, where many are isolated without access to markets or other resources. One of the biggest challenges is the "first mile," that is, the distance over which goods need to be moved to reach established transportation channels. Richard Seshie had an idea. If motorbikes and drivers could be strategically positioned in an organized network, they could transport farmers' products to markets and deliver supplies in return, increasing financial returns to the farmers and providing employment for the drivers. By 2013, he had completed a successful pilot project and was preparing to take his idea to scale across Ghana (Ashoka, n.d.-d).

Environment. In Mumbai, India, as in many urbanizing areas, noise is a major problem, causing hearing loss and other health issues. Working through the Awaaz Foundation, Sumaira Abdulali works to increase public awareness of noise pollution as a public health problem and to monitor and report noise problems. She developed a system for tracking the locations of excessive noise and engaged volunteers to help encourage government and businesses to take steps to reduce the risks (Ashoka, n.d.-e).

Health. In 2003, an outbreak of malaria killed 267 people in South Halmahera, Indonesia. Mohammad Alhabsyi, a physician, realized that the top-down approach to preventing and treating malaria followed by the government just was not working. Malaria prevention needed to involve everyone and be centered at the local level. He founded the Malaria Center, which organized communities to identify and prevent outbreaks. Village Malaria Committees take the lead and provide a channel of communication to the government when further support is needed. He also initiated a curriculum to educate children on the causes of malaria and promote immunization. He established treatment centers, gaining support for them from government at various levels, and set up Internet cafés, which generated revenue to support the centers while also increasing Internet access in the villages (Ashoka, n.d.-f).

Human Rights. In 2013, nearly 11,000 people were sentenced to prison in Costa Rica, many of them for relatively minor offenses. Rather than rehabilitating inmates, the prisons were continuing a cycle of crime; many of those sentenced were recidivists, meaning that they had been in prison before. Lauren Diaz Arias founded Fundacion Nueva Oportunidad, which began operations in 2013, aiming to "empower inmates, decrease recidivism and develop a more empathic society that understands and reintegrates ex-convicts, keeping them away from crime" (Ashoka, n.d.-c). Fundacion Nueva Oportunidad works with prison staff as well as inmates who have committed minor crimes and are nearing the end of their sentences, to help them develop a plan for a business that will provide self-employment upon release. Seven inmates completed the program in the first year, and Diaz developed plans to expand the program to serve 200 prisoners eventually, while also advocating for changes in public policy that would support their integration back into society (Ashoka, n.d.-c).

Learning/Education. Even in an affluent country like the United States, classroom teachers often go without needed supplies for which public funds are not available. In 2000, Charles Best, a history teacher in the Bronx started paying for some supplies from his own pocket. He then had the idea to create a website through which anyone with as little as $5 could also help teachers obtain needs materials. He called it "Donors Choose." Best's initiative took off when Oprah Winfrey identified it as an innovative organization, and by 2007, it had gone national. Most donors permit Donors Choose to keep 15 percent of their gift, providing earned income to maintain the organization, with the balance going to meet classroom needs. By 2015, Donors Choose had over 1.6 million donors, had funded over 225,000 teachers, and had reached over 14 million students (Donors Choose, n.d.).

The examples above illustrate some points expressed earlier in this chapter. All of the cases involve innovative ideas for addressing social problems. Some involve earned income, but others do not; some rely on philanthropy, government support, or both. Some use business methods, but others achieve results primarily by building communities and engaging volunteers. As the examples also demonstrate, social entrepreneurship extends beyond the United States to all parts of the world. Indeed, some people argue that social entrepreneurship that incorporates business approaches is even more important in parts of the world outside the United States and Western Europe, where traditional philanthropy may be less a part of cultures and where governments may be less prepared to address social problems. In such circumstances, social entrepreneurship may provide a more realistic strategy than philanthropic fundraising or government social programs based on Western models. For example, Muhammad Yunus (2007), founder of *microfinance* pioneer Grameen Bank, makes the case that business, government, and the nonprofit sector as we know it are not able to meet the challenges and advocates for creating *social businesses* as an alternative strategy.

Yunus (2007) argues that "Unfettered markets in their current form are not meant to solve social problems and instead may actually exacerbate poverty, disease, pollution, corruption, crime, and inequality" (p. 5). Nor, says Yunus, can government be the solution. Government provides public goods such as national defense, central banking, public schools, and public health services, and sets the rules by which markets work. But governments in developing nations are too often slow and bureaucratic, prone to corruption, and controlled by vested interests that resist change (p. 9). Yunus also questions whether nonprofits alone can solve the problem of poverty. Echoing Bill Shore and others who advocate more reliance on nonprofit earned income, he considers the voluntary giving that supports nonprofits to be a form of "trickle-down economics"; in other words, nonprofits receive only the economic surplus that affluent people voluntarily give and do not have a sustainable revenue model of their own. Yunus agrees that corporate social responsibility may be a good thing, but is doubtful that social goals can ever trump the drive for profit, since corporate directors have an obligation to shareholders to maximize financial returns. Nor does he believe that hybrid organizations can overcome the ultimate pressure to favor profit over social impact. Multinational institutions dedicated to poverty alleviation, such as the World Bank, have focused on the development of infrastructure (e.g., roads, dams, and airports) in the belief that such projects will stimulate economic development, but Yunus sees two problems. First, this approach is also a form of "trickle down," and the poor are not actors. "The poor can be actors themselves," he writes. "The poor can be self-employed entrepreneurs and create jobs for others" (p. 12).

Although he generally adopts the social innovation perspective on social entrepreneurship, Yunus's (2007) advocates the creation of social businesses, of which he identifies two types. The first type operate as businesses, but with a positive social impact; that is consistent with the idea of social enterprises as many people use the term. The second type are owned by individuals who are poor, helping them to achieve economic independence.

Building High-Impact Nonprofits

If social impact is a defining characteristic of social entrepreneurship, what do we know about organizations that achieve it? What makes them different from others?

In research that was reported in an influential 2008 book, revised and updated in 2012, Leslie Crutchfield and Heather McLeod Grant (2012) describe characteristics of nonprofit organizations that they identify as representing "a new cadre of entrepreneurial nonprofits [that have] created extraordinary levels of social impact" (p. 13). They argue that entrepreneurial nonprofits will define the future:

> If the 1980s and early 1990s were all about replicating programs and the [2000s] was about building effective organizations, we believe the next leap is to see nonprofits as *catalytic agents of change* [italics original]. We must begin to study and understand nonprofits not merely as organizations housed within four walls, but as catalysts that work within, and change, entire systems. The most effective of these groups employ a strategy of leverage, using government, business, the public, and other nonprofits as *forces for good,* [italics original] helping them deliver even greater social change than they could possibly achieve alone. (p. 18)

Crutchfield and Grant (2012) examined hundreds of nonprofits using two criteria: (1) Did the organization achieve substantial and sustained results at the national level? (2) Did the organization have an impact on an entire system? After extensive research, the authors identified 12 organizations—in various subsectors—that they determined to be exemplary (although not an exhaustive list of organizations that might meet their criteria). The 12 organizations—some of which have already been mentioned in this text—are listed in Table 16.2.

According to Crutchfield and Grant (2012), these entrepreneurial nonprofits shatter "myths" of "perceived wisdom in the field [of nonprofit management]" (p. 30). Many are not perfectly managed and do not have low overhead. Many do not have prominent brand names. Not all are based on a breakthrough new idea. Not all have textbook mission statements or large budgets. Moreover, many do not rate highly on conventional metrics. Rather, the authors identified six practices common to all 12 organizations:

1. *Advocate and serve.* Some began by offering programs, and others began as advocacy organizations, but over time, all evolved to include both types of activity.

2. *Make markets work.* Some have corporate partnerships or earned income, while others rely primarily on philanthropy, but all have used market forces and use private sector methods in their work.

TABLE 16.2 ■ **High-Impact Nonprofits Identified by Crutchfield and Grant (2012)**

- Center on Budget and Policy Priorities
- City Year
- Environmental Defense Fund
- Exploratorium
- Feeding America (formerly America's Second Harvest)
- Habitat for Humanity
- The Heritage Foundation
- National Council of La Raza
- Self-Help
- Share Our Strength
- Teach for America
- YouthBuild USA

3. *Inspire evangelists.* All have created committed advocates on their behalf.

4. *Nurture nonprofit networks.* All form partnerships with other nonprofits as well as government.

5. *Master the art of adaptation.* All are capable of adjusting their strategies to environmental changes.

6. *Share leadership.* The CEOs of these organizations empower others and delegate authority within their organizations.

Sustaining Innovation

Again, social entrepreneurship is not synonymous with founding new organizations and social innovation may occur in various settings, including established organizations. As James Phills, Kriss Deiglmeier, and Dale Miller (2008) point out, "Innovation can emerge in places and from people outside the scope of social entrepreneurship and social enterprise. In particular, large, established nonprofits, businesses, even governments are producing social innovations." But what determines the capacity for innovation and what can organizations do to enhance it?

There is an extensive research literature on innovation, but most of it relates to businesses rather than nonprofit organizations. In a study funded by the Rockefeller Foundation and discussed in a 2012 report, Christian Seelos and Johanna Mair surveyed the literature on innovation in nonprofits and offered a model of organizational capacity for continuous innovation (OCCI), which leaders may apply to analyzing their own organizations (Seelos & Mair, 2012a). The authors emphasize that innovation should be thought about as a *process* rather than just an outcome. In other words, innovations don't just happen; there are steps through which new ideas are generated, analyzed, tested, and eventually formalized as ongoing new programs (pp. 8–9). What are the factors that either hinder or promote innovation? Seelos and Mair (2012a) identify some factors that involve the organization's relationships with the outside world and others that are related to internal realities. An organization's capacity for innovation may be hindered or enhanced by its relationships with funders, competitors, collaborators, customers, and communities. But internal factors are important, too, including creativity, strategy, structure, culture, leadership, vision, and mission (p. 11). Warren Nilsson and Tana Paddock (2014) also studied innovative organizations and, like Seelos and Mair, they emphasize the importance of both external relationships and internal factors, writing "The organizations that we worked with . . . have in common one apparently simple practice: They pay a great deal of attention to the inner experiences of the people who work in them. The key to changing the world may have less to do with understanding far-flung stakeholders than with understanding the person who sits at the desk right next to us" (p. 48).

So, exactly what should nonprofits do to increase their capacity for innovation? There is no shortage of practical advice, most directed at organizational leaders. The following provide a sampling of common points:

• Create a "vision for innovation," defining what it means to people throughout the organization (Robertson, 2011).
• Align innovation systems with organizational strategy (Robertson, 2011; Emmons, Hanna, and Thompson, 2012).
• Listen and stay open, both to internal and external sources of possible new ideas (Hoque, 2014).

- Engage in collaboration, since partners bring new perspectives and ideas (Hoque, 2014).
- Maintain a flat organizational structure, facilitating communication and a quick approval process for new initiatives (Hoque, 2014).
- Define jobs around innovation (Emmons et al., 2012).
- Build a culture that embraces failure (Hoque, 2014).

But despite the abundance of advice offered in the literature, Seelos and Mair (2012a) do not endorse easy formulas and, like Crutchfield and Grant, they challenge some established wisdom. First, they emphasize, social innovation may not even be necessary for an organization to create social value. Maintaining effective programs over time, with incremental improvements, may be sufficient and, indeed, bring less risk. Second, while the literature offers many recommendations, there is no unified theory of how to build an innovative organization; there is no one right way. As Seelos and Mair (2012b) explain:

Easy recipes in "three steps to better innovation," often at the core of popular innovation books, are not justified, no matter how tempting they may be or how plausible they may sound ... Innovation is a complex process and depends on the unique constellation of many organizational factors.... Serious engagement with existing organizational theories and knowledge requires that we deal with innovation in all of its complexity, and case by case.

Seelos and Mair's conclusion is thus consistent with the observation offered elsewhere in this book with regard to other topics. Nonprofit managers need to maintain a balanced perspective, avoid one-right-way prescriptions, and select strategies and methods that are best adapted to their particular organizations and circumstances.

The Future of Social Entrepreneurship

Social entrepreneurship has become a subject that is not only of worldwide interest to philanthropists and nonprofit leaders; in recent years, it also has been adopted as a key strategy of the U.S. government to promote social goals both at home and around the world. The Edward M. Kennedy Serve America Act, signed by President Barack Obama in 2009, created a federally funded Social Innovation Fund to provide grants to funding intermediaries in local communities, which would in turn use them to "identify high-performing nonprofit organizations working in low-income communities that have innovative solutions with evidence of compelling results" (Corporation for National and Community Service, 2014a). The grants required matching with private funds, and many have been accompanied by technical assistance to help nonprofits increase their impact. In its first three years, the SIF and private matching donors provided over one-half billion dollars in support of innovative programs targeting community problems (Corporation for National and Community Service, 2014a). Similarly, the European Commission embraced social innovation and established programs to provide both funding and support for such efforts (European Commission, 2014).

But some observers offer a somewhat critical assessment regarding the impact of social entrepreneurs. Some views reflect political perspectives, especially regarding the efficacy of government and markets. Public administration scholar Paul Light writes that "At best, social entrepreneurship creates the fantasy that solving intractable problems is only one mad scientist away; at worst, it reinforces the budget-cutter's illusion that anything old cannot be worth saving." Light acknowledges the importance of social entrepreneur as

Websites

Ashoka Foundation: http://www.ashoka.org/

Aspen Institute Program on Philanthropy and Social Innovation: http://www.aspeninstitute.org/policy-work/nonprofit-philanthropy

Duke Center for the Advancement of Social Entrepreneurship: http://www.caseatduke.org/

Echoing Green: http://www.echoinggreen.org/

Social Enterprise Alliance: http://www.se-alliance.org/

Companion Website

Visit study.sagepub.com/worth4e for access to certain full-text SAGE journal articles and links to relevant video and multimedia content.

chapter 17

Unlike a century ago, when most people lived in rural areas or small communities and had little awareness of events in other parts of the world, we now live in a globalized society. The pace of globalization appears to be accelerating, and technological, economic, political, and cultural changes have created a world in which the greatest threats and the most promising opportunities require cooperation among nations and people from all parts of the world.

Photo: Thinkstock/Comstock/Thinkstock

Learning Objectives

After reading this chapter, students should be able to:

1. Define various types of *international organizations*.

2. Summarize trends in international philanthropy and fundraising.

3. Describe various models for governing international and global organizations.

4. Identify unique considerations in managing international organizations.

5. Analyze cases, applying principles from the chapter.

Governing and Managing International and Global Organizations

17

A century ago, an increasing number of people were employed in industrial settings, including factories and mines, but most people still lived and worked on farms or in small communities. Travel was expensive, and communication was slow. The Wright Brothers' first flight had just occurred in 1903, and the majority of American homes would not have electricity until 1930. Television, the Internet, and space travel were still decades in the future.

Events in other parts of the world had little impact on most Americans' lives and, indeed, seldom intruded on their thinking, which was focused on the communities in which they lived and worked. Philanthropy included giving to one's church and an occasional campaign to build a new fire house, hospital, or school. The greatest threats to human health included common diseases for which there were yet no cures: The life expectancy for Americans at birth was less than 50 years (Shrestha, 2006).

Over the past 100 years, the pace and magnitude of change have been staggering. Today, the greatest threats facing humanity, including disease, terrorism, climate change, and natural disasters, are ones that cannot be confined within national boundaries nor isolated by the oceans that separate the continents. Instant communications and frequent travel transmit ideas, images, news, even diseases, as rapidly as people a century ago could cross the town squares of their small communities. At the same time, the greatest opportunities for technological and economic advancement lie in cooperative efforts that engage people, and minds, across the globe. Philanthropy, once primarily an American phenomenon, now flows in significant amounts all around the world, and a gift requires only the click of a computer mouse or a touch to a tablet's screen to complete. While the nonprofit sector in the United States remains the largest and philanthropy on a large scale remains predominantly American, similar organizations are increasing in number and importance in many nations and on a global basis, and many of these are turning to fundraising in the American style.

Why has the world become smaller? And why have nonprofit organizations come to play an important role on the world stage? The answer lies in advances in communication technology as well as changes in political, cultural, and economic realities. One reason is the end of the Cold War and the spread of a democratic and capitalist philosophy across the globe. This change removed political barriers to economic interaction and to nonprofit organizations, which had often been viewed as threats by repressive governments. The establishment of free-trade areas and organizations in the 1990s, including the World Trade Organization (WTO), the European Union (EU), and the North American Free Trade Agreement (NAFTA), led to greater economic integration across national boundaries (Thomas, 2002). At the same time, the movement toward devolution of government services and outsourcing to the private sector that has occurred in the United States has also been seen in other nations, which have sought to lower tax rates in order to encourage economic and business growth. As in the United States, private organizations have been called on to replace services previously provided through government programs and to seek financial support from the private sector, leading to the growth of fundraising as a worldwide profession. This new philosophy also has been reflected in the management of international aid programs, with governments preferring to deliver assistance through private organizations rather than directly (Anheier & Themudo, 2005).

Among the most powerful forces for change has been technology. The development of the Internet, the World Wide Web, satellite communications, social media, and social networks has made global communication instantaneous. It has driven international economic competition in a "flat" world, in which national borders prevent no barrier to entry into the mainstream of business life (Friedman, 2006). It has become a force in political struggles around the world and is used by groups of all ideologies. And it has been raising the awareness of people in developed nations about the needs of others on the planet, stimulating unprecedented global responses to humanitarian needs.

The pace of globalization appears to be accelerating, presenting all of American society with significant challenges. Those who will live their lives—and manage nonprofit organizations—in the balance of the 21st century will need to understand, accept, and be prepared to work with different mind-sets and different skills than have ever been required before.

In this chapter, we will consider some basic definitions and concepts related to international and global organizations and some of the unique considerations in governing, managing, and fundraising in the international arena. In the next chapter, we will discuss the growth of social entrepreneurship, a phenomenon that has influenced the nonprofit sector in the United States, but especially in other parts of the world.

Definitions and Scope of International Organizations

As in the United States, the terminology used to discuss organizations across the world is sometimes inconsistent and confusing. The term *international organization* is used as an umbrella term that encompasses two types—*international institutions* and *international nongovernmental organizations* or NGOs. International institutions include, for example, the United Nations, the World Bank, and the International Monetary Fund, which have governments as members and are controlled by agreements among those governments (Missoni, 2014a). There are also *transnational hybrid organizations (THOs)*, such as the International Committee of the Red Cross, which have government members but also an independent status of their own (Missoni, 2014c). But our focus in this chapter is on the type of international organization usually called a *nongovernmental organization* or *NGO*.

The term *nonprofit organization* is not widely used in the international environment, although there are organizations in many countries that fit the definitions of nonprofit that were considered in Chapter 2. Although the term has different meanings in different parts of the world, what we call a nonprofit in the United States is elsewhere most commonly referred to as a *nongovernmental organization* (or NGO). The term nongovernmental organization has its origins in the United Nations system, and, indeed, the United Nations (UN) has formal consultative relationships with many such organizations engaged in economic development activity (United Nations, 2004). Unlike international institutions, NGOs are chartered under the law of one nation and are not recognized under international law (Bongiovanni, Missoni, & Alesani, 2014).

There are different types and classifications of NGOs, some analogous to those in the United States that we discussed in Chapter 2. They include *public interest NGOs (PINGOs)*, which provide a public benefit, and *business interest NGOs (BINGOs)*, which are similar to trade and professional associations in the United States and advance the agenda of business industries or sectors (Missoni, 2014b). Some NGOs operate within one country and engage in activities similar to those of U.S. nonprofits, but they vary widely in the legal frameworks within which they exist, the sources of their funding, and especially their relationships with government. Some organizations are indeed operated by government and are known by the acronym *GONGOs—government-operated nongovernmental organizations.* There is no concept quite like the U.S. "nonprofit sector" in most parts of the world. In the international context, some scholars refer to the collection of organizations that reside between government and the private sector as the "civil society sector" (Salamon, Sokolowski, & Associates, 2004, p. 11).

The best-known NGOs are the *international nongovernmental organizations* (or INGOs). These are organizations whose activities are not confined to a single country. They "make significant operating expenditures across national borders and do not identify themselves as domestic actors [within one nation]" (Anheier & Themudo, 2005, p. 102). In addition, they are sometimes said to be *transnational* because, as the term implies, they "organize . . . in pursuit of goals and purposes that transcend the boundaries of national territories and state jurisdictions" (Boli, 2006, p. 333). Until recent decades, most INGOs were based in the United States or Western Europe, but they are now more diffused around the world (Anheier & Themudo, 2005). INGOs include the large brand-name organizations that most people know, including, for example, the Red Cross, Oxfam, Friends of the Earth, Greenpeace, Amnesty International, CARE International, and Save the Children.

Bonnie Koenig (2004) describes a continuum along which some nonprofits have evolved. They start as local organizations with local interests. Then they begin to develop an international awareness, perhaps including international topics in their conferences and published materials. They may then move along to develop some international programs, possibly hosting conferences attended by people from around the world or publishing materials in various languages. At this point along the continuum, they have started to become *international organizations.* At a later point in their evolution, such organizations may begin to admit international members, open offices or form chapters in other countries, and enter alliances or partnerships with organizations in other nations. Finally, some ultimately may evolve into *global organizations* "with members, programs, or operations in many different regions around the world and having a multinational board of directors or other decision-making group" (p. 5). Some INGOs were created as global organizations from the beginning. For example, CIVICUS, an international alliance that works to strengthen civil society around the world, was founded in 1993 with a multinational board—it was global from the beginning, both in its purposes and its governance (Koenig, 2004).

It is important to clarify the distinction between organizations that are international and those that are global, especially since the terms are sometimes used interchangeably. An *international* organization is somewhere along Koenig's continuum: It may have some programs in other countries, but it is governed within and maintains a focus on its home country. A *global* organization is one that has activities throughout the world and probably has a governance structure that places decision making in the hands of individuals from multiple countries. Today, most American national nonprofits are at least international. The large brand-name INGOs are global organizations.

INGOs have grown in number, especially within recent decades. The *Yearbook of International Organizations,* published by the Union of International Associations, identifies more than 67,000 organizations in its 2015 edition (Union of International Associations, 2015). The INGOs are often large and visible, but it is a more complex challenge to track NGOs within various countries around the world. There is no single source of comprehensive data, although research interest has increased in recent years. One of the most ambitious efforts, begun in 1991, is the Johns Hopkins Comparative Nonprofit Sector Project, a collaborative investigation led by Lester Salamon at The Johns Hopkins University. The project began with teams of local researchers in 13 countries. Now working in 45 countries, the project has developed extensive comparative data on civil society organizations, philanthropy, and voluntarism and has produced several books, more than 60 published papers, and the Johns Hopkins Global Civil Society Index. The index makes it possible to access more than 300 research products, including many focused on global civil society and others related to the U.S. nonprofit sector (ccss.jhu.edu).

Like nonprofits in the United States, NGOs in other nations engage in a variety of activities. According to the Johns Hopkins project research, the largest number provide services, including education and social services. Another significant percentage are engaged in what Salamon and S. Wojciech Sokolowski (2004) call "expressive functions," including arts, culture, recreation, and professional associations. Others are *advocacy organizations* that bring social and human problems to public attention and work for change— for example, to protect human rights, preserve the environment, and other goals.

The World Bank divides INGOs into two basic types: advocacy INGOs and operational NGOs. *Advocacy INGOs* are organizations that promote a cause or issue on a multinational basis. In the World Bank's definition, *operational INGOs* are those whose primary purpose is to design and implement economic development projects. However, the mission of other INGOs that also operate programs, for example, the Red Cross, is to provide immediate and short-term relief from human suffering, rather than support economic or infrastructure development over the long run. The latter distinction is analogous to the differences between charity and philanthropy that we discussed earlier in this book.

Many development INGOs, working in partnership with the UN and the World Bank, are focused on accomplishment of economic development goals. The *UN Millennium Development Goals,* adopted by world leaders in 2000, included specific targets for the reduction of poverty, disease, illiteracy, environmental degradation, and discrimination against women to be achieved by 2015. A 2014 report by the secretary general of the United Nations indicated that some of the goals had been accomplished ahead of schedule. However, the report also identified remaining challenges (United Nations, 2014). In 2015, the U.N. announced sustainable development goals for 2030, which envision an even larger role for nonprofits (O'Neil, 2015). Most efforts in pursuit of U.N. development goals are funded by governments, although philanthropy has played an increasing role.

International Philanthropy and Fundraising

Recall from our discussion in Chapter 2 that nonprofit organizations in the United States have varied patterns of revenue. Some organizations are highly dependent on philanthropy, while others may be more reliant on government support or earned income. The revenue strategies of international NGOs are similarly diverse (Stroup, 2012). For example, CARE USA relies mostly on grants from the U.S. government and receives only 17 percent of its revenue from American individual donors. In contrast, Oxfam in Great Britain receives most of its revenue from private gifts and Médecins Sans Frontières (MSF; Doctors Without Borders in the United States), based in France, receives only private support—about half from French donors and half from other parts of the world, including the United States (p. 81). This reflects in part the sources of support that are available in their home countries as well as differences in the causes that the organizations address. Individual donors may be drawn to giving to MSF in disasters and emergencies, but perhaps not to the long-term programs of CARE, for which government support is more appropriate. But there are also issues related to resource dependency. (Remember the discussion back in Chapter 3 of this book.) For example, some are critical of CARE's reliance on government, charging that it limits the organizations' independence. MSF's sections hold different views on whether to accept government funds, for reason of similar concern (p. 86). But MSF is limited in its ability to raise funds in France, where individual giving in not substantial, and relies on its U.S. section for about of a third of its revenue (p. 87).

International Giving

Global poverty and health have become the focus of a growing number of substantial gifts and priorities for foundation grant programs. U.S.-based donors are the largest source of international giving; for example, the largest U.S. foundation, the Bill and Melinda Gates Foundation, is primarily concerned with global health and global economic development and has given nearly $32 billion to those purposes since 1994 (Bill & Melinda Gates Foundation, 2015). Other developed nations have given more as their economies have expanded in recent years (Hudson Institute, 2013).

Developing reliable data on international philanthropy faces significant challenges of methodology as well as definition; the totals reported by various researchers differ widely and are likely understated (Hudson Institute, 2013). For example, as measured by the Lilly Family School of Philanthropy at Indiana University (2014) and reported by the Giving USA Foundation, American philanthropy directed to international programs and purposes totaled $14.9 billion in 2013. But the data do not include funds spent on international activities by U.S.-based nonprofits in fields such as education, health care, arts and culture, youth development, and religion, which are reported in other categories; they do not capture all foundation and corporate giving; and they do not include gifts that individuals made to organizations based in other countries that are not chartered in the United States. Unless the recipient organization is registered in the United States, the donor cannot claim a tax deduction for the gift. Some organizations headquartered abroad establish U.S.-based nonprofits, often called a *foundation* or *friends of* in order to qualify to receive deductible gifts from U.S. citizens. Gifts to those organizations could be captured in the Giving USA totals, but gifts that Americans make directly to organizations abroad could not be, since the estimates are based on tax data. Giving USA data also do not include the substantial payments made by private individuals, including recent immigrants to the United States, who send funds directly to their home countries to support either families or projects. Such payments are called *remittances* rather than gifts. By one estimate, such payments emanating from the United States alone totaled over $100 billion in 2011 (Hudson Institute, 2013, p. 30).

Global Fundraising

At the same time that international giving from the United States and other developed countries has increased, NGOs in many parts of the world have been required to pursue new sources of revenue. For example, governments in many nations have reduced funding for higher education institutions, forcing them to institute or increase tuition charges and to look to U.S.-style fundraising for their future growth. Nonprofits in other fields, facing limited resources and growing needs, also have adopted and adapted many of the techniques of organized fundraising that were discussed in Chapter 13.

Fundraising and philanthropy face obstacles in many nations. First, philanthropy requires the presence of surplus income or wealth, which does not exist within many nations. It is illogical to assume that a country in which most individuals are desperately poor will be able to generate a level of giving that can sustain the growth of local organizations sufficient to have an impact on the country's overwhelming problems, and the competition for international giving is difficult for small organizations without internationally recognized brand names.

Second, while most religions and cultures include expectations of altruistic behavior beyond one's family, not all cultures support organized fundraising or voluntarism on the U.S. model (Wagner, 2004). For example, in some cultures, it would be deemed inappropriate to ask another for funds to support an organization on whose board the solicitor served. For another example, in Japan there historically has been no tradition of charitable bequests, with estates going only to families. Only 10 percent of individuals make a will, and inheritance is distributed among family members according to the law (Cagney & Ross, 2013, p. 57). There are legal obstacles in some nations, which have inhibited the growth of independent nongovernmental organizations. For instance, until recently, China required organizations to work through a dual registration and management system, which made it difficult to become registered. Organizations were required to obtain a government agency to sponsor them and then also a second government agency to monitor and audit them (Cagney & Ross, 2013, p. 25).

Even the desirability of philanthropy is a subject of debate in many nations. Some people are concerned about the potential for philanthropy to undermine the responsibility of the state to meet social needs. Others view philanthropy as extending control by wealthy elites, and some governments view NGOs as threats to their authority. For example, anti-NGO legislation was passed or proposed in 2013 in Russia, Ethiopia, and Rwanda and some prodemocracy organizations were shut down after the Arab

Spring uprisings in Egypt (Cagney & Ross, 2013, pp. 4–6). In addition to cultural barriers, few national tax systems include benefits for giving as generous as those available to donors in the United States, although some have increased incentives in recent years (Cagney & Ross, 2013).

There are also technical obstacles to the implementation of U.S.-style fundraising techniques; for example, telephone and mail systems may not support sophisticated telemarketing or direct-mail solicitation, and some countries have low rates of connectivity to the Internet. However, the Internet also has greatly increased the ability of NGOs to reach potential donors on a global basis at minimal cost and has enabled donors in developed countries to learn about needs abroad and make gifts to support their needs. For example, GlobalGiving, a 501(c)(3) U.S. nonprofit, operates a website through which donors can make gifts to support specific projects listed by organizations throughout the world. Projects can be selected by country, theme (e.g., children, women, the environment), and other criteria. By 2015, almost 422,000 donors had provided gifts totaling nearly $166 million to 11, 685 projects (GlobalGiving, 2015).

Despite obstacles, fundraising has grown in nations around the world. Some have adopted U.S.-style methods and strategies, including direct mail, phone solicitation, and campaigns, but others have developed methods more suited to their unique traditions and environments. A comprehensive overview is beyond the scope of this chapter, but few selected highlights provide a rich tasting of the varied methods in use:

- Argentina has a poor postal system but high levels of online giving (Cagney & Ross, 2013, p. 4).
- Ethiopia has mounted some of the largest mass participation events (Cagney & Ross, 2013, p. 4).
- In Japan, most individual donors use giving boxes or respond to face-to-face solicitations on the street (Uo, 2013, p. 50).
- Although Latin America is a diverse region encompassing diverse cultures, historically, fundraising from individuals has surrounded events, including galas and sporting events (Galafassi, 2013, p. 68).
- Western Europe also is a diverse region, each with different traditions. In some, many of the fundraising methods developed in the United States also are common; for example, direct mail is used in continental Europe. Raffles are popular in the United Kingdom, and individuals in Spain and Italy can make gifts via their tax returns (Carnie, 2013, pp. 98–99).
- In Australia and New Zealand, fundraisers use a method known as the two-step. Street canvassers collect information from individuals that is then used for a follow-up contact by phone, Internet, or mail (Triner, 2013, p. 147)
- A technique used in India is, in essence, the opposite of the two-step. Called *telefacing*, it involves a phone call that sets up an appointment for a face-to-face solicitation (Menon & Tiwari, 2013, p. 283).
- In Kenya, fundraising follows the tradition of *Harambee*, which means "all pull together." Harmabee events include small and large events and are often advertised on social media (Muchilwa, 2013, p. 193).

There have been examples of successful U.S.-style campaigns in other countries, especially in higher education. For example, the Universidad de Monterrey in Mexico launched the first capital campaign in Latin American higher education in 1995 and raised $27 million (Cagney & Ross, 2013, p. 71). Campaigns have become standard practice at universities in the United Kingdom. The University of Oxford announced a £1.25 billion campaign in 2008, with £575 million already having been committed, and in 2013 increased its goal to £3 billion (www.campaign.ox.ac.uk/oxford-thinking/about).

Fundraising as a professional field has emerged in the United States primarily over the past 40 years and more recently internationally. Professional associations, like the Association of Fundraising Professionals (AFP) in the United States, have developed in a number of countries, and some have relationships with AFP and the Fund Raising School, part of the Lilly Family School of Philanthropy at Indiana University. The Mexican Center for Philanthropy (Centro Mexicano para la Filatropía) was founded in 1988 and provides fundraising courses, conducts research, and fosters voluntary service. By 2012, AFP had established

11 chapters outside of the United States and Canada, including those in Mexico, Southeast Asia, Puerto Rico, and Egypt. AFP also maintains alliances with other fundraising association around the world and established international growth as one of the priorities of its 2011–2013 strategic plan (Association of Fundraising Professionals, 2009). The Council for Advancement and Support of Education (CASE) opened a London office in 1994, a Singapore office in 2007, and a Latin American office in 2011 (Council for Advancement and Support of Education, n.d.). In 2015, its membership included more than 3,400 higher education institutions in 74 countries, according to the CASE website (www.case.org). In 2014, CASE appointed as its president a fundraising professional whose primary experience had been in the United Kingdom and Australia, rather than an American college or university (Council for Advancement and Support of Education, 2014).

International Nonprofit Governance and Management

Managing an international or global organization combines the complexities of nonprofit management that have been discussed throughout this book with the additional challenges of working across legal systems, languages, cultures, and geographic distances.

Just as there has been a revolution in nonprofit management in the United States in recent decades, as discussed in Chapter 1 of this book, management is becoming more important for international and global organizations. Daniele Alesani and Eduardo Missoni (2014) argue that "a management approach [to international organizations] only recently started surfacing" and that the development of management practices is still developing (p. 1). A full discussion of international NGO management could easily follow the same sequence of chapters as that of this book and identify unique considerations of international management related to virtually every topic—governance, leadership, accountability, staff and volunteer management, fundraising, communications and marketing, and so forth. Many of the pressures facing nonprofit organizations in the United States—including growing needs for services amidst declining government support, call for strengthened governance and accountability, and the need to balance commitment to mission with competition for resources—are all present in the international environment. Thus, with globalization, "international managers [both in business and NGOs] face an external environment more complex, more dynamic, more uncertain, and more competitive than ever before" (Thomas, 2002, p. 10). Space does not permit a full discussion of all these topics in this chapter, but let's consider briefly some issues related to managing across cultures, governance of international and global organizations, and models for organizational structure in the global environment.

Managing Across Cultures

NGO managers must accommodate national and regional differences in legal systems, political environments, and culture. Among the three, David Thomas (2002) argues, culture is uniquely important for three reasons. First, "the economic, legal, and political characteristics of a country are a manifestation of a nation's culture." Second, while the legal and political characteristics of nations are explicit and observable, culture is often invisible, especially to those who have grown up in different environments. "The influence of culture is difficult to detect and managers therefore often overlook it" (p. 19). Finally, the practice of management often focuses on interpersonal relationships—with staff, volunteers, donors, and others—and it is in such interactions that cultural differences may be most manifest. It affects such ordinary events as how individuals greet each other, how directions are communicated, and other everyday interactions.

elect to join AFP and vice versa. Linked through the Web, members of both partners can access each other's members, databases, publications, and other information resources (Koenig, 2004, p. 101).

As in national nonprofits within the United States, achieving the proper balance between centralized control and local autonomy in an international organization requires careful calibration. Historically, many NGOs had centralized structures that were pushed out to chapters as they were established, but as growth extends into more geographically remote regions and diverse national and cultural settings, there is a trend toward greater autonomy for regional chapters or affiliates. The challenge is to determine what policies and what functions need to be retained centrally in order to maintain ethical standards, quality of programs, and adherence to a common mission, and which decisions can be left to local organizations. For example, Oxfam International is a confederation of national groups that was created in its present form in the mid-1990s. At the international level, the groups work together in advocacy, program harmonization, and emergency response. Local affiliates are responsible for allocating resources and managing their own programs (Koenig, 2004).

Regarding the balance between centralization and decentralization, Koenig (2004) offers three pragmatic standards:

- The more parts of the world in which an organization has interactions or activities, the more it will want to determine which practices need to be standardized among its local entities or partners and which can vary or be locally determined.
- The larger an organization's international presence is, the more flexible it should be in looking at options for its operations.
- Organizations that want to grow internationally and develop sustainable structures must be willing to review their progress in relation to their organizational goals and make modifications as needed (p. 126).

It is ironic that in a period of time when increasing calls for accountability may suggest tighter centralized controls and when concern about image and control of the message also would dictate more uniform standards, the realities of communications technology and internationalization pull in the opposite direction. Access to the Internet provides local organizations with control over messages seen around the world, and the need to adapt to widely diverse laws, cultures, and economic realities increases the benefits of a decentralized approach.

Questions about centralization and decentralization are, of course, familiar ones even in national nonprofits within the United States. But working across legal, cultural, and language differences and considerable geographic distances makes them even more complex and delicate in the international environment, placing a premium on communication, flexibility, and a tolerance for ambiguity. In the nonprofit world, as in business, "conventional organizational forms are giving way to networks of less hierarchical relationships and cooperative strategic alliances with other [organizations]" (Thomas, 2002, p. 5). Managing such enterprises is likely to be a challenging task for "control freaks" or those who do not possess or acquire communication skills, trust in others, and sophisticated cultural understanding. For nonprofit managers of the 21st century, developing such skills and qualities is essential to effective leadership.

Chapter Summary

Unlike a century ago, when most people lived in rural areas or small communities and had little awareness of events in other parts of the world, we now live in a globalized society. Technological, economic, political, and cultural changes have created a world in which the greatest threats and the most promising opportunities require cooperation among nations and people from all parts of the world. Nonprofit organizations are playing an increasing role in global affairs and in efforts to address such problems as poverty and health. Those who will manage nonprofit organizations in the balance of the 21st century need to understand, accept, and be prepared to work with different mind-sets and different skills than have ever been required before.

As within the nonprofit sector in the United States, the terminology used to discuss organizations across the world is inconsistent and can be confusing. In most parts of the world, such organizations are known as *nongovernmental organizations* (NGOs) rather than nonprofits. NGOs that work within a single nation vary widely in the legal frameworks within which they exist, the sources of their funding, and especially their relationships with government. The best-known NGOs are the *international nongovernmental organizations* (or INGOs). They are organizations that have activities not confined to a single country and that usually reflect a global approach to governance. Some organizations have been global since the beginning, while others were national nonprofits that became *internationalized* by opening chapters abroad or forming alliances with organizations abroad that pursue similar missions or causes.

The number of INGOs has increased exponentially in recent decades. Although there is no single source of comprehensive data on NGOs around the world, one of the most ambitious research efforts was the Johns Hopkins Comparative Nonprofit Sector Project, which developed the *International Classification of Nonprofit Organizations* and a *global civil society index.*

NGOs in other nations engage in a variety of activities, including educational and social services, arts, culture, recreation, and professional activities. Others are advocacy organizations that bring social and human problems to public attention and work for change. The World Bank divides INGOs into two basic types: *operational NGOs* and *advocacy INGOs.* Operational NGOs of interest to the bank are those engaged in economic development. However, other NGOs are limited to providing temporary relief, for example, to victims of disasters or wars.

International philanthropy, especially that flowing from the United States and Western Europe to the rest of the world, has grown rapidly in recent years. Some of the largest U.S. foundations, including the Gates Foundation, have been focused on global health and poverty and on achievement of the UN's Millennium Development Goals.

Fundraising and philanthropy of the type known in the United States face obstacles in many countries, including culture, tax laws, and technical issues. However, NGOs are adopting and adapting U.S.-style fundraising, and there have been some notable successes as a culture of philanthropy is developing around the world. Some countries have developed fundraising methods that are unique and reflect their particular environments. Fundraising is emerging as a worldwide profession, through efforts by the Association of Fundraising Professionals, the Center on Philanthropy at Indiana University, the Council for Advancement and Support of Education, and professional associations that have been established in other nations.

Managing an international or global organization combines the complexities of nonprofit management that have been discussed throughout this book with the additional challenges of working across legal systems, languages, cultures, and geographic distances. Culture may be the most important variable, since the economic, legal, and political characteristics of a country reflect its culture; culture is invisible and may be overlooked by managers; and much of managers' work involves personal interactions with people, in which cultural differences may be highly relevant.

As organizations evolve from local or national to international and global in scope, they need to adapt their governance structures to accommodate board members from various parts of the world. There are various models for doing so, each of which offers advantages and disadvantages. Another question that arises as a nonprofit begins to operate in various regions is how centralized or decentralized its policies and operations should be, that is, which matters need to be determined by headquarters and which can be left to local groups. The trend appears to be toward greater decentralization, and that presents challenges in terms of accountability and communication of an integrated message.

Managing nonprofit organizations or NGOs in the international environment requires skills in communication, flexibility, and a tolerance for ambiguity. Managers of the 21st century need to possess or develop these qualities in order to be effective leaders.

Conclusion

Readers who have persisted through this entire text hopefully will have learned many things. Even those who may have had some prior experience working in a nonprofit organization may have found some new theory, some new concept, or some new data that added to their existing body of knowledge or understanding. Those for whom this book has been an initiation into the subject will have learned even more. But some may be wondering, "So exactly what have I learned?" "What *is* the right way to manage a nonprofit organization?" "Is there a future for nonprofit management as a distinct profession? And, if so, what qualities, skills, and perspectives are needed to pursue a career in the field during the decades ahead?"

This book has no simple answers to offer. The nonprofit sector is so diverse that no specific approach can be equally effective in all organizations. Some of the skills needed to manage a university may be quite different from those required to manage an international nongovernmental organization or a community-based nonprofit serving low-income citizens of one particular city. Indeed, when I began writing the first edition of this textbook, some friends advised me that the diversity of the nonprofit sector would render the task of writing a broadly useful book about nonprofit management far too challenging. Rather, they suggested, there should be a series of books on nonprofit management, each focused on a particular type of organization, such as universities, hospitals, arts institutions, human services organizations, and others. Of course, many such specialized books already exist; indeed, there are academic programs of study that focus on each of those areas. But the wide acceptance of the first three editions of this book demonstrated that there are commonalities that run across the management of nonprofit organizations and institutions and thus some basic principles on which individuals seeking to lead such organizations should be well informed. This fourth edition has attempted to address shortcomings in the first three and to provide a balanced perspective that may be of benefit to students and future nonprofit executives in all types of organizations.

The rationale for this book lies with the management commonalities we have discussed. These include the need to balance mission and money—to measure success by a double bottom line—and the need to manage relationships with multiple constituents who may hold competing or conflicting views of what the organization should be and do, and who are both free and motivated to express them. There is also a political dimension to the job of a nonprofit manager. Thus, two constants of nonprofit management would be a highly nuanced leadership ability and—even for the commercialized and hybrid nonprofits—the deep underlying commitment to a mission that differentiates good managers of nonprofits from good managers in organizations guided by the pursuit of wealth or constrained by the limits of political feasibility.

It remains true that such wide variation among organizations and the rapid pace with which the sector is changing suggest that there can be no one right way to manage a nonprofit that students can learn today and then apply throughout their careers. Rather, as it has been said at various points in the book, successful management in this sector and in this period of history requires an approach that is pragmatic, eclectic, and flexible. Successful managers select the tools and approaches that best fit the circumstances and needs of their organizations, ever mindful of the overriding and immutable centrality of the mission. That may suggest the application of commercial methods or the exercise of charismatic leadership to inspire philanthropy. It may call for a strategic management approach or for creating an entrepreneurial culture. Indeed, it may call for founding a new organization or leading a transformational process that brings systemic change. It may require seeking government funds or working to develop earned income or philanthropy to diversify support and preserve greater autonomy. Or it may require doing all these things—and others—at the same time.

While contemporary concerns such as accountability and compliance, effectiveness and performance, capacity and strategic management, earned income, and collaborations and mergers are all important, it is also essential not to become too committed to the management fads or buzzwords of the day. Of course, no manager can ignore current legal, social, and financial pressures; deny the realities of competition; or pretend that organizations can be managed as they may have been at some earlier time. Rather, students and future nonprofit managers need to maintain both openness to new ideas and a healthy skepticism about those that are offered as one-right-way prescriptions.

In his conclusion to the 2005 edition of the *Jossey-Bass Handbook of Nonprofit Leadership and Management,* its editor, Robert Herman, asks the question of whether nonprofit management as a distinct profession will continue to exist in the future. He concludes that it will, because the nonprofit sector will continue to exist. Herman (2005) bases this optimistic prediction on the supply-side theories about "the motives and desires of those who actually take the time and effort to create and sustain an organization" (p. 733).

But Herman's (2005) tone is one of cautious optimism rather than conviction. He emphasizes commercialism as a threat that could turn nonprofits into nothing more than businesses and government contractors, requiring nothing distinctive from their managers and causing some to question whether they should continue to exist in nonprofit form at all (pp. 733–734). Indeed, the growing literature regarding hybrid organizations and the Fourth Sector, discussed earlier in this text, could portend that Herman's caution was prescient and that nonprofit organizations as we traditionally have defined them may become less a part of the mix. Perhaps social needs and problems will increasingly be addressed by for-profit social enterprises that are integral to the market economy. It is, as Yogi Berra is reported to have said, difficult to make predictions, especially about the future. But my view is that the nonprofit sector is likely to survive and thrive in the decades ahead, providing unprecedented opportunities for professional managers, volunteer leaders, and philanthropists alike.

Commercialism in the nonprofit sector is not new. It has existed in education and the arts for decades, yet most institutions in those fields continue to exhibit cultures and qualities that affirm their nonprofit identities. Of course, many authors who express concern about commercialism are primarily focused on the human and social service organizations, which constitute the largest number of organizations in the sector. Critical observers worry that some of those organizations have become almost exclusively government contractors or that philanthropists have come to see their support of them as a form of investment requiring a measurable return, transplanting the culture of capital markets into the nonprofit arena. Such concerns are not without foundation, but they may sometimes overshadow more promising developments and trends.

Concerns that there are too many nonprofit organizations are often expressed. Some believe, and not without any foundation, that limited resources, duplication of management infrastructure, and inefficiencies should be addressed by consolidation within the nonprofit sector. Calls for such change likely will continue, and increasing collaboration, even mergers, may be driven by even tighter financial conditions in future years. However, nonprofit organizations are also differentiated, including many whose mission statements may make them sound alike. Just as there is a place for McDonalds and Burger King, as well as Five Guys—because their burgers are all a little different—many nonprofits represent a particular theory of change or philosophy of action, and many reflect the emotional commitment of donors and volunteers to their unique characteristics and cultures. Some who see too many nonprofits may be undervaluing the hold of such distinctions on the hearts of those who staff and support many organizations—and that undeniably drive the creation of new organizations every year.

Indeed, one of the joys of teaching nonprofit management at a university is the opportunity to interact with students who are not only aspiring social entrepreneurs, savvy in the methods of the marketplace but also driven by compassion, conscience, and commitment to a social mission. Some will create new organizations or try; some will succeed and others fail. Others will bring change to existing organizations and increase their impact. There is no reason to believe that the numbers of such individuals will diminish; indeed, their numbers may be growing in response to increasing awareness of the social, economic, and environmental problems that will occupy future generations of people worldwide. The energy of young people—and the sustained commitment of older people, who may find that their life priorities turn increasingly toward a broader engagement with society—will continue to add new nonprofit organizations to the mix and to drive renewal of existing ones—redefining the sector over and over again.

Even those philanthropists who emphasize measurable results and think like investors are not primarily interested in a financial bottom line. To be sure, many expect and demand that their resources be used efficiently and effectively, but in all cases, their involvement is driven by a passion for a cause, not by the desire to make a profit. Genuine philanthropists are motivated by emotion, however rational their methods. It is still true, as Seymour (1966) wrote in his classic book on fundraising, that "the heart has to prompt the mind to go where logic points the way" (p. 29). Some social entrepreneurs and contemporary philanthropists may apply the tools and techniques of business to their endeavors, but their motivations still relate to the social missions of the organizations they support.

It is certain that nonprofit managers of the future will need to be able to implement business judgments and methods in their work. Skills in marketing, financial management, strategic planning, and other business techniques will become ever more essential, and students are strongly encouraged to pursue knowledge in these and other areas far beyond the brief introduction that this book provides. Nonprofit managers of the future will need to accept and master new organizational forms and new methods with an open mind and a willingness to adapt to changing principles, values, and norms. But also essential will be the ability to envision and to inspire, as well as the qualities of effective leadership that can only derive from deep personal commitment. Nonprofit management is likely to remain a distinct field because the nonprofit sector is likely to remain distinctive. It reflects the noble impulses and humane instincts that are the best elements of human nature and that cannot be fulfilled or expressed as fully anywhere else.

Appendix: Cases for Discussion

APPENDIX Case 1
New York City Opera

Relevant chapters:

Chapter 4 (Nonprofit Governing Boards); Chapter 5 (Executive Leadership); Chapter 7 (Developing Strategy and Building Capacity); Chapter 10 (Marketing and Communications); Chapter 12 (Financial Management); Chapter 13 (Philanthropic Fundraising); Chapter 14 (Earned-Income Strategies).

"Throughout its history as The People's Opera, the New York City Opera (NYC Opera) has made opera accessible and affordable. And now NYC Opera needs help to produce its upcoming season," read the funding appeal (New York City Opera, 2013). This seemingly commonplace request for donations did not take the form of an e-mail to longtime patrons or a glossy brochure mailed to established donors. Instead, in September 2013, the NYC Opera—one of the city's premier cultural institutions—took the unprecedented step of attempting to fund its upcoming season by turning to Kickstarter, a crowdfunding website used by amateur musicians, artists, theater troupes, filmmakers, inventors, and others to collect small donations from the public to fund their projects.

The fundraising strategy was a failure. The NYC Opera needed to raise $7 million to fund its upcoming season, $1 million of which it hoped to raise via Kickstarter. The organization brought in only $300,000 from about 2,100 Kickstarter donors, in addition to $1.5 million in other funds (New York City Opera, 2013). After this last-ditch attempt fell far short of the mark, on October 3, 2013, NYC Opera filed for Chapter 11 bankruptcy protection, effectively closing its doors after 70 years of operations (Cooper, 2013).

How could one of New York City's most lauded and beloved cultural assets have reached such an unfortunate situation? Was it the result of the fundraising challenges in an economy that was still recovering from the financial crisis of 2008? Were demographic changes to blame, with younger New Yorkers perhaps having less interest in opera than previous generations? Or could the organization's collapse have been the result of poor decisions made by its management and board of directors? Or was it a combination of these reasons?

Background and History

NYC Opera was established in 1943 with the assistance of New York City Mayor Fiorello La Guardia, who deemed it "The People's Opera." In keeping with this characterization, the organization's mission was "to inspire audiences with innovative and theatrically compelling opera, to nurture the work of promising American artists, and to build new audiences through affordable ticket prices and extensive outreach and education programs" (Guidestar, 2013).

The scope of NYC Opera's activities was consistent with this mission. For example, it presented a variety of operas each season and performed a wide range of distinguished compositions. At its peak, each season NYC Opera presented 12 to 16 different operas and gave 130 performances (Associated Press, 2013). Its repertoire encompassed 275 works spanning from Baroque compositions to modern-day operas, including 29 world premieres and 61 American or New York premieres. NYC Opera also remained true to its mission by attracting and promoting high-caliber artists. It launched the international careers of 3,000 singers, including for example, noted artists Reneé Fleming, José Carreras, Beverly Sills, Plácido Domingo, and Frederica von Stade (New York City Opera, 2010). The organization also sought to bring diversity to the world of opera, which it achieved by giving the first starring opera role to an African American singer, giving the first regular opera contract to an African American singer, and premiering the first opera written by an African American composer (National Public Radio, 2013).

NYC Opera further achieved its mission by making opera more accessible to New Yorkers. For example, in 1983 it was the first U.S. opera company to use supertitles. That means it projected onto a screen the text of the opera in English, allowing audiences to more easily follow the plot. Today this is a standard feature of operatic performances. NYC Opera also strove to keep its performances affordable, with ticket prices beginning at a relatively low $25 in its 2013 season (Iaboni, 2013). Additionally, NYC Opera sought to cultivate future opera audiences through its in-school NYC Opera Education program, which introduced thousands of public school students in the New York metropolitan area to opera each year and took them behind the scenes of opera productions (New York City Opera, 2013).

The NYC Opera had years of great success. For example, during the 1980s, it was led by Beverly Sills, an international opera star who got her start with NYC Opera. During her tenure from 1979 to 1989, her tireless fundraising and prodigious promotion of the organization led to an increase in its budget from $9 million to $26 million, and turned a $3 million deficit into a $3 million surplus. According to Kevin Russell, who served as NYC Opera's director of special events under Sills, "She knew who had money and knew who would give it. And she had no problem asking anybody for it" (Godfrey & Schneiderman, 2013). But when Sills left her position, "she also left behind a daunting problem: NYC's fundraising success had been mostly dependent on her. Sills was the very face of American opera; many donors who gave to the New York City Opera were giving money to *her*" (Cohn, 2012).

By the 2000s, NYC Opera faced a series of crises that culminated in its closure. It began running large deficits in 2003, and its funding was hit hard by the 2008 financial crisis. The organization offered no performances in its 2008–2009 season and thus earned no ticket revenue, due to the renovation of its performance venue, the New York State Theater (now named the David H. Koch Theater) at Lincoln Center. Also in 2008 and 2009, NYC Opera invaded its endowment to cover operating expenses and pay down debt. In 2011, in an effort to trim fixed costs, NYC Opera moved out of Lincoln Center yet did not secure a permanent performance venue, resulting in the loss of a major component of the organization's identity. Throughout the decade, NYC Opera responded to financial difficulties by reducing its performance schedule, such that it gave just 16 performances of four different operas in 2012, compared with 115 performances of 17 different operas a decade prior (Cooper, 2013a).

Years of Crisis and Decline

While a key player in the cultural life of New York City, NYC Opera was unable to raise funds adequate to carry it into its 71st year. The organization experienced financial instability throughout much of its history, but this instability was especially pronounced in the final decade before its bankruptcy (Cooper & Pogrebin, 2013). The elements of NYC Opera's decline include an unstable funding model heavily dependent upon grants and gifts, multiple invasions of the organization's endowment, and a series of strategic decisions that may have exacerbated the problems.

Unsustainable Revenue Model

A key contributing factor to NYC Opera's closure was its unsustainable revenue model, particularly in the years leading up to its bankruptcy filing. NYC Opera began running dangerously high deficits beginning in 2003 (Cooper & Pogrebin, 2013). Its accumulated deficit in 2012 reached $44 million (Cooper, 2013a). NYC Opera's revenue model lacked diversification, relying significantly on gifts and grants. Until its 2000–2001 season, the organization had operated as a "50/50" company; that is, it derived its revenue equally from contributed income (gifts and grants) and from earned income (ticket sales) (Cohn, 2012). However, this changed after the September 11 terrorist attacks, which resulted in a decline in performing arts attendance throughout New York City. For NYC Opera, this decline was permanent (Cohn, 2012). Consequently, ticket sales contributed less and less to the organization's bottom line, while gifts and grants became increasingly important.

And although New York's mayor and the city's commissioner of cultural affairs served as ex-officio members of the NYC Opera board and sent representatives to its meetings (Stewart, 2013), the organization reported only $153,000 in government grants in 2011.

As a point of comparison with other New York City organizations, in 2011 the Metropolitan Opera had program service revenue roughly equal to its contribution and grant revenue (at about $141 million and $137 million, respectively) (Metropolitan Opera Association 2011 Form 990). Likewise, in 2010 the New York Philharmonic had program revenue of roughly $28 million and contribution and grant revenue of nearly $35 million (New York Philharmonic 2010 Form 990).

The growing reliance on philanthropy, rather than earned income, may have reflected NYC Opera's commitment to its mission as the "People's Opera" and its reluctance to increase ticket prices. Keeping prices so low may have been a strategic error. However, given the relatively high demand elasticity of luxury goods, such as opera tickets, it is also possible that doubling or tripling ticket prices would have lowered revenue even further. In other words, any additional money earned from higher ticket prices might have been more than offset by fewer tickets being sold.

In addition, NYC Opera curtailed its performance schedule precipitously in an effort to rein in costs. That action reduced costs, but it also reduced revenue. Severely reducing the number of performances may have had the effect of sending NYC Opera into a downward spiral, wherein fewer performances led to fewer tickets sold, thereby further reducing revenues and necessitating even fewer performances. It also may have reduced the donor base, as it made NYC Opera less effective in achieving its mission and weakened its organizational identity. When coupled with large deficits, insufficient diversification of revenue sources eventually made the organization's financial situation untenable.

Endowment Invasions

In the face of financial pressures, the NYC Opera board repeatedly drew upon the organization's endowment to cover routine expenses and pay down debt, a practice known as "endowment invasion"

(Godfrey & Schneiderman, 2013). NYC Opera gained approval from the courts and the New York attorney general to withdraw about $24 million from its endowment, $17.5 million in 2008 and $6.6 million in 2009. In 2001, its endowment stood at $51.6 million; by June 2013, it totaled just $5.2 million. The reduction reflects investment losses as well as the endowment invasions (Stewart, 2013).

The principal of most endowments is not intended to be spent, but rather to ensure the existence of the institution in perpetuity, especially during financially tumultuous times. Indeed, the Lila Acheson and DeWitt Wallace Fund for Lincoln Center, the source of most of NYC Opera's endowment, mandated the funds be maintained "in perpetuity as an endowment fund" (Stewart, 2013). However, the income the endowment generates *can* be used to cover current operating expenses. By depleting the principal of its endowment, NYC Opera also reduced the future income that it would receive from endowment earnings. Its endowment once returned $3 million annually in investment income to the organization, but after the $24 million in withdrawals, that amount dwindled to under $200,000—less than the revenue NYC Opera earned from a thrift store it managed in Manhattan (Cooper, 2013b).

The endowment invasions made it possible for NYC Opera to cover immediate funding shortfalls, but those decisions undermined the organization's ability to meet future funding needs. According to Manuela Hoelterhoff, a well-known opera critic and executive editor of the arts and culture section of Bloomberg News, drawing down its endowment "was a suicidal thing to do" (Stewart, 2013).

Another financial decision made by the board was to switch the endowment's investments from stocks to cash in response to the 2008 financial crisis. While this was intended to shield the organization's endowment from the stock market selloff during that period NYC Opera failed to switch back to stocks as the market recovered in 2009. Consequently, it realized a $9.5 million investment loss in fiscal 2008 (which ended in June 2009), at a time that coincided with the decision to raid its endowment. It was reported that the board did not have an investment committee to oversee investment of the endowment (Stewart, 2013).

Critical Leadership Decisions

In its last several years before entering bankruptcy, the NYC Opera board made a series of key decisions. These included the 2007 hiring of Gerard Mortier as general manager and artistic director, essentially the CEO; the decision to offer no performances during the 2008–2009 season due to the renovation of its performance venue; the 2009 appointment of George Steel as CEO; and NYC Opera's 2011 move out of its newly renovated performance space at Lincoln Center without first securing a new permanent venue.

Susan Baker became chair of the NYC Opera board in 2004. In 2007, general manager Paul Kellogg announced his departure. Baker was reported by some to be a hands-on board chair, frequently in the company's offices and involved in management decisions. Some said that Kellogg retreated in the face of Baker's forceful presence, which created confusion on the part of staff about who was really in charge (Cohn, 2012).

Belgian opera maestro Gerard Mortier was hired to replace Paul Kellogg as general manager and artistic director. Mortier, who was concluding his tenure at the Paris Opera, had made his name with elaborate, iconoclastic productions, and the board thought he could inject new energy and vitality into NYC Opera. He effectively ended NYC Opera's ongoing search for a more suitable performance venue by pushing for the renovation of its longtime concert hall, New York State Theater at Lincoln Center, although some said that it was both too large and too close to the Metropolitan Opera, which was also housed at Lincoln Center. The renovation helped improve the hall's acoustics, but it did not address the fact that the venue was too large to allow for smaller scale, more intimate performances that donors and audiences desired. Additionally, some said that it prevented NYC Opera from clarifying its identity by physically distancing itself from its rival, the Metropolitan Opera (Pogrebin, 2009).

Renovating New York State Theater led to the cancellation of NYC Opera's 2008–2009 season, as the musicians had nowhere to perform. This inflicted an additional financial wound. For calendar year 2008, NYC Opera had program revenue of only $922,000 (New York City Opera 2009 Form 990). In short, the "missing season caused a loss in revenue and momentum from which the company . . . never recovered" (Cohn, 2012). Mortier stepped down in late 2008 upon his discovery that the $60 million budget he had requested from the board—an amount he felt necessary to achieve his artistic vision—would not be granted.

Indeed, he would receive only $36 million (Cohn, 2012). His departure introduced additional uncertainty into an organization contending with severe financial challenges, a cancelled performance season, and the renovation of its performance hall. In addition to creating a leadership vacuum, Mortier's resignation compounded NYC Opera's financial difficulties by making it impossible for the board to capitalize on his name recognition among donors to raise additional funds (Pogrebin, 2009).

Some board members and others thought that Mortier's appointment had been a mistake. His experience had been in Europe, where the arts receive generous government support. Some people said that his unfamiliarity with fundraising in the private sector was a shortcoming in the NYC Opera's environment and in view of its financial problems. Additionally, some said, Mortier's artistic vision proved too large for NYC Opera's financial capabilities, as evidenced by his request for a $60 million budget that the board was simply unable to provide (Godfrey & Schneiderman, 2013).

Following Mortier's departure, the NYC Opera board appointed George Steel to become NYC Opera's general manager and artistic director. Steel had for 11 years served as executive director of Columbia University's Miller Theater, a small musical theater that he reinvigorated with innovative performances of both contemporary and early music. Aside from a few months as head of the Dallas Opera, the position he held at the time of his appointment to NYC Opera, he had no experience running an opera company. For these reasons, some observers were surprised by his being named to the post (Cohn, 2012).

Steel's tenure was defined by two moves he made in an attempt to shore up the organization's finances. The first of these was the curtailing of NYC Opera's season; it gave just 16 performances in 2012. The second was the controversial decision in 2011 to move NYC Opera out of its longtime home at Lincoln Center—which had just been renovated—without first securing a new permanent performance venue.

While the move helped to save the fixed costs of renting and operating an enormous venue, it relegated the NYC Opera to a nomadic troupe that performed at various locations scattered throughout Manhattan and Brooklyn. Julius Rudel, general director and principal conductor of NYC Opera from 1957 to 1979, argued that the organization's Lincoln Center home conferred upon it a high degree of respectability and prestige and helped it attract top-shelf talent. In arguing against the 2011 move, he wrote that "Lincoln Center solidified the company's place not as New York's *second* opera company, but as New York's *other* opera company" (Rudel, 2011). The move out of Lincoln Center was seen as a highly visible symbol of NYC Opera's grave financial situation. Steel's decision was sharply criticized by the musicians' unions, which picketed his press conference announcing the decision. Former opera company members also spoke out and a *New York Times* op-ed criticized the move (Cohn, 2012). The decision also alienated donors, further compounded NYC Opera's fiscal woes (Cooper & Pogrebin, 2013).

The New York City Opera was not the only arts organization facing challenges during the years of its decline and eventual failure. Organizations in New York City and across the country have had to contend with audiences' changing tastes and with a difficult fundraising environment due to the economy. These factors were especially pertinent to NYC Opera; the organization suffered from the 2008 financial crisis, and opera had traditionally struggled to attract the younger audiences whose patronage was becoming increasingly important to performing arts nonprofits. But some saw other factors at work in the case of the NYC Opera. One reviewer described the events as "an epic saga of economic hardship, mismanagement, and just plain bad luck" (Cohn, 2012). Others criticized the board. John Godfrey and Jason Schneiderman (2013) reflect the views of some critics, arguing that "Amongst the board's chief roles are to appoint the CEOs and to have fiduciary responsibility toward the company's donors," adding that "the board of the New York City Opera appears to have failed at both."

The opera *Anna Nicole* is based on the life of Anna Nicole Smith, who gained notoriety for her marriage to her wealthy and much-older husband, J. Howard Marshall II, and for the bitter dispute between Marshall's family and Smith regarding her inheritance from his estate. *Anna Nicole* was NYC Opera's final performance before slipping into bankruptcy and closing down. There is a scene in which the star's elderly husband collapses of what appears to be a heart attack. But he quickly rises and delivers the line "I'm not dead yet." When "Not Dead Yet" was sung by tenor Robert Brubaker in NYC Opera's final performance in 2013, the irony could not have been fully appreciated by the audience that night (Maloney, 2013). Some people were still determined to revive the historic organization.

Bidding for Rebirth

When an organization files for bankruptcy, the court is responsible for dividing up whatever assets may remain and settling claims by its creditors. Usually, the courts will sell the assets to the highest bidder. But in 2014, a group known as NYCO Renaissance, led by former NYC Opera board member and investor Roy Niederhoffer, bid $1.25 million for the remaining assets and the name of NYC Opera, intending to bring it back to life. The opera's board requested that the court approve the offer, although some creditors pressured the court to approve a rival, higher offer for the opera's assets that also had been presented (Cooper, 2015). While awaiting the court's decision, NYCO Renaissance moved forward with plans to relaunch NYC Opera with a benefit performance at the Rose Theater in Lincoln Center, honoring the memory of Julius Rudel, the opera's former director (Cooper, 2014). Held in March, 2015, the benefit raised $800,000. But legal questions remained under consideration by the court (Tommasini, 2015).

Some questioned the financial viability of the NYCO Renaissance plan as well as the need for NYC Opera in a changed environment. They argued that other organizations had come to play the role that had for many years belonged exclusively to NYC Opera (Milnes, 2015). Smaller opera companies, including the Gotham Chamber Opera and Loft Opera, were selling out shows and receiving favorable reviews (Milnes, 2015). Moreover, New York's major opera company, the Metropolitan Opera, also had evolved.

During the years of NYC Opera's decline, the Metropolitan Opera faced some of the same external realities of a struggling economy and changing audience preferences. Of course, the Metropolitan Opera had greater resources than the NYC Opera, which enabled it to better weather challenging economic conditions. However, in recent years, the Metropolitan Opera also brought opera to new audiences through various innovative endeavors. Since 2006, the year Peter Gelb became the organization's general manager, it set fundraising records, nearly doubling the number of new annual productions, brought younger audiences to its performances, started a 24-hour channel on Sirius XM radio, and created an iPad app (Brown, 2013). Additionally, the Metropolitan Opera made its performances available to audiences across the country and around the world through its "Live in HD" program, which broadcasts opera performances in high definition to movie theaters. As of 2012, it reached 1,700 theaters in 54 countries and had begun to turn a profit. In short, Gelb "[had] guided the opera company into the digital age and . . . put an art form long associated with aristocratic privilege on a more populist footing" (Brown, 2013).

During the years that NYC Opera floundered, the Metropolitan Opera was able to thrive in a challenging fundraising and artistic environment. Crucially, through its embrace of technology, it helped to democratize opera by making it accessible to millions of people in dozens of countries. Had the Metropolitan Opera, once a symbol of elitism and privilege, come to fulfill the purposes of what once had been the "People's Opera"?

NOTE: This case was written by Michael McCarthy, a graduate student at The George Washington University in fall, 2013. It has been adapted and expanded by the textbook author, including sections related to events after 2013.

CASE 1: QUESTIONS FOR DISCUSSION

1. How do decisions made by the NYC Opera board relate to the responsibilities of nonprofit governing boards discussed in Chapter 4?

2. Did NYC Opera exhibit symptoms of founder syndrome during some periods of its history, even when led by executives who were not literally the founder?

3. What are some strategies that NYC Opera might have pursued to broaden its source of revenues beyond gifts and grants in order to have avoided bankruptcy in 2013?

4. Did the NYC Opera appear to have a strategy, as defined in Chapter 7? If so, how would you summarize it? If not, what strategy might you have recommended during its final decade?

5. What principles of financial management, discussed in Chapter 14, might have made a difference to the fate of NYC Opera?

6. Which principles of marketing discussed in Chapter 10 are most relevant to the case of New York City Opera?

7. What do efforts to revive New York City Opera after its bankruptcy suggest about its brand? In what ways is its brand different from that of other operas?

8. In your opinion, and based on the limited information provided in the case, who or what is responsible for the failure of the NYC Opera? Did the board fail or did it take what few actions were available in the face of external circumstances that would have eventually brought down the NYC Opera no matter what was done?

APPENDIX Case 2
Share Our Strength/No Kid Hungry

Relevant chapters:

Chapter 7 (Developing Strategy and Building Capacity); Chapter 8 (Collaborations, Partnerships, and Mergers); Chapter 9 (Managing Staff and Volunteers); Chapter 10 (Marketing and Communications); Chapter 11 (Advocacy and Lobbying); Chapter 12 (Financial Management); Chapter 13 (Philanthropic Fundraising); Chapter 14 (Earned-Income Strategies); Chapter 15 (Government Grants and Contracts); Chapter 16 (Social Entrepreneurship and Social Innovation).

Bill Shore grew up in a working-class neighborhood of Pittsburgh, where his father instilled in him a concern for the plight of people who were facing challenges in their lives. Motivated by those values and by the social activism of the 1960s, he had gravitated toward politics and by 1984 held a staff position in the first presidential campaign of Senator Gary Hart. Following the senator's withdrawal from the race and a brief vacation, Shore was on his way back to work in the senator's office when he saw a headline in the *Washington Post*: "200,000 to Die this Summer in Ethiopia." The threat of imminent famine that would claim so many lives caused Shore to reflect on his own life's work. As Shore recalls,

> I sat thinking about what the famine meant, what it would be like for the ravaged families who lived there. For the first time since my involvement in the presidential campaign, I really felt something about world events; I made an emotional connection to something beyond the usual calculations of how they could be turned to political advantage. It just seemed that since I felt so strongly about it, I ought to pay attention to that impulse. ("More Than Food," 1998)

Later that year, working in the basement of a row house in Washington's Georgetown neighborhood, Shore and his sister Debbie acted on the impulse by founding a new nonprofit organization, using a $2,000 cash advance on a credit card ("Q&A," 2015). Believing that "everyone has a strength to share in the global fight against hunger and poverty," they named the new organization Share Our Strength (SOS). (Share Our Strength, n.d.)

Creating Community Wealth

By 1986, the Shores were again working for Senator Hart while running SOS on the side. Their fundraising for SOS consisted primarily of mailings to chefs and restaurant owners, whom they thought might have a particular interest in food. But the results from this traditional method were modest. Then, while working for Hart in Denver, the Shores persuaded local chefs to participate in a special event to benefit their young organization. The chefs would offer a sampling of gourmet dishes to guests, with the ticket fees going to benefit SOS. The event raised $10,000, and the Shores calculated that the chefs had given far more in the form of gifts-in-kind and their own time and effort than they ever would have given in cash in response to direct-mail solicitations. This success provided an important insight: "[N]onprofits needed to move away from seeking charitable contributions and toward building *strategic partnerships* with companies . . . " [italics original] (Crutchfield & Grant, 2012, p. 91).

Despite numerous historical antecedents, the terms *social enterprise* and *social entrepreneur* were not as widely used in 1984 as they are today; but Shore became convinced that organizations working for social change needed to pursue a new model. He argued that too many nonprofits were dependent on traditional sources of revenue, primarily philanthropy, and were struggling to achieve impact. Too many CEOs were distracted from building programs by the constant need to engage in fundraising. Traditional revenue sources were insufficient to bring successful programs to a scale that they could achieve lasting change or assure the sustainability of even successful organizations. Wealth was being created at a historic rate in the business sector, but "nonprofit organizations [had] been left behind" (Shore, 1999, p. 212). Most were "wed to practices that rely on redistributing wealth, rather than committed to the entrepreneurial activities that create wealth" (p. 212). SOS would join other pioneering nonprofits taking a different approach: "creating *community wealth* through business enterprise, cause-related marketing partnerships, and licensing—directing profits back into the community" [italics added] (p. 143).

Partnering With Business

For its first twenty years, Share Our Strength operated primarily as a funding intermediary that raised funds and made grants to other nonprofits providing direct services, including food banks and other emergency food assistance programs (Crutchfield & Grant, 2012). The funds were raised by mobilizing the food and restaurant industry through sponsored events.

Based on the Shores' experience in Denver, Taste of the Nation was launched in 1988. The event brought together dozens of chefs and charged diners an entry fee to sample the fare of participating restaurants. The first event, held simultaneously in several cities, raised nearly $250,000 in one day (Share Our Strength, n.d.). Over the next two years, Taste of the Nation expanded to 18 American cities (Crutchfield & Grant, 2012). By 2013, there were 35 Taste of the Nation events, attracting more than 20,000 guests, engaging more than 1,200 chefs and restaurants, and raising over $4 million (Share Our Strength, 2013). The events were mutually beneficial to all participants, providing funds for SOS, helping chefs and restauranteurs to associate with SOS's cause, and providing corporate sponsors, such as Anheuser-Busch, opportunities to develop relationships with participating chefs and restaurants who might sell their products.

In 1993, a partnership between Share Our Strength and American Express achieved breakthrough success and became a widely studied example (Crutchfield & Grant, 2012). Share Our Strength already had established relationships with restaurants through Taste of the Nation and other programs. The Charge Against Hunger campaign leveraged those relationships to provide another source of revenue for SOS and a marketing benefit for its corporate partner. Consumers were encouraged to dine out at participating restaurants to help fight hunger. American Express donated three cents from every transaction during October, November, and December from 1993 to 1996 (Nelson, Kanso, & Levitt, 2007). Over the four-year period, Charge Against Hunger raised $21 million for Share Our Strength, as well as increasing awareness of hunger issues and raising the profile of American Express, which was working to improve its image within the restaurant industry (Nelson et al., 2007). The campaign was lauded as a model for future cause-marketing endeavors. Other corporation-sponsored events were developed, including the Great American Bake Sale, Restaurants for Relief, and A Tasteful Pursuit. Although not all events succeeded, SOS became a "cause-marketing machine" (Crutchfield & Grant, 2012).

Community Wealth Ventures

By 1998, SOS had attracted wide attention for its fundraising success and other nonprofits were calling for advice on how they could create successful commercial partnerships with businesses and start their own revenue-generating enterprises. SOS decided to leverage that visibility by establishing its own for-profit subsidiary, to provide consulting services to other nonprofits desiring to establish cause-marketing partnerships and earned-income ventures. The new consulting firm, Community Wealth Ventures (CWV), would generate profits to help support SOS.

Community Wealth Ventures refined and expanded Shore's concept of community wealth and developed materials for nonprofits to use in planning commercial partnerships and earned-income ventures (including some content that was included in Chapter 14 of this text). Community Wealth Ventures returned $1 million in profits to SOS in its first eight years and successfully partnered with hundreds of organizations, including high-profile clients such as City Year, KaBOOM!, and the Campaign for Tobacco-Free Kids.

In 2013, Community Wealth Ventures changed its name to Community Wealth Partners, reflecting a shift in emphasis from commercial partnerships and earned-income ventures to a broader relationship with nonprofit clients, related to achieving social change. This refocus was consistent with new directions adopted by its parent, SOS, which are discussed in the next section of this case (Community Wealth Partners, n.d.).

Refocusing for Greater Impact

By most measures, Share Our Strength's first 20 years in operation were a success. By 2004, it had raised more than $200 million for thousands of hunger and poverty organizations, received positive media attention, and had created a widely emulated model for successful cause-marketing initiatives with major corporate sponsors. But it became clear to Shore that SOS's activity as a grantmaker was not achieving the broader impact that was needed. As Shore observed, "we made grants to thousands of organizations around the United States, all of which were doing an impressive job of feeding hungry people, but few of which were focused on ending hunger . . . much of the focus, internally and externally, was on the entrepreneurial ways it [SOS] generated funds (through innovations in cause-related marketing) rather than on how it [SOS] used the funds to advance its mission" (Shore, Hammond, & Celep, 2013).

Indeed, despite the efforts of Share Our Strength and public programs such as the Supplemental Nutrition Assistance Program (SNAP), hunger in America persisted. As Shore explained, "It was … unsatisfying that we could not quantify our impact. Was the funding we provided equal to 1 percent of what was needed, or was it 50 percent? When was our job done? Without a specific measure of success it was impossible to know" (Shore et al., 2013). Additionally, after years of growth, SOS's fundraising totals were flat (Blum, 2012a).

Shore knew that a new approach was essential. The only way to maximize impact was to markedly change how the organization was approaching the hunger problem. SOS needed to develop a vision of what success would look like, develop a scalable model that would permanently change the system, and define what its impact would be. Perhaps most importantly, SOS would need to leverage its strong existing assets to challenge the root of the hunger problem in new, significant ways (Shore, 2013). Shore recognized that SOS would need to "go big or go home" (Blum, 2012a). He concluded that the answer would lie in shifting activities from broad anti-hunger issues to a specific problem and with a specific achievable goal: *end childhood hunger in America by 2015* (Shore et al., 2013).

The problem of childhood hunger is widespread. Nearly half of the 47 million people receiving support through the SNAP program (sometimes referred to as "food stamps") are children. One in five American children do not consistently receive the nutritious food they need. All American children are eligible for school breakfasts, but only 11 million receive them ("Q&A," 2015). The effects of childhood hunger are profound. A study conducted by the consulting firm Deloitte (Augustine-Thottungal, Kern, Key, & Sherman, 2013) found hungry children under age three suffer from cognitive impairment that limits their future educational and economic success. In addition, hungry children are 31 percent more likely to be hospitalized and are 3.4 times more likely to be overweight or obese (Augustine-Thottungal et al., 2013). A lack of nutritious food leads kids to higher levels of anxiety and aggressive behavior, and hungry teens are more likely to be suspended from school and suffer from difficulty in interpersonal relationships (Share Our Strength, 2011).

To achieve its new goal, SOS would launch a new nationwide campaign: *No Kid Hungry*. Its strategy would shift from funding programs that provided food to connecting kids in need with existing programs that provide food but remain underutilized, such as the School Breakfast Program (SBP) and the Summer Meals programs. It also would launch the Cooking Matters program to provide low-income families with food skills to stretch their food budgets, use nutrition information to make healthier food choices, and cook affordable meals (Augustine-Thottungal et al., 2013). But No Kid Hungry would become more than just a slogan, a campaign, or a collection of programs—it would become the rebranded face of Share Our Strength.

No Kid Hungry

No Kid Hungry would focus on initiatives state-by-state and on building cross-sector collaborations in order to achieve scale, consistent with the concept of collective impact (Shore et al., 2013). The campaign operated under the premise that American children are not hungry because of a lack of available food in society or a lack of nutrition programs intended to provide this food to children. Rather, kids lack access to these programs ("Q&A," 2015). So, instead of focusing on providing food, Share Our Strength became an organization that served as a connector—connecting children to federal nutrition programs; connecting state agencies, nonprofits, and donors in order to achieve state-level solutions; and connecting federal food dollars with states. SOS's role would be to provide the coordination and resources each community needed to remove the roadblocks that were keeping children from participating in food and nutrition programs (Shore et al., 2013).

Share Our Strength developed a network of state- and city-based No Kid Hungry campaigns to achieve these purposes ("Q&A," 2015) and, by 2014, operated campaigns in 16 states and the District of Columbia. The campaign was addressed to both children and parents through a number of new and existing programs, in order to increase the number of kids who were eating three nutritious meals a day.

Implementing No Kid Hungry

The new strategy would require additional investments and entail some risks. As Shore explains, "The challenge is: Are you willing to do less program and less service in the short term if that frees up money to allow you to make the investments you need to do even more program and service in the long term" (Blum, 2012a). SOS spent $300,000 to develop the new brand identity (Blum, 2012b), introducing a new name, tagline, and logo. As illustrated in Figure 1, No Kid Hungry became SOS's primary consumer-facing brand, with the original name of the organization reduced to the equivalent of a tagline (Shore et al., 2013).

With its new strategy, Share Our Strength needed to build its internal capacity, and it grew quickly, hiring nearly 100 additional employees and increasing its operating budget from $6 million in 2009 to $14 million in 2013. The new staff members included individuals with strengths in advocacy, marketing, accounting, public policy, and program management (Blum, 2012b). This change was not easy for existing staff, some of whom had to train for new roles, change their working style, or even transition out of the organization (Shore et al., 2013). The growth included the hiring of a chief strategy officer, who was responsible for removing established silos among Share Our Strength's fundraising, administration, and program initiatives in order to leverage all of the organization's assets together. This focus on capacity was also reflected in changes to SOS's board of directors, which began to include more individuals with diverse business and political experience (Blum, 2012b).

The strategic shift also posed several challenges for internal communications. Share Our Strength's leaders knew it was vital that each employee could explain the organization's new goal and inspire others to join the cause, so staff spent several weeks on efforts to ensure message cohesion (Shore et al., 2013). In some cases, new employees hired to implement the new direction brought work styles and experiences that were different from those of the existing SOS team, which led to some initial tensions. For example, new political campaign operatives were accustomed to operating in fast-paced, urgent environments, while some existing staff had been accustomed to working at a more deliberate pace (Shore et al., 2013). These styles needed to be reconciled before moving forward.

Share Our Strength's leadership understood that it was important to build national awareness around childhood hunger, both to inspire the public and increase political support for food programs. Though its new branding helped, SOS would need to reframe the discussion around hunger, both to show that it was a solvable problem and to build a bigger network of support. Instead of talking about hunger on its own, SOS sought to connect it with other problems that resonated in communities across the nation, presenting childhood hunger as an education issue, a health issue, and an economic issue.

In some cases, SOS's new strategy caused discomfort and misalignment with existing nonprofit partners. As Shore explains, "Some of our nonprofit partners were nervous about being held accountable for ending childhood hunger by 2015" (Shore et al., 2013). Some corporate partners also failed to make the transition to the new approach and discontinued their support (Shore et al., 2013).

FIGURE 1 ■ No Kid Hungry Branding

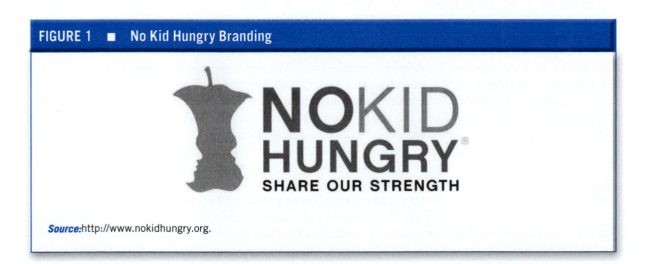

*Source:*http://www.nokidhungry.org.

Expanding School Breakfasts

Working with the consulting firm Deloitte, SOS began to identify the barriers to receiving school breakfasts. One problem they discovered was that this meal was typically served in the school cafeteria before the first morning bell rang (Augustine-Thottungal et al., 2013). With variable bus schedules and busy parents, students often missed the school's breakfast. Additionally, research found that the notion of school breakfast holds a stigma—the idea that "poor kids" must go to the cafeteria to get an extra meal; therefore, some hungry children would avoid going. SOS's solution was to take breakfast out of the cafeteria and make it part of the school day so that more children would have the chance to participate. The organization created a model for students to eat together in the classroom after the bell rang (Augustine-Thottungal et al., 2013).

In order to make this delivery model effective, SOS needed to capitalize on one of its own strengths—the ability to build partnerships. Instead of just relying on corporate partners as it had in the past, the No Kid Hungry campaign would require SOS to reach into its networks to achieve a multisector approach—using private money to collaborate with governments and local nonprofits to unlock the government funds that were available but untapped (Blum, 2012b).

In the school breakfast program's pilot state of Maryland, Share Our Strength reached out to then Governor Martin O'Malley, who, in 2008, declared that his state would be the first to end childhood hunger (Share Our Strength Center for Best Practices, n.d.). O'Malley brought together school superintendents from throughout the state to urge them to adopt breakfasts in the classroom, as well as increasing funding for Maryland Meals for Achievement, a state-run program that connects high-need schools with resources to provide free and reduced-price meals for students (Maryland State Department of Education, n.d.). Additionally, Share Our Strength recruited a core advisory group, made up of state offices and corporate and nonprofit partners, such as Kellogg, Kaiser Permanente, the Walmart Foundation, Maryland Hunger Solutions, and faith-based and food-focused organizations (Share Our Strength Center for Best Practices, n.d.). These collaborations helped provide funding, food resources for meals, school access, and awareness. Following the Maryland pilot, the No Kid Hungry School Breakfast Program was expanded to a number of states, including Colorado, Texas, and Minnesota (Share Our Strength, n.d), where the campaign often works with small community nonprofits and state legislatures to advance its efforts (Shore et al., 2013).

Team No Kid Hungry

Although Bill Shore had a background in politics, lobbying and advocacy were not a major emphasis for SOS during its first 20 years. With the introduction of No Kid Hungry, advocacy efforts became a central part of SOS's strategy. Share Our Strength has sought to influence food-based legislation, including reauthorization of the Child Nutrition Act, which provides funding for School Breakfast, National School Lunch, Child and Adult Care Food, Summer Food Service, and the Fresh Fruit and Vegetable programs. It also has lobbied for funding of SNAP and the U.S. Department of Agriculture's Special Supplemental Nutrition Program for Women, Infants, and Children (WIC). Advocacy activities have included visits to Capitol Hill by SOS leaders, prominent celebrities, and children affected by hunger. SOS also has arranged multiple advocacy days and flooded congressional offices with meetings, calls, and e-mails. (Share Our Strength, n.d).

As evidenced in Maryland's school breakfast program, Share Our Strength has met with governors to unlock state and local funding on anti-hunger initiatives (Crutchfield & Grant, 2012). With the support of elected officials, Maryland, Colorado, and Arkansas increased aid for school breakfasts in thousands of schools. After-school snacks and summer meals are also a target area for SOS's state advocacy (Shore et al., 2013).

SOS also used its new strategy to create a nationwide grassroots advocacy campaign to mobilize individuals to take action in their own states. Its Team No Kid Hungry initiative enlists volunteers to speak out for childhood hunger issues by attending town hall meetings, e-mailing and calling legislators, and recruiting additional members through social media efforts. Team No Kid Hungry has sent hundreds of thousands of letters, e-mails, and calls to advocate in support of the goal to end childhood hunger in America, including more than 40,000 pieces of correspondence in 2013 alone (Share Our Strength, n.d.).

Growth and Impact

Though it had already been a leader in fundraising efforts, No Kid Hungry provided SOS with a new platform for support from diverse audiences, including additional corporate sponsors, government, and individual donors. Following the launch of the No Kid Hungry campaign, revenues more than tripled. As depicted in Figure 2, revenue increased from $13 million in 2008 to nearly $45 million in 2013, despite a national recession that intervened (Blum, 2012b; Share Our Strength 2013 Form 990).

Some fundraising programs that previously had floundered achieved new success. For example, in 1996, Share Our Strength had partnered with chain restaurants to launch a program called Dine Across America, in which the restaurants would donate a portion of their proceeds. Dine Across America's goal was to raise $1 million in 1996, but instead it produced only $250,000. In view of this disappointment, SOS had abandoned the program (Crutchfield & Grant, 2012). But the idea was resurrected in 2008 as Dine Out for No Kid Hungry. The new weeklong, annual event is sponsored by well-known industry names, such as the Food Network and Open Table, and includes national participants, such as Corner Bakery, Shake Shack, Arby's, and Denny's (Share Our Strength, n.d.). Share Our Strength supports Dine Out at participating restaurants by providing marketing materials, online fundraising widgets, and talking points. Dine Out for No Kid Hungry has brought together millions of consumers to raise a total of more than $18 million since 2008 (Share Our Strength, n.d.).

No Kid Hungry relies on its highly visible partnerships, an area in which SOS has succeeded through-out its history. From celebrities such as Jeff Bridges and Rachael Ray to corporations such as Citigroup, JCPenney, and the Arby's Foundation, SOS has been successful in leveraging collaborations for fundraising,

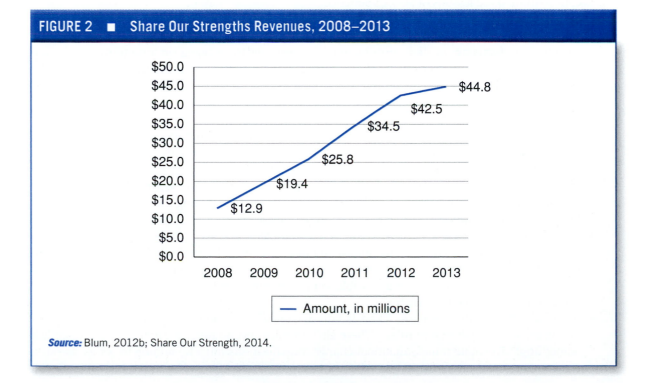

FIGURE 2 ■ Share Our Strengths Revenues, 2008–2013

Source: Blum, 2012b; Share Our Strength, 2014.

visibility, and advocacy efforts. But along with growing revenues from corporate partnerships, SOS also has worked to increase giving by individual donors, which reached $7 million in 2012, up from $4 million in 2008 (Blum, 2012b). A No Kid Hungry pledge, asking people to sign up online to show support for the campaign, collected more than 280,000 signatures, and SOS stepped up its efforts to raise online gifts from individual donors (Blum, 2012b).

No Kid Hungry has connected children with more than 107 million meals, including a 1.9 million-meal increase in summer lunches from 2010 to 2011 (Blum, 2012b). Hundreds of thousands of children have also started in nutrition programs for the first time. The school breakfast program in Maryland was associated with a 7.2 percent decrease in chronic absenteeism (Shore et al., 2013). The No Kid Hungry campaign invested $1.1 million to unlock $33 million in federal funds, which allowed for the purchase of 67,000 more breakfasts daily in the state. Success has been comparable in other states in which No Kid Hungry works with school breakfast and summer lunch programs, with millions of meals and snacks served in California, Colorado, New York, and Florida (Share Our Strength, n.d.). SOS's Cooking Matters program has helped more than 265,000 low-income American families learn how to cook and eat more nutritious and affordable meals (Share Our Strength, n.d.).

Why has Share Our Strength achieved success with No Kid Hungry? Co-founder and CEO Bill Shore attributes it to the clear goal the campaign has set. "Holding ourselves accountable to a specific outcome that was bold but believable inspired our stakeholders and gave them confidence that we merited their investment" (Shore et al., 2013).

Lessons Learned

In 2013, Bill Shore reflected on SOS's transition from its traditional mission to the focused goal of No Kid Hungry. In an article coauthored with another nonprofit CEO whose organization had experienced similar change, he identified the lessons of SOS' experience:

- Focus: Set a Bold Goal. Solving a social problem at the magnitude it exists requires an organization to shift from focusing on short-term incremental progress to focusing on long-term transformational change. The latter is risky, hard to measure, and even harder to achieve, but it provides the inspiration that generates motivation, resources, and a new sense of what is possible. This means developing a goal so bold that achieving it means a social ill has been eradicated.
- Stakeholders: Open Up Your Circle. Transformational change requires an organization to look outside of its core group of true believers and put greater emphasis on mobilizing those less engaged. Every leader trying to solve a problem at the magnitude it exists must ask the simple question: Who has a role to play in solving this problem? The answer often includes cross-sector stakeholders, and those making transformational change are particularly adept at moving beyond their core champions and engaging seemingly unlikely partners. They excel at converting the "maybes"—by far the largest stakeholder group for any social goal—into "yeses."
- Communication: Change the Conversation. Solving problems at scale requires an organization to do more than open up the circle of champions. At times, it requires leaders not just to join a conversation but to actually change the conversation. Changing the conversation can broaden the base of support for an idea by making it accessible to more people and interests or helping others better understand its connection to them.
- Approach: Disrupt the Norms. As Thomas Edison famously quipped in response to a new employee's inquiry about laboratory rules, "There ain't no rules around here. We're trying to accomplish something!" To create transformational change, organizations must be willing to act as skeptics, questioning—and often disrupting—the norms among those affected by and those who affect a

social problem. Norms are standards or patterns of social behavior that are typical or expected of a group. Ultimately, the reason to disrupt norms is to motivate a critical number of people to change their behavior, leading to a new norm, and then to advocate for standards or policies that will enforce the new norm (Shore et al., 2013).

Continuing Challenges

The No Kid Hungry campaign has shifted the way SOS looks, how it conducts business, and the strategies it employs to end childhood hunger. By many measures, it has been a success. However, key questions and challenges remain.

Some critics charge that SOS is feeding hungry children on a daily basis but still not getting to the underlying problem of hunger in America (Shore et al., 2013). Shore acknowledges that getting to the root causes of hunger and poverty is essential, but argues that school breakfasts and lunches are a bridge toward the goal, since these nutrition programs enable children to become self-sufficient and remove barriers to learning (Shore et al., 2013).

Other questions apply to the future of SOS itself. For example, No Kid Hungry was always intended to be a *campaign*, not the new name of the organization. But has the No Kid Hungry brand effectively replaced the brand of Share Our Strength? If Share Our Strength succeeds in achieving its goal, that is, if childhood hunger is eventually eliminated, then the rationale for No Kid Hungry will cease to exist and the organization will need to redefine its mission. SOS could become a victim of its own success. If it decides to change its focus in future years, will it ever be able to reestablish its original brand?

SOS receives a significant portion of revenue from corporate marketing partnerships (Blum, 2012b). The No Kid Hungry rebrand became a more recognizable, and therefore attractive, prospect to corporate sponsors, which has caused SOS's revenues to surge. However, could this resource dependency prove to be a vulnerability should corporate priorities shift or a new recession affect companies' ability to provide sponsorship support? Or, again, if childhood hunger someday ceases to be a national problem?

The number of children receiving meals at school increased every year from 2007 through 2014. Looking just at free school breakfasts, participation increased by at least 300,000 to 400,000 students per year (Food Research and Action Center, n.d.). But hunger in America remains as a broader problem. In a 2014 survey, 17 percent of American households reported that they were experiencing food hardship (Food Research and Action Center, 2015). This was the lowest rate reported since 2008, but it had declined only to about the same level that existed before the Great Recession. Moreover, increasing national awareness of hunger remained a challenge. As the Food Research and Action Center observed in 2015, hunger is often an invisible problem:

Americans do not always recognize how pervasive struggles against hunger are or that hunger is a problem where they live. In our communities it is often hidden by families that do not want to share their economic struggles. Sometimes it hides behind doors of nice houses with mortgages in default, or the heat turned off, or all the income going to housing costs, leaving little or none for food. Sometimes it hides behind the stoic faces of parents who skip meals to protect their children from hunger. It goes unseen by those not looking for it. (p. 2)

NOTE: This case was written by Gretchen Wieland, a graduate student in the Trachtenberg School of Public Policy and Public Administration at The George Washington University in spring, 2015. It has been adapted and expanded by the textbook author.

CASE 2: QUESTIONS FOR DISCUSSION

1. Leslie Crutchfield and Heather McLeod Grant (2012) write:

   If the 1980s and 1990s were all about replicating programs and the [decade of the 2000s] was all about building effective organizations, we believe the next leap is to see nonprofits as catalytic agents of change. We must begin to study and understand nonprofits not merely as organizations housed within in four walls, but as catalysts that work within, and change, entire systems. (p. 16) Does Share Our Strength illustrate this point, and If so, explain how.

2. What principles of marketing discussed in Chapter 10 are illustrated in the case of Share Our Strength?

3. The No Kid Hungry campaign has achieved wide brand awareness. If that campaign were to come to conclusion, what steps would Share Our Strength need to take to reassert its organizational brand?

4. Is Bill Shore a *social entrepreneur*? If so, which definitions of that term seem to apply most closely?

5. Many factors affect the prevalence of hunger, including general economic conditions, the commitment of state officials, and political support for government food programs. In light of these various factors, how might Share Our Strength try to evaluate its own impact on the problem?

6. What changes in internal culture may have been required when Share Our Strength shifted its strategy from funding other nonprofits that provided food toward advocacy to increase funding for government food programs?

7. Go back to Chapter 14 and review materials created by Community Wealth Ventures regarding non-profit earned-income strategies. What assets did Share Our Strength leverage in creating partnerships with corporations and other businesses?

8. Go back to Chapter 6 of this text. How do the key terms related to the outcome model discussed there apply to the case of Share Our Strength?

9. If Share Our Strength desired to diversify its revenues in order to reduce its dependence on events and corporate sponsors, which fundraising strategies and methods discussed in Chapter 13 do you think might hold promise? Explain.

APPENDIX Case 3
The Y

Relevant chapters:

Chapter 1 (Nonprofit Management as a Profession and a Field of Study); Chapter 3 (Theories of the Nonprofit Sector and Nonprofit Organizations); Chapter 6 (Ensuring Accountability and Measuring Performance); Chapter 7 (Developing Strategy and Building Capacity); Chapter 10 (Marketing and Communications); Chapter 13 (Philanthropic Fundraising); Chapter 14 (Earned-Income Strategies).

The Y

The Young Men's Christian Association (YMCA) was founded in London in 1844 by George Williams. During that period of history, young men were migrating in large numbers from rural parts of England to the cities and Williams was concerned about the "bleak landscape of tenement housing and dangerous influences" that they faced in the urban environment. The YMCA would engage young men in Bible study and prayer, in order to provide an "escape from the hazards of life on the streets" (YMCA website). Several years later, Thomas Valentine Sullivan, a retired sea captain, became concerned about the welfare of sailors and merchant seamen in Boston and founded the first YMCA in the United States, adopting the English model (YMCA website).

The early YMCAs in the United States were not open to African Americans. Anthony Brown, a freed slave, founded the first Y for African American men in Washington, DC, in 1853 (YMCA website). African American YMCAs became common meeting places during the Civil Rights movement in the 1960s. A national YMCA resolution in 1946 had banned segregation, but some local Ys continued to exclude African Americans. Stronger action to ban discrimination was taken by the national organization in 1967. Remaining segregated Ys were subsequently closed, although some local Ys continued to serve predominantly African American communities (A brief history of the YMCA and African American communities, 2010).

The YMCA is a federation of independent local associations. The YMCA of the USA, headquartered in Chicago, is a national resource office serving affiliated local associations across the country. In 2014, that included 2,700 Ys in the United States, employing 19,000 full-time staff members, and serving nine million youth and 13 million adults each year (YMCA website). The Y's mission is "To put Christian principles into practice through programs that build healthy spirit, mind, and body for all" (YMCA of the USA, 2014).

From Evangelism to General Service

In its early years, the YMCA was an interdenominational Protestant organization, with an evangelical purpose. YMCA workers distributed religious materials and worked actively to convert young men to Christianity (Miller & Fielding, 1995). But this focus presented some challenges. For one, local YMCA associations had considerable autonomy and held various viewpoints on the appropriate balance of evangelism and service programs. Second, the emphasis on religious conversion did not necessarily hold the interest of young men, limiting membership and thus revenue (Miller & Fielding, 1995). And, third, reliance on philanthropy placed the Y's revenue in jeopardy in economic downturns, when it was especially difficult to compete with churches for members and gifts. The YMCA began new programs that would generate earned income, while also remaining consistent with its mission (Minkoff & Powell, 2006).

Among the new programs were lectures and educational programs. For example, the first known course on English as a second language was offered by the YMCA in Cincinnati, Ohio, in 1856 to serve German immigrants (YMCA website). In the 1860s, beginning in Chicago, the YMCA began to build residential dormitories for men. Its inventory totaled 100,000 rooms by 1940, making it larger than any hotel chain at the time (YMCA website).

Development of residential facilities was given impetus by the growth of railroads in the late 19th century. Beginning, in 1872, the YMCA initiated programs to serve railroad workers, who were often young men away from their homes. "Railroad YMCAs" were established at major points along rail lines, and the Y's transportation department worked directly with the railroad companies, which provided 40 percent of the financial support for these facilities and their programs. "The railroad Ys provided practical things, such as clean beds, good meals, and hot showers, but also addressed the educational, spiritual, and recreational needs of the workers with Bible study, instructional courses on a variety of subjects, organized sports, and other activities" (History of Transportation Department, 2005). The need for the railroad Ys diminished with changes in the railroad industry, and the transportation department was disbanded in 1989 (History of Transportation Department, 2005).

YMCA dormitories came to include gymnasiums. That attracted new members and also was consistent with the philosophy of serving the whole person, including physical and other dimensions. Physical activities became an increasing emphasis, perhaps driven in part by the boards of local YMCAs, which included businessmen with an interest in that area (Miller & Fielding, 2005). In 1881, a YMCA staff member in Boston coined the term *body building* and developed exercise classes that presaged today's fitness movement (YMCA website).

Despite its roots as a religious institution, the YMCA evolved toward becoming a nonprofit that provided services. Once dependent on gifts, earned income became the primary source of revenue for some YMCAs—in other words, they became commercialized. Fees for service diminished the need for gifts and also required that the Y become more responsive to the "demands of its clientele," that is, more like a secular business organization (Minkoff & Powell, 2006, p. 590).

Positioning for Growth

In the twentieth century, the increased reliance on earned income led the Y's leaders to identify new target markets for growth. The focus of programs extended beyond men to families. Although the Y had been founded to serve young urban working men, it reached out to a more affluent clientele. Starting as early as the 1920s, some Ys offered a more expensive and exclusive "second tier" of membership, called Business Men's Clubs or Men's Health Services, which featured such amenities as private lockers and steam rooms. With the migration of middle class families to the suburbs during the 1950s and 1960s, more branches were built in suburban areas and the Y's membership became increasingly affluent. By the 1970s, even some urban Ys were building state-of-the-art new facilities to attract downtown business professionals (Stern, 2011).

Y membership continued to grow as a result of the national fitness boom that began in the 1970s. But so did the number of commercial health clubs, which presented direct competition to the Ys. In 1968, there were only 350 commercial gyms in the United States. That number grew to over 2,000 by 1976 and to more than 15,000 by 2000 (Stern, 2011). There was internal debate among Y officials about whether to emulate the features and practices of new competitors, and some were concerned about the possible impact of a more commercial image on fundraising. However, the Ys responded to the challenge from for-profit gyms by continuing to upgrade their own facilities.

By the 1980s, the Y's competition with for-profit gyms had become controversial. Some began to question whether the Y was truly a nonprofit and whether it should remain tax exempt (Stern, 2011). The executive director of the International Health, Racquet, and Sportsclub Association (IHRSA), which represented the for-profit gyms, wrote in 2000 that the industry's main enemy was "a rogue charity that is often . . . no charity at all" (Stern, 2011, p. 1). The debate came to include fundamental questions about the very definition and purpose of a nonprofit organization.

Defining *Nonprofit*

In the view of the commercial health club industry, the YMCA presented unfair competition because of the benefits conferred by its nonprofit status. The IHRSA argued that tax exemptions represented a subsidy to the Y that lowered its operating costs. Some of that subsidy was passed along to members in the form of lower prices that the for-profit clubs could not match. At the same time, the industry argued, the Y was serving a middle-class clientele that did not need subsidies and that represented the same target market that for-profit clubs were pursuing (Miller & Fielding, 1995). Moreover, the commercial clubs argued, the Y's expansion into new competitive markets was relatively easy, given its brand recognition, ability to receive charitable gifts toward capital projects, and the requirement that its profits be reinvested in the organization rather than distributed to stakeholders, consistent with the non-distribution constraint that faces all nonprofits (Miller & Fielding, 1995).

Criticisms of the Ys went to the very justification for nonprofit organizations' tax exempt status. Some said that the purpose of nonprofits is to "provide goods and services that the for-profit sector is not interested in providing . . . hence, the need for government subsidies if the product is to be provided at all" (Miller & Fielding, p. 89). In other words, they cited market failure as a justification for the nonprofit sector (Hansmann, 1987; Weisbrod, 1975, 1988). Defining a public good narrowly as "[providing] food, shelter, and/or clothing . . . for those incapable of providing for themselves or their children," critics argued that the commercialized Ys did not meet the test, since most of their members were middle- and upper-class people, who could well afford the dues of a for-profit health club (Miller & Fielding, p. 90).

These arguments and others led some to propose that the YMCA should pay unrelated business income tax (UBIT) on *all* of its revenue derived from activities that compete with the private sector and that the IRS standard of exempting commercial revenue that is "substantially related" to the charitable mission should be repealed (Miller & Fielding, p. 95). In essence, this could have subjected *all* of the Y's earned income to taxation.

Y leaders met with the IHRSA and agreed to not market their associations as purely health or athletic facilities, but rather as human service agencies. But they also maintained that "proposals to restrict nonprofits to serving the poor exclusively . . . are unacceptable" (Stern, 2011, p. 9).

Challenges to its tax exempt status "posed an existential threat to the Y" (Stern, 2011, p. 12). But in the view of some observers, the challenges also strengthened the Y as a national organization, by forcing it to "respond and rethink its practices, its mission, and its presentation of itself as a community organization and presence in American society" (Stern, 2011, p. 1).

Rebranding and Focusing on Mission

By the 2000s, the Y was facing increasing challenges. The challenges went beyond the criticisms of the for-profit health club industry. Membership and fundraising were stagnant and The Y had acquired a "stodgy image" (Daniels, 2014a). Y leaders began exploring new strategies for refocusing and expanding its mission, improving its image, and generating new strategies for revenue and growth (Daniels, 2014a).

The transformation began with a 10-year planning cycle initiated in 2007. Strategic plans developed for the YMCA of the USA, the national organization, established broad goals and directions to serve as guidelines for local associations in developing their own plans. Within the 10-year cycle, the first of a series of three-year plans was developed to cover the period of 2007 to 2010. Titled Mission Impact, the plan focused on strengthening the capacity of the national office. The second three-year plan (2011–2013) was titled Advancing Our Cause. It focused on increasing visibility and enhancing the capacity of local associations, following the roll-out of a new branding program in 2010.

The Y's image was a common element in many of the challenges it faced. As Amber Stephenson (2013) describes the situation, "The general public, stakeholders, and organization influencers perceived the YMCA as a fitness facility that offered *some other programs*" [italics added] (n.p.). This did not accurately reflect the wide-ranging impact of Y programs in communities. Changing public perceptions would be necessary to attract more membership and more philanthropic support and to expand the Y's impact (Daniels, 2014a).

The rebranding included a new logo and slogan. Instead of *YMCA*, the new official name would be what many people had always called the organization—*the Y.* The national organization would be known as *Y-USA*. This new name would be used in conjunction with a new slogan: "The Y. So much more" (Daniels, 2014a). The intended message was that "The Y isn't just a place to work out; it's a force for change" (Daniels, 2014a).[1]

The Y's transformation would require more than rebranding; it would include a refocusing and expansion of its mission and a plan for growth (Daniels, 2014a). Given its federated structure, development of the Y's 2014–2017 strategic plan required a participative process, which began in 2012. Engagement in various aspects of the process included 1,701 individuals and 459 local YMCAs. This was necessary to achieve buy-in from the local associations and greater consistency in the Y's image and programs. Many of the ideas included in the plan came from local Y leaders. (Daniels, 2014a) As the head of the Y-USA explained it, the re-engineering came from the national organization listening to the voices of the affiliates, not by using "carrots and sticks" (Daniel, 2014a). But local Ys would be required to align their branding and programs with national priorities and to cooperate in some activities, including fundraising, with changes to be phased in over five years (Daniels, 2014a).

The strategic plan for 2014–2017 defined desired outcomes for the entire Y movement in three program areas: *youth development, healthy living*, and *social responsibility* (YMCA of the USA, 2014). Youth development initiatives include summer camps for children, which the Y has offered for many years. The Y also provides leadership-training courses and other educational programs for young people. Healthy living programs include exercise and cooking classes, designed to prevent chronic diseases. The Y also is encouraging communities to develop farmer's markets, build pathways that people can use for exercise, and take other actions to promote good health. And the Y created a Community Health Living Index to rate communities on such variables as bike paths, produce stands, and the number of fast-food restaurants. Under the rubric of social responsibility, the Y advocates for food banks and operates programs that provide after-school meals, adult literacy training, and preparation for high-school equivalency (GED) testing ("3 Causes the Y Hopes Will Attract," 2014).

The plan for achieving the stated outcomes in all three program areas included three "strategic imperatives"—elevate membership and improve program efficacy, build organizational capacity, and generate the awareness and financial resources needed to sustain the Y cause (YMCA of the USA, 2014). Specific objectives and related metrics were identified for each strategic imperative, to be achieved by 2017 (YMCA of the USA, 2014).

Just as the need for diversified revenue had influenced the Y's evolution from evangelism to general services in its early years, new strategies implemented since 2007 were related to revenue needs as well as mission. One strategy was to increase fundraising through a more coordinated effort. The decentralized structure of the Y and autonomy of local associations had sometimes resulted in disjointed fundraising initiatives. For example, before 2015, Ys in Massachusetts conducted their annual giving solicitations according to their own calendars, at various times. Beginning in 2015, Ys were to be grouped together within states or regions and would run their annual programs simultaneously. They also would work together in planning their annual campaigns and share data regarding their fundraising costs and results. The national office would increase its support of local fundraising, distributing a "Red Book" of tips and ideas (Daniels, 2014a).

New programs also held the potential for new sources of earned income. For example, the diabetes prevention program, implemented in 2005, would have an impact on community health, but objectives also included increasing Y membership among participants in the program by 30 percent. And the Y advocated new federal legislation that would provide reimbursement for its service to pre-diabetes clients under Medicare and Medicaid (Daniels, 2014b; YMCA of the USA, 2014).

As Daniels observed in 2014, "The story of the Y's transformation is still unfolding . . . [and] it holds lessons about how both rewarding and tough it can be to remake a large and traditional nonprofit organization." But the Y had transformed itself before, from an evangelical organization established to protect young men from the dangers of urban life to a nonprofit serving 10,000 communities, both urban and rural, with a range of programs for young people and families. It had evolved from an organization mostly dependent on philanthropy to one with substantial earned income—a hybrid organization. And it had helped shape American culture. The Y "launched the first basketball teams and group swim lessons . . . popularized exercise classes and created the oldest summer camp still in operation" (Weeks, 2015). As the Y's CEO Kevin Washington stated in 2015, "Innovation and impact are in the Y's DNA" (quoted in Weeks, 2015).

Note

1. The Y's style guidelines state that "The Y" is to be used to refer to the collective organization and "The YMCA of (Location)" is to be used in referring to a local association.

CASE 3: QUESTIONS FOR DISCUSSION

1. Is access to a health club a public good, a private good, or a common good? How about access to programs that provide education about health and fitness?

2. Should a nonprofit that competes with a for-profit business be taxed just to level the playing field, even if its earned income is related to its mission?

3. How are models of organizational life cycles, discussed in Chapter 7 of this text, reflected in the history of the Y?

4. As discussed in Chapter 1 of this text, Robert Herman (2010) observes that nonprofit management uniquely requires the ability to integrate mission, the acquisition of resources, and strategy. How are those points reflected in the case of the Y?

5. How does resource dependency theory relate to the case of the Y?

6. How does the process followed in developing the Y's 2014–1017 strategic plan compare with the process followed by Brian Gallagher at United Way, discussed in Case 5.2? How is it similar and how is it different? How would you explain any similarities or differences?

7. What might have been some variables identified in the Y's SWOT analysis that are reflected in its strategic plan?

8. How does the Y's plan to implement a more coordinated approach to fundraising relate to trends discussed in Chapter 13?

9. Review the Y's strategic plan (www.ymca.net/sites/default/files/organizational-profile/Delivering-Our-Cause-Strategic-Plan-Online.pdf). How does it reflect the concept of a double bottom line?

10. The vocabulary used in the Y's strategic plan is somewhat different from the terminology used in Chapter 7 of this text, although key concepts are the same. Read the Y's plan online and see how the various elements of the plan match up against the concepts discussed in Chapter 7 (www.ymca.net/sites/default/files/organizational-profile/Delivering-Our-Cause-Strategic-Plan-Online.pdf).

References

Abelson, R. (1998, March 27). At Minnesota Public Radio, a deal way above average. *New York Times*. Retrieved from http://www.nytimes.com/1998/03/27/business/at-minnesota-public-radio-a-deal-way-above-average.html

Adams, J. S. (1965). Inequity in social exchange. In L. Berkowitz (Ed.), *Advances in experimental psychology* (vol. 2, pp. 267–299). New York, NY: Academic Press.

Adelman, K. (2005, September 1). Bricks tell a story. *Washingtonian.com*. Retrieved from http://www.washingtonian.com/articles/people/1757.html

Adizes, I. (1999). *Managing corporate lifecycles*. Paramus, NJ: Prentice Hall.

Air Wick partners with National Park Foundation to launch new collection. (2012, March 15). *Business Wire*. Retrieved from http://www.businesswire.com/news/home/20120315005287/en/Air-Wick%C2%AE-Partners-National-Park-Foundation-Launch

Aldrich, H. E. (1999). *Organizations evolving*. Thousand Oaks, CA: Sage.

Alesani, D., & Missoni, E. (2014). Introduction. In E. Missoni & D. Alesani (Eds.), *Management of international institutions and NGOs* (pp. 1–10). New York, NY: Routledge.

Allison, M. (2002). Into the fire: Boards and executive transitions. *Nonprofit Management & Leadership, 12*(4), 341–351.

Allison, M., & Kaye, J. (2015). *Strategic planning for nonprofit organizations: A practical guide for dynamic times* (3rd ed.). Hoboken, NJ: Wiley.

America's top donors. (2006). *Chronicle of Philanthropy*. Retrieved from http://philanthropy.com/stats/topdonors/index.php?page=2&year=2006&donorstate=All states&recipientstate=All states&donorsource=All sources of wealth&order=pledged

American Cancer Society. (2008). ACS Mission Statement. Retrieved from http://www.cancer.org/aboutus/whoweare/acsmission-statements

American Heart Association. (2015). *Heart-check mark*. Retrieved from http://www.heart.org/HEARTORG/GettingHealthy/NutritionCenter/HeartSmartShopping/Heart-Check-Mark-Nutritional-Guidelines_UCM_300914_Article.jsp

American Red Cross responds to latest ProPublica and NPR coverage [statement by the American Red Cross]. (2015, June 3). Retrieved from http://www.redcross.org/news/press-release/American-Red-Cross-Responds-to-Recent-ProPublica-Report-on-Haiti

Andrea Mitchell interviews Susan G. Komen's Nancy Brinker. (2012). Retrieved from http://firstread.nbcnews.com/_news/2012/02/02/10303379-andrea-mitchell-interviews-susan-g-komens-nancy-brinker?lite

Andreasen, A. R. (2006). *Social marketing in the 21st century*. Thousand Oaks, CA: Sage.

Andreasen, A. R. (2009). Cross-sector marketing alliances: Partnerships, sponsorships, and cause-related marketing. In J. Cordes & E. Steuerle (Eds.), *Nonprofits and business* (pp. 155–191). Washington, DC: Urban Institute.

Andreasen, A. R., & Kotler, P. (2008). *Strategic marketing for nonprofit organizations* (7th ed.). Upper Saddle River, NJ: Prentice Hall.

Andresen, K. (2006). *Robin Hood marketing: Stealing corporate savvy to sell just causes*. San Francisco, CA: Jossey-Bass.

Anheier, H. K. (2014). *Nonprofit organizations: Theory, management, policy* (2nd ed.). New York, NY: Routledge.

Anheier, H. K., & Themudo, N. (2005). The internationalization of the nonprofit sector. In R. D. Herman & Associates (Eds.), *The Jossey-Bass handbook of nonprofit leadership and management* (2nd ed., pp. 102–127). San Francisco, CA: Jossey-Bass.

Anthony, R. N., & Young, D. W. (2005). Financial accounting and financial management. In R. D. Herman & Associates (Eds.), *The Jossey-Bass handbook of nonprofit leadership and management* (2nd ed., pp. 466–512). San Francisco, CA: Jossey-Bass.

Arizona Humane Society. (2014). History, mission, and values. Retrieved from http://www.azhumane.org/arizona-humane-society-about-us/arizona-humane-society-history-mission-values/

Arnsberger, P., Ludlum, M., Riley, M., & Stanton, M. (2011). A history of the tax-exempt sector: An SOI perspective. In J. S. Ott & L. A. Dicke (Eds.), *The nature of the nonprofit sector* (2nd ed., pp. 125–150). Boulder, CO: Westview Press.

Ashoka. (n.d.-a). About us. Retrieved from https://www.ashoka.org/about

Ashoka. (n.d.-b). *What is a social entrepreneur?* Retrieved from http://www.ashoka.org/social_entrepreneur

Ashoka (n.d.-c). Profile of Lauren Diaz Arias. Retrieved from https://www.ashoka.org/fellow/lauren-diaz-arias

Ashoka (n.d.-d). Profile of Richard Seshie. Retrieved from https://www.ashoka.org/fellow/richard-seshie

Ashoka (n.d.-e). Profile of Sumaira Abdulali. Retrieved from https://www.ashoka.org/fellow/sumaira-abdulali

Ashoka (n.d.-f). Profile of Mohammad Alhabsyi. Retrieved from https://www.ashoka.org/fellow/mohammad-alhabsyi

Aspire CoffeeWorks Website. Retrieved from https://www.aspirecoffee-works.com/learn/company/

Aspire of Illinois 2013 Form 990. Retrieved from http://www.guidestar.org/FinDocuments/2014/362/654/2014-362654558-0b1d398b-9.pdf

Associated Press. (2013, October). New York City Opera to shut down after failing to meet $7m funding goal. Retrieved from http://www.the-guardian.com/world/2013/oct/01/new-york-opera-files-bankruptcy

Association of Fundraising Professionals. (2009). International growth and development. Retrieved from http://www.afpnet.org/About/content.cfm?ItemNumber=5373&navItemNumber=5374

Augustine-Thottungal, R., Kern, J., Key, J., & Sherman, B. (2013). *Ending childhood hunger: A social impact analysis. Deloitte and Share Our Strength /No Kid Hungry Center for Best Practices*. Retrieved from https://www.nokidhungry.org/pdfs/school-breakfast-white-paper.pdf

Aviv, D., & Bass, G. D. (2013, December 3). IRS plan on nonprofit political work undermines democracy. *Chronicle of Philanthropy*. Retrieved from http://philanthropy.com/article/IRS-Plan-on-Nonprofit/143351/

Avner, M. (2010). Advocacy, lobbying, and social change. In D. O. Renz & Associates (Eds.), *The Jossey-Bass handbook of nonprofit leadership and management* (3rd ed., pp. 347–374). San Francisco, CA: Jossey-Bass.

B Lab website (https://www.bcorporation.net/what-are-b-corps/about-b-lab). accessed 1/6/16

Baruch, Y., & Ramalho, N. (2006, March). Communalities and distinctions in the measurement of organizational performance and effectiveness across for-profit and nonprofit sectors. *Nonprofit and Voluntary Sector Quarterly, 35*(1), 39–61.

Bass, B. M. (1985). *Leadership and performance beyond expectations*. New York, NY: Free Press.

Bass, B. M., & Avolio, B. J. (Eds.). (1994). *Improving organizational effectiveness through transformational leadership*. Thousand Oaks, CA: Sage.

Battilana, J., Lee. M., Walker, J., & Dorsey, C. (2012, Summer). In search of the hybrid ideal. *Stanford Social Innovation Review*. Retrieved from http://www.ssireview.org/articles/entry/in_search_of_the_hybrid_ideal

Beaubien, J. (2015, June 5). Behind the story: What made NPR look into Red Cross efforts in Haiti? NPR. Retrieved from http://www.npr.org/sections/goatsand-soda/2015/06/05/412071811/behind-the-story-what-made-npr-look-into-red-cross-efforts-in-haiti

Bekkers, R., & Wiepking, P. (2011, October). A literature review of empirical studies of philanthropy: Eight mechanisms that drive charitable giving. *Nonprofit and Voluntary Sector Quarterly, 40*(5), 924–973.

Benefit Corp Information Center. (n.d.). Benefit corp vs. certified B corp. Retrieved http://www.benefitcorp.net/what-makes-benefit-corp-different/benefit-corp-vs-certified-b-corp

Bennis, W. G., & Nanus, B. (1985). *Leaders: The strategy for taking charge*. New York, NY: Harper & Row.

Berger, P. L., & Neuhaus, J. (1977). *To empower people: The role of mediating structures in public policy*. Washington, DC: American Enterprise for Public Policy Research.

Berkshire, J. C. (2011, October 2). Mergers are just one way charities find to team up and battle a tough economy. *Chronicle of Philanthropy*. Retrieved from http://philanthropy.com/article/CollaborationsMergers-Get/129197/

Bermudez, C., Daniels, A., & Wallace, N. (2013, December 19). Zuckerberg commits $1 billion more to Silicon Valley community fund. *Chronicle of Philanthropy*. Retrieved from http://www.philanthropy.com/article/Zuckerberg-Gives-1-Billion/143691

Berry, J. M. (2003, November 27). Nonprofit groups shouldn't be afraid to lobby. *Chronicle of Philanthropy, 16*(4), 33.

Better Business Bureau Wise Giving Alliance. (2003). *Standards for charity accountability*. Retrieved from http://www.bbb.org/us/standards-for-charity-accountability/

Bibb, E., Fishberg, M., Harold, J., & Layburn, E. (n.d.). *The blended value glossary*. Retrieved from http://www.blendedvalue.org/wp-content/uploads/2004/02/pdf-blended-value-glossary.pdf

Bill & Melinda Gates Foundation. (2015). Foundation fact sheet. Retrieved from http://www.gates-foundation.org/Who-We-Are/General-Information/Foundation-Factsheet

Bixler, M. (2005, April 16). Habitat founder forms rival group. *Atlanta Journal-Constitution*, A1.

Blackwood, A. S., Dietz, N., & Pollack, T. (2014). *The state of nonprofit governance*. Washington, DC: Urban Institute.

Blackwood, A. S., Roeger, K. L., & Pettijohn, S. L. (2012). *The nonprofit sector in brief: Public charities, giving, and volunteering, 2012*. Washington, DC: Urban Institute.

Blake, R. R., & Mouton, J. S. (1985). *The managerial grid III: A new look at the classic that has boosted productivity and profits for thousands of corporations worldwide*. Houston, TX: Gulf Publishing.

Blended Value. (2004, January). *Blended value map*. Retrieved from http://www.blendedvalue.org/wp-content/uploads/2004/02/pdf-bv-map.pdf /

Block, S. R. (2001). A history of the discipline. In J. S. Ott (Ed.), *The nature of the nonprofit sector* (pp. 97–111). Boulder, CO: Westview Press.

Block, S. R., & Rosenberg, S. (2002). Toward an understanding of founder's syndrome: An assessment of power and privilege among founders of nonprofit organizations. *Nonprofit Management & Leadership, 12*(4), 353–368.

Blum, D. E. (2012a, December 2). Go big or go home: Tips from Share Our Strength. *Chronicle of Philanthropy*. Retrieved from http://philanthropy.com/article/Go-Big-or-Go-Home-and/135990/

Blum, D. E. (2012b, December 2). Bigger staff and bolder goals turn around a quiet hunger-fighting charity. *Chronicle of Philanthropy*. Retrieved from http://philanthropy.com/article/Bold-Goals-Turn-Around-a-Quiet/135988/

BoardSource. (2005). *The source: Twelve principles of governance that power exceptional boards.* Washington, DC: Author. Retrieved from http://pipertrust.org/wp-content/uploads/2011/05/ExceptionalBoards.pdf

BoardSource. (2010). *The handbook of nonprofit governance.* San Francisco, CA: Jossey-Bass.

Bolder Advocacy. (2015). Comparison of 501(c)(3)s, 501(c)(4)s, and Political (526) organizations. Retrieved from http://bolderadvocacy.org/resource/comparison-of-501c3s-501c4s-and-political-527-organizations

Boli, J. (2006). International nongovernmental organizations. In W. W. Powell & R. Steinberg (Eds.), *The non-profit sector: A research handbook* (2nd ed., pp. 333–354). New Haven, CT: Yale University Press.

Bolman, L. G., & Deal, T. E. (2003). *Reframing organizations: Artistry, choice, and organizations* (3rd ed.). San Francisco, CA: Jossey-Bass.

Bongiovanni, I., Missoni, E., & Alesani, D. (2014). Governance models and reforms. In E. Missoni & D. Alesani (Eds.), *Management of international institutions and NGOs: Frameworks, practices and challenges* (pp. 215–238). New York, NY: Routledge.

Bonk, K., Tynes, E., Griggs, H., & Sparks, P. (2008). *Strategic communications for nonprofits* (2nd ed.). San Francisco, CA: Jossey-Bass.

Boris, E. T., deLeon, E., Roeger, K. L., & Nikolova, M. (2010). *Human service nonprofits and government collaboration: Findings from the 2010 national survey of nonprofit government contracting and grants.* Washington, DC: Urban Institute. Retrieved from http://www.urban.org/uploadedpdf/412228-nonprofit-government-contracting.pdf

Bornstein, D. (2007). *How to change the world: Social entrepreneurs and the power of new ideas.* New York, NY: Oxford University Press.

Bornstein, D. (2011, March 7). Coming together to give schools a boost.

New York Times. Retrieved from http://opinionator.blogs.nytimes.com/2011/03/07/coming-together-to-give-schools-a-boost/

Boston Consulting Group. (2011, October 3). Brian Gallagher on uniting United Way: An interview with the President and CEO. Bcg.perspectives. Retrieved from https://www.bcgperspectives.com/content/videos/leadership_transformation_brian_gallagher_uniting_united_way/

Bowman, W. (2011). *Finance fundamentals for nonprofits: Building capacity and sustainability.* Hoboken, NJ: Wiley.

Bowman, W., & Fremont-Smith, M. R. (2006). Nonprofits and state and local governments. In E. T. Boris & C. T. Steuerle (Eds.), *Nonprofits and government: collaboration and conflict* (pp. 181–218). Washington, DC: Urban Institute.

Boy Scouts of America. (2014). Mission & vision. Retrieved from http://www.scouting.org/scoutsource/Media/mission.aspx

Bradshaw, P. (2009, fall). A contingency approach to nonprofit governance. *Nonprofit Management & Leadership, 20*(1), 60–81.

Bray, I. (2013). *Effective fundraising for nonprofits: Real-world strategies that work* (4th ed.). Berkeley, CA: Nolo.

Brest, P. (2012, Spring). A decade of outcome-oriented philanthropy. *Stanford Social Innovation Review, 10*(2), 42–47.

Bridgespan Group. (2012, February 6). *Case study: Cincinnati, Covington, and Newport.* Retrieved from http://www.bridgespan.org/getmedia/67713826-a5f8-4eb7-bf51-bc4113aaec1e/Community-Collaboratives-CaseStudy-Cinncinnati.pdf.aspx

A brief history of the YMCA and African American communities. (2010). Minneapolis, MN: University of Minnesota Libraries Kautz Family YMCA Archives. Retrieved from https://www.lib.umn.edu/ymca/guide-afam-history

Brinkerhoff, D. W., & Brinkerhoff, J. M. (2011). Public-private partnerships: Perspectives on purposes, publicness, and good governance. *Public Administration and Development, 31*(1), 2–14.

Broce, T. E. (1986). *Fund raising: The guide to raising money from private sources* (2nd ed.). Norman: University of Oklahoma Press.

Brooks, A. C. (2009). *Social entrepreneurship: A modern approach to social value creation.* Upper Saddle River, NJ: Prentice Hall.

Brooks, D. (2009, May 7). The Harlem miracle [op-ed]. *New York Times.* Retrieved from http://www.nytimes.com/2009/05/08/opinion/08brooks.html

Brothers, J., & Sherman, A. (2012). *Building nonprofit capacity: A guide to managing change through organizational lifecycles.* San Francisco, CA: Jossey-Bass.

Brown, C. (2013, March 21). The epic ups and downs of Peter Gelb. *New York Times* Magazine. Retrieved from http://www.nytimes.com/2013/03/24/magazine/the-epic-ups-and-downs-of-peter-gelb.html

Bruce, M. (2010, June 9). Taking a chance; public boarding school reaps great success. Retrieved from http://www.seedfoundation.com/wp-content/uploads/2010/06/06_09_2010-ABC-News.pdf

Brudney, J. L. (2010). Designing and managing volunteer programs. In D. O. Renz & Associates (Eds.), *The Jossey-Bass handbook of nonprofit leadership and management* (3rd ed.). San Francisco, CA: Jossey-Bass.

Bryman, A. (1992). *Charisma and leadership in organizations.* London, UK: Sage.

Bryson, J. M. (2011). *Strategic planning for public and nonprofit organizations* (4th ed.). San Francisco, CA: Jossey-Bass.

Bureau of Labor Statistics. (2014). *Volunteering in the United States, 2013.* Retrieved from http://www.bls.gov/news.release/volun.nr0.htm

Burnett, J. J. (2007). *Nonprofit marketing: Best practices.* Hoboken, NJ: Wiley.

Burns, J. M. (1978). *Leadership.* New York, NY: HarperCollins.

Cagney, P., & Ross, B. (2013). *Global fundraising: How the world is changing the rules of philanthropy.* Hoboken, NJ: Wiley.

Caligiuri, P. (2012, August 14). When Unilever bought Ben & Jerry's: A story of CEO adaptability. *Fastcompany*. Retrieved from http://www.fastcompany.com/3000398/when-unilever-bought-ben-jerrys-story-ceo-adaptability

Canada, G., & Williams-Isom, A. (2014, October 5). How Harlem Children's Zone spent a decade preparing for new leadership. *Chronicle of Philanthropy*. Retrieved from http://philanthropy.com/article/How-Harlem-Children-s-Zone/149157/

Capps, K., & Montgomery, D. (2014, April 25). The great divide. *Washington City Paper*. Retrieved from http://www.washingtoncitypaper.com/articles/45699/the-great-divide-22-questions-for-the-corcoran/

Carlson, M., & Donohoe, M. (2003). *The executive director's survival guide: Thriving as a nonprofit leader*. San Francisco, CA: Jossey-Bass.

Carnegie, A. (1889, June). Wealth. *North American Review, 148*(391), 653–665.

Carnie, C. (2013). Western Europe. In P. Cagney & B. Ross, *Global fundraising: How the world is changing the rules of philanthropy* (pp. 89–107). Hoboken, NJ: Wiley.

Carson, E. (2012a, August 31). Rethinking collective impact [Web log comment]. *Huffington Post*. Retrieved from http://www.huffingtonpost.com/emmett-d-carson/rethinking-collective-imp_b_1847839.html

Carson, E. (2012b, September 5). Rethinking collective impact: Part two [Web log comment]. *Huffington Post*. Retrieved from http://www.huffingtonpost.com/emmett-d-carson/collective-impact-_b_1847972.html

Carver, J. (1990). *Boards that make a difference: A new design for leadership in nonprofit and public organizations*. San Francisco, CA: Jossey-Bass.

Carver, J. (1997). *Boards that make a difference: A new design for leadership in nonprofit and public organizations* (2nd ed.). San Francisco, CA: Jossey-Bass.

Carver, J. (2006). *Boards that make a difference: A new design for leadership in nonprofit and public organizations* (3rd ed.). San Francisco, CA: Jossey-Bass.

CASA. (2014). Annual Report. Retrieved from http://casademaryland.org/casa-2014-annual-report/

CASA in Action. (2015). About us. Retrieved from http://casainaction.org/about-us/

Cash, S. (2002, April). Smithsonian $35m gift. *Art in America, 90*(4), 33.

CBS News. (2014, September 18). "Three Cups of Tea" author Greg Mortenson plans reluctant return. Retrieved from http://www.cbsnews.com/news/three-cups-of-tea-author-greg-mortenson-plans-reluctant-return/

CBS News. (2015, January 12). 5 years after devastating earthquake, Haiti in political turmoil. Retrieved from http://www.cbsnews.com/news/5-years-after-devastating-earthquake-haiti-in-political-turmoil/

Cellini, S. R., & Kee, J. E. (2010). Cost-effectiveness and cost-benefit analysis. In J. S. Wholey, H. P. Hatry, & K. E. Newcomer (Eds.), *Handbook of practical program evaluation* (3rd ed., pp. 493–530). San Francisco, CA: Jossey-Bass.

Center on Philanthropy at Indiana University. (2012, November). *The 2012 Bank of America study of high net worth philanthropy*. Indianapolis: Author.

Chait, R. P., Holland, T. P., & Taylor, B. E. (1999). The new work of the nonprofit board. In *Harvard Business Review on Nonprofits* (pp. 53–75). Boston, MA: Harvard Business School Press. (Reprinted from *Harvard Business Review,* September/October, 1996)

Chait, R. P., Ryan, W. P., & Taylor, B. E. (2005). *Governance as leadership: Reframing the work of nonprofit boards*. Hoboken, NJ: BoardSource/Wiley.

Charity Navigator. (n.d.). Haiti earthquake: One year later. Retrieved from http://www.charitynavigator.org/index.cfm?bay=content.view&cpid=1194#.VXdRf3kcGcw

Charity Navigator. (2014). How do we rate charities? Retrieved from http://www.charitynavigator.org/index.cfm?bay=content.view&cpid=1284#.VF1K03lMucw

Chen, C.-A. (2014). Nonprofit managers' motivational styles: A view beyond the intrinsic-extrinsic dichotomy. *Nonprofit and Voluntary Sector Quarterly, 43*(4), 737–758.

Chen, L., & Chen, J. (2011). The motivations and expectations of international volunteer tourists. *Tourism Management, 32*, 435–442.

Chhichhia, B. (2015, January 8). The rise of social stock exchanges. *Stanford Social Innovation Review*. Retrieved from http://www.ssireview.org/blog/entry/the_rise_of_social_stock_exchanges?utm_source=Enews&utm_medium=Email&utm_campaign=SSIR_Now&utm_content=Read_More

Child, C. D., & Grønbjerg, K. A. (2007, March). Nonprofit advocacy organizations: Their characteristics and activities. *Social Science Quarterly, 88*(1), 259–281.

Child, C. D., Witesman, E. M., & Braudt, D. B. (2014, July 17). Sector choice: How fair trade entrepreneurs choose between nonprofit and for-profit forms. *Nonprofit and Voluntary Sector Quarterly, 44*, 832–851.

Choi, J. (2006). A motivational theory of charismatic leadership: Envisioning, empathy, and empowerment. *Journal of Leadership & Organizational Studies, 13*(1), 24.

Citizens United v. FEC, 558 U.S. 50 (2010)

Clegg, S., Kornberger, M., & Pitsis, T. (2005). *Managing and organizations: An introduction to theory and practice*. Thousand Oaks, CA: Sage.

Coe, C. K. (2011). *Nonprofit financial management: A practical guide*. Hoboken, NJ: Wiley.

Cohn, F. (2012, January). The ballad of NYCO. *Opera News*. Retrieved from http://www.operanews.com/Ballad_of_NYCO.html

Cohen, R. (2014, July 15). For-profit health clubs challenge nonprofit YMCAs' tax exempt status. *Nonprofit Quarterly*. Retrieved from http://nonprofitquarterly.org/2014/07/15/for-profit-health-clubs-challenge-nonprofit-ymcas-tax-exempt-status/

Collins, J. C. (2001). *Good to great: Why some companies make the leap . . . and others don't*. New York, NY: HarperCollins.

Collins, J. C. (2005). *Good to great and the social sectors: A monograph to accompany Good to Great.* New York, NY: Harper.

Collins, J. C., & Porras, J. L. (1994). *Built to last: Successful habits of visionary companies.* New York, NY: Harper Business.

Commission on Private Philanthropy and Public Needs. (1975). *Giving in America: Toward a stronger voluntary sector.* Washington, DC: Author.

Community Wealth Partners. (n.d.). About us. Retrieved from http://communitywealth.com/about-us/

Community Wealth Ventures (now Community Wealth Partners). (2001). *The community wealth seeker's guide.* Washington, DC: Author.

Community Wealth Ventures (now Community Wealth Partners). (2004). *Evaluating a social enterprise opportunity.* Washington, DC: Author.

Community Wealth Ventures (now Community Wealth Partners). (2010). *Social enterprise: A portrait of the field.* Retrieved from http://communitywealth.com/social-enterprise-a-portrait-of-the-field/

Condon, S. (2012). Susan G. Komen reverses course, will keep funding Planned Parenthood. *CBS News.* Retrieved from http://www.cbsnews.com/8301-503544_162-57371169-503544/susan-g-komen-reverses-course-will-keep-funding-planned-parenthood/

Cone Communications. (n.d.). *2013 Cone Communications impact study: The next cause evolution.* Retrieved from http://www.conecomm.com/stuff/contentmgr/files/0/e3d2eec1e15e858867a5c-2b1a22c4cfb/files/2013_cone_comm_social_impact_study.pdf

Cone Communications. (2010, March 19). Top ten types of cause promotions. Retrieved from http://www.conecomm.com/top-10-types-of-cause-promotions

Connolly, P., & Lukas, C. (2002). *Strengthening nonprofit performance: A funder's guide to capacity building.* Saint Paul, MN: Amherst H. Wilder Foundation & Grantmakers for Effective Organizations.

Coombs, W. T. (2007). Protecting organization reputations during a crisis: The development and application of situational crisis communication theory. *Corporate Reputation Review, 10,* 163–176.

Coombs, W. T. (2011). Crisis management and communications. Retrieved from http://www.instituteforpr.org/crisis-management-and-communications/

Cooney, K., Koushyar, J., Lee, M., & Murray, H. (2014, December 5). Benefit corporation and L3C adoption: A survey. *Stanford Social Innovation Review.* Retrieved from http://www.ssireview.org/blog/entry/benefit_corporation_and_l3c_adoption_a_survey

Cooper, M. (2013a, October 3). New York City Opera files for bankruptcy. *New York Times.* Retrieved from http://www.nytimes.com/2013/10/04/arts/music/new-york-city-opera-files-for-bankruptcy.html

Cooper, M. (2013b, September 26). For City Opera, the talk turns to a shutdown. *New York Times.* Retrieved from http://www.nytimes.com/2013/09/27/arts/music/city-opera-board-says-it-may-enter-bankruptcy.html

Cooper, M. (2014, December 10). Tribute to Julius Rudel aims to aid City Opera. *New York Times.* Retrieved from http://artsbeat.blogs.nytimes.com/2014/12/10/tribute-to-julius-rudel-aims-to-aid-city-opera-revival/?_r=0

Cooper, M. (2015, January 20). Potential buyers of New York City Opera hold a bidding war in court. *New York Times.* Retrieved from http://www.nytimes.com/2015/01/21/nyregion/potential-buyers-of-new-york-city-opera-hold-a-bidding-war-in-court.html?_r=0

Cooper, M., & Pogrebin, R. (2013, October 4). The frenzied last-act effort to save City Opera, *New York Times.* Retrieved from http://www.nytimes.com/2013/10/05/arts/music/the-frenzied-last-act-effort-to-save-city-opera.html

Copilevitz & Canter. (2014). *Working with commercial co-venturers.* Retrieved from http://www.copilevitz-canter.com/working-with-commerical-co-venturers/

Corporation for National and Community Service. (2006, December). *Volunteer growth in America: A review of trends since 1974.* Retrieved from http://www.nationalservice.gov/pdf/06_1203_volunteer_growth.pdf

Corporation for National and Community Service. (2014a). *Social innovation fund.* Retrieved from http://www.nationalservice.gov/programs/social-innovation-fund

Corporation for National and Community Service. (2014b). *The state of volunteering in America, 2014.* Retrieved from http://www.volunteeringinamerica.gov/infographic.cfm

Council for Advancement and Support of Education. (n.d.). International Initiatives. Retrieved from http://www.case.org/About_CASE/International_Initiatives.html?site=desktop

Council for Advancement and Support of Education. (2014, November 20). Council for Advancement and Support of Education Announces New President: Sue Cunningham will join education association. Retrieved from http://www.case.org/About_CASE/Newsroom/Press_Release_Archive/Council_for_Advancement_and_Support_of_Education_Announces_New_President.html

Cravens, J., & Ellis, S. J. (2014). *The last virtual volunteering guidebook: Fully integrating online service into volunteer involvement.* Philadelphia, PA: Energize.

Crutchfield, L. R., & Grant, H. M. (2008). *Forces for good: The six practices of high-impact nonprofits.* San Francisco, CA: Jossey-Bass.

Crutchfield, L. R., & Grant, H. M. (2012). *Forces for good: The six practices of high-impact nonprofits* (2nd ed.). San Francisco, CA: Jossey-Bass.

Curto, V. E., & Fryer, R. G., Jr. (2012). *The potential or urban boarding schools for the poor: Evidence from SEED.* Retrieved from http://scholar.harvard.edu/

fryer/publications/potential-urban-boarding-schools-poor-evidence-seed

Daniels, A. (2014a, April 20). YMCA sheds 'gym' image to focus more on youths and health. *Chronicle of Philanthropy*. Retrieved from http://philanthropy.com/article/YMCA-Sheds-Gym-Image-to/146115/?cid=pt&utm_source=pt&utm_medium=en

Daniels, A. (2014b, April 20). Nonprofit seeks a niche, and revenue, in helping Americans prevent diabetes. *Chronicle of Philanthropy*. Retrieved from http://philanthropy.com/article/Y-Seeks-Revenue-by-Helping/146101

Daniels, A. (2015, January 22). Advocates poised for Capitol Hill battle on donor-advised funds. *Chronicle of Philanthropy, 27*(5), 31–33.

Dansereau, F., Graen, G. B., & Haga, W. (1975). A vertical dyad linkage approach to leadership in formal organizations. *Organizational Behaviour and Human Performance, 13*, 46–78.

Daring to lead 2011: a national study of nonprofit executive leadership. (2011). A Joint Project of CompassPoint Nonprofit Services and the Meyer Foundation. Retrieved from http://daringtolead.org/wp-content/uploads/Daring-to-Lead-2011-Main-Report-online.pdf

Dees, J. G. (1998). Enterprising nonprofits. In *Harvard Business Review on Nonprofits* (pp. 135–166). Boston, MA: Harvard Business School Press. (Reprinted from *Harvard Business Review,* January/February, 1998)

Dees, J. G. (2004). Putting nonprofit business ventures in perspective. In S. Oster, C. Massarsky, & S. Beinhacker (Eds.), *Generating and Sustaining Nonprofit Earned Income*. San Francisco, CA: Jossey-Bass.

Dees, J. G., & Anderson, B. B. (2006). Framing a theory of social entrepreneurship: Building on two schools of practice and thought. In R. Mosher-Williams (Ed.), *Research on social entrepreneurship: Understanding and contributing to an emerging field* (pp. 39–66). [ARNOVA Occasional Paper Series, *1*(3)]

Dees, J. G., Emerson, J., & Economy, P. (2001). *Enterprising nonprofits: A toolkit for social entrepreneurs*. New York, NY: Wiley.

Denhardt, R. B., Denhardt, J. V., & Aristigueta, M. P. (2013). *Managing human behavior in public and nonprofit organizations* (3rd ed.). Thousand Oaks, CA: Sage.

Dixon, J., & Keyes, D. (2013, Winter). The permanent disruption of social media. *Stanford Social Innovation Review*. Retrieved from http://www.ssireview.org/articles/entry/the_permanent_disruption_of_social_media

Dollery, B. E., & Wallis, J. L. (2003). *The political economy of the voluntary sector*. Northampton, MA: Edward Elgar.

Donors Choose. (n.d.). Story. Retrieved from http://www.donorschoose.org/about/story.html#in5years

Donovan, D. (2012, September 30). New United Way USA leader to urge autonomous groups to work together. *Chronicle of Philanthropy*. Retrieved from https://philanthropy.com/article/New-United-Way-USA-Leader/156031

Douglas, J. (1983). *Why charity? The case for a third sector*. Beverly Hills, CA: Sage.

Douglas, J. (1987). Political theories of nonprofit organization. In W. W. Powell (Ed.), *The nonprofit sector: A research handbook* (pp. 43–54). New Haven, CT: Yale University Press.

Driessen, K. (2012, March 16). District opens new permanent-housing complex for homeless women. *Washington Post*. Retrieved from http://www.washingtonpost.com/local/district-opens-first-permanent-housing-complex-for-homeless-women/2012/03/14/gIQAtfLkGS_story.html

Drucker, P. (1990). *Managing the nonprofit organization: Principles and practices*. New York, NY: HarperCollins.

Duke Center for the Advancement of Social Entrepreneurship. (2008). Developing the field of social entrepreneurship. Retrieved from http://entrepreneurship.saddleback.edu/Resources/Social%20Entrepreneurship%20Field%20of%20Social%20Entrepreneurs.pdf

Dunlop, D. (1993). Major gift programs. In M. J. Worth (Ed.), *Educational fund raising: Principles and practice* (pp. 97–116). Washington, DC/Phoenix, AZ: American Council on Education/Oryx Press.

Durand, C., & Cici, K. (2011, Fall/Winter). Four reason why not to use social media . . . and why to use it anyway. *Nonprofit Quarterly*. Retrieved from http://nonprofitquarterly.org/2011/12/20/four-reasons-why-not-to-use-social-media-and-why-to-use-it-anyway/

Durham, S. (2010). *Brandraising: How nonprofits raise visibility and money through smart communications*. San Francisco, CA: Jossey-Bass.

Dym, B., & Hutson, H. (2005). *Leadership in nonprofit organizations*. Thousand Oaks, CA: Sage.

Ebrahim, A., & Rangan, V. K. (2010, July 9). The limits of nonprofit impact: A contingency framework for measuring social performance (Harvard Business School working paper). Retrieved from http://hbswk.hbs.edu/item/6439.html

Echoing Green. (n.d.-a). About us. Retrieved from http://www.echoinggreen.org/about/history

Echoing Green. (n.d.-b). Work on purpose. Retrieved from http://www.echoinggreen.org/work-on-purpose

Edgers, G. (2004, January 25). MFA's Monets: Dicey deal? *Boston Globe*, A1.

Edna McConnell Clark Foundation. (2014). *Grantee portfolio*. Retrieved from http://www.emcf.org/our-grantees/our-grantee-portfolio/youth-villages/overview/

Egger, R. (2002). *Begging for change*. New York, NY: HarperCollins.

Eikenberry, A. M., & Kluver, J. D. (2004, March/April). The marketization of the nonprofit sector: Civil society at risk? *Public Administration Review, 64*(2), 132.

Eisenberg, P. (2007, June 28). Charities should remain nonpolitical. *Chronicle of Philanthropy, 19* (18), 53.

Elliott, S. (2006, June 5). Seeking a distinctive sound for people of a certain age. *New York Times*, C7.

Elliott, J., & Sullivan, L. (2015, June 3). How the Red Cross raised half a billion dollars for Haiti and built six homes. ProPublica. Retrieved from https://www.propublica.org/article/how-the-red-cross-raised-half-a-billion-dollars-for-haiti-and-built-6-homes

Emmons, G., Hanna, J., & Thompson, R. (2012, May 23). Five ways to make your company more innovative (Harvard Business School, Research and Ideas). Retrieved from http://hbswk.hbs.edu/item/6982.html

Environmental Defense Fund. (2014). *Corporate donation policy.* Retrieved from http://www.edf.org/approach/partnerships/corporate-donation-policy

Erikson, E. (1959). *Childhood and society.* New York, NY: Norton.

European Commission. (2014). Social innovation. Retrieved from http://ec.europa.eu/growth/industry/innovation/policy/social/index_en.htm

Evans, M. G. (1970). The effects of supervisory behavior on the path-goal relationship. *Organizational Behavior and Human Performance, 5,* 277–298.

Ex-official at medical charity accused of $1.8-million theft. (2014, November 19). *Chronicle of Philanthropy.* Retrieved from http://philanthropy.com/blogs/philanthropytoday/ex-official-at-medical-charity-accused-of-1-8-million-theft/93573

Explore Endowment Data. (2014, November 16). *Chronicle of Philanthropy.* Retrieved from https://philanthropy.com/interactives/endowments

Facebook's Mark Zuckerberg gives $500 million. (2012, December 19). *Chronicle of Philanthropy.* Retrieved from https://philanthropy.com/article/Facebooks-Mark-Zuckerberg/218313

Fain, P. (2005a, September 2). Board suspends American U. president. *Chronicle of Higher Education, 52*(2), A58.

Fain, P. (2005b, October 21). Trustees at American U. fire president but remain divided over severance. *Chronicle of Higher Education, 52*(9), A36.

Fain, P. (2005c, November 4). Ladner resigns as president of American U. and agrees to $950,000 settlement. *Chronicle of Higher Education, 52*(11), A24.

Fain, P. (2006, June 2). American U.'s chastened trustees approve wide-ranging reforms. *Chronicle of Higher Education, 52*(39), A25.

Fiedler, F. E. (1967). *A theory of leadership effectiveness.* New York, NY: McGraw-Hill.

Field, A. (2012, October 22). Ben & Jerry's, poster child for the B Corp movement, becomes a B Corp. *Forbes.* Retrieved from http://www.forbes.com/sites/annefield/2012/10/22/ben-jerrys-poster-child-for-the-b-corp-movement-becomes-a-b-corp/

Financial Accounting Standards Board. (1993). *Statement of financial accounting standards, no. 116.* Retrieved from http://www.fasb.org/pdf/fas116.pdf

Fine, A. (2011, August 21). It's time to get serious about using social media. *Chronicle of Philanthropy.* Retrieved from http://philanthropy.com/article/Social-Media-Are-No-Longer/128749/

Fiscale, A., & Missoni, E. (2014). General coordination of responses to crisis situations. In E. Missoni & D. Alesani (Eds.), *Management of international institutions and NGOs* (pp. 181–202). New York, NY: Routledge.

Fisher, J. L. (1984). *Power of the presidency.* New York, NY: American Council on Education/Macmillan.

FitzGerald, K. (2013, June 26). Successful mergers: Two CEOs talk shop. (Interview with Schroeder Stribling and Kelly Sweeney McShane). Retrieved from http://meyerfoundation.org/successful-mergers-two-ceos-talk-shop

Flandez, R. (2012a, February 6). Some charities find text-pledging events can bring large donations. *Chronicle of Philanthropy.* Retrieved from http://philanthropy.com/article/Mobile-Philanthropy-Goes-Big/130637/

Flandez, R. (2012b, March 6). Nature conservancy faces flap over fundraising deal to promote swimsuit issue. *Chronicle of Philanthropy.* Retrieved from http://philanthropy.com/article/Swimsuit-Deal-Causes-Flap-at/131084/

Flannery, H., & Harris, R. (2011). *2011 donor Centrics Internet and multichannel giving benchmarking report.* Target Analytics (a Blackbaud Company). Retrieved from https://www.blackbaud.com/files/resources/downloads/WhitePaper_MultiChannelGivingAnalysis.pdf

Folino, L. (2010, February 18). The great leaders series: Ben Cohen and Jerry Greenfield, co-founders of Ben & Jerry's Homemade. *Inc.com.* Retrieved from http://www.inc.com/30years/articles/ben-and-jerry.html

Food Research and Action Center. (n.d.). *School breakfast program: Trends and factors affecting student participation.* Retrieved from http://frac.org/pdf/school_breakfast_trends_and_factors2015.pdf

Food Research and Action Center. (2015, April). *How hungry is America?* Retrieved from http://frac.org/pdf/food_hardship_2014.pdf

Forbes, K .F., & Zampelli, E. M. (2014). Volunteerism: The influences of social, religious, and human capital. *Nonprofit and Voluntary Sector Quarterly, 43*(2), 227–253.

Forrer, J. J., Kee, J. E., & Boyer, E. (2014). *Governing cross-sector collaboration.* San Francisco, CA: Jossey-Bass.

Foster, W., & Bradach, J. (2005, February). Should nonprofits seek profits? *Harvard Business Review, 83*(2), 92–100.

Fox, R. C. (2014). *Doctors Without Borders: Humanitarian quests, impossible dreams of Médecins Sans Frontiéres.* Baltimore, MD: Johns Hopkins University Press.

Fourth Sector Network. (2014). Retrieved from http://www.fourthsector.net/

Frechette, H. (2011, July 11). Aspire CoffeeWorks: A paradigm of social entrepreneurship. *Citizen polity.* Retrieved from http://citizenpolity.com/2011/07/11/aspire-coffee-works-a-paradigm-of-social-entrepreneurship/

Fremont-Smith, M. R., & Cordes, J. (2004). *What the ratings revolution means for charities.* Washington, DC: Urban Institute.

Friedman, T. L. (2006). *The world is flat: The globalized world in the twenty-first century.* London, UK: Penguin Books.

Froelich, K. A. (1999, September). Diversification of revenue strategies: Evolving resource dependence in nonprofit organizations. *Nonprofit and Voluntary Sector Quarterly, 28*(3), 246–268.

Froelich, K., McKee, G., & Rathge, R. (2011). Succession planning in nonprofit organizations. *Nonprofit Management & Leadership, 22*(1), 3–20.

Frumkin, P. (2002). *On being non-profit: A conceptual and policy primer.* Cambridge, MA: Harvard University Press.

Frumkin, P., & Imber, J. B. (2004). *In search of the nonprofit sector.* New Brunswick, NJ/London, UK: Transaction.

Gadsden, C. H. (2002, November 11). The Hershey power play. *Trusts and estates.* Retrieved from http://wealthmanagement.com/asset-protection/hershey-power-play

Gainer, B., & Moyer, M. S. (2005). Marketing for nonprofit managers. In R. D. Herman & Associates (Eds.), *The Jossey-Bass handbook of nonprofit leadership and management* (pp. 277–309). San Francisco, CA: Jossey-Bass.

Galafassi, N. (2013). Latin America. In P. Cagney & B. Ross, *Global fundraising: How the world is changing the rules of philanthropy* (pp. 59–87). Hoboken, NJ: Wiley.

Galaskiewicz, J., & Colman, M. S. (2006). Collaboration between corporations and nonprofit organizations. In W. W. Powell & R. Steinberg (Eds.), *The non-profit sector: A research handbook.* New Haven, CT: Yale University Press.

Gallagher, B. (2005, April 5). *Statement of Brian A. Gallagher, President and CEO United Way of America, April 5, 2005, United States Senate Committee on Finance.* Retrieved from http://www.finance.senate.gov/imo/media/doc/bgtest040505.pdf

Gallagher, L. (2001, August 6). Prairie Home Commercial. *Forbes, 168*(3). Retrieved from http://www.forbes.com/forbes/2001/0806/054.html

Gammal, D. L. (2007, Summer). Before you say "I do." *Stanford Social Innovation Review, 5*(3), 47–51.

Gamwell, F. I. (1984). *Beyond preference: Liberal theories of independent association.* Chicago, IL: University of Chicago Press.

Gazley, B. (2008). Beyond the contract: The scope and nature of informal government-nonprofit partnerships. *Public Administration Review, 68*(1), 141–154.

Gazley, B. (2015). Nonprofit human resources. In R. C. Kearney & J. Coggburn (Eds.), *Public human resource management: Problems and prospects* (6th ed., Chap. 7). Thousand Oaks, CA: CQ Press.

Gazley, B., & Brudney, J. L. (2007). The purpose (and perils) of government-nonprofit partnership, *Nonprofit and Voluntary Sector Quarterly, 36*(3), 389–415.

Gifts that can warp a museum [Editorial]. (2001, May 31). *New York Times.* Retrieved from http://www.nytimes.com/2001/05/31/opinion/gifts-that-can-warp-a-museum.html

Giving USA. (2014). *The annual report on philanthropy for the year 2013.* Chicago, IL: Giving USA Foundation.

Glenn, B. (2007, January 18). Aspire of Illinois CEO. Retrieved from http://www.chicagobusiness.com/article/20070118/NEWS01/200023520/aspire-of-illinois-ceo

GlobalGiving. (2015). Homepage. Retrieved from http://www.globalgiving.org/

Global Impact Investing Network (GIIN). (n.d.). Impact investing. Retrieved from http://www.thegiin.org/impact-investing/

Godfrey, J., & Schneiderman, J. (2013, October 10). Should New York City Opera board be held accountable? *Nonprofit Quarterly, 15*(12). Retrieved from https://nonprofitquarterly.org/governancevoice/23048-should-new-york-city-opera-board-be-held-accountable.html

Gose, B. (2005, January 6). America's charity explosion. *Chronicle of Philanthropy, 17*(6), 6–9.

Gose, B. (2006, October 26). Former financial officer faces charges in museum debt crisis. *Chronicle of Philanthropy, 19*(2), 17. Retrieved from http://philanthropy.com/premium/articles/v19/i02/02006201.htm

Gose, B. (2012, April 19). $1 million settlement in "three cups" scandal offers warning to boards. *Chronicle of Philanthropy, 24*(11), 15.

Grameen America. (n.d.). About us. Retrieved from http://grameenamerica.org/about-us

Grant Thornton. (2012). *2012 National Board governance survey for not-for-profit organizations.* Chicago, IL: Author.

Greene, S. G. (1999, May 20). Trustees ousted in Hawaii. *Chronicle of Philanthropy, 11*(15), 30.

Greene, S. G. (2004, April 15). Hostile takeover or rescue? *Chronicle of Philanthropy, 13*(13), 24–27.

Greenleaf, R. K. (1977). *Servant leadership: A journey into the nature of legitimate power and greatness.* Ramsey, NJ: Paulist Press.

Griswold, J., & Jarvis, W. (2009, July/August). Underwater funds: UPMIFA throws a lifeline to drowning endowments. *Currents.* Retrieved from https://www.case.org/Publications_and_Products/2009/JulyAugust_2009.html

Grønbjerg, K. A., & Salamon, L. M. (2002). Devolution, marketization, and the changing shape of government–nonprofit relations. In L. M. Salamon (Ed.), *The state of nonprofit America* (pp. 447–470). Washington, DC: Brookings Institution.

Grunfeld, D., & Lash, D. (2012, March 18). Komen's crisis came not from politics but from poor management decisions. *Chronicle of Philanthropy.* Retrieved from http://philanthropy.com/article/Don-t-Blame-the-Culture-Wars/131191/

GuideStar. (2013, November). New York City Opera Inc. Retrieved from http://www.guidestar.org/organizations/13-2974347/new-york-city-opera.aspx

GuideStar. (2015). Wecome to charting impact. Retrieved from http://www.guidestar.org/rxg/update-nonprofit-report/charting-impact.aspx?gclid=CLmgwLrL6cECFbHm7AodWcAhw

Guo, C., & Acar, M. (2005, September). Understanding collaboration among nonprofit organizations: Combining resource dependency, institutional, and network perspectives. *Nonprofit and Voluntary Sector Quarterly, 34*(3), 340–353.

Guo, C. & Saxton, G. D. (2014). Tweeting social change: How social media are changing nonprofit advocacy. *Nonprofit and Voluntary Sector Quarterly, 43*(1), 57–79.

Gural, N. (2010, January 22). Hershey loses taste for Cadbury. Forbes.com. Retrieved from http://www.forbes.com/2010/01/22/hershey-cadbury-kraft-markets-equities-offer-withdrawn_print.html

Habitat for Humanity International. (2015). *Habitat for humanity : About*. Retrieved from http://www.habitat.org/how/about_us.aspx

Hager, M. A., & Flack, T. (2004, August). *The pros and cons of financial efficiency standards* (Brief No. 5). Washington, DC/Indianapolis : Urban Institute/Indiana University Center on Philanthropy.

Haider, D. (2007, Summer). Uniting for survival. *Stanford Social Innovation Review, 5*(3), 52–55.

Haiti telethon haul put at $57 million so far. (2010, January 23). NBCNEWS.com. Retrieved from http://today.msnbc.msn.com/id/35023278/ns/today-entertainment/t/haiti-telethon-haul-put-million-so-far/

Hall, H. (2005, January 6). Fund-raising association clarifies stand on fees. *Chronicle of Philanthropy, 17*(6), 47.

Hall, H. (2006, July 20). Nonprofit-marketing experts outline hot trends, discuss challenges. *Chronicle of Philanthropy, 18*(19), 29.

Hall, H. (2007, November 1). Public radio network has a script for success. *Chronicle of Philanthropy, 20*(2).

Hall, J. L. (2010). *Grant management: Funding for public and nonprofit programs*. Sudbury, MA: Jones & Bartlett.

Halloran, T. (2013, September 20). Defining nonprofit political activity through bright lines and safe harbors. *The Hill*. Retrieved from http://thehill.com/blogs/congress-blog/economy-a-budget/323461-defining-nonprofit-political-activity-through-brightl-lines-and-safe-harbors

Hammack, D. C. (1998). *Making the nonprofit sector in the United States*. Bloomington: Indiana University Press.

HandsOn Network. (2010). Volunteers versus paid employees. Retrieved from http://www.handsonnetwork.org/files/resources/TLK_VolunteersVSPaidEmployees_2010_HON.pdf

Handy, F., & Mook, L. (2010). Volunteering and volunteers: Benefit-cost analyses. *Research on Social Work Practice, 21*(4), 412–420.

Hansmann, H. (1987). Economic theories of nonprofit organization. In W. W. Powell (Ed.), *The nonprofit sector: A research handbook* (pp. 27–42). New Haven, CT: Yale University Press.

Harlem Children's Zone. (2014). History. Retrieved from http://hcz.org/about-us/history

Hatry, H. P. (2014). *Transforming performance measurement for the 21st century*. Washington, DC: Urban Institute.

Hauser, J. (2003, June). Organizational lessons for nonprofits. *McKinsey Quarterly, 2003*(2), 52–59. Retrieved from http://dheise.andrews.edu/Content/leadership/comps/3a/4reflection/OrganizationalLessonsForNonprofits.htm

Hayes, C. L. (1998, May 22). Getting serious at Ben & Jerry's; Cherry Garcia and friends trade funky for functional. *New York Times*. Retrieved from http://www.nytimes.com/1998/05/22/business/getting-serious-ben-jerry-s-cherry-garcia-friends-trade-funky-for-functional.html?pagewanted=all&src=pm

Hayes, C. L. (2000, April 13). Ben & Jerry's to Unilever, with attitude. *New York Times*. Retrieved from http://www.nytimes.com/2000/04/13/business/ben-jerry-s-to-unilever-with-attitude.html?pagewanted=all&src=pm

Held, T. (2014, July 13). Charities like Facebook for rallying support but not much for fundraising. *Chronicle of Philanthropy*. Retrieved from https://philanthropy.com/article/Charities-Like-Facebook-for/150511

Herman, R. D. (2005). Conclusion. In R. D. Herman & Associates (Eds.), *The Jossey-Bass handbook of nonprofit leadership and management* (2nd ed., pp. 731–736). San Francisco, CA: Jossey-Bass.

Herman, R. D. (2010). Executive leadership. In D. O. Renz & Associates (Eds.), *The Jossey-Bass handbook of nonprofit leadership and management* (3rd ed., pp. 157–177). San Francisco, CA: Jossey-Bass.

Herman, R. D., & Heimovics, D. (2005). Executive leadership. In R. D. Herman & Associates (Eds.), *The Jossey-Bass handbook of nonprofit leadership and management* (2nd ed., pp. 153–170). San Francisco, CA: Jossey-Bass.

Herman, R. D., & Renz, D. O. (2002). *Nonprofit organizational effectiveness: Practical implications of research on an elusive concept* (Occasional paper). Kansas City: University of Missouri-Kansas City, Henry W. Bloch School of Business and Public Administration.

Herman, R. D., & Renz, D.O. (2008). Advancing nonprofit organizational effectiveness research and theory: Nine theses. *Nonprofit Management and Leadership, 18*(4), 399–415.

Hersey, P., & Blanchard, K. H. (1969). Life-cycle theory of leadership. *Training and Development Journal, 23*, 26–34.

Herzberg, F. (1968). One more time: How do you motivate employees? *Harvard Business Review, 46*, 36–44.

Hessekiel, D. (2013, September 17). Cause marketing coopetition on the rise. *Forbes*. Retrieved from http://www.forbes.com/sites/davidhessekiel/2013/09/17/cause-marketing-coopetition-on-the-rise/

Hessenius, B. (2007). *Hardball lobbying for nonprofits: Real advocacy for nonprofits in the new century*. New York, NY: Palgrave/Macmillan.

History of Transportation Department. (2005). Minneapolis: University of Minnesota Libraries, Kautz Family YMCA Archives. Retrieved from http://special.lib.umn.edu/findaid/html/ymca/yusa0032.phtml

Hochberg, E. (2002, August 8). Business ventures go beyond the bottom line. *Chronicle of Philanthropy, 14*(20), 35.

Hochberg, E., & Wise, A. (2005, March 3). Don't give up on charity-run businesses. *Chronicle of Philanthropy, 17*(10), 49–50.

Hopkins, B. R. (2003). *Legal responsibilities of nonprofit boards*. Washington, DC: BoardSource.

Hopkins, B. R. (2005). *Nonprofit law made easy*. Hoboken, NJ: Wiley.

Hoque, F. (2014, June 4). How to create a culture of innovation. *Fast Company*. Retrieved from http://www.fastcompany.com/3031092/how-to-create-a-culture-of-innovation-in-the-workplace

House, R. J. (1976). A 1976 theory of charismatic leadership. In J. G. Hunt & L. L. Larson (Eds.),

Leadership: The cutting edge (pp. 189–207). Carbondale: Southern Illinois University Press.

Howe, F. (2002). Nonprofit accountability: The board's fiduciary responsibility. In V. Futter (Ed.), *Nonprofit governance and management* (pp. 29–38). Chicago, IL: American Bar Association and American Society of Corporate Secretaries.

Howe, F. (2004). *The nonprofit leadership team: Building the board–executive director relationship.* San Francisco, CA: Wiley.

Hrywna, M. (2007, January 2). Extreme makeover: Girl Scouts shrink councils. *The NonProfit Times.* Retrieved from http://www.the-nonprofittimes.com/article/detail/extreme-makeover-1981

Hudson, M. (2005). *Managing at the leading edge.* San Francisco, CA: Jossey-Bass.

Hudson Institute. (2013). *Index of glocal philanthropy and remittances, 2013.* Washington, DC : Author. Retrieved from http://www.hudson.org/research/9914-2013-index-of-global-philanthropy-and-remittances-with-a-special-report-on-emerging-economies

Huget, J. J. (2010, May 4). Is buying KFC by the bucket a good way to fight breast cancer? *Washington Post.* Retrieved http://www.washingtonpost.com/wp-dyn/content/article/2010/04/30/AR2010043001971.html

Iaboni, R. (2013, October 1). New York City Opera sings the blues over finances, plans to file for bankruptcy. CNN.com. Retrieved from http://www.cnn.com/2013/10/01/us/new-york-city-opera/

Idealist. (2014a). *Volunteer management as a career.* Retrieved from http://www.idealist.org/info/VolunteerMgmt/Career

Idealist. (2014b). *What is volunteer management?* Retrieved from http://www.idealist.org/info/VolunteerMgmt/What

Independent Sector. (2005). *Panel on the Nonprofit Sector: Strengthening transparency, governance, accountability of charitable organizations* (A final report to Congress and the nonprofit sector). Washington, DC: Author.

Independent Sector. (2007). *Principles for good governance and ethical practice: A guide for charities and foundations.* Washington, DC: Author. (See also Panel on the Nonprofit Sector, 2007)

Independent Sector. (2009a). *Facts and figures about charitable organizations.* Retrieved from http://www.independentsector.org/economic_role?s=facts%20and%20figures

Independent Sector. (2012a). *The nonprofit lobbying guide* (2nd ed.). Retrieved from http://www.independentsector.org/lobby_guide?s=Nonprofit%20advocacy%20and%20lobbying

Independent Sector. (2012b). *Scope of the nonprofit sector.* Retrieved from http://www.independentsector.org/scope_of_the_sector

Independent Sector. (2012c). *The sector's economic impact.* Retrieved from http://www.independentsector.org/economic_role

Independent Sector. (2014). *National value of volunteer time.* Retrieved from http://www.independentsector.org/volunteer_time

Independent Sector. (2015a). Lobbying guidelines for public charities. Retrieved from http://www.independentsector.org/lobbying_guidelines_public_charities?s=lobbying%20guidelines%20for%20public%20charities

Independent Sector. (2015b). Political activity of 501(c)(4) tax exempt organizations. Retrieved from https://www.independentsector.org/501c4_organizations

Independent Sector. (2015c). IRS controversy: Scrutiny of tax exempt applications. Retrieved from http://www.independentsector.org/irs_controversy

Independent Sector. (2015d). *Principles for good governance and ethical practice: A guide for charities and foundations.* Washington, DC: Author.

Independent Sector. (2015e). Lobbying guidelines for private foundations. Retrieved from https://www.independentsector.org/lobbying_guidelines_private_foundations

Ingram, R. T. (2003). *Ten basic responsibilities of nonprofit boards.* Washington, DC: National Center for Nonprofit Boards (now BoardSource).

Internal Revenue Service. (n.d.-a). *Exemption requirements—Section 501(c)(3) organizations.* Retrieved from http://www.irs.gov/Charities-&-Non-Profits/Charitable-Organizations/Exemption-Requirements-Section-501(c)(3)-Organizations

Internal Revenue Service. (n.d.-b). *Social welfare organizations.* Retrieved from http://www.irs.gov/Charities-&-Non-Profits/Other-Non-Profits/Social-Welfare-Organizations

Internal Revenue Service. (2005a). *"Substantially related" defined.* Retrieved from http://www.irs.gov/Charities-&-Non-Profits/Substantially-related

Internal Revenue Service. (2005b). *U. museum retailing: UBIT issues.* Retrieved from http://www.irs.gov/pub/irs-tege/eotopicu79.pdf

Internal Revenue Service. (2013, July). *Form 990, Part VI—Governance, management, and disclosure: Frequently asked questions and tips.* Washington, DC: Author.

Internal Revenue Service (2015). «Direct» and «grass roots» lobbying defined. Retrieved from http://www.irs.gov/Charities-&-Non-Profits/Direct--and--Grass-Roots--Lobbying-Defined

Jaffee, H. (2006, April). Let them eat truffles. *Washingtonian, 41*(7), 76–79, 116, 123, 131–133.

James, E. (1987). The nonprofit sector in comparative perspective. In W. W. Powell (Ed.), *The nonprofit sector: A research handbook* (pp. 397–415). New Haven, CT: Yale University Press.

Javits, C. I. (2008). *REDF's current approach to SROI.* San Francisco, CA: REDF.

Jensen, B. (2005, February 17). Housing group fires its founder. *Chronicle of Philanthropy, 17*(9), 26.

Jensen, B. (2006a, September 14). NAACP cleared by federal tax agency. *Chronicle of Philanthropy, 18*(23), 13. Retrieved from http://philanthropy.com/article/NAACP-Cleared-by-Federal-Ta/58506/

Jensen, B. (2006b, September 28). Grants to help charities improve operations are on the decline. *Chronicle of Philanthropy.*

Retrieved from http://philan-thropy.com/article/Grants-to-Help-Charities/57895/

Jensen, B. (2008, September 9). The controversy of charity endorsements of corporate products. *Chronicle of Philanthropy*. Retrieved from https://philanthropy.com/article/The-Controversy-of-Charity/192601

Jewell, J. (2005). New times, new leaders. *Christianity Today, 49*(4), 24.

Johnson, E. M. (2006). *The Pension Protection Act of 2006 and non-profit reforms*. Washington, DC: ASAE and The Center for Association Leadership.

Joslyn, H. (2004, January 8). Young people fuel demand for nonprofit study. *Chronicle of Philanthropy, 16*(6), 6–10. Retrieved from http://philanthropy.com/article/Young-People-Fuel-Demand-for/62104/

KaBOOM! (n.d.). *Play matters: A study of best practices to inform local policy and process in support of children's play*. Washington, DC: Author. Retrieved from http://kaboom.org/docs/documents/pdf/playmatters/Play_Matters_Case_Summaries.pdf

KaBOOM! (2013). Our story. Retrieved from http://kaboom.org/about_kaboom

Kania, J., & Kramer, M. (2011, Winter). Collective Impact. *Stanford Social Innovation Review, 9*(1). Retrieved from http://www.ssireview.org/articles/entry/collective_impact

Kania, J., & Kramer, M. (2013, January 21). Embracing emergence: How collective impact addresses complexity. *Stanford Social Innovation Review*. Retrieved from http://www.ssireview.org/blog/entry/embracing_emergence_how_collective_impact_addresses_complexity

Kania, J., Hanleybrown, F., & Juster, J. S. (2014, Fall). Essential mindset shifts for collective impact. *Stanford Social Innovation Review*. Retrieved from http://www.ssireview.org/articles/entry/essential_mindset_shifts_for_collective_impact

Kaplan, R. S., & Norton, D. (1992). Using the balanced scorecard as a strategic management system. *Harvard Business Review, 70*(1), 71–79.

Karnani, A. (2010, August 23). The case against corporate social responsibility. *Wall Street Journal*. Retrieved from http://www.wsj.com/articles/SB10001424052748703338004575230112664504890

Katz, D., & Kahn, R. L. (1966). *The social psychology of organizations*. New York, NY: Wiley.

Katz, D. (1955). Skills of an effective administrator. *Harvard Business Review, 33*(1), 33–42.

Kearns, K. P. (2000). *Private sector strategies for social sector success*. San Francisco, CA: Jossey-Bass.

Kearns, K. P., Bell, D., Deem, B., & McShane, L. (2014). How nonprofit leaders evaluate funding sources: An exploratory study of nonprofit leaders. *Nonprofit and Voluntary Sector Quarterly 43(1)*, 121–143.

Kee, J. E., & Newcomer, K. E. (2008). *Transforming public and non-profit organizations: Stewardship for leading change*. Vienna, VA: Management Concepts.

Kelly, K. S. (1998). *Effective fund-raising management*. Mahwah, NJ: Erlbaum.

Kennicott, P. (2009, November 4). National Trust's chief retiring. *The Washington Post*, C12.

Kibbe, B. D. (2004). Investing in nonprofit capacity. In Grantmakers for Effective Organizations (Eds.), *Funding effectiveness: Lessons in building nonprofit capacity* (Chap. 1). San Francisco, CA: Wiley.

King, K. T. (2006, April 6). The limits of usefulness. *Chronicle of Philanthropy, 18*(12), 63–65.

Kirkpatrick, K. T. (2007, Summer). Go ahead: Pop the question. *Stanford Social Innovation Review, 5*(3), 3–46.

Klintsov, V., & von Löhneysen, E. (2001). Shall we dance? *McKinsey Quarterly, 2001*(4, Special Ed.), 6–9. Retrieved from https://www.questia.com/library/journal/1G1-80118067/shall-we-dance

Koenig, B. L. (2004). *Going global for the greater good: Succeeding as a nonprofit in the international community*. San Francisco, CA: Jossey-Bass.

Komen gifts plunged in year after planned parenthood flap. (2014, January 6). Retrieved from http://philanthropy.com/blogs/philanthropytoday/komen-gifts-plunged-in-year-after-planned-parenthood-flap/79705

Komen has 'moved past' planned parenthood flap, leader says. (2014, July 21). Retrieved from http://philanthropy.com/blogs/philanthropytoday/komen-has-moved-past-planned-parenthood-flap-leader-says/88265

Koteen, J. (1997). *Strategic management in public and nonprofit organizations* (2nd ed.). Westport, CT: Praeger.

Kotter, J. P. (1996). *Leading change*. Boston, MA: Harvard Business School Press.

Koulish, J. (2013, May 15). Rules governing nonprofits and political activity: A brief overview. Retrieved from http://www.urban.org/urban-wire/rules-governing-non-profits-and-political-activity-brief-overview

Kylander, N., & Stone, C. (2012, Spring). The role of brand in the nonprofit sector. *Stanford Social Innovation Review*. Retrieved from http://www.ssireview.org/articles/entry/the_role_of_brand_in_the_non-profit_sector

LaBarre, P. (2006, November/December). How do you transform a 95-year-old organization? Ask the girls. *The Merrill Lynch Leadership Magazine*, 44–50.

Lampkin, L. M., Winkler, M. K., Kerlin, J., Hatry, H. P., Natenshon, D., Saul, J., . . . & Seshadri, A. (2006). *Building a common outcome framework to measure nonprofit performance*. Washington, DC: Urban Institute. Retrieved from http://www.urban.org/sites/default/files/alfresco/publication-pdfs/411404-Building-a-Common-Outcome-Framework-To-Measure-Nonprofit-Performance.PDF

La Piana, D. (2008). *The nonprofit strategy revolution: Real-time strategic planning in a rapid-response world*. Saint Paul, MN: Fieldstone Alliance.

La Piana, D. (2010, Spring). Merging wisely. *Stanford Social Innovation Review, 8*(2), 28–33.

La Piana Consulting. (2014). The Partnership Matrix. Retrieved from http://www.lapiana.org/insights-for-the-sector/insights/collaboration-and-strategic-restructuring/partnership-matrix.aspx

Larkin, E. D. (2002, November 28). A dangerous precedent for donors.

Chronicle of Philanthropy, 15(4). Retrieved from http://www.danlarkinlaw.com/backend/files/A%20Dangerous%20Precedent%20For%20Donors.doc

Lee, J. (2009, May 6). *What is the social innovation fund?* Retrieved from http://www.whitehouse.gov/blog/what-is-the-social-innovation-fund/

Lee, M. (2010). The role of the YMCA in the origins of U.S. nonprofit management education. *Nonprofit Management and Leadership, 20*(3), 277–293.

Lee, Y., & Wilkins, V. M. (2011). More similarities or more differences? Comparing public and nonprofit managers' job motivations. *Public Administration Review, 71*(1), 45–56.

Leonard, R. W. (2013). Nonprofit motivation behavior and satisfaction. *Journal of Business and Behavioral Sciences, 25*(1), 81–93.

Letson, P. (2010, July 11). After helping Haiti at its worst, a need for economic development grows clearer. *Chronicle of Philanthropy.* Retrieved from http://www.acdivoca.org/site/ID/news-Haiti-six-months-later-Chronicle-of-Philanthropy/

Letts, C. W., Ryan, W., & Grossman, A. (1997, March/April). Virtuous capital: What foundations can learn from venture capitalists. *Harvard Business Review, 75*(2), 36–44.

Letts, C. W., Ryan, W. P., & Grossman, A. (1999a). *High performance nonprofit organizations: Managing upstream for greater impact.* New York, NY: Wiley.

Letts, C. W., Ryan, W. P., & Grossman, A. (1999b). Virtuous capital: What foundations can learn from venture capitalists. In *Harvard Business Review on Nonprofits* (pp. 91–110). Boston, MA: Harvard Business School Press. (Reprinted from *Harvard Business Review,* March/April, 1997).

Levine, H., & Zahradnik, A. (2012). Online media, market orientation, and financial performance in nonprofits. *Journal of Nonprofit & Public Sector Marketing, 24*(1), 26–42.

Leviner, N., Crutchfield, L. R., & Wells, D. (2006). Understanding the impact of social entrepreneurs: Ashoka's answer to the challenge of measuring effectiveness. *Research on Social Entrepreneurship* [ARNOVA Occasional Paper Series, *1*(3), 89–104]. Indianapolis, IN: Association for Research on Nonprofit Organizations and Voluntary Action. Retrieved from http://www.ashoka.org/printroom

Lewis, N. (2002, February 21). Controversy over donor's role causes Smithsonian to lose $36.5 million. *Chronicle of Philanthropy, 14*(9), 16.

Levy, R. (2008). *Yours for the asking.* Hoboken, NJ: Wiley.

Libby, P., & Associates (2012). *The lobbying strategy handbook.* Thousand Oaks, CA: Sage.

Light, P. C. (2000). *Making nonprofits work: A report on the tides of nonprofit management reform.* Washington, DC: Brookings Institution.

Light, P. C. (2002). *Pathways to nonprofit excellence.* Washington, DC: Brookings Institution.

Light, P. C. (2004a, Spring). Capacity building and the national infrastructure to support it. *Nonprofit Quarterly,* 36–41.

Light, P. C. (2004b). *Sustaining nonprofit performance: The case for capacity building and the evidence to support it.* Washington, DC: Brookings Institution.

Light, P. C. (2011, May 15). Social entrepreneurs are visionaries—but not wizards. *Chronicle of Philanthropy.* Retrieved from http://philanthropy.com/article/Social-Entrepreneurs-Aren-t/127504/

Likert, R. (1967). *The human organization.* New York, NY: McGraw-Hill.

Liket, K. C., & Maas, K. (2015). Nonprofit organizational effectiveness: Analysis of best practices. *Nonprofit and Voluntary Sector Quarterly, 44*(2), 268–296.

Lilly Family School of Philanthropy at Indiana University. (2014). *Giving USA: The annual report on philanthropy for the year 2013.* Glenview, IL: Giving USA Foundation.

Lipke, D. J. (2000, September). Fountain of youth: AARP woos reluctant boomers with a high-priced makeover. *American Demographics, 22*(9), 37–39.

Lipman, H. (2006, August 17). A record fund-raising feat. *Chronicle of Philanthropy, 18*(21), 2. Retrieved from http://www.philanthropy.com/premium/articles/v18/i21/21002201.htm

Lipman, H., & Williams, G. (2002, August 8). D.C. United Way's troubles cause concern elsewhere. *Chronicle of Philanthropy, 14*(20), 30.

Locke, E. A. (2000). Motivation by goal setting. In R. T. Golembiewski (Ed.), *Handbook of organizational behavior* (2nd ed., pp. 43–56). New York, NY: Marcel Dekker.

Lohmann, R. A. (1992). *The commons.* San Francisco, CA: Jossey-Bass.

Lubell, S. (December, 2005). Katrina and heritage: Richard Moe, president of the National Trust for Historic Preservation. *Architectural Record, 193*(12), 32.

Lyons, T.S., Townsend, J., Sullivan, A.M., & Drago, T. (2010, February). Social enterprise's expanding position in the nonprofit landscape. Retrieved from http://www.nesc.org/download/social-enterprises-expanding-position-in-the-nonprofit-landscape.pdf

MacLaughlin, S. (2011, December, 27). How much money is raised through online giving? *Np Engage* [Blog, published by Blackbaud]. Retrieved from http://www.nptrends.com/nonprofit-trends/how-much-money-is-raised-through-online-giving.htm

MacMillan, I. C. (1983). Competitive strategies for nonprofit organizations. *Advances in Strategic Management, 1,* 61–82.

Maddox, D. (1999). *Budgeting for not-for-profit organizations.* Hoboken, NJ: Wiley.

Make-a-Wish. (2015). About us. Retrieved from http://wish.org/about-us/our-story/local-and-global-structure

Maloney, L. (2013, September 29). Do you think the fat lady has really sung? *The Wall Street Journal.* Retrieved from http://online.wsj.com/news/articles/SB10001424052702304373104579105721040672260?mg=reno64-wsj&url=http%3A%2F%2Fonline.wsj.com%2Farticle%2FSB10001424052702304373104579105721040672260.html

Mangan, K. S. (1999, November 12). Stanford's health system ends merger with University of California at San Francisco. *Chronicle of Higher Education, 46*(12), A43.

Martin, R. L., & Osberg, S. (2007, Spring). Social entrepreneurship: The case for definition. *Stanford Social Innovation Review,* 28–39.

Maryland State Department of Education. (n.d.). Meals for Achievement. Retrieved from http://www.marylandpublicschools.org/MSDE/programs/schoolnutrition/meals_achieve.htm

Maryland Nonprofits. (2014). *Standards for excellence.* Retrieved from http://www.marylandnonprofits.org/NonprofitResources/StandardsforExcellence/The-StandardsforExcellenceCode.aspx

Maslow, A. H. (1954). *Motivation and personality.* New York, NY: Harper.

Mattocks, R. (2008). *Zone of insolvency: How nonprofits avoid hidden liabilities and build financial strength.* Hoboken, NJ: Wiley.

MAXIMUS. (2014). Our philosophy. Retrieved from http://maximus.com/our-philosophy

McCambridge, R. (2011, February 18). Acting human pays off in $$$ in wake of rogue beer tweet. *Nonprofit Quarterly.* Retrieved from https://nonprofitquarterly.org/index.php?option=com_content&view=article&id=9791:acting-human-pays-off-in--in-wake-of-rogue-beer-tweet&catid=155:nonprofit-newswire&Itemid=986

McCambridge, R. (2012, January 11). Two years after Haiti's earthquake, the U.S. has delivered on only 30% of its pledge. *Nonprofit Quarterly.* Retrieved from http://www.nonprofitquarterly.org/philanthropy/19041-two-years-after-haitis-earthquake-the-us-has-delivered-on-only-30-of-its-pledge.html

McCausland, C. (2008). Planting a SEED in Baltimore. *Baltimore Magazine.* Retrieved from http://www.baltimoremagazine.net/old-site/this-month/2008/07/planting-a-seed-in-baltimore

McClelland, D. C. (1961). *The achieving society.* New York, NY: Free Press.

McCormick, D. H. (2001). *Nonprofit mergers: The power of successful partnerships.* Gaithersburg, MD: Aspen.

McCracken, J. (2009, November 27). Hershey Trust seeks Cadbury-bid blessing. WSJ.com (*Wall Street Journal* online). Retrieved from http://online.wsj.com/article/SB10001424052748704499880457455760962471292.html

McCurley, S. (2005). Keeping the community involved: Recruiting and retaining volunteers. In R. D. Herman & Associates (Eds.), *The Jossey-Bass handbook of nonprofit leadership and management* (2nd ed., pp. 587–622). San Francisco, CA: Jossey-Bass.

McCurley, S., & Lynch, R. (2006). *Volunteer management: Mobilizing all the resources in the community* (2nd ed.). Kemptville, ON, Canada: Johnstone Training and Consultation.

McDill, V. (2006, August). Preventing cultural catastrophe. *OAH Newsletter* (Organization of American Historians), p. 7.

McGinnis, J. (2011). The young and the restless: Generation Y in the nonprofit workforce. *Public Administration Quarterly, 35*(3), 342–362.

McGregor, D. (1960). *The human side of enterprise.* New York, NY: McGraw-Hill.

McKeever, B.S., & Pettijohn, S.L. (2014). *The nonprofit sector in brief 2014.* Washington, DC: Urban Institute. Retrieved from http://www.urban.org/UploadedPDF/413277-Nonprofit-Sector-in-Brief-2014.pdf

McKinsey & Company. (2001). *Effective capacity building in nonprofit organizations.* Washington, DC: Venture Philanthropy Partners. Retrieved from http://www.vppartners.org/sites/default/files/reports/full_rpt.pdf

McKinsey & Company. (2013). The organizational capacity assessment tool (OCAT): 2.0. Retrieved from http://mckinseyonsociety.com/ocat./

McLaughlin, T. A. (2010). *Nonprofit mergers and alliances* (2nd ed.). Hoboken, NJ: Wiley.

McLaughlin, J. A., & Jordan, G. B. (2010). *Using logic models.* In J. S. Wholey, H. P. Hatry, & K. E. Newcomer (Eds.), *Handbook of practical program evaluation* (3rd ed., pp. 55–80). San Francisco, CA: Jossey-Bass.

McMillan, E. J. (2003a). *Not-for-profit accounting, tax, and reporting requirements.* Hoboken, NJ: Wiley.

McMillan, E. J. (2003b). *Not-for-profit budgeting and financial management.* Hoboken, NJ: Wiley.

Médecins Sans Frontières. (2005, February 9). *MSF Greece reintegrated into the MSF international movement.* Retrieved from http://www.msf.org/article/msf-greece-reintegrated-msf-international-movement

Médecins Sans Frontières. (2011, July 3). *MSF reforms its highest international governance Structures* [Press release]. Retrieved from http://www.doctorswithoutborders.org/news-stories/press-release/msf-reforms-its-highest-international-governance-structures

Médecins Sans Frontières. (2013). *International activity report 2013—The year in review.* Retrieved from http://www.msf.org/international-activity-report-2013-year-review

Médecins Sans Frontières (2015). The MSF movement. Retrieved from http://www.msf.org/msf-movement

Memmott, M. (2012, March 9). *NPR CEO Vivian Schiller resigns after board decides she should go.* Retrieved from http://www.npr.org/blogs/thetwo-way/2011/03/10/134388981/npr-ceo-vivian-schiller-resigns

Mendel, S.C. (2014, winter). A field of its own. *Stanford Social Innovation Review, 12*(1), 61–62.

Menon, U., & Tiwari, A. (2013). India. In P. Cagney & B. Ross (2013), *Global fundraising: How the world is changing the rules of philanthropy* (pp. 267–289). Hoboken, NJ: Wiley.

Metropolis Coffee Website. Retrieved from https://www.metropoliscoffee.com/

Metropolitan Opera Association 2011 Form 990. Retrieved from http://www.guidestar.org/FinDocuments/2011/131/624/2011-131624087-08604420-9.pdf

Meyer, M. W. (2002). *Rethinking performance measures: Beyond the balanced scorecard*. Cambridge, UK: Cambridge University Press.

Mildenberg, D. (2013, December 12). Private toll-road investors get low-risk deals from states. *Bloomberg Business News*. Retrieved from http://www.bloomberg.com/bw/articles/2013-12-12/private-toll-road-investors-get-low-risk-deals-from-states

Miller, J. P. (1998, March 24). Public radio outlet reaps $120 million for direct marketer. *Wall Street Journal*, B9.

Miller, L. K., & Fielding, L. W. (1995, February 1). The battle between the for-profit health club and the "commercial" YMCA. *Journal of Sport and Social Issues, 19*(1), 76–107.

Milnes, S. E. (2015, February 2). Should New York City Opera just stay dead? *Daily Beast*. Retrieved from http://www.thedailybeast.com/articles/2015/02/02/should-new-york-city-opera-just-stay-dead.html#

Milward, H. B., & Provan, K. G. (2012). A manager's guide to choosing and using collaborative networks. In J. S. Ott & L. A. Dicke (Eds.), *Understanding nonprofit organizations* (2nd ed., Ch. 19). Boulder, CO: Westview Press.

Milway, K. S., Orozco, M., & Botero, C. (2014, March 6). Why nonprofit mergers continue to lag. Retrieved from http://www.bridgespan.org/Publications-and-Tools/Strategy-Development/Why-Nonprofit-Mergers-Continue-to-Lag.aspx

Minkoff, D. C., & Powell, W. W. (2006). Nonprofit mission: Constancy, responsiveness, or deflection? In W. W. Powell & R. Steinberg (Eds.), *The non-profit sector: A research handbook* (2nd ed., pp. 591–611). New Haven, CT: Yale University Press.

Minor, E. (2005, February 3). Habitat for Humanity volunteers urge reinstatement of founder and president. *Associated Press*. Retrieved from http://legacy.utsandiego.com/news/nation/20050203-0124-habitatfounder.html

Minzner, A., Klerman, J. A., Markovitz, C. E., & Fink, B. (2014). The impact of capacity-building programs on nonprofits: A random assignment evaluation. *Nonprofit and Voluntary Sector Quarterly, 43*(3) 547–569.

Mirabella, R. M. (2007, December). University-based educational programs in nonprofit management and philanthropic studies: A 10-year review and projections of future trends. *Nonprofit and Voluntary Sector Quarterly, 36*(4), Supplement, 11S–27S.

Mirabella, R. M., & Young, D. R. (2012, Fall). The development of education for social entrepreneurship and nonprofit management: Diverging or converging paths? *Nonprofit Management and Leadership, 23*(1), 43–56.

Miriam's Kitchen. (n.d.). Miriam's Kitchen. Retrieved from http://www.guidestar.org/organizations/52-1331552/miriams-kitchen.aspx

Missoni, E. (2014a). International institutions: Classification and main characteristics. In E. Missoni & D. Alesani (Eds.). *Management of international institutions and NGOs: Frameworks, practices, and challenges* (pp. 13–48). New York, NY: Routledge.

Missoni, E. (2014b). International non-governmental organizations: Definitions, classification, and relation with the UN system. In E. Missoni & D. Alesani (Eds.), *Management of international institutions and NGOs: Frameworks, practices, and challenges* (pp. 49–76). New York, NY: Routledge.

Missoni, E. (2014c). Transnational hybrid organizations: Global public-private partnerships and networks. In E. Missoni & D. Alesani (Eds.). *Management of international institutions and NGOs: Frameworks, practices, and challenges* (pp. 77–102). New York, NY: Routledge.

Mitchell, G. E. (2012, February). The construct of organizational effectiveness: Perspectives from leaders of international nonprofits in the United States. *Nonprofit and Voluntary Sector Quarterly, 42*(2), 324–345.

Montgomery, D. (2012a, December 11). After months of turmoil, Corcoran to keep its home. *Washington Post*, A1.

Montgomery, D. (2012b, July 20). Corcoran gallery: Why don't donors give? *Washington Post*. Retrieved from https://www.washingtonpost.com/entertainment/museums/corcoran-gallery-why-dont-donors-give/2012/07/19/gJQAJkNGyW_story.html

Montgomery, D. (2013a, March 5). Wayne Reynolds, former Ford's Theatre chair, pitches to save the Corcoran. *Washington Post*. Retrieved from https://www.washingtonpost.com/entertainment/museums/wayne-reynolds-former-fords-theatre-chair-pitches-to-save-corcoran-gallery/2013/03/05/e4937706-85a5-11e2-999e-5f8e0410cb9d_story.html

Montgomery, D. (2013b, April 3). Corcoran, University of Maryland agree to explore partnership. *Washington Post*. Retrieved from https://www.washingtonpost.com/entertainment/museums/corcoran-university-of-maryland-agree-to-explore-partnership/2013/04/03/b2fb57d6-9c6b-11e2-9bda-edd1a7fb557d_story.html

Montgomery, D. (2014, February 19). Corcoran Gallery of Art and college agrees to takeover by the National Gallery of Art, GWU. *Washington Post*. Retrieved from http://www.washingtonpost.com/entertainment/museums/corcoran-gallery-of-art-and-college-to-be-taken-over-by-the-national-gallery-of-art-and-george-washington-university/2014/02/19/a236132e-9994-11e3-b88d-f36c07223d88_story.html

Montgomery, D., & Judkis, M. (2014, August 18). Judge approves Corcoran Gallery of Art plan to partner with National Gallery, GWU. *Washington Post*. Retrieved from http://www.washingtonpost.com/lifestyle/style/judge-approves-corcoran-gallery-of-art-plan-to-partner-with-national-gallery-gwu/2014/08/18/18eefdbc-2326-11e4-8593-da634b334390_story.html

More than food: Bill Shore's vision of sharing strength to fight hunger. (1998, Winter). Penn Arts & Sciences. Retrieved from http://www.sas.upenn.edu/sasalum/newsltr/winter98/shore.html

Morino, M. (2010, January). "Social outcomes": Missing the forest for the trees? *VPP News*. Retrieved from http://www.vppartners.org/learning/enews/archive/january-2010

Morino, M. (2011). *Leap of reason*. Washington, DC: Venture Philanthropy Partners.

Mortenson, Greg. (2011, April 14). Response to 60 Minutes. Retrieved from http://www.cbsnews.com/htdocs/pdf/MORTENSONSTATEMENT.PDF

Moyers, R. L. (2011). *Daring to lead 2011* [Brief 3: The board paradox]. CompassPoint and the Meyer Foundation. Retrieved from http://daringtolead.org/wp-content/uploads/Daring-Brief-3-080511.pdf

Moyers, R. L. (2012, February 27). Hull House collapse is a cautionary tale for boards and executives. *Chronicle of Philanthropy*. Retrieved from http://philanthropy.com/blogs/against-the-grain/hull-house-collapse-is-a-wake-up-call-for-boards-and-executives/28045

Moyers, R. L. (2013). *The nonprofit chief executive's ten basic responsibilities (2nd ed.)*. Washington, DC: BoardSource.

Muchilwa, M. (2013). Africa. In P. Cagney & B. Ross (2013), *Global fundraising: How the world is changing the rules of philanthropy* (pp. 179–222). Hoboken, NJ: Wiley.

Mullins, L. (2012, December). Crisis at the Corcoran. *Washingtonian, 48*(3), 64–71.

Murray, V. (2010). Evaluating the effectiveness of nonprofit organizations. In D. O. Renz & Associates (Eds.), *The Jossey-Bass handbook of nonprofit leadership and management* (3rd ed., pp. 431–460). San Francisco, CA: Jossey-Bass.

Museums and money [Editorial]. (2001, May 31). *The Washington Post*, A24.

Nanus, B., & Dobbs, S. M. (1999). *Leaders who make a difference: Essential strategies for meeting the nonprofit challenge*. San Francisco, CA: Jossey-Bass.

National Center for Charitable Statistics. (n.d.). Quick facts about nonprofits. Retrieved from http://nccs.urban.org/statistics/quickfacts.cfm

National Council for Public-Private Partnerships. (2012). Retrieved from http://www.ncppp.org/howpart/index.shtml

National Geographic. (n.d.). *National Geographic, NBC, and Fox Entertainment Group announce worldwide venture to expand the National Geographic Channel*. Retrieved from http://www.prnewswire.com/news-releases/national-geographic-nbc-and-fox-entertainment-group-announce-worldwide-venture-to-expand-the-national-geographic-channel-74397542.html

National Public Radio. (2013, October 7). The fat lady sings for New York City Opera. Retrieved from http://www.npr.org/templates/story/story.php?storyId=230126261

National Trust for Historic Preservation. (2008). *2008 annual report*. Washington, DC: Author.

National Trust for Historic Preservation. (2013). *2013 annual report*. Washington, DC: Author.

The nation's attic: Secret contracts, soaring salaries—they don't belong at the Smithsonian [Editorial]. (2006, April 24). *The Washington Post*, A16.

Nee, E., & Jolin, M. (2012, Fall). Roundtable on collective impact. *Stanford Social Innovation Review*. Retrieved from http://www.ssireview.org/articles/entry/roundtable_on_collective_impact

Neibauer, M. (2012, March 15). N Street Village moving homeless women into new apartments. *Washington Business Journal*. Retrieved from http://www.bizjournals.com/washington/blog/2012/03/n-street-village-moving-homeless-women.html?page=all

Nelson, L. A. (2012, June 26). Missing the mark on gainful. *Inside Higher Education*. Retrieved from http://www.insidehighered.com/news/2012/06/26/education-department-releases-data-gainful-employment-rule

Nelson, R. A., Kanso, A. M., & Levitt, S. R. (2007). Integrating public service and marketing differentiation: An analysis of the American Express Corporation's "Charge Against Hunger" promotion program. *Service Business, 1*(4), 275–293.

Network for Good. (2014). *The 2014 online fundfaising survival guide*. Retrieved from http://www.fundraising123.org/files/2014%20Online%20Fundraising%20Survival%20Guide%20--%20March.pdf

Newcomer, K. E., Hatry, H. P., & Wholey, J. S. (2010). Planning and designing useful evaluations. In J. S. Wholey, H. P. Hatry, & K. E. Newcomer (Eds.), *Handbook of practical program evaluation* (3rd ed., pp. 5–29). San Francisco, CA: Jossey-Bass.

New Hope Housing. (2014). Strategic plan: New Hope Housing Strategic Plan 2011–2016. Retrieved from http://www.newhopehousing.org/about/strategic-plan/

Newman, A. A. (2012, July 18). In AARP's view, advertisers need to focus. *New York Times*. Retrieved from http://www.nytimes.com/2012/07/19/business/media/aarp-campaign-tries-to-persuade-advertisers.html?_r=0

New York City Opera. (2010, March 9). 20th-century opera takes center stage in New York City Opera's 2010–2011 season. Retrieved from http://pressroom.nycopera.com/pr/nycopera/news/20th-century-opera-takes-center-154809.aspx

New York City Opera. (2013). The people's opera: New York City Opera's 2013–2014 season. Retrieved from http://www.kickstarter.com/projects/1551842735/the-peoples-opera-new-york-city-operas-2013-2014-s

New York City Opera 2009 Form 990. Retrieved from http://www.guidestar.org/FinDocuments/2010/132/974/2010-132974347-07353053-9.pdf

New York Philharmonic 2010 Form 990. Retrieved from http://www.guidestar.org/FinDocuments/2011/132/974/2011-132974347-0856fa0f-9.pdf

New York Times. (2010, December 10). Geoffrey Canada. Retrieved from http://topics.nytimes.com/topics/reference/timestopics/people/c/geoffrey_canada/index.html

Nilsson, W., & Paddock, T. (2014, Winter). Social innovation from the inside out. *Stanford Social Innovation Review, 12*(1), 46–52.

Nobbie, P. D., & Brudney, J. L. (2003, December). Testing the implementation, board performance, and organizational effectiveness of the policy governance model in nonprofit boards of directors. *Nonprofit and Voluntary Sector Quarterly, 32*(4), 571–595.

Nolo. (2014). Sexual orientation discrimination: Your rights. Retrieved from http://www.nolo.com/legal-encyclopedia/sexual-orientation-discrimination-rights-29541.html

Nonprofit Integrity Act, SB 1262. (2004).

Norris-Tirrell, D., & Clay, J. A. (Eds.). (2010). *Strategic collaboration in public and nonprofit administration.* Boca Raton, FL: CRC Press.

NPR State Impact. (2012, June 26). Paving the way for Ohio's first public boarding school. Retrieved from http://stateimpact.npr.org/ohio/2012/06/26/paving-the-way-for-ohios-first-public-boarding-school/

The nonprofit sector in brief. (2013). Washington, DC: Urban Institute. Retrieved from http://www.urban.org/uploadedpdf/412923-the-nonprofit-sector-in-brief.pdf

Northouse, P. G. (2013). *Leadership: Theory and practice.* Thousand Oaks, CA: Sage.

N Street Village. (n.d.). About us. Retrieved from http://www.nstreetvillage.org/about/

N Street Village. (2011, November 2). N Street Village wins board leadership award [press release]. Retrieved from http://www.nstreetvillage.org/news/36/

N Street Village (2014a). Keeping our promise: The 40th anniversary capital campaign for N Street Village [brochure]. Washington, DC: N Street Village.

N Street Village. (2014b). *Annual Report July 1, 2012–June 30, 2013.* Retrieved from http://www.nstreetvillage.org/_attachments/docs/form990%20fy13%20n%20street%20village.pdf

Ogden, T. (2008, July 21). Interview: United Way of America CEO Brian Gallagher. *Philanthropy Action.* Retrieved from http://philanthropyaction.com/articles/interview_united_way_of_america_ceo_brian_gallagher/

O'Neil, M. (2014, November 16). An unexpected online success offers a blueprint for other nonprofits. *Chronicle of Philanthropy.* Retrieved from http://philanthropy.com/article/An-Unexpected-Online-Success/150023/

O'Neil, M. (2015, September 28). $3-trillion U.N. development plan sets ambitious agenda for nonprofits. *Chronicle of Philanthropy.*

Retrieved from https://philanthropy.com/article/3-Trillion-UN-Development/233451?cid=pt&utm_source=pt&utm_medium=en

O'Neill, M. (2002). *Nonprofit nation: A new look at the third America.* San Francisco, CA: Jossey-Bass.

O'Neill, M. (2007, December). The future of nonprofit management education. *Nonprofit and Voluntary Sector Quarterly, 36*(4), Supplement, 169S–176S.

Oostlander, J., Güntert, S.T., van Schie, S., & Wehner, T. (2014). Leadership and volunteer motivation: A study using self-determination theory. *Nonprofit and Voluntary Sector Quarterly, 43*(5), 869–889.

Oster, S. M. (1995). *Strategic management for nonprofit organizations.* New York, NY: Oxford University Press.

Oster, S. M., Massarsky, C. W., & Beinhacker, S. L. (Eds.). (2004). *Generating and sustaining nonprofit earned income.* San Francisco, CA: Jossey-Bass.

Ostrower, F., & Stone, M. M. (2010, September). Moving governance research forward: A contingency-based framework and data application. *Nonprofit and Voluntary Sector Quarterly, 39*(5), 901–924.

Ott, J. S. (2012). Perspectives on organizational governance: Some effects on government-nonprofit relations. In J. S. Ott & L. A. Dicke (Eds.), *The nature of the nonprofit sector* (2nd ed., 249–256). Boulder, CO: Westview Press.

Ott, J. S., & Dicke, L. A. (Eds.). (2012). *The nature of the nonprofit sector* (2nd ed.). Boulder, CO: Westview Press.

Overhead Myth. (2013). Letter to the donors of America. Retrieved from http://overheadmyth.com/letter-to-the-donors-of-america/

Page, A., & Katz, R. A. (2012, Fall). The truth about Ben & Jerry's. *Stanford Social Innovation Review, 10*(4), 39–43.

Pallotta, D. (2010). *Uncharitable: How restraints on nonprofits undermine their potential.* Lebanon, NH: Tufts University Press.

Pallotta, D. (2013). The way we think about charity is dead wrong (TED Talk). Retrieved from http://www.ted.com/talks/dan_pallotta_

the_way_we_think_about_charity_is_dead_wrong?language=en

Panel on the Nonprofit Sector. (2005). *Strengthening transparency governance accountability of charitable organizations: Final report to Congress and the nonprofit sector.* Washington, DC: Independent Sector. Retrieved from http://www.nonprofitpanel.org/Report/final/Panel_Final_Report.pdf

Panel on the Nonprofit Sector. (2007). *Principles for good governance and ethical practice: A guide for charities and foundations.* Washington, DC: Independent Sector.

Panepento, P. (2012, February 1). Social media fuel debate as big charity cuts off Planned Parenthood aid. *Chronicle of Philanthropy.* Retrieved from http://philanthropy.com/blogs/social-philanthropy/social-media-fuel-debate-as-a-big-charity-cuts-off-planned-parenthood-aid/29976

Paton, R. (2003). *Managing and measuring social enterprises.* Thousand Oaks, CA: Sage.

Payton, R. L. (1988). *Philanthropy: Voluntary action for the public good.* New York, NY: Macmillan.

Pekkanen, R. J., & Smith, S. R. (2014). Nonprofit advocacy: Definitions and concepts. In R. J. Pekkanen, S. R. Smith, & Y. Tsujinaka (Eds.), *Nonprofits and advocacy: Engaging community and government in an era of retrenchment* (pp. 1–20). Baltimore, MD: Johns Hopkins University Press.

Peloza, J., & Steel, P. (2005). The price elasticities of charitable contributions: A meta-analysis. *Journal of Public Policy & Marketing, 24,* 260–272.

Peng, S., Pandey, S. K., & Pandey, S. (2015, Fenruary 16). Is there a nonprofit advantage? Examining the impact of institutional context on individual–organizational value congruence. *Public Administration Review.* Retrieved from http://onlinelibrary.wiley.com/doi/10.1111/puar.12357/pdf

Penn, S. (2015, June 9). Our cross to bear. *Huffington Post.* Retrieved from http://www.huffingtonpost.com/sean-penn/haiti-red-cross_b_7548084.html

Peregrine, M. (2012, February 19). Steps charity leaders can take to avoid "getting Komened." *Chronicle of Philanthropy*. Retrieved from http://philanthropy.com/article/article-content/130829/

PerformWell. (n.d.). Helping practitioners deliver more effective programs. Retrieved from http://nccsdataweb.urban.org/kbfiles/1772/PerformWell_V2.pdf

Perry, S. (2009, May 8). Obama proposes $10 million to expand Harlem Children Zone's approach. *Chronicle of Philanthropy*. Retrieved from http://philanthropy.com/blogs/government-and-politics/obama-proposes-10-million-to-expand-harlem-childrens-zone-approach/11008

Perry, S. (2010, February 7). Supreme Court ruling raises concern for nonprofit advocacy groups. *Chronicle of Philanthropy*. Retrieved from http://philanthropy.com/article/Supreme-Court-Ruling-Raises/63911/

Perry, S. (2011, December 16). Nonprofits see mixed results in federal budget deal. *Chronicle of Philanthropy*. Retrieved from http://philanthropy.com/article/Nonprofits-See-Mixed-Results/130114/

Perry, S. (2012a, August 23). Nonprofit inquiry reignites debate on fundraising costs. *Chronicle of Philanthropy, 24*(16), 1.

Perry, S. (2012b, August 23). Senate inquiry raises questions about a fundraising company's approach. *Chronicle of Philanthropy, 24*(16), A8.

Perry, S. (2014, April 7). Despite attempts to boost volunteerism, rate hits a new low. *Chronicle of Philanthropy*. Retrieved from htpp://www.philanthropy.com

Perry, S., & Wilhelm, I. (2006, July 20). Contribution to history. *Chronicle of Philanthropy, 18*(19), 6. Retrieved from http://www.philanthropy.com/premium/articles/v18/i19/19000601.htm

Peters, T. J., & Waterman, R. H. (1982). *In search of excellence*. New York, NY: Harper & Row.

Pettijohn, S. L. (2013a). *The nonprofit sector in brief: Public charities, giving, and volunteering, 2013*. Retrieved from http://www.urban.org/uploadedpdf/412923-the-nonprofit-sector-in-brief.pdf

Pettijohn, S. L. (2013b). Federal government contracts and grants for nonprofits (Brief 01). Washington, DC: Urban Institute. Retrieved from http://www.urban.org/UploadedPDF/412832-federal-government-contracts.pdf

Pfeffer, J. (2003). Introduction to the classic edition. In *External control of organizations: A resource dependence perspective* [Classic ed.]. Palo Alto, CA: Stanford University Press.

Pfeffer, J., & Salancik, G. R. (1978). *The external control of organizations: A resource dependence perspective*. New York, NY: Harper & Row.

Philanthropy News Digest. (2007, August 15). Brian Gallagher, President/CEO, United Way of America. Retrieved from http://www.philanthropynewsdigest.org/newsmakers/brian-gallagher-president-ceo-united-way-of-america

Phills, J. A., Jr. (2005). *Integrating mission and strategy for nonprofit organizations*. New York, NY: Oxford University Press.

Phills, J. A., Jr., & Chang, V. (2005, Spring). The price of commercial success. *Stanford Social Innovation Review, 65–72*. Retrieved from http://www.ssireview.org/articles/entry/the_price_of_commercial_success

Phills, J. A., Jr., Deiglmeier, K., & Miller, D. T. (2008, Fall). Rediscovering social innovation. *Stanford Social Innovation Review*. Retrieved from http://www.ssireview.org/articles/entry/rediscovering_social_innovation/

Pidgeon, W. P. Jr. (2004). *The not-for-profit CEO: How to attain and retain the corner office*. Hoboken, NJ: Wiley.

Pierce, J. (2004). Habitat founder and board disagree on his retirement date. *Christian Century, 121*(20), 15.

Pioneer Human Services. (2015). Manufacturing & assembly. Retrieved from http://pioneerhumanservices.org/business/manufacturing/manufacturing-assembly/

Pogrebin, R. (2009, June 17). City Opera tries to hold off the ultimate finale. *New York Times*. Retrieved from http://www.nytimes.com/2009/06/18/arts/music/18city.html

Poister, T. H., Aristigueta, M. P., & Hall, J. L. (2015). *Managing and measuring performance in public and nonprofit organizations* (2nd ed.). San Francisco, CA: Jossey-Bass.

Pollack, A. (2014, November 19). Deal by Cystic Fibrosis Foundation raises cash and some concern. *New York Times*. Retrieved from http://www.nytimes.com/2014/11/19/business/for-cystic-fibrosis-foundation-venture-yields-windfall-in-hope-and-cash.html?_r=0

Porter, M. E., & Kramer, M. R. (2011, January). Creating shared value. *Harvard Business Review*. Retrieved from https://hbr.org/2011/01/the-big-idea-creating-shared-value

Powell, W. W., & DiMaggio, P. J. (1991). *The new institutionalism in organizational analysis*. Chicago, IL: University of Chicago Press.

Preston, C. (2010, January 15). Social media aid efforts to help Haiti earthquake victims. *Chronicle of Philanthropy*. Retrieved from http://philanthropy.com/article/Social-Media-Aid-Efforts-to/63566/

Preston, C., & Wallace, N. (2011, January 6). Charities report slow progress in Haiti, despite $1.4 billion raised in a year. *Chronicle of Philanthropy*. Retrieved from http://philanthropy.com/article/Charities-Face-Struggles-to/125847/

A primer on risk management. (2007). Retrieved from http://www.handsonnwnc.org/express/nccenteron-riskmanagement.pdf

Prince, R. A., & File, K. M. (1994). *The seven faces of philanthropy*. San Francisco, CA: Jossey-Bass.

Public Relations Society of America. (n.d.). What is public relations? Retrieved from http://www.prsa.org/AboutPRSA/PublicRelationsDefined/

Putnam, R. (1995, January). Bowling alone: America's declining social capital. *Journal of Democracy, 6*(1), 65–78.

Pynes, J. E. (2013). *Human resources management for public and nonprofit organizations* (4th ed.). San Francisco, CA: Jossey-Bass.

Q&A with Share Our Strength Founder Billy Shore. (2015, September 9).

Retrieved from http://blog.williams-sonoma.com/qa-with-share-our-strength-founder-billy-shore/

Quotah, E. (2009, October 15). Two national youth charities strike partnership to share resources. *Chronicle of Philanthropy*. Retrieved from http://philanthropy.com/article/article-content/57780/

Rainey, H. G. (2014). *Understanding and managing public organizations* (5th ed.). San Francisco, CA: Jossey-Bass.

Raymond, J. (2009, October 13). Seeing red in pink products: One woman's fight against breast cancer consumerism. Newsweek.com. Retrieved from http://www.newsweek.com/seeing-red-pink-products-one-womans-fight-against-breast-cancer-consumerism-222566

Raynor, J. (2014, November 19). The return of capacity building. *Stanford Social Innovation Review*. Retrieved from http://www.ssireview.org/blog/entry/the_return_of_capacity_building

Regenovich, D. (2011). Establishing a planned giving program. In E. R. Tempel, T. L. Seiler, & E. E. Aldrich (Eds.), *Achieving excellence in fundraising* (3rd. ed., 139–158). San Francisco, CA: Jossey-Bass.

Rehberg, W. (2005, June). Altruistic individualists: Motivations for international volunteering among young adults in Switzerland. *Voluntas: International Journal of Voluntary and Nonprofit Organizations, 16*(2), 109–122.

Rich, C. (2014, October 15). 10 reasons for nonprofits to move to a revenue-driven model. *Forbes*. Retrieved from http://www.forbes.com/sites/yec/2014/10/14/10-reasons-for-nonprofits-to-move-to-a-revenue-driven-model/

Robbins, K. C. (2012). The nonprofit sector in historical perspective: Traditions of philanthropy in the West. In J. S. Ott & L. A. Dicke (Eds.), *The nature of the nonprofit sector* (2nd ed., pp. 88–107). Boulder, CO: Westview Press.

Robertson, L. L. (2011, July). How to create a culture of innovation. *Associations Now* (Publication of ASAE/Center for Association Leadership). Retrieved from http://www.asaecenter.org/Resources/ANowDetail.cfm?ItemNumber=98669

Rockefeller Foundation gives $500,000 to develop "social" stock market. (2008, March 24). *Chronicle of Philanthropy*. Retrieved from http://philanthropy.com/blog-Post/Rockefeller-Foundation-Gives/14716/

Roeger, K. L., Blackwood, A. S., & Pettijohn, S. L. (2012). *The nonprofit almanac 2012*. Washington, DC: Urban Institute.

Rogers, J. L. (2006, April 16). Foundations are burning out charity CEOs. *Chronicle of Philanthropy, 18*(10), 45–46.

Rogers, K. (2014, September 13). Tax-exempt? The NFL's nonprofit status by the numbers. CNBC Sports Business. Retrieved from http://www.cnbc.com/id/101996109#.

Romero, S., & Lacey, M. (2010, January 12). Fierce quake devastates Haitian capital. *New York Times*. Retrieved from http://www.nytimes.com/2010/01/13/world/americas/13haiti.html?_r=1

Ronquillo, J. (n.d.). Aspire: Building partnerships through social entrepreneurship and empowerment (e-case). The Hubert Project. Retrieved from http://www.hubertproject.org/hubert-material/322/

Rose-Ackerman, S. (1996). Altruism, nonprofits and economic theory. *Journal of Economic Literature, 34,* 701–728.

Rudel, J. (2011, June 6). The people's opera, in peril. *New York Times*. Retrieved from http://www.nytimes.com/2011/06/07/opinion/07rudel.html

Ruiz, R. R. (2015, May 19). 4 cancer charities are accused of fraud. *New York Times*. Retrieved from http://www.nytimes.com/2015/05/20/business/4-cancer-charities-accused-in-ftc-fraud-case.html?_r=0

Rural Assistance Center Website. (2014). Retrieved from http://www.raconline.org/topics/federally-qualified-health-centers

Ryan, W. P., Chait, R. P., & Taylor, B. E. (2013, January 2). Problem boards or board problem? *Nonprofit Quarterly*. Retrieved from http://www.aspeninstitute.org/sites/default/files/content/docs/pubs/4th%20sector%20paper%20-%20exec%20summary%20FINAL.pdf

Sabeti, H. (with the Fourth Sector Network Concept Working Group). (2009, September 9). *The emerging fourth sector: Executive summary*. Washington, DC: Aspen Institute. Retrieved from http://www.aspeninstitute.org/publications/emerging-fourth-sector-executive-summary

Sagawa, S., & Segal, E. (2000). *Common interest, common good: Creating value through business and social sector partnerships*. Cambridge, MA: Harvard Business School Press.

Salamon, L. M. (1999). *America's nonprofit sector: A primer* (2nd ed.). New York, NY: Foundation Center.

Salamon, L. M. (2012a). *America's nonprofit sector: A primer* (3rd ed.). New York, NY: Foundation Center.

Salamon, L. M. (2012b). *The state of nonprofit America* (2nd ed.). Washington, DC: Brookings Institution.

Salamon, L. M., & Geller, S. L. (2005). *Nonprofit governance and accountability* [The Johns Hopkins Nonprofit Listening Post Project Communique No. 4]. Baltimore, MD: Johns Hopkins University Center for Civil Society Studies/Institute for Policy Studies.

Salamon, L. M., Sokolowski, S. W., & Associates. (2004). *Global civil society: Dimensions of the nonprofit sector* (Vol. 2). Bloomfield, CT: Kumarian Press.

Salmon, J. L. (2006, June 27). Chapter overhaul adds to Red Cross turmoil. *The Washington Post*, A27.

Sander, T. H., & Putnam, R. D. (2005, September 10). September 11 as civics lesson. *The Washington Post,* A23.

Sargeant, A. (2005). *Marketing management for nonprofit organizations*. New York, NY: Oxford University Press.

Sargeant, A. (2010, April 10). Making fund raising a real profession: Next steps. *Chronicle of Philanthropy*. Retrieved from http://philanthropy.com/article/Making-Fund-Raising-a-Real/64903

Sargeant, A., Shang, J., & Associates. (2010). *Fundraising principles and practice*. San Francisco, CA: Jossey-Bass.

Sataline, S. (2011, October 16). From mergers that didn't stick, lessons emerge for other charities. *Chronicle of Philanthropy.* Retrieved from http://philanthropy.com/article/Avoiding-Messy-Breakups-/129370/

Sawhill, J., & Williamson, D. (2001). Measuring what matters most in nonprofits. *McKinsey Quarterly, 2001*(2), 16–25.

Schein, E. H. (2010). *Organizational culture and leadership: A dynamic view* (4th ed.). San Francisco, CA: Jossey-Bass.

Schervish, P. G., & Havens, J. J. (2001). The new physics of philanthropy: The supply-side vectors of charitable giving—Part 2: The spiritual side of the supply side. *CASE International Journal of Educational Advancement, 2*(3), 221–241.

Schervish, P. G. (2009). Beyond self-interest and altruism: Care as mutual nourishment. In *Conversations on Philanthropy* (Vol. VI, pp. 33–44). Alexandria, VA: DonorsTrust. Retrieved from http://www.conversationsonphilanthropy.org/wp-content/uploads/2009_entire_journal.pdf

School of Philanthropy To Be Named After Lilly Family (2013, April 9). *The Nonprofit Times.* Retrieved from http://www.thenonprofittimes.com/news-articles/school-of-philanthropy-to-be-named-after-lilly-family/

Schwinn, E. (2002, November 14). How '96 law on financial abuses has been applied by IRS in four cases. *Chronicle of Philanthropy, 15*(3), 32.

Schwinn, E. (2006a, September 28). IRS warns charities to avoid electioneering. *Chronicle of Philanthropy, 18*(24), 18. Retrieved from http://philanthropy.com/article/IRS-Warns-Charities-to-Avoid/57914/

Schwinn, E. (2006b, January 26). Two churches in Ohio accused of playing politics. *Chronicle of Philanthropy, 19*(3), 18. Retrieved from http://philanthropy.com/article/Two-Churches-in-Ohio-Accused/57864/

Schwinn, E. (2007, May 17). Seven American Lung Association affiliates sever ties with national charity. *Chronicle of Philanthropy.* Retrieved from http://philanthropy. com/article/Seven-American-Lung-Associa/55124/

Schwinn, E. (2008, May 15). United Way of America outlines 10-year plan. *Chronicle of Philanthropy.* Retrieved from https://philanthropy.com/article/United-Way-of-America-Outlines/163103

Sciolino, E. (2001a, May 10). Smithsonian is promised $38 million, with strings. *New York Times,* A20.

Sciolino, E. (2001b, May 26). Smithsonian group criticizes official on donor contract. *New York Times,* A8.

Sciolino, E. (2001c, May 30). Citing differences, director of a Smithsonian museum resigns. *New York Times,* A20.

Scott, W. R. (1995). *Institutions and organizations.* Thousand Oaks, CA: Sage.

Scully, S. (2009, December 15). In Hershey's possible Cadbury bid, a school's fate. *Time.com.* Retrieved from http://www.time.com/time/printout/0,8816,1947492,00.html

SEED Foundation. (2014a). History. Retrieved from http://www.seedfoundation.com/index.php/about-seed/history

SEED Foundation. (2014b). Results. Retrieved from http://www.seedfoundation.com/index.php/about-seed/results

SEED Foundation. (2014c). South Florida. Retrieved from http://www.seedfoundation.com/index.php/plans-for-future-schools/south-florida

Seelos, C., & Mair, J. (2012a). What determines the capacity for continuous innovation in social sector organizations (Rockefeller Foundation Report). Stanford University Center on Philanthropy and Civil Society. Retrieved from http://pacscenter.stanford.edu/practitioners/published-papers

Seelos, C., & Mair, J. (2012b, Fall). Innovation in not the holy grail. *Stanford Social Innovation Review.* Retrieved from http://www.ssireview.org/articles/entry/innovation_is_not_the_holy_grail

Seiler, T. L. (2011). Plan to succeed. In E. R. Tempel, T. L. Seiler, & E. E. Aldrich (Eds.), *Achieving excellence in fund raising* (3rd ed., pp. 10–17). San Francisco, CA: Jossey-Bass.

Senge, P. M. (1990). *The fifth discipline: The art and practice of the learning organization.* New York, NY: Doubleday.

Senge, P. M. (1994). *The fifth discipline fieldbook: Strategies and tools for building a learning organization.* New York, NY: Currency.

Seo, M. G., Barrett, L. F., & Bartunek, J. M. (2004, July). The role of affective experience in work motivation. *Academy of Management Review, 29*(3), 423–439.

Seymour, H. J. (1966). *Designs for fundraising.* New York, NY: McGraw-Hill.

Share Our Strength Website. Retrieved from https://www.nokidhungry.org/

Share Our Strength. (2011). Facts on Childhood Hunger. Retrieved from https://www.nokidhungry.org/sites/default/files/2011-childhood-hunger-facts.pdf

Share Our Strength. (2013). Share Our Strength annual report 2013. Retrieved from http://www.nokidhungry.org/annual-2014/Annual-Report-2013.pdf

Share Our Strength Center for Best Practices (n.d.). *No Kid Hungry Case Study: The Partnership to End Childhood Hunger in Maryland.* Retrieved from http://bestpractices.nokidhungry.org/sites/default/files/resources/NKH%20Maryland%20Case%20Study.pdf

Share Our Strength 2013 Form 990. Retrieved from http://www.nokidhungry.org/pdfs/SOS_2013-12_TAX_Form_990.pdf

Shin, A. (2013, July 21). Gentrification in overdrive on 14th Street. *Washington Post.* Retrieved from http://www.washingtonpost.com/...entrification-in-overdrive-on-14th-street/2013/07/21/d07d344e-ea5b-11e2-a301-ea5a8116d211_story.html

Shin, S., & Kleiner, B. H. (2003). How to manage unpaid volunteers in organisations. *Management Research News, 25*(2/3/4), 63–71.

Shogren, E. (2011). BP: A textbook example of how not to handle PR. NPR (Morning Edition). Retrieved from http://www.npr.org/2011/04/21/135575238/bp-a-textbook-example-of-how-not-to-handle-pr

Shoham, A., Ruvio, A., Vigoda-Gadot, E., & Schwabsky, N. (2006,

About the Author

Michael J. Worth is professor of nonprofit management in the Trachtenberg School of Public Policy and Public Administration at The George Washington University in Washington, DC. He teaches graduate courses related to the governance and management of nonprofit institutions and organizations and to philanthropic fundraising.

Dr. Worth served as vice president for development and alumni affairs at The George Washington University for 18 years and previously served as director of development at the University of Maryland College Park. Earlier in his career, he was assistant to the president at Wilkes University and director of development at DeSales University, both in Pennsylvania. As vice president at The George Washington University, he planned and directed two major campaigns and provided support to the board of trustees for board development programs.

Dr. Worth has served as a member of the Commission on Philanthropy of the Council for Advancement and Support of Education (CASE) and as editor of the CASE International Journal of Educational Advancement, a peer-reviewed scholarly journal focused on the practice of institutional advancement in educational institutions.

He has written or edited ten books, including: Public College and University Development (1985); The Role of the Development Officer in Higher Education (1994, 2000); Educational Fund Raising: Principles and Practice (1993); New Strategies for Educational Fund Raising (American Council on Education and Praeger Publishers, 2002); Securing the Future (Association of Governing Boards of Universities and Colleges, 2005); Sounding Boards (Association of Governing Boards of Universities and Colleges, 2008); Nonprofit Management: Principles and Practice (SAGE Publications: 1st edition, 2009; 2nd edition, 2012, 3rd edition, 2013); Leading the Campaign (American Council on Education and Rowman and Littlefield, 2010); and Foundations for the Future (Association of Governing Boards of Universities and Colleges, 2012).

Among other voluntary services, Dr. Worth has been a member of the board of directors of Miriam's Kitchen, an organization providing services to homeless individuals in Washington, DC, and a member of the advisory board of the Young Nonprofit Professionals Network, Washington, DC, chapter.

Dr. Worth consults widely with nonprofit institutions and organizations in the areas of fundraising, board development, and management.

He holds a BA in economics from Wilkes College, an MA in economics from The American University, and a PhD in higher education from the University of Maryland.